MCSE Complete: Core Requirements

San Francisco ▸ Paris ▸ Düsseldorf ▸ Soest ▸ London

Associate Publisher: Guy Hart-Davis

Contracts and Licensing Manager: Kristine O'Callaghan

Acquisitions Editor: Neil Edde

Developmental Editor: Linda Lee

Compilation Editor: Bronwyn Shone Erickson

Project Editors: Lisa Duran, Kelly Winquist

Editors: Davina Baum, Marie Dolcini, Lawrence Frey, Ronn Jost

Technical Editors: Jim Cooper, Ron Reimann, Paul Scott

Book Designer: Maureen Forys

Graphic Illustrators: Michael Gushard, Tony Jonick, Michael Parker

Electronic Publishing Specialist: Kris Warrenburg

Project Team Leader: Leslie Higbee

Proofreaders: Jeffry Chorney, Kathy Draski, Andrea Fox, Rich Ganis, Bonnie Hart, Leslie Higbee, Sandy Young

Indexer: Nancy Guenther

Cover Designer: Design Site

Cover Illustrator: Design Site

Screen reproductions produced with Collage Complete.

Library of Congress Card Number: 99-62997

ISBN: 0-7821-2583-2

Printed in Canada.

10 9 8 7 6 5 4 3

TRADEMARKS

SYBEX has attempted throughout this book to distinguish proprietary trademarks from descriptive terms by following the capitalization style used by the manufacturer.

The author and publisher have made their best efforts to prepare this book, and the content is based upon final release software whenever possible. Portions of the manuscript may be based upon pre-release versions supplied by software manufacturer(s). The author and the publisher make no representation or warranties of any kind with regard to the completeness or accuracy of the contents herein and accept no liability of any kind including but not limited to performance, merchantability, fitness for any particular purpose, or any losses or damages of any kind caused or alleged to be caused directly or indirectly from this book.

Microsoft, the Microsoft Internet Explorer logo, Windows, Windows NT, and the Windows logo are either registered trademarks or trademarks of Microsoft Corporation in the United States and/or other countries.

SYBEX is an independent entity from Microsoft Corporation, and not affiliated with Microsoft Corporation in any manner. This publication may be used in assisting students to prepare for a Microsoft Certified Professional Exam. Neither Microsoft Corporation, its designated review company, nor SYBEX warrants that use of this publication will ensure passing the relevant exam. Microsoft is either a registered trademark or trademark of Microsoft Corporation in the United States and/or other countries.

ACKNOWLEDGMENTS

This book incorporates the work of many people, inside and outside Sybex.

Guy Hart-Davis, Neil Edde, and Linda Lee defined the book's overall structure and adapted its contents, and Bronwyn Shone Erickson compiled all the material for publication in this book.

A large team of editors, developmental editors, project editors, and technical editors helped to put together the various books from which *MCSE Complete: Core Requirements* was compiled: Neil Edde handled developmental tasks; Davina Baum, Marie Dolcini, Lawrence Frey, Ronn Jost, and Emily K. Wolman all contributed to editing or project editing; and Jim Cooper, Ron Reimann, and Paul Scott provided technical edits. Susan Berge, Lisa Duran and Kelly Winquist deserve special thanks for their care in preparing this book for production.

The *MCSE Complete: Core Requirements* production team of electronic publishing specialist Kris Warrenburg and project team leader Leslie Higbee worked with speed and accuracy to turn the manuscript files and illustrations into the handsome book you're now reading.

Finally, our most important thanks go to the contributors who agreed to have their work excerpted in *MCSE Complete: Core Requirements*: James Chellis, Gary Govanus, Robert King, Glenn Madow, Lance Mortensen, and Rick Sawtell. Without their efforts, this book would not exist.

Contents at a Glance

Table of Contents

INTRODUCTION

M*CSE Complete: Core Requirements* is a one-of-a-kind book—valuable both for the breadth of its content and for its low price. This thousand-page compilation of information from five Network Press Exam Notes books provides comprehensive coverage of all the core MCSE exams.

If you've purchased this book, you are probably chasing one of the Microsoft professional certifications: MCP, MCSE, or MCT. All of these are great goals, and they are also great career builders. Glance through any newspaper and you'll find employment opportunities for people with these certifications—these ads are there because finding qualified employees is a challenge in today's market. The certification means you know something about the product, but more importantly, it means you have the ability, determination, and focus to learn—the greatest skill any employee can have!

You've probably also heard all the rumors about how hard the Microsoft tests are—believe us, the rumors are true! Microsoft has designed a series of exams that truly test your knowledge of their products. Each test not only covers the materials presented in a particular class, it also covers the prerequisite knowledge for that course. This means two things for you—that first test can be a real hurdle and each test *should* get easier since you've studied the basics over and over.

Is This Book for You?

MCSE Complete: Core Requirements was designed to be a portable exam review guide that can be used either in conjunction with a more complete study program (book, CBT courseware, classroom/lab environment) or as an exam review for those who don't feel the need for more extensive test preparation. It isn't our goal to "give the answers away," but rather to identify those topics on which you can expect to be tested and to provide sufficient coverage of these topics.

Perhaps you've been working with Microsoft networking technologies for years now. The thought of paying lots of money for a specialized MCSE exam preparation course probably doesn't sound too appealing. What can they teach you that you don't already know, right? Be careful, though.

Many experienced network administrators have walked confidently into test centers only to walk sheepishly out of them after failing an MCSE exam. As they discovered, there's the Microsoft of the real world and the Microsoft of the MCSE exams. It's our goal with this book to show you where the two converge and where they diverge. After you've finished reading through this book, you should have a clear idea of how your understanding of the technologies involved matches up with the expectations of the MCSE test makers in Redmond.

Or perhaps you're relatively new to the world of Microsoft networking, drawn to it by the promise of challenging work and higher salaries. You've just waded through an 800-page MCSE study guide or taken a class at a local training center. Lots of information to keep track of, isn't it? Well, by organizing this book according to the Microsoft exam objectives, and by breaking up the information into concise manageable pieces, we've created what we think is the handiest exam review guide available. As you read through the book, you'll be able to identify quickly those areas you know best and those that require more in-depth review.

NOTE

The goal of the Exam Notes series, on which *MCSE Complete: Core Requirements* is based, is to help MCSE candidates familiarize themselves with the subjects on which they can expect to be tested in the MCSE exams. For complete, in-depth coverage of the technologies and topics involved, we recommend the MCSE Study Guide series from Sybex.

How Is This Book Organized?

This book has five parts and two appendices.

Part 1: Networking Essentials Covers objectives for exam 70-058.

Part 2: NT Server 4 Covers objectives for exam 70-067.

Part 3: NT Workstation 4 Covers objectives for exam 70-073.

Part 4: NT Server 4 in the Enterprise Covers objectives for exam 70-068.

Part 5: Windows 98 Covers objectives for exam 70-098.

Appendix A Answers to the Practice Exam section of each unit.

Appendix B A comprehensive glossary of terms.

As mentioned above, this book is organized according to the official exam objectives list prepared by Microsoft for the 70-058, 70-067, 70-073, 70-068, and 70-098 exams. The parts coincide with the different exams, and the chapters coincide with the broad objectives groupings, such as Planning, Installation and Configuration, Monitoring and Optimization, and Troubleshooting. These groupings are also reflected in organization of the MCSE exams themselves.

Within each chapter, the individual exam objectives are addressed in turn. And in turn, the objectives sections are further divided according to the type of information presented. For each objective, you'll find all the critical information you need to know, followed by key procedures. Each part ends with a selection of questions similar to those you'll encounter on the actual MCSE exam. Answers and explanations are provided in Appendix A so you can gain some insight into the test-taking process.

In Appendix B, the glossary, you'll find the most important terms and concepts related to each objective brought together in a comprehensive glossary. You'll understand what all those technical words mean within the context of the related subject matter.

For a more comprehensive collection of exam review questions, check out the MCSE Test Success series, also published by Sybex.

How Do You Become an MCSE?

Attaining Microsoft Certified Systems Engineer (MCSE) status is a challenge. The exams cover a wide range of topics and require dedicated study and expertise. This is, however, why the MCSE certificate is so valuable. If achieving the MCSE were too easy, the market would be quickly flooded by MCSEs and the certification would become meaningless. Microsoft, keenly aware of this fact, has taken steps to ensure that the certification means its holder is truly knowledgeable and skilled.

To become an MCSE, you must pass four core requirements and two electives. Most people select the following exam combination for the MCSE core requirements for the most current track:

Client Requirement

70-073: Implementing and Supporting Windows NT Workstation 4.0 *or*

70-098: Implementing and Supporting Microsoft® Windows 98®

Networking Requirement

70-058: Networking Essentials

Windows NT Server 4.0 Requirement

70-067: Implementing and Supporting Windows NT Server 4.0

Windows NT Server 4.0 in the Enterprise Requirement

70-068: Implementing and Supporting Windows NT Server 4.0 in the Enterprise

Electives

Some of the more popular electives include:

70-059: Internetworking Microsoft TCP/IP on Microsoft Windows NT 4.0

70-087: Implementing and Supporting Microsoft Internet Information Server 4.0

70-081: Implementing and Supporting Microsoft Exchange Server 5.5

70-026: System Administration for Microsoft SQL Server 6.5

70-027: Implementing a Database Design on Microsoft SQL Server 6.5

70-028: System Administration for Microsoft SQL Server 7

70-088: Implementing and Supporting Microsoft Proxy Server 2.0

70-079: Implementing and Supporting Microsoft Internet Explorer 4.0 by Using the Internet Explorer Administration Kit

TIP

The source books for *MCSE Complete: Core Requirements* are part of a series of MCSE Exam Notes books, published by Network Press (SYBEX). These cover the core requirements and your choice of several electives—the entire MCSE track!

NOTE

You can also check out *MCSE Complete: Electives*, which will help you prepare for some of the most popular electives exams. These include: Internetworking Microsoft TCP/IP on Microsoft Windows NT 4.0, Implementing and Supporting Microsoft Internet Information Server 4.0, Implementing and Supporting Microsoft Exchange Server 5.5, System Administration for Microsoft SQL Server 7, and Implementing and Supporting Microsoft Internet Explorer 4.0 By Using the Internet Explorer Administration Kit.

Where Do You Take the Exams?

You may take the exams at any one of more than 800 Sylvan Prometric Authorized Testing Centers around the world or through Virtual University Enterprises (VUE).

For the location of a Sylvan testing center near you, call (800) 755-EXAM (755-3926). Outside the United States and Canada, contact your local Sylvan Prometric Registration Center. You can also register for an exam with Sylvan Prometric via the Internet. The Sylvan site can be reached through the Microsoft Training and Certification site or at `http://www.slspro.com/msreg/microsoft.asp`.

To register for an exam through VUE, call 888-837-8616 (North America only) or visit their web site at `http://www.vue.com/ms/`.

NOTE

At the time of this writing, the exams are $100 each.

When you schedule the exam, you'll be provided with instructions regarding appointment and cancellation procedures, ID requirements, and information about the testing center location.

How Microsoft Develops the Exam Questions

Microsoft's exam development process consists of eight mandatory phases. The process takes an average of seven months and contains more than 150 specific steps. The phases of Microsoft Certified Professional exam development are listed here.

Phase 1: Job Analysis Phase 1 is an analysis of all the tasks that make up the specific job function based on tasks performed by people who are currently performing the job function. This phase also identifies the knowledge, skills, and abilities that relate specifically to the certification for that performance area.

Phase 2: Objective Domain Definition The results of the job analysis provide the framework used to develop exam objectives. The development of objectives involves translating the job function tasks into a comprehensive set of more specific and measurable knowledge, skills, and abilities. The resulting list of objectives, or the objective domain, is the basis for the development of both the certification exams and the training materials.

NOTE

The outline of all Exam Note books is based upon the official exam objectives lists published by Microsoft. Objectives and are subject to change without notification. We advise that you check the Microsoft Training & Certification Web site (`www.microsoft.com\train_cert\`) for the most current objectives list.

Phase 3: Blueprint Survey The final objective domain is transformed into a blueprint survey in which contributors—technology professionals who are performing the applicable job function—are asked to rate each objective. Based on the contributors' input, the objectives are prioritized and weighted. The actual exam items are written according to the prioritized objectives. The blueprint survey phase helps determine which objectives to measure, as well as the appropriate number and types of items to include on the exam.

Phase 4: Item Development A pool of items is developed to measure the blueprinted objective domain. The number and types of items to be written are based on the results of the blueprint survey. During this phase, items are reviewed and revised to ensure that they are:

- Technically accurate
- Clear, unambiguous, and plausible
- Not biased toward any population, subgroup, or culture
- Not misleading or tricky
- Testing at the correct level of Bloom's Taxonomy
- Testing for useful knowledge, not obscure or trivial facts

Items that meet these criteria are included in the initial item pool.

Phase 5: Alpha Review and Item Revision During this phase, a panel of technical and job function experts reviews each item for technical accuracy, then answers each item, reaching consensus on all technical issues. Once the items have been verified as technically accurate, they are edited to ensure that they are expressed in the clearest language possible.

Phase 6: Beta Exam The reviewed and edited items are collected into a beta exam pool. During the beta exam, each participant has the opportunity to respond to all the items in this beta exam pool. Based on the responses of all beta participants, Microsoft performs a statistical analysis to verify the validity of the exam items and to determine which items will be used in the certification exam. Once the analysis has been completed, the items are distributed into multiple parallel forms, or versions, of the final certification exam.

Phase 7: Item Selection and Cut-Score Setting The results of the beta exam are analyzed to determine which items should be included in the certification exam based on many factors, including item difficulty and relevance. Generally, the desired items are answered correctly by 25 percent to 90 percent of the beta exam candidates. This helps ensure that the exam consists of a variety of difficulty levels, from somewhat easy to extremely difficult.

Also during this phase, a panel of job function experts determines the cut score (minimum passing score) for the exam. The cut score differs from exam to exam because it is based on an item-by-item determination of the percentage of candidates who would be expected to answer the item correctly. The experts determine the cut score in a group session to increase the reliability.

Phase 8: Live Exam Once all the other phases are complete, the exam is ready. Microsoft Certified Professional exams are administered by Sylvan Prometric.

Tips for Taking an MCSE Exam

Here are some general tips for taking an exam successfully:

- Arrive early at the exam center so you can relax and review your study materials, particularly tables and lists of exam-related information.
- Read the questions carefully. Don't be tempted to jump to an early conclusion. Make sure you know *exactly* what the question is asking.
- Don't leave any unanswered questions. They count against you.
- When answering multiple-choice questions you're not sure about, use a process of elimination to get rid of the obviously incorrect questions first. This will improve your odds if you need to make an educated guess.
- Because the hard questions will eat up the most time, save them for last. You can move forward and backward through the exam.
- This test has many exhibits (pictures). It can be difficult, if not impossible, to view both the questions and the exhibit simulation on 14- and 15-inch screens usually found at the testing centers. Call around to each center and see if they have 17-inch monitors available. If they don't, perhaps you can arrange to bring in your own. Failing this, some have found it useful to quickly draw the diagram on the scratch paper provided by the testing center and use the monitor to view just the question.
- Many participants run out of time before they are able to complete the test. If you are unsure of the answer to a question, you may want to choose one of the answers, mark the question, and go on—an unanswered question does not help you. Once your time is up, you cannot go on to another question. However, you can remain on the question you are on indefinitely when the time

runs out. Therefore, when you are almost out of time, go to a question you feel you can figure out–given enough time–and work until you feel you have got it (or the night security guard boots you out!).

- You are allowed to use the Windows calculator during your test. However, it may be better to memorize a table of the subnet addresses and to write it down on the scratch paper supplied by the testing center before you start the test.

Once you have completed an exam, you will be given immediate, online notification of your pass or fail status. You will also receive a printed Examination Score Report indicating your pass or fail status and your exam results by section. (The test administrator will give you the printed score report.) Test scores are automatically forwarded to Microsoft within five working days after you take the test. You do not need to send your score to Microsoft. If you pass the exam, you will receive confirmation from Microsoft, typically within two to four weeks.

Contact Information

To find out more about Microsoft Education and Certification materials and programs, to register with Sylvan Prometric, or to get other useful information, check the following resources. Outside the United States or Canada, contact your local Microsoft office or Sylvan Prometric testing center.

Microsoft Certified Professional Program—(800) 636-7544 Call the MCPP number for information about the Microsoft Certified Professional program and exams, and to order the latest Microsoft Roadmap to Education and Certification.

Sylvan Prometric testing centers—(800) 755-EXAM Contact Sylvan to register to take a Microsoft Certified Professional exam at any of more than 800 Sylvan Prometric testing centers around the world.

Microsoft Certification Development Team—Web:
`http://www.microsoft.com/Train_Cert/mcp/examinfo/certsd.htm`
Contact the Microsoft Certification Development Team through its Web site to volunteer for participation in one or more exam development phase or to report a problem with an exam. Address written correspondence to

Certification Development Team, Microsoft Education and Certification, One Microsoft Way, Redmond, WA 98052.

Microsoft TechNet Technical Information Network—(800) 344-2121
This is an excellent resource for support professionals and system administrators. Outside the United States and Canada, call your local Microsoft subsidiary for information.

How to Contact the Publisher

Sybex welcomes reader feedback on all of their titles. Visit the Sybex Web site at `www.sybex.com` for book updates and additional certification information. You'll also find online forms to submit comments or suggestions regarding this or any other Sybex book.

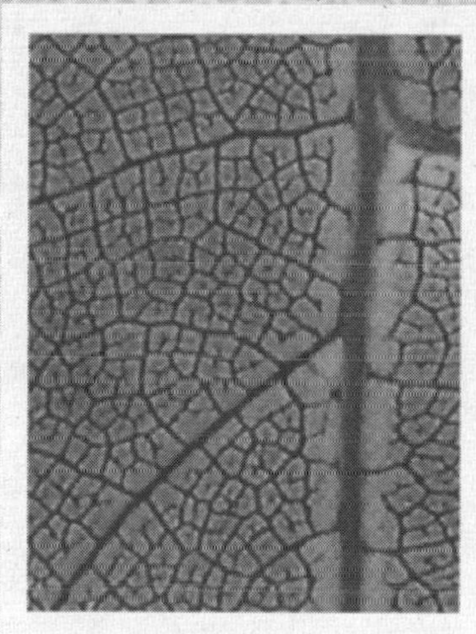

PART I

Networking Essentials

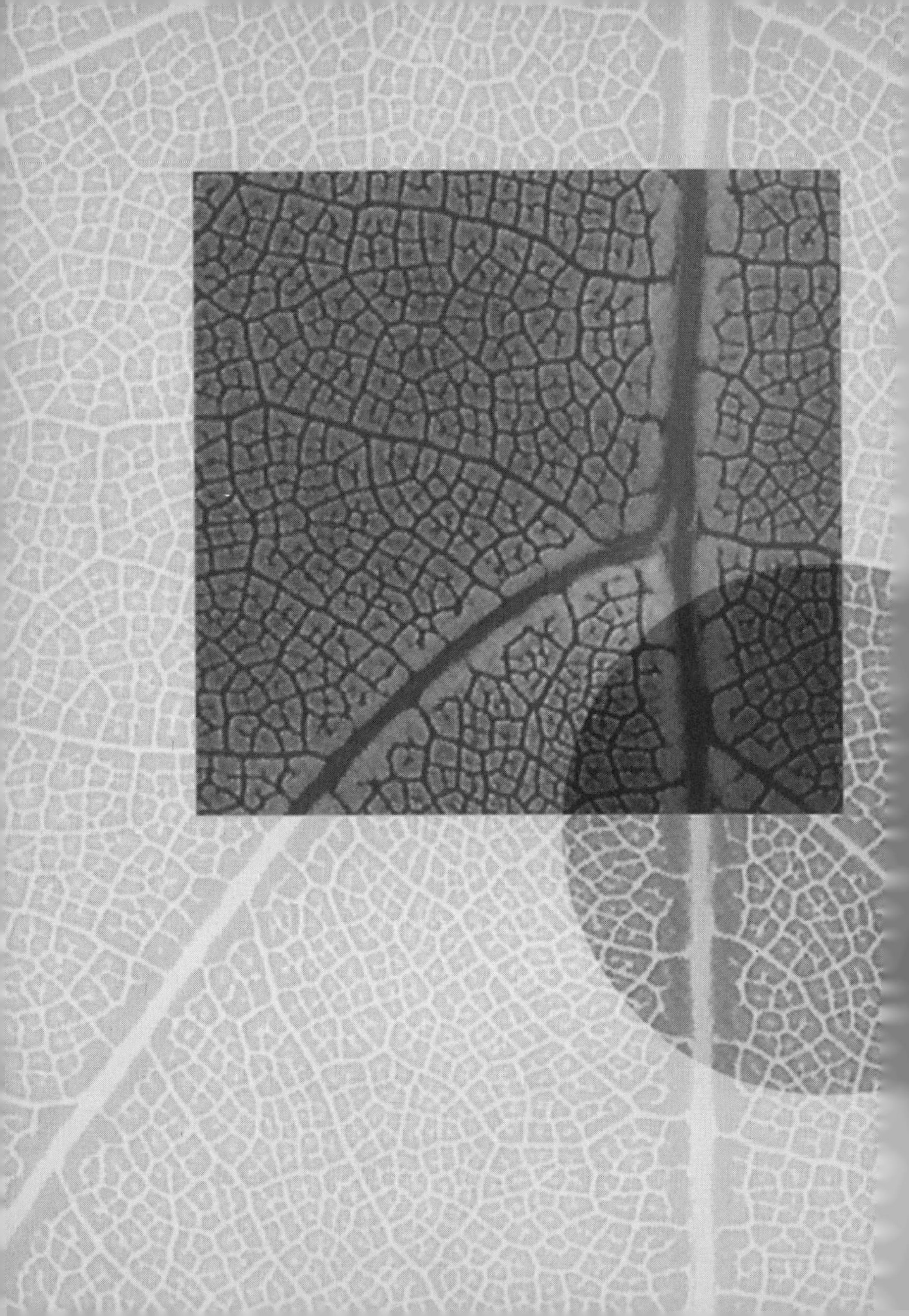

Chapter 1

Standards and Terminology

The purpose of networking is to share information and resources. This chapter provides information about basic networking concepts while it builds a foundation for understanding the balance of information contained in this book. The focus of this chapter is on making decisions about basic networking alternatives.

Adapted from *MCSE Exam Notes: Networking Essentials*
by Glenn Madow and James Chellis
ISBN 0-7821-2291-4 320 pages $19.99

Most of the information presented in this chapter is conceptual and built on models. In order to understand networking you need an appreciation for the theories that explain and guide networks. It can be stated quite simply: Networking is based on theoretical models, these models are rooted in standards, and finally, these standards depend on specific terminology.

The chapter starts by describing networks and what they do. It covers the fundamental terms associated with local area networks (LANs) and wide area networks (WANs). The next section begins with a discussion about the difference between connection-oriented communications and connectionless communications and how each handles transmission errors on a network.

The terms related to a network's remote transport capabilities come next. Knowing the difference between SLIP and PPP, two WAN transport protocols, provides an introduction to WAN technology presented later in Chapter 2.

Finally, you need to be familiar with how a network is divided both physically and logically. The last part presents two models: the OSI reference model and the IEEE 802 family, IEEE 802.3 and 802.5 standards. The OSI model creates a logical design that segments networking into distinct tasks: sending and receiving messages. The IEE 802.3 and 802.5 standards explain the physical end of networking and specify wiring and hardware requirements.

Define common networking terms for LANs and WANs.

A computer network is a group of computers that have been connected together in some fashion so these two things can be shared:

- Information (all data stored on individual hard drives)
- Resources (all expensive hardware and software at each computer)

The design and implementation of a network requires that three components be present:

- Something that needs to be shared (resources, information)
- A physical pathway between network "nodes" (transmission media)
- Rules to control communication along the pathway (protocols)

Different computer networks provide distinct and sometimes separate functions. Classification of computer networks and their services can help describe the functionality of any particular network. This section introduces a few common distinctions, including the difference between LANs and WANs, and the comparison of various computing models including centralized processing, distributed processing, and cooperative processing.

In addition, networks are described by the services their operating systems provide, and this section will describe important network services including file, print, application, and messaging.

Types of Networks

Based largely on a network's geographic size, you can divide networks into two categories:

- Local Area Networks (LANs)
- Wide Area Networks (WANs)

NOTE

The differences here lie in the geographical area covered and the types of connections used to establish communication. Different types of transmission media and protocols are used in WANs as compared to LANs.

LANs

A *local area network* (LAN) is a number of computers connected to each other by cable in a single location, usually a single floor of a building or all the computers in a small company. LANs are perfect for sharing resources within a building or campus but are inadequate for connecting computers from distant sites.

LANs were first implemented in the late 1960s. They developed from point-to-point connections, where a single wire joined the two systems. It was not uncommon to see this wire running a few hundred feet.

There are many different topologies, the most popular being the star and the linear bus configurations. In the star configuration, each workstation is connected to a central hub with its own cable. In the linear bus topologies, the cable goes through the location from one workstation to another. Ethernet takes advantage of both of these topologies.

There are three common topologies used for creating LANs: bus, star, and ring. Figure 1.1 illustrates a typical LAN topology.

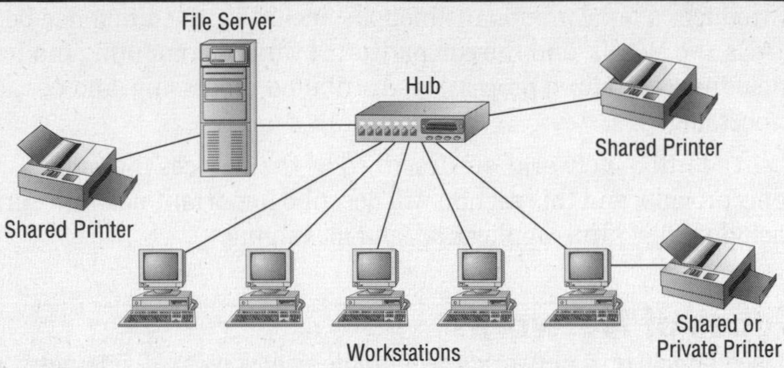

FIGURE 1.1: A typical LAN topology

LANs typically have the following characteristics:

- Small geographical area (single building to small campus)
- Cabled with twisted-pair wire, coaxial cable, or fiber-optic cable

WANs

Wide area networks (WANs) are sets of connecting links between local area networks. Larger companies have their offices throughout a large region. For example, Microsoft has a headquarters site and offices throughout the nation, states, and cities. Wide area networks address the needs of such an organization.

Connecting links are made over telephone lines leased from the various telephone companies. In some cases, WANs are created with satellite links, packet radio, or microwave transceivers. Most WANs are privately owned by the businesses that use them. The Internet has become the largest and least expensive WAN in the world. Many companies now form private WANs by way of encrypted communications over the Internet.

WANs suffer from extremely limited bandwidth. The fastest commercially feasible wide area data links are many times slower than the slower local area links, making the sharing of resources over a WAN difficult. Generally, WAN links are used only for inter-process communications to route short messages, such as e-mail or HTML (World Wide Web) traffic. Figure 1.2 diagrams a typical WAN.

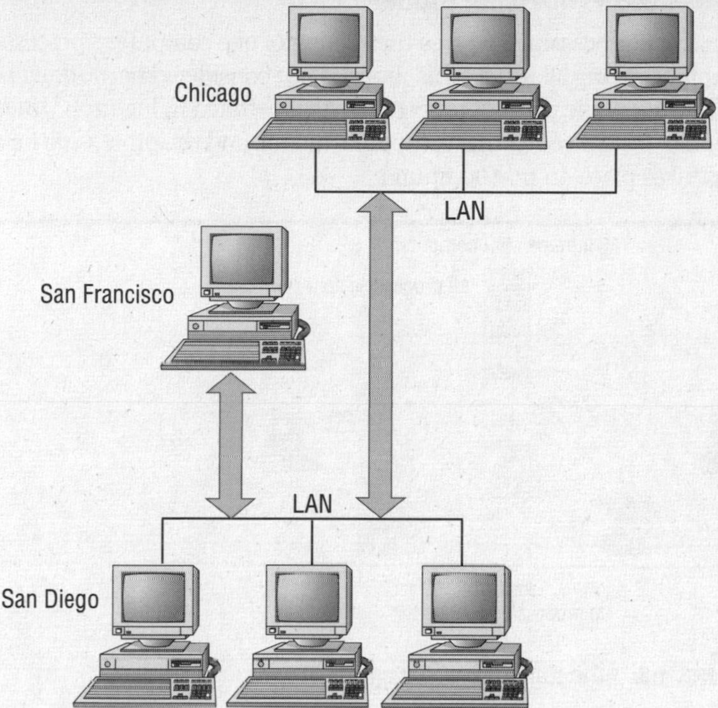

FIGURE 1.2: A typical WAN

WANs typically have the following characteristics:

- Geographical coverage that can span metropolitan areas, states, and even countries
- Links between sites are typically leased services

NOTE

Despite the differences in geographical area and links, a WAN is still one network, and access to the network is the same whether the user is part of a LAN or WAN. The biggest difference the user will see is that communication speed will typically be slower across leased communication services.

Computing Models

It will be helpful to discuss ways or models for computing to get a comprehensive view of how computers have been and are being used.

Centralized Processing Model

Centralized processing involves the sharing of one computer's processing capability among all users. This model is not considered networking because it involves a single point of processing. As illustrated in Figure 1.3, only one computer is involved in this computing model, and the processing for all users takes place on that computer.

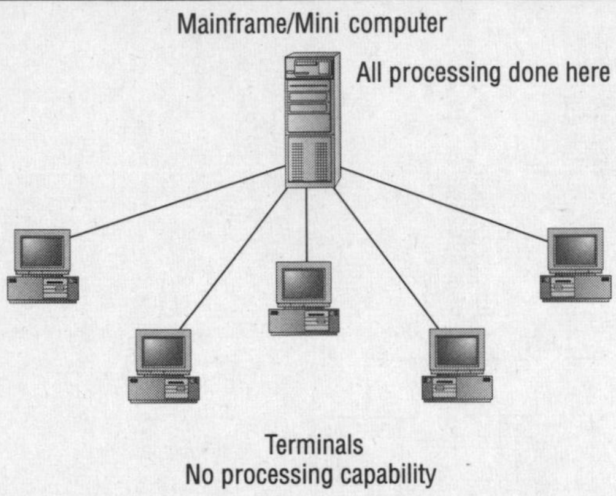

FIGURE 1.3: Centralized processing model

Distributed Processing Model

This model describes a network with several computers. There may be some centralization of processing, but the entire processing does not exist on one computer. Each workstation or client is an independent computer. This computing model can have a file server that shares resources and information with the rest of the network. In this case, the network would be considered a "centralized system," which is different from the term *centralized processing*. (See Figure 1.4.)

NOTE

A client/server network can use both distributive and cooperative models. When it uses the term *centralized system,* to describe the client/server network, the exam is referring to the Distribution model. Client/server networks are discussed later in this chapter.

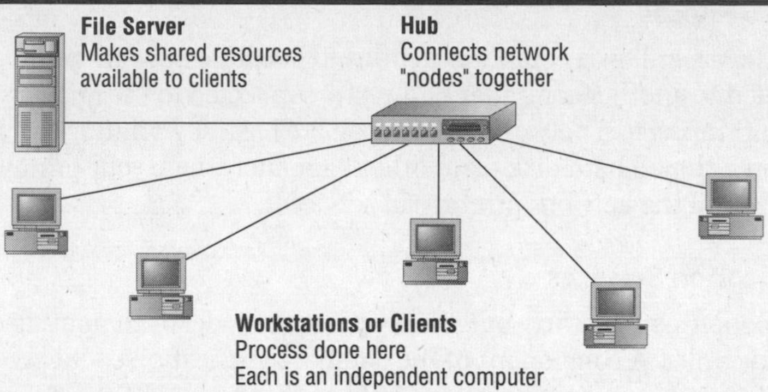

FIGURE 1.4: Distributed processing model

Cooperative Processing Model

This model (not shown) looks much like the distributed processing model in Figure 1.4, except that the workstations and clients would not always be working independently. In this model, the client and a server, or several clients and servers, could work together on performing a common processing task. Different parts of a program can run on separate computers. Each program part runs on the most appropriate computer, while other computers can cooperate to perform the necessary processing.

Network Services

In order for resources to be shared, the network operating system must provide *services* to allow this to happen. Some of the services that provide access to shared resources are file services, print services, application services, and messaging services.

File Services

Information is stored on the hard disk in the form of a file. *File services* provide the means to share the files and folders on a computer's hard disk with several network computers. File services give access to files and folders despite the location of another computer. The file or folder from a sharing computer will appear as another drive letter (F:, H:, or Z:) or as a UNC name at the computer doing the borrowing. Assuming that a user has the correct network permissions, file services provide the ability to read, write, change, copy, delete, and execute these files from a remote computer.

Print Services

Print services allow a computer to print to a remote network printer attached to another computer or directly connected to the network. When printing to a network printer, you are basically printing to a location on a shared hard disk on another computer where your print job is stored until the network printer can service it.

Application Services

Application services carry out the cooperative model of computing discussed earlier. A component of the database application could be installed on an application server, such as Windows NT Server. The server would perform processing on the database data such as database queries, updating, and maintenance. Client computers would also run a portion of the database application. This part of the application would allow them to have efficient access to the database by having their client program component communicate with the server program component.

Messaging Services

Messaging services enable users to use several programs to transfer information in various forms (text, graphics, voice, and video) across the network to other users. Electronic mail (e-mail) is the most common example of how message services can be used.

Messaging services must coordinate the complex interactions between users, documents, and applications. For example, with messaging services, you can send an electronic note, attached to a voice-mail message, to another user on a network.

There are four main types of message services: electronic mail, workgroup applications, object-oriented applications, and directory services.

Electronic mail With e-mail, you can easily send a message to another user on the network or other networks, including the Internet.

Workgroup applications Workgroup applications process common sets of tasks among multiple users. There are two types of workgroup applications: workflow management applications and linked-object documents. Workflow management applications coordinate documents, forms, and notices. Scheduling programs are examples of workflow applications. Linked-object documents provide compound documents with links to separate files that are displayed inside the compound document but can be edited and updated separately. An example of a linked-object document would be an HTML document with links to objects such as graphic images, ActiveX components, and ODBC-compatible databases.

Object-oriented applications Object-oriented applications are programs that can accomplish complex tasks by combining smaller applications, called *objects*, into large tasks. Message services facilitate communication between these objects by creating agents that pass the data between objects.

Directory services Directory services is a network application that allows easy lookup of usernames and services. A typical directory service is organized into a hierarchical tree made up of many OUs (organizational units). An OU is a container that holds other objects that contain users, printers, and other services.

Compare a file-and-print server with an application server.

Because the tasks involved in a server-based network are typically complex and varied, the ability to add servers that are configured to perform specialized functions is a distinct advantage that client/server networks have over peer-to-peer networks.

There are three main types of specialized (dedicated) servers: file servers, print servers, and application servers.

With this objective, Microsoft introduces the concept that various special servers require different amounts of individual resources. Knowing the functions and resource requirements for different special servers is a prerequisite skill for performing server optimization. Server optimization is a skill covered in the Microsoft's Implementing and Supporting Windows NT Server 4.0 exam.

File Servers

File servers offer services that allow network users to share files. File services are the network applications that store, retrieve, and move data. When using network file services, users can exchange, read, write, and manage shared files and the data contained in them. File servers are designed specifically to support the file services for a network. Because of constant file access, file servers place great demands on their hard drives. These servers need to contain several fast hard drives.

Print Servers

An important feature of networking is the ability to share printers. *Print servers* manage and control printing on a network, allowing multiple and simultaneous access to printing facilities. The network operating system achieves this by using print queues, which are special storage areas where print jobs are stored and then sent to the printer in an organized fashion.

The following are characteristics of print servers:

- Allow users to share printers
- Allow you to place printers where they are convenient, not just near individual computers
- Achieve better workstation performance by using high-speed network data transfer, print queues, and print spooling
- Allow users to share network fax services

Application Servers

An *application server* is the "server" portion of what is known as a client/server application. With this type of application, the client portion or "front end" of the program runs on the client computer and provides the user interface to allow the user to interact with the server portion of the program. The server portion or "back end" of the program runs on an application server and provides most of the data processing for a particular task.

Having application servers allows for complex data processing tasks to be centralized on a high-performance computer for better performance, control, and manageability of the application and its data. A key to understanding client/server applications is to remember that processing is taking place on at least two computers cooperatively: the client computer and the server computer.

Application servers can be dedicated servers set up specifically for the purpose of providing application services, or they can serve multiple functions. A single server, for example, can provide file, print, communication, and database services.

NOTE

Examples of Microsoft application servers are Microsoft SQL Server and Microsoft Exchange Server.

Besides file, print, and application servers, it is not unusual to find other server types on a network. Below are a few examples.

Mail servers Processing for e-mail and other types of electronic messaging is centralized on this type of server. The hard drive for a mail server can store the different types of message data and can also run the software for routing the messages to the proper destination.

Fax servers These servers can provide the capability to share fax modems with everyone on the network and provide management over outgoing and incoming faxes. Incoming faxes can be routed to the proper recipient, in much the same way as e-mail.

Communication servers These server types handle data flow between the server's network and other networks. They often handle incoming and outgoing remote user and Internet traffic. Servers that handle access to centralized network resource databases (Windows NT domain controllers, for example) can also be considered communication servers. Communication servers that handle remote user access often contain a modem and provide a dial-up destination for remote users as well as a point at which access to the network by these users can be controlled.

Management servers A management server collects hardware and software inventory information, distributes and installs software, shares network applications, and troubleshoots hardware and software problems. A management server can provide centralized administration of computers in a WAN situation. Microsoft's Systems Management Server (SMS) is an example of a management server.

Compare a client/server network with a peer-to-peer network.

In a peer-to-peer network all computers are equal, and no computer has centralized control over resources such as files and printers. Each computer acts as a client using resources from other computers and as a server providing resources to other computers. A client/server network consists of dedicated servers that perform centralized functions such as database storage and retrieval, authorization of network permissions, and printing.

NOTE

Although Microsoft tests your knowledge about these two distinct network models, many network environments are actually a combination of client/server and peer-to-peer networks. Because of this real-world fact, Microsoft does include at least one question that recognizes their compatibility.

Networks are typically divided into one of two broad categories, client/server networks and peer-to-peer networks.

Client/Server Networks (Server-Based Networks)

Client/server or *server-based networks* use dedicated servers that provide resources to the rest of the network. These networks can grow or "scale" to fit the increased demand of a growing number of users and increasing resource requirements.

Client/server networks define how programs will distribute the processing load between a client computer and a server computer. The client/server approach is the most efficient way to provide database management and centralized file storage. In a client/server environment, all tasks are divided between a back end (the server), which stores and distributes data, and a front end (the client), which requests specific data from the server.

Client/server networks are characterized by the following:

- A client/server network can cover a much larger geographical area, from a one-building LAN to an international WAN.

- The cabling scheme can range from the very simple to very complicated.
- A client/server network can have specialized servers to meet specific services.
- Users typically are not involved in network administration; trained network administrators perform it.
- Security and performance are important issues.
- Growth of the network is typically planned for and implemented by adding new servers when necessary.
- Cost can range from low to extremely expensive depending on the resource, security, management, and connectivity requirements.
- Reduced network traffic.
- Centralized data and security.

Peer-to-Peer Networks

A *peer-to-peer* (or *peer*) *network* has no servers and uses the network to share resources among its independent peers. These networks are usually small networks made up of "peers" in which each node can be either a client or a server, or both. Peer networks are for file sharing, printer sharing, e-mail, tight budgets, and easy installation. They usually consist of two to ten users.

There are no servers in peer networks; users simply share disk space and resources, such as printers and faxes, as they see fit. Peer networks are organized into workgroups. Workgroups have very little security; there is no central logon process. If you have logged into one peer on the network, you will be able to use any resources on the networks that are not controlled by a specific password.

Access to individual resources can be controlled if the user who shared the resource requires a password to access it. The user cannot specify which users on the network can access the resource. Any users on the network who know the password can access the resource. Because there is no central security trust, you will have to know the individual password for each shared resource you wish to access. Peers are also not optimized to share resources. Generally, when a number of users are accessing resources on a peer, the user of that peer will notice significantly degraded performance.

Peer-to-peer networks are characterized by the following:

- Small geographical area covered (small office, single floor, or part of a floor)
- Simple cabling scheme (usually twisted-pair cable with a small hub)
- Users typically perform most administration duties themselves
- Performance is not an important issue
- Growth of the network is anticipated to be fairly limited
- There is no central administrator who sets network policies
- Inability of peers to handle as many network connections as servers
- Typically support fewer than ten people in organization
- The people in your organization are sophisticated computer users
- Security is not an issue, or the users can be trusted to maintain good security
- No extra investment in server hardware or software is required.
- Lower cost for small networks

Table 1.1 compares peer-to-peer and client/server networks according to several network characteristics.

TABLE 1.1: Server-Based / Peer-to-Peer Comparison

Network Characteristic	Peer-to-Peer	Server-Based
Size	Small geographical area	Any size geographical area
Cabling scheme	Typically twisted-pair wire with a small hub to connect the network. Coaxial cable is also used.	From simple to very complex utilizing cable and wireless media as well as leased WAN services
Who administers the network?	Users	Trained network administrators

TABLE 1.1 continued: Server-Based / Peer-to-Peer Comparison

NETWORK CHARACTERISTIC	PEER-TO-PEER	SERVER-BASED
Centralized administration capability	Not possible. Administration for each computer is performed on that computer.	Administered centrally
Security	Limited Share-level	High levels possible User-level
Network expansion capabilities	Limited	Fewer limitations
Cost	Inexpensive	From inexpensive to very expensive, depending on the requirements of the network

Compare user-level security with access permission assigned to a shared directory on a server.

Network security should provide protection from both intentional and unintentional acts that could prove harmful to the network and/or its shared information and other resources. Each network's security needs are different and range from very little need for security of any kind to a need for the most stringent levels of security.

This objective involves two different kinds of security models: share-level and user-level. Share-level security is only capable of assigning a password to a file or folder and lacks the flexibility for providing various levels of security, which is available with user-level security. In the real world, user-level security is used more often. As a network administrator you will need to know how to provide various levels of security for different networking situations, which can only be supplied by user-level security.

Microsoft considers this an important objective because it relates to concepts and skills involving the domain security accounts database. You will learn concepts in this section that are prerequisite to the concepts and skills needed for maintaining an accounts database, an objective in Microsoft's Implementing and Supporting Windows NT Server 4.0 exam.

Security Models

Implementing network access security is commonly done using one of two security models depending on the network's security needs:

- Share-level security
- User-level security

Share-Level Security (Password-Protected Network Shares)

The *share-level security* model requires that a separate password be assigned to each shared resource. Access to this resource can be achieved by providing the correct password. It does not make use of user authentication through a network logon. In addition, many systems provide share permissions that allow the owner of the resource to specify the type of access that is being provided. Common share permissions are read-only and full access. These permissions can be assigned based on the password provided, so that there could exist a read-only access password and a full access password to the same resource.

User-Level Security (Access Permissions with Authentication)

User-level security involves requiring an initial logon authentication by each user where a user ID and password will have to be provided. The user ID is stored in one large accounts database for the entire network; Windows NT calls this database SAM (Security Account Manager), and it is accessed through the User Manager for Domains utility. With user-level security, the user enters a name and password combination when logging on, and this logon determines access to shared resources. User-level security is a more extensive security model and provides a higher level of control over access rights and permissions.

Network resources under this security model have their own access lists. Users and groups of users can be placed in the access list for a resource and provided with only the necessary access permissions. In this way each resource can be protected individually with only appropriate users granted access. Windows NT implements this security model through logical collections of computers called *domains*. Within a domain, a computer known as a *domain controller* stores all account and security information and authenticates all logons.

The security advantage of peer-to-peer networking is that each user controls access to their own resources; the disadvantage is that they cannot differentiate among network users when they allow access to a resource. The security advantage of server-based networking is that each user is allowed access to only those resources that the user has the privilege to access. A disadvantage is that someone must centrally administer the security on the network.

In Windows 95, for example, the user of a computer can allow any other computer on the network to access a shared directory or device. The user can assign a password to the shared resource if some degree of security is required. However, the user cannot specify which users on the network can access the resource; any user on the network who knows the password can access the resource.

Another limitation of peer-to-peer (implemented in this manner) is that each shared resource that you wish to control access to must have its own password. The number of passwords to resources that you must remember can quickly grow unwieldy in a large network.

Under Windows 95 and Windows for Workgroups 3.11, File Manager or Explorer provides you with the ability to assign a password for each shared resource. Access to these resources is only granted when the user enters the appropriate password. Under Windows NT, all permissions are assigned to users and groups. When sharing a resource under Windows NT, you cannot specify an access password for that particular resource. Instead, you must specify the users and groups who can access the resource. Access permissions assigned to users and groups are defined by the domain.

A Windows 95 computer can be a client in a network with user-level security. User-level security allows you to grant access to Windows 95 resources for users and groups defined in a Windows NT domain security accounts database. Such a database can only be created on a Windows NT Server domain controller.

When a shared folder is referenced by another computer in a domain, the UNC (Universal Naming Convention) method is used for naming that shared resource. The UNC is a path name that includes the computer name and the name of the share. For example, a shared folder named *customers* residing on a computer named *Server-2* in a domain called *Alpha* is referenced as:

```
\\Server-2\customers
```

The domain name is not used in a UNC name. The computer name must be unique on the entire network, with no two domains or two computers having the same name. The shared folder name does not have to be unique. The same name can exist on different computers.

NOTE

A diskless computer is a computer without a floppy disk drive or hard drive. Only diskless computers can insure that no data can be removed from a network after access to that data has been granted.

You need to understand when a Windows NT workstation is considered to be participating in a peer-to-peer network and when it participates in a client/server network.

Logging on to a Windows NT Workstation as a Peer in a Peer-to-Peer Network

1. If a workstation is a member of a peer-to-peer workgroup, you will not be able to log on to a domain. You will only have the local logon option.
2. In the box labeled Domain, you will only see the name of the workstation and not any domain name. This option lets you log on by using the workstation's local account database, and it gives you access to the local computer.
3. As with any logon procedure, you need to type in a username and password for the local account.
4. After you have successfully logged on to the local workstation account, you are operating as a peer in a peer-to-peer network. If you try to access a shared folder on another Windows NT computer, that computer will ask you for a legal username and password specific to that computer's account database.

▶ Distinguish whether SLIP or PPP is used as the communications protocol for various situations.

This is the first of several objectives in this chapter that deal with network standards. *SLIP* (Serial Line Internet Protocol) and *PPP* (Point-to-Point Protocol) are two WAN protocol standards established by the network industry that provide remote access for dial-up users. Microsoft places a great deal of emphasis on this objective because it relates to remote access, specifically Windows NT's Remote Access Server (RAS) and its remote access client software. Remote access allows mobile users, such as accountants using laptop computers, the capability to dial-up and have easy access to network resources. Microsoft values its RAS and devotes several questions to it in the Implementing and Supporting Windows NT Server 4.0 exam. Because knowing when to use SLIP and PPP is a prerequisite concept to using RAS, there are many questions on SLIP and PPP in the Networking Essentials exam.

Remote Access Protocols

SLIP and PPP are two very common protocols used to transmit IP (Internet Protocol) packets over serial line and telephone connections, most often as part of a dial-up connection. Windows NT supports both SLIP and PPP from the client end using the Dial-Up Networking application. On the server end, Windows NT RAS (Remote Access Service) supports PPP only. Windows NT cannot act as a SLIP server.

PPP

PPP is a multiprotocol transport mechanism that can transport LAN protocols such as TCP/IP, IPX, AppleTalk, and other types of traffic simultaneously on the same connection. These LAN protocols will be discussed in Chapter 2.

In addition to offering enhanced security, PPP offers two methods for automating logins: Password Authentication Protocol (PAP) and Challenge-Handshake Authentication Protocol (CHAP).

NOTE

These authentication methods are covered in greater depth in Sybex's *MCSE: NT Server 4 Study Guide, 2nd edition* (1998).

In recent years, PPP has slowly replaced SLIP; PPP was developed as an improvement over SLIP.

SLIP

There are a number of drawbacks inherent with SLIP. *SLIP* is a simple protocol that functions at the Physical layer, whereas PPP is a much more enhanced protocol that provides Physical layer and Data Link layer service. Unlike PPP, SLIP does not have authentication or encryption. Instead, SLIP transmits data in plain text only.

SLIP does not allow the assignment of IP addresses. With SLIP, you must know both the IP address assigned to you by an Internet service provider (ISP) and the IP address of the remote system your computer will be dialing into.

SLIP is older than PPP and was originally used in Unix. This is why SLIP supports the TCP/IP transport protocol only.

WARNING

You can use SLIP or PPP with a client computer dialing into a server that uses SLIP or PPP. However, the Windows NT Remote Access Service only uses PPP. Consequently, a client accessing a Windows NT server can only be configured for using PPP.

Configuring a Windows NT Workstation with SLIP or PPP

By performing the following procedure, the differences between SLIP and PPP will be more evident. However, you will not be tested on these specific screen displays and inputs on the exam.

1. The client version of Windows NT RAS is called Dial-Up Networking, and it can be used for both SLIP and PPP.

2. You need to configure Dial-Up Networking to be able to have your computer connect to a WAN server or Internet provider when using a modem. You start by selecting Dial-Up Networking from the Accessories group on a Windows NT computer. The Dial-Up Networking application allows you to connect to a server as a dial-up client using SLIP or PPP.

3. After creating a New Phonebook Entry, a dialog box appears with several tabs. When you click the Server tab, you can choose SLIP or PPP as the dial-up server type.

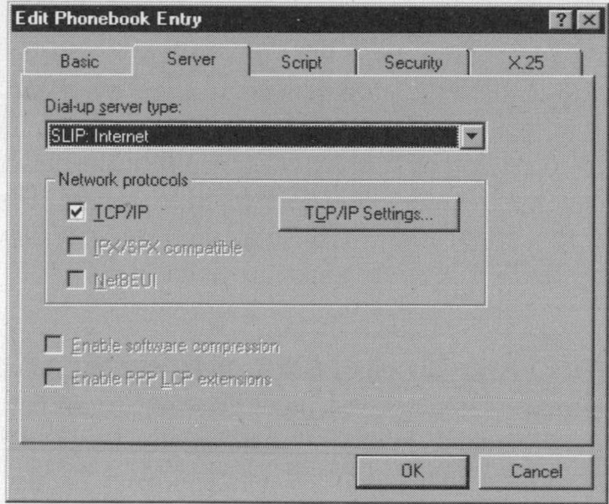

4. If you select SLIP, only TCP/IP appears as a transport protocol. Both IPX/SPX and NetBEUI are not available and are grayed out. The software compression option is also grayed out. All these options are available if you select PPP as the dial up server type.

Compare the implications of using connection-oriented communications with connectionless communications.

A connection-oriented communication link is a network connection that requires more network attention and resources, while a connectionless communication link is faster because of little overhead. This is an important distinction in networking, because most protocols can be classified as providing one or the other. The use of these terms helps to clarify how different protocols transfer data and what kind of data is best suited for each protocol. Microsoft's operating systems require that networking protocol suites be able to provide both connectionless and connection-oriented communications, because most transmissions on a network require both types of communications at the same time.

There are two ways that communications between computers can be arranged, connectionless and connection-oriented. Each method can be identified by the protocols being used.

Connectionless Communications

Connectionless communication systems optimistically assume that all data will get through, so there's no protocol overhead for guaranteed delivery or sequential packet ordering. This makes them fast. Error detection and correction are not handled by any of the network nodes; rather, the decision to retransmit is performed by higher order protocols closer to the actual application. User Datagram Protocol (UDP/IP) is an example of connectionless Internet transport protocol.

Connection-Oriented Communications

Connection-oriented systems pessimistically presume that some data will be lost or disordered in most transmissions. Connection-oriented protocols guarantee that transmitted data will reach its destination in sequential order by retaining the data and negotiating for retransmission until sequential data can be handed to higher level protocols. Connection-oriented mode relies on internal nodes within the network to detect errors and retransmit if necessary. This means that any application can rely on a connection-oriented transport to reliably deliver data as it was transmitted. The application is relieved of this task. Transmission Control Protocol (TCP/IP) is an example of a connection-oriented Internet protocol.

▶ Define the communication devices that communicate at each level of the OSI model.

The International Standards Organization (ISO) began developing the Open Systems Interconnections (OSI) reference model in 1977, and it has become the most widely accepted model for understanding network communication. The IEEE 802s are enhancements to the OSI model. The OSI model will help you identify the various parts that make up networks and understand how they all work together. It is the best tool available to people hoping to learn about network technology.

This section will present material that describes the function of each OSI layer, although the objective emphasizes connectivity devices and does not specifically state function.

NOTE

Each network device, its function, and an explanation of where the selected layer operates are presented in the objective on connectivity devices in Chapter 2.

The exam uses two types of questions involving the OSI model. There are questions about the function of each layer that leave out connectivity devices; other questions ask you to match connectivity devices to their appropriate OSI layer.

The OSI reference model describes how information makes its way from application programs (such as spreadsheets) through a network medium (such as wires) to another application program in another computer.

The seven layers of the OSI model are as follows:

- Physical
- Data Link
- Network
- Transport
- Session
- Presentation
- Application

The OSI Model at Work

Before discussing the individual layers, you need to know how the model works. Each computer on the network needs to have a protocol stack, or protocol suite. A *protocol stack* is a group of protocols arranged on top of each other as part of a communication process. An example of a protocol stack is TCP/IP, which is widely used for Unix and the Internet for two computers to communicate (the same protocol stacks must be running on each computer). These stacks are made of several different protocols that perform the functions of the various layers of the OSI reference model. Each protocol layer has a peer or equivalent on each computer so that communication can occur between systems.

When a message is sent from one computer to another, it travels down the layers of one computer and then up the layers of the other. This route is illustrated in Figure 1.5. Each layer can only communicate with the layer above and below it.

As the message travels down the first stack, each layer it passes through (except the Physical layer) adds a header. These headers contain pieces of control information that are read and processed by the corresponding layer on the receiving stack. As the message travels up the stack of the other machine, each layer strips the header added by its peer layer. (See Figure 1.6.)

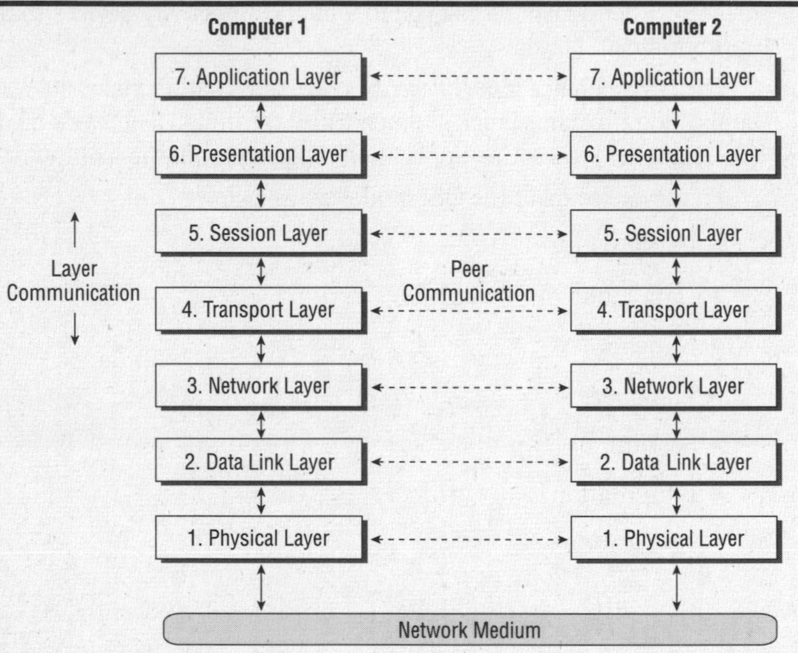

FIGURE 1.5: OSI reference model

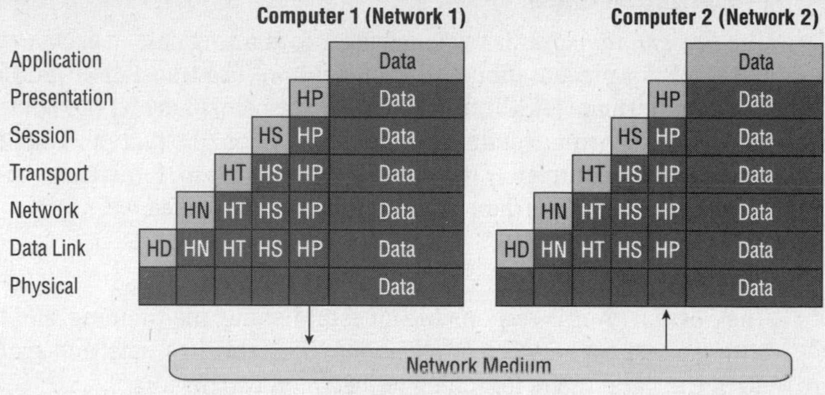

FIGURE 1.6: OSI model showing the building of packets

The Layers of the OSI Model

Now that the basic features of the OSI layered approach have been described, each individual OSI layer and its functions can be discussed in greater depth. Each layer has a predetermined set of functions it must perform for communication to occur.

There are several mnemonics that help candidates remember the names of the layers of the OSI model:

All **P**eople **S**eem **T**o **N**eed **D**ata **P**rocessing

People **D**on't **N**eed **T**o **S**ee **P**aula **A**bdul

Application Layer

The *Application layer* is responsible for giving applications access to the network. Examples of application layer tasks include file transfer, elec tronic mail services, and network management. The data units here are real user data. The *gateway* connectivity device can be used at this layer for sharing data between different networks.

NOTE

Although the term *gateway* can be applied to Transport through Application layers, gateways are more commonly used at the Application layer. The Networking Essentials exam may ask a question where either usage is the correct answer, but a single question will never have both together as possible choices.

Presentation Layer

The *Presentation layer* is responsible for formatting data in such a way that it is ready for presentation to the application. The translation of different character formats (ASCII/EBCDIC) is done here, plus text (de)compression, virtual terminal emulation, and encryption/decryption. The Presentation layer is completely responsible for translation, formatting, and the syntax selection. The data units on this layer are called *messages*.

Session Layer

The *Session layer* is responsible for establishing, maintaining, and terminating a session between applications. It establishes, sets, and synchronizes the parameters for dialogues between two devices.

This layer provides session control between the two computers by placing checkpoints in the data stream. If the transmission fails, only the data after the last checkpoint has to be retransmitted.

Transport Layer

The *Transport layer* is responsible for a guaranteed delivery of data. It provides a reliable service. It takes care of the setup, maintenance, and shutdown of virtual circuits, and it is responsible for fault detection, error recovery, and flow control. Data units on this layer are referred to as *datagrams*.

The boundary between the Session layer and the Transport layer can be thought of as the boundary between Application-layer protocols and lower-layer protocols. Whereas the Application, Presentation, and Session layers are concerned with application issues, the lower four layers are concerned with data transport issues. The Transport layer attempts to provide a data transport service that shields the upper layers from transport implementation details.

Network Layer

The *Network layer* is a complex layer that provides connectivity and path selection between two end systems that may be located on geographically diverse subnetworks. A *subnetwork*, in this instance, is essentially a single network cable (sometimes called a segment). Because of substantial geographic distance, many subnetworks can separate two end systems desiring communication. The Network layer uses routing protocols. Routing protocols select optimal paths through the series of interconnected subnetworks. Traditional Network-layer protocols then move information along these paths. The information is broken into messages that contain computer addresses. The Network layer is responsible for assigning addresses to these messages and translating logical addresses and names into physical addresses.

There is no guarantee of correct data delivery, because the Network layer does not provide error correction. The devices active on this layer are called *routers*, and the data units are referred to as *packets*.

Data Link Layer

The *Data Link layer* provides reliable transit of data across a physical link. In so doing, the Data Link layer is concerned with physical (as opposed to network, or logical) addressing, network topology, line discipline (how end systems will use the network link), error notification, ordered delivery of frames, and flow control.

The Data Link layer is responsible for the physical addressing of the data. This means its addressing is based on the true network interface card addresses, also known as MAC (media access control) addresses. The Data Link layer is also responsible for error notification, ordered delivery of frames, and flow control.

The IEEE has split this layer up into MAC and LLC (logical link control). The MAC sublayer is network-specific. Ethernet and Token Ring have different MAC protocols (CSMA/CD and Token passing) but the same LLC (IEEE 802.2). It's on the MAC part of the Data Link layer where bridges are active. The data units related to this layer are called *frames*.

Physical Layer

The *Physical layer* defines the electrical, mechanical, procedural, and functional specifications for activating, maintaining, and deactivating the physical link between end systems. Such characteristics as voltage levels, timing of voltage changes, physical data rates, maximum transmission distances, physical connectors, and similar attributes are defined by Physical layer specifications. Devices active on this layer are called repeaters. The units transmitted are bits (1 or 0).

Communication Devices and OSI Layers

Network devices enhance communications for LANs and WANs. These devices provide routing and rebuilding services along paths and junctions within a network. Chapter 2 will discuss in detail each device and how its operation contributes to a network's performance. For now you need to memorize the OSI layer at which each device operates. To fully understand each device's layer assignment, you may turn to the section, "Select the Appropriate Connectivity Devices for Various Token Ring and Ethernet Networks" in Chapter 2. Use Table 1.2 as a quick reference. Try memorizing each device and its associated OSI layer before further inquiry in Chapter 2.

TABLE 1.2: Quick Reference: Device/OSI Layer

Connectivity Devices and OSI Layers	
Device	**OSI Layer**
Repeater	Physical
Bridge	Data Link
Router	Network
Brouter	Network and Data Link
Gateway	Transport to Application

Describe the characteristics and purpose of the media used in IEEE 802.3 and IEEE 802.5 standards.

The IEEE 802 family of standards gathers and quantifies the capabilities and limitations of related network components such as various cables, different network adapter cards and their transceivers, matching cable connectors, and connectivity devices like hubs. The capabilities and limitations involve transmission speed, network access, cable distance, and allowable concentrations of computers. As a network administrator you will need to design and implement networks based on an organization's needs while accommodating these physical constraints. Knowing the specific elements of the 802 family of standards becomes a useful reference for this task.

The 802 standard defines network standards for the physical components of the network that include the interface card and the cable. The 802 standard is actually an enhancement to the Physical and Data Link layers of the OSI model and divides the Data Link layer into two sublayers, the Data Link MAC sublayer and the Data Link LLC sublayer.

The two most important members of the 802 family of standards are the 802.3 Ethernet standards and the 802.5 Token Ring standards. Table 1.3 illustrates the 802 family of standards.

TABLE 1.3: IEEE 802 Specifications

IEEE 802 SPECIFICATIONS	
802.1	Internetworking
802.2	LLC (logical link control)
802.3	CSMA/CD – Ethernet
802.4	Token Bus LAN
802.5	Token Ring LAN
802.6	MAN (metropolitan area network)
802.7	Broadband Technical Advisory Group
802.8	Fiber-Optic Technical Advisory Group
802.9	Integrated Voice / Data Networks
802.10	Network Security
802.11	Wireless Networks
802.12	Demand Priority Access LAN, 100 Base VG

IEEE 802.3 (Ethernet)

Xerox Corporation's Palo Alto Research Center (PARC) developed Ethernet in the 1970s. Ethernet was the technological basis for the IEEE 802.3 specification, which was initially released in 1980. Shortly thereafter, Digital Equipment Corporation, Intel Corporation, and Xerox Corporation jointly developed and extended the Ethernet specification into the IEEE 802.3 specifications. Today the terms Ethernet and IEEE 802.3 are basically the same.

Ethernet is a bus- or star-based topology that uses Baseband signaling and the Carrier Sense with Multiple Access with Collision Detection (CSMA/CD) to arbitrate network access. CSMA/CD allows only one computer to use the network at a time. Before sending data, CSMA/CD stations "listen" to the network to see if it is already in use. If it is, the station wishing to transmit waits. If the network is not in use, the station transmits. A collision occurs when two stations listen for network traffic, "hear" none, and transmit simultaneously. In this case, both transmissions are damaged, and the stations must retransmit at some later time. Backoff algorithms determine when the colliding stations retransmit. CSMA/CD stations can detect collisions, so they know when they must retransmit.

Ethernet LANs are broadcast networks. In other words, all stations see all frames, regardless of whether they represent an intended destination. Each station must examine received frames to determine if the station is a destination. If so, the frame is passed to a higher protocol layer for appropriate processing.

Ethernet Cabling Systems

The five commonly used Ethernet cabling systems are 10Base2, 10Base5, 10BaseT, 10BaseFL, and 100BaseT.

10Base5 (Thicknet) Ethernet

The original wiring used for Ethernet is called *Thicknet*, or 10Base5. The 5 stands for its maximum length, 500 meters (about 1650 feet). The coaxial (coax) cable is marked every 2.5 meters (8.25 feet) for connection points so you don't try to connect devices closer than 2.5 meters—a shorter distance degrades the signal. A transceiver and a transceiver cable attach each computer on a Thicknet network. The cabling used for Thicknet is a 50-ohm, 0.4 inch-diameter coaxial cable, which is stiffer than the transceiver cable.

10Base5 (Thicknet) Ethernet has the following specifications:

- Maximum segment length: 500 meters (1650 feet)
- Maximum taps: 100
- Maximum segments: 5
- Maximum segments with nodes: 3
- Minimum distance between taps: 2.5 meters (8.25 feet)

- Maximum repeaters: 4
- Maximum overall length with repeaters: 2.5 kilometers (1.5 miles)
- Maximum AUI drop cable length: 50 meters (165 feet)
- Topology: Bus
- Cable type: 50-ohm Thicknet
- Connector type: N-Series with vampire taps
- Media access method: CSMA/CD
- Transmission speed: 10Mbps

You normally use a device called a *vampire tap* to connect new connections to the Thicknet. To do so, use a tool that drills a small hole into the coaxial cable. Then attach the tap and tighten it down, with its connector, into the hole. Although in some cases you can tap coaxial cable with users up and running, you should try to do it after working hours. A mistake can short the center conductor with the shielding and take down the entire segment.

The tap includes a *transceiver*, a device that handles transmission data signal generation and reception. A transceiver cable usually comes with a transceiver unit. A male and a female N-Series type connector is mounted on either end of the cable, along with transceiver connectors and slide locks to lock the cable to the network interface card. Thicknet uses N-Series barrel connectors to attach two trunk cables. Thicknet cables are terminated with 50-ohm N-Series terminators. At both ends of the cable, you must install a terminator to complete the electrical circuit and to cut down on signal reflections. Figure 1.7 shows some components of Thicknet Ethernet.

NOTE

The advantages of Thicknet cabling are few for today's networks, but many Thicknet networks are still in use and are reliable. Most books on networking no longer cover Thicknet.

TIP

The exam covers very little on Thicknet. You might get one question on Thicknet, if any. You need to know the term Thicknet and the 500m maximum length.

NOTE

The 10Base5 wiring specification allows you to increase the length of the overall network by using *repeaters*, which are devices that pick up signals and repeat them to another segment of the cable. You may use a maximum of four repeaters on one network, with only three of the segments populated with nodes. Thus, the overall length of a network that implements repeaters to extend the length is 2.5 kilometers (1.5 miles).

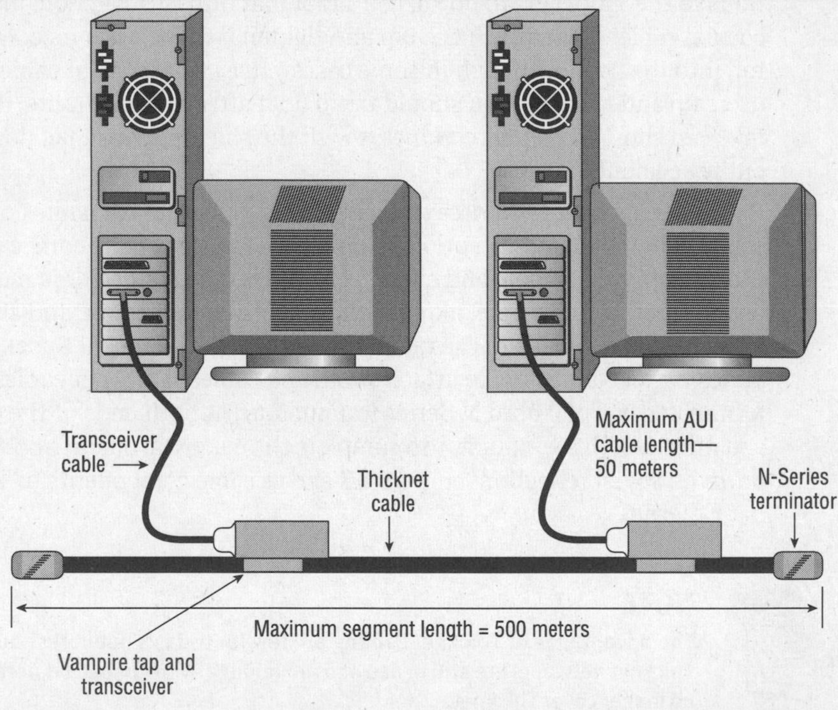

FIGURE 1.7: Thicknet cable, transceiver, transceiver cable, N-Series terminator

10Base2 (Thinnet Coax) Ethernet

When *Thinnet coax* (10Base2) cable was introduced, it quickly became a popular choice of network cabling. Because of its low cost, it is sometimes referred to as Cheapernet.

10Base2 has the following specifications:

- Maximum segment length: 185 meters
- Maximum segments: 5
- Maximum segments with nodes: 3
- Maximum repeaters: 4
- Maximum devices per segment: 30
- Maximum overall length with repeaters: 925 meters (3052.5 feet)
- Topology: Bus
- Cable type: 50-ohm Thinnet – RG-58 A/U and RG-58 C/U
- Connector type: BNC
- Media access method: CSMA/CD
- Transmission speed: 10Mbps

The specification for Thinnet is 50-ohm RG-58 A/U or RG-58 C/U coaxial cable. RG-58 A/U is the most widely used type. You should avoid using RG 59 cable, which is intended for television signals. Another type of cable you may see is RG-58U. Installing this type of wiring is a mistake because it does not meet the IEEE specification for 10Base2.

You use BNC (British Naval Connector) connectors for Thinnet, along with the T connectors required to connect to the BNC female connectors on the LAN card. As with 10Base5 (Thicknet), each end of the cable must have a terminator. Only one end of the cable must be grounded. (See Figure 1.8.)

The 10Base2 wiring specification differs significantly from 10Base5 in that the transceiver is built into the LAN card itself and is not a device you must attach to the cable. A cable connecting the T connector to the workstation, called a *pigtail*, cannot be used with this standard. The T connector must connect directly to the back of the card in a daisy-chain fashion. If it doesn't connect this way, the network connections will fail.

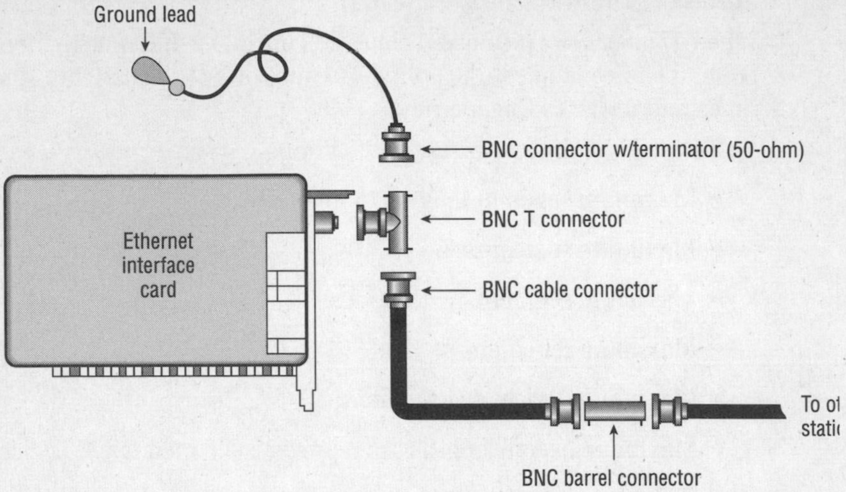

FIGURE 1.8: BNC T connector, BNC terminator, BNC barrel connector, BNC cable connector, ground

As with 10Base5, you can use up to four repeaters on a network, with only three of the segments populated with nodes. You can mix 10Base2 and fiber-optic cabling by using a fiber/Thinnet repeater.

NOTE

There is a rule called the "5-4-3" rule, which states that an Ethernet network can have up to five segments with four repeaters where only three segments can have computers. The 5-4-3 rule does not apply to UTP or fiber-optic cable. With UTP, hubs act as repeaters and you cannot have two devices separated by more than four hubs.

The disadvantages of Thinnet include the high cost compared to UTP cable and the fact that the bus configuration makes the network unreliable. If any node's cable is broken, the entire segment, and probably the entire network, will be affected. Nevertheless, because it was the most economical solution for a long time, Thinnet is used in many existing installations.

10BaseT (Twisted-Pair) Ethernet

The use of *unshielded twisted-pair* (*UTP*) cable is now a well-established trend in Ethernet network wiring schemes. UTP costs less and is more flexible than 10Base5 or 10Base2 cabling. The IEEE 802.3 subcommittee created the specification for UTP in the 1980s. Do not substitute shielded twisted-pair (STP) cable for UTP; the IEEE 10BaseT specification is for UTP only. STP is discussed in Chapter 2.

10BaseT (twisted-pair) Ethernet has the following specifications:

- Maximum segments: 1024
- Maximum segments with nodes: 1024
- Maximum segment length: 100 meters (330 feet)
- Maximum nodes per segment: 2
- Maximum nodes per network: 1024
- Maximum hubs in a chain: 4
- Topology: Star
- Cable type: UTP (categories 3-5)
- Connector type: RJ-45
- Media access method: CSMA/CD
- Transmission speed: 10Mbps

10BaseT is wired as a star, which means that each device has its own set of wires connected directly to a hub. Although the physical topology of 10BaseT is a star, its logical topology is a bus, giving you the advantages of a star wiring scheme and a bus in one specification. 10BaseT is easy to troubleshoot because problems on one segment of wiring usually do not affect the other segments. (Each node uses its own separate segment.)

You can also isolate a device that is causing problems by just disconnecting its cable from the hub. Some hubs have built-in management capabilities that will report errors or problems, as well as allow you to disconnect remotely the devices from the hub. These types of hubs are known as *intelligent hubs*.

The connection to the hub and the LAN cards is made with an RJ-45 connector. You can also connect 10BaseT to a DIX connector or an AUI connector by using a transceiver or twisted-pair access unit (TPAU). Thinnet connections on LAN cards can also be used with special transceiver devices.

UTP cable is classified in categories defined by the Electrical Industries Association. Categories 1 and 2 are voice-grade cable. Categories 3, 4, and 5 are data-grade. Be sure to ask the vendor for a performance specification sheet when you purchase category 5 cable to be sure it meets the specifications for your network. (See Figure 1.9.)

There are also Teflon-coated versions of UTP cable for areas that require plenum-rated wire. The cable is light and flexible, which makes it easy to pull through during construction. The cable should be 22-, 24-, or 26-gauge AWG (American Wire Gauge), with an impedance (resistance based on signal frequency) of 85 to 110 ohms at 10MHz.

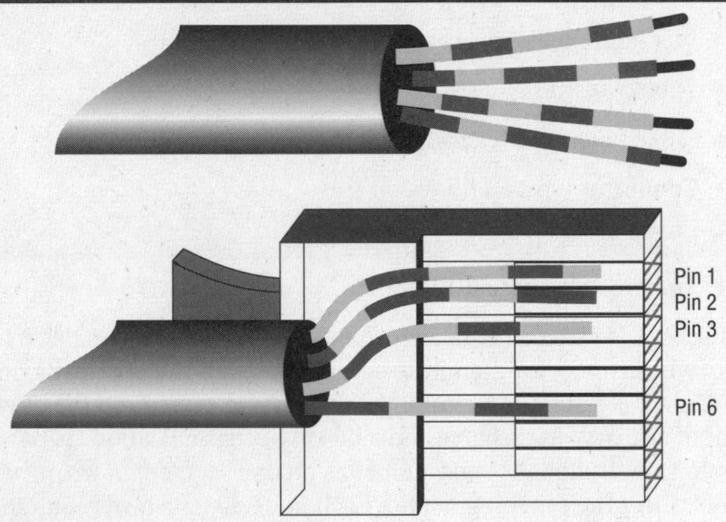

FIGURE 1.9: Unshielded twisted-pair cable and RJ-45 connector

10BaseFL Ethernet

10BaseFL (10Mbps data rate, Baseband signaling over a fiber-optic cable) uses light rather than electricity to transmit Ethernet frames. 10BaseFL is a star-wired network because it requires a network hub (also called a *concentrator*) to receive the light signal from each network station and send the same signal to all stations. The hub can be either active, with electronics to detect and retransmit the signal, or passive, with optics to split the light and reflect or guide it out to all the network stations.

10BaseFL Ethernet has the following specifications:

- Maximum segments: 1024
- Maximum segments with nodes: 1024
- Maximum segment length: 2000m
- Maximum nodes per segment: 2
- Maximum nodes per network: 1024
- Maximum hubs in a chain: 4
- Topology: Star
- Cable type: Fiber-optic
- Connector type: Distinct
- Media access method: CSMA/CD
- Transmission speed: 10Mbps

100Mbps Ethernet

For some networking applications, a 10Mbps data rate is not enough. Two competing standards extend traditional Ethernet to 100Mbps:

- 100VG-AnyLAN
- 100BaseT Ethernet, also known as Fast Ethernet

100VG-AnyLAN combines elements of traditional Ethernet and Token Ring and supports both Ethernet and Token Ring packets. It uses demand priority access method and not CSMA/CD. You can use 100VG-AnyLAN over categories 3, 4, and 5 twisted-pair and fiber-optic cable.

100BaseT, also known as Fast Ethernet, is simply regular Ethernet run at a faster data rate over category 5 twisted-pair cable. 100BaseT uses CSMA/CD protocol in a star wired bus 10BaseT.

100BaseT has been specified for three media types:

- 100BaseT4 (four pairs of categories 3, 4, or 5 UTP or STP)
- 100BaseTX (two pairs of category 5 or STP)
- 100BaseFX (two-strand fiber-optic cable)

Token Ring IEEE 802.5

IBM's Token Ring implementation has been the most popular implementation of the IEEE 802.5 standard. Token Ring is more complex than Ethernet. It uses a physical star topology but is logically a ring. Workstations connect to the network by means of individual cables that connect to a Multistation Access Unit (MSAU) or Controlled Access Unit (CAU). These devices act like hubs.

The main purpose of Token Ring cabling is to connect the workstation's LAN card to the MSAU and connect other MSAUs with each other.

In a ring topology, each computer is connected to the next computer, with the last one connected to the first. Only a computer holding a token (a special packet) can send data. If the computer does not have data, it sends the token to the next computer. In this way, every computer has equal access to the network.

Every computer is connected to the next computer in the ring and each computer retransmits what it receives from the previous computer. The data flows around the ring in one direction. Each computer retransmits what it receives and is not subject to the signal loss problems a bus experiences. There is no need to terminate the ring because there is no end to the ring.

All computers on a Token Ring network are responsible for monitoring the token passing process. When a computer detects a serious error, it sends a signal called a *beacon* onto the network. The beaconing process is used to isolate errors on the network.

Token Ring has the following specifications:

- Cable type: UTP, STP, or fiber-optic
- Maximum MSAUs: 33
- Maximum nodes: 260
- Maximum distance between node and MSAU: 45.5 meters (150 feet) for UTP cable; up to 100 meters (330 feet) for STP or fiber-optic
- Maximum patch cable distance connecting MSAUs: 45.5 meters for UTP cable; 200 meters (650 feet) with STP; 1 kilometer (.6 miles) for fiber-optic cable
- Minimum patch cable distance connecting MSAUs: 2.5 meters (8 feet)

- Maximum cumulative patch: 121.2 meters (400 feet) with UTP cable; cable distance connecting all MSAUs: fiber-optic cabling can span several kilometers
- Transmission speed: 4 or 6Mbps

TIP

Other 100BaseT characteristics depend on the type of cable used. The exam only asks about its transmission speed, 100Mbps.

Explain the purpose of NDIS and Novell ODI network standards.

The NDIS and the ODI standards act as the common foundation for all other major protocol stacks including TCP/IP, IPX, and NetBEUI/NetBIOS. These standards take form as drivers that act as middlemen between protocol stacks and various network adapter cards. If the objective is studied by itself, it has limited scope. The topic is introduced again within the objective on protocols in Chapter 2. You can refer to this objective as you study the material in this section.

NDIS (Network Device Interface Specification) and *ODI* (Open Driver Interface) were created to allow multiple network drivers to be bound to multiple transports; this allows you to use both TCP/IP and IPX on a single network adapter or to use four network adapters all with the same TCP/IP stack.

The drive interface you use is determined by the network operating system you select. Windows NT networking products use NDIS rather than ODI. For most other network products, such as Novell NetWare, you will be using ODI.

NDIS defines the communications interface between the MAC sublayer and the driver. The purpose of NDIS is to allow NICs (Network Interface Cards) to use multiple protocols simultaneously. NDIS was developed by Microsoft; ODI was developed by Apple, Novell, and other major networking companies. ODI eliminates the need for custom drivers for every protocol and NIC combination.

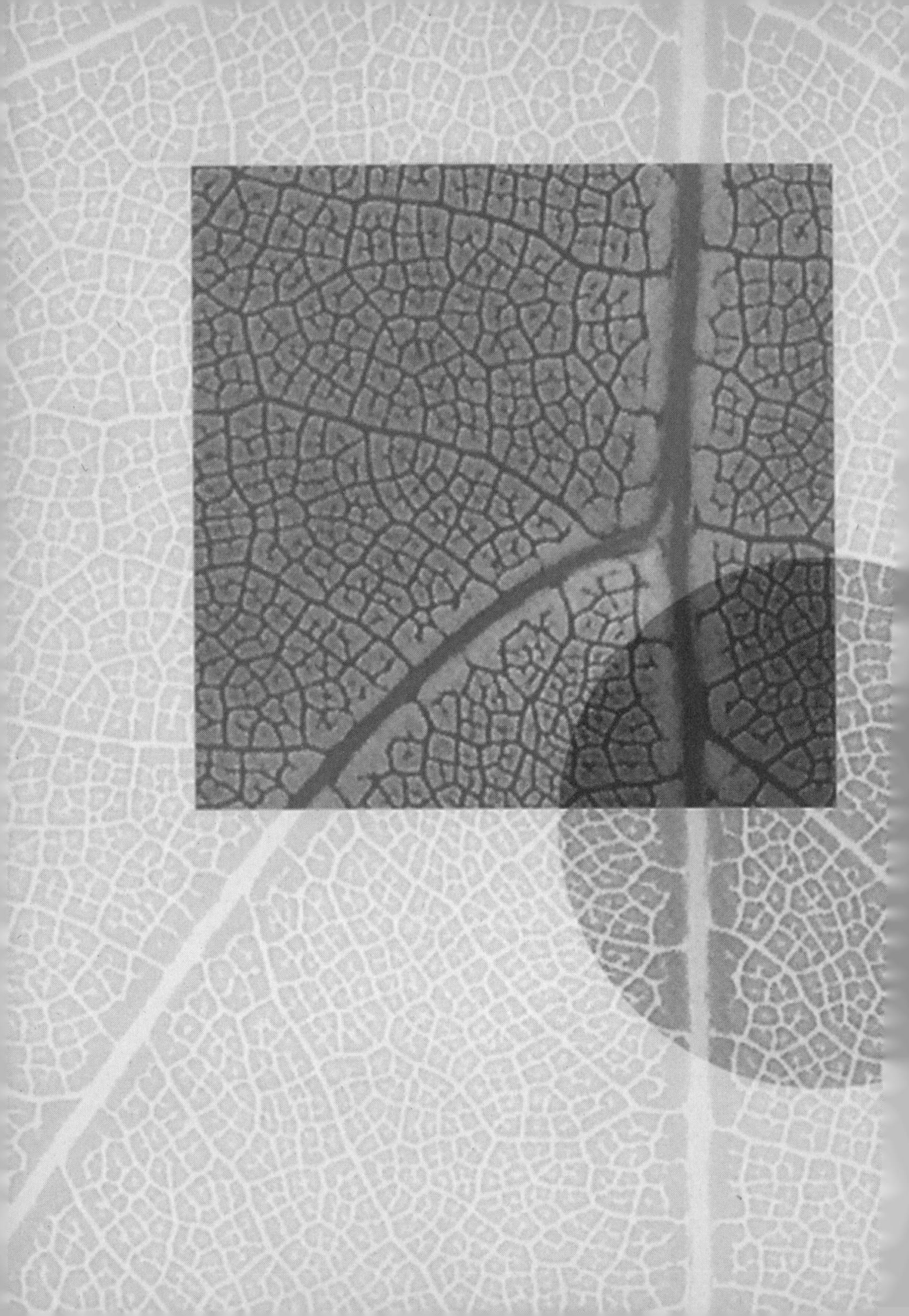

Chapter 2

Planning

Network design depends on the selection of several network elements: type of media (cable), type of topology, types of protocols, and types of connectivity devices. When planning a network, choices in each area will have an effect on all the network needs. For example, selecting a bridge instead of a router will limit your ability to extend the network in the future. In addition, the design of a network must consider all these ingredients simultaneously, because the choice of each ingredient is interdependent on the selection of all other components. For example, if a star topology were selected for a network, then the connectivity device would most likely have to be a hub, which would necessitate the use of category 5 unshielded twisted-pair cable.

Adapted from *MCSE Exam Notes: Networking Essentials*
by Glenn Madow and James Chellis
ISBN 0-7821-2291-4 320 pages $19.99

Select the appropriate media for various situations.

Media choices include:

- Twisted-pair cable
- Coaxial cable
- Fiber-optic cable
- Wireless

Situational elements include:

- Cost
- Distance limitations
- Number of nodes

When planning a network, the most important element to consider is the choice of transmission media. At least eighty to ninety percent of all network installation problems involve wiring. The importance of knowing about various cables and wireless methods cannot be stressed enough. There are many cable types and wireless media to choose from, and several influential variables need to be considered including distance limitations, environmental interference, node capacity, and cost.

This section focuses on information needed to make appropriate decisions for selecting media types. In so doing, the section concentrates on the situational elements of cost, bandwidth capacity, node capacity, installation and cabling scheme, attenuation, and EMI resistance. Currently, the most widespread media type for connecting networks is cable. There is a vast array of cable types to choose from; the following three types connect the majority of networks today:

- Coaxial cable including thin (Thinnet) and thick (Thicknet)
- Twisted-pair, including shielded (STP) and unshielded (UTP)
- Fiber-optic

Evaluation Criteria

In considering these different cable types, it is useful to have some method of comparing and classifying their characteristics:

Cost Rather than trying to give a cost per foot, the focus will be the cost of one type of cable relative to the other types.

Bandwidth capacity Capacity or bandwidth, for the purposes of this discussion, is the number of bits per second (bps) or, more commonly, megabits per second (Mbps) that can be accommodated by the cable.

Node capacity Two specifications for node capacity are discussed, the maximum number of nodes per segment and the maximum number of nodes per network.

Installation and cabling scheme In this category, how easy the cable is to install and the method used to cable a network using the given cable type are considered. Some of the standard physical topologies, such as bus and star, are introduced to describe the cabling schemes. In addition, the section will cover any additional hardware necessary, such as hubs that are required to connect network computers. Again, relative comparisons with the other cable types will be used.

Attenuation Attenuation refers to the tendency of a signal to weaken as it travels through a transmission medium. Signal attenuation is one of the reasons that network cabling standards specify maximum cable lengths for the various types of cables.

EMI resistance Because signals are transmitted through cables using electricity, they are susceptible to interference from outside electromagnetic sources such as lightning, fluorescent lights, electric motors, or any other power source strong enough to interfere with the electrical signal traveling through the cable. Some cable types have shielding incorporated into the cable to increase resistance to interference.

A type of interference known as *crosstalk* will also be considered, where applicable. Crosstalk involves interference produced by adjacent cables and can be a problem where a large number of cables have been run very close together in a big bundle.

Coaxial Cable

Coaxial cable, commonly called *coax*, has two conductors that share the same axis. A solid copper wire (or stranded wire) runs down the center of the cable. This wire is surrounded by a plastic foam insulation, which is surrounded by a second conductor, a wire mesh tube, metallic foil, or all three. The wire mesh protects the wire from EMI (electromagnetic interference). It is often called a shield. A tough plastic jacket forms the cover of the cable, providing protection and insulation.

Coaxial cable comes in different sizes. It is classified by size (RG) and by the cable's resistance to direct or alternating electric currents (measured in ohms) also called impedance. The important thing is that you must use cable that is rated at the proper impedance for the devices that will be attached to it.

There are two types of coaxial cable:

- Thin coax (often called Thinnet)
- Thick coax (often called Thicknet)

Thin Coax (Thinnet)

Thinnet is lighter and more flexible than Thicknet and is inexpensive and easy to install. The type of Thinnet used in networks is a type of RG-58 cable that has a 50-ohm impedance. It is approximately 0.25 inches thick. Figure 2.1 is an example of thin coax.

FIGURE 2.1: Thin coax (Thinnet)

Thick Coax (Thicknet)

Thicknet is about twice the diameter of Thinnet (0.5 inches). The type of Thicknet used in networks is a type of RG-11 or RG-8 cable that has a 50-ohm impedance. Sometimes referred to as Standard Ethernet cable, it is often used as a backbone for connecting Thinnet LANs into a larger network. See Figure 2.2 for an example of thick coax.

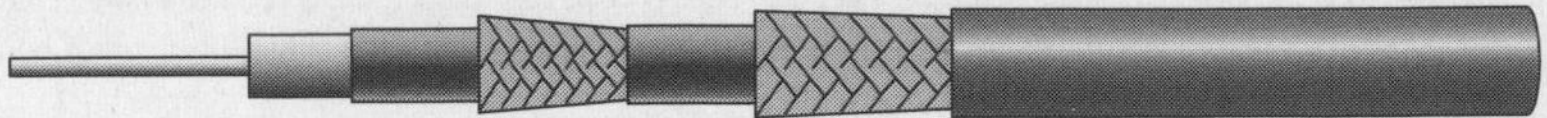

FIGURE 2.2: Thick coax (Thicknet)

As you might suspect, Thicknet is more rigid, heavier, and harder to work with than Thinnet, and it is also more expensive.

Coaxial cable has the following characteristics:

Cost Coax is relatively inexpensive. The cost for thin coaxial cable is less than STP or category 5 UTP; thick coaxial is more expensive than STP or category 5 UTP but less than fiber-optic cable.

Bandwidth capacity A typical data rate for today's coaxial networks is 2.5Mbps for ARCnet to 10Mbps for Ethernet, although the potential is higher. Coaxial cable's bandwidth potential increases as the diameter of the inner conductor increases.

Node capacity The specified maximum number of nodes on a Thinnet segment is 30 nodes; on a Thicknet segment it is 100 nodes.

Installation It's easy. With a little practice, installing the connectors becomes simple and the cable is resistant to damage. Coaxial cable is most often installed either in a device-to-device daisy-chain (Ethernet) or a star (ARCnet). Coaxial cable is used to connect computers together in a bus topology. Each computer is connected to the next in a serial fashion. The interface may involve 'T' connectors or vampire clamps (or taps). Coaxial cable must be grounded and terminated. Grounding completes the electrical circuit. Termination keeps the signals that reach the end of the cable from reflecting and causing interference.

Attenuation Because it uses copper wire, coaxial cable suffers from attenuation, but much less so than twisted-pair cable. Coaxial cable runs are limited to a couple thousand meters. Thinnet cable is rated for a maximum cable run of about 185 meters (about 607 feet). To run a longer segment risks attenuation to the point of signal loss. With a thicker copper core, Thicknet suffers less attenuation and has a maximum segment length of 500 meters (about 1650 feet).

EMI resistance Coaxial cabling is still copper wire and vulnerable to EMI—and eavesdropping. However, the shielding provides much better resistance to EMI's effects. It is considered to be much more resistant to EMI than unshielded twisted-pair cable and comparable to shielded twisted-pair cable.

Fire codes and coaxial cable grades Coaxial cable comes in two grades, polyvinyl chloride (PVC) and plenum. Which grade of cable you use depends on where you are going to run the cable. PVC cable has its outer jacket and insulation layer constructed of polyvinyl chloride. This grade of cable is light and flexible and is useful for routing cable in exposed areas. It should not, however, be used to run cable through the space in buildings called the plenum.

The *plenum* is the narrow empty space in many buildings between the suspended ceilings, structure, and floor above. It is usually used to circulate return air through the building. Fire codes specify that PVC cable cannot be used in this area because when PVC cable burns it produces poisonous gases and, because the cable was routed through the plenum, these gases would be transported to the rest of the building.

If cable is to be routed through the plenum, then plenum-grade cabling should be used. This grade of cable is constructed of fire resistant materials that produce a minimum amount of smoke when burned, which reduces poisonous fumes. Plenum cable can be used in the plenum area and in vertical runs within a wall without having to use conduit. On the downside, plenum-grade cabling is more expensive than PVC cable.

NOTE

All the cable types discussed come in both PVC and plenum grades.

Table 2.1 outlines some coaxial cables commonly used in networking.

TABLE 2.1: Common Coaxial Cables

Cable	Description
RG-8 and RG-11	Thicknet cable
RG-58 /U	Solid copper core (not good for networks)
RG-58 A/U	Stranded copper core (used for Thinnet networks)
RG-58 C/U	Military version of RG-58 A/U (used for Thinnet networks)
RG-59	Cable TV cable
RG-62	A cabling option for ARCnet networks

Twisted-Pair Cable

In its simplest composition, twisted-pair cable consists of two insulated strands of copper wire twisted around each other. There are two types of twisted-pair cable, unshielded twisted-pair (UTP) and shielded twisted-pair (STP).

Unshielded Twisted-Pair (UTP)

Unshielded twisted-pair (*UTP*) cable consists of a number of twisted pairs with a simple plastic casing. UTP is commonly used in telephone systems. There is a tendency for each wire to produce interference, called *crosstalk*, in the other. To decrease the amount of crosstalk and outside interference, the wires are twisted. This allows the emitted signals from one wire to cancel out the emitted signals from the other, and protects them from outside noise. Figure 2.3 shows an example of UTP.

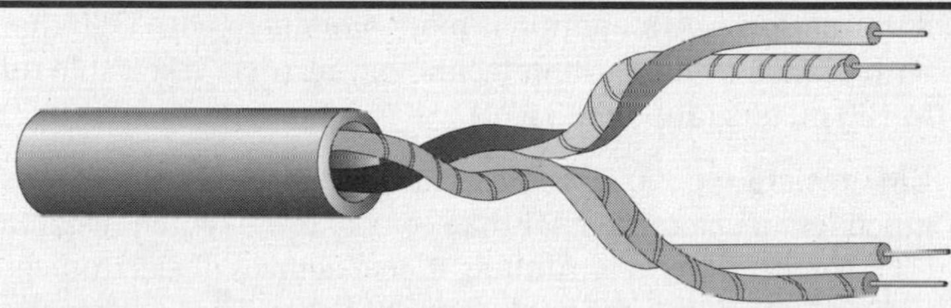

FIGURE 2.3. UTP cable

NOTE

Crosstalk is a potential problem with all types of cabling. Signals from one line can be mixed with signals from an adjacent wire if there is not proper shielding. UTP cables are most susceptible to crosstalk. STP uses a woven copper braid jacket with foil wraps between and around the wire pairs to reduce crosstalk. Each RG-58 A/U and RG-58 /U coaxial cable has one layer of foil insulation and one layer of braided metal shielding and, therefore, is less susceptible to interference than twisted-pair cables.

UTP has the following characteristics:

Cost UTP is the least costly cable type discussed in this chapter. Because many new buildings are pre-wired with UTP cable, the cabling cost of setting up a network using UTP is greatly reduced.

Bandwidth capacity Common UTP data rates range from 4Mbps to 10Mbps, which is currently very common. A 100Mbps data rate using category 5 UTP is quickly becoming the standard for networks where high performance is preferred.

Node capacity There is only one node per segment leading to a hub. An entire network can have 1024 nodes.

Installation and cabling scheme UTP cabling is very easy to work with. It is light, flexible, and the connectivity devices (connectors and hubs) are easy to configure. UTP cables are connected to network devices using RJ-45 connectors. These connectors are similar to RJ-11 phone connectors, but are larger and contain eight wires (four pairs) instead of four (two pairs) for the RJ-11. The RJ-45 connector is not compatible with the RJ-11 telephone jack.

Attenuation Attenuation is more prominent with UTP than with coaxial cable. Current technology restricts UTP cable runs to 100 meters (about 328 feet).

EMI resistance UTP cable lacks a shield and is, therefore, much less resistant to EMI than coaxial cable. When installing UTP you need to avoid running it near sources of electromagnetic interference such as fluorescent lights. The "noisier" the environment in which the cable is run, the shorter the effective cable lengths will be. UTP has the same susceptibility to electronic eavesdropping as coaxial cable. Electronic eavesdropping devices can detect and pick up radiated signals from the cable if they are in close proximity to the cable.

NOTE

Most new network installations are using category 5 UTP cable because it can support transmission speeds up to 100Mbps. UTP should be your first choice when choosing your network media.

Shielded Twisted-Pair (STP)

Shielded twisted-pair (STP) cable is similar in construction to UTP except that the twisted pairs are enclosed in a woven copper and foil wrap shield. See Figure 2.4 for an example of STP cable.

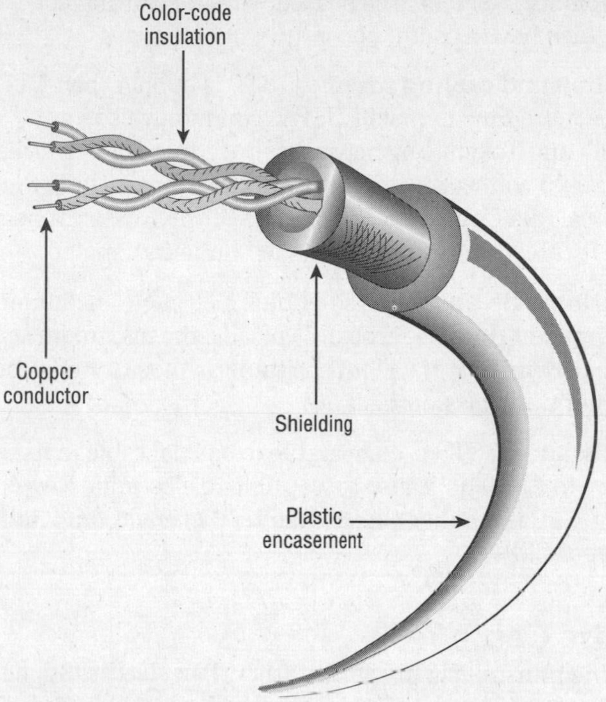

FIGURE 2.4: STP cable

The shielding is used in STP for the same purpose it is used in coaxial cable—to reduce the effects of electromagnetic interference. The shielding allows clearer signals with higher transmission rates over longer distances. STP shielding is more bulky than UTP. STP cable has been categorized by IBM into several types for specifying different STP characteristics. IBM Type 1 cabling is the most common STP used.

STP has the following characteristics:

Cost STP cable is more costly than either UTP or Thinnet cable. However, it is less costly than Thicknet cable or fiber-optic cable.

Bandwidth capacity STP is capable of transmission speeds of up to 500Mbps. Current implementations using STP typically do not exceed 155Mbps. The most common transmission rate currently in use is 16Mbps on IBM Token Ring networks.

Node capacity STP is usually used with Token Ring networks, which have a useful upper limit of 260 nodes.

Installation and cabling scheme STP is bulkier than UTP and takes more time to install. STP is commonly used in AppleTalk and Token Ring networks. Both types of networks can use RJ-45 connectors. Older connector types include the Apple LocalTalk Connector and the IBM Type 1 data connector. STP is cabled using a physical star configuration.

Attenuation Because of its shielding, STP cable encounters less attenuation than UTP cable. Typically, the maximum segment lengths for STP are about the same as those for UTP, but with higher transmission rates.

EMI resistance STP is comparable to coaxial cable in its resistance to EMI and is also susceptible to electronic eavesdropping. STP is a better choice than UTP in environments with a lot of EMI.

Fiber-Optic Cable

Fiber-optic cable transmits light signals rather than electrical signals. It is much more efficient than other network transmission media. Fiber-optic cable uses light to transmit digital data signals. There are two "strands" of fiber, one strand for each direction of transmission. Figure 2.5 shows an example of fiber-optic wire.

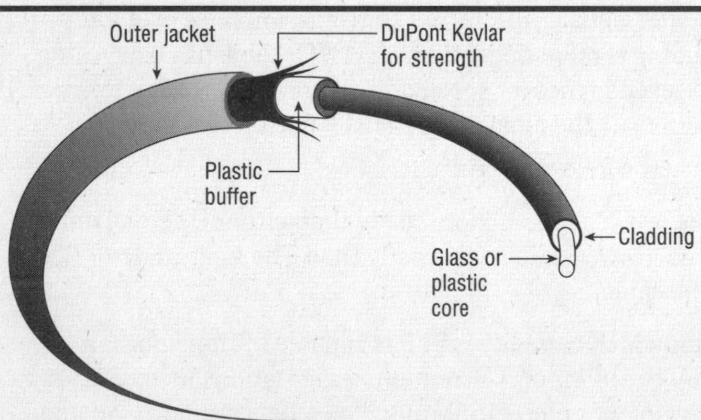

FIGURE 2.5: Fiber-optic cable

Fiber-optic has the following characteristics:

Cost Fiber-optic cable is slightly more expensive than copper cable, but costs are falling. Associated equipment costs can be much higher than for copper cable, making fiber-optic networks far more expensive.

Bandwidth capacity Because it uses light, which has a much higher frequency than electricity, fiber-optic cabling can provide extremely high bandwidths. Current technologies allow data rates from 100Mbps to 2Gbps.

Node capacity Because only two computers can be connected together by a fiber-optic cable, the number of computers in a fiber-optic network is not limited by the cable. The number of computers is limited by the hub(s) that connects the cables together. In an Ethernet network the useful upper limit is around 75 nodes on a single collision domain. Fiber-optic networks using other protocols, such as FDDI, usually use the fiber cable as a backbone between slower LANs.

Installation Fiber-optic cable is more difficult to install than copper cable. Every fiber connection and splice must be carefully made to avoid obstructing the light path. Also, the cables have a maximum bend radius, which makes cabling more difficult.

Attenuation Fiber-optic cable has a much lower attenuation than copper wires, mainly because the light is not radiated out in the way the electromagnetic field is radiated from the copper cables. The cables can carry signals over distances measured in kilometers. Fiber-optics suffer very little from attenuation but have instead a different problem—chromatic dispersion.

EMI resistance Fiber-optic cable is not subject to electrical interference. In addition, it does not leak signals, so it is immune to eavesdropping. Because it does not require a ground, fiber-optic cable is not affected by potential shifts in the electrical ground, nor does it produce sparks. This type of cable is ideal for high-voltage areas or in installations where eavesdropping could be a problem.

TIP

Using fiber-optic cable offers several advantages such as tremendous bandwidth, the ability to go great distances, and no interference from EMI or EMF; however, it is difficult to install and is more expensive.

Wireless Networks

Wireless technology has not progressed to the point of replacing cabled media because of high prices and low bandwidth. However, there are situations where wireless connections are justified.

Types of wireless networks:

- Local area networks (LANs)
- Extended local area networks
- Mobile computing

Local Area Networks (LANs)

There are various transmission methods used with LANs:

- Infrared
- Laser-based
- Narrow-band radio
- Spread-spectrum radio

Infrared Devices utilizing infrared transmissions operate in much the same way as a television remote control. An infrared beam is used to carry signals from device to device. Devices using infrared signals to communicate must be relatively close together, usually within about 100 feet, and can operate with data transmission rates up to 10Mbps.

There are four types of infrared networks: line-of-sight, scatter infrared, reflective infrared, and broadband optical telepoint.

Line-of-sight This method requires the sending and receiving devices be in clear sight of one another.

NOTE

The expression *line-of-sight* should not be confused with *point-to-point connections*. Point-to-point connections differ from the other types of wireless connectivity in that they transmit data between only two devices instead of communicating between several network devices. An example of a point-to-point connection would be transferring data between a laptop computer and a desktop computer using infrared technology or transferring data between a computer and a printer.

Scatter infrared The infrared transmissions are broadcast, with any reflection off walls and ceilings, before eventually hitting the receiver. The effective area is limited to about 100 feet and the data transmission rate is relatively slow because of the signal bouncing.

Reflective infrared In this case, computers transmit toward a central hub transceiver, which redirects the transmissions toward the receiving computer.

Broadband optical telepoint This version of infrared technology provides broadband technology. This category is capable of achieving transmission rates comparable to those of cabled networks.

Laser-based This wireless technology uses high-powered laser beams to transmit a signal if a line-of-sight can be established.

Narrow-band radio This method uses single-frequency radio to broadcast, which is similar to the way broadcasts are made from a radio station. The broadcast range is approximately 5000 square feet. Line-of-sight positioning is not required because the signal can bounce off walls and buildings. However, the signal cannot go through steel or other heavy walls. Transmission rates are relatively slow at less than 5Mbps.

Spread-spectrum radio The spread-spectrum uses a technique that spreads signals over a range of frequencies. This method uses a method known as *frequency hopping* where the transmission switches or hops among several frequencies, broadcasting over each for a specified time period. The receiving device is aware of the hop timing and can correctly receive the transmission. Because the message is spread among multiple frequencies, it is difficult to eavesdrop unless the hopping sequence is known. Typical transmissions speeds for spread-spectrum radio are up to 250Kbps. The effective transmission distances range from 400 feet indoors to two miles outdoors.

Extended Local Area Networks

This use of wireless technology allows for the connection of one LAN to another without having to make a long cable run, such as between two buildings. An example of this technology is a wireless LAN bridge. Wireless bridges typically utilize spread-spectrum radio to provide a connection between devices.

For making connections that involve more distance than is possible with the wireless bridge, a long-range wireless bridge can provide bridging for distances up to 25 miles.

Mobile Connections

This technology makes it possible to build wireless mobile networks and involves utilizing telephone carriers and public communications services to establish connectivity. This type of communication enables traveling users with laptop computers or personal digital assistants (PDAs) to connect to the network and process e-mail, exchange files, and perform other standard networking tasks.

There are three ways mobile connections can be established: packet-radio connections, cellular network connections, and satellite-based connections.

NOTE

Transmission rates for mobile connections such as these typically range from 8Kbps to 19.2Kbps.

Packet-radio connections This mobile system breaks the transmission into network-style packets that are transmitted to satellites to be broadcast to the destination.

Cellular network connections This mobile networking method uses cellular phone technology to send and receive cellular digital packet data (CDPD) over the cellular phone network. This option offers fast communication speeds.

Satellite microwave With this method, the use of microwave technology establishes a satellite to ground link, allowing mobile devices to communicate through the satellite uplink.

NOTE

Microwave communication technology can play a role in wireless LANs and connecting LANs, as well as mobile connections. Microwave communication falls into two categories, terrestrial microwave links (used between two buildings) and satellite microwave links (used between satellites and ground links).

Select the appropriate topology for various Token Ring and Ethernet networks.

A network's topology directly affects its capabilities and the way the network is managed. Although real-world network designs can be very complex, they all stem from four basic topologies: bus, star, ring, and mesh. The choice among topologies depends on reliability, redundancy, scalability, responsiveness to troubleshooting, and cost.

The way in which connections are made is called the *topology* of the network. Network topology specifically refers to the physical layout of the network, especially the locations of the computers and how the cable is run between them. It is important to select the right topology for how the network will be used. Each topology has its own strengths and weaknesses. Four of the most common topologies are bus, star, ring, and mesh.

Bus Topology

The bus topology is often used when a network installation is small, simple, or temporary. Figure 2.6 illustrates an example of a bus topology. A bus is one wire with many computers attached to it. It usually relies on CSMA/CD to regulate network traffic.

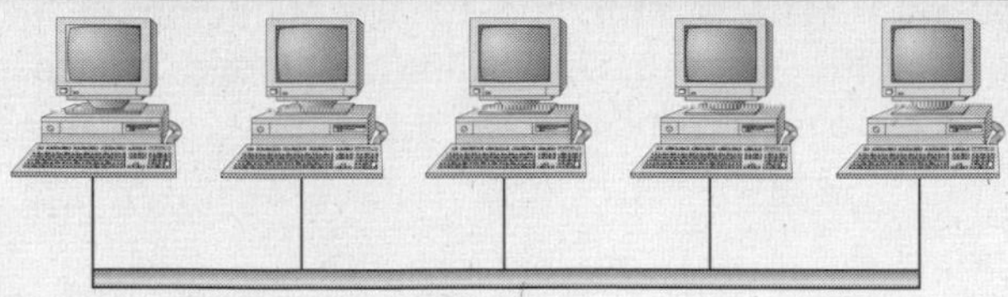

FIGURE 2.6: Bus topology

There are several advantages to a bus topology:

- The bus is simple, reliable (in very small networks), easy to use, and easy to understand.
- The bus requires the least amount of cable to connect the computers together and is, therefore, less expensive than other cabling arrangements.
- It is easy to extend a bus. Two cables can be joined into one long cable with a BNC barrel connector, making a longer cable and allowing more computers to join the network. A repeater can also be used to extend the bus; a repeater boosts the signal and allows it to travel a longer distance.

There are also several disadvantages to a bus topology:

- Heavy network traffic can slow a bus considerably. Because any computer can transmit at any time and computers on most bus networks do not coordinate with each other to reserve times to transmit, a bus with a lot of computers can spend a lot of its bandwidth with computers interrupting each other instead of communicating.
- Each barrel connector weakens the electrical signal, and too many prevent the signal from being correctly received all along the bus.
- It is difficult to troubleshoot a bus. A cable break or loose connector will cause reflections and bring down the whole network.

Star Topology

In a star network, all cables run from the computer to a central location, where they are all connected by a device called a hub. Figure 2.7 illustrates a star topology. Stars are used in concentrated networks, where the endpoints are directly reachable from the central location.

There are several advantages to a star topology:

- It is easy to modify and add new computers to a star network without disturbing the rest of the network. You simply run a new line from the computer to the central location and plug it into the hub. When the capacity of the central location hub is exceeded, you can replace it with one that has a larger number of ports to plug lines into.
- The center of the star is a good place to diagnose network problems. Intelligent hubs also provide for central monitoring and management of the network.
- Single computer failures do not necessarily bring down the whole star network. The hub can detect a network fault and isolate the problematic computer or network cable and allow the rest of the network to continue functioning.

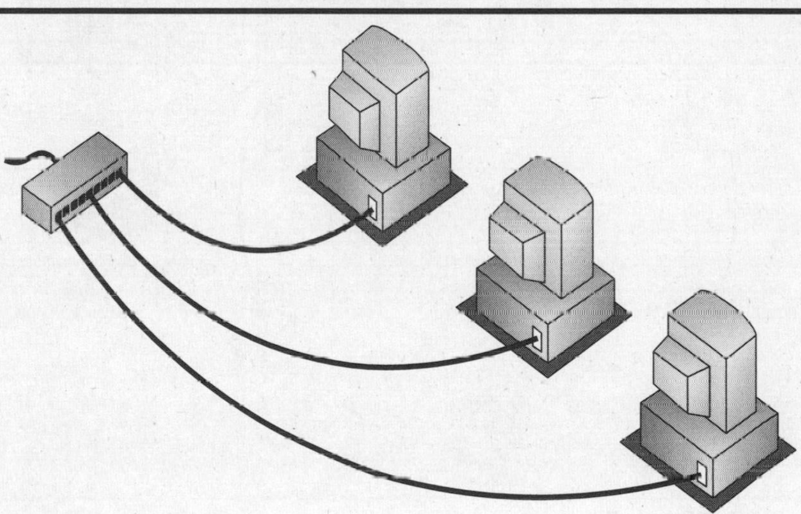

FIGURE 2.7: Star topology

NOTE

The star topology is the easiest in which to diagnose network problems.

There are also several disadvantages to a star topology:

- If the central hub fails, the whole network stops.
- It costs more to cable a star network because all network cables must be pulled to one central point, requiring more cable than other network topologies.

Ring Networks

In a ring topology, each computer is connected to the next computer with the last one connected to the first. The ring topology provides equal access for all computers on the network. A ring network usually needs more cabling than a bus network. See Figure 2.8 for an example of a ring topology.

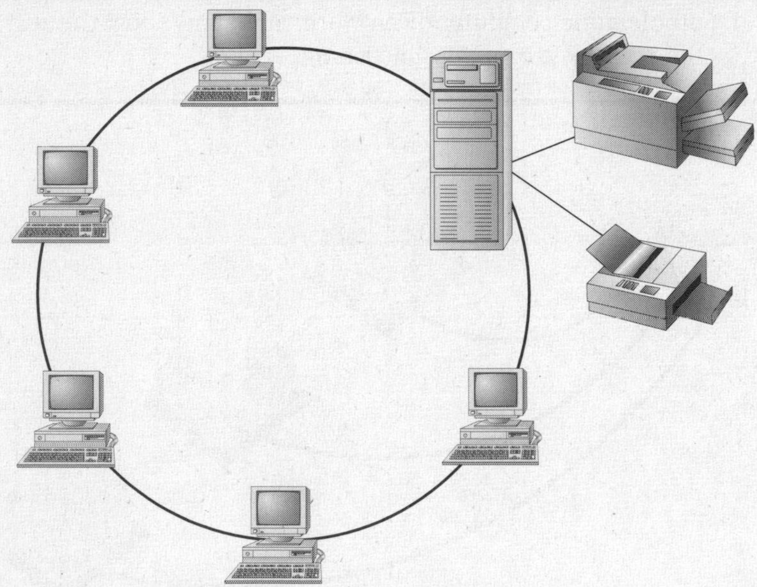

FIGURE 2.8: Ring topology

There is one major advantage to a ring topology:

- Because every computer is given equal access to the token, no one computer can monopolize the network.

There are several disadvantages to a ring topology:

- Failure of one computer on the ring can affect the entire network.
- It is difficult to troubleshoot a ring network.

- Adding or removing computers disrupts the network.
- More cabling is needed than in a bus network.

Physical Mesh Topology

A mesh topology is a network where computers are linked to each other through intermediate nodes with redundant paths. Between any two computers are a number of other nodes not arranged in a straight line. Because the nodes are scattered, alternative paths can be created that eventually connect the two computers. If you are using a WAN and routers to search among multiple active paths to determine the best path for a particular moment, then you need to use a mesh topology. Figure 2.9 is an example of a mesh topology. The Internet is an example of a large mesh topology.

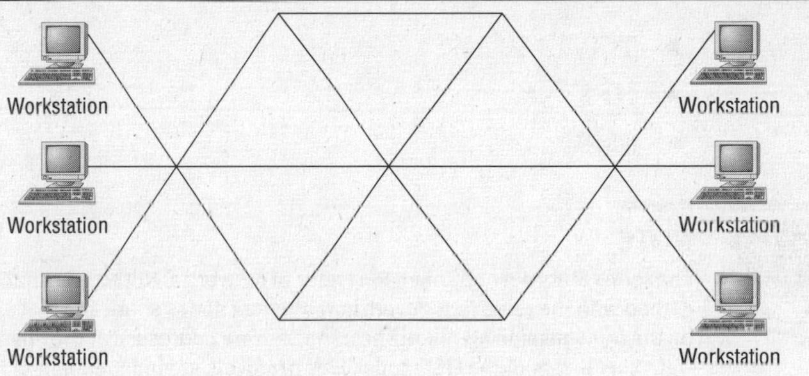

FIGURE 2.9: Mesh topology

There are several advantages to a mesh topology:

- The major advantage of the mesh is fault tolerance.
- Communication channel capacity is guaranteed.
- It is easy to troubleshoot.

There are two main disadvantages to a mesh topology:

- Difficulty of installation and reconfiguration.
- Cost of maintaining redundant links.

Select the appropriate network and transport protocol or protocols for various Token Ring and Ethernet networks.

Protocol choices include:

- DLC
- AppleTalk
- IPX
- TCP/IP
- NFS
- SMB

NOTE

The terms Ethernet and Token Ring refer to network architectures that are concerned with the rules that govern how network nodes share and place packets on the transmission medium. These matters are addressed at the Physical and Data Link layers of the OSI model. LAN protocols are independent of Network architectures and are associated with higher layers, the Network layer to Application layer. Each protocol mentioned in this chapter can be used with both architectures unless otherwise cited.

Protocols are rules that enable two nodes on a network to communicate. These rules are incorporated into small software programs that perform communication links. Each protocol has a particular function and that function is associated with the OSI reference model. Protocols are grouped together in stacks and work together to accomplish the entire communication process as represented by all the OSI layers. Like anything else involving networking, utilizing protocols requires decisions. Selecting which protocol stack to use in a particular situation requires knowing the advantages and disadvantages of each protocol stack. Knowing how to install and configure protocols is an important survival skill for any network administrator. Recognizing each protocol's purpose is a necessary skill for future network design and troubleshooting. As a related skill, you need to know how packets and addresses work with protocols. Protocols prepare messages by using packets or datagrams. These packets use network addressing and computer name resolution to find their way from computer to computer.

NOTE

Microsoft only mentions a sampling of what the candidate needs to know in each objective. There are many questions in the exam that include several other protocols, and some of these protocols are more important than the ones listed in the objective, as far as the exam appears. Two examples are NetBIOS and NetBEUI.

When two computers wish to exchange information over a network, there are several components that must be in place before the data can actually be sent and received. Of course, the physical hardware must exist, which typically includes network interface cards (NICs) and wiring of some type to connect them. Beyond this physical connection, however, computers also need to use a protocol that defines the parameters of the communication between them. In short, a protocol defines the rules that each computer must follow so that all the systems in the network can exchange data.

Application Protocols

Application protocols work at the upper layer of the OSI model. They provide application-to-application interaction and data exchange. Popular application protocols include:

APPC (Advanced Program-to-Program Communication) IBM's peer-to-peer

SNA A protocol, mostly used on AS/400s

FTAM (File Transfer Access and Management) An OSI file access protocol

X.400—A CCITT A protocol for international e-mail transmissions

X.500—A CCITT A protocol for file and directory services across several systems

SMTP (Simple Mail Transfer Protocol) An Internet protocol for transferring e-mail

FTP (File Transfer Protocol) An Internet file transfer protocol

SNMP (Simple Network Management Protocol) An Internet protocol for monitoring networks and network components

Telnet An Internet protocol for logging on to remote hosts and processing data locally

Microsoft SMBs (Server Message Blocks) Client shells or redirectors

NCP (Novell NetWare Core Protocol) Used for Novell client shells or redirectors

AppleTalk and AppleShare Apple's networking protocol suite

AFP (AppleTalk Filing Protocol) Apple's protocol for remote file access

DAP (Data Access Protocol) A DECnet file access protocol

Transport Protocols

Transport protocols provide for communication sessions between computers and ensure that data is able to move reliably between computers. They are not concerned with the specific software programs that generated the request for information. Specific application file formats and data types are dealt with by application protocols. Popular transport protocols include:

TCP Transmission Control Protocol for guaranteed delivery of sequenced data

SPX Part of Novell's IPX/SPX (Internetwork Packet eXchange/Sequential Packet eXchange) protocol suite for sequenced data

NetBEUI NetBIOS establishes communication sessions between computers

ATP (AppleTalk Transaction Protocol), NBP (Name Binding Protocol) Apple's communication session and data transport protocols

Network Protocols

Network protocols provide what are called link services. These protocols handle addressing and routing information, error checking, and retransmission requests. Network protocols also define rules for communicating in a particular networking environment such as Ethernet or Token Ring. Popular network protocols include:

IP The Internet Protocol for packet forwarding and routing

NWLink The Microsoft implementation of the IPX/SPX protocol

NetBEUI A network (and transport) protocol that provides data transport services for NetBIOS sessions and applications

DDP (Datagram Delivery Protocol) An AppleTalk data transport protocol

DLC (Data Link Control) A Network layer protocol used mainly by Hewlett-Packard network attached printers and IBM mainframes

TCP/IP Protocol Suite

One of the most popular protocols in use today is *TCP/IP*, which stands for Transmission Control Protocol/Internet Protocol. Applications developed for TCP/IP generally use several of the protocols in the suite. Program applications communicate with the top layer of the protocol suite. The top-level protocol layer on the source computer passes information to the lower layers of the stack, which in turn pass it to the physical network. The physical network transfers the information to the destination computer. The lower layers of the protocol stack on the destination computer pass the information to higher layers, which in turn pass it to the destination application.

The advantages of TCP/IP include:

- Broad connectivity among all types of computers and servers
- Direct access to the Internet
- Strong support for routing
- Support for SNMP (Simple Network Management Protocol)
- Support for DHCP (Dynamic Host Configuration Protocol)

- Uses hierarchical network naming for effective internetwork addressing

The disadvantages of TCP/IP include:

- Difficulty of setup
- Relatively high overhead to support connectivity and routing
- Slower speed than NWLink and NetBEUI

Each TCP/IP protocol functions at a particular layer and is independent of the other protocols. However, each protocol expects to receive certain services from the protocol beneath it, and each protocol provides certain services to the protocol above it.

Application Layer Protocols

Below are the more important TCP/IP protocols arranged by layer, starting with higher layers first.

SNMP (Simple Network Management Protocol) A TCP/IP protocol for monitoring Windows NT networks. You must install SNMP before you can use TCP/IP performance counters in Windows NT Performance Monitor.

Telnet A protocol that is mostly used to provide connectivity between dissimilar systems including Unix and VMS, PC and VMS, and PC and routers. Telnet is also used for accessing special sites on the Internet.

FTP (File Transfer Protocol) Provides file transfer service.

SMTP (Simple Mail Transfer Protocol) A protocol for routing e-mail messages. SMTP uses TCP and IP to route the mail messages across the internetwork.

Transport Layer—TCP and UDP Protocols

The Transport layer of the TCP/IP protocol suite consists of two protocols, the User Datagram Protocol (UDP) and the Transmission Control Protocol (TCP). UDP provides an unreliable connectionless delivery service to send and receive messages from specific processes on the sending and receiving nodes. TCP adds reliable byte stream-delivery services on top of the IP datagram delivery service.

TCP For applications that must send or receive large volumes of data, unreliable datagram delivery can become troublesome. The TCP/IP suite of protocols avoids this problem by using TCP, a reliable byte stream-delivery protocol. TCP is known as a connection-oriented protocol. In other words, before two programs can begin to exchange data they must establish a "connection" with each other. Once the connection has been established, both sides may send and receive data until the connection is closed.

The TCP protocol uses full-duplex transmission, which means two data streams can flow in opposite directions simultaneously. Thus, the receiving application can send data or control information back to the sending application while the sending application continues to send data. The TCP protocol gives each segment a sequence number. At the receiving end of the connection, the application checks successive sequence numbers to ensure that all the segments are received and processed in the order of the sequence numbers. The receiving end sends an acknowledgment to the sender for the segments received.

UDP Unlike TCP, UDP does not present data as a stream of bytes, nor does it require that you establish a connection with another program in order to exchange information. Data is exchanged in discrete units called datagrams, which are similar to IP datagrams. The sender and receiver must administer their own application protocol on top of UDP. When using UDP, much of the work that TCP performs, such as creating checksums, acknowledging the receipt of packets, and retransmitting lost packets, must be performed by the application itself. Because of this, UDP doesn't have the overhead that TCP has and is much faster than TCP. UDP is the solution when speed is most important, or when the number of packets sent over the network must be kept to a minimum.

Network Layer Protocols

Following are five network layer protocols.

IP (Internet Protocol) When a system sends data over the network using the Internet Protocol, it is sent in discrete units called datagrams, also commonly referred to as packets. A datagram consists of a header followed by message data. Packet delivery is not guaranteed by this service. A packet can be interrupted, duplicated, or lost on the way to its destination. The service is connectionless because all packets are transmitted independently of any other packets, not in a stream.

An IP datagram has a header section containing the sender's and the receiver's IP addresses and a data section. The IP address for a node is a logical address and is independent of any particular hardware or network topology. It is a 4-byte (32-bit) numeric value that identifies both a network and a local host or node (computer or other device) on that network. The 4-byte IP address is usually represented in dotted decimal notation. Each byte is represented by a decimal number, and dots separate the bytes: for example, 129.47.6.17.

An important function of this layer is the routing function of IP. Internetworks are typically connected in a maze-like structure with routers as intermediate nodes and the physical networks between them. When there is more than one unique route to choose from, the best route must be selected for the packets to reach the destination address.

ICMP (Internet Control Message Protocol) ICMP packets contain information about failures on the network: inoperative nodes and gateways, packet congestion at a gateway, and so on. The IP software, rather than the application, interprets an ICMP message, then takes the appropriate action with respect to the ICMP message independently of the application. Because an ICMP message might need to travel across several networks to reach its destination, it is encapsulated in the data portion of an IP datagram. ICMP is also used to test connectivity between two nodes. The originating node sends an ICMP echo request, or ping, and waits for an ICMP echo response from the destination.

ARP (Address Resolution Protocol) Each node has a physical address for the specific hardware device that connects it to a network. The physical addresses have different forms on different networks, and they are assigned in different ways. For instance, a physical address on an Ethernet network is a 6-byte numeric value, such as 08-00-14-57-69-69. An

IP address is mapped to a physical address using the ARP on broadcast networks such as Ethernet, Token Ring, or ARC-net. Nodes using the TCP/IP protocols translate the destination IP addresses to the physical addresses of MAC hardware to send packets to other nodes on the network. Each time the node broadcasts an ARP request and receives a response, it creates an entry in its address resolution cache. The entry maps the IP address to the physical address.

RIP (Routing Information Protocol) RIP is a distance-vector routing protocol, which means it periodically broadcasts routing tables across the internetwork. This is similar to NetWare's RIP. RIP can cause bottlenecks in WANs and is being replaced by OSPF.

OSPF (Open Shortest Path First) OSPF is a link-state routing protocol. It was developed to create less overhead than RIP.

NOTE

Physical addresses are also called media access control (MAC) addresses.

TCP/IP steps for passing packets between two computers:

1. The Application layer passes a stream of bytes to the Transport layer on the source computer. The Transport layer divides the stream into TCP segments, adds a header with a sequence number for that segment, and passes the segment to the Internet (IP) layer. The checksum is computed.
2. The IP layer creates a packet with a data portion containing the TCP segment. The IP layer adds a packet header containing source and destination IP addresses. The IP layer also determines the physical address of the destination computer or intermediate computer on the way to the destination host. It passes the packet and the physical address to the Data Link layer. The checksum is computed again.
3. The Data Link layer transmits the IP packet in the data portion of a Data Link frame to the destination computer. If the destination is an intermediate computer or node, then step 3 happens again until the final destination is reached.

4. At the destination computer, the Data Link layer discards the Data Link header and passes the IP packet to the IP layer. The IP layer checks the IP packet header. If the checksum contained in the header does not match the checksum computed by the IP layer, it discards the packet.
5. If the checksums match, the IP layer discards the IP packet header and passes the TCP segment to the TCP layer. The TCP layer checks the sequence number to determine whether the segment is the correct segment in the sequence.
6. The TCP layer computes a checksum for the TCP header and data. If the computed checksum does not match the checksum transmitted in the header, the TCP layer discards the segment. If the checksum is correct and the segment is in the correct sequence, the TCP layer sends an acknowledgment to the source computer.
7. The TCP layer discards the TCP header and passes the bytes in the segment just received to the application. The application on the destination computer receives a stream of bytes, just as if it were directly connected to the application on the source computer.

Other TCP/IP Protocols and Related Services

Following are additional protocols and options to consider.

DHCP (Dynamic Host Configuration Protocol) The DHCP is a mechanism that automates the assignment and reassignment of IP addresses to network computers. DHCP comes with Windows NT and uses a database to provide IP addresses to computers for a set period of time. This is called a lease and is used to economize the use of IP addresses in a TCP/IP network. DHCP is capable of dynamically assigning IP addresses to computers and reassigning IP addresses for computers that are moved between subnets.

Three main benefits of DHCP are automated reconfiguration of TCP/IP information for computers that are moved between subnets, automatic configuration of WINS and DNS server addresses, and improved control of IP addresses through a lease-management algorithm.

Subnet mask Subnet masks enable the user of a single TCP/IP network address to split the network into multiple subnets. Without a subnet mask each broadcast message sent from a computer (host) on this network would have to be processed by every other computer on the same subnetwork. The 32-bit values are broken into 8-bit groups called octets to form a subnet mask. Setting the first eight bits to all ones creates the subnet mask 255.0.0.0 and signifies that the first octet of an IP address (102.54.94.97) will indicate the network number (102 in this case), and that the last three octets will indicate the host number (54.94.97). If another computer on the same subnet wants to send a message to this computer, it must have the same subnet mask. If the second computer has a different subnet mask, it might not be able to communicate with the first computer. For example, if the second computer has a subnet mask of 255.255.0.0, it will evaluate the IP address 102.54.94.97 as having a network address equal to 102.54 and a host address equal to 94.97. This is the wrong host address for the first computer and messages sent to this computer using the network address 102.54 and the host address 94.97 will never get to this computer.

NOTE

In order for two computers using TCP/IP on the same subnet to communicate with each other, they must have the same subnet.

WINS (Windows Internet Server) and DNS (Domain Name Server) The TCP/IP protocol does not use NetBIOS names to identify computers; it uses IP addresses instead. When one Windows computer needs to contact another using TCP/IP, it must find the IP address associated with a NetBIOS computer name. Usually the best way to do this is to use a WINS server. The key limitation of WINS is that it requires each client machine to know its server's IP address.

When a computer name includes Internet style domain and subdomain names using periods (as in station1.netsys.com), a DNS is used for resolving IP addresses. HOSTS and

LMHOSTS files are used when a name server (WINS or DNS service) is not available to resolve DNS (HOSTS) or NetBIOS (LMHOSTS) names. NetBIOS host names (such as NASHVILLE) are resolved using LMHOSTS files and WINS servers. Hierarchical host names (such as Nashville.Commerce.com) are resolved using HOSTS files and DNS servers.

NWLink (IPX/SPX)

NWLink is Microsoft's implementation of Novell's IPX/SPX protocol stack, used in Novell NetWare. IPX/SPX is included with Microsoft Windows NT primarily to support interconnection to Novell NetWare servers. Microsoft clients and servers can then be added to existing network installations for migrating between platforms. NWLink by itself does not allow file and print sharing to be accessed from NetWare servers by NT workstations. Those functions are assisted by the Client Services for NetWare (CSNW) redirector that comes with Windows NT.

Application-Session Layer

At the Session layer, SAP (Service Advertising Protocol) is concerned with session administration for file transfer. At the Application layer, SAP provides active service advertisement. File servers and print servers use SAP to advertise their services on the network.

Transport Layer-SPX

NetWare's Transport layer SPX protocol provides a connection-oriented link between nodes. A connection-oriented protocol is one that establishes a connection between sender and receiver, then transmits the data, and finally breaks the connection. All packets in the transmission are sent in order, and all take the same path. This is in contrast to a connectionless service in which packets may use different paths.

The SPX protocol ensures that packets arrive at their destination with enough sequence information to reconstruct the message at the receiving end and also to maintain a connection at a specific level of quality. To accomplish this, SPX is responsible for flow control, packet acknowledgment, and similar activities.

Network Layer-IPX

IPX is a Network layer protocol, and it is responsible for addressing and routing packets to nodes on other networks. IPX assigns and works with Network layer addresses, as opposed to Physical layer addresses, which are assigned by network interface card manufacturers. The IPX protocol uses the services of the Data Link layer, and it provides services to the SPX protocol in the next higher layer.

The IPX protocol is a connectionless protocol, which means that it doesn't need a fixed connection between source and destination. The protocol can send different packets along different routes and doesn't need to worry about sequencing.

RIP (Routing Information Protocol) RIP is the default protocol for NetWare using routing in a LAN environment. RIP uses the distance-vector route-discovery method to determine hop counts. The hop count is the number of intermediate routers a packet must cross to reach a particular device.

The advantages of NWLink include:

- Intended for medium-size networks (in a single facility) or for networks that require access to Novell NetWare file servers
- Support for routing between networks
- Speeds greater than TCP/IP
- Ease of connection with NetWare

The disadvantages of NWLink include:

- Lack of effective network addressing for hierarchical network
- Slower than NetBEUI
- Doesn't support standard network management protocols

NetBEUI/NetBIOS

NetBEUI and NetBIOS can work with other protocol suites. For example, NetBIOS can be transported over TCP/IP. The two protocols can work together and can be considered a protocol suite. Both NetBEUI and NetBIOS were created by IBM and Microsoft. They are sometimes referred to as the Microsoft protocol suite, because Microsoft has made great use of both protocols in Windows NT.

Application Layer

Following are two application layer protocols.

SMB (Server Message Block) The SMB protocol is used to transmit server message blocks (SMBs). It is an application protocol that defines a series of commands passed from a redirector on a client machine to a service on a server machine. A server message block usually contains data that is used by a remote device (such as a hard drive controller when accessing remote files).

NFS (Sunsoft's PC Network File System) NFS is an application protocol. Windows NT provides file services to Unix environments through the NFS file system or through FTP. FTP and NFS are not installed by default on Windows NT. If you want Unix workstations to be able to see your Windows NT Server files, you must install them.

Upper Layers-NetBIOS (Network Basic Input/Output System)

NetBIOS provides a standard interface to the lower networking layers. The protocol itself functions at a range above the top three layers (Session, Presentation, Application) of the OSI model. The protocol provides higher layer programs with access to the network.

NetBIOS can also act as an API (application program interface) for data exchange. It provides programmers with access to resources for establishing a connection between two computers or between two applications on the same computer.

Lower Layers-NetBEUI (Network Basic Extended User Interface)

NetBEUI implements the NetBIOS Frame (NBF) transport protocol. Unlike IBM's original NetBIOS implementation, which used proprietary lower-layer protocols, NetBEUI was designed to communicate with standard LLC (logical link control) protocols at the lower layers. NetBEUI protocols are used in Microsoft's operating systems. NetBEUI is intended for small, single-server networks. NetBEUI cannot be routed between networks, so it is constrained to small local area networks.

Some advantages of NetBEUI:

- High speed on small networks
- Ease of implementation
- Self-tuning features
- Good error protection
- Small memory overhead

Some disadvantages of NetBEUI:

- Cannot be routed between networks
- Few tools for analyzing its performance
- Very little cross-platform support

AppleTalk

AppleTalk is the name given to the protocol suite designed for the Apple Macintosh.

Upper Layers

These AppleTalk protocols work at the upper layers of the OSI model:

ADSP (AppleTalk Data Stream Protocol) Responsible for transmitting information in byte streams.

ASP (AppletTalk Session Protocol) Provides Session layer services by establishing, maintaining, and releasing connections. It works in conjunction with ATP to provide reliable packet delivery.

PAP (Printer Access Protocol) A Session layer protocol that permits sessions to be initiated by both service requesters and service providers. PAP provides more than just printing service.

ZIP (Zone Information Protocol) Allows devices to be organized into logical groups called zones. A zone can reduce the apparent complexity of an internetwork by limiting the number of service providers viewed to the subset the user needs to see. Routers and other network nodes use ZIP to map between zone and network names.

AFP (AppleTalk Filing Protocol) AFP was developed to facilitate file sharing. It works at the Session and Presentation layers to translate local file system commands into a format that can be used for network service.

AppleShare A suite of three protocols or applications (AppleShare File Server, AppleShare Print Server, AppleShare PC) that provide AppleTalk's Application layer services.

Middle Layers

The AppleTalk protocols at the middle layers of the OSI model include:

DDP (Datagram Delivery Protocol) For datagram packet delivery; provides connectionless service at the Network layer.

RTMP (Routing Table Maintenance Protocol) A distance-vector routing protocol similar to RIP.

NBP (Name Binding Protocol) Used to map logical names to addresses.

ATP (AppleTalk Transaction Protocol) A Transport layer protocol that uses acknowledgments to keep track of transactions. A transaction is similar in meaning to a connection. A transaction consists of a request followed by a response and is identified by a transaction ID.

Lower Layers

The lower layer protocols of AppleTalk include Apple's original LocalTalk, as well as Ethernet and Token Ring. Another good protocol included here is the AppleTalk Address Resolution Protocol (AARP), which functions at the OSI model's Data Link and Network layers.

LocalTalk (LLAP) Apple's original Data Link and Physical layer protocol. LocalTalk was developed for small workgroups. It is slow, at 230Kbps, and is limited to 32 devices and 300 meter segment lengths. It is still useful for small offices.

EtherTalk (ELAP) ELAP (EtherTalk Link Access Protocol) is an implementation of AppleTalk that uses Ethernet protocol (contention access, collision detection, and star bus topology).

TokenTalk (TLAP) TLAP (TokenTalk Link Access Protocol) is an adaptation of AppleTalk at the Physical and Data Link layers. It uses Token Ring protocol.

AARP (AppleTalk Address Resolution Protocol) Maps AppleTalk addresses to Ethernet and Token Ring physical addresses. AARP allows upper layer protocols to use Data Link layer protocols other than LocalTalk.

Other Protocol Issues

Binding Order

When using multiple transport protocols on a Windows NT workstation computer, you should always place the most frequently used transport protocol at the top of the binding order. Doing so will reduce network response time and speed up network connections.

Interconnectivity

In order for NetWare clients to access resources on a Windows NT server, the Windows NT server must have both the NWLink protocol and File and Print Services for NetWare (FPNW) installed. Client Service for NetWare is required on a Windows NT workstation to connect to a NetWare server.

In order for Windows 95 computers to access files on a NetWare server, the IPX/SPX compatible protocol stack must be installed. Microsoft Client for NetWare Networks must also be installed for Windows 95 computers to access file and print resources on NetWare servers. An alternative to having the Microsoft Client for NetWare service installed on each client is to install the Windows NT Gateway Services for NetWare (GSNW) on a Windows NT server. This service allows all Windows NT workstations to access a NetWare server by going through the GSNW on the Windows NT server.

To allow the NetWare clients to access file and print resources on the Windows NT server, there are two options, client-based or server-based. You can either install additional redirectors on the NetWare clients, or you can install File and Print Services for NetWare on the Windows NT server, which is an add-on and is not included with NT. Each of the options can allow the NetWare clients to access volumes, files, and printers on the Windows NT server.

Installing TCP/IP

Microsoft TCP/IP on Windows NT enables enterprise networking and connectivity on your Windows NT-based computer. Installing TCP/IP is simple and straightforward. Although TCP/IP is one of the default protocols installed during Windows NT installation, it may need to be removed and then reinstalled if the network interface card is replaced with a new one. The following procedure explains how TCP/IP can be installed onto a Windows NT Server 4.0 computer.

1. From the Control Panel, double-click the Network icon, and then select the Protocol tab.
2. Click the Add button to display the protocols that can be added from the Select Network Protocol window.
3. Select TCP/IP from the window and click the OK button. Make sure the Windows NT Server 4.0 installation disk is in the CD-ROM drive.
4. After the necessary files are copied to the server, TCP/IP will appear in the Network window under Network Protocols.
5. Next, you will need to configure the protocol. Select TCP/IP from the Network window and click the Properties button, which displays the Microsoft TCP/IP Properties dialog box.
6. There are five tabs at the top of this dialog box, and each contains settings that can be configured for a particular network. Click the IP Address tab.
7. You will either allow an IP address to be obtained from a DHCP server, or you will manually enter an assigned address with at least its subnet mask.

8. The two tabs to the right, DNS and WINS address, can be configured if a DHCP server will not provide their addresses. The DHCP Relay tab allows you to configure your server as a DHCP relay agent. The Routing tab allows your server to act as router if it contains at least two network interface cards and operates as a multihomed server.

9. Finally, click the OK button to close the Microsoft TCP/IP Properties dialog box, and then the Close button to exit the Network window. The closing of the window will cause a binding procedure that attaches this new protocol and its configuration settings to lower layer drivers and the NIC.

Select the appropriate connectivity devices for various Token Ring and Ethernet networks.

Connectivity devices include:

- Repeaters
- Bridges
- Routers
- Brouters
- Gateways

This section introduces several connectivity devices that allow for the expansion of a network both locally and as a WAN. In the real world, a network administrator will be planning a network that meets the needs of an organization with a large number of computer users who will need access to the network. The planning stage needs to consider network speed, reliability, scalability, and management. The following connectivity devices provide the instrumentality to increase the size of a network.

Repeaters

All transmission media attenuate (weaken) the electromagnetic waves that travel through them. *Attenuation*, therefore, limits the distance any medium can carry data. Adding a device that amplifies the signal can allow it to travel farther, increasing the size of the network. The repeater's job is merely to boost a weak signal back to its original strength and send it on its way. A *repeater* operates at the Physical layer of the OSI model. You use repeaters to extend the length of segments on your LAN. Repeaters are generally used on bus topologies; of course, you can extend your backbone by using repeaters connected to hubs connecting star, bus, or Token Ring topologies to the backbone. See Figure 2.10 for an illustration of a repeater.

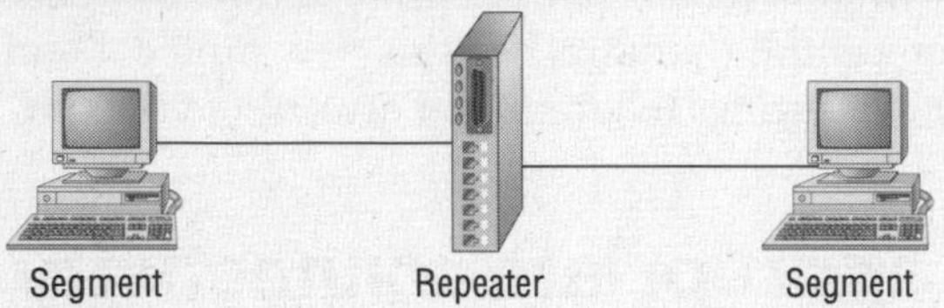

FIGURE 2.10: Repeater

Your system can have a maximum of four repeaters connecting five segments. Only three of these segments can contain devices. This is called the "5-4-3 rule." Ethernet LAN segments connected via repeaters can be a maximum of 2500 meters long, and the length depends on the type of cable being using.

Repeaters don't filter out any data, and each segment connected with a repeater must have the same access method and LLC (logical link control) mechanism. The LLC layer translates the different access methods it receives from the MAC layer allowing different MAC methods to be used. Because repeaters operate only at the Physical layer, they are unable to employ the benefits provided by the Data Link layer.

This homogeneity allows the repeater to send data to the same or different physical media, but the LLC and packets from the source segment to the target segment must be the same. Bridges can perform this important conversion because they operate at the Data Link layer.

NOTE

An *amplifier* is a device that amplifies electrical signals so they can travel on additional cable length for broadband networks. Amplifiers strengthen broadband signals that are weakened by attenuation.

A passive hub simply combines the signals of network segments. There is no signal processing or regeneration. Because it does not boost the signal and, in fact, absorbs some of the signal, a passive hub reduces by half the maximum cabling distances permitted.

Active hubs are like passive hubs except that they have electronic components that regenerate or amplify signals. Because of this, the distances between devices and computers can be increased. An active hub can be described as a multiport repeater.

Intelligent hubs perform some network management and intelligent path selection, besides performing signal regeneration. One type of intelligent hub is a switching hub. A *switching hub* chooses only the port of the device where the signal needs to go, rather than sending the signal along all paths. Figure 2.11 is an example of a switching hub.

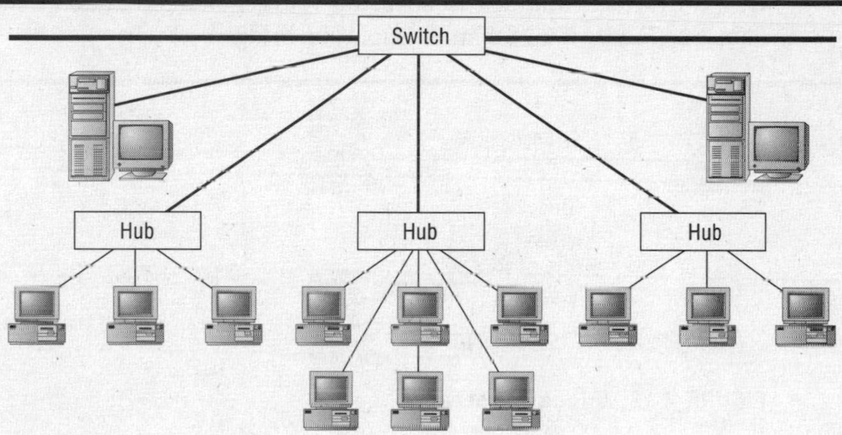

FIGURE 2.11: Switching hub

Bridges

Bridges can do all that repeaters can and more. They're not subject to the 5-4-3 rule because each segment that a bridge connects is considered to be from a different network. Bridges connect network segments, and the use of a bridge increases the maximum possible size of your network. Unlike a repeater, which simply passes on all the signals it receives, a bridge selectively determines the appropriate segment to which it should pass a signal. It does this by reading the address of all the signals it receives. The bridge reads the physical location of the source and destination computers from this address. Bridges are used to decrease network traffic by dividing a network into segments, which increases the maximum possible size of your network.

Repeaters operate on the Physical layer; bridges operate on the Data Link layer. The Data Link layer contains the MAC sublayer. Each computer has a MAC address, which is a unique hardware address specifically assigned to each computer's network card. Bridges determine the location of computers and which segments they're on via their MAC addresses. That way, they can keep traffic local that wasn't intended for other segments. Bridges build a routing table of the computers on the local segment by collecting and associating computers with their MAC addresses and the segments they're on. The bridges discard packets' sources and destination MAC addresses that are contained on the same physical segment, sending all nonmatching packets to neighboring segments and devices. As you can see, this can reduce network traffic significantly by keeping local traffic local and not broadcasting it to segments that don't need the data. See Figure 2.12 for an example of a bridge.

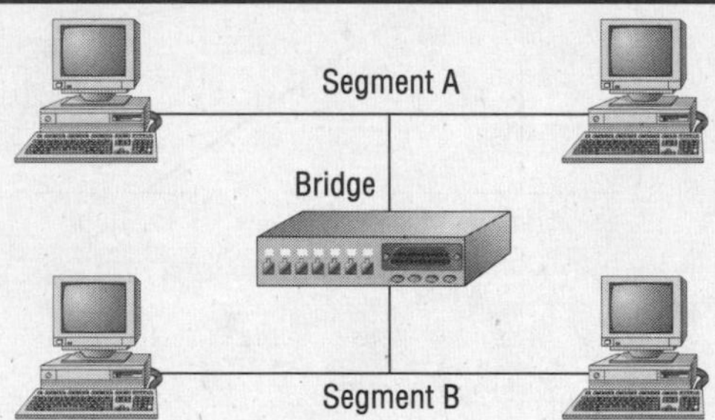

FIGURE 2.12: Bridge in a network

Bridges should not be joined on a network to create loops of any kind. Connecting them would create a circular connection between all the bridges, which would cause bottlenecks from never-ending data transmissions. A network should use bridges in a hierarchical pattern to avoid this problem. Some bridges prevent this from happening with the use of a technique called STA (spanning tree algorithm). These types of bridges act like routers to determine the best path for data to travel.

WARNING

Although bridges use tables, you should associate the use of routing tables with routers and not bridges, when sitting for the exam.

Bridges are incapable of connecting LAN segments with different architectures. For example, an Ethernet segment and a Token Ring segment normally cannot be connected with a bridge because each network type uses different physical addressing. However, a special bridge called a "translation bridge" allows you to connect different network types.

Routers

Routers are devices that connect two or more networks. Routers include the physical interfaces to the various networks in the internetwork. These interfaces can be Token Ring, Ethernet, T1, Frame Relay, Asynchronous Transfer Mode (ATM), or any number of other technologies.

Similar to bridges, routers can be used to segment a busy network to reduce network traffic by filtering network messages. However, routers can do more than bridges by using network addresses instead of MAC hardware addresses. A network address consists of two parts, where one part of the address identifies an entire network segment, and the other part identifies a node such as a computer residing on that network segment. Where bridges use routing tables containing individual computers' MAC addresses, routers store network locations.

Routers work at the Network layer, where they work with packets and protocols, whereas bridges work with MAC addresses and frames at the Data Link layer. Routers match packet headers to a LAN segment and choose the best path for the packet, optimizing network performance. Routers are capable of determining the best path for data to follow, but bridges usually can't. By not working at the Data Link layer, they can operate with different media access methods and network architectures, such as Ethernet and Token Ring.

Routers pass packets to other routers. When packets are passed from router to router, the routers need to see the network addresses so they can send a packet across different network architectures. In order to see the network addresses, they strip off and recreate Data Link layer source addresses and destination addresses. Remember, the Data Link layer portion of the packet is added on last, so it forms its outer layer. This outer layer will need to be "peeled" off to reveal the Network layer address. Once the Network address is read and ready to be routed, the Data Link layer addresses (MAC addresses) can be put back. Figure 2.13 is an example of a router.

WARNING

Routers don't *translate* between different protocols— they just *route* different protocols at the same time. When sitting for the exam, remember: *Only gateways translate protocols.*

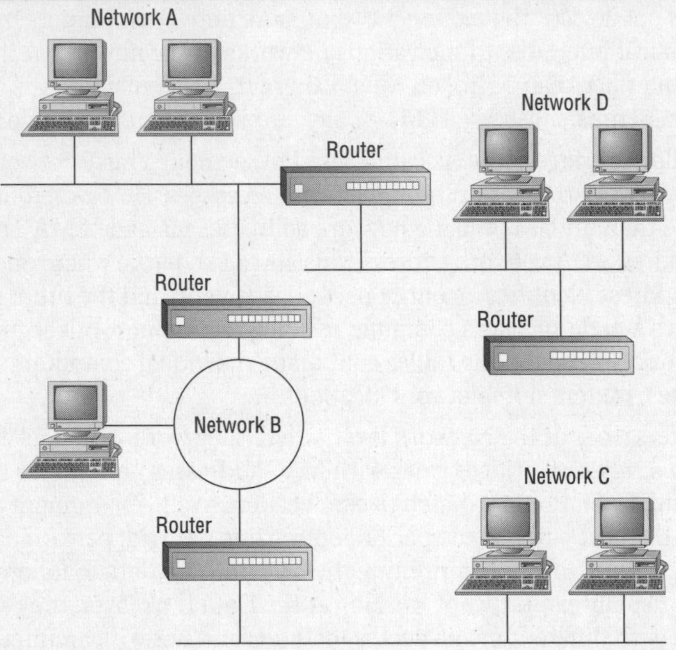

FIGURE 2.13: Router in a network

WARNING

Routers can connect different network architectures with different access methods, such as connecting a Token Ring network to an Ethernet network, but routers can't connect totally different networks, such as connecting an IBM SNA network to an Ethernet network.

Although routers don't rely on MAC addresses, they do inspect packets for broadcast storms. A *broadcast* is a normal event where a computer announces itself on a network. This happens periodically, especially on a Windows NT network. However, a *broadcast storm* is an overload of these announcements. Broadcast storms are usually caused by faulty network cards. Routers prevent broadcast storms using a process called flow control.

Because routers operate at the Network layer of the OSI model, they interpret packets at the Protocol level, which means that the protocols used with a router must be routable and capable of being sent through multiple routers. The following protocols are routable:

- DECnet
- TCP/IP
- NWLink IPX (SPX/IPX)
- DDP (AppleTalk)
- OSI and XNS

NetBEUI, DLC, and LAT (from Digital Equipment Corporation) are examples of nonroutable protocols. The packets that NetBEUI sends don't contain the structure that can store routing information.

Routers can even share paths and other kinds of information with other routers, so they can work together to provide the best solution. Routers can be categorized when examining this feature.

Static and dynamic routers With static routers you can manually program routes into a router to create a static routing table. More recently, routers can automatically create dynamic routing tables based on the data they receive from other routers.

Distance-vector and link-state protocols Routers use several methods to determine the best path for data to follow. In distance-vector routing, each router advertises its presence to other routers on the network along with the information in its own routing table, allowing all routers to update their own tables. The following are examples of distance-vector routing protocols:

- RIP (Routing Information Protocol)
- IGRP (Interior Gateway Routing Protocol)
- RTMP (Routing Table Maintenance Protocol)

Because distance-vector routing generates too much network traffic to cause a problem on internetworks that have a lot of routers, link-state routing was developed as an improvement. Link-state routers broadcast their complete routing tables only at startup and at certain intervals, which is much less frequently than distance-vector broadcasts. Thus, this type of routing generates less network traffic than the distance-vector method. An example of link-state routing is Open Shortest Path First (OSPF).

Brouters

A *brouter* is a router that can also be a bridge. A brouter first tries to deliver the packet based on network protocol information. Brouters can transmit both routable and nonroutable protocols with the same device. These devices route whatever protocols they can and bridge the rest. If the brouter does not support the protocol the packet is using or cannot deliver the packet based on protocol information, it bridges the packet using the physical address. True routers simply discard a packet if it doesn't have a correct logical address. A brouter can be a more affordable option than having both a router and a bridge. It can also make network management simpler.

Gateways

A *gateway* is a device that can interpret and translate the different protocols that are used on two distinct networks. Gateways are used to connect mainframes and LANs.

Gateways can be comprised of software, dedicated hardware, or a combination of both. A gateway can function at the upper layers of the OSI model, but it does so more often at the Application layer. You can connect systems with different communication protocols, languages, and architecture using a gateway.

NOTE

Although gateways can function at the network layer, for the exam, think of gateways as operating at the upper layers of the OSI model, above the Network layer. In other words, they function at the Transport, Session, Presentation, and Application layers.

Multiplexers

Multiplexers allow you to use more bandwidth of the medium by combining two or more separate signals and transmitting them together. The original signals can then be extracted at the other end of the medium. This is called *demultiplexing*. Multiplexing provides a way of sharing a single medium segment by combining several channels for transmission over that segment.

List the characteristics, requirements, and appropriate situations for WAN connection services.

WAN connection services include:

- X.25
- ISDN
- Frame Relay
- ATM

It has become increasingly necessary for network engineers to understand telecommunications as well as data communications. More companies are extending the reach of their networks into diverse geographical locations, and the popularity of the World Wide Web has made remote access to global information a modern expectation. This section provides you with the basic knowledge of various WAN services, and it provides a beginning framework for making these decisions. Microsoft wants you to know the features of each WAN technology and how they influence the variables of speed, flexibility, and expense.

WAN Connections

A *wide area network* (WAN) provides data communication services between geographically separated areas. A WAN can interconnect not only separate nodes but also multiple LANs. Examples of WAN links are Frame Relay, X.25, Switched 56, T1, SMDS, and ATM. In addition, the dial-up telephone connections discussed in Chapter 1 are considered WAN links. Most of the time WANs are separate from local area networking technologies. On the other hand, some technologies, such as ATM, can be applied to both LAN and WAN situations. For example, wiring two ATM switches locally is a typical LAN solution. By expanding the cable length and moving one switch to a geographically separated area, the same ATM networking configuration becomes a WAN solution.

There are two general alternatives in building a WAN environment:

- Point-to-point connections
- Packet switching connections

Point-to-Point Connections

A *point-to-point connection* is a network configuration in which a connection is established between only two points. There are generally two ways to make a point-to-point connection.

Connecting two points using a network cable is the selection most often used because of the distance limitation of twisted-pair, coaxial cable, and fiber-optic cable (especially the single-mode fiber).

Connecting two points by leasing a dedicated line from a telephone company is the other. A dedicated line is one that is always open, whether you're transmitting data or not. The disadvantages of the dedicated line are that you cannot "hang-up" the line, and you need to pay for the time you are not connected. Nevertheless, a dedicated line saves the time of establishing the connection and guarantees the line is always there.

A point-to-point connection guarantees the connection between two nodes is the shortest route. However, because any two nodes must be connected, any new added node will double your total line cost.

Switching Connections

User stations are not connected directly to each other. Rather, they communicate with each other by sending data through a *switch* (or set of switches). The switch relays the data to the receiving computer terminal, telephone, or some other component.

When you send a packet from one network to another, you just send the packet to the switch. The switch will find the routing information for you and transmit the packet to the destination network. A switching network simplifies the network structure and, hence, increases the network performance.

There are three kinds of switching technologies:

Packet Switches Packet switching has become the prevalent switching technique for data communications networks. It is used in such diverse systems as private branch exchanges (PBXs), local area networks (LANs), and even multiplexers.

Packet switching is so named because a user's data (such as messages) are separated and transmitted in small units called *packets*. Each packet occupies a transmission line only for the duration of the transmission; the line is then made available for another user's packet. Packet size is limited so that those packets do not occupy the line for extended periods. A packet-switched network uses multiple routes (paths) between the packet switches within the network. The packets are routed across the paths in accordance with traffic congestion, error conditions, the shortest end-to-end path, and other criteria.

Many packet switching networks employ *virtual circuits*. Virtual-circuit packet switching establishes a logical connection between the sending and receiving devices, a virtual circuit. After the sending and receiving devices agree on communication parameters, a virtual circuit is established. This circuit lasts as long as the two devices are communicating. With this method, all the packets follow the same route. This feature increases speed and bandwidth.

Packet switching also provides an attractive feature for connecting the DTEs for a session. In a circuit-switched (telephone) system, the time to set up a connection is often lengthy (sometimes, several seconds). In contrast, a packet-switching system uses dedicated leased lines, which are immediately made available to users.

By definition, a packet switched network provides "any-to-any" connectivity. That is, any station can transmit to any other station on the network over a wide variety of possible paths. This is different from point-to-point connectivity.

Circuit Switches In a circuit switching technology, a direct connection is created through the switches that reside between the communicating stations. Originally, it was designed for voice traffic, which needs a dedicated line for conversation between two people. However, the two users do not have direct wires through a circuit-switched network. Instead, the intervening switches have electronic connectors that couple the communications links directly to each other.

NOTE

Circuit switching is used for point-to-point connections. Do not confuse circuit switching with packet switching. For exam purposes, think of these two switching technologies as complete opposites.

Message Switches Message switching is designed specifically for data traffic. As with circuit switching, the communications lines are connected to a switching facility, but the end users do not have a direct physical connection to each other. Rather, the message is transmitted to the switch and stored on direct access media (such as a disk) for later delivery. The term *store-and-forward* is associated with message switching networks.

Examples of Point-to-Point Connections

Leased, or dedicated, lines provide the permanent end-to-end connection between two nodes.

Leased Lines

Generally a leased line operates at the bandwidth of 56Kbps or 1.544Mbps, which is somewhat higher than the telephone network. Moreover, a leased line provides a fixed amount of bandwidth at a fixed speed and is most suitable for the locations with amounts of steady data traffic. The tariffs of a leased line are based on a combination of the line bandwidth and the distance between two points. Therefore for the bursty traffic applications, which are usually underutilized and often running at less than 20 percent of total capacity, the leased line solution seems to be an expensive one. However, some applications, such as connecting a web server to the Internet, need a continuous connection, and the dedicated lines are commonly used. T-carrier services deliver digital data and voice transmission at rates as high as 45Mbps. Although packet switching such as Frame Relay is a lot less expensive than T-carrier services, companies need T1/T3 lines to provide dedicated connections where there is constant steady traffic.

Switched 56 Services Switched 56 is a digital communication technology for transporting data over switched synchronous lines at 56Kbps and is based on circuit-switching technology. The channels are dial-up, allowing customers to use the service only when needed. Switched 56 requires a modem-like device called a channel service unit (CSU/DSU) to connect to a router attached to a LAN and, at the other end, attached to the Switched 56 phone line. Switched 56 is less expensive than T1 and fractional T1 services.

T-Carrier Service The T-carrier service, originally introduced by the Bell System in the 1960s, was the first successful dedicated line solution that supports both the data and voice transmission. A T-carrier system consists of multiple channels that are multiplexed to create higher transmission rate. Table 2.2 shows the typical features of the T-carrier systems.

TABLE 2.2: T-Carrier Systems

Signal	T-Carrier	Voice Channels	Bit Rate (Mbps)
DS-1	T1	24	1.544
DS-2	T2	96	6.312
DS-3	T3	672	44.736
DS-4	T4	4032	274.760

Each channel operates at 64Kbps. However, you will find the bit rates of T-carriers are not exactly the same as the product (64Kbps times the channel number). For example, T1 consists of 24 channels, which should equal 1.536Mbps (64Kbps * 24); however, the T1 line is 1.544Mbps. In fact, the extra 8Kbps is used for signaling.

A number of variations on the number and use of channels are possible in T-carrier systems. You can also lease the subdivisions of a full T-carrier service, which is known as fractional T services.

Examples of Packet Switching Connections

Following are eight examples of packet sweitching connections.

X.25

X.25 is the CCITT-recommended standard for packet-switched networks for communication between DTE and DCE. The user end of the network is known as Data Terminal Equipment (DTE), and the carrier's equipment is Data Circuit-terminating Equipment (DCE).

The X.25 standard has three layers—the Physical, the Data Link, and the Network layers.

X.25 is a standard packet-switching communication protocol (or transport) developed during the 1970s by CCITT (called ITU, International Telecommunication Union, since 1993). Due to the unreliable transmission media at that time, people implemented redundant error checking and flow control to assure successful delivery. Because the error checking mechanism occupies quite a few bits in a X.25 packet, the X.25 network is relatively slower compared to other technologies such as Frame Relay, which provide less error checking in transmission. X.25 is somewhat obsolete nowadays because more reliable media is available.

X.25 utilizes connection-oriented service, which asks for call establishment. This service ensures that packets are transmitted in order. Chapter 1 discussed the two types of services, the connection-oriented and the connectionless services. Connection-oriented service requires a call establishment before data can be transmitted between DTE and DCE. It takes care of transmitting data by requesting acknowledgment from both sides. In contrast, connectionless service requires no call establishment. Both ends can transmit data whenever they like. One bad thing about connectionsless service is that packets may arrive out of sequence.

X.25 and OSI Layers X.25 encompasses the first three layers of the OSI seven-layered architecture as defined by the International Standards Organization (ISO):

The Physical layer (X.21) is responsible for the physical transmission of the packets offered to it by the layer above. It specifies the electrical and physical interface between DTE and X.25 networks. Sometimes RS232-C or V.75 might substitute for X.21.

The Data Link layer (LAP-B: Link Access Protocol-Balanced) guarantees error-free transfer of the packet offered to it by the layer above from one end of a physical connection to the other. It might have to retransmit a packet several times to achieve such a transfer.

The Network layer (PLP: Packet Level Procedure) is involved in routing packets from source to destination. This third layer of X.25 has additional functionality. It is also involved in flow control and error control. Flow control involves controlling the rate of arrival of packets so that congestion does not take place. Error control ensures that all of the packets are received as they are sent without any error.

DTE and DCE Contacts The X.25 PLP permits a DTE user on an X.25 network to communicate with a number of remote DTEs simultaneously. Connections occur on logical channels of two types:

Switched virtual circuits (SVCs) SVCs are very much like telephone calls; a connection is established, data are transferred, and then the connection is released. Each DTE on the network is given a unique DTE address, which can be used much like a telephone number.

Permanent virtual circuits (PVCs) A PVC is similar to a leased line in that the connection is always present. The logical connection is established permanently by the Packet Switched Network administration. Therefore, data may always be sent, without any call setup.

Modems are used to let computers have access to telephone networks. Similarly, PADs (Packet Assemblers/Disassemblers) and X.25 Smart Cards can be used for X.25 connections. A PAD is comparable to an external modem while a X.25 Smart Card (a hardware card with a PAD embedded) resembles an internal modem. A PAD converts non-packet data streams, such as start-stop bits of an asynchronous transmission, into packets that can be transmitted over an X.25 packet-switching network. A PAD at the other end disassembles the packets.

NOTE

X.25 is an older technology that, for the most part, has been phased out. However, the Networking Essentials exam contains at least two questions involving X.25.

Some advantages and disadvantages of X.25:

- X.25 is cheaper than dedicated lines. X.25 gives you a virtual high-quality digital network at low cost.
- Another useful feature is speed matching. Because of the store-and-forward nature of packet switching, plus excellent flow control, DTEs do not have to use the same line speed. So you can have, for instance, a host connected at 56Kbps communicating with numerous remote sites connected with cheaper 19.2Kbps lines.
- There is an inherent drawback caused by the store-and-forward mechanism. On most single networks the turn-around delay is about 0.6 seconds. This has no effect on large block transfers, but in flip-flop types of transmissions the delay can be very noticeable. Frame Relay (also called Fast Packet Switching) does not store-and-forward, but simply switches to the destination part way through the frame, reducing the transmission delay considerably.

- Another problem for the networks is a large requirement for buffering to support the store-and-forward data transfer. One of the reasons that Frame Relay is so cost effective is that storage requirements are minimal.

Frame Relay

Frame Relay is a simplified form of packet switching, similar in principle to X.25, in which synchronous frames of data are routed to different destinations depending on header information. Frame Relay typically provides bandwidth from 56Kbps to 1.544Mbps. Most of the major carriers, such as AT&T, MCI, US Sprint, and the Regional Bell Operating Companies (RBOCs), offer Frame Relay. Frame Relay uses PVCs between communication devices, where the same path is used for all communications, to ensure proper delivery and high bandwidth rates.

Compared to X.25 network, Frame Relay uses fast packet technology that eliminates the error checking service and leaves error checking to the higher level protocols or applications. This design was fostered by changes in technology within the last two decades; transmission media are much faster and more reliable, and computers are much more powerful and less expensive. Computers can now perform error checking, and WANs can concentrate on utilizing the speed offered by transmission media. Frame Relay simplifies its protocol by reducing unnecessary overhead and eliminating error correction. Frame Relay provides the minimal services for the connection. If a bad frame is received, Frame Relay does nothing except discard it. Both flow control and the re-sending mechanism are handled by software application performed by computers.

Because of its bandwidth-on-demand capability, Frame Relay can handle bursty traffic and provide increased bandwidth as needed. When you consider real voice and video applications, which require a steady flow of transmissions, Frame Relay is not recommended.

Frame Relay uses other connection types to perform the physical transmission, while Frame Relay itself handles the logical connections. When setting up a Frame Relay connection, you have a choice of access speeds. You can select 56Kbps by using a Switched 56 service, or you can select 128Kbps by using ISDN, or you can select 384Kbps to 1.544Mbps by using T1 or fractional T1 lines.

ATM

ATM (Asynchronous Transfer Mode) is an example of cell switching that is a form of fast packet switching. Cell switching can transmit data at megabit and gigabit per second rates. Switched Multimegabit Data Service (SMDS) is another example of cell switching.

With ATM, information is chopped up into small, fixed-length cells (53 bytes) to transmit different types of traffic simultaneously, including voice, video, and data. Cells are reassembled at the destination point. It is because each cell is transported in this predictable way that multiple traffic types can be accommodated on the same network.

Each cell is broken into two main sections, header (5 bytes) and payload (48 bytes). The header contains information that allows the cell to be forwarded to its destination. The payload is the portion that carries the actual information—whether it be voice, data, or video.

The header is used to identify cells belonging to the same virtual channel and to perform the appropriate routing. To guarantee fast processing in the network, the ATM header has very limited function. Its main function is the identification of the virtual connection by an identifier that is selected at call set-up and guarantees a proper routing of each packet. In addition, it allows easy multiplexing of different virtual connections over a single link.

ATM is a transport protocol that operates at the MAC sublayer of the Data Link layer in the OSI model. Because of this, it operates above several Physical layer topologies and converts any kind of packet into its 53-byte cell. ATM can be used on existing T1 lines and T3 lines. However, industry experts are endorsing the Synchronous Optical Network (SONET) as the ATM physical transport for both WAN and LAN applications.

ATM provides cell sequence integrity. That is, cells arrive at the destination in the same order as they left the source. This may not be the case with other packet-switched networks.

Cells are much shorter than in standard packet-switched networks, reducing the value of delay variance, and making ATM acceptable for timing sensitive information like voice.

The quality of transmission links has lead to the omission of overheads, such as error correction, in order to maximize efficiency.

Cells are transported at regular intervals. There is no space between cells. At times when the network is idle, unassigned cells are transported.

The advantages of ATM:

- This technique provides great flexibility because it can match the rate at which it transmits cells to the rate at which the information is generated. This is important for many of the new high-bit-rate services that are being developed, particularly those with a video component, because they are variable-bit-rate services. ATM is made for data, voice, and video, providing flexibility for different application scenarios.
- ATM allows multiplexing multiple streams of traffic on each physical facility (between the end user and the network or between network switches).
- Bandwidth is allocated on demand by the network as users have traffic to transmit. Most applications are or can be viewed as inherently bursty; data applications are LAN-based and are very bursty; voice is bursty because both parties are either speaking at once or not at all; video is bursty because the amount of motion and required resolution varies over time.
- ATM provides scalability in speed and network size as it supports link speeds of T-1/E-1 to OC-12 (622Mbps) today and will support into the multi-Gbps range before the end of the decade.
- ATM can be used consistently from one desktop to another because it supports both LAN to WAN and WAN to LAN architectures.

The disadvantages of ATM:

- ATM is still very expensive.
- Networks must use ATM compatible switches, routers, and other connectivity devices. This means that switching to ATM would require all new equipment.

ISDN

ISDN (Integrated Services Digital Network) is a switched digital communications network designed to bring the power of the digital network directly to the desktop. One of the original goals of ISDN developers was to have ISDN replace all current phone lines.

There are two basic types of ISDN service, Basic Rate Interface (BRI) and Primary Rate Interface (PRI). *BRI* consists of two 64Kbps B channels and one 16Kbps D channel for a total of 144Kbps. This basic service is intended to meet the needs of most individual users.

PRI is intended for users with greater capacity requirements. Typically the channel structure is 23 B channels plus one 64Kbps D channel for a total of 1536Kbps. In Europe, PRI consists of 30 B channels plus one 64Kbps D channel for a total of 1984Kbps. It is also possible to support multiple PRI lines with one 64Kbps D channel using Non-Facility Associated Signaling (NFAS).

ISDN uses multiplexing mechanisms to merge different channels. Some standardized channel types are shown below.

A–4KHz analog telephone channel

B–64Kbps digital channel for voice or data

C–16Kbps digital channel

D–16Kbps digital channel for out-of-band signaling

E–64Kbps digital channel for internal ISDN signaling

H–384, 1536, or 1920Kbps digital channels

Three combinations have been standardized by CCITT so far:

Basic rate: 2B + 1D

Primary rate: 23B + 1D (USA), 30B + 1D (Europe)

Hybrid: 1A + 1C

To access BRI service, it is necessary to subscribe to an ISDN phone line. Customers must be within 18,000 feet (about 3.4 miles or 5.5 km) of the telephone company central office for BRI service; beyond that, expensive repeater devices are required, or ISDN service may not be available at all.

B-ISDN (Broadband-ISDN) is a third version that can offer bandwidth rates over 155Mbps and is used with ATM and SONET. The underlying transfer mode for delivering B-ISDN is cell switching. ATM is the switching technology for B-ISDN. SONET will be explained later in this chapter.

The advantages of ISDN include:

- ISDN is as easy to use as analog but offers much more. ISDN, BRI's two 64Kbps B channels, can be used as separate links for simultaneous voice and data, or they can be combined into a single 128Kbps pipeline. This makes it ideal for large-scale data transfer, video teleconferencing, imaging, and other information intensive applications. Even with data compression, a 28.8Kbps modem can reach 115.2Kbps only when line conditions are ideal and data is highly compressible. With ISDN bonding you get true 128Kbps every time, all the time.

- Voice, data, and video can be sent over a single ISDN line.
- ISDN connections are made almost instantly (typically, less than a second), unlike analog modems and analog lines, which can require 30 to 60 seconds before any data can be transmitted.
- Because it's a digital service, ISDN offers near-perfect line quality that is far superior to analog, so line conditions never force you to fall back to a slower speed.

Switched Multimegabit Data Service (SMDS)

Switched Multimegabit Data Service (SMDS) is a telecommunications service that provides connectionless, high performance, packet-switched data transport. It is neither a protocol nor a technology. Rather, it supports standard protocols and communications interfaces using current and future technology.

SMDS has been defined by the IEEE 802.6 Metropolitan Area Network (MAN) standard, as implemented by Bellcore. It can use a variety of technologies, including Broadband-ISDN (B-ISDN) and Distributed Queue Dual Bus (DQDB). Current North American implementations utilize DQDB with DS1 (1.5Mbps) or DS3 (45Mbps) lines. Other implementations utilize E1 lines at speeds in excess of 1.9Mbps or E3 lines. Future SMDS networks will couple B-ISDN with SONET OC3 at 155Mbps.

The development of this service has paralleled the emerging Asynchronous Transfer Mode (ATM) standards. Like ATM, SMDS uses cell relay transport. Both services use 53-octet cells for transport; however, the maximum length for SMDS is 9188 octets, and the maximum length for ATM is 65,535 octets. Because of this, SMDS is considered to be an intermediate between the packet-switched services offered today and the ATM service of the future.

WAN Physical Transport for High Performance Links

ATM and SMDS are two high performance Data Link layer protocols that use packet switching and cell switching. They can be constructed on top of several Physical layer protocols that define physical media, especially fiber. Although most high performance networks use T3 lines, FDDI and SONET are being used for local metropolitan environments.

Fiber Distributed Data Interface (FDDI) *FDDI* is a topology standard that transmits information packets using light produced by a laser or LED (light-emitting diode) and offers tremendous speed. FDDI uses fiber-optic cable and equipment to transmit data packets. Typical data rates are around 100Mbps. Cable lengths can easily be up to 100 kilometers (with repeaters at least every two kilometers).

This topology uses IEEE 802.5 and is similar to Token Ring with the additional feature of using *two* rings instead of one. FDDI uses a primary ring to move data and a second ring to provide system fault tolerance and backup. The two send messages in opposite directions, although the second ring is inactive until it is needed.

FDDI is an excellent technology to interconnect relatively close LANs, as in one metropolitan area. FDDI is one of several transport services used by ATM and SMDS.

Synchronous Optical Network (SONET) *SONET* is a high-speed fiber-optic data transmission system. It can move data at rates faster than 1Gbps. SMDS is an LEC (local exchange carrier) service for building local area networks in a city-wide area. It is a connectionless, cell-based service that can provide any-to-any connections between a variety of sites.

Although SONET is not a standard for packet or cell switching, it is used at the Physical layer for both ATM and SMDS. SONET defines how fiber-optic technologies can deliver data, video, and voice over a network at speeds over 1Gbps. SONET is a set of physical standards for high speed WANs, the same way Ethernet is a set of physical standards for LANs.

The following are standard SONET transmission rates:

OC Level	Line Rate
OC-1	51.8Mbps
OC-3	155.5Mbps
OC-9	466.5Mbps
OC-12	622.0Mbps
OC-18	933.1Mbps
OC-24	1.24Gbps
OC-36	1.86Gbps
OC-48	2.48Gbps

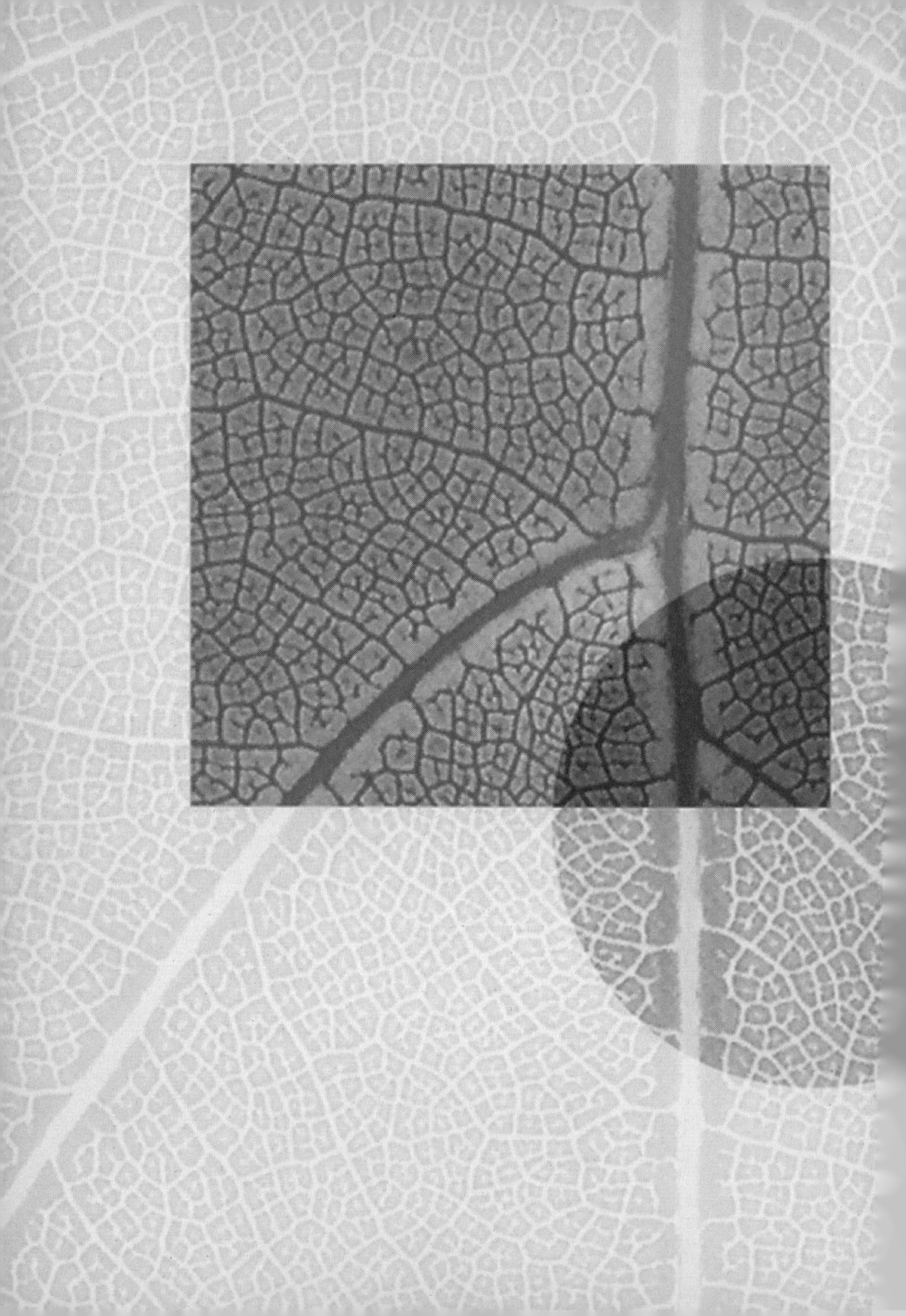

Chapter 3
Implementation

Implementing a network implies the actual installation of network software and all ongoing configuration activity. A network's life depends on the network administrator keeping it healthy, safe, and in good working order. Immediately after a network operating system is installed, an administrative plan needs to be implemented that provides techniques for preventing problems and reducing the effects of possible disasters. Most of these techniques involve organizational procedures that keep intentional and unintentional human activity from destroying or removing sensitive data. For example, creating user and group accounts and then allowing these accounts to access only certain network resources keeps a network functioning the way it was intended. Other techniques are concerned with minimizing the effects of hardware failures such as recovering data in case of hard drive destruction.

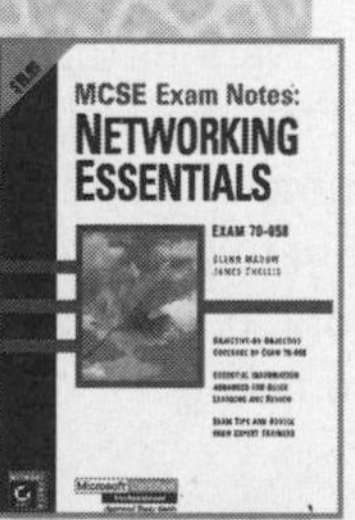

Adapted from *MCSE Exam Notes: Networking Essentials*
by Glenn Madow and James Chellis
ISBN 0-7821-2291-4 320 pages $19.99

Choose an administrative plan to meet specific needs, including performance management, account management, and security.

An organization should not grant all members immediate permission to use its network. As soon as network hardware is in place and the network operating system has been installed, a network administrator assigns network accounts to designated employees only. So, account management is at the center of any security policy. Before the administrator creates these user accounts, he needs to determine which network resources need to be available for each user. Establishing which shared resources should have general access and those that need limited access continues to shape a network's security policy. The security policy goes on to include a plan that protects passwords from theft. In Windows NT, the Accounts Policy helps to guard passwords from getting into the hands of unlawful intruders.

Security is an essential part of network management. Small networks can use password-protected shares, but access permissions provide a much more flexible and secure way of protecting data. Passwords should be carefully protected, and a network that needs greater security can also use data encryption, auditing, diskless computers, and virus protection software.

Sharing Data

The primary reason for installing a network with a file server is that you can store files on the server and share these files with network users. Shared files and directories can exist on one computer in a network, which can be accessed from other computers. These shared directories facilitate the completion of group activities where several people in an organization can work on one set of files at the same time. By storing different files in various directories you can contain sensitive data in certain locations, and these directories can restrict access to only a few users or groups. At the same time, other directories can be designed to offer full access for everyone. Sharing printers operates the same way. Printers can be shared across a network, but access to a network printer can be restricted to certain users and groups.

User Accounts and Groups

Users' account names and passwords identify them to the network and are the basis for all accounting and security with regard to users on the network. You can assign users to groups, and you can give both users and groups access rights to resources on the network. With careful planning, you can use groups to make administering a large number of users much easier. Windows NT enables you to create user accounts and group accounts that are stored in one database owned by a domain. A *domain* is a group of computers that share the same security and logon authentication database.

User Accounts

Every network user needs an *account*. A user account identifies the user to the network. This way, the server can give users access to their own files and can regulate each user's access to other files and services. Every network operating system has a program or utility to help you manage user accounts. The Windows NT utility is called User Manager for Domains. (See Figure 3.1.) It resides in the Administrative Tools program group in Windows NT.

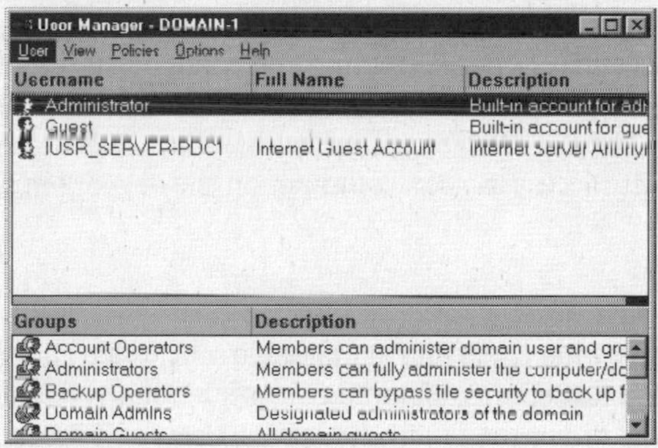

FIGURE 3.1: User Manager

Removing accounts from the network is just as important as creating them; every account you create may eventually have to be deleted as the people in your organization change. Schools and universities, for instance, create and remove hundreds of accounts every semester. On the other hand, some companies never need to delete an account. You can choose to either disable an account or delete it. An account you disable will appear not to exist, which means no one can use that account to log in. However, it does still exist in the network operating system database. If the account is needed later, you can un-disable to reinstate it. Also, accounts can become locked-out due to several unsuccessful logon attempts. If someone is trying an unlawful logon by using random passwords, Windows NT will detect this action after several unsuccessful logon attempts and automatically lock the account.

NOTE

If a user is unable to log on to a server, the user could be using the wrong password, the password could have expired, the account could have been locked out, or the account could have been disabled.

NOTE

Deleting an account removes it from the network database. If a deleted account is needed in the future, you will have to create it again. Thus you should disable the account, not delete it.

There are two default accounts created by Windows NT during installation; the Administrator account and the Guest account. The *Administrator account* manages the overall configuration of the server and can be used for managing security policies, creating and changing user and group accounts, creating shared directories for the network, and maintaining software and hardware. The *Guest account* enables one-time users or users with low or no security access to use a computer on the network in a limited fashion.

Group Accounts

Groups are created to gather users into manageable sets, which allows for efficient configuration and control of numerous user accounts. Permissions are assigned to groups rather than individual users. Users who are members of a group have all the permissions assigned to that group. Window NT supports two types of groups: global, or network groups, and local groups that apply only to a single computer. Windows NT Server, acting as domain controller, creates global groups with the User Manager for Domains. Windows NT Workstations can only create groups local to that workstation. *Local groups* are assigned permissions to use resources and contain global groups for members. *Global groups* are not assigned permissions to use resources; instead they are added as members to local groups and receive their authority from the local groups to which they belong.

Built-In Groups

Windows NT comes with some groups predefined for your convenience in having to assign network rights to certain users. These groups, called *built-in groups* are those found in most networks; they correspond to common network functions. Built-in groups are divided into three categories:

Administrators Members of this group have access rights to everything on the server.

Operator-type groups Members of these groups can perform specific tasks on the network. One example is the Print Operators group, which can manage printers on the network.

Other Members of these groups can do other specialized tasks on the network.

Microsoft Windows NT comes with the built-in groups defined in Table 3.1.

TABLE 3.1: Groups Built in to Microsoft Windows NT Server

Group	Initially Contains	Group Modifiers	Rights and Other Capabilities
Local Groups (The Real Power Holders)			
Administrators	Domain Admins (global group), Administrator (user account)	Administrators	Create, delete, and manage user accounts, global groups, and local groups. Share directories and printers. Grant resource permissions and rights. Install operating system files and programs.
Users	Domain users (global group)	Administrators, account operators	Normal user rights and permissions.
Guests	Guest (user account)	Administrators, account operators	Guest user rights and permissions.
Server Operators	None	Administrators	Share and stop sharing resources. Lock or unlock server. Format server disks. Back up and restore server. Shut down server.
Print Operators	None	Administrators	Shared and unshared printers. Manage printers.

TABLE 3.1 continued: Groups Built in to Microsoft Windows NT Server

Group	Initially Contains	Group Modifiers	Rights and Other Capabilities
LOCAL GROUPS (THE REAL POWER HOLDERS)			
Backup Operators	None	Administrators	Back up and restore servers. Shut down server.
Account Operators	None	Administrators	Perform user and group management functions for users and groups other than administrator or server operator groups.
Replicator	None	Administrators, account operators, server operators	Perform directory replication functions.
GLOBAL GROUPS			
Domain Admins	The initial Administrator user account	Administrators	Receive their rights from the local groups they are members of.
Domain Users	The initial Administrator user account	Administrators, account operators	Receive their rights from the local groups they are members of.
Domain Guests	Guest	Administrators, account operators	Receive their rights from the local groups they are members of.

Implementing Security on Windows NT

Network security involves protecting network resources from internal and external intruders, as well as intentional and unintentional damage. Your role as a network administrator includes the following security tasks:

- Creating a security policy
- Distributing appropriate access permissions to network resources and rights to network functions
- Auditing and monitoring network resource usage

Security Policy Including Password Security

The most important part of any security policy is password security. In Windows NT password security is created in the Account Policy (see Figure 3.2), which is included in the User Manager for Domains. The following features found in the Windows NT Account Policy help to prevent passwords from being stolen:

- Requires users to have unique passwords with a minimum length
- Requires users to have regular, frequent password changes
- Requires new passwords with each change of password and limit the use of old passwords

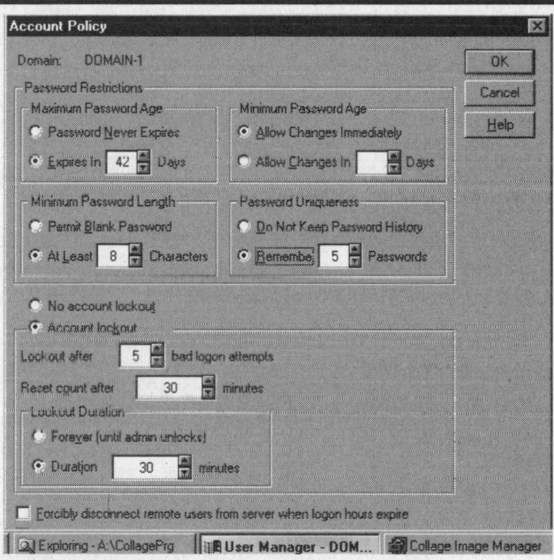

FIGURE 3.2: Account Policy dialog box

Other security policy features:

- Restricts logon times
- Carefully limits guest accounts
- Provides secure physical locations for servers that can be locked
- Protects equipment against fire and natural disasters
- Uses fault-tolerance techniques and keeps adequate backups

- Protects the network against viruses
- Audits (monitors) network resources

Permissions and Rights

After you have created users and groups and have established a security policy, you need to assign appropriate permissions and rights to network resources.

Share permissions and file permissions By creating shared resources on a network, you are permitted to establish a set of rules that determines who will have access to each share. These rules or sets of permissions become part of the network's security policy and are assigned to individual users and groups. Windows NT implements two types of sharing, share permissions and file permissions. *Share permissions* only operate at the folder or directory level and work regardless of the file system being used, so you can use them on both NTFS and FAT shared volumes. *File permissions* work only with NTFS volumes and limit access on a directory or file basis. Only file permissions can provide security to a local shared folder when a user logs on locally to that computer. When a computer only uses share permission security, a user logged on locally can gain access to any shared folder at that machine regardless of his/her assigned permissions.

A shared folder can use both share permissions and file permissions. These sets of permissions include standard permissions, such as read, write, delete, and no access. Both sets of permissions are usually assigned to local groups, and a user's group membership determines his/her permissions for any particular shared folder. One individual user can belong to many groups creating a situation where the user would have multiple and different permissions for a particular shared folder. Sometimes multiple permissions are complementary and cumulative. For example, a user who belongs to two groups might have the read permission to a particular shared folder from one group and the write (change) permission from another group. In this case, the two permissions are cumulative and the user is allowed to read and write to files in this folder.

Rights *Rights* are abilities that a user can use to control the system. Rights apply to the system as a whole, rather than to specific objects, which are controlled by permissions. Table 3.2 shows a list of rights available with Windows NT.

TABLE 3.2: Windows NT Rights

Windows NT Rights	
Access the computer from the network	Log on locally
Add workstations to a domain	Manage auditing and security log
Backup files and directories	Restore files and directories
Change the system time	Shut down the system
Force shutdown from a remote system	Take ownership of files and other directories
Load and unload device drivers	

Auditing

Another element of a good security plan for a network is auditing security events. *Auditing* refers to the tracking of activities caused by users and other system incidents.

Auditing can track the following events:

- Success and failures of logon attempts
- Success and failures of opening or closing files
- Changes to files or folders
- Password changes
- Changes to user or group accounts
- Changes to permissions to files or folders

In the Audit Policy dialog box of the User Manger for Domains, you can specify which events you want to audit. Notice Audit These Events has been checked in Figure 3.3, and several checks have been applied to the Success and Failure tracking for certain events.

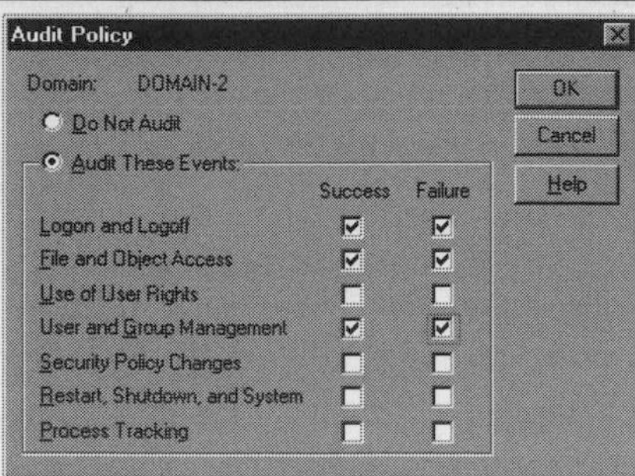

FIGURE 3.3: Audit Policy dialog box

You can view the events you selected to track by using Windows NT Event Viewer's Security Log.

Data Encryption

If a network is using sensitive data and you want to prevent anyone from stealing information, you will need to employ data encryption. *Encryption* is a process in which ordinary text or numerical information is converted into an unintelligible form called *ciphertext* using a well-defined and reversible conversion algorithm and a predefined bit value known as a key.

Virus Protection

A *virus* is a small bit of computer code that is self-replicating and designed to hide inside other programs. The virus travels with these programs, and it is invoked whenever the program is launched. Because the virus is self-replicating, it will make a copy of itself whenever the program is invoked, and it can then infest other files, disks, computers, and an entire network. There are many third-party virus protection programs that can check storage media throughout an entire network on a regular basis.

Diskless Workstations

Diskless workstations are inexpensive computers without floppy disk drives. They provide users with network access at a reasonable price while providing data security, because users are unable to download data to a floppy disk and walk away. Diskless workstations are good for unsupervised areas.

WARNING

You will see at least one question on the exam that includes all the security measures discussed in this section: auditing, assigning permissions, password protection, virus protection, diskless workstations, and data encryption. The question is not a difficult one; Microsoft just wants you to be aware of these techniques and their definitions.

Choose a disaster recovery plan for various situations.

This objective is a continuation of the previous one. Every security policy needs to include provisions for recovering data in case of predictable hardware failure or unpredictable destruction. You must ensure that the network is reliable. A regular data backup is a good first line of defense, and an uninterruptable power supply (UPS) for the network servers is a wise investment. Environments where continuous operation is critical can invest in RAID (Redundant Arrays of Independent Disks).

Tape Backup

Every network should have some form of backup. The most common form is backup on magnetic tape. If you have a *tape backup* of your important data files and something does happen to your file server, you can restore the data to that server or to another server. Without a tape backup, the data could be lost permanently.

A tape backup of your data can also be useful when data files are inadvertently or intentionally deleted. You can restore those deleted files from the backup tape. You will lose any changes that were made since the files were last backed up, but the files themselves will be restored.

You will need two things to protect your data with tape backups:

- A tape drive
- A backup policy

The Backup Policy

When you back up your data, you can use one of the methods described in Table 3.3.

TABLE 3.3: Backup Methods

METHOD	DESCRIPTION
Full backup	Backs up and marks files as having been backed up.
Copy	Backs up and does not mark files as having been backed up.
Incremental backup	Backs up the files if they have changed since the last backup. Marks those files as having been backed up.
Daily copy	Backs up files that have changed that day. Does not mark those files as having been backed up.
Differential copy	Backs up files if they have changed since the last full backup. Does not mark those files as having been backed up.

You should perform a full backup of your server data fairly often. The full backup will store all your data, whereas the incremental backups store only what has changed since your last backup. If your network holds critical data that changes often, you may wish to perform a full backup every night and several incremental backups during the day to minimize the amount of data that can be lost. If even that is not sufficient, you should consider fault-tolerant systems, as described a little later in this chapter.

It is important to keep a log of tape backups. It will help you retrieve the right files from the backup tape if an emergency occurs. Here are some items you should record:

- Date and time the backup was performed
- Tape number or description
- Type of backup
- Who performed the backup operation
- Which computer was backed up
- Which files were backed up
- Location of the tapes

Connecting the Backup System

You can either connect the tape drive directly to the server or connect it to a client computer that will run the backup program and back up the server. The advantage of connecting the tape drive to the server is that backups are quicker when the data does not have to be transmitted over the network. A disadvantage is that, if the server has difficulties, you must repair the server before you can retrieve data from the tape backup.

An advantage of connecting the tape drive to a client computer is that the client computer can still operate while the server is out of commission, allowing you to get at the data while the server is down and restore the data to another server, if possible. Another advantage is that it is easier to back up multiple servers using a client computer. A disadvantage is that all the data being backed up must be transferred over the network to the client computer.

Networks with several servers often have an isolated segment for backup, and all data for backup is transferred over that segment. This arrangement frees other network segments from the load of backing up the data, and it isolates the data backup from the effects of network use.

Uninterruptible Power Supply (UPS)

Your file server is an electrical device; when the power fails, so does your server. One way to protect your computer from power failure is with an *uninterruptible power supply* (*UPS*). A UPS stores electricity while your computer and the power supplying it are acting normally. When a power failure occurs, the UPS continues to provide power to your computer for a period of time. How long it provides power depends on the UPS you purchase; it can range from several minutes to several hours. Five or ten minutes are common UPS capacities. The UPS will signal your file server that power has failed and that it may be necessary for the file server to save its data and shut down. The UPS allows the file server operating system to shut down when power fails instead of being halted in the middle of an important operation, which might cause data to be lost.

Your UPS should protect your equipment from power spikes as well as power failures and brownouts. The UPS should come with software to communicate with the server and notify it of a power problem. It should also be powerful enough to drive all the devices that will depend on it if a power failure occurs, and it should give the network systems enough time to shut down.

For critical network operations, you may wish to consider an independent source of power, such as a gasoline-powered generator. The UPS can provide electrical power until the generator comes online. This way your network can continue to function even when the power is out for an extended period of time.

Disk Fault-Tolerant Systems

If you have critical network functions that must continue to operate even in the event of hardware failure on the network, consider using *fault-tolerant systems* in your network. These are systems that can continue to operate even when one part of them fails. RAID is one example of a fault-tolerant system.

Redundant Arrays of Independent Disks

Redundant Arrays of Independent Disks (*RAID*) is a system of using several hard disks to allow a computer to recover from the failure of any one disk without losing data, to provide greater speed accessing data on disks, or both. RAID can be hardware- or software-based. Windows NT implements RAID in software, so you do not need an expensive RAID card to have the benefits of RAID in your system. RAID comes in five levels. The RAID software provided by Microsoft implements levels 0, 1, and 5.

Level 0—Disk Striping Disk striping combines several physical disk partitions (called a *stripe set*) into one logical drive. Data stored to the logical drive is distributed across all partitions in 64K chunks. The advantage of this type of distribution is that data from several physical hard drives can be transferred to and from each of the hard drives simultaneously, which makes file storage and retrieval faster. Disk striping is more convenient than having several separate drives because it combines all the storage space into one large logical drive. Disk striping does not, however, provide greater reliability. In fact, if any one of the drives fails, the data on all of them will be lost. RAID level 0 does not store parity information that would allow the computer to recover from a drive failure.

In Windows NT a stripe set can consist of 2 to 32 physical drives. The physical drives can be of different types (SCSI, IDE, ESDI, and so on) and sizes.

WARNING

Don't get caught off guard—RAID 0 includes NO fault tolerance.

Level 1—Disk Mirroring Disk mirroring simply keeps a complete copy of one hard drive partition on another hard drive partition on another physical hard drive. This is the simplest method of fault tolerance in a RAID system. If there is a failure on the first partition, the second partition can take over.

When a second hard drive controller is used to control the second hard drive, the process is called *duplexing*. Duplexing is faster than regular disk mirroring because the computer can talk to both drives at the same time, through each one's adapter, rather than sending the data to one drive and then sending the data again to the second drive.

NOTE

Disk duplexing is a modification of disk mirroring where each disk drive has its own drive controller.

Level 2—Disk Striping Disk Striping with ECC Level 2 distributes data across all the disks, just as level 0 does, but it also stores error correction code (ECC) with the data. The ECC allows the computer to reconstruct the data on one of the disk drives if the disk drive fails. ECC uses more disk space than parity methods do (see levels 3 through 5), so it is not used very often.

Level 3—ECC Stored as Parity Level 3 is like level 2 except that it stores parity information instead of ECC to recover information when any one disk dies. *Parity* refers to an error-checking mechanism in which all binary 1s in the stored data must always be the same—odd or even. Parity is used to recreate missing data in the event of a failed disk. Level 3 uses one of the disks used in the RAID system to store parity information and results in about 85 percent of disk space available for data storage when seven drives or a multiple of seven is used (the optimal number of drives in a RAID system).

Level 4—Disk Striping with Large Blocks Level 4 uses large blocks (larger than the 64K blocks used in other striping levels) to speed up operations on large files. The parity information is stored on one of the disks in the RAID system. Because the whole large block must be read and modified whenever there is even a small change, Level 4 is slower than other levels when working with small files.

Level 5—Striping with Parity Striping with parity is the most popular form of fault-tolerant RAID. It uses from 3 to 32 hard drives and writes the parity information across all drives in the array. The data information and parity information for any one stripe (row of 64K blocks) is always on different disks.

NOTE

Stripe sets with parity have better read performance than disk mirroring.

WARNING

Windows NT supports RAID levels 0, 1, and 5 directly. These are strictly software-based solutions, which are supported by the Windows NT operating system itself. You can employ the other RAID levels with Windows NT, if you desire a hardware-based solution. For the exam, however, consider levels 2, 3, and 4 to be incorrect answers.

Sector Sparing

Windows NT also uses a technique called *sector sparing* (also called hot-fixing) to detect and work around bad spots in hard drives. This technique requires hard disk drives that can support this feature. Currently, Windows NT only supports sector sparing using SCSI drives. When a disk operation fails for a sector on the hard drive, Windows NT marks that sector as bad and designates a different sector to store data.

TIP

Some types of hard drives can perform sector sparing on their own (SCSI is one such type), while other types, such as IDE and ESDI, cannot.

Given the manufacturer's documentation for the network adapter, install, configure, and resolve hardware conflicts for multiple network adapters in a Token Ring or Ethernet network.

Network interface cards (NICs) in the computer place the information on the network. Over fifty percent of all network problems are related to inoperative network interface cards. Faulty NICs are the result of either physical deterioration of the card itself, loose connections, or improper configuration. This section is concerned with the last two.

A network adapter card must match both the bus of the computer it is placed in and the network to which it will be attached. In addition, the card must be configured to communicate with the computer by installing the correct drivers and making sure that certain settings are selected properly. The network administrator must be careful to avoid possible conflicts between NIC settings and similar settings of other computer hardware.

Network adapter cards in IBM-compatible computers must be configured to operate correctly. The four most common items requiring configuration are:

- The interrupt
- The base I/O port
- The base memory address
- The transceiver

TIP

Adapter cards now are usually software configured, but many older network adapter cards required that they be configured by setting jumpers or dip switches.

Interrupt

Interrupts are the means by which a device in a computer signals the computer that it requires servicing. For example, a network adapter card will interrupt the computer when data has arrived to notify the computer that it has more data to process. Each device must have its own interrupt. The interrupts are assigned different priority levels so that the most important will be serviced first.

Table 3.4 lists the IRQs (Interrupt ReQuest lines) a network adapter can use if they are not already being used by another device.

TIP

IRQs 3 and 5 are the most commonly used for network adapters and are usually available. You can use the MSD (Microsoft Diagnostic) program to determine which IRQs are already being used. For the exam, you should memorize the default IRQ settings listed in Table 3.4; you may be asked questions about the interrupts assigned to devices in a standard PC.

TABLE 3.4: IRQs in a Computer

IRQ	Computer with an 80286 Processor or Higher
2	EGA/VGA (enhanced graphics adapter/video graphics adapter)
3	Available unless used for second serial port (COM2, COM4, or bus mouse)
4	COM1/COM3
5	Available unless used for second parallel port (LPT2) or sound card
6	Floppy disk controller
7	Parallel port (LPT1)
8	Real-time clock
9	Available
10	Available
11	Available
12	Mouse (PS/2)
13	Math coprocessor
14	Hard disk controller
15	Available

Base I/O Port

The *base input/output port* specifies an I/O location through which the computer communicates with the card. The base I/O port must be different for each device in the computer. You may need to check your computer documentation to see which addresses are already in use in your system.

Base Memory Address

The computer talks with the adapter card through the base I/O port, but it places the data to be transmitted in its own memory in the location specified by the *base memory address*. The adapter reads from this area as it prepares data to be sent out to the network cable, and it places incoming information in this area. The base memory address is sometimes called the RAM start address. Somc adapter cards do not have a base memory address because they do not use any of the computer's RAM to store or buffer data.

NOTE

A common base address for network adapters is D8000. Sometimes the final digit is dropped, so you will see it as D800. You must select a base address that no other device is using.

Transceiver

A *transceiver* is a device that can both receive and transmit a signal. Transceivers can be part of a network card or an external component. Some adapter cards have several transceivers. For instance, the Allied Telesyn ATI 1500T has both fiber-optic and twisted-pair ports. Also, many Ethernet cards contain 10BaseT and 100BaseT capabilities. Y may need to select which port will be used in your network and co the adapter card to match. You can do this by means of either ju software.

Data Bus

There are five common bus types in PC-compatible cor network interface card must be of the type your comp

ISA The bus introduced by IBM with the IB it was an 8-bit bus; it was extended to 16 bits the IBM PC AT. The 8-bit cards could still work in the 16-bit slots, but 16-bit cards could not work in the 8-bit slots of the original PC. The ISA bus is slow; it is limited to 8 or 12MHz (megahertz).

EISA An expansion on the ISA bus standard. It extends the ISA bus to 32 bits. It also has some of the improvements found in Micro Channel (described below). A consortium of hardware vendors introduced the EISA standard to compete with IBM's Micro Channel architecture. ISA cards can still be put in EISA slots, but not vice versa.

Local bus Another extension to the ISA standard. In addition to expanding that standard to 32 bits, it speeds it up considerably. Local bus cards run at the processor's bus speed (not to be confused with the processor's internal clock speed), which can be as high as 33MHz.

Micro Channel IBM's attempt at a new bus standard for personal computers. Micro Channel is not electrically compatible with ISA; an ISA card cannot be put into a Micro Channel slot. Micro Channel runs at a higher speed than ISA and can be a 16- or 32-bit bus. Micro Channel also supports advanced features, such as bus mastering.

PCI A bus standard used with computers based on the Pentium chip and in Apple Computer's Power Macintoshes. Only PCI cards can be placed in a PCI slot. PCI was designed for Plug and Play, which is a philosophy and a set of specifications designed to make configuring computers easier. Ideally, a user would not have to configure a PCI card when installing it in a personal computer; it would configure itself automatically.

Sometimes more than one bus type is supported in the same computer. In such cases you can decide to use a more expensive and powerful card (such as PCI) or a less expensive card (usually ISA).

Cabling Connectors

The network interface card must support the type of cable used in your network. Some network standards—for example, Ethernet—can use one of several cable types, so your Ethernet card must support the cable type you chose to install.

The card must perform three functions in relation to the cabling:

- Make the physical connection to the cable
- Generate the electrical (or optical) signals on the cable
- Follow specific rules controlling access to the cable

Some cards support several connector types, providing greater flexibility in cabling choice.

Network Optimization

Your network adapter cards affect network performance in a big way. All the data in your network flows through the network adapter cards. Not only can one slow card make one workstation slow, it can slow all the other computers on the network while waiting for the slow card to finish transmitting. A number of things can speed up communication over a network adapter card. The following are features that can speed network communications:

Direct Memory Access (DMA) Bypasses the computer's microprocessor, moving data directly from the card to the computer's system memory.

Shared adapter memory With this feature the memory on the card also appears in the computer's main memory space.

Shared system memory In this case the adapter card selects and uses a portion of the computer's main memory to store and buffer data.

Bus mastering With bus mastering, the adapter card can take control of the computer's bus and place the data directly in the computer's memory. This method avoids certain setup and data-movement inefficiencies that DMA experiences. EISA and Micro Channel can do bus mastering, but cards that support it are often expensive.

RAM buffering This feature uses extra memory on the card to buffer data while previous data is still being transmitted or the network is otherwise busy.

Onboard microprocessor An onboard microprocessor can speed network operations by performing, by itself, calculations that might otherwise require the computer's CPU.

The highest-performing cards should go in the server because the speed of the server affects all clients on the network. You may wish to use other, less expensive cards for client computers, depending on the nature of the computing and communication each client computer is handling.

NOTE

Shared memory (either shared adapter memory or shared system memory) is a faster memory transfer method than the basic I/O method or DMA (Direct Memory Access). In general, network adapter cards using the EISA, PCI, or the Micro Channel architecture bus type are faster than cards using the ISA bus type.

Implement a NetBIOS naming scheme for all computers on a given network.

Windows NT Server 4 is required to use NetBIOS names for its computers, which is an asset because it facilitates the sharing of network resources and network security. However, NetBIOS names are also handicapped because they are limited to 15 characters. Microsoft realizes this limitation and wants Windows NT administrators to be able to work around this restriction. This objective and the questions produced from it concentrate on the NetBIOS 15-character limitation.

The NetBIOS naming scheme was covered in Chapter 1, "Standards and Terminology." You may want to review that section in addition to the information given here.

NetBIOS Name Resolution

NetBIOS provides an upper-layer application programming interface (API) for applications to use to communicate with network resources. One thing that NetBIOS does is to identify each computer on the network with a unique 15-character name. An extra 16th character is used to provide additional system information about the name. NetBIOS names cannot contain spaces or backslash characters. A NetBIOS name is added to a computer when its operating system is installed. Whenever a computer is connected to the network, it broadcasts its name to other nodes on the network.

Select the appropriate hardware and software tools to monitor trends in the network.

You will want to keep your network running smoothly so that network users can perform their jobs. To do this you must watch your network's performance, staying alert to bottlenecks and network trouble spots. Ideally, you will be able to anticipate network problems and prevent them from occurring. Tools like the Windows NT Performance Monitor can be useful in gauging the health of the network. During the beginning stages of a network, Performance Monitor is used to gather statistics in the form of charts, reports, and logs for establishing a baseline. Baselines or reference points are used to compare future network performance to a previous healthy state when the baseline statistics were gathered. Network documentation can help you keep track of the network and make the task of fixing, expanding, or handing over administration of the network to another individual much easier. Tools such as the Microsoft Systems Management Server (SMS) software can help you work with a large network and keep track of the state of that network.

Bottlenecks

When a problem with a device slows the whole network, it is called a *bottleneck*. If one of the devices in your network cannot transfer information as quickly as other devices, the whole network slows down. Bottlenecks can originate at a server and at network media or network devices, such as routers and hubs. One of your functions is to observe the various devices that cooperate to make a network and observe when one is causing the rest to slow down.

Devices that can experience bottlenecks include:

Servers

- CPU
- Memory
- Network interface cards
- Disks and disk controllers

Network

- Network media
- Network connectivity devices

A device can cause a bottleneck if it is old or slow, functioning marginally (in which case it might soon fail completely), set up improperly, given insufficient resources to perform its job, or inappropriate for the type of network you are using.

Windows NT Performance Monitor

Windows NT provides a utility to help you monitor your network server. Windows NT Performance Monitor can graph many aspects of network performance that involve a server, including:

- Processors
- Hard disks
- Memory
- Network utilization

In addition to displaying and recording data, Performance Monitor can send you an alert when a resource, such as disk space, exceeds a threshold. This way you can take care of network problems before they become critical. Performance Monitor can also automatically start up certain programs (such as disk compression or archive programs) that may bring the network back within normal parameters when a threshold is exceeded.

Your first task with Performance Monitor is to become familiar with network performance while the network is performing well. Later you will be able to recognize an anomalous network condition, such as unusual disk activity or exceptionally high memory usage, and take steps to correct these situations.

You must install Simple Network Management Protocol (SNMP) before you can use TCP/IP performance counters in Windows NT Performance Monitor.

NOTE

You may see a question on the exam that asks you to select multiple tools that can gather baseline information. Besides the Performance Monitor, protocol analyzers including the Windows NT Network Monitor can gather networking performance statistics by examining packets captured on the network. A protocol analyzer is a device used to capture and decode network packets. The Network Monitor is a software example of a protocol analyzer. Protocol analyzers are known more for detecting problems with network media and are discussed in the next chapter.

SNMP

While Windows NT Performance Monitor helps you monitor the network server, the Simple Network Management Protocol (SNMP) is a standard protocol for monitoring other devices on your network. Any network device that has an SNMP agent (a software program within the device) can monitor network traffic and report the behavior of the device to a central monitoring program. This data is stored in a Management Information Base (MIB).

Network devices that commonly have SNMP management include:

- Hubs
- Servers
- Interface cards
- Routers and bridges
- Printer network adapters

The central monitoring program (usually a program run on the server) regularly connects to the SNMP agents and gathers statistical information about the network device. That information is stored in the MIB and can be displayed on a monitor or printed as text. SNMP software can also present the information in the form of graphs, maps, and charts. A central monitoring program can also export the data to other programs to be analyzed. The central program can be set to alert the network administration staff when certain network conditions occur, such as a fault or overload. Network staff can then solve the problem. This alert is especially useful in large networks where the network staff cannot observe all computers all the time.

Documenting the Network

Your network should be well documented. Network documentation not only helps you keep track of your network, it becomes indispensable if someone else needs to perform your network administration duties. Network documentation makes it easier for several people to perform network tasks, because it is a written record of what each individual has done. Valuable time is saved because you don't have to figure out what your coworker has done, it is all there, written down. Be sure to keep all network information in one log and make all changes in that log. You can, of course, make copies of the log, but there should be only one place to record new network information.

You need network documentation because your network will almost certainly not stay the same as when you installed it. Eventually your network will grow, and you will add equipment. You will also do maintenance tasks and reinstall or upgrade the server and client systems. By documenting what you did the first time, you can perform these tasks more easily the next time you need them.

Here are some useful items to include in your network documentation:

- Purchase dates and item descriptions
- Vendor and warranty information
- Serial numbers
- The location of product documentation (manuals, and so on)
- The installation process and results
- The initial network configuration
- A diagram of the network
- Subsequent network changes
- Network drive assignments
- Shared network resources (printers, and so on)
- Listings and locations of copies of critical files (such as config.sys)
- Shared software on the server
- The number of software licenses for each application and the location of the license certificates
- A history of network problems and their solutions

If you keep your documentation as a network file, it is a good idea to print it out and to store the file away from the network—you may need to use the information when the network is not functioning.

Automated Network Management

Software packages are available to help you manage your network. One such software package is Microsoft's Systems Management Server (SMS). It can help you keep track of the hardware and software on your network and can automate the process of updating application software and client station computers. Functions provided by SMS include:

Inventory management SMS can query client station computers and store an inventory of the client station's hardware and software. This inventory list is stored on the server in a SQL server database.

Software distribution SMS can distribute software to client stations and update client station software. You can also use it to run commands on client computers to do tasks such as virus scanning.

Shared application management SMS can make shared network programs available to client computers dynamically by building a program group for the client that will allow users to select the shared program by clicking an icon on their desktop.

Remote control and network monitor SMS allows you to interrogate client computers, diagnose client problems remotely, and analyze traffic on the network.

SMS does not provide virus protection or an SNMP management interface, but it allows third-party products to interface with it in order to provide these services.

Using Windows NT Performance Monitor

Windows NT Performance Monitor is used to monitor common network bottlenecks that are server related. Performance Monitor offers four ways to represent the captured data: charts, reports, logs, and alerts.

1. From the Administrative Tools group, select Performance Monitor and notice under the View menu that Chart has been selected by default.

2. Choose Add To Chart from the Edit menu to display the Add To Chart dialog box.
3. Before you can select a specific data counter, you first need to choose a set of data counters. Select Processor.
4. Next, scroll within the Counter window and select % Processor Time, then click the Explain button. Notice that the explanation says that this counter represents the percentage of non-idle time the processor needs to work. A continuous percentage of over 80% may mean you need an upgrade or additional processors.
5. Next, click the Add button, then click the Done button. You will now notice the graphing taking place. (See Figure 3.4.)

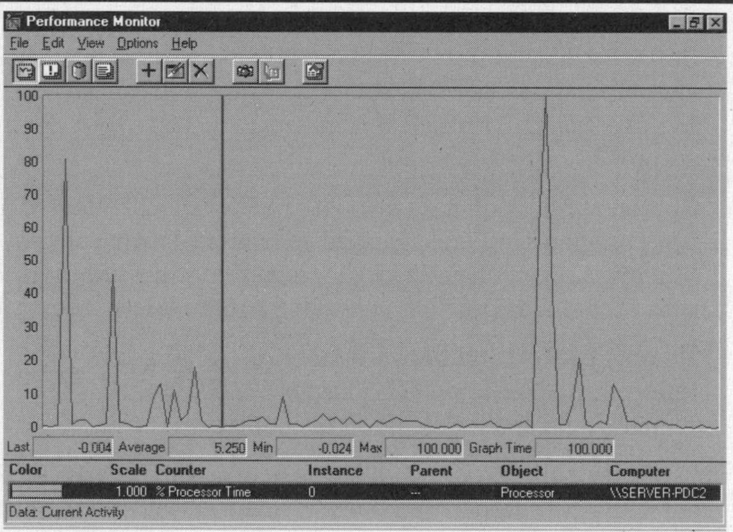

FIGURE 3.4: Performance Monitor chart

6. Try starting another application and watch the counter's line rise and fall when performing some action.
7. Notice the Average box with the present average % Processor Time. This is another indication of whether there is a processor need or not.

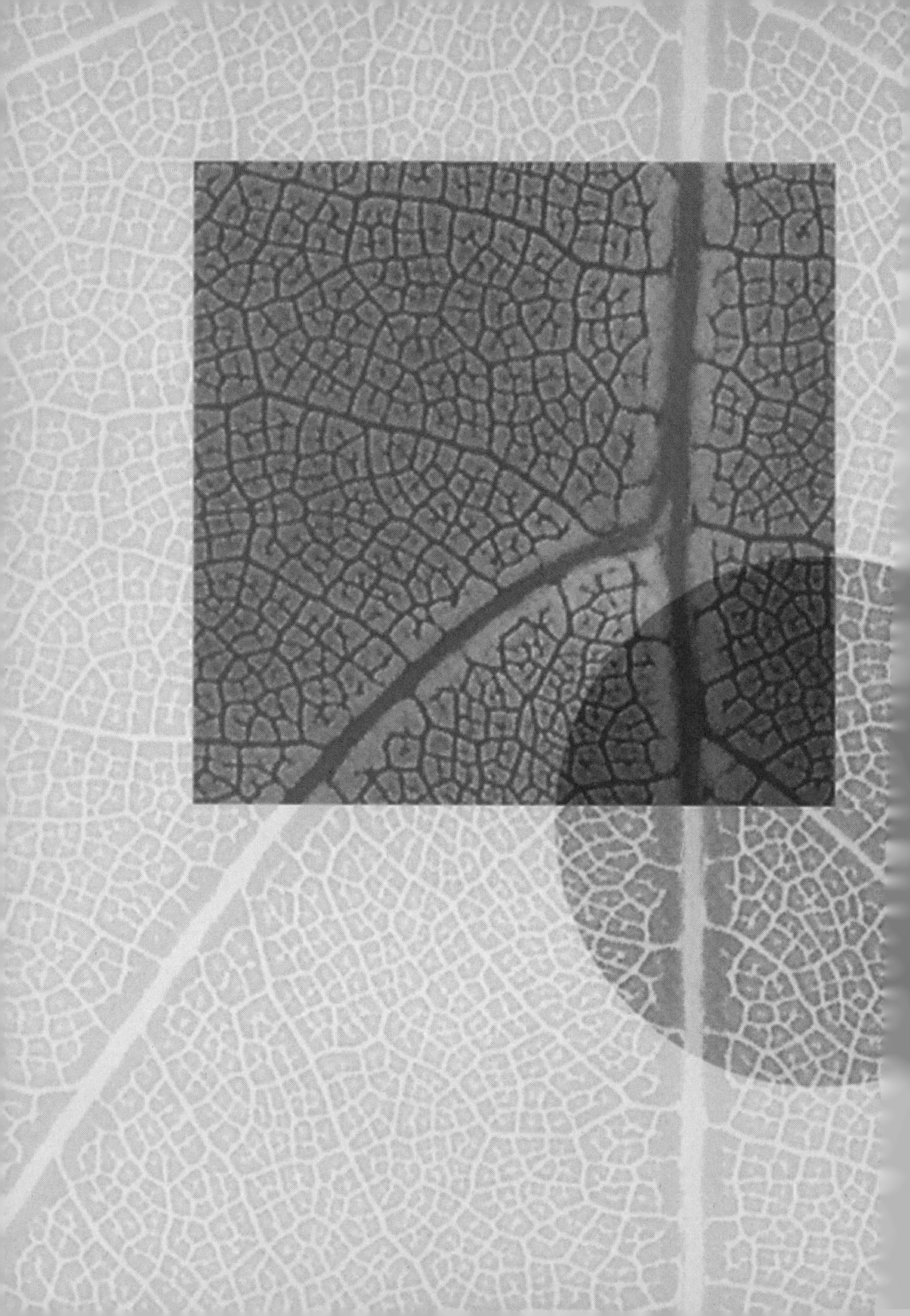

Chapter 4

TROUBLESHOOTING

Troubleshooting is one of the primary tasks of the network administrator. Troubleshooting is the art of seeking out the cause of a problem and eliminating or controlling that problem. This chapter discusses troubleshooting techniques for solving problems related to network cabling, adapter cards, and other important connectivity devices. In addition, you will learn some guidelines for troubleshooting network performance. To be able to recognize the source of network problems, you will need to understand how a normal network operates based on the characteristics of healthy network components and baseline information. Of course, knowing what to look for from having previously experienced the same problem is the best preparation for any problematic situation. But as a brand new network administrator you need to read and talk about network problems as much as possible.

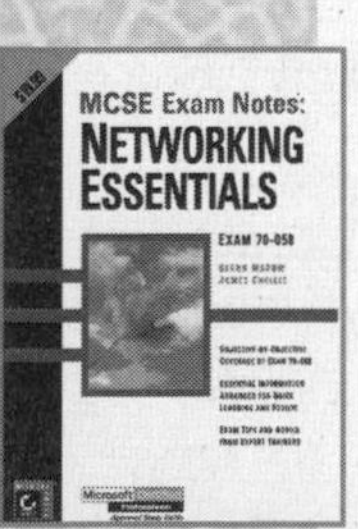

Adapted from *MCSE Exam Notes: Networking Essentials*
by Glenn Madow and James Chellis
ISBN 0-7821-2291-4~MS320 pages $19.99

Identify common errors associated with components required for communications.

This objective and the next one are much alike at first glance; however, Microsoft considers problems involving network software to be more common than problems that involve network hardware. Therefore, this objective covers issues related to client and server software problems, while the next objective deals mostly with hardware-related problems. Discussed under this objective are strictly software problems and not faulty software symptoms caused by related hardware problems. Microsoft is concerned about a network administrator being able to diagnose protocol mismatches, mismatched IPX/SPX frame types, and poorly configured TCP/IP utilities.

Identifying Protocol Problems

The following information discusses three areas of protocol problems that are very common in newly installed networks:

- Incompatible IPX/SPX frame types
- Incompatible protocols
- TCP/IP-related problems

Incompatible IPX/SPX Frame Types

Unlike TCP/IP or NetBEUI, the IPX protocol cannot automatically determine the packet type. The IPX protocol supports four different frame types in an Ethernet environment and two different frame types in the Token Ring environment. Each of the four Ethernet frame types is incompatible with the others:

- Ethernet 802.3: Used mostly in Novell NetWare 2.2 and 3.*x* networks.
- Ethernet 802.2: Default frame type for Novell NetWare 3.12 and 4.*x*.
- Ethernet SNAP: Used in some AppleTalk networks.
- Ethernet II: Used in TCP/IP networks.

Normally, you must specify the correct frame type to be used. Incorrect frame types cause many problems on IPX networks. For two IPX (or NWLink) computers to communicate they must use the same frame type. The frame type is the format used to put together packet header and data information for transmission on the data link. The 802.2 frame type is the default and most commonly used frame type in Windows NT networks. If only one computer on the network is affected, then it would almost always be more appropriate to change its frame type rather than change the frame type of the server and all the other computers on the network.

NOTE

Windows NT and Windows 95 can auto-detect frame types, but they can only detect one frame type automatically. In a multiple frame network, when auto-detection is selected it can only recognize the first frame type the computer encounters.

NOTE

For communication to occur between two computers on an Ethernet network, they both must use the same frame type. On a network with multiple frame types, the Windows NT server will need to be configured with all possible frame types that are being used by different clients.

If your IPX/SPX network uses more than one frame type, you will want to tell the driver which frame type to anticipate. You can specify a frame type for the IPX/SPX-compatible protocol by choosing the Advanced tab on its property sheet.

Incompatible Protocols

If two machines are active on the same network but still cannot communicate, it may be that they are using different protocols. For successful communications to occur, both must be using the same protocol. If machine A is only speaking NetBEUI and machine B is only speaking TCP/IP, the two machines are not able to establish a successful connection. Use the network control panel to determine which protocols are supported.

NOTE

Windows NT does not use the DLC protocol to establish workstation or server sessions. DLC is only used for mainframe and network printer traffic.

NOTE

If a Unix machine cannot access shared folders on an NT server, there is a protocol mismatch between the server and Unix computers.

TCP/IP-Related Problems

DNS Many connection problems are the result of improperly configured utilities that perform name resolution. Computers communicate with each other by using numbers for machine identification. Because humans use computer names and not numbers, there is a need to change computer names to numbers. There are two main utilities that convert computer names to number IDs (IP addresses). DNS (Domain Name Service) converts Internet type domain names to IP addresses, and the WINS (Windows Internet Naming Service) can convert regular NetBIOS names to IP addresses. In addition, there are several utilities that test their operations. *Ping* is a diagnostic software tool used to verify the connection to one or more remote hosts. You can ping a computer, which means you enter the command "Ping" along with another computer's IP address (example: Ping 126.34.56.101). If you receive the reply "Reply from 126.34.56.101...," the connection between your computer and this machine is a good one. Similarly, you can ping a computer by using its NetBIOS name or domain name (example: Ping computerone.comp.com). If you ping in this manner and you receive the reply "Time out...," it could mean that the connection is bad. More likely, this reply means that the domain name was not resolved to its IP address and your computer has no access to a DNS.

NOTE

If your machine can ping the NT server with the IP address but not with the domain name, your computer has no access to a Domain Name Server.

WINS When one computer needs to contact another computer and uses its NetBIOS name and wants to know its IP address, the best way to resolve IP addresses with NetBIOS names is to use a WINS server. If a computer is not configured properly and doesn't know the IP address of the WINS server, the computer will not be able to use the WINS server. As a result the computer will then send a broadcast to every computer on the same subnet asking for the right computer to respond with its IP address. If the receiving computer is not in the same subnet, the sending computer will not receive an answer. Broadcasts remain in a single subnet. Also, if a broadcast is not sent for some reason, the sending computer will not be able to communicate with the intended-receiving computer.

NOTE

If a client computer does not know the IP address of a WINS server, it will not be able to use WINS service.

Choosing the Correct IPX/SPX Frame Type

If your IPX/SPX network uses more than one frame type, you will want to tell the driver which frame types to anticipate. You can specify a frame type using the Network icon in the Control Panel. You will need a Windows NT server in order to complete this exercise. You will not be able to add multiple frame types using Windows NT Workstation.

1. Open up the Control Panel and double-click the Network icon.
2. Select the Protocols tab and then choose NWLink IPX/SPX Compatible Transport. Notice the setting in this dialog box; return the setting to the original status after this exercise.
3. Next, check Manual Frame Type Detection instead of Auto Frame Type Detection, which can only detect one frame type.
4. Click the Add button at the bottom to display the Manual Frame Detection window.
5. From the pull-down menu you can select one of four frame types. Select Ethernet 802.2 and enter any eight-digit network number (for example, 56120019) under Network Number (you will remove this later).
6. Click the Add button; you should see this frame type and the network number listed in the NWLink IPX/SPX Properties dialog box.

7. Repeat the same steps and add the other three frame types.
8. Remove all frame types and configure the NWLink IPX/SPX Properties dialog box the way it was before this exercise.

Diagnose and resolve common connectivity problems with cards, cables, and related hardware.

This objective covers three areas. First, it discusses troubleshooting procedures. Next, it describes several troubleshooting tools and explains their use. Finally, some common hardware-related network problems that employ the troubleshooting procedures and tools are described.

Troubleshooting Procedures

Problem prevention reduces the number and types of problems that occur, but things will still go wrong with the network. When they do, it's time to do some troubleshooting. Troubleshooting usually involves applying a combination of knowledge and experience.

Isolating the Problem

Troubleshooting requires the ability to separate a problem into smaller parts and see how all the parts relate to one another. Breaking down a problem allows you to test individual guesses at what went wrong. To help isolate a problem, follow these steps:

- Eliminate the possibility of user error.
- Check the physical site. Is everything that should be there present and connected correctly?
- Back up data if there is a possibility that storage media (hard drive or disk drives) may be the problem.
- Turn everything off and back on again. (This solves a number of problems.)
- Simplify the system. Remove unnecessary elements and isolate the problem by involving a minimum number of factors.

These steps can be useful for solving a number of network problems. For more complex and persistent problems, however, turn to the troubleshooting model described next.

A Troubleshooting Model

Microsoft's troubleshooting model generally has five steps:

1. Set the problem's priority.
2. Collect information to identify the symptoms.
3. Develop a list of possible causes.
4. Test to isolate the cause.
5. Study the results of the test to identify a solution.

The following sections look at these steps in detail.

Setting Your Priorities Network problems always have different levels of priority. John and Frank's inability to play Doom across the network is probably not going to be as important as ensuring that the accounting server doesn't have a virus. For this reason, before you begin work on a network problem, you must assess its priority. At times you will need to let a problem wait while you deal with more urgent matters.

Collecting Basic Information The first step in collecting information is to discover what you can through communication with users and other sources of information. Find out the extent of the problem (what has been affected), what problems the end user is experiencing, and what the computer was doing when the problem occurred.

Ask network users experiencing a particular problem several questions as you begin the troubleshooting process. For example, the following questions may provide a wealth of information:

When was the last time it worked? Have they used it recently or has it sat dormant for a period of time? This question is particularly pertinent to hardware problems. If the last time users used this modem was two years ago, it can make a difference in how you approach the problem.

What changes have been made since the last time it was used? Have there been new hardware additions? Software additions? Has anything on the network been rearranged?

When you have talked to the users, check your documentation to find out how the network usually operates. When you know what is normal for the network, you can compare that performance with what is occurring now.

Developing a List of Possible Causes After you have gathered some basic information, use that information and your own knowledge to formulate an idea about what the problem is most likely to be. Break the problem into smaller parts. Is the problem in the area of user error, application software, operating system software, or equipment? Then prioritize your hypotheses according to their chance of success and the cost of attempting the solution. Remember that cost involves more than hardware; you must factor in network downtime and technician time as well. This prioritization will help you decide which solution to work on first.

If you are having a hard time determining the exact location of a network problem, try separating the network into parts and testing those parts individually. Try workstations on a stand-alone basis.

Testing to Isolate the Cause When you have a good idea of where the problem is, you are ready to test your hypotheses. First, determine which hypothesis is most likely to be successful and cost the least. Then test each part of your hypothesis, one element at a time.

To identify the problem as efficiently as possible, make only one change at a time. Making several at once won't help you determine the exact problem. (Would you want a mechanic to replace your starter motor and your battery before knowing which was faulty?)

Be sure to use reliable procedures, testing equipment, and software when you are testing. Otherwise, you may become confused trying to determine what the original problem was and what new problems have been introduced.

It may be best to begin testing your hypothesis using *forward chaining*, which is the technique of beginning with the source device and moving toward the destination device. Investigating in the reverse fashion, from the destination device to the source device, is called reverse chaining.

Studying the Results to Identify the Solution After you have tested the system, you will either have a better idea of what the problem is, or you will have to go back a couple of steps (or to the beginning) and start again.

Now that you have looked at the five steps of the Microsoft troubleshooting model, consider some other important aspects of network troubleshooting.

Diagnostic Tools

As you grapple with more and more network problems, you'll probably discover that cabling, cable connectors, and network adapter cards are the home of most network hardware problems. Cable breaks, shorts, bad connectors, and faulty adapter cards are common. To handle these problems, you might want to try some of the approaches described in the following sections.

There are several important tools you can use to diagnose network problems. Many network engineers use these tools when they are not able to solve hardware problems otherwise. You may wish to purchase the tools for use, depending on how often you run into hardware problems. Keep in mind, however, that prices for this equipment range from $50 to $25,000.

Some of the most useful tools are:

- Terminators
- Time-domain reflectometers (TDRs)
- Digital voltmeters (DVMs)
- Continuity testers
- Cable testers
- Protocol analyzers
- Oscilloscopes

Terminators

If you suspect that there is a break in a cable, you can use a *terminator* to narrow down the problem. By dividing a piece of cable and putting a terminator in its place, you can see whether the problem is at that point in the cable or somewhere earlier. If you find the general portion of the network where the problem resides, you can repeatedly divide the cable, using the terminator to further isolate the problem.

Time-Domain Reflectometers (TDRs)

Time-domain reflectometers work by emitting short pulses of known amplitude that travel down a cable. A TDR analyzes the time delay associated with the resultant signal reflections. The TDR is then able to help you determine whether there are any shorts or open cable sections. If the TDR you are using is good, it will also be able to give you a pretty clear idea of where the problem is located. TDRs are available for all LAN types. Optical TDRs provide a similar test capability for fiber cable. Here is how a TDR is typically used: An end of a network cable is connected to a TDR device. The type of device must be selected on the TDR. For example, if you are testing a coaxial cable, you need to select "coaxial." If there is a problem with the cable, a message should indicate whether the cable is "open" or "short" and how far down the cable the problem resides.

TIP

To help ensure that your TDR works as effectively as possible, be sure to connect the TDR to the end of a segment. Also, turn off any repeaters and bridges you have connected to the local network before attaching the TDR to the cable.

TDRs typically use a positive electric pulse. Because transceivers do not have positive voltage protection, power down the network while doing a TDR test unless you are sure your TDR is specially designed for testing with the power on. (See Figure 4.1.)

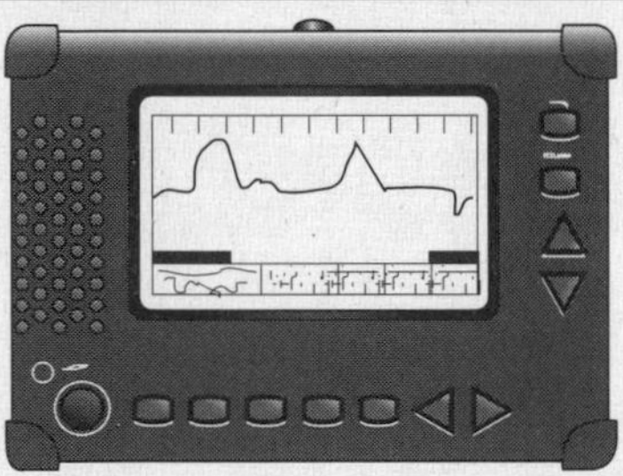

FIGURE 4.1: Time-domain reflectometer (TDR)

Digital VoltMeters (DVMs)

Digital voltmeters can help you find a break or a short in a network cable by checking the voltage being carried across a network cable. A DVM (see Figure 4.2) is a hand-held unit with which you can measure both the continuity of a cable and whether or not there is a short. Digital voltmeters are used with Thinnet and Thicknet.

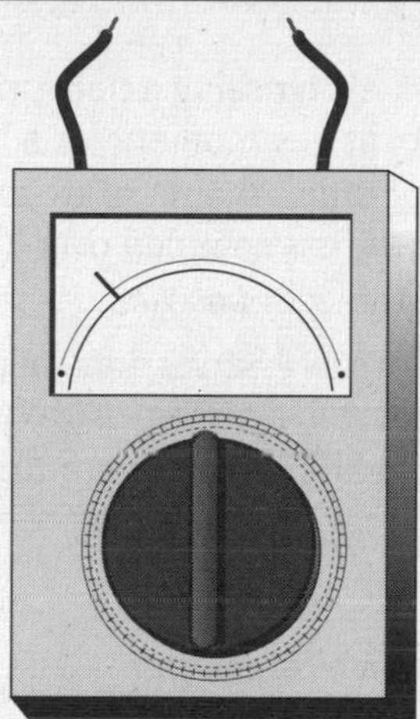

FIGURE 4.2: Digital voltmeter

Continuity Testers

A *continuity tester* is similar to a DVM. Continuity testers usually come in pairs. You insert one end of a cable in the first tester and the other end in the second tester. Each tester has two or more RJ-45 female ports and four lights. Each pair of twisted wires is associated with a corresponding LED. When a cable is connected to both testers, LED lights should be active at one tester. If the corresponding LED light does not come on for a specific pair, then that cable has a break. Continuity testers are used with UTP.

Protocol Analyzers (Network Analyzers)

A *protocol analyzer* (or network analyzer) is a very powerful tool for troubleshooting a network. It can provide detailed, real-time network traffic analysis. Protocol analyzers also typically have time-domain reflectometers built in. More importantly, they can capture packets, decode them, and determine which components of a network are generating errors. Another feature of some protocol analyzers is an alarm that alerts you if network traffic exceeds the limits you set. Some of the problems that these tools can identify include LAN bottlenecks, traffic fluctuations, and unusual network utilization patterns.

Protocol analyzers can help you to avoid having to shut down servers or routers when troubleshooting problems such as broadcast storms. A protocol analyzer monitors network activity, gathers statistics, and provides guidelines for optimizing performance.

Protocol analyzers continuously track packets crossing a network, providing an accurate picture of network activity at any moment, or a historical record of network activity over a period of time. Analyzers are useful for baselining, in which the activity on a network is sampled over a period of time to establish a normal performance profile, or *baseline*.

The Network Monitor that is on the Windows NT Server 4 installation disk is a low level protocol analyzer. Other protocol analyzers use a combination of software and hardware to ensure that all frames are captured.

NOTE

Windows NT Network Monitor is a software protocol analyzer.

WARNING

Protocol analyzers can be used for collecting *baseline* information, although their main purpose is for troubleshooting. If an exam question asks for multiple baseline tools, select Network Monitor (protocol analyzer) along with Performance Monitor.

WARNING

TDRs can test the bandwidth CAPACITY of a cable in conjunction with a built-in oscilloscope. To measure the current bandwidth UTILIZATION as a percentage of available bandwidth, you use a protocol analyzer. The exam may ask which tool measures the bandwidth of a network without specifying capacity or utilization. In this case, assume the question means utilization.

Cable Testers

A *cable tester* is an instrument for testing the integrity of a stretch of cable. (See Figure 4.3.) Cable testers run tests to determine a cable's attenuation, resistance, and other characteristics.

FIGURE 4.3: Cable tester

If you're going to use a previously installed cable for your network, make sure all of it works properly before you begin. A cable tester can provide detailed information about the cable's physical and electrical properties. When you're dealing with a long cable system, the chances are good that at least parts of it will be faulty.

NOTE

High-end cable testers can determine conformity to network architecture specifications. Some can even identify cable types. These cable testers are used as certification tools that can assign a specific category to a cable.

Advanced cable testers can be used to identify a wide range of problems including congestion errors. Some cable testers provide information that goes beyond that which relates only to the Physical layer of the OSI model. These devices are able to display information about frame counts, collisions, and beaconing (a method of isolating serious failures in token passing networks). Advanced cable testers can also indicate if a particular network adapter card is causing problems.

Oscilloscopes

An *oscilloscope* (see Figure 4.4) is an electronic device with a CRT used to measure voltage in relationship to time. It can also be used with TDRs to determine crimps and sharp bends in cabling, shorts, breaks, and problems with attenuation.

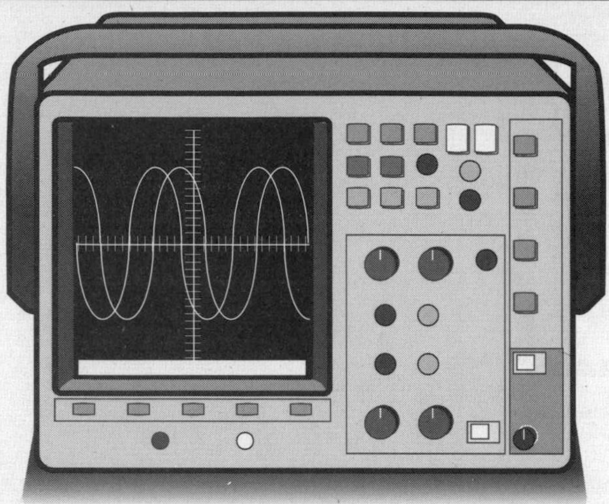

FIGURE 4.4: An oscilloscope

Troubleshooting Problems

10Base2 Problems

If your 10Base2 network goes down, it is likely that the bus continuity has been damaged or disconnected (perhaps someone moved a PC). Check terminators at both ends of the cable with a volt-ohm meter to be sure they still read 50 ohms resistance. Check the resistance of the entire segment of cable by using the center conductor of a T and the T's outside shield. It should measure 25 ohms or slightly above. If it measures close to 50 ohms, you may have a faulty terminator, a missing terminator, a break in the wire, or a missing T connector. Also, check that one end of the cable is still grounded.

If you are working with 10Base2, make sure the cable has not grown too long as a result of the addition of users without consideration of wiring lengths. This is a very common problem with bus topology networks.

Because some people see no difference between RG-59, RG-58A/C, and RG-62, make sure someone did not add a black piece of coax to extend or repair the cable. Also, check for the wrong connector types on your cable.

TIP

If only one workstation is having a problem on a 10Base2 or 10Base5 network, you can be pretty sure it is not the cabling but the LAN card, the transceiver, or the AUI connector (if it is 10Base5). You will probably need to swap out the card to nail this one down, so make sure you have a spare. Remember to configure the card before you attempt this solution.

Terminators and Ground Problems A *terminator* is a resistor used at each end of an Ethernet cable to ensure that signals do not bounce back and forth. The terminator at one end of the cable needs to be attached to an electrical ground. (See Figure 4.5.) Terminator resistance must match the network architecture specification; otherwise, it may cause the network to fail. RG-58 A/U Thinnet cable requires a 50-ohm resistor in the terminator. A 75-ohm terminator will not work.

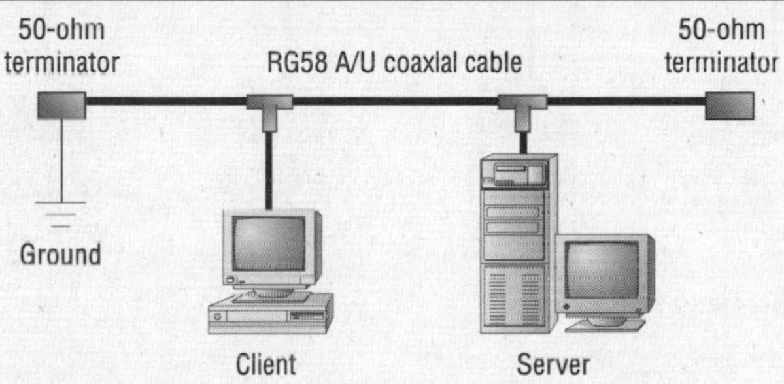

FIGURE 4.5: Correct configuration of terminators and ground

Faulty ground connections, especially where there is more than one ground connection, result in voltage measurements that relate to the difference in ground potentials between two points on the same cable. Ethernet tries to overcome this problem by specifying that only one end of the cable is to be grounded. In practice, however, installers tend to ignore this specification and wire the shield of the conductor cable to main ground or some nearby metal. This type of wiring can create differences in voltage between the various ground points. As a result, voltage travels down the cable and flows into the network cards, causing either damage to the card, intermittent faults, or errors on the network. By inserting the meter into the earth shield and measuring the current flowing (or voltage difference), this type of fault is easily identified. There should be no voltage difference.

There are two common problems with terminators and grounds. Because you can only have two terminators per cable (one at each end), you cannot connect a second cable to a midpoint on another cable. Figure 4.6 diagrams the problem of having too many terminators on a cable. Figure 4.7 diagrams the problem of too many grounds (two) attached to one cable.

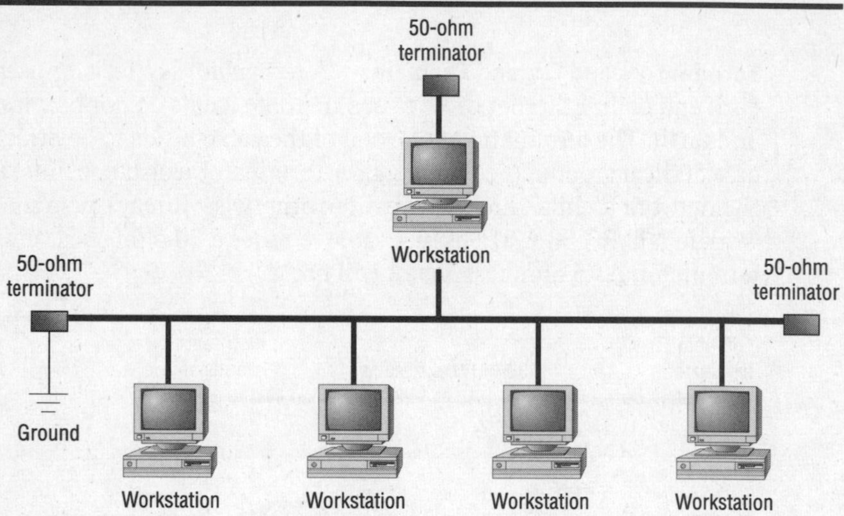

FIGURE 4.6: Too many terminators

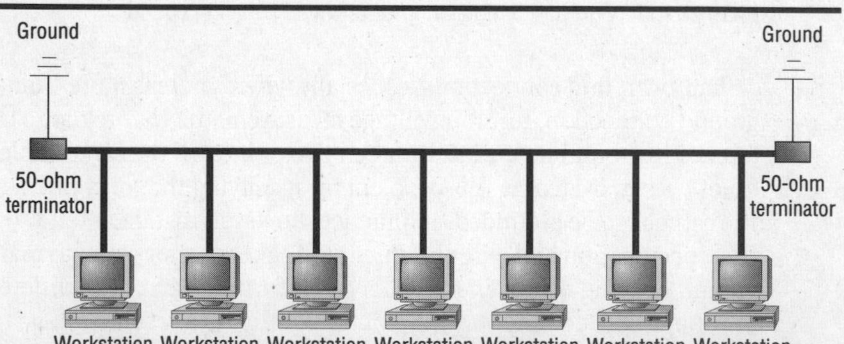

FIGURE 4.7: Too many grounds

When testing for faulty terminators, you can use an *Ohmmeter*. Make sure the meter is switched to resistance. When testing a cable with one good terminator at each end, your reading should be 25 ohms. Remember, the golden rule of resistance in parallel is that the resultant resistance is

$$R = (R1 * R2) / (R1 + R2)$$

So, where the two resistors (terminators) are equal, the value given equals one half of any one resistor. In our case, this is equal to 25. On the other hand, if a terminator at one end is bad and the other terminator is good, it is like having only one good terminator on the cable. Applying an Ohmmeter to this cable would give a reading of 50 ohms and indicate a faulty terminator at one end.

To test a terminator by itself, you need to remove it from the cable and test it separately. In this case, getting a reading of 50 ohms is good. A good Ethernet system has two 50-ohm terminators, one at each end of the cable. They appear in parallel. Thus, a good system will measure 25 ohms; a shorted system less than 25 ohms; and a break, open circuit, or poor connection is greater than 25 ohms. If both terminators are missing or faulty, the resistance reading will be very high. These tests should be performed on a network where all workstations and servers are turned off.

Cable Problems and Cable-Testing Tools

Check to make sure the cabling does not run near high-voltage cables or is wrapped in cable trays. Fluorescent lights can also cause electromagnetic interference (EMI). Check that the wires are not run against or across these lights. Electrical motors also cause EMI if wires are run across them.

Network cable testing equipment can locate wiring faults quickly. If you suspect you will be troubleshooting on a regular basis, a network cable tester is a good investment.

A TDR is a cable-testing device that can tell you whether the cable is shorted, broken, or crimped. The device sends a signal down the wire and measures the characteristics of the reflected signal. From the reflection it can determine the type of problem with the cable. (This is like throwing a rock down a well and determining how long it takes before you hear it hit the bottom, as well as sensing whether it hit water, dirt, or other rocks.)

When testing for breaks or shorts in a coax cable, you need to understand the reading of infinity on a DVM. *Infinity* is a very high number of ohms caused by an enormous amount of resistance. A break in a cable introduces an endless amount of resistance, which can cause a measurement of infinity ohms. However, a very high reading of ohms is expected when testing a good cable from core to shield. Because the core and shield should not be touching, there should be much resistance as a result of the open space. If there is a low reading of ohms when testing core to shield, there is a short in the cable. A short happens when the wrong electronic components come into contact with each other and results in a condition with little resistance.

WARNING

There are two diagnoses that can be performed when testing a cable: end-to-end and core-to-shield. If an exam question does not specify how the cable is being tested, assume the question refers to end-to-end diagnosis.

NOTE

First, always measure the resistance of your cables, terminators, and T connectors separately. Unplug them from cards, hubs, and each other. Then you can measure them together.

Summary of good ohm readings:

RG-48 cable–measuring shield-to-core should read infinity ohms. If not infinity there could be a short.

RG-58 cable–measuring end-to-end at core should read 0 ohms. If it reads infinity there may be a break.

RG-58 terminator–measuring pin-to-body should read 50 ohms. Infinity or anything other than 50 ohms could indicate a bad terminating resistor. A reading of 75 ohms indicates the wrong terminator.

RG-58 with two terminators–measuring cable from end-to-end should read 25 ohms.

Other good ohm readings include:

RG-58 T connector (BNC T connector)–measuring pin-to-body should be infinity ohms. If the reading is not infinity ohms, there is a bad T connector.

UTP cable–measuring one wire end-to-end should be 0 ohms. If the reading is very high there could be a break.

NIC Problems Revisited

When a workstation's NIC goes out and begins to talk continuously and incoherently on the network, it creates packets that are larger than 1518 bytes and has CRC errors. This type of packet is called a *jabber packet.* To find the faulty card, disconnect workstations or hubs one at a time until you pinpoint the rogue card.

In some cases, resource conflicts can cause network communications problems. You may need to take all the boards out of your system except the network adapter. When you have it working, add one board in at a time until you find the board that has the conflicts. Reconfigure and continue adding cards until the system is up and running.

Remember that COM1 uses IRQ4 and COM2 uses IRQ3. Try to avoid these when configuring IRQ's because they are commonly used by a serial mouse and modem. Sometimes, just the presence of the serial port will interfere with these IRQ's.

Check for the frequent error of not having common frame types bound to the workstation and the file server. If they are not bound, your workstation will respond with the message, "File server not found."

Some network adapter cards do not make a very good connection in the card socket. Cleaning the card connector and resetting the card can usually solve this problem. (Don't be tempted to use an eraser to clean the connector–it will leave grit on the card.) If you have checked the settings and cleaned the card and it still doesn't work, replace it with a spare that you know is functional.

If only one computer is affected, then the problem is local. In this case, the problem is likely to be caused by the network adapter card on the client computer. A network adapter card could have I/O address conflicts, interrupt conflicts or memory conflicts with other devices and prevent the computer from connecting to the network. A faulty cable terminator or a faulty network adapter card on the domain controller usually affects all computers on the network.

A NIC can be configured for using the wrong transceiver if there are two or more transceivers attached to the card. If the network adapter in the affected client computer is configured to use the wrong transceiver, it will not be able to communicate on the network.

Same MAC Addresses The manufacturer creates the default MAC address on a network, and on some cards the address can be changed. No two cards can have the same MAC on a network and communicate with the network. This address created by the manufacturer follows an industry standard set by the IEEE where the actual address is a hexadecimal number of six two-digit pairs separated by colons; for example, 01:99:40:55:A1:C4 is a MAC address.

Token Ring Card Problems The following are additional problems that can occur on a Token Ring network:

> **Card has wrong configuration** You need to be sure that all Token Ring cards are configured for the same speed. In other words, if a network is set for 16Mbps, make sure that the card you are troubleshooting is configured for 16Mbps as well.
>
> **MSAUs are from different vendors** Operating like an Ethernet hub, the Multiple Station Access Unit (MSAU) has several computers attached to it. MSAUs from different vendors have different internal electrical characteristics. Having a mixed set of MSAUs can cause problems on the Token Ring network.

The Windows NT Network Monitor is an example of a software protocol analyzer. You can use the Network Monitor to capture and display frames or packets in order to identify and troubleshoot problems on local area networks. The Network Monitor can diagnose hardware and software problems that prevent communication between two or more computers. When diagnosing packets, the length of a particular packet can be very informative. Faulty packets can be too long or too short. You can use the Network Monitor to capture packets between the server and another computer to examine that computer's messages and its packet length. You will need to use a Windows NT server for this exercise.

1. From the Administrative Tools group select Network Monitor (see Figure 4.8).
2. From the Capture menu, select Start. Wait two minutes and then select Stop and View from the File menu to display three capture windows with the Summary window at the top. The Summary window lists all packets captured for every computer communicating with the server.
3. Double-click any packet line to open the contents of that packet.

4. Look for Ethernet, UDP, or IP frames and double-click them to display information about each frame. Find the line that contains the frame length.

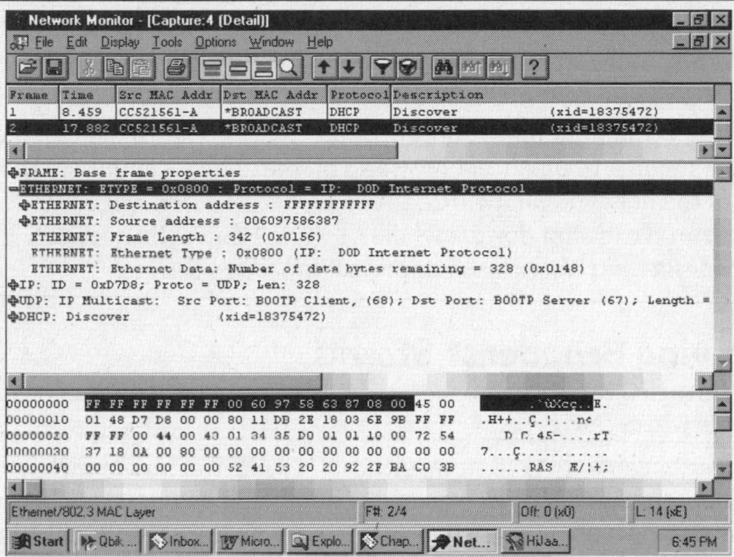

FIGURE 4.8: Windows NT Network Monitor

5. Return to the Summary window and repeat the procedure for several packets. Notice the range of frame lengths and compare frame lengths between Ethernet, UDP, IP, and so on.

Resolve broadcast storms.

Broadcasts are an intricate part of all Microsoft networks. Almost all Microsoft networks use NetBIOS names and the resulting broadcast requirements. There are basically three methods for reducing broadcast storms:

- Replace any bad network interface cards causing broadcast storms
- Disable rarely used network interface cards
- Implement a segmented network with the use of routers

What Are Broadcasts and Broadcast Storms?

Computers that use NetBIOS names and name resolution will perform many broadcasts on a network. A *broadcast* is a message sent by a computer that either announces and registers that computer with a network service that collects computer names, or a message is sent to retrieve the name of another computer from this same service and list. Announcement-type broadcasts are performed more often on a network.

Every computer on the network must process each broadcast message. If the number of broadcast messages on the network surpasses the capacity of the network bandwidth, then a *broadcast storm* will occur. A broadcast storm can shut down a whole network. Routers do not pass broadcasts and can be used to prevent broadcast storms.

Solving Broadcast Storms

A faulty NIC can spew broadcasts. You can use a protocol analyzer to locate which card is bad.

Disabling rarely used network adapter cards can improve overall network performance by decreasing the number of broadcast packets on the network. Because every active adapter card on the network must process each broadcast packet, the more adapter cards on the network, the longer the connection time.

Routers do not pass broadcasts, and they can be used to prevent broadcast storms. Routers interconnect networks and provide filtering functions. They work at the Network layer to route packets across multiple networks based on specific network addresses. Routers can be used to prevent broadcast storms because broadcasts are not forwarded. Although bridges can segment network traffic, they cannot filter broadcasts. If the destination address of a packet is not in the bridge's routing table (as in the case of a broadcast), the bridge forwards the packets to all its nodes and, therefore, possibly creates broadcast storms.

TIP

If you are using brouters on the network and you are experiencing broadcast storms, turn off the bridging feature on all brouters.

NOTE

If you are using NetBEUI as the only protocol and you want to solve broadcast storms, you will need to switch to TCP/IP before implementing a plan that includes segmenting the network and introducing routers.

Identify and resolve network performance problems.

Diagnosing and eliminating bottlenecks at the server is a primary concern and should be investigated first. Improving network bandwidth on the LAN is the second important area to be analyzed. This is different from exploring ways to improve WAN bandwidth, which needs to be investigated separately. In the real world, the network administrator is investigating all three areas simultaneously by constantly collecting ongoing performance statistics. The Networking Essentials exam is not complicated in this objective and only tests your knowledge of each area separately. However, the questions can be tricky because many of them cover information that is not found in regular texts. An example would be the formula for determining the cumulative bandwidth of a multi-modem WAN link.

There are three areas of concern when dealing with the issue of network performance:

- Eliminating performance bottlenecks at the network server(s)
- Improving network bandwidth on the LAN
- Improving the bandwidth of WAN links

Eliminating Bottlenecks at the Server

The Performance Monitor can investigate four major areas in which bottlenecks at the server can occur:

- Processor performance
- Memory performance
- Disk performance
- Network performance

Processor Performance

There are three counters that you can use to examine a possible microprocessor bottleneck:

- % Processor Time
- Processor Queue Length
- Interrupts/Sec

The % Processor Time measures the percentage of time the microprocessor is performing during non-idle work. Consistent measurements over 80% indicate a need for upgrading the processor or adding additional processors.

The Processor Queue Length counts the number of threads or tasks waiting to be processed from the processor. A persistent queue length greater than two indicates a possible need for upgrading the processor.

The Interrupts/Sec counter measures the rate of service requests from devices that need the attention of the CPU. If this counter value increases dramatically without a corresponding increase in system usage, it could indicate a faulty hardware device and not the microprocessor. The counter should operate between 100 and 1000, but it can spike up to 2000.

Disk Performance

There are two main counters for detecting possible disk bottlenecks:

- % Disk Time
- Avg. Disk Queue Length

If % Disk Time for any drive climbs above 90% or the Avg. Disk Queue Length consistently rises above two, you need to consider spreading your disk access load to other drives.

Memory Performance

Memory performance is measured mainly by the following counters:

- Available Bytes
- Pages/Sec
- Avg. Disk Sec/Transfer

Available Bytes should be 4MB or more. If it falls below 4MB, it means that most of your memory is being used. Paging is a related memory area that causes a bottleneck. No matter how much physical memory (RAM) you have in a computer, Windows NT needs to use a certain amount of virtual memory or paging file. The process of swapping information back and forth between physical memory and virtual memory is called *paging*. You can examine excess paging using the Avg. Disk Sec/Transfer and the Pages/Sec counter. If the product of the two counters consistently exceeds 0.1, paging is taking more than 10% of the disk access time and your server needs physical memory.

Network Performance

Two very good counters for measuring network performance are:

- Bytes Total/Sec
- % Network Utilization

Bytes Total/Sec measures the number of bytes the server has sent to and received from the network, which indicates how busy the server is. The % Network Utilization counter gives you another running snapshot of current network usage and should remain below 30% on an Ethernet network and below 90% on a Token Ring network.

NOTE

If the network has a performance problem and every performance counter has a measurement in an acceptable range, then the problem is not related to the server, and most likely there is a need for segmenting the network or upgrading network components.

Improving Network Bandwidth

If a network is very slow after adding several clients, there are a number of things you can do:

- Replace all of the Ethernet concentrators with Ethernet switches.
- Replace all of the 10BaseT hubs with 100BaseT hubs.
- Replace all category 3 UTP cables with category 5 UTP cables.
- Replace all 10BaseT network adapters with 100BaseT network adapters.
- Replace the topology with FDDI (Fiber Distributed Data Interface). FDDI is essentially 100Mbps Token Ring over fiber-optic

cable with a second counter-rotating ring that provides a measure of fault tolerance in case a cable fails.

NOTE

All of the above methods are expensive and would not reduce the cost if included in a plan. Refer to Chapters 1 and 2 for more information.

- Increase TCP window size from 4096 to 16384 bytes. TCP window size is a count of bytes that a sender is allowed to send before receiving an acknowledgment from the receiver. The send TCP window size should be greater than the receive window size. Both recommendations will ensure that the sender will not be idle while waiting for an acknowledgment.
- Change the maximum packet size on all the computers from 576 bytes to 1514 bytes. By increasing the size of the packet, you can reduce the number of read and write operations that are performed on a network.

NOTE

If a Token Ring network (4Mbps) is connected to a 10BaseT (10Mbps) Ethernet, a 5Mbps file will need two minutes to travel from the Token Ring segment to the Ethernet segment while the same file will only need 30 seconds traveling from Ethernet to Token Ring. This is because the packet size on a Token Ring network is larger. This is similar to pouring water between a bucket and several small bottles. Pouring water from the bucket to the bottles will take more care and ultimately more time. On the other hand, pouring water from the bottles to the bucket needs less mental concentration and is faster because the target is much wider.

When using multiple transport protocols such as TCP, NetBEUI, and SPX you need to reorder the binding order at the workstation (not the server). The most frequently used protocol should be the top of the binding order to reduce network response time and speed up network connections.

Improving WAN Bandwidth

If a WAN connection is very slow, there are a number of things you can do:

- If a network uses a 56K leased line where people need to access a database and there are many complaints that the network is slow, you need to upgrade the WAN to a faster connection such as a T1 (1.544Mbps).

- When replacing 56K leased lines with T1 lines you need to provide redundancy. For example, if you connect three cities with T1 lines, then you need to use three connections that form a triangle as in Figure 4.9. In this case, if one connection goes down all three cities can still communicate with each other.

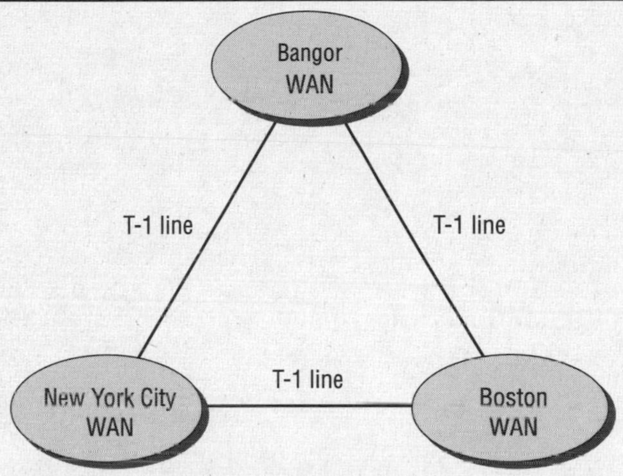

FIGURE 4.9: Three cities connected by T1 lines

- Regular analog modems can be used together on a V.35 combined circuit link to provide throughput rates, which are higher than the rates that could be obtained using a single modem. To figure out the maximum possible throughput rate, divide Kbps by 8 and multiply by 100 and by the number of modems. An example when using four 28.8 modems:

  28.8 Kbps/8 * 100 * 4 = 1.44Mbps

WARNING

Know the formula for combining the speed of multiple modems: *(modem Kbps)/8 * 100 * (number of modems).*

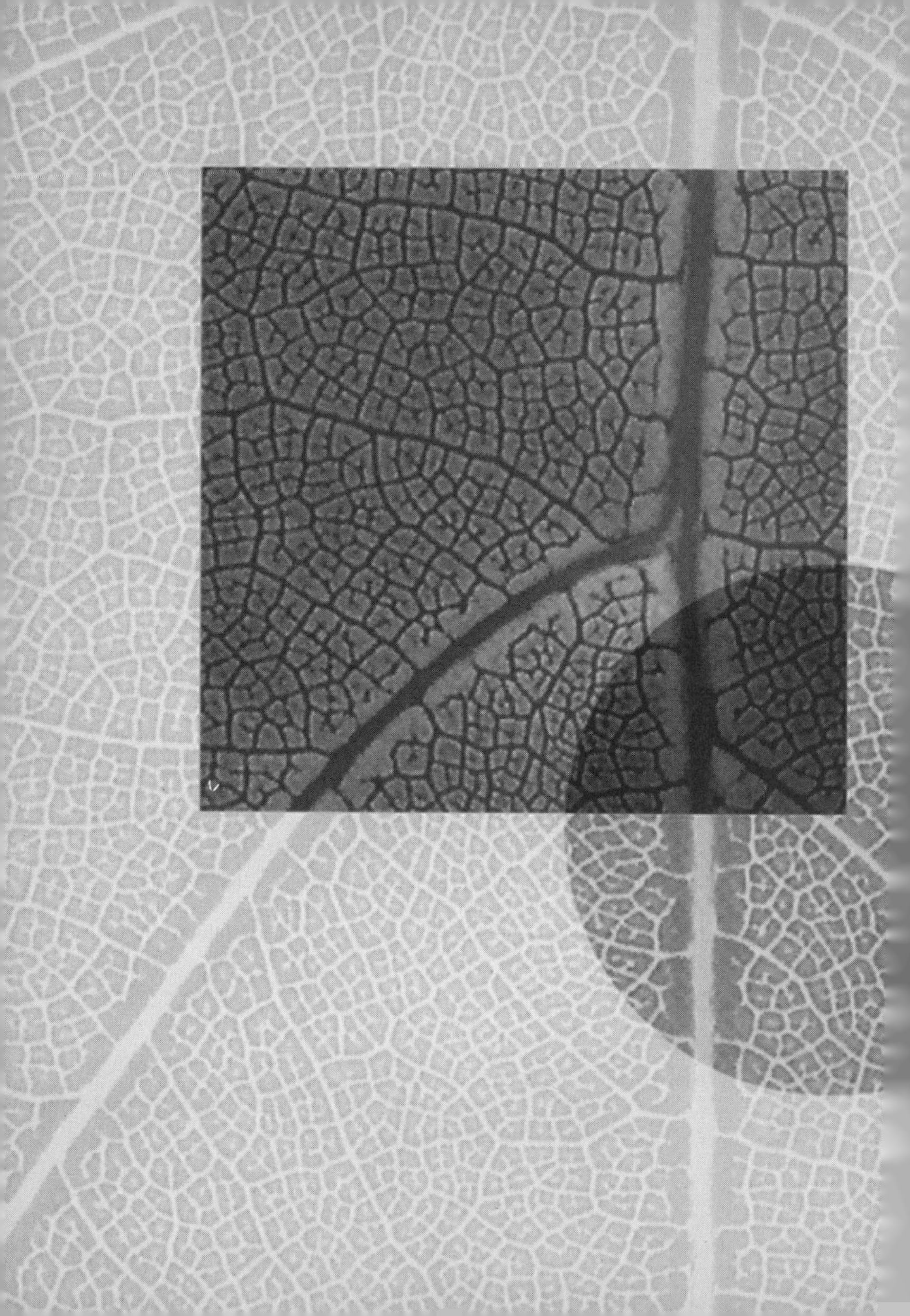

Part I

Networking Essentials Practice Exam

1. Which of the following best describes the function of the token in a Token Ring network?

   A. Only the station that holds the free token is allowed to transmit a message on the network.

   B. The station that holds the token has the highest priority on the network.

   C. A token contains the routing information for the network.

   D. Token passing provides greater transfer speed than Thicknet.

2. As a consultant, you have been asked to design a network for a mid-sized accounting firm. Because of the data handled by the company, security is extremely important. The network must support 80 computers with easy expandability to more than 100 in the next few months. What type of network would be best for you to install at your client's office?

   A. Internet

   B. Mainframe/terminal

   C. Peer-to-peer

   D. Server-based

3. Which one of the following roles does the server play in a system that uses the client/server architecture?

   A. The server fulfills the requests from the client computer for data and other processing resources.

   B. The server stores the data for the client, but all the data processing occurs on the client computer.

   C. The server stores data and performs all the data processing, so that the client computer functions primarily as an intelligent display device.

   D. The server fulfills the requests from the client for remote processing resources, but the data is stored on the client computer.

4. Security is not a major concern in your company network. However, your boss wants to protect several resources with special passwords. Which of the following security models should you implement to accomplish this task?

A. Share-level security

B. User-level security

C. Domain-level security

D. Server-level security

5. Which of the following is associated with connection-oriented communication?

A. Fast but unreliable delivery

B. Assured delivery

C. Fiber-optic cable

D. Infrared

6. Which of the following connectivity devices work at the Data Link layer of the OSI model?

A. Router

B. Bridge

C. Repeater

D. Gateway

7. Which type of media access method is commonly used by Ethernet networks?

A. Token passing

B. CSMA/CA

C. CSMA/CD

D. Demand priority

8. Which of following statements shows the benefits of both NDIS and ODI?

A. They allow network adapters to be used in any compliant computer.

B. They allow network adapters to transmit information over a greater distance than non-compliant network adapters can.

C. They allow network adapters to communicate with other compliant network adapters.

D. They allow network adapters to be independent of any particular transport protocol.

9. Which of the following cable types can be used for 100BaseT networks?

   A. RG-58 A/U

   B. RG-58 /U

   C. Category 3 UTP

   D. Category 5 UTP

10. Which of the following refers to the signal overflow from an adjacent wire?

   A. Attenuation

   B. Crosstalk

   C. Beaconing

   D. Jitter

11. Which of the following are true of 10BaseT networks? (Choose all that apply.)

   A. They use fiber-optic cable

   B. They use hubs as the central point of connection

   C. They must be terminated at each end

   D. They utilize category 3 UTP

12. Which of the following protocols cannot be routed? (Choose all that apply.)

   A. XNS

   B. DLC

   C. LAT

   D. NetBEUI

   E. DECnet

13. Match the definition to the networking term: This high-level network protocol provides file-sharing services on a network that uses NetBIOS.

A. IPX/SPX

B. TCP/IP

C. DLC

D. PPP

E. NetBEUI

F. Server message block (SMB)

G. Routing information protocol (RIP)

H. AppleTalk filing protocol (AFP)

I. Network core protocol (NCP)

14. Which of the following connectivity devices works at the Data Link layer of the OSI model?

A. Router

B. Bridge

C. Repeater

D. Gateway

15. Which of the following describes the difference between bridges and routers?

A. Bridges can choose between multiple paths

B. Routers can choose between multiple paths

C. Bridges support Ethernet but not Token Ring environments

D. Routers support Ethernet but not Token Ring environments

16. Which of the following best describes Frame Relay technology?

A. It is a point-to-point system that transmits fixed-length frames at the Data Link layer.

B. It is a point-to-point system that transmits variable-length frames at the Data Link layer.

C. It is a point-to-point system that transmits fixed-length packets at the Network layer.

D. It is a point-to-point system that transmits variable-length packets at the Network layer.

17. Which of the following should you implement to ensure that the data on a server is easily and quickly available in case of a server disk crash?

    A. Disk encryption

    B. Disk monitoring

    C. RAID level 0

    D. RAID level 1

18. What can you do to make sure the data on a server is easily and quickly available in the event of a server disk crash with minimum down time?

    A. Implement RAID level 0

    B. Implement RAID level 1

    C. Implement RAID level 5

    D. Implement daily backup

19. Al has just plugged a new network adapter card into his computer, but the operating system failed to detect the network adapter card. Which of the following is the most likely cause of the problem?

    A. The IRQ setting of the adapter card

    B. The protocol setting of the adapter card

    C. The transceiver setting of the adapter card

    D. The frame type of the adapter card

20. Lorraine's computer consists of COM1, COM2, LPT1, and LPT2 with their default IRQ settings. The NE-2000 network adapter card is using IRQ3 and 0x300 as I/O port address. Which of the following devices is conflicting with the network adapter card?

    A. LPT1

    B. LPT2

    C. COM1

    D. COM2

21. Which of the following uses 15-character names to identify computers on a network?

    A. NetBIOS

    B. IPX/SPX

    C. AppleTalk

    D. TCP/IP

22. Examine the following situation, desired result, and solutions:

    You are designing a NetBIOS naming scheme for all the servers and client computers in your company. In the next two years, your company will install a WAN that will connect all its networks.

    Required result: You need to setup a NetBIOS naming scheme for all the servers and client computers in one company's networks. The NetBIOS naming scheme at your location must continue to work after the WAN is connected.

    Optional desired results: You want the NetBIOS name for each server to describe the server's department or function. You want each client computer's NetBIOS name to describe the computer's primary user or function.

    Proposed solution: Assign each server a NetBIOS name that consists of the first eight characters of the server's department name, a five-character location code, plus a two-digit identifier to distinguish between multiple servers within the department. Assign each client computer a NetBIOS name that corresponds to the e-mail address of the computer's principal user.

    Which result does the proposed solution produce?

    A. The proposed solution produces the required result and produces both of the optional desired results.

    B. The proposed solution produces the required result and produces only one optional desired result.

    C. The proposed solution produces the required result and produces none of the optional desired results.

    D. The proposed solution does not produce the required result.

23. Which of the following functions is provided directly by Systems Management Server (SMS)?

    A. Virus protection

    B. SNMP services

    C. Remote control of client machines

    D. Gateway services for mainframes

24. There is a frame type mismatch on your Novell NetWare network. It is only affecting one computer. Which of the following needs to be reconfigured?

    A. The frame type on the client machine

    B. The frame type on the server machine

    C. The frame binding setting on the client machine

    D. The frame binding setting on the server machine

25. You added one client machine on an IPX network, but the new machine cannot communicate with the other machines on the network. What may be causing the problem?

    A. TCP/IP

    B. CPU type

    C. Frame type

    D. PPP

26. After a long holiday, Barry reported that his computer is no longer connected to the network and he cannot get through. However, he can log on to the network on a coworker's PC. What should you check first?

    A. The network cable is detached from Barry's computer

    B. Incorrect frame type of network protocol

    C. The terminator of cable is disconnected

    D. The network cable is broken

27. The following is the configuration of a new computer on your network:

    Pentium-200 CPU MMX

32 MB of RAM

A 3.5GB IDE hard disk

A parallel port configured as LPT1

A mouse on COM1

A modem on COM2

SCSI host adapter for a scanner is using IRQ5

Sound card using IRQ11

Amy needs to add a new network adapter card into her computer. When Amy looks in her reference manual, the network adapter card will support only IRQs 2, 3, 4, 5, 10, and 11. Which IRQ should Amy use for the network interface card without creating an IRQ conflict with another device?

A. IRQ2

B. IRQ3

C. IRQ4

D. IRQ10

28. Your network has been very slow for the past two days. You check the computer systems, cables, and the hub. You do not find any problems. You have concluded that the problem is broadcast storms. Which of the following tools can confirm your guess and troubleshoot the problem?

A. Digital voltmeter

B. TDR

C. Ohmmeter

D. Protocol analyzer

29. Why does a high number of broadcast messages degrade overall network performance?

A. Broadcast messages are processed by every computer on the network.

B. Broadcast messages are automatically routed to every LAN segment.

C. Broadcast messages are passed by routers using multiple paths simultaneously.

D. Broadcast messages require acknowledgment packets from every computer on the network.

30. Only Laura's computer on your network cannot connect to the network, but all other computers can access all network resources. Which of the following is the most likely cause of the problem?

A. The terminator is disconnected from the cable

B. Excessive media collisions

C. The network card on the server computer is faulty

D. The network card on the client computer is faulty

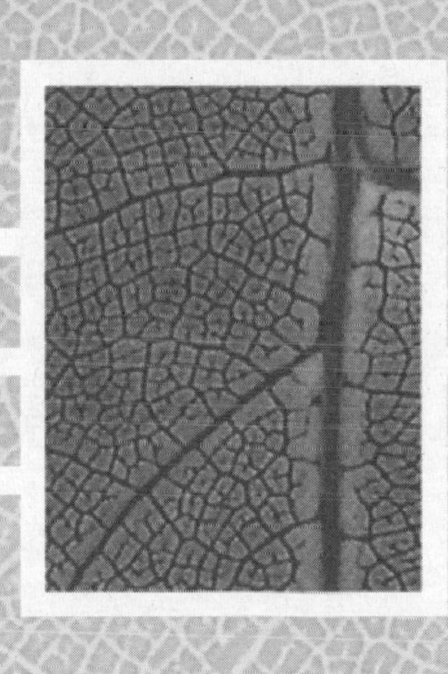

PART ii

NT Server 4

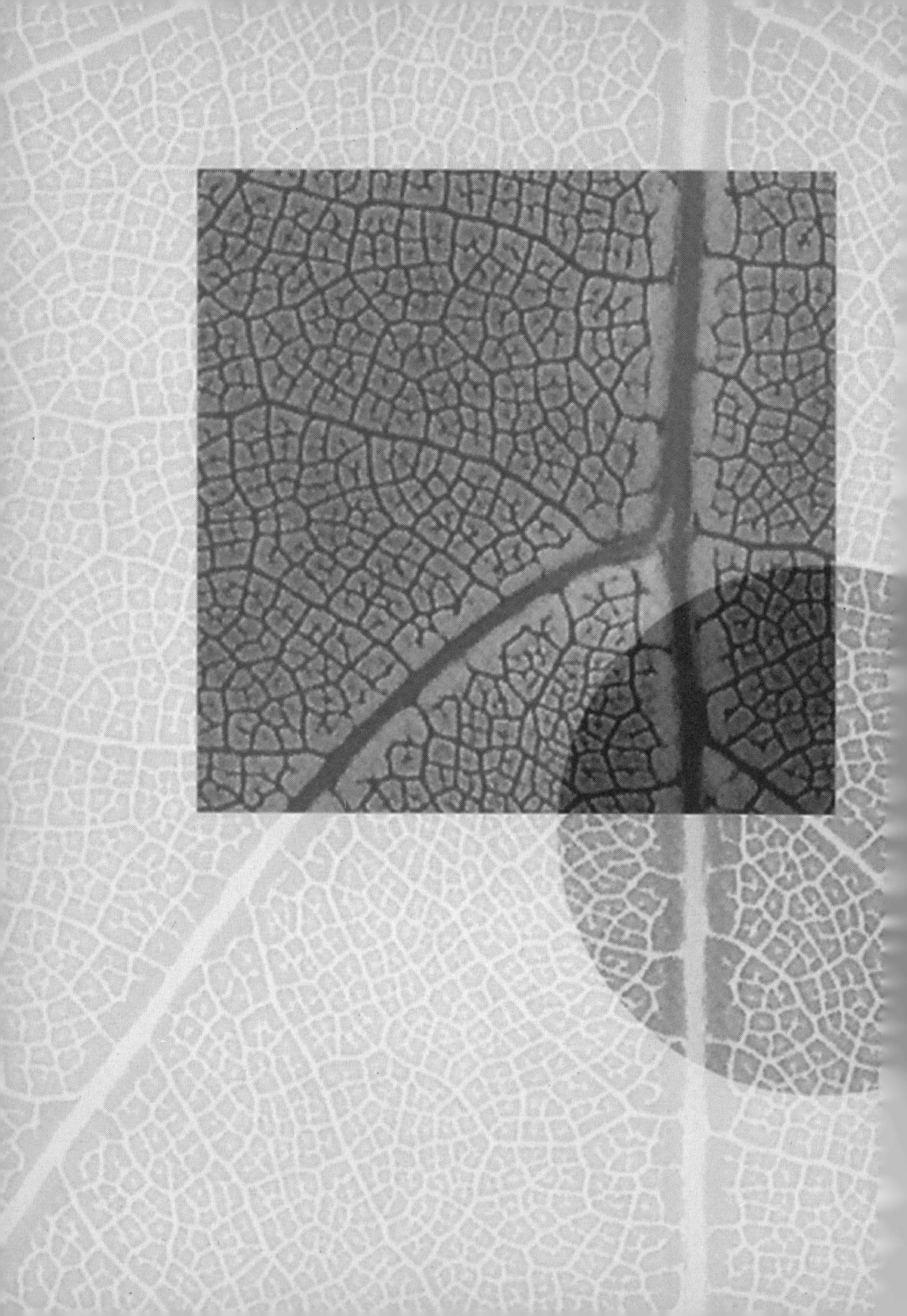

Chapter 5

Planning

Someone very wise once said that proper planning prevents poor performance. Planning can be time consuming. It starts with questioning and goal setting. First, determine the goal of the network. This goal will drive many of the questions that follow. If your network is to provide file, print, application, and messaging services to an office of 20 people, the questions take one form. If your network is to provide communication services for a network of 20,000 people spread over several continents, the questions take an entirely different form. The NT Server exam assumes that the network you will work with is relatively small.

Adapted from *MCSE Exam Notes: NT Server 4* by Gary Govanus and Robert King

ISBN 0-7821-2289-2 360 pages $19.99

Plan the disk drive configuration for various requirements.

Requirements include:

- Choosing a file system
- Choosing a fault-tolerance method

Planning your hard drive configuration starts with the purchase of your server. As you begin to contemplate the data and applications that you will store on the server, you will get an idea of the overhead involved. If you purchase hardware that can support the expected workload, it will have a positive impact on your users.

NOTE

Even though this is a "short" objective, there is a lot of information. Disk technology is an ever-growing arena. The information presented here (or in any written materials) represents the technology that was current at the time of writing. As a systems engineer, you will be responsible for keeping up to date on new advances in disk subsystems.

Controller Choices

There are numerous disk technologies on the market today, with more on the horizon. Table 5.1 lists some of the more common technologies used in servers, with their data transfer rates, advantages, and disadvantages.

TABLE 5.1: Comparison of Disk Technologies

Type	Approximate Data Transfer Rate	Advantages	Disadvantages
IDE/EIDE	Up to 8.3MB per second (IDE) and 16.6MB per second (EIDE)	Included on most modern motherboards; Easy to configure; (just add drive to CMOS); Least expensive hardware	Limit of two drives per controller; Traditional IDE drives were limited to 540MB; enhanced IDE has a work-around for larger drives, but not all BIOS will recognize large drives

TABLE 5.1 continued: Comparison of Disk Technologies

Type	Approximate Data Transfer Rate	Advantages	Disadvantages
SCSI	5MB per second	Standard, mature technology; Moderately expensive hardware	Must understand SCSI installation, termination, and IDs
FAST SCSI	10MB per second	Speed	Little more expensive
FAST-20 or ULTRA SCSI	20MB per second	More speed	More expensive
ULTRA SCSI-2	40MB per second	Most speed	Most expensive next to RAID drives

Busmaster Controllers

Some controllers have an on-board processor designed to off-load processing from the CPU. The CPU passes a data or write request to the controller and can then continue with another task. The controller's processor handles the details of the request and interrupts the CPU only when the requested function has been completed. Busmastering is very common on high-end (SCSI) controllers, and is often used on servers.

Caching Controllers

Some controllers have their own memory. When the CPU needs to write data to disk, the data can be written into this memory. This process is extremely fast. The controller then writes the data to disk on its own. As in busmastering, the goal is to free up the CPU as quickly as possible.

WARNING

It is imperative to have a good UPS (uninterruptable power supply) on a server using a caching controller. Once the CPU has finished passing the data to the controller, it considers the data to have been written to disk. If power is lost before the data are flushed from the cache, no fault-tolerance system would be aware of the problem. This is usually not a big issue since most controllers have limits on how long data can sit in cache—but it's better to be safe than sorry.

Hardware-Controlled RAID (Redundant Array of Inexpensive Disks)

RAID technology is designed to add fault tolerance to a disk subsystem. In a RAID system, a duplicate of all data is stored on another disk (this is a simplification–RAID will be discussed in more detail later in the "Choosing a Fault-Tolerance Method" section). If one disk dies, the data can be rebuilt on the fly. Some controllers have RAID technologies built into the hardware.

Once you have chosen a type of disk subsystem and installed the hardware, you must configure those disks for NT. So, the discussion will now focus on partitioning your disks and choosing a file system.

Partitioning

Before a hard disk can be used by an operating system, the hard disk must be partitioned. When you partition a hard disk, you define the boundaries of a physical area on the disk. This area can then be formatted for use by an operating system such as Microsoft Windows NT. You can use partitioning to organize your data by creating a "boot" partition that contains only NT system files, and another partition to hold your data. On a dual-boot computer, you can create separate partitions for each operating system so that each system file has its own physical space. An organized hard disk makes it easier to find your data.

On the physical level, a disk must be partitioned before an operating system can use its storage space. A partition is made up of unused space on the drive. The unused space will be used to form either a primary or an extended partition. You can create a maximum of four partitions on each disk. A primary partition has the necessary configuration to be used by an operating system for the boot process. You can create up to four primary partitions on a single disk. This allows you to isolate the system files from multiple operating systems on a single drive. One of the primary partitions will be marked as active–this is the partition that will be booted from.

Once a partition is created, it must then be formatted. Formatting sets up the basic housekeeping or accounting system on the partition to allow files to be stored and retrieved successfully by the operating system. While several formats exist, the most popular is file allocation table (FAT). Almost every operating system can read FAT, including DOS, Windows 95, Windows NT, UNIX, and Macintosh.

In addition to FAT, advances in the file systems have developed more mature formats such as HPFS, FAT32, and NTFS. High performance file systems (HPFS) was developed for use with OS/2, and NT file system (NTFS) was developed for use with Windows NT. However, these file systems are not designed to be read by other operating systems such as DOS.

You can set up a computer to dual-boot NT and Windows 95. To accomplish this, the partition must be formatted with the FAT file system (which will be discussed later in the "Choosing a File System" section). Note that NT cannot read a partition formatted with FAT32 (a file system available on Windows 95 SR2), so do not use this file system on machines on which you intend to dual-boot NT and Windows 95.

One way to get around the four-partition limit is to use an extended partition. There can be one extended partition on each disk (it *does* count against the four-partition limit). The extended partition can be subdivided into multiple logical disks, each of which will be given a drive letter by the system.

NT dynamically assigns drive letters to each partition using the procedure shown in Figure 5.1 and listed below.

1. Beginning with disk zero, the first primary partition on each drive is assigned a consecutive letter (starting with the letter *C*).
2. Beginning with disk zero, each logical drive is assigned a consecutive letter.
3. Beginning with disk zero, all other primary partitions are assigned a letter.

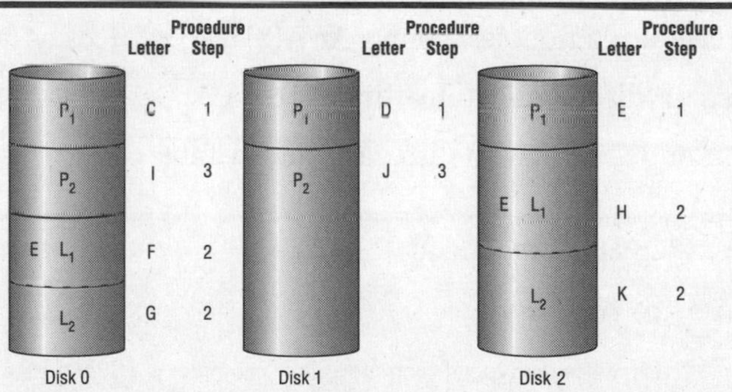

FIGURE 5.1: Assigning drive letters

You can override these default assignments in the Disk Administration tool by choosing Tools ➢ Assign Drive Letter.

Understanding Partition Numbering and ARC Paths

Windows NT assigns each partition an identification number, as shown in Figure 5.2. NT uses the partition number in an ARC path (defined later in this section) to locate the needed area on a disk for read and write operations. For troubleshooting, you need to know how NT assigns partition numbers.

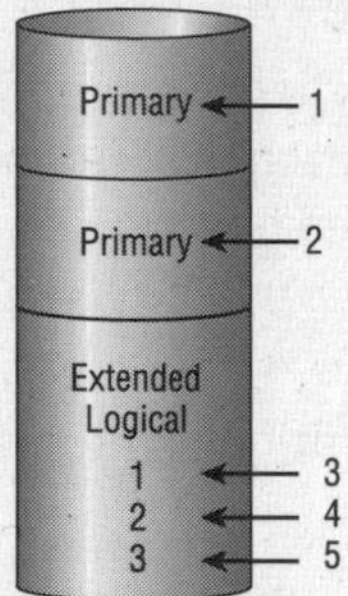

FIGURE 5.2: Assigning partition numbers

NT assigns a number to all primary partitions first, starting with the number *one,* and then assigns an ID to each logical drive in the extended partition (if one exists).

NT uses the partition numbers in an ARC (advanced RISC computing) path to find the partition. You must understand ARC paths, both for the exam and for real-world troubleshooting. An ARC path will look as follows:

multi/scsi(a)disk(b)rdisk(c)partition(d)

Each *a, b, c,* and *d* will have a value, as listed in Table 5.2.

TABLE 5.2: ARC Path Components

Component	Definition
multi/scsi	Identifies the type of controller. If the controller is a SCSI device with the BIOS *not* enabled, this value will be *scsi* ; for all others, it will be *multi* .
(a)	The ordinal value of the controller. As each controller initializes, it is given a value—the first will be given a value of *zero*, the next *one*, etc.

TABLE 5.2 continued: ARC Path Components

COMPONENT	DEFINITION
disk(b)	SCSI bus number; for multi, this value is always *zero* .
rdisk(c)	For non-SCSI disks, this will be the ordinal value of the disk. It is assigned in the same way as (*a*) above.
partition(d)	The ordinal value of the partition (as described above).

Planning Disk Drive Configuration

Following are procedures for planning disk drive configuration.

Choosing a File System

NT supports three different file systems:

- FAT (file allocation table)
- NTFS (NT file system)
- CDFS (CD-ROM file system)

NOTE

Since CDFS is a specialized file system used for CD-ROMs, it will not be discussed here.

FAT File System The FAT file system has been used since the earliest days of DOS computers. FAT has minimal overhead (less than 1MB) and is the most efficient file system for partitions smaller than 400MB. Since it is the only file system that DOS, Windows 95, and Windows NT have in common, the system partition must be a FAT partition on dual-boot machines. RISC-based computers will boot only from a FAT partition, so all RISC systems must have a small FAT partition to hold boot files.

On the downside, performance decreases as the number of files in a partition increases due to the way files are tracked. Another downside is that the FAT file system has no features to prevent file fragmentation, which can affect performance. As a security feature, Windows NT prevents a deleted file from being undeleted, but on a FAT partition (if the computer is booted to DOS), undelete tools might be able to recover deleted files. Also, there is no file- or directory-level security available on a FAT partition. The only security is that available through directory-level sharing supplied by the operating systems.

The version of the FAT file system included with Windows NT has been enhanced to support long filenames. Filenames adhere to the following criteria:

- Can be up to 255 characters (including the full path)
- Must start with a letter or number, and can include any characters except for quotation marks (""), forward and backward slashes (/ \), brackets ([ ]), semicolons (;), colons (:), equal signs (=), commas (,), carets (^), asterisks (*), and question marks (?)
- Can include multiple spaces
- Can include multiple periods, but the last period denotes the file suffix, which is similar to DOS 8.3 naming conventions (for example, .EXE, .COM)
- Preserve case, but are not case sensitive

TIP

As an aid to troubleshooting, many administrators create a FAT partition and place the NT boot files there. In the event of a problem, they can then boot to DOS and access the files on the partition, replacing corrupt files or using DOS-based disk diagnostic tools.

NTFS NTFS is the file system specifically designed for use on a Windows NT–based computer. NTFS offers many advantages over the older FAT file system:

- File- and directory-level security.
- Larger file and partition sizes. Theoretically, both the maximum file and the maximum partition size is 16 exabytes. Functionally, with today's hardware, the limit is 2 terabytes.
- Built-in file compression.
- A recoverable file system. It uses a transaction log for disk activity. The log file can be used to redo or undo operations that failed.

- Bad-cluster remapping. If a write error occurs, the file system will move the data to another sector of the disk.
- Support for Macintosh files. (You must install Services for Macintosh.)
- Support for POSIX.1-compliant software.
- Reduced file fragmentation.

There are only two, small drawbacks to NTFS—since it has a fairly high overhead (approximately 50MB), floppy disks cannot be formatted with NTFS. Also, NTFS does not support removable media (when using removable media formatted with NTFS, you must restart the computer to change disks).

Managing Hard Disks

The next step in planning your disk drive configuration is to determine how those disks will act together to store your data. NT offers many configuration options—you must be able to determine which option is right for your environment.

Volume Sets You can add together areas of free space on your hard disks to create one logical drive—thus creating a volume set. Once created, this area must then be formatted with either FAT or NTFS. Once you have created the volume set, it will appear as one drive to the system. When using a volume set, NT will fill each segment, before starting to use the next.

You can also add space to an existing NTFS volume by choosing Extend Volume Set from the Partition menu in Disk Administrator. Once free space has been added to a volume set, you cannot take it back. The only way to reclaim that space is to delete the *entire* volume set (and thus any data stored there).

TIP

If you need to extend a volume set formatted with the FAT file system, first convert it to NTFS using the CONVERT.EXE command-line tool. Remember that this is a one-way operation—once you have converted to NTFS, you cannot go back to FAT.

Stripe Sets Like a volume set, a stripe set adds free space on two or more hard drives to one logical drive. Unlike a volume set, however, a stripe set must include space on at least 2 drives (up to a maximum of 32 drives). The areas created must be approximately the same size (if they are not, Disk Administrator will adjust the size for you).

When data are placed in a stripe set, the data are written evenly across all physical disks in 64KB "stripes." While a stripe set does not provide fault tolerance, it can improve I/O performance.

Choosing a Fault-Tolerance Method

Because of the critical nature of most data stored on servers, the disk subsystem must be fault tolerant. A *fault-tolerant disk system* can survive the death of a single hard drive, with the data still accessible. The fault-tolerant features of Windows NT are managed through the Disk Administrator tool.

NT provides fault tolerance through software-controlled implementation of redundant array of inexpensive disks (RAID). There are seven primary levels of RAID in the industry; NT Server can implement software versions of three RAID levels–0, 1, and 5. Level 0 (disk striping) is just the ability to create a volume set that spans multiple hard drives. Since this provides no fault tolerance, it will be ignored in this discussion.

Level 1 RAID is commonly referred to as disk mirroring. In a *mirror system,* there is a redundant copy of all data on the partition. With mirroring, if the primary disk dies, the system can switch over to the redundant disk–the users will not notice the hardware failure.

Disk duplexing is a subset of mirroring in which the disks are accessed through separate controllers. In mirroring, if the controller dies, there is no way to access the redundant disk. Since you have multiple controllers in a duplexed system, the server can survive a controller failure–the users will not notice a problem.

Level 5 RAID consists of disk striping (as discussed above) with the addition of a parity set. The *parity set* is a calculation of the contents of the data, placed on another disk in the set. If one disk dies, the RAID system can use the parity information to recreate the missing data on the fly.

Level 1 RAID (mirroring) is an efficient way to provide fault tolerance (especially if you upgrade it to duplexing). Since an entire copy of the data exists on another hard drive, the user will not notice any difference in performance in the event of a hardware failure. However, mirroring is more expensive than level 5 RAID–in mirroring, only 50 percent of the disk space is usable, since the other half is used to maintain redundancy. Mirroring is also the only way to make your system and boot partitions fault tolerant. These two partitions cannot be part of a volume set, stripe set, or stripe set with parity.

Level 5 RAID is very common in today's business environments. It actually increases I/O performance by splitting the work across the hard disks. It is also more cost effective than mirroring. In a level-5 implementation, the more disks involved in the stripe set, the lower the percentage of disk space used for the fault-tolerant information. In mirroring, one-half of the total disk space is used to provide fault tolerance. In a level-5 implementation with the minimum of three disks, only one-third of the space is used to hold the parity information (one-fourth with four disks, one-fifth with five disks, etc.). Level 5 RAID can support up to 32 disk partitions. Keep in mind, though, that level 5 RAID can survive the loss of only one disk. If you lose more than one disk, all the information on the disk array becomes inaccessible and useless.

NOTE

Windows NT provides software-controlled RAID. Although this is an inexpensive way to achieve fault tolerance, it is not necessarily the correct choice. Some hardware has been specifically designed to provide RAID functions. In most cases, hardware-based RAID will be faster than software-based RAID.

Reassigning Drive Letters

You reassign disk drive letters by using the Disk Administrator tool. Click the partition you want to reassign, choose Tools ➢ Assign Drive Letter, and change the letter.

Creating a Volume Set

In Disk Administrator, Ctrl-click all of the partitions that should be included and choose Partition ➢ Create Volume Set.

Creating a Stripe Set

In Disk Administrator, Ctrl-click all of the partitions (2–32) that should be included in the set. Remember that the segments must be approximately the same size (Disk Administrator will adjust the size for you if they are not). Choose Partition ➢ Create Stripe Set.

Creating a Mirror Set

In Disk Administrator, Ctrl-click the two partitions that will make up the set (they must be on different hard drives) and choose Fault Tolerance ➢ Establish Mirror.

Creating a Stripe Set with Parity

In Disk Administrator, Ctrl-click the partitions (3–32) that will make up the segments of the set. Remember that these must be approximately the same size (Disk Administrator will adjust the size as appropriate). Choose Fault Tolerance ➢ Create Stripe Set with Parity.

Choose a protocol for various situations.

Protocols include:

- TCP/IP
- NWLink IPX/SPX Compatible Transport
- NetBEUI

In its simplest sense, *protocol* can be defined as a set of rules that govern behavior. If you understand how communication protocols work, it will help you choose the protocols you want to implement in your environment. Implementing too many protocols on the network is probably the most common cause of slow performance. As a systems engineer, you need to understand when each protocol is appropriate and when it is not. You need to know how you can use a single protocol to provide as many services as possible, and you need to know how to choose that protocol for a given environment. Also, you need to know how to configure each protocol and implement it in the most efficient manner. In other words, you need to understand how computers talk to each other.

NOTE

The objectives in this section are designed to test your ability to choose the right protocols based upon the needs of the network.

Over the course of your MCSE studies, you will be presented with a lot of different protocols. The most important one is probably TCP/IP, because it is the protocol of the Internet. Some of the other protocols commonly used on NT networks will also be discussed. Each protocol has strengths and weaknesses of which you will need to be aware.

TCP/IP

TCP/IP is a hot topic in today's networking world. If you pick up any of the industry magazines, you'll find at least one story about the installation, management, or new developments of the TCP/IP suite. TCP is regarded as the future of networking–you will need to understand it to work with the networks of today and tomorrow.

TCP/IP is really a suite of protocols, each piece of which provides a very specific service to the network. The name TCP/IP will be used to refer to the entire suite. If you understand what each piece does, it can greatly increase your ability to solve network-related problems. TCP/IP is also a protocol created, maintained, and advanced by committee. TCP/IP is based upon a complex set of RFCs (requests for comments)–documents that propose additions to the suite and changes to existing protocols. Just about anyone can submit an RFC. It then goes through a series of revisions, until it either gets pushed aside (this happens to most RFCs), gets made an optional piece of a TCP/IP environment, or gets added as part of the standard.

The best way to start when learning TCP/IP is to get a feel for the entire suite. Table 5.3 lists some of the more common protocols in the suite and their functions.

Part II

TABLE 5.3: Common TCP/IP Protocols and Their Functions

Protocol	Function
TCP (transmission control protocol)	Used for connection-oriented, reliable transport of packets
UDP (user datagram protocol)	Used for connectionless, nonreliable transport of packets
IP (Internet protocol)	Provides addressing and routing functions
ICMP (Internet control message protocol)	Used for protocol-level management messages between hosts
ARP (address resolution protocol)	Used to obtain the hardware address of a host. "Resolves" a known IP address to a physical MAC (media access control) address

TABLE 5.3 continued: Common TCP/IP Protocols and Their Functions

Protocol	Function
NetBT (NetBIOS over TCP/IP)	Used by NetBIOS applications to communicate over a TCP/IP-based network
SNMP (simple network management protocol)	An industry standard method of monitoring and configuring hardware or software over a TCP/IP-based network

Windows NT ships with a series of utilities that provide network services on a TCP/IP network. Table 5.4 lists the more commonly used (and tested upon) utilities and their functions.

TABLE 5.4: Common TCP/IP Utilities and Their Functions

Utility	Function
PING (packet Internet groper)	Tests IP connections
FTP (file transfer protocol)	Bidirectional file transfer services. Requires user to log onto the host providing FTP services, even if anonymous
TFTP (trivial file transfer protocol)	Bidirectional file transfer services. Usually used for UNIX system code files
Telnet	Terminal emulation to a host offering Telnet services
RCP (remote copy protocol)	File transfer services
RSH (remote shell)	Runs commands on a UNIX host
REXEC (remote execution)	Runs a process on a UNIX host
FINGER	Retrieves system information from the host running the finger service
Microsoft Internet Explorer	Browser software
ARP	Displays local ARP cache
IPCONFIG	Displays your current IP configuration
NBTSTAT	Displays cached information for connections using NetBIOS over IP
Netstat	Protocol statistics and connections
ROUTE	Works with the local routing table
Hostname	Displays the host name of your computer
Tracert (trace route)	Displays the route to a remote host

NOTE

For this exam, you will not be expected to be an expert in many of these utilities, but you might be expected to know what functions they perform.

Now for the meat of this objective—how does one know if TCP/IP is the right choice? The following bulleted list describes the benefits of TCP/IP.

- TCP/IP was specifically designed to allow diverse computing systems to communicate. No network operating system can hope to make it in the market unless it provides a common protocol that allows communication with existing systems. Most medium or larger-sized systems are made up of a mixture of hardware and operating systems, and it is not economically feasible to migrate *everything* to NT at once.
- TCP/IP was specifically designed for a routed network. It is the most routable protocol in use today. If you plan on connecting through any type of WAN link, TCP/IP will give you the best performance, the most control, and the least congestion.
- TCP/IP has SNMP (simple network management protocol). This is the industry standard protocol for use in managing routers, bridges, gateways, and all the other components that make up a network. Just about every network-management software package can use the SNMP protocol, and there is no indication that this will change. The bottom line—if you want to manage your network, TCP/IP will be your protocol of choice.
- TCP/IP is the protocol of the Internet. If you plan on connecting to the Internet, creating a Web site, or using e-mail, you will be using TCP/IP.
- A whole slew of tools is available to make TCP/IP more manageable—not only for managing pieces of your network, but for managing the protocol itself. These tools include DHCP (dynamic host configuration protocol), WINS (Windows Internet name service), DNS (domain name service), and others. These tools take the headache out of installing and configuring TCP/IP hosts (more on these tools later in this section).

TCP/IP with DHCP and WINS

As mentioned earlier, numerous tools are available to help manage the TCP/IP protocols. Two of the most commonly implemented tools are DHCP and WINS. Each of these tools is designed to alleviate some of the more common headaches encountered in a TCP/IP network.

DHCP (Dynamic Host Configuration Protocol)

To really appreciate the value of DHCP, you must understand a little more about how TCP/IP works. In an IP network, each host has a unique identifier called an IP address. This address must be unique when compared to all other hosts that are attached to any network with which the local host can communicate. (Stop and think about this–if you are connected to the Internet, your computer must have an address that is different from the addresses of millions of other hosts that can attach to the Internet.)

TRADITIONAL IP HEADACHES

Here is a list of some traditional IP headaches:

- Configuring each host takes time—and lots of it! Each host was configured by hand, which meant that either someone from the IS department went to each device in turn or you trained your users. Neither solution is an efficient use of time and resources.
- Configuration by hand means mistakes! It does not matter how well you type—if you are configuring 500 machines, you are bound to make at least a couple of mistakes. At best, duplicate or invalid addresses will affect only the host where the mistake was made; at worst, they can affect communication across your network.
- Change is problematic. There is a very strict and complicated set of rules for addressing in an IP network. Networks will grow, and sometimes you have to change your addressing scheme. This means changing the configuration at *all* hosts.
- If you add a new IP-based service, you may need to add or change a configuration parameter at each host.

CONTINUED ➔

▸ If you physically move a device within your environment, you may need to change its IP configuration. Usually, when you move a machine, the last thing on your mind is its configuration (you are thinking about what a pain users are, you are griping about a management team that can't leave well enough alone, or you have a list of more important things that you should be doing). Even worse—users occasionally take it upon themselves to move a device without letting you know. In this case, you have addressing problems and don't even know what has changed.

Why DHCP? Using traditional methods to manage an IP network was a hassle, but it was necessary. DHCP was designed to overcome some of these hassles. The theory behind DHCP is fairly simple–DHCP is a protocol specifically designed to configure IP hosts as they attach to the network. DHCP runs as a service on an NT server. This service manages a pool of IP addresses and configuration parameters. When a DHCP client boots, one of the first things it does is try to find a DHCP server. If it finds one, the DHCP sends it all of the TCP/IP configuration information necessary to function on the network. From a management perspective, this means you have only one place to manage your TCP/IP environment. You assign addresses appropriately, make changes, and add configuration parameters to the "pool"–these changes are reflected every time a client boots on your network.

WINS (Windows Internet Name Service)

Another tool designed to ease the management of a Windows-based network that uses the TCP/IP protocol is WINS. Once again, to really appreciate WINS, you have to delve a little deeper into how IP and NetBIOS work. (NetBIOS is the upper-level protocol that Windows-based networks use to communicate.) WINS adds two basic services to your network–NetBIOS name registration and name resolution.

Name registration In a NetBIOS-based network (any Windows network), each computer is given a unique name–the NetBIOS name. Since NetBIOS uses this name to communicate between machines, these names *must* be unique. In a traditional NetBIOS network, each machine sends a NetBIOS broadcast that announces its name as it boots. If another host already exists with that name, it will send a message to thc new client saying that the name is in use. If it doesn't get a message back, the client assumes that the name is available.

This process works OK on a single-segment network. Unfortunately, most routers do not pass NetBIOS broadcast traffic. This means that there is no mechanism to prevent two computers from having the same name if they are on different network segments. Duplicate names *will* cause communication errors somewhere down the line!

While routers can be set up to pass these broadcasts, there is a more elegant and effective solution–the Windows Internet naming service (WINS). In a WINS environment, each client is configured with the IP address of the WINS server. When the client boots, it sends a message to this server–a request to use a name. The WINS server keeps a database of all the NetBIOS names that are in use–if the name is *not* already in use, it returns an acknowledgement; if the name *is* already in use, it returns a denial. If the name is approved, the WINS server places a record for that client (made up of its NetBIOS name and IP address) in its database.

WINS clients send a name release to the WINS server when they are properly turned off. This allows the WINS server to update its database so that it contains only names for computers that are currently available on the network.

Name resolution Users shouldn't be forced to remember complicated IP addresses for all of the machines with which they need to communicate. Unfortunately, acquiring this address is mandatory before communication can happen. You should give your computers names that are easy to remember so that users can use a "friendly" name to represent a computer.

First, the NetBIOS name (the name you gave the computer when you installed NT) must be resolved into an IP address. Traditionally, this is done by broadcasting a request on the network. Basically, the computer shouts on the wire, "Hey, I'm looking for a computer named XYZ." If computer XYZ receives the request, it will send a message back that contains its IP address. There are two problems with this technique. First, broadcast traffic must be analyzed by *every* computer on the network, adding overhead to machines that are not involved in the communication. Second, most routers are configured *not* to pass broadcast traffic, so your request will be fulfilled only if you are attempting to communicate with a device on your own network segment.

To get around the broadcast problem, you could create a text file named LMHOSTS on every computer. This text file would contain the NetBIOS name and IP address of every computer with which you are going to communicate. What a hassle! Every time you add a new computer to your network, you will have to update the LMHOSTS file on all other computers in your network.

If you have implemented WINS, though, you already have a database that contains the names and IP addresses of all computers available on the network. In a WINS environment, when your computer wants to communicate with another computer, it sends a name-resolution request to the WINS server. This request contains the NetBIOS name of the machine to which you wish to connect. The WINS server looks through its database. If it finds a matching NetBIOS name, it returns the IP address of that machine.

Why WINS? WINS saves time and traffic on your network, therefore helping to keep it efficient. Without WINS, many of the procedures for establishing a connection with another machine are based upon broadcast traffic. Broadcast traffic is the bane of systems engineers. When a packet is broadcast, all computers that receive it must stop what they are doing and waste time reading the packet to determine if they should respond. In a WINS environment, all of this traffic is directed to the WINS server. It is the only computer that will analyze these packets, while all others continue processing without interruption.

NWLink IPX/SPX Compatible Transport

NWLink is Microsoft's implementation of the IPX/SPX protocol suite used by Novell's NetWare products. On most NT networks, you will implement NWLink only if you need to communicate with a NetWare server. As far as the protocol suite goes, IPX/SPX has some advantages and disadvantages of which you will need to be aware. For that reason, NWLink is not installed by default on an NT machine, Server, or Workstation.

IPX/SPX is easy to implement and manage. There are no complex addressing schemes. Each computer gets its unique identifier from its network interface card. This means that you do not have to configure any unique parameters at each computer for communication to occur. Further advantages include:

- IPX/SPX supports routing between networks.

- IPX/SPX allows you to easily connect your NT environment to your NetWare environment. You can slowly integrate NT servers into your network, without having to replace your existing resources.

NOTE

Installing NWLink is only the first step in integration. The rest of the process will be discussed in Chapter 8, "Connectivity."

Although there is no address configuration at each computer, you do have to give unique identification values to each network segment. Unlike TCP/IP, there is no addressing scheme to these addresses. The LAN administrator comes up with a segment-numbering plan and implements it. Other disadvantages include:

- Until recently, there was no way to register your IPX network addresses. This made it difficult to connect to any kind of central network or shared wiring scheme.
- IPX/SPX is not used on the Internet. If you intend to connect to the Internet, you must use TCP/IP.
- IPX/SPX does not support SNMP.
- IPX/SPX uses more broadcast-based traffic to organize the network. Although the process is automatic, it increases the traffic on your network.

NOTE

On the exam, you will implement NWLink only if you need to communicate with Novell NetWare-based file servers.

NetBEUI

NetBIOS extended user interface (NetBEUI) is a protocol that was originally developed for small departmental LANs (with less than 200 computers). It is fast enough for most small networks. Unfortunately, NetBEUI cannot be routed, so it is not suited to any kind of WAN environment. NetBEUI relies on broadcast-based traffic for many of its functions, so it can place more overhead on the network than other protocols. The Windows NT implementation of NetBEUI provides interoperability with Microsoft LAN Manager and Windows for Workgroups networks. NetBEUI provides the following benefits:

- Both connection and connectionless communication
- Self configuration and self timing
- Error protection against corruption on the wire
- Because of its limited function set, requires a very small amount of memory

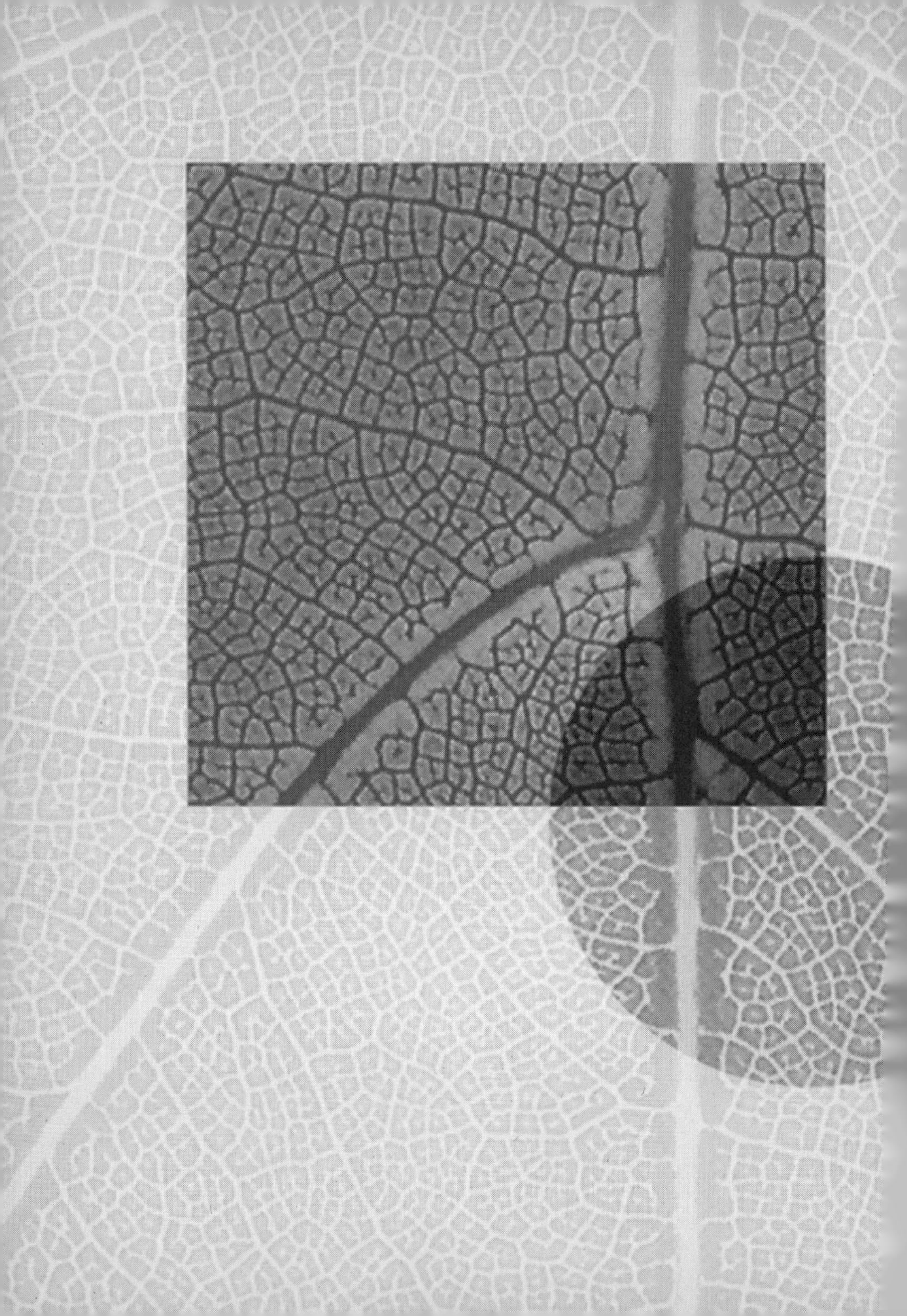

Chapter 6

Installation and Configuration

In Chapter 5, you developed a task list and made decisions on how to implement and provide the basic services your customers will need. By the end of this chapter, you will learn how to update your network to meet the demands of everyday life.

Adapted from *MCSE Exam Notes: NT Server 4*
by Gary Govanus and Robert King
ISBN 0-7821-2289-2 360 pages $19.99

Your task list will grow to include the following items:

- Communications
- Adding disk space while allowing for future growth
- Upgrading the tape backup unit
- Adding an uninterruptible power supply
- Upgrading the mouse and video cards
- Putting in a new printer

Some of the objectives in this chapter are stressed heavily on the exam. For example, if you know several of the command-line switches used during an installation, it will be more helpful than knowing how to configure certain peripherals and devices. You will need to understand the differences between a PDC, BDC, and member server. Study the objective on hard disk space, and understand the different types of redundancy. Also, questions about minimum requirements for disk striping with parity will pop up in the most unexpected places.

NOTE

The objective on printing is crucial.

Install Windows NT Server on Intel-based platforms.

This objective is a behind-the-scenes look at what happens during the installation process. It is not only important to know which and how many pieces to use, but how the pieces will work together to provide the desired results. This section describes how the installation process will work and what NT will do each step along the way. Some installations fail, and it is far easier to troubleshoot problems when you know what was supposed to happen next.

Installation Requirements

NT 4 can be installed on a variety of platforms, including the Intel *x*86, Pentium-based computers, and RISC-based computers. NT 4 will even run on the MIPS R4x00-based microprocessor or higher, the Digital

Alpha AXP-based microprocessor, and the PReP-compliant PowerPC-based microprocessor. This book (and the exam) concentrates on the Intel platform.

Microsoft lists minimal hardware requirements that must be met before the installation begins. The official requirements for Windows NT Server 4, as published in Microsoft's TechNet, are as follows:

- 16MB of RAM
- VGA-level video support
- Keyboard
- IDE, EIDE, SCSI, or ESDI hard disk
- 486/33 processor or better
- CD-ROM drive, 1.44MB or 1.2MB floppy disk drive, or active network connection

Microsoft has also released a *suggested minimum* list:

- 486DX2/50 processor or better
- 32MB of RAM
- 28.8 v.34 external modem, for remote debugging and troubleshooting
- Windows NT–compatible CD-ROM drive

The folks from Redmond also forgot to mention a network interface card (NIC). You must have one, and it must be on Microsoft's NT hardware compatibility list (HCL). You can find the HCL at Microsoft's NT Web site. How much disk space will an NT installation take? It depends on the accessories that you install, but the minimum space requirements for Windows NT Workstation and Server, as listed on TechNet, are as follows:

- Standard installation: 124MB of free disk space
- WINNT /b: an additional 24MB of free disk space
- Copying I386 folder to hard disk: 223MB more free disk space

These disk space requirements assume that you have a standard hard disk controller, not an enhanced integrated device electronics (EIDE) hard disk controller.

NOTE

Some 486 computers operate under the assumption that integrated device electronics (IDE) drives can be a maximum of 504MB. However, translation mode fakes out the system—the inner workings of the computer may think that the new EIDE drive is only 504MB, when in reality it might be 5GB.

Make sure that the disk is partitioned and formatted. Here are the recommendations from Microsoft on the disk configurations:

- The root folder (the folder to which you will install NT 4) should be on a disk formatted with either the original FAT 16 format (translated to NTFS during installation) or NTFS from NT version 3.51 or 4. If you are using NTFS, the drive can be compressed. NT will not install on a hard drive that has been compressed with any other utility.
- If your target drive uses address translation, it should use: logical block addressing (LBA); ONTrack Disk Manager; EZDrive; and extended cylinder head sector.

If you make sure that your BIOS and hard drive support these translations, you should be in good shape.

Keep in mind that these are the recommended *minimum* requirements. NT will make use of all of the tools you give it, so give it as much as you can. The more advanced the processor and the more memory you give the server, the better.

Installation Procedures

Microsoft provides three preconfigured setup scenarios, as well as a Custom option. If you select the Custom option, it gives you the right to install NT Workstation just the way you want it. With NT Server, there are no preconfigured methods of installation–you will perform a custom installation. Most of the decisions that you will need to make were covered in Chapter 5 and are available in your working papers.

The installation is really quite elegant and is carried out in four easily definable steps, each with its own set of tasks to accomplish. Working together, these tasks lay the foundation on which your network will be built. The four steps are: initializing installation; gathering information; installing NT networking; and finishing setup.

Initializing Installation

A complete installation will be covered later in this chapter. For now, it is important to know what you will face as you go through the installation. During the initialization phase:

- NT checks for previous versions of NT. Will this be a new install or an upgrade? If it is an upgrade, NT will ask you some pointed questions about the directory into which you will put the operating system. NT 4's default root folder is WINNT (this is a change from previous versions).
- NT examines your computer to see what hardware it recognizes. It will then check whether what it found corresponds to what you think it should have found.
- NT looks for a formatted disk partition. If you plan to dual boot between DOS and NT, you must have at least 200MB of free disk space in the DOS partition so that NT can use it for temporary file storage. The Installation Wizard will copy files to the DOS partition before the installation process continues.
- The Installation Wizard will ask you which file system you will use–NTFS or FAT. NTFS is more effective for drives over 400MB.
- The initialization phase completes when NT asks you where you want to put the program files.

Gathering Information

This phase is as simple as it sounds. The progressive information screens will ask for the following items:

- Name and organization of the person to whom the copy of NT is licensed. At this point, do you enter your own name, or the name of the MIS director, the CEO, or the CIO?
- Licensing mode: Per Server or Per Seat.
    - Per Server licensing–With Per Server licensing, each client access license (CAL) is assigned to a specific server for the basic file and print services. Once a CAL has been assigned to a server, that user can access any file or share on that server. The number of CALs must equal the maximum number of clients that will connect to that server at the same time. If your server reaches the maximum number of licensed connections and another client

attempts to connect, NT will issue an error message and not allow the connection.

- Per Seat licensing–With Per Seat licensing, a CAL applies to a specific seat or client. With this licensing mode selected, an unlimited number of clients can attach to your server, as long as each of the clients has a license. This is an NT Server CAL. A Windows 95 workstation does not necessarily have the right to attach to the server.

NOTE

If you are not sure which licensing mode to choose, use Per Server. You can convert from Per Server to Per Seat one time only at no cost. It is not possible to convert from Per Seat to Per Server.

- Computer name. This name must be 15 characters or less and unique among all computers, workgroups, and domain names on the network. You can change it later.
- The type of server to install: primary domain controller (PDC), backup domain controller (BDC), or member server.
- A password for the administrator account.
- Optional components to install. Here, you will have to make some decisions. For the most part, though, these are not installation-critical decisions–if you decide to skip this phase, you can always install the optional components later. Optional components include:
    - Accessibility options–These options make running your server easier for the physically challenged.
    - Accessories such as WordPad, Paint, Clock, and Calculator.
    - Communications programs for rudimentary modem communications.
    - Games, such as FreeCell and Solitaire.
    - Windows messaging, which will give you an e-mail client.
    - Multimedia programs.

Also, have a 3.5-inch floppy disk handy. You may want to create an emergency repair diskette, which can come in handy in times of crisis.

Installing NT Networking

The purpose of buying and installing NT Server is to enable users to share information and resources. To make that happen, you have to install NT networking. This piece of the puzzle provides the communication link between the server and all of the resources on the network. It is a subsystem that can consist of NICs, modems, software services, and protocols. You will have to provide information about the following items:

- Whether the computer will be on a LAN, dialed into remotely, or both.
- Which network adapter cards are installed and the configuration parameters for each.
- Which protocols to install–for example, TCP/IP, NetBEUI, or NWLink.
- Whether any additional network services need to be installed–for example, Internet Information Server, proxy services, or DHCP.
- Which domain the computer will join. You have already chosen the role that the server will play in the domain.

Finishing Setup

To finish setup, you need to provide the following information to the new NT server:

- The date, time, and time zone in which the server will reside.
- Statistics about the video card driver and its configuration. Be aware of the optimum resolution of the card/monitor combination.

Install Windows NT Server to perform various server roles.

Server roles include:

- Primary domain controller
- Backup domain controller
- Member server

When you install an NT server, you should have a clear idea of the services that it will provide to your network clients. An NT server can provide numerous services–from DHCP and WINS to acting as a domain controller and your e-mail server. Each of these services will add overhead to a server. This overhead will be characterized in Chapter 9, "Monitoring and Optimization." For now, the discussion will be limited to the first service-related decision you have to make during the installation–whether a server should be a domain controller?

Understanding Server Roles

One of the first things that you do when planning a network is determine the role each server will perform. This decision will influence your purchase plans, network design, and long-term management.

Primary and Backup Domain Controllers

Primary and backup domain controllers are similar–they both hold a copy of the SAM and are used for authentication during the logon process. Since they are alike in their duties, their hardware needs are similar. Before their function is examined, hardware will be discussed.

Necessary Hardware Before you buy your server, you need to know the load. Load is mainly determined on a domain controller by the size of the SAM. The bigger the SAM, the bigger the load. A big SAM indicates a large number of users, and the more users there are, the more logons the server will have to authenticate and the more changes there will be to the database. Before you can determine the minimum requirements for a domain controller, you need to approximate the size of the SAM it will support.

The number of objects you define determines the size of the SAM. Each object represents a record in the database; each type of object has a record of a different size. Table 6.1 describes the sizes of the various records in the SAM.

TABLE 6.1: Objects in the SAM

Object Class	Size
User account	1KB
Computer account	.5KB
Global group account	512 bytes plus 12 bytes for every member
Local group account	512 bytes plus 36 bytes for every member

You need to estimate the number of user and computer accounts that you will create. This *should* be easy—determine how many users and NT-based servers and workstations are in your company. Next, you need to estimate the number of groups that you will create. Analyze the resources you will share, then come up with a plan for sharing each resource. This will tell you approximately how many groups you will need to create. Once you have the number of groups, estimate how many users will be members of each group. Take the numbers and do a little math.

Once you've calculated the size of the database, use the information in Table 6.2 to determine the minimum hardware needed to support it.

TABLE 6.2: Hardware Requirements Based upon SAM Size

Number of Users	SAM Size (MB)	CPU Needed	RAM Needed (MB)
3,000	5	486DX/33	16
7,500	10	486DX/66	32
10,000	15	Pentium, MIPS, or Alpha	48
15,000	20	Pentium, MIPS, or Alpha	64
30–40,000	40	Pentium, MIPS, or Alpha	128

WARNING

These numbers were obtained from Microsoft's TechNet Technical Information Network (Article Q130914). They are probably a little low for most installations, because Microsoft assumes that the server will be dedicated to the task of acting as a domain controller.

When planning your domain, you should compare the estimated size of the SAM with the hardware you will have available as a server. If the hardware won't support the SAM, buy a more robust server. The only other option is to split the domain into multiple domains, until the hardware *will* support the SAM, which can make for a long-term administrative headache.

Now that you have chosen your hardware, the functions of domain controllers can be discussed. The primary responsibility of domain controllers is user authentication. Since domain controllers are the only computers that hold the accounts database, all users must access them when logging onto the network. When the user logs onto the network, their name and password are compared to information in the SAM. If the name and password match an existing account, the domain controller creates the SID (system identification) for that user. The SID contains the identification and the access control elements of the user and any groups of which the user is a member. This information will be used when the user tries to access a resource, so copies of the accounts database must be synchronized on a regular basis. If it isn't, information about the user might not be current at the domain controller to which the user attaches during the logon process.

Synchronizing Primary and Backup Domain Controllers The primary domain controller holds the main copy of the accounts database. All changes to the SAM must be made on the primary domain controller (PDC), which then updates the copies stored on the backup domain controllers (BDC). This is known as a *single master model*, because all changes are made to the master copy and then synchronized with all other copies. The process of synchronization is fairly simple. Every time a backup domain controller comes online, one of the first things it does is try to find the primary domain controller (PDC) to verify that its user accounts database is up to date. The PDC keeps a log of all changes to the database. Each change that has been made is given a version ID–think of this as a counter. When the PDC updates a BDC, it records the highest version ID (counter) on the updated records. The next time the PDC checks for changes, it compares the highest version ID of the last synchronization with the version IDs in the change log. If anything in the change log has a higher value than the last recorded update of the BDC, that change has not been synchronized on the BDC. The PDC will then synchronize the changes on the BDC.

By default, the PDC checks the BDC version IDs against the change log every five minutes. This time period is referred to as the pulse. There are two types of updates–partial and complete. In a partial update, only the changed information is synchronized. In a complete update, the entire database is sent to the BDC. From an optimization perspective, it is preferable to do a partial update rather than send the entire database.

A complete update might occur for various reasons:

- Every time a new BDC is brought online.
- When the change log fills up (it has a specific size), the PDC starts writing over the oldest change records. If there are enough changes in a pulse, the last known version ID for a BDC will no

longer be in the change log. In this case, the PDC can no longer be sure of exactly which changes have been synchronized and which have not. At this point, a complete update must occur.

- When an error occurs during a partial update.
- When the administrator forces a complete update. (Use Server Manager to accomplish this task.)

This synchronization traffic can have an impact on where you physically place domain controllers on the network backbone. If you place a backup domain controller on the other side of a WAN link, the synchronization traffic will have to cross that link–this could affect the link's ability to support other types of traffic. On the other hand, if you don't place a BDC across the wire, all logon traffic will have to cross the link to find a domain controller for authentication.

Microsoft expects you to understand the trade-off between synchronization traffic and logon traffic. For faster synchronization, put all domain controllers in a central location. For faster logons, put the domain controllers near the users so that logons can be done locally.

WARNING

Most consultants consider synchronization traffic to be a reasonable cost of business. You don't optimize for background traffic—you optimize for your users.

Most of the time, you will distribute domain controllers across your network so that users don't have to cross any slow links to log on, which means that the synchronization traffic *will* have to cross those links. If you are short on bandwidth, you can change a couple of registry parameters to control the amount and frequency of traffic generated.

Synchronization Parameters in the Registry There are two ways to control synchronization traffic–controlling how often it happens and/or controlling how much traffic is generated. Both of these methods are accomplished through a parameter called the ReplicationGovernor. This parameter is set to a percentage. By default, it is set to 100 percent, which means that the PDC can take up to 100 percent of the available bandwidth and buffer 128KB of data at a time. This can greatly affect a slow link where users are also competing for a limited amount of bandwidth. If you set the ReplicationGovernor to 50 percent, the NetLogon service can buffer only 50 percent as much data (64KB) for each transmission and can have synchronization messages on the network only 50 percent of the time. This will spread out the traffic over twice as much time.

WARNING

If you set this value too low, it can prevent synchronization from completing.

You can also change the timing of the pulse. By default, the PDC checks for changes every five minutes. You can increase this time by increasing the pulse parameter–to a maximum value of 48 hours. (Once again, though, if you check for changes less frequently, it is more likely that you will be forced to do a complete update.)

To increase the odds of being able to do partial updates, increase the size of the change log by changing the ChangeLogSize parameter. By default, the change log is 64KB, which is enough room to record approximately 2,000 changes. You should make changes to the pulse and the ChangeLogSize in parallel.

Member Server

A *member server* is any NT server that was not installed as a domain controller. Unlike domain controllers, member servers are not involved in the management of the domain accounts database, which means that the processing power and memory will be more fully utilized by functions other than domain administration. You might install a server as a member server for three reasons:

- You already have enough domain controllers for your environment. Microsoft recommends that you have at least one backup domain controller for fault tolerance, and one backup domain controller for every 2,000 users. If you have 5,000 users and 10 servers, Microsoft would recommend one PDC (mandatory for each domain) and three backup domain controllers, for a total of four domain controllers.
- A server performs a function that is so processor or memory intensive that no resources are left for the overhead of acting as a domain controller.
- Member servers can be moved from domain to domain. Domain controllers, on the other hand, cannot be moved from the domain into which they were installed.

Install Windows NT Server by using various methods.

Installation methods include:

- CD-ROM
- Over the network
- Network Client Administrator
- Express versus custom

Before you can start working on the rest of your wish list, you have to install NT on the first computer. To do this, you will perform a CD-ROM installation. You can install from it directly or copy the directory to a network share and make sure that the installation files are always available. NT installation files, like those for Windows 95, should be available on the network. When something new is added to an NT server, it needs to access information on the installation CD. If you make these files available on the network, you won't have to carry around a CD.

Installation Methods

Before you begin the installation process, look very closely at your new server and make sure that every component is on the NT hardware compatibility list (HCL). If you aren't sure what you have in your computer, NT can help—with a handy utility called the NTHQ tool. This tool is stored on the NT Server CD-ROM in \Support\HQTool. Put a formatted floppy disk in drive A: and run the MAKEDISK tool. Once MAKEDISK has finished, restart the computer with the diskette in the drive. Keep in mind that this is not the most sophisticated diagnostic tool. For example, if you have 128MB of RAM in your system, the tool will report it as >=64MB. When you run the tool, it will show you only what is in your computer that NT recognizes and cares about.

If you know that there are SCSI devices in your system, try running SCSITOOL, which is in the \Support\SCSITool folder of the NT Server CD-ROM. Insert a floppy disk in drive A:, run the MAKEDISK utility, and reboot with the floppy disk still in the drive. SCSITOOL will check your system and report on any SCSI controllers that it finds.

The NT installation program works fastest from an NT environment, but how do you install from an NT environment without having NT installed? Microsoft's solution: Use the three 3.5-inch diskettes that came with NT Server to boot the computer. As part of the boot process, the system hardware is analyzed and the CD-ROM is recognized, providing the medium for the installation program.

CD-ROM

If you have the licenses and the CD-ROM, but seem to have misplaced the diskettes, you can re-create them by doing as follows:

1. Put the NT Server CD-ROM in a CD-ROM drive and open a command prompt. The type of operating system on the computer you are using for this procedure does not matter. You need to have a computer with working CD-ROM and 3.5-inch disk drives.
2. Select the drive that contains the CD-ROM. For example, the D: drive.
3. Select the i386 directory. You will see a file called WINNT.EXE.
4. Type **WINNT /?** at the command prompt and then press Enter.

When you press Enter, you will be presented with a list of all the command-line switches for the NT installation program. The proper syntax for utilizing these switches is as follows:

```
WINNT.EXE [/S[:]sourcepath] [/T[:]tempdrive] [/I[:]inffile]
[/X | [/F] [/C] [/D[:]winntpath]]
```

Table 6.3 describes the functionalities of the command-line switches.

TABLE 6.3: Command-Line Switches and Their Functionalities

Switch	Functionality
/S[:] source path	Specifies where the NT files are located.
/T[:] temp drive	Specifies where NT stores temp files during the installation.
/I[:]inf file	Tells NT where the information files (.INF) are located. If you are really creative, you can automate this process.
/OX	Creates boot floppy disks for CD-ROM installation.

TABLE 6.3 continued: Command-Line Switches and Their Functionalities

Switch	Functionality
/X	Specifies to not create the boot floppy disks, because you already have them.
/F	Specifies that you will create the boot floppy disks, but will not verify the files that are being copied to those floppy disks.
/C	Skips the free-space check on those floppy disks, because you know that they are empty and formatted.
/B	Provides floppy disk-less operation. Requires the /S parameter.
/U:script file	Provides unattended operation. Also requires /S.
/R:directory	Specifies optional directory to be installed.
/RX:directory	Specifies optional directory to be copied.
/E:command	Specifies command to run at the end of the GUI setup.

To create a set of installation diskettes, your command-line syntax will be WINNT /OX (that's "o" as in "orange").

Over the Network

You can provide access to the files from the NT 4 CD-ROM in two ways. First, you can put the NT CD-ROM into a CD tower or shared CD-ROM drive, and share various folders. Another method, if you have the available disk space, is to use XCOPY to copy the NT CD-ROM to a drive and share the various folders. If you choose this method, be sure to use the /S parameter with the XCOPY command to copy all of those pesky subfolders. In reality, though, you don't have to copy over the whole CD, just the \i386 and \Drvlib folders.

TIP

You can also use NT Explorer to copy the folders to the disk. Be sure that the default settings are changed to allow files with extensions such as .DLL, .SYS, and .VXD to be displayed and copied. Select View ➢ Options, and then in the Hidden Files list, click Show All Files.

Network Client Administrator

If you access the installation files from the server's hard disk, your installation will be faster than if you share a CD. In either case, your computer must be able to access the share point on an NT server somewhere on the network. To connect to that share point, the new computer must have a configured network client or redirector to communicate with the server. To configure the network client, use the Network Client Administrator, which is located in the Network Administration group on an existing NT server.

You can use the Network Client Administrator for four tasks: to make installation startup disks to download network client software; to make the setup disks for the client software; to copy administration tools to a server and create a share; and to view remote-boot client information.

To use the Network Client Administrator, you must first copy and share the tools. Start the Administrator, select Copy Client-Based Tools, and specify a path to the server files. You can either choose to share those files or create a new folder, copy the files to the folder, and then share the folder.

Express versus Custom

If you have to perform multiple NT Server installations on a corporate-standard file server that is always configured exactly the same way, you can simplify your life by automating the installation process. You can configure two files to make the automated installation process work really well. You can also automate the installation process to perform an *unattended* installation. If your servers are configured exactly the same way, you can create an unattended answer file to mirror the setup configurations in your organization. These files are just text files with section names and keys that can be edited. You can access these files from any text editor. There is a sample unattended .TXT file in the NT Server Resource Kit; or, use the Setup Manager utility on the NT CD-ROM.

The other file is called a uniqueness database file (UDF). While the UNATTEND.TXT file is generic and relates to several computers, the UDF is unique and provides answers for a specific computer.

Miscellaneous NT Upgrade Paths

Although upgrading various operating systems (MS-DOS, Windows 95, NT 3.51) to NT 4 is not covered in the objectives, it is covered on the exam.

How do you upgrade DOS to NT Server? This is straightforward–perform a complete installation.

There is a pseudo-upgrade path from Windows 95 to Windows NT: installing Windows NT into a separate directory on your Windows 95 machine. In other words, don't put the program files in the \Windows directory. Reinstall all applications so that the information gets written to the NT registry. The lack of a true upgrade path is due to fundamental structural differences between the Windows 95 and Windows NT registries.

To upgrade from NT 3.51 to NT 4 (assuming you followed all of the defaults in your 3.51 installation), start the upgrade process by putting the NT 4 CD-ROM in the 3.51 server CD-ROM drive. In the \i386 directory of the Windows NT 4 CD-ROM, you will find a file named WINNT32.EXE. Run this executable instead of WINNT. Place the NT 4 server files in the \WinNT35 directory instead of the default \WinNT directory. If you place the files in any other directory, you will have a dual-boot situation, not an upgrade situation.

Installation Procedures

Now that you have a broad overview of what happens, let's examine the step-by-step process.

Installing NT Server 4

The system is booting, it's using the three diskettes you created, the NT installation CD-ROM is in the CD-ROM drive, and the drivers necessary to access the CD-ROM are loading.

1. Watch the screen while the system is booting from the three diskettes. The setup program does a cursory investigation of your computer before starting to load the NT Executive and creating the hardware abstraction layer.
2. Insert setup disk number two when prompted. The second disk starts with Windows NT setup, and provides support for PCMCIA, SCSI, keyboard, and video drivers, and the FAT/NTFS file systems. A setup screen will give you four options:
   - Learn more about NT setup
   - Set up NT now
   - Repair a damaged NT installation
   - Quit without installing

3. Press Enter to continue with the installation. At this point, NT setup is looking for drives. It looks for only ESDI and IDE drives. If you have SCSI controllers and devices in your system, be sure to RTFS (read the fine screen), because you can bypass this section by typing **S** and make manual selections later. If you have IDE drives in your system, press Enter and let the setup program take care of things for you.

4. Once you make your selection, the Wizard prompts you to put in setup disk number three and then looks for all of the different adapters. Do not get impatient at this point. Just let NT do its thing.

5. After NT is finished searching the system, it presents you with a list of the adapters–PCI, IDE, and SCSI–it has found. The designers of the Installation Wizard recognized that there would be hardware NT could not recognize, so you also have the opportunity to make further selections. If there is a card in your system that does not show up on the drop-down list and you have the driver diskettes provided by the hardware manufacturer, you can choose to install support now. To install support for a special mass-storage device, type **S** and make your selection, or provide the appropriate diskette. Otherwise, hit Enter to proceed.

6. The system loads the disk drivers and the device driver for the NT file system (NTFS). It also has to go through other device drivers before letting you know what it found.

7. Type **C** to continue.

8. Page down through the license agreement–you are prompted to press F8 to continue.

9. Once you press F8, the standard hardware summary screen appears. Make sure it matches your computer (or at least comes close–you can make changes later). You will see the phrase, "The above list matches my computer." If it does, press Enter to go to the next screen.

10. If you are installing NT on a computer that already has a hard drive installed and partitioned, the next screen shows the current drive partitions for all devices located. Highlight the partition where you will install NT and press Enter to continue.

11. The system asks whether you want to use the FAT file system or the NTFS. The features of these two files systems are reviewed in Table 6.4.

TABLE 6.4: Features of the FAT File System and the NTFS

FAT 16 File System	NTFS
Accessible through NT, Windows 95, MS-DOS, and OS/2	Accessible through NT
Does not support file compression	Supports file compression
Does not support local security	Supports local security
Maximum file/partition size of 4GB	Maximum file/partition size of 16 exabytes—2 terabytes actual

NOTE

FAT has minimal file system overhead and is most efficient for file system partitions under 400MB.

12. After the drives have been formatted, NT is ready to begin the most time-consuming part of the process—copying the files. First, it needs to know where to put them. The default is C:\WINNT. This is called the root directory. The partition in which this directory is located is known in NT terminology as the system partition.
13. Before NT copies files, it wants to check your drive for corruption. Press Enter to continue with the check or Esc to skip it. After the check, the copying begins.
14. Once the copying has been completed, it is time to pull the NT setup disk from the floppy disk drive and the NT CD-ROM from the CD-ROM drive, and press Enter to restart the computer. When the system finally boots, NT is now actually running in a reduced configuration. The operating system says that it wants to check things over. In addition, you have to start entering some system-unique information. First, enter your name and company.
15. Enter the CD key number from your CD-ROM case.

16. Review the first section of this chapter–about licensing modes–and choose the appropriate mode.

TIP

When in doubt, choose Per Server.

17. NT wants to know what you will name this server. The name must be unique on the network. If you are not sure what name to enter, be sure to ask someone.

18. Grab your notes from Chapter 5–it is time to tell NT what you want it to do. Will it be a primary domain controller (PDC), a backup domain controller (BDC), or a stand-alone member server?

19. Enter the administrator password. It can have a maximum of 14 characters, and like most passwords, you have to reenter it once you've typed it the first time. Don't forget that unlike other NT data, the password is case sensitive.

20. Now that the system knows who the administrator is and what the password is, you can begin to select components to install, such as the accessibility components for the keyboard layout, sound cards, etc. You can choose to install the calculator, wallpapers, mouse pointers, screen savers, and all of the items that will personalize your server so that it reflects your tastes. You will also be able to select communications for some rudimentary dial-up tools, games so that you can play FreeCell while waiting for the backups to finish, multimedia drivers, and MAPI (mail application programming interface) tools for Windows messaging.

NOTE

If you choose to install all of the accessories, it will take up another 26MB of disk space.

21. It is time to start installing networking. Select whether your server will be wired to the network or need remote access to the network.

22. The next screen asks whether you want to install Microsoft Internet Information Server. Unless this server will be a Web or FTP server on the Internet or an intranet, clear the Default Install checkbox. (A different exam covers IIS, so this screen will not be discussed here.)

23. The system now needs to find out whether it can talk to the network. This is a physical-layer task that requires a network interface card. NT will now try to find your network card, or you can choose to select it from a list.

24. After the network card has been discovered, it is time to select protocols. By default, NT selects TCP/IP and NWLink IPX/SPX Compatible Transport. The defaults will work with the Internet and Novell networks. You can also choose to install NetBEUI.

25. The next choice you are given concerns the services, such as server or workstation, which you want your server to start. Stay with the defaults.

26. After you choose the services, you can select the protocol bindings and the order in which the system will access them.

27. At this point, NT is ready to start the network so that the rest of the installation can be completed. However, before that, if you have chosen to install a PDC, NT wants to know the name of the domain. Be really careful when entering the domain name. You can change it later, but if too much time passes before you do, the ramifications can be significant.

28. The next choice is the date, time, and time zone. This should be set to where the server will actually reside. If you are in Minneapolis and prepping a server for Reno, choose PST. After you figure out the date and time, choose OK.

29. The final choice is your display properties. Pick the one that is right for you and be sure to test it, because NT will not let you get by with just a wild guess. Even if you know for sure what display you will use, NT will still make you test it, just to be sure.

Once you have done all of this, click OK—NT finally starts to configure itself. When it restarts, it will come up as a happy server, with the default operating system (in the case of a computer with multiple operating systems) as NT Server. If not, check Chapter 10, "Troubleshooting."

Installing NT Server over the Network

How does the installation process vary if the files are being accessed from a share point rather than a CD-ROM? In reality, there are not many differences. You configure the potential server to access the network. Once you have accessed the network, you can authenticate and access the share where WINNT.EXE is located. Run WINNT.EXE from the share–it will install the OS to the new server. In effect, you are using a share point on another server as the NT Server installation server.

You can also automate the installation process to perform an unattended installation. When you save the answer file, it does not have to bear a special name. The command syntax to run a setup using an answer file is as follows:

```
WINNT /U:AnswerFilename
```

Your potential server must be able to access the network to get to the share point. To communicate with the server, the potential server (and all workstations) must be running a network client.

Creating Network Client Diskettes

Once your original NT server is installed, you can create a set of network client diskettes. This will provide the basic communications to the network. Choose Administrative Tools ➢ Network Client Administrator.

To create the diskette:

1. Select Make Network Installation Startup Disk and click Continue. This brings up the Share Network Client Installation Files dialog box.
2. Enter the path to the client files. If you are using the CD-ROM, as shown in the screen shot above, the path will point to the \Clients directory. This is where the system will copy files *from*.
3. Now, you have to make a decision. Are you going to leave the CD-ROM on the server and share the CD, are you going to copy the client files to a folder on the server hard drive and then create a share pointing to the folder, or do you already have a folder set up? Make your decision. The client folder on the target server will be located at C:\Clients. A share

name called Clients will be created, and it will take up to 64MB of disk space to accomplish this task. After you have made your decision, click OK.

4. Now that the server is configured to work with the clients, you need a diskette to use on all of the workstations. After all the information is copied to your server folder, you will see a handy message that tells you 254 directories were just added and 1,141 files have been copied. Click OK to continue.
5. The Target Workstation Configuration dialog box comes up and offers another set of pretty obvious choices—the size of the diskette, the network client to install (either Network Client 3 for DOS/Windows or the Windows 95 client). The final section asks about the NIC that is installed in your workstations. Once you have made your choices from the drop-down menu, click OK to continue.

NOTE

If you have a NIC that isn't listed, you should not attempt this method of installation. Use the Installation Disk Set method.

6. A dialog box appears with the Network Startup Disk Configuration selections. This allows you to enter a computer name, user name, domain, and network protocol. You can specify whether this computer will use DHCP to acquire its IP address or have a static IP address. You can also specify the destination for the new diskette. After filling in the appropriate selections, click OK.
7. The confirmation screen appears, reiterating all of the information you have just entered. Before clicking OK, make sure the diskette in the A: drive has been formatted with the appropriate version of DOS and is a system diskette. If all of the above criteria are met, click OK to continue. This will create the startup disk.

It might be easier to create a set of diskettes to carry around with you, especially if you need only one or two clients. In that case, select Make Installation Disk Set from the Network Client Administrator screen. You will be prompted for the client or service and the drive on which to create the diskettes. Once you have provided that information, you will be told how many diskettes you really need. Click OK to continue.

If you choose the third selection from the Network Client Administrator screen, it will allow you to copy administration tools to a client workstation. The tools you can copy depend on the operating system your client is configured to use. For example, between NT and Windows 95, tools such as Server Manager and User Manager for Domains are shared. With NT Workstation, you can manage DHCP, DNS, and WINS; from Windows 95, you can look at the event viewer, and check file and print security.

Configure protocols and protocol bindings.

Protocols include:

- TCP/IP
- NWLink IPX/SPX Compatible Transport
- NetBEUI

In this section, the installation and configuration of the protocols discussed in Chapter 5 will be examined. For each protocol, the tools used for installation and the configuration parameters available will be discussed.

Protocol Choices

Unfortunately, you will probably encounter a number of questions on the exam in which the answers are a list of menu choices. This is why you will see a lot of lists and screen captures in this chapter.

TPC/IP

Numerous configuration options are available with the TCP/IP protocol. Fortunately, only a few are absolutely necessary for communication. The first choice you will have to make is whether this machine should get its IP configuration from a DHCP server. In most cases, you will want to manually configure the IP information at NT servers just in case the DHCP server goes off-line.

WARNING

If you configure your servers as DHCP clients, you could be asking for a big problem. Suppose that a storm knocks out power at your office. When the power comes back on, all of your servers will power up and boot. (Of course, if you have a proper UPS, this wouldn't be an issue.) When they boot, they will look for the DHCP server to configure them. If that server either didn't boot properly or booted slow, your other servers won't get IP addresses. However, don't take this to mean that DHCP isn't the right tool for client workstations.

You can set three IP addressing parameters: the IP address, the subnet mask, and the default gateway.

If this server is to be a DHCP client, click Obtain IP Address from DHCP Server on the Properties page for the TCP/IP protocol; if not, you need to configure the parameters described in Table 6.5.

TABLE 6.5: IP Parameters

Parameter	Description
IP address	A 32-bit unique identifier for each host on an IP network. The four-octet address is made up of two parts—a network address and a host or node address.
Subnet mask	Used to identify which portion of the IP address represents the network and which portion represents the host. Most IP networks are divided into subnets to help control traffic on the wire.
Default gateway	Identifies a router address to send all packets that are not local (the destination is not on the local subnet).

If your environment includes WINS servers, your server needs the IP address of your WINS servers. If you use DNS (domain name service) on your network, you will need to configure the DNS information for this server. DNS will be discussed in Chapter 8, "Connectivity."

NWLink IPX/SPX Compatible Transport

You will need to configure only two parameters: internal network number and frame type. The internal network number is used to identify servers on an IPX/SPX network. In the case of NT, you might set this if your server is running a program that can be directly accessed by clients. (In an NT environment, this would probably be SQL Server or Microsoft SNA Server.) In other words, the program can be accessed *without* logging onto the NT domain. This allows Novell clients to access the service without loading Microsoft Windows client software. The internal network number is a hexadecimal value that must be unique across your entire IPX/SPX network.

The frame type defines how IPX/SPX packets will be formed for transmission on the physical wiring of the network. Each packet transmitted on the network has a series of headers attached to the data. These headers identify items such as the sender of the packet, its intended recipient, a checksum (calculation against the contents that can be re-created at the destination to see whether the packet has been corrupted in transit), or other information defined by the protocol. The definition of how these headers are organized is called the frame type. Many frame types are defined to be used in an IPX/SPX network.

The nice thing about NT is that it will pick a packet off the network and determine its frame type for you. To configure this, click Auto Frame Type Detection on the Properties page for the NWLink protocol. Unfortunately, NT will detect only one packet type in the automatic mode. So, if you are using multiple frame types on your network, you will have to manually configure them. On the same page, click the Add button and pick the frame type(s) in use from the drop-down list.

NetBEUI

No configurable options are associated with the NetBEUI protocol.

Protocol Bindings

In the most generic sense, to *bind* is to link components at different levels to enable communication. The architecture of NT is made up of various layers—each layer provides a certain type of service. Some of these services will need to communicate with the services on another layer. The process of binding enables this communication. In the discussion of protocols, binding referred to establishing a communication channel between the network adapter card driver and a protocol.

On a simple server, you don't need to worry too much about protocol bindings. By default, each protocol you install will be bound to all network adapters installed in the computer. In a more complex environment, though, you can control the use of the binding of protocols to increase security or performance.

Increasing Performance

In the Network applet on the Binding tab, you can manage the protocol bindings. The protocols are bound to both server and workstation services. The order in the list of bindings affects the efficiency of network communication. When an NT-based computer attempts to communicate with another device on the network, it will try to communicate using the protocols in the binding list—in the order that they are listed. If you have multiple protocols in the list, make sure that the most commonly used protocol is listed first.

As an example, assume that you have a TCP/IP-based network. Because of a few legacy NetWare servers, you added the NWLink protocol to your NT servers. If NWLink is listed first in your binding list, all communication attempts will try to use IPX/SPX first, and switch to TCP/IP only after IPX fails. You can decrease connection time to most hosts by moving TCP/IP to the head of the list.

The MCSE exams are designed to determine a candidate's ability to perform administrative tasks associated with an NT network. Protocol management is a big part of those tasks. Be comfortable with the various procedures listed for this objective before you take the exam.

Increasing Security

Binding enables communication between the adapter's driver and a protocol. If you do *not* bind a protocol to an adapter, that card cannot communicate using that protocol. You can use binding to control traffic on your network and provide increased security.

Configuring Protocols

You install all of the protocols discussed in this chapter from the same location.

Installing a Protocol

To install a protocol, do as follows:

1. Right-click the Network Neighborhood icon on your desktop and choose Properties (or open the Network control panel).
2. Click the Protocols tab.

3. Click the Add button. You will see the following list:

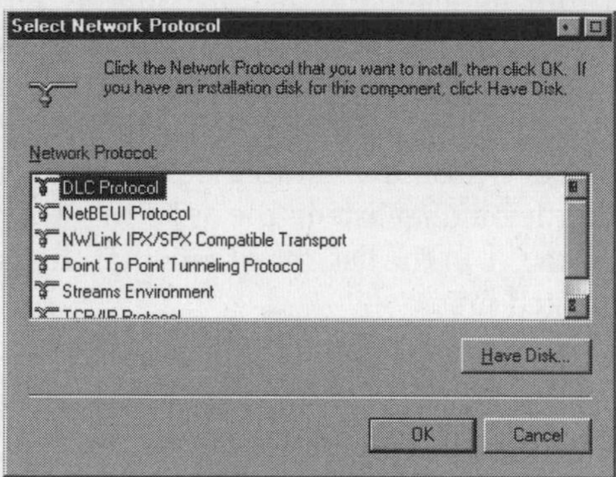

Installing a Service

The network services discussed in this section are installed in a similar manner:

1. Right-click the Network Neighborhood icon on your desktop and choose Properties (or open the Network control panel).
2. Click the Services tab.
3. Click the Add button. You will see the following list:

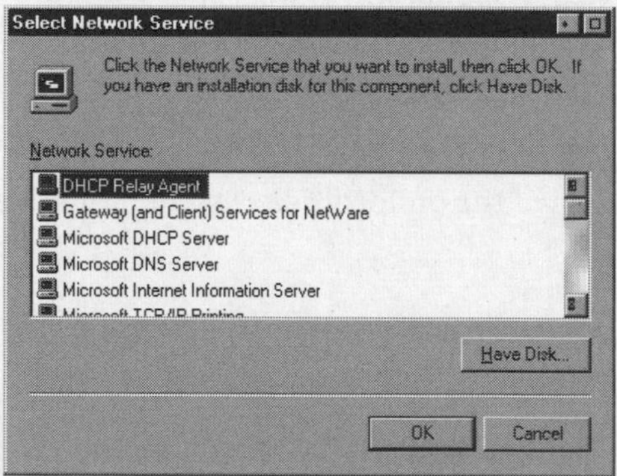

Setting the IP Addressing Information

You can configure the following addressing parameters: IP address, subnet mask, and default gateway.

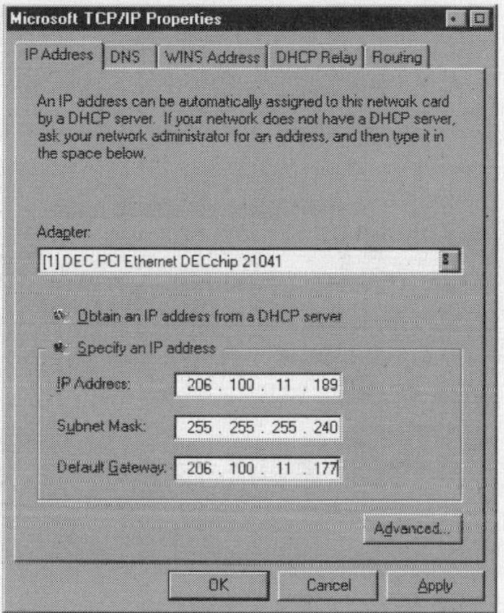

Setting the WINS Server Address

Access the configuration screen by clicking the WINS Address tab on the protocol's Properties page. Add the primary (and secondary) WINS server IP addresses.

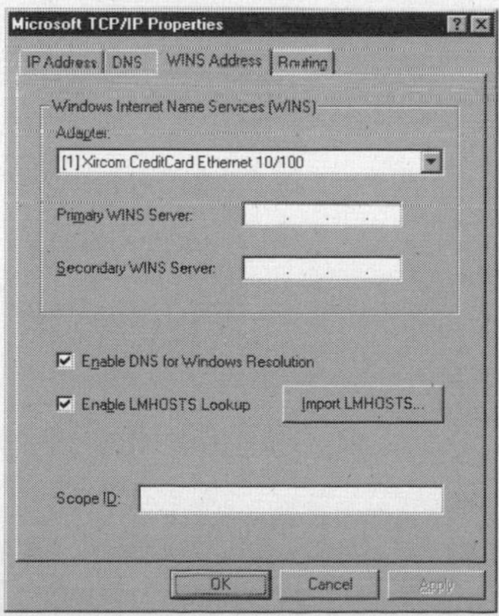

Setting the DNS Client Information

Enter the host name for this computer (in most cases, it will be the same as the NetBIOS name) and the IP addresses of your DNS servers.

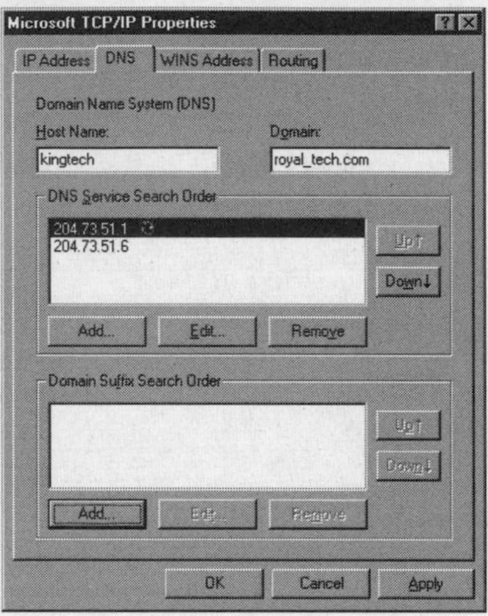

Configuring NWLink

Open the Network control panel. On the Protocols tab, highlight NWLink IPX/SPX Compatible Transport and click the Properties button. Unless you need to change the default values, leave the Internal Network Number set to 00000000 and Auto Frame Type Detection selected.

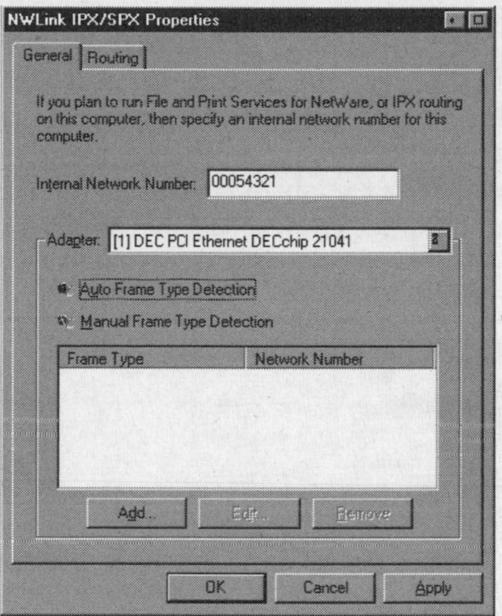

▶ Configure network adapters.

Considerations include:

- Changing IRQ, I/O base, and memory addresses
- Configuring multiple adapters

Essentially, there are only three ways to configure network adapters: put one in during NT installation, put several in during installation, or put a card in after installation. With the advent of multipurpose cards, it can be challenging to find the hardware resources. The configuration of the computer's current network cards is usually readily available. If the PC is up and working, and already configured with Windows 95 or Windows 3.1, you can get this information from the Network Tools control panel or Windows setup. If it is a DOS machine, check whether the card came with a diskette. If it did, the card is probably software configurable and has a utility to read the settings. Once you have the settings, write them down.

Changing IRQ, I/O Base, and Memory Addresses

Your network card's settings are the resources that this card uses, and they cannot conflict with anything else in the computer. In the Network control panel, there are lots of choices for each setting on a network card. Figure 6.1 shows the settings available for a Xircom CreditCard 10/100 network card.

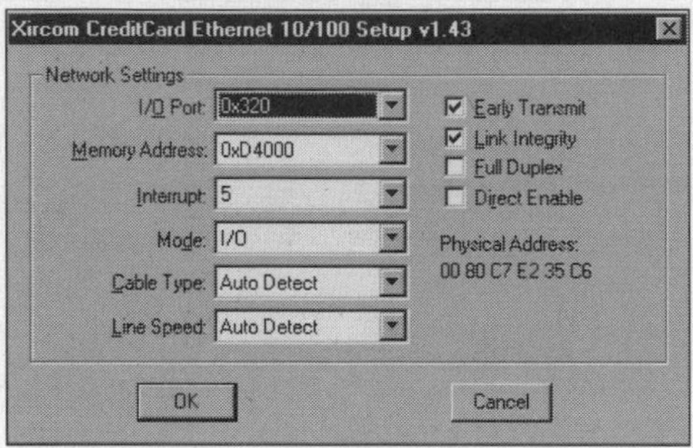

FIGURE 6.1: PC card setup

The large number of settings implies that there may be a right or a wrong setting. However, that is not the case. There is no right or wrong, just used and unused. Computers of all shapes and sizes can be really stupid. If you configure peripherals within your computer to use some of the same resources, strange things happen. The quick and easy resolution to this problem is to make sure that the new piece of hardware has the interrupt set to something that is not currently being used.

Pentium-based computers now come equipped with several peripheral component interconnect (PCI) slots. The slots are designed to provide faster throughput to the CPU. As computer people, we all know that faster is *always* better. By purchasing a network card that is a PCI card, you eliminate the interrupt problem. Each PCI slot has the intelligence to assign an unused interrupt and address. The card takes its settings from the slot, not the other way around. Since the slot manages the address and interrupt, there should be no conflicts.

Configuring Multiple Adapters

NT, as an operating system, can handle an unlimited number of adapters. Your server hardware may not be as flexible. Each time you add a new adapter to the system, you must adhere to the basics. Adapters cannot share resources and must have a unique IRQ, I/O base, and memory address. Remember to read your system documentation and the information on the utilities discussed in the objective on installations, such as the NTHQ tool and SCSITOOL.

Changing IRQ, I/O Base, and Memory Addresses

To change settings on an existing network card:

1. Open the Network control panel. Click the Adapters tab and highlight the adapter. Click Properties.
2. From the Properties page, select the drop-down menu for the setting you need to change.
3. Click the new selection.
4. Make any other necessary changes (IRQ, memory address, etc.).
5. Click OK.
6. Click Close to shut the Network window.
7. Select Yes to restart the computer.

WARNING

When you change the settings on cards that are currently installed and configured, it can lead to unexpected network problems. This should be attempted only by a competent hardware technician and then, only as a last resort.

Configuring Multiple Adapters

If you are installing multiple cards as part of the installation process, once NT finds the first card, you can click a button to tell it to look for more. NT will continue looking for cards until it doesn't find anymore or you run out of manufacturer's diskettes. What if you want to add a new NIC to an existing system?

If you are installing a new PCI card into an available slot:

1. Shut down the server.
2. Install the hardware per the manufacturer's directions.
3. Open the Network control panel.

4. Click the Adapters tab.
5. Click Add.
6. From the Select Network Adapter window, select the appropriate network card and click OK, or click Have Disk. If you clicked Have Disk, insert the disk in drive A:, or provide the appropriate path, and click OK.
7. When you choose a network card, you will be prompted for the path to Windows NT system files–from either the CD-ROM or a location to which the files have been copied. After providing the path, click Continue.
8. The files will be copied, and a default binding will be provided.
9. Close the dialog boxes and restart the system when prompted.

If you do not have an open PCI slot, you will have to install an ISA-compatible card. Each card has its own installation routine. So, before you begin any installation, be sure to RTFM (read the fine manual). As an example of installing a card, the steps necessary to install a plug and play–compatible LinkSys 16-bit ISA-compatible Ethernet card are listed below.

To install the card:

1. Turn off the PC.
2. Remove the cover.
3. Physically install the card.
4. Cable the card to the concentrator.
5. Turn the server back on and log on as administrator.

The card is now physically installed. The next step is to configure the card to work in your server. Because the card in the example went into an ISA slot, you have to run the setup utility. Boot your server to DOS and run setup, which shows the default parameters–an IRQ setting of 3 and memory address of 300. If you choose to let the final IRQ and memory address be plug and play compatible, the operating system should handle the actual settings.

To install the new card and driver for NT:

1. Open the Network control panel.

2. Click the Adapters tab.
3. Click Add, which will bring up the Select Network Adapter dialog box.
4. Choose Have Disk.
5. In the Insert Disk window, add the path to the software drivers–A:\WINNT, in this case.
6. Select the card by highlighting the card name and click OK.
7. Enter an open I/O port or choose Auto, depending on the capabilities of the card.
8. Enter an open IRQ number or choose Auto, depending on the capabilities of the card.
9. Enter a network address, if necessary.
10. Click OK. The system begins to examine the network subsystem to make sure that everything is just the way it is supposed to be.
11. Since IP is loaded by default, the first glitch the system will find is that the new card does not have a working IP address. The Microsoft TCP/IP Properties dialog box is displayed—you can choose to receive your IP address from a DHCP server or static address. Since this is a server, you opt for a static address.
12. Enter DNS and WINS information, if necessary. Click OK.
13. Restart the computer.

Configure Windows NT Server core services.

Services include:

- Directory Replicator
- License Manager
- Other services

NT can be configured to work on a small scale, but it is also flexible enough to expand to an enterprise. Microsoft knows that you don't want to work any harder than necessary, so they have provided core services to alleviate some of the pain of routine and mundane tasks. Windows NT Server core services are as follows:

Directory Replicator Provides the ability to automatically move logon scripts, policies, folders, and files from one server to another.

License Manager Provides a way to manage and track NT licenses and BackOffice application licenses.

Computer Browser Services Makes it possible to see network resources from the Network Neighborhood utility. Computer Browser Services establishes the hierarchy of how search tasks are divided and which domain controller will fill which role.

NT Server Core Services

You can assign the server that will keep track of information and replicate it. The replicating server can service several other servers. Not every server needs to receive the same information—you can be selective. Backup domain controllers can either participate in the browser election process or wait for the results to determine their place in life.

Directory Replicator

Directory replication is a method of copying files and folders containing commonly used information from one NT server to another. This can also be referred to as an update. The most common items that need to be replicated are logon scripts, system policies, and information commonly shared across the network. In addition, you can use replication for load balancing by choosing which information to send to a server at a certain time of day or night.

Directory replication has several components. You must have an export server, an import computer, and export and import directories.

Export server This is the single point of administration for the shared files, but a network can have as many exporters as they have servers. Changes you make to this server will be replicated throughout the system, as you designate. The export server must be running NT Server.

Import computer You can't export without something willing to import. The import computer can be running NT Server, NT Workstation, or Microsoft LAN Manager OS/2 servers. These machines receive the information from the export servers. An import computer can receive updates from more than one export server, just like an export server can export to multiple import servers.

Export and import directories How does the export server know what to export to each import computer? This is done through a series of folders and subfolders that each of the computers knows about and agrees on. For example, by default, information to be exported will be placed in subfolders of the \Winnt\System32\Repl\Export folder. As a system administrator, you will create subfolders and files under this folder for each group of files that need to be exported.

Each import computer will have a directory that corresponds to the export server's export directory.

TIP

If you want to set a default import and export path, use Server Manager. These folders must be manually configured. Files stored directly under the export directory will not be exported.

Now that the folders are in place, here is a broad overview of how the system works:

- Information that needs to be passed to other servers is saved to the Export folder on Server-1. The replication service on Server-1 checks occasionally to determine whether there is anything that needs to be replicated. When it finds new information, it sends an update notice to all the computers or domains that are configured to import from the INF folder.
- Once the import computer has received the update notice, it checks the export server's directory structure.
- The import computer will now copy any new or changed files to its import directory. In addition, it will do some housecleaning—it will delete any files or subfolders that are no longer present in the export directory.

License Manager

Every client connection to an NT server needs a client access license (CAL). There are two types of NT Server CALs: Per Server and Per Seat. The client workstation receives the CAL, not the person using the workstation.

Per Server Licensing In Per Server licensing, CALs are associated with a specific server. If Server-1 is configured to 50 connections, it may maintain 50 simultaneous connections. When you configure an NT server to use Per Server mode, you must take into account the maximum number of concurrent connections that will be made to that server, and purchase the appropriate number of licenses.

When should you use Per Server mode? Per Server mode is ideal for special-use servers, such as a remote access server (RAS) or Internet Information Server (IIS). In both cases, clients will attach to the server for a relatively short period of time and then disconnect. If you have the Per Server license mode selected, it also serves as a kind of heavy-handed approach to load balancing. If you feel this server can adequately handle 25 connections and you have 25 CALs allocated, when user number 26 tries to connect, the connection is refused.

Per Seat Licensing When you license your network on a Per Seat basis, you walk around the office counting computers. If you come up with 500 computers, you should buy 500 CALs. Every time you buy a new computer, you need to buy a new CAL. With the Per Seat licensing mode, a client can access any resource on the network and may be connected to multiple servers at the same time.

Choosing the Right Licensing Method If there is only one server on your network, select the Per Server mode and specify the maximum number of client connections. If the company grows to the point that Per Seat mode becomes more economical, a one-time change from Per Server to Per Seat is allowed.

Tracking Licenses How do you keep track of all these licenses? NT Server provides two tools to help in that effort. The first is the Licensing program in Control Panel; the other is the License Manager program on the Administrative Tools (Common) menu. By using these tools, licensing information will be replicated from the PDC to a centralized database on a server that you designate.

Using the Licensing Program to Track Licenses

If you go into Control Panel and select Licensing, you will bring up the Choose Licensing Mode screen. At this point, you choose between Per Server and Per Seat; if you have designated Per Server, you can add or remove licenses. There is also a Replication selection. When you choose Replication, you will be allowed to designate whether the master server to hold the database will be a domain controller or one of the servers in the enterprise. If you select the Enterprise radio button, it gives you the opportunity to specify the server. This server will then act as a master license replication server for two or more domains.

The Licensing program also gives you the opportunity to specify how often the replication takes place. You can specify whether you want the replication to start at a certain time every day or after so many hours. The range of hours is between 1 and 72.

Using License Manager to Track Licenses

The other option is go into Administrative Tools (Common) and select License Manager (see Figure 6.2).

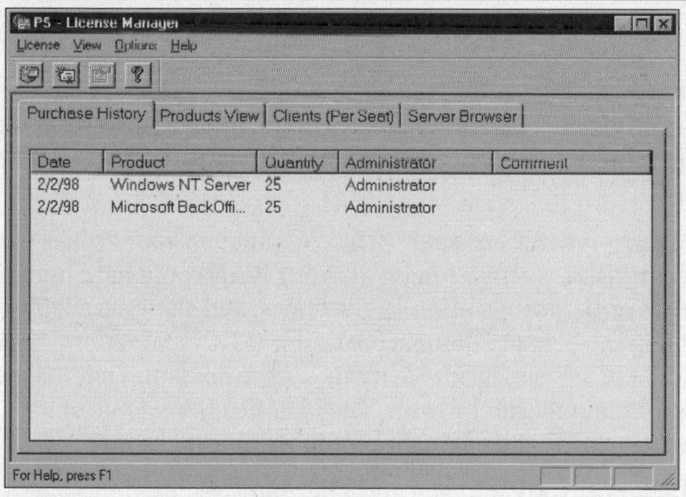

FIGURE 6.2: License Manager

This utility will allow you to track a purchase history of licenses needed on your network—not just for NT Server, but for things such as BackOffice and some third-party applications. You can also keep track of Per Seat or Per Server licensing. You can browse the servers in your domain. Double-click a server to bring up the Licensing Mode screen for that server. You can add or remove licenses, and switch between Per Seat and Per Server licensing.

Other Services

NT offers several other services that may be of use to your network.

DHCP Service By starting the dynamic host control protocol (DHCP) service, you can choose to make your NT server either a DHCP client or a DHCP server. As a DHCP client, your server will be dynamically assigned an IP address by a DHCP server. The DHCP server service will allow your NT server to manage and assign IP addresses.

DNS Service When you start the domain name service (DNS), it allows you to configure your server to resolve DNS names to IP addresses. As a DNS resolver, it will take the DNS name `www.microsoft.com` and resolve it to an IP address.

WINS Service Windows Internet name service (WINS) resolves NetBIOS computer names to IP addresses. WINS resolution specifies that computer name WS1, for example, is at a specific IP address.

Browser Service This service allows workstation and server computers to use Network Neighborhood to see other resources. There are five types of browsers:

> **Domain master browser** The computer on your desk is part of a massive computer network. Your WAN could have hundreds or thousands of servers, services, and shares available to users. The primary domain controller (PDC) maintains a master list of services available for the entire domain. That makes it the domain master browser. The PDC delegates some of its chores. The first delegation goes to the master browser.
>
> **Master browser** In any network, there is at least one workgroup. If you have a larger network, you may have several workgroups. If you have several network cards in your file server and are using the TCP/IP protocol, you will have several subnets in your network. Each of these workgroups or subnets must have a master browser. If there is another NT server on the subnet or in the workgroup, when that server comes up, it will check in

with the master browser and tell it what services the newcomer has to offer. When you open your Network Neighborhood, the new server and its services will magically appear. The master browser passes that list up to the domain master browser.

Backup browser The backup browser acts as a kind of backstop for the master browser. The master browser is always trying to keep track of all the services on the subnet or in the workgroup. The backup browser gets its list from the master browser.

Potential browser The potential browser is otherwise known as the browser wanna-be. This computer just hangs out while waiting to become a browser.

Nonbrowser The name says it all. This computer cannot act as a browser. Actually, it is probably too busy doing other things to be bothered with answering browser requests.

How does a master browser get to be a master browser while a potential browser waits around with all of its potential going to waste? Computer networking is really much more democratic than you may have thought—the systems can call for an election. The election is somewhat weighted. For example, if a computer is running NT Server, it gets more votes than a computer running NT Workstation. If a computer is just running Windows 95—you get the picture. If there is a tie, the backup browser will get a higher vote than the potential browser.

You can rig the election by tweaking the HKEY_Local_Machine\System\CurrentControlSet\Services\Browser\Parameter setting. If you set the parameter to Yes, the system will always try to become a browser. If you set the parameter to No, the system will sit on the sidelines and watch the elections go by. If you set the parameter to Auto (the default), it ensures that the server is at least a potential browser.

Configuration Procedures

Following are the configuration procedures for the replication service, the export server, the import computer, running a license manager, and for configuring a computer to participate in browser elections.

Configuring the Replication Service

Before you start configuring directory replication, review the basics:

- You need something to share.
- You must configure the replication service.
- You must configure an export server.
- You must configure an import server.
- Information stored in the \Winnt\System32\Repl\Export root folder will not be exported. You must manually create subfolders to share information.

To configure directory replication:

1. The replication service needs a user account. This account is set up just like any other user account–using User Manager for Domains. The account must meet the following criteria:
   - All logon hours are allowed.
   - The User Must Change Password at Next Logon check box must be cleared.
   - The user must be a member of Backup Operators and the Replicator group for the domain.
   - The Password Never Expires check box must be selected.
2. Open the Services control panel. Click Directory Replicator Service to open the Directory Replicator Service window.
3. The Directory Replicator Service window is used to configure Directory Replicator to start automatically and to log on using the account you just created. You will have to enter the password and a confirmation for the password.

Configuring the Export Server

To configure the export server:

1. Create the folders that will be replicated. These folders must be created in the folder \Winnt\System32\Repl\Export.
2. Start Server Manager by selecting Start ➢ Programs ➢ Administrative Tools ➢ Server Manager.

3. Highlight the Export Server and press Enter.
4. Choose Replication.
5. Select Export Directories and click Manage.
6. Click Add.
7. Type in the name of the subdirectory and click OK to call up the Manage Exported Directories window.

You will notice several check boxes at the bottom of the window and selections to add or remove a lock.

- Add Lock prevents the directory from being exported.
- Wait Until Stabilized makes the file remain in the subdirectory for a set period of time before being exported.

After clicking OK, you can choose to which computers you want to export these files:

1. Select Add (located under To List:).
2. Highlight and select the computers to which you want the information copied.
3. Click OK.
4. Click OK again—replication services will start.

Configuring the Import Computer

To configure the import computer:

1. Open the Services control panel. Configure the Directory Replicator to start automatically and log on using the account you just created.
2. From Server Manager, configure the import computer to import files from other computers or domains.

To manage the import process:

1. Start Server Manager.
2. Highlight the import computer and press Enter.
3. Choose Replication, which will bring up the Directory Replication window.

4. Select Import Directories and click Manage.
5. Click Add.
6. Type in the name of the subdirectory and click OK.

After clicking OK, you can choose the computers from which you want to import:

1. Click the Add button under From List:.
2. Highlight and select the computers from which you want the information copied.
3. If you click Manage, it will allow you to enter specific subdirectories from which you will be importing. You will also be given information on whether the subdirectory is locked, the status of the master file, when the last update has been received, and how long the folder has been locked. You can also use the Manage screen to lock the receiving folder.
4. Click OK.
5. Click OK again–replication services will start.

All information that is placed in these subfolders will be replicated to other servers. Policies and logon scripts will be covered in more detail later in the book.

Running License Manager

To start License Manager:

1. Choose Start ➢ Programs ➢ Administrative Tools (Common) ➢ License Manager.
2. From the menu, select License.
3. Select New License–this will bring up a dialog box. Select Windows NT Server in the Product dialog box within the New Client Access License dialog box.
4. Enter the appropriate quantity.
5. Click OK.
6. Check that you understand the Microsoft licensing agreement. Click OK.

7. Verify that the licenses showed up under the Product History tab.

Configuring a Computer to Participate in Browser Elections

To configure a computer to participate in the browser elections, you must modify the \HKEY_LOCAL_MACHINE\SYSTEM\CurrentControlSet\Services\Browser\Parameters\MaintainServerList parameter:

1. Start \WINNT\System32\Regedt32.EXE.
2. Select the HKEY_LOCAL_MACHINE hive.
3. Double-click SYSTEM.
4. Double-click CurrentControlSet.
5. Double-click Services.
6. Double-click Browser.
7. Double-click Parameters.
8. Click MaintainServerList. At this point, you can enter three values: Yes, No, or Auto.
   - Yes–Computer will be a master or backup browser.
   - No–Computer will not be a browser.
   - Auto–Computer can be a master, backup, or potential browser.

If your computer is on a network that does not have a PDC (such as a workgroup), you can force a computer to be the master browser by changing the key \HKEY_LOCAL_MACHINE\SYSTEM\CurrentControlSet\Services\Browser\Parameters\IsDomainMaster to True. It is set to False by default, even on a PDC.

Configure peripherals and devices.

Peripherals and devices include:

- Communication devices
- SCSI devices
- Tape device drivers

- UPS devices and UPS service
- Mouse drivers, display drivers, and keyboard drivers

First, you will install and configure a communication device. This is your basic modem. Next, the backup subsystem is discussed. This subsystem consists of the tape backup device and the software that actually archives the data; the discussion will be limited to the installation and configuration of tape device drivers. Many people look at a UPS as a method for users to save their data before the server has to go down because of a power outage. Finally, there are the routine, mundane tasks such as driver upgrades. Many of the devices used daily are driven by software drivers.

Peripheral Options

Installing and configuring peripherals can be rather tricky topics to discuss. The answer to many of these questions is the same—it depends. The best way to be sure about the installation of any device is to read the manual.

Communication Devices

Modem installation and configuration can be a big job if you are installing a system that works with multiple COM ports and processors. Some manufacturers make systems that will integrate with NT and handle up to 256 ports, each with its own CPU. If you don't have the problem of remote users who need to dial into your system, you may be able to get by with a single modem. Modem selection has gotten more complicated in recent years—you have to make some difficult decisions. For example, will it be a "regular" modem to handle dial-up features over everyday phone lines, or will it be a modem designed to work with the latest and greatest ISDN lines?

SCSI Devices

SCSI (pronounced scuzzy) stands for *small computer system interface*, which is a standard high-speed parallel interface defined by the American National Standards Institute (ANSI). A SCSI interface is used for connecting microcomputers to peripheral devices such as hard disks. All sorts of devices—plotters, scanners, tape devices, and manufacturing devices—use SCSI interfaces, because SCSI is a very flexible technology. SCSI can address anything from disk and tape drives to CD-ROMs, scanners, printers, and even other computers. However, with flexibility and intelligence, there comes a price—that price can be steep.

Tape Device Drivers

It is not a question of *if* your storage devices will fail, it is a question of *when* your storage devices will fail. Windows NT comes with a utility called NT Backup that will allow you to archive your data to an off-line device such as a tape storage unit. Before NT Backup can send the data to that tape, you must add a tape backup device and drivers. All configuration of tape devices and the associated drivers is handled through the Tape Devices control panel.

UPS Devices and UPS Service

UPS stands for uninterruptible power supply. UPSs come in a variety of shapes, sizes, and configurations. Some will keep the server up for only 10 to 15 minutes after the power goes out. Some can keep it up for hours. Others will not only ensure that the system will not crash due to a power outage, but will condition the power that comes into your place of business. This provides a constant flow of even current, without the spikes and valleys that can ruin even the best servers.

UPS technology varies. UPSs with more features are more costly. Some UPSs will shut down the system. Some will send out broadcast messages saying that the system is coming down. Others will page you before the system goes down. When it is time to configure your new UPS, you do it through the UPS control panel.

Mouse Drivers

While most people view the mouse as a useful device, many people don't realize that it is configurable. The Mouse control panel gives you the opportunity to configure the mouse to meet your specifications. Users who are left handed can swap the buttons on the mouse. You can even choose the time between clicks that constitutes a double-click.

Display Drivers

Display drivers drive your video display. Depending on the type of video card in your computer and the amount of memory it has, you can configure your monitor to display millions of different colors, with clarity that will surpass your television set. The display driver gives you all sorts of options to personalize your computer, from wallpapers to screen savers that deliver a message for the day.

Keyboard Drivers

Keyboard drivers are used to customize the keyboard so that it meets the individual user's preferences. Some users are very fast typists and need to alter the repeat rate for keys. The keyboard driver also customizes the keyboard layout for languages other than English. For systems with multiple users who speak multiple languages, you can configure the keyboard for several different languages, as long as one is the default.

Configuring Peripherals

If you paid close attention to the section above, you would have noticed a theme running through all of the discussions–in each case, the configuration is handled by a control panel.

Installing Communication Devices

Since communication devices are the first selection on the objectives list, installing a modem will be the first priority:

1. Physically install the modem. If you have a problem with your internal modem, check the interrupt and COM port settings (how they are set on the modem compared to what you have available). COM1 and COM3 share an interrupt, COM2 and COM4 share an interrupt, and interrupt 3 is a common choice among network cards. When in doubt, read the manual.
2. Once the modem is installed, open the Modems control panel.
3. If this is the first modem in the system, the Installation Wizard will open. The Installation Wizard will search for the modem and return the brand and type of the modem. If the brand and type don't match what you have, use the Change button–a drop-down menu with a long list of modem manufacturers and models will appear. Choose the one that matches your needs. If your modem still does not show up, check the modem's manual for a compatible model.
4. Once the hardware is recognized, you will be presented with a Modems Properties screen. This screen lists the modems that are installed. Highlight a specific modem and choose Properties to bring up a rather generic screen. The General tab allows you to select the volume of the modem speaker and the speed of the modem.

5. The Connection tab will allow you to change the connection preferences, if necessary, and determine how to handle outgoing calls. There are several check boxes at the bottom of the screen—Wait for Dial Tone before Dialing, Cancel the Call If Not Connected within *x* Seconds, and Disconnect a Call If Idle for More Than *x* Minutes. The interesting options appear when you click the Advanced button on the Connection tab.

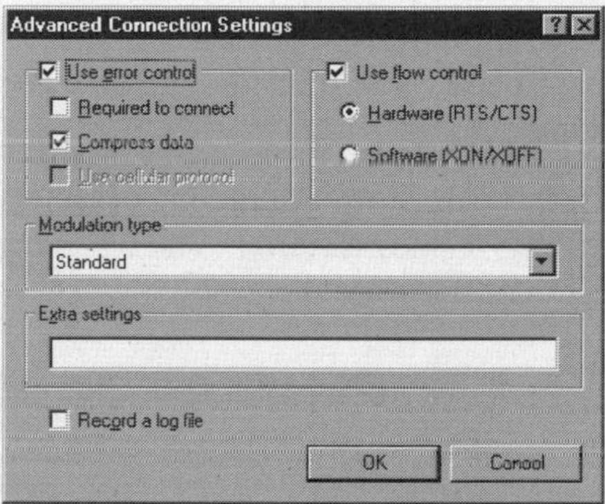

6. The Advanced Connection Settings screen (shown above) allows the administrator to choose how to handle error control and flow control, and the type of modulation. For error control, you can require error control to connect, you can choose to compress data, and you can use the cellular protocol for users dialing in with cell phones.

NOTE

You may have to remember the Compress Data tab, not for testing purposes, but for real life. Some software communications programs compress the data before they get to the modem. If the modem tries to compress them again, data corruption can occur.

7. Use Flow Control tells the modem how to determine the speed at which data are sent. Your two choices are Hardware and Software.

TIP

Unless you are told otherwise, keep modems set to the defaults.

Installing SCSI Devices

Before the computer can access SCSI devices, you must install a controller. The installation varies with manufacturer and type, but some common threads run through the process:

1. Install the SCSI adapter and driver as instructed by the manufacturer.
2. Open the SCSI Adapters control panel. Each SCSI controller system will look different. The following screen is a sample of all of the installed devices.

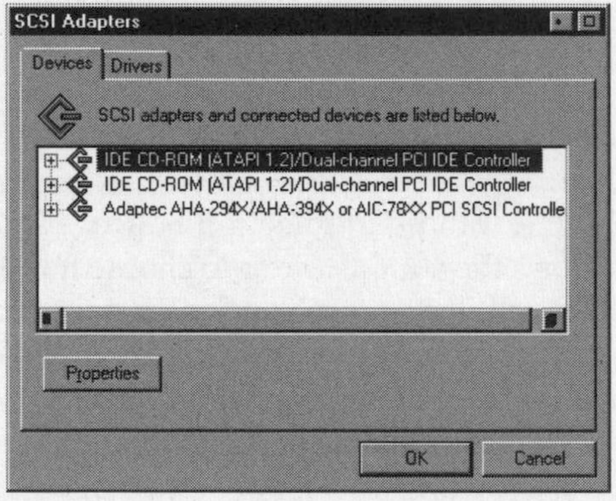

On this screen, there are two entries for the Dual-Channel PCI IDE Controller, which say that these devices are ATAPI compliant. The ATAPI standard is a subset of SCSI drivers. When the designers of NT needed a place to put them, this is where the designers decided they should go.

The Dual-Channel PCI IDE Controller was installed as part of the NT installation process. NT found the controller and loaded the drivers, and everything worked. The other driver listed is the Adaptec AHA-294X/AHA-394X driver. This card was installed after the server was configured. The installation went as follows:

1. Shut down the server.

2. Install the controller card and the SCSI device (in this case, an external CD-ROM), ensuring that SCSI IDs are properly set and cable termination requirements are met.
3. Restart NT and log on as administrator.
4. Open the SCSI Adapters control panel.
5. Choose the Drivers tab.
6. Click Add.
7. Choose the controller manufacturer and select Have Disk.
8. Put the disk in the A: drive.
9. Click OK.
10. Restart the computer when prompted.
11. Open My Computer to observe the new CD-ROM device. Create a share so that the second CD-ROM can be shared throughout the network.

Other than the Add/Remove button on the Drivers tab, there is not much to configure here. If you highlight a driver under the Devices tab and click Properties, you will get an information screen on the card. You will also be able to see an information screen on the driver. If you are curious, open the Resources tab of the Properties screen to see which IRQ and memory settings the card is using. Since the demonstration card is a PCI card, there are no changeable settings on this screen.

Configuring Tape Device Drivers

Configuring a tape drive is a two-step process. You configure the driver and then make NT discover the tape device. There are default drivers for some of the more common tape devices, but you might want to have any software drivers that came with the controller and tape drive handy, just in case. To install a tape backup unit:

1. Install the necessary hardware, as described by the hardware vendor.
2. Once the hardware has been installed and the computer has been restarted, log on as an administrator.
3. Open the Tape Devices control panel.
4. Select the Drivers tab and click Add.

5. Choose from the list of manufacturers and tape devices, or select Have Disk.

6. Click OK. At this point, the Installation Wizard will copy and install the device drivers. You will be prompted to restart your computer.

7. After the computer restarts, reenter the Tape Devices control panel.

8. With the Device tab selected, choose Detect to have NT find and configure the tape device.

Installing UPS Devices and Services

To install UPS devices and services:

1. Install the hardware according to the vendor's specifications.

2. Make sure that you attach a serial cable (usually nine pin) from the UPS to an available COM port. Make note of the port.

3. Open the UPS control panel.

4. Select the Uninterruptible Power Supply Is Installed On: check box and add the appropriate COM port.

5. You can now configure your UPS to recognize the loss of power. The configuration is accomplished by selecting one or more check boxes.

NOTE

When power is lost, an event is logged and no new connections can be made to the server. However, existing connections can continue. Warning messages will be broadcast according to the parameters you specify.

6. When the Power Failure check box is selected, you can choose how you want NT to react to a loss of power. By selecting Execute a Command File, you can write a series of commands for the system to carry out before shutting down.

   - If you opt not to write a command file, you can manually configure the UPS characteristics. Service characteristics include the time between power failure and initial warning message. The default is five seconds. If you live in an area with frequent storms that cause power outtages, you may want to change that setting. You can also specify how often you want the message to be rebroadcasted. The default is every two minutes.

- The other manually configured options revolve around what happens when the power comes back on. The first is the Expected Battery Life. This tells NT how long the UPS is rated to keep the computer up and working before shutting things down. You can also provide an informational selection, showing how long the battery must be recharged for each minute it is run. The default is 100 minutes per minute of downtime.
- You can configure NT to issue a Low Battery Signal warning at least two minutes before shutdown. After the server runs on batteries for a while, the system will signal when it is two minutes away from shutdown. If the administrator decides to select the Low Battery Signal option, the UPS characteristics remain grayed out.
- The final configuration is remote UPS shutdown. This signals NT to start shutting itself down.

You can also configure a command file to execute before shutdown. You can design this command file to shut down services and send out notifications to end users of the pending shutdown.

Changing or Updating a Mouse Driver

To change or update a mouse driver:

1. Log onto the computer as an administrator.
2. Open the Mouse control panel.
3. Select the General tab.
4. Click Change.
5. Choose the appropriate driver, or select Have Disk.
6. Click OK after the file copy and installation has been completed.
7. Restart the computer when prompted.

Changing or Updating a Display Driver

To change or update a display driver:

1. Log onto the computer as an administrator.
2. Open the Display control panel.
3. Select the Settings tab.
4. Click Display Type. If you know the type of adapter you are using and have the diskettes, click Change. Otherwise, click Detect.
5. Highlight the appropriate manufacturer and model number of your video card.
6. Click OK.
7. Click OK again.
8. When you return to the Settings tab, click Test. If the test is completed successfully, click OK and restart the computer if prompted.

Changing or Updating Keyboard Drivers

Keyboard drivers are also configured through the control panel.

1. Log on as administrator.
2. Open the Keyboard control panel.
3. Click General.
4. Click Change.
5. Choose the appropriate driver, or select Have Disk. Click OK.
6. When you return to the Select Device screen, click OK.
7. Click OK at the Keyboard General screen and restart the computer when prompted.

Configure hard disks to meet various requirements.

Requirements include:

- Allocating disk space capacity
- Providing redundancy
- Improving performance
- Providing security
- Formatting

Before you can make any decisions regarding the configuration of your disk storage environment, you need to know the options that are available. This objective walks through the various choices you can make once the disks are physically installed on your server.

Allocating Disk Space Capacity

Before a hard disk can be used by an operating system, it must be partitioned. When you partition a hard disk, you define the boundaries of a physical area on the disk. You can then format this area for use by an operating system such as Microsoft Windows NT.

You can use partitioning as a method of organizing your data by creating a boot partition that contains only NT system files, and another partition to hold your data. On a dual-boot computer, you could create separate partitions for each operating system so that each system file has its own physical space.

On the physical level, you must partition a disk before an operating system can use its storage space. A partition is made up of unused space on the drive. That free space will be used to form either a primary or an extended partition. You can create a maximum of four partitions on each disk.

A primary partition has the necessary configuration to be used by an operating system for the boot process. You can create up to four primary partitions on a single disk. A primary partition allows you to isolate the system files from multiple operating systems on a single drive. One of the primary partitions will be marked as active–this is the partition that will be booted from.

You can set up a computer to dual boot NT and Windows 95. To accomplish this, the partition must be formatted with the FAT file system. It is important to note that NT cannot read a partition formatted with FAT32 (a file system available as an option in Windows 95), so do not use this file system on machines on which you intend to dual boot NT and Windows 95.

Primary partitions cannot be further subdivided. One way to get around the four-partition limit is to use an extended partition. There can be one extended partition on each disk (it *does* count against the four-partition limit). You can subdivide the extended partition into multiple logical disks, each of which will be given a drive letter by the system.

Like a primary partition, an extended partition is created from unused space on the drive. Since there can be only one extended partition, you usually create it last and use all of the remaining space on the drive. You can then divide into logical drives for management purposes.

NT will dynamically assign drive letters to each partition using the procedure shown in Figure 6.3.

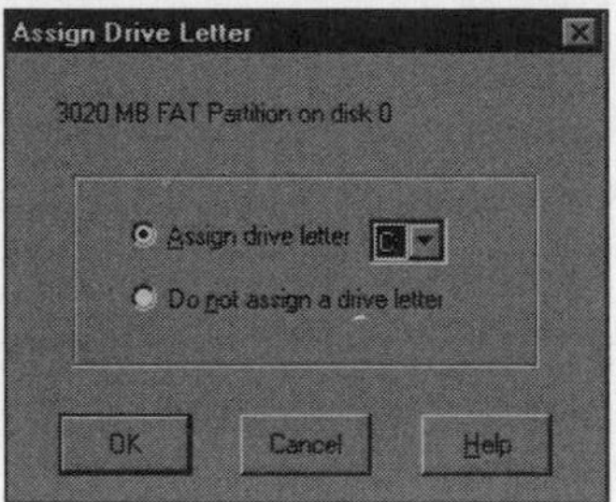

FIGURE 6.3: Assigning drive letters

1. Beginning with disk 0, the first primary partition on each drive is assigned a consecutive letter (starting with the letter *C*).
2. Beginning with disk 0, each logical drive is assigned a consecutive letter.
3. Beginning with disk 0, all other primary partitions are assigned a letter.

You can override these default assignments in the Disk Administration tool, by choosing Tools ➢ Assign Drive Letter.

Understanding Partition Numbering and ARC Paths

Windows NT assigns each partition an identification number, as described below. NT uses the partition number in an ARC path (defined later in this section) to locate the area on a disk needed for read and write operations. For troubleshooting purposes, you need to know how NT assigns partition numbers. NT assigns a number to all primary partitions first, starting with the number *1*, and then assigns an ID to each logical drive in the extended partition if one exists. NT uses the partition numbers in an ARC (advanced RISC computing) path to find the partition. You must understand ARC paths, for the exam and real-life troubleshooting. An ARC path will look as follows:

multi/scsi(a)disk(b)rdisk(c)partition(d)

Each *a, b, c,* and *d* will have a value, as described in Table 6.6.

TABLE 6.6: ARC Path Components

ARC Convention	Definition
multi/scsi	Identifies the type of controller. If the controller is a SCSI device with the BIOS *not* enabled, this value will be scsi; for all others, it will be multi.
(a)	The ordinal value of the controller. As each controller initializes, it is given a value; the first controller will be given a value of 0, the next 1, etc.
disk(b)	The SCSI bus number; for *multi*, this value is always 0.
rdisk(c)	For non-SCSI disks, the ordinal value of the disk. It is assigned in the same way as (a).
partition(d)	The ordinal value of the partition (it starts at 1 instead of 0).

Volume Sets

You can add together areas of free space on your hard disks to create one logical drive—thus creating a volume set. The process will be discussed later in this section. Once created, you must format this area with either FAT or NTFS. Once you have created the volume set, it will appear as one

Part II

drive to the system. When using a volume set, NT will fill each segment before starting to use the next.

You can also add space to an existing NTFS volume by choosing Partition ➢ Extend Volume Set in Disk Administrator. Once you have added free space to a volume set, you cannot take it back. The only way to reclaim that space is to delete the *entire* volume set (and thus any data stored there but not backed up).

TIP

If you need to extend a volume set formatted with the FAT file system, first convert it to NTFS using the CONVERT.EXE command-line tool. Remember that this is a one-way operation—once you have converted to NTFS, you cannot go back to FAT.

Stripe Sets

Like a volume set, a stripe set combines free space on two or more hard drives into one logical drive. Unlike a volume set, however, a stripe set must include space on at least 2 drives (up to a maximum of 32 drives). The areas created must be approximately the same size (if they are not, Disk Administrator will do this for you).

When you place data in a stripe set, the data are written evenly across all physical disks in 64KB stripes. While a stripe set does not provide fault tolerance, it can improve I/O performance, especially if the drives are on separate controllers.

Providing Redundancy

Because of the critical nature of most data stored on servers, it is important that the disk subsystem be fault tolerant. A fault-tolerant disk system is one in which the system can survive the death of a hard drive, while the data remain accessible. You manage the fault-tolerant features of Windows NT through Disk Administrator.

NT provides fault tolerance through software-controlled RAID. NT supports internal software implementations of RAID levels 0, 1, and 5. Level 0 is the ability to create a volume set that spans multiple hard drives. Since this provides no fault tolerance, it will be ignored in this discussion.

RAID level 1 is commonly referred to as disk mirroring. A mirror system is one in which there is a redundant copy of all data on the partition. The point of mirroring is that if the primary disk dies, the system can switch over to the redundant disk so that the users will not notice the hardware failure.

Disk duplexing is a subset of mirroring in which the disks are accessed through separate controllers. In mirroring, if the controller dies, there is no way to access the redundant disk. Since you have multiple controllers in a duplexed system, the server can survive a controller failure without the users noticing a problem.

RAID level 5 consists of disk striping (as discussed above), with the addition of a parity set. The parity set is a calculation of the contents of the data, placed on another disk in the set. If one disk dies, the system can use the parity information to re-create the data on the fly.

RAID level 1 (mirroring) is an efficient way to provide fault tolerance (especially if you upgrade it to duplexing). Since an entire copy of the data exists on another hard drive, the user will not notice a difference in performance in the event of a hardware failure. However, mirroring is more expensive than RAID level 5—in mirroring, one-half of the disk space is redundant. Mirroring is also the only way to make your system and boot partitions fault tolerant. These two partitions cannot be part of a volume set, stripe set, or stripe set with parity.

RAID level 5 is very common in today's business environments. It increases I/O performance by splitting the work across hard disks. It is also more cost effective than mirroring. In a level-5 implementation, if more disks are involved in the stripe set, the percentage of disk space used for the fault-tolerant information will be lower. In mirroring, one-half of the total disk space is used to provide fault tolerance. In a level-5 implementation with three disks, only one-third of the space is used to hold the parity information (one-quarter for four disks, one-fifth for five disks, etc.). Keep in mind, though, that RAID level 5 can survive the loss of only one disk. If you lose more than one, the parity information becomes useless. However, the likelihood of more than one drive failing simultaneously is much more remote than that of just one, making RAID level 5 an effective insurance policy.

Improving Performance

Once the disks have been installed, you can use a few optimization techniques to get the most performance from your hardware. First, you need to analyze your disk storage trends. If you have multiple disk controllers, try to place heavily used data on separate drives. You should try to split the load equally across all of the physical devices.

If you have two heavily used databases and two disk controllers, give each one its own path to a hard drive. In other words, split them across drives attached to the different controllers. When you plan your disk storage strategy around this philosophy, it can dramatically affect disk drive performance.

Another suggestion is to watch the placement of the paging file (PAGEFILE.SYS). The paging file is used as virtual memory–effectively allowing your NT server to allocate more memory than there is physical RAM in the computer. When the operating system detects a need for more memory, but there is no RAM available, it will move portions of RAM into the paging file until they are needed again. A small amount of paging is normal on an NT server. However, this process is disk intensive. If you place the paging file on a disk that is busy performing other functions, you will notice a decline in overall server performance. Microsoft suggests that you move the paging file off the disk that contains the NT system files. If possible, you should create paging files on multiple disks to spread the workload.

Providing Security

If security is a major concern in your environment, you should probably use NTFS. NTFS provides file- and directory-level security–FAT does not. To put it another way, any user who can log on at a computer can access any files on that computer that are stored on a FAT partition. Files stored on an NTFS can be secured using NT permissions.

NOTE

You can secure files on a FAT partition if those files are being accessed remotely. When you create a share point, you can assign permissions to the data stored there. Security is an issue on FAT partitions only when the user logs onto the computer locally—not from across the network.

Formatting

Before you can use a partition to store data, it must be formatted. In NT, you can format a partition in two ways–through Disk Administrator or using the command-line utility FORMAT.

Hard Disk Configuration Procedures

Most servers act as repositories of data that are to be accessed by end users. NT administrators must be able to configure and manage the disks on their servers. The procedures covered for this exam objective concern the skills necessary to manage the disk configuration of an NT server.

Reassigning Drive Letters

You reassign disk drive letters using the Disk Administrator tool. Click the partition you want to reassign, choose Tools ➢ Assign Drive Letter, and change the letter.

Creating a Volume Set

In Disk Administrator, Ctrl-click all of the partitions that should be included and choose Partition ➢ Create Volume Set.

Creating a Stripe Set

In Disk Administrator, Ctrl-click all of the partitions that should be included in the set. Remember that the segments must be approximately the same size (Disk Administrator will adjust the size for you if they are not). Choose Partition ➢ Create Stripe Set.

Creating a Mirror Set

In Disk Administrator, Ctrl-click the two partitions that will make up the set (they must be on different hard drives) and choose Fault Tolerance ➢ Establish Mirror.

Creating a Stripe Set with Parity

In Disk Administrator, Ctrl-click the partitions that will make up the segments of the set. Remember that they must be approximately the same size (Disk Administrator will adjust the size as appropriate). Choose Fault Tolerance ➢ Create Stripe Set with Parity.

Formatting a Partition

In NT, you can format a partition in two ways—both ways can format the partition with either the FAT file system or NTFS.

From a command prompt, you can use the FORMAT command. The syntax is as follows:

```
FORMAT Drive: [fs:file-system] [/v:label]
```

The other option is to use Disk Administrator. Highlight the partition to be formatted and choose Tools ➢ Format.

Configure printers.

Tasks include:

- Adding and configuring a printer
- Implementing a printer pool
- Setting print priorities

In MicroSpeak, the object you load paper into is called a *printing device.* A *printer* is the software interface that takes the information from your application and redirects it to a printing device. A *print driver* is the piece of software that translates application information into the printer-specific commands that are passed to the actual print device. The printing objective receives *lots* of attention on the exam.

Printing Fundamentals

In the NT print architecture, the application that you use to generate the output does not care about the kind of printer you are using. It just sends the job off to the printer, and the print job magically appears. This magic is made up of many processes that work together to give your users the desired results.

Adding and Configuring a Printer

Printing is an ever-evolving process. You will constantly add or upgrade printers to make sure that your users have access to the appropriate resource. Printer configuration has many aspects, depending on the driver that is supplied with the printer. Usually, you will be able to configure paper size, input trays, duplexing, fonts, and paper layout. You can also specify default settings for specialty printers. To understand the complexities of printing, you must understand the entire printing process–from the selection of Print to the final output.

An application creates an application print request and passes that request to the graphics device interface (GDI). The GDI is the first of several "translation" pieces. The GDI takes the application print request and translates it into device driver interface (DDI) calls. When the DDI gets done with the file, it can now be called a print job. There are two types of print jobs:

Raw print job–A set of commands that the printer will understand to produce the final product.

Journal file print job–A list of DDI calls that can be used to come up with a raw print job. This is used when the printer is directly attached to the workstation printing the job.

The print job still isn't printer specific. Now that the DDI calls have been stored in the print job, the print driver comes into play. It takes these generic calls and turns them into printer-specific commands.

The print job is basically complete. It just needs to find its way to the right printer. So, the printer router takes over. When the printing device is ready, a print monitor takes the job from the print spooler and feeds it to the printing device.

NOTE

The print monitor is actually three DLL files. One handles local printing devices through the parallel and serial ports. This is the LOCALMON.DLL. The HPMON.DLL sends jobs to HP printers hooked directly to the network rather than to a computer. The LPRMON.DLL (LPR stands for line printer) sends jobs to UNIX print daemons.

Printing devices come in several categories:

- Network printing device–A printing device hooked directly to the network cable.
- Local printing device–To be local, the printing device must be hooked directly to the server computer.
- Remote printing device–Any printing device hooked to another computer on the network.

In this book, connecting a network printing device to the system will not be discussed. If you are configuring a network printing device, you are using a third-party printing solution. Follow the manufacturer's installation instructions.

Implementing a Printer Pool

Every network administrator reaches the time in their professional life when the amount of paper to be generated by a specific department is greater than the capacity of a single print device. A decision must be made—upgrade to a bigger, faster print device, or just add another print device of the same type to take up the slack. If you decide to add another printer of the same type, you can create a printer pool to double your output. With a printer pool, one printer controls multiple printing devices. While this concept sounds appealing, there are some catches. First, the printing devices in the printer pool must be the same type—they must use the same driver. For the sake of logistics, it is also a good idea to have all of the devices located in the same area.

Setting Print Priorities

To set a print priority, you must first configure two printers for the printing device in question. One of the printers is granted a higher priority. When two print jobs hit the printers at the same time, the printer with the higher priority will print and the other job will wait.

Printer Procedures

You will install several different kinds of printers and printing devices, create a printer pool, and set up print priorities.

Creating a Local Printer

Here, you are creating a local *printer*. Before you can send tasks to a local *print device*, you have to configure a local printer.

To create the local printer:

1. Log on as an administrator on the computer.
2. Choose Start ➢ Settings ➢ Printers.
3. Double-click the Add Printer icon.
4. Because you are creating a local printer, check the My Computer radio button. Click Next.
5. Choose the port to which the printer will be attached. Click Next.
6. You will see two lists. The one on the left allows you to select the manufacturer of your printer. The one on the right lets you pick the model of your printer. Make your choices and click Next.

7. Give your printer a name. If it will be the default printer (the one you usually print to), select the Yes check box; otherwise, select No. Click Next.
8. If you want to share the printer, enter a share name. What if you want the printer to be shared by something other than a Windows product? Hold down the Ctrl key and click all of those other operating systems with which you want to work. Then, click Next to continue.
9. The Wizard will let you print a test page. This is usually a good idea, because it helps in troubleshooting. If there is a problem, it is good to find it early.
10. Make sure that you have your NT Server installation CD-ROM handy. NT may ask for it to copy some files.
11. If you look closely at the Printer window, you should notice a new icon for your printer. You can use the icon to make changes to the printer.
12. Click OK to exit the Install a Printer Wizard.

Configuring a Local Printing Device

Now that the printing device is installed, it is time to configure it. Configuration is done from the Printers control panel. Choose the printer you want to configure, highlight it, right-click, and select Properties.

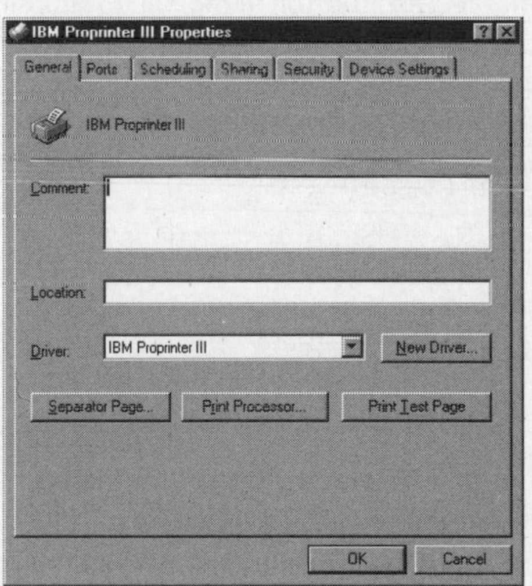

As you can see, there is plenty to play with on this page. The properties shown here are a function of the particular print driver, so your Properties page may not look like the one shown.

General Tab Under the General tab, you will see the New Driver button. If you click it, the first screen will warn you that changing the drivers may change the Properties screen. If you agree to the warning, the system reopens the Add Printer Wizard to the driver's page. Make your selection here, or use the Have Disk function.

Back to the General tab. If you click Separator Page, it will allow you to put a page between each document or switch printing modes from PCL to PostScript. You can create a document for this purpose and browse to it. Once you have found the document you want, click OK. This option is important in the following situations:

- In a busy office where many people share the same printer. The separator page will let your end users know when they have grabbed someone else's document.
- If you are using a laser printer that can handle both PostScript and PCL languages, but cannot automatically sense the change. This was the case in early versions of the HP III SI. Most printers that can use both PCL and PostScript can automatically sense—the printing device recognizes the PostScript header and switches to PostScript mode automatically.

The Print Processor button allows you to choose the way you want jobs processed. The print processor is the rendering piece of the printing puzzle—it is where the print job is completed before being sent to the print monitor. NT provides two generic processors, with selections for each.

- Windows print processor:
    - RAW—Set of instructions that will result in a printed document.
    - RAW (FF Appended)—Puts a form feed at the end of the job, if one is not already there.
    - RAW (FF Auto)—Automatically puts a form feed at the end of a print job.
    - NT EMF 1.003—When you print a document that contains a read-only embedded font not listed as an installed font in the Fonts folder, Windows NT uses a substitute

font if the printer is set to use NT EMF 1.003 mode. Windows NT prints the font correctly in RAW mode.

- Text–Prints documents in Text mode.

- Macintosh print processor:
    - Handles jobs sent from a Macintosh workstation to a non-PostScript printer attached to an NT computer. In other words, this processor translates PostScript code into something the designated printer can understand.

The last selection on the General tab is self explanatory–Print Test Page. This is a great place to start troubleshooting.

Ports Tab While looking at the Ports tab, you will notice all of the standard ports that any good computer should have. There is LPT1 to LPT3 for your parallel printing devices, COM1 to COM4 for serial printing devices, and the FILE selection so that you can print to a file rather than a real printing device. If this does not give you enough choices, you can always add your own port by clicking the Add Port button. If you click Add Port, you can add specialty ports, such as a digital network port, DLC ports, TCP/IP ports, or a local port. When you configure the port, it will set the Transmission Retry parameter. The Transmission Retry parameter sets the amount of time the user must wait before NT reports that the printer is not available. This setting not only affects the specific printer, but all printers using the same driver.

Don't overlook the two check boxes at the bottom of the screen. The top check box allows you to enable or disable bidirectional support. The bottom check box allows you to enable printer pooling.

NOTE

A printer pool is defined as multiple print devices of the exact same type that work together.

Scheduling Tab On the Scheduling tab, you determine when this printing device will be available to actually print. You can choose to have the printing device always available, or you can specify certain hours when the print device will be available. You can also use this tab to specify a priority to jobs going to the printing device.

Once you decide whether this device will have a special schedule or priority, you can decide how you want it to handle print jobs. It can spool documents so that the program finishes faster or print directly to the printer. If you choose to spool documents, you can make the system wait to start printing until the last page is spooled, or you can start printing immediately.

The check boxes at the bottom of the screen are as follows:

Hold Mismatched Documents–Suppose that the Accounting department has only one printer. That printer can be used to print both checks and memos. You have mismatched documents when checks and memos are sent to the printer at the same time. In this case, the printer will expect you to manually change the paper.

Print Spooled Documents First–This option groups the documents together by type. In the case mentioned above, all checks would be printed, and then all memos would be printed.

Keep Documents After They Have Printed–When a job moves through the printing process and is finally output on the printing device, the print job is deleted. Usually, this is not a problem, because you have a copy of the document stored somewhere on the system. However, some applications will generate a report, send it to the printer, and then delete the report. This option allows you to keep the print job in the spooler until you are sure it has printed correctly, and then you must manually delete it.

Sharing Tab The next tab available on the Properties screen is the Sharing tab. It is a fallback to the Sharing tab from the Install Wizard. Here, you can select the drivers that you want the printer to make available. You can choose from a variety of alternate drivers, depending on the operating systems your clients are running.

Security Tab The Security tab will allow you to manage who can use the printer. By clicking Permissions, you can grant users the right to use or manage the printer, or take away their right to even see the printer.

From the Security tab, you can select from Permissions, Auditing, and Ownership.

Permissions—This button is for user permissions. User permissions define who can print to this printer and who can manage the documents submitted to this printer. By default:

- Administrators have full control.
- The creator or owner of the document has the permission to manage documents.
- Everyone can print.
- Print operators have full control.
- Server operators have full control.

Auditing—This button allows the administrator to track the success or failure of various print functions.

Ownership—This button allows a user to take ownership of a printer.

Device Settings Tab The final tab is the Device Settings tab. This tab is driver/printing device specific. It lets you define which paper tray will be used for which form, how much memory is installed in the printer, if there are any font cartridges installed, and what soft fonts are accessible.

Installing a Remote Printer

A remote printer is a printing device that is attached to another computer on the network. It is not physically attached to your NT server. When the print job is sent to the remote printer, the job is first sent to the remote printer, where it is spooled for the printer.

For your users to share the printer, do as follows at the workstation that needs access to the printer:

1. Choose Start ➢ Settings ➢ Printers.
2. Click Add Printer. This will begin the Add Printer Wizard.
3. Choose Network Printer instead of Local Printer.
4. Browse the network to find the appropriate printer.
5. Select the printer you want and click OK in the Connect to Printer dialog box. You may be asked to install a print driver if one is not available from your operating system.

6. You will be asked whether this printing device will be your default printer. This is your call–it is a Yes or No decision.
7. Click Finish.

Implementing a Printer Pool

To create a printer pool:

1. Open the Printers control panel.
2. Highlight the printer that will be part of the pool and right-click.
3. Select Properties and then choose the Ports tab.
4. Check the Enable Printer Pooling option.
5. Select the ports that also have printing devices of the same type attached to them.
   - If the printing devices are attached to physical ports (LPT2 and LPT3 as well as LPT1), select those ports.
   - If the printing devices are remote printers, connected through an LPR port, select each network printer port. Use this selection if you are using TCP/IP printing.
6. Select OK.

Setting Print Priorities

Once you have put the pieces together, you can change the priority of one printer to a higher setting:

1. Create two printers connected to the same printing device.
2. In the Printers control panel, highlight the printer that will receive the higher priority, right-click, and choose Properties. Select the Scheduling tab.
3. Change the priority to the highest setting.

NOTE

The default priority setting is Lowest. So, when you simply change the priority on one printing device, it accomplishes the task as outlined.

4. Click OK.

TIP

For more information on printing, check out *MCSE: NT Server 4 Study Guide, Second Edition,* by Matthew Strebe and Charles Perkins with James Chellis, published by Sybex.

Configure a Windows NT Server computer for various types of client computers.

Client computer types include:

- Windows NT Workstation
- Microsoft Windows 95
- Microsoft MS-DOS based

Now that the network is configured, you can tweak the configuration to make the server more accessible to various client types. If you work in a mixed environment (and most people do), this section can help alleviate the complaint that the network is slow on a given day.

In Chapter 5, there was a section devoted to protocols. In that section, you were shown how to configure your server to communicate with different clients utilizing different protocols. Depending on the client computers that your network is servicing, it is important to provide the right protocol. As you saw in Chapter 5, some of the protocols supported by NT Server are NetBEUI, TCP/IP, IPX/SPX, DLC, and AppleTalk (also DHCP, WINS, and DNS, but these are really services). Not all of the clients that you attach to the network will have the flexibility to connect using each of these protocols. Table 6.7 lists the protocols or services that can be used with various operating systems.

TABLE 6.7: Operating System Protocols and Services

Client	NetBEUI	NWLink IPX/SPX	TCP/IP	DLC	DHCP	WINS	DNS	AppleTalk
MS-DOS	Yes	Yes	Yes	Yes	Yes			
LAN MAN for DOS	Yes	Yes	Yes	Yes				
LAN MAN for OS/2	Yes		Yes					
Windows 95	Yes	Yes	Yes		Yes	Yes	Yes	
Macintosh								Yes
NT Workstation	Yes	Yes	Yes	Yes	Yes	Yes	Yes	

Once you have configured the server to support the protocols, you can enhance client operation by changing the binding order on client machines–it is the client that chooses the protocol it will use to "talk" with the server. If you place the more frequently used protocols at the top of the binding order, performance will increase. Working with binding order at the workstation machine may affect how quickly it communicates over the network.

Changing the Binding Order of Protocols

To change the binding order of protocols for a client machine using Windows NT Workstation:

1. Highlight Network Neighborhood.
2. Right-click and select Properties.
3. On the Network screen, select the Bindings tab.
4. Expand Workstation.
5. Highlight the chosen protocol and use the Move Up or Move Down button.

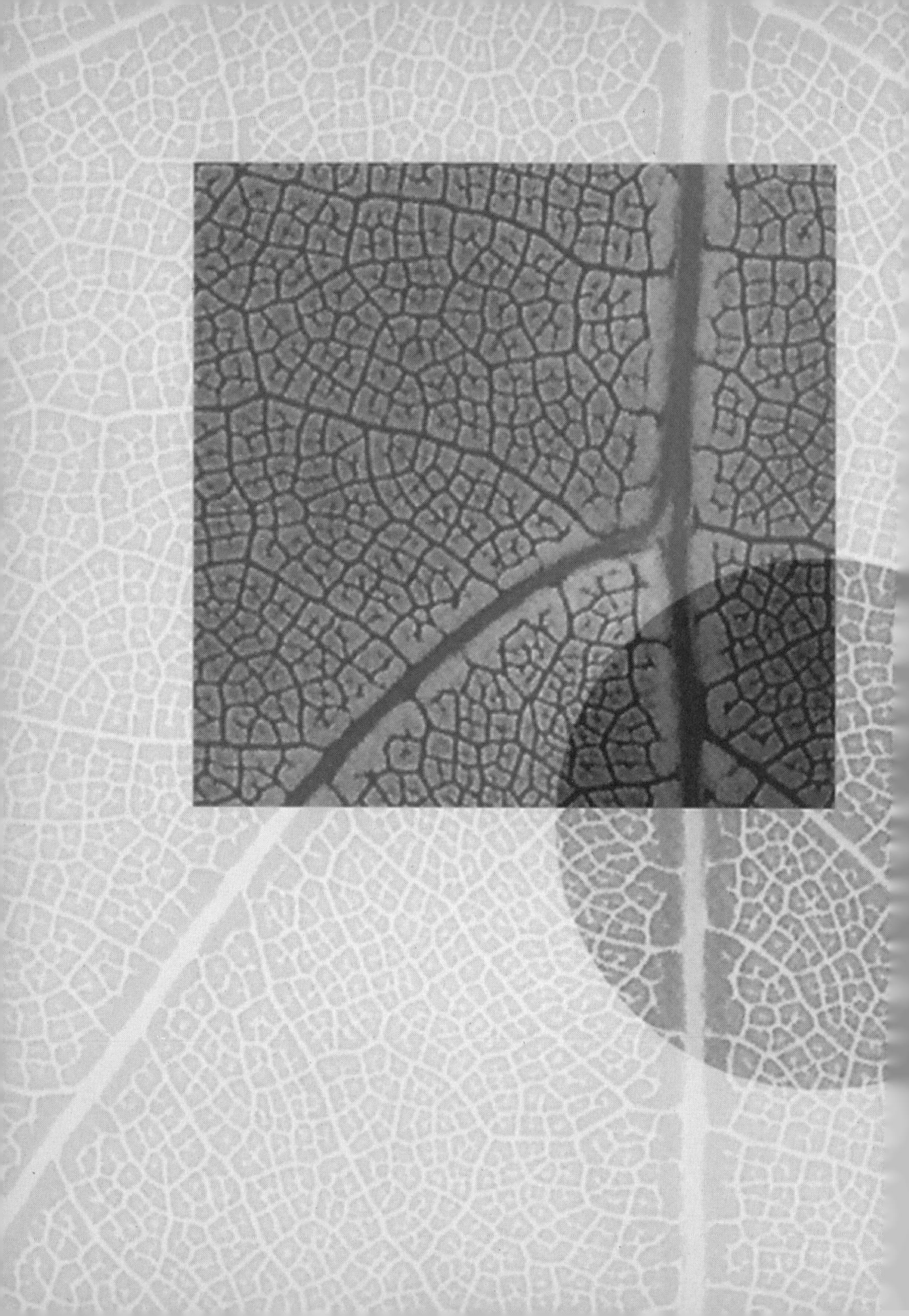

Chapter 7
Managing Resources

One of the best definitions of a network is having two or more people with information to share, a communication medium to send the information, and rules to govern the communication. The whole reason for having a computer network is sharing—sharing information, sharing resources, and sharing applications. That very broad overview tends to get complicated really quickly when the amount of people with something to share grows to 50, 100, 1000, or more. It is especially complicated when *you* have to provide others with the opportunity to share files and peripherals throughout the entire company. It can be a daunting task. However, it doesn't have to be that way. As you study this chapter, you will find ways to cut that task down to size.

Adapted from *MCSE Exam Notes: NT Server 4*
by Gary Govanus and Robert King
ISBN 0-7821-2289-2 360 pages $19.99

While the first objective groups users together and handles them *en masse*, the second objective starts to give the user some human characteristics. The third objective pertains to remote server administration. The fourth objective on managing disk resources shows how to manage the information stored on the disks. Lots of exam questions will be asked about the material covered in this chapter–be sure to pay close attention to the concepts of local groups and global groups. Questions on groups will haunt you during the NT Server test, the NT Enterprise test, and beyond.

Manage user and group accounts.

Considerations include:

- Managing Windows NT user accounts
- Managing Windows NT user rights
- Managing Windows NT groups
- Administering account policies
- Auditing changes to the user account database

To break down this objective, remember one of the commandments of LAN administration–do unto many. Anytime you can group users together as one entity, it will make your life much easier. As you try to see the "big picture" of your network, you look around at all those users, running all those applications, printing to all those printers, and you have to wonder how you can manage all of that. The more you look, the more you realize these people can be grouped by the tasks they perform and the resources they require.

Managing Windows NT User Accounts

The more users you group together, the less work for the administrator or Information Services team. Who wants to work harder? The NT domain model provides security for the files and resources on your network. This security is implemented by assigning permissions to four types of objects: the local user, the global user, the global group, and the local group. Are you wondering how each is used? Let's start the discussion small–with the user. With Windows NT, there are two kinds of users, local users and global users. Each has separate roles to fill. In addition, NT creates a set of default users that you can use as templates or role models.

Local User Account

Sometimes, naming can be tricky. This is one of those times. A local user account is created on an NT computer via an NT domain, and its purpose is to serve a single user on just that server. That user account can enable access for local users in addition to those from other NT domains. For example, assume that you have a diverse network made up of NT servers and Windows 95 clients. A user who primarily logs on and uses the services of the NT network could have direct server login authentication provided through a local user account–without a local account, they would not.

NOTE

Local accounts can access services only from within the NT server (or workstation) where they reside, since they are in the local (via domain) SAM. They are created in the individual computer SAM by using the User Manager utility as opposed to the User Manager for Domains utility.

Global User Account

Because global user accounts are the most commonly created, they are generally referred to as just "user accounts." A global user account differs from a local account in that it can provide permissions to access resources in any domain, beginning with the domain in which it was created. As long as there is a trust relationship between domains, these accounts can utilize resources in any trusting domains. Global user accounts can receive these permissions either individually or through membership in a group. A global user account is created with User Manager for Domains.

As mentioned, two default user types are created with the NT installation:

- **Administrator** User account for administering the computer and/or domain
- **Guest** User account for providing guest access to the computer and/or domain

A local user account is designed for the user who will log onto the computer itself. A global user is someone who is allowed to log on and access resources from the domain. Local accounts are created using User

Manager if the NT computer is designed as a part of a peer-to-peer network or standalone system. Local users can be implemented regardless of whether the server is being used in an NT domain environment. Otherwise, global users are created using User Manager for Domains.

User accounts can be created two ways—you can create a new user account or you can copy an existing user account. No matter which way you choose to create the account, you can still make changes in three key areas—user account information, group membership information, and user account profile information.

The New User dialog box is shown in Figure 7.1.

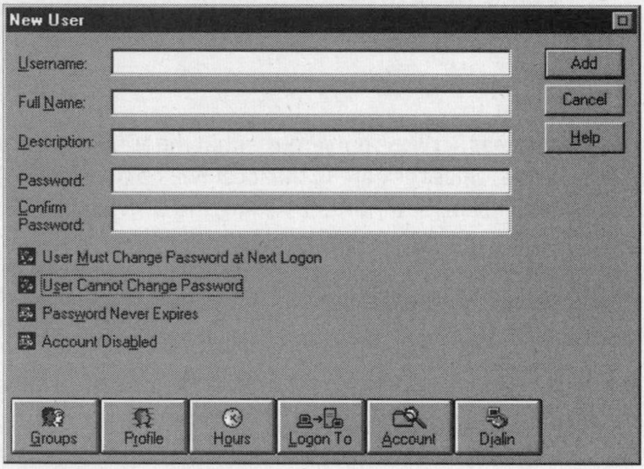

FIGURE 7.1: New User dialog box

What do you do with the users once they have been created?

Managing Windows NT User Rights

Now that the users have been created, you have to give them permission to do something. Usually, you will plan for your groups first. In most cases, rights and permissions can be assigned at the group level, leaving user accounts to be assigned to global groups. Even if you have laid out a security plan in which all rights and permissions are assigned to groups, there are still some universal settings you may want to set for all users, such as using the corporate logo as wallpaper or making sure the network hookup is just the way you want it. You can make these edits on the User

Environment Profile screen. The User Environment Profile screen is shown in Figure 7.2.

FIGURE 7.2: User Environment Profile

This screen allows you to point to where you have stored the user profile and the name of the logon script that the user should execute. You can give a user a path to their home directory, where they can store all that really private user stuff. This directory can be on any server or share.

User profiles contain those settings and configuration options specific to the user–installed applications, desktop icons, color options, and so forth. This profile is built from system policy information (for example, those things that a user has access to and those things that a user can and cannot change), the default user profile, and permitted, saved changes that a user makes to customize their desktop.

Remember that mandatory profiles can be created by changing the profile suffix from .DAT to .MAN. This resets profile settings to the mandatory values each time a user logs on. While it saves time and prevents users from mangling their desktop settings on a permanent basis, the downside to this implementation is that if the domain controllers are unavailable, users cannot log on, even with cached profile information.

NOTE

User profiles deal with a specific user. User policies deal with all users of a domain.

The Group Memberships screen (see Figure 7.3) shows you which groups a user is a member of and to which groups a user can be added.

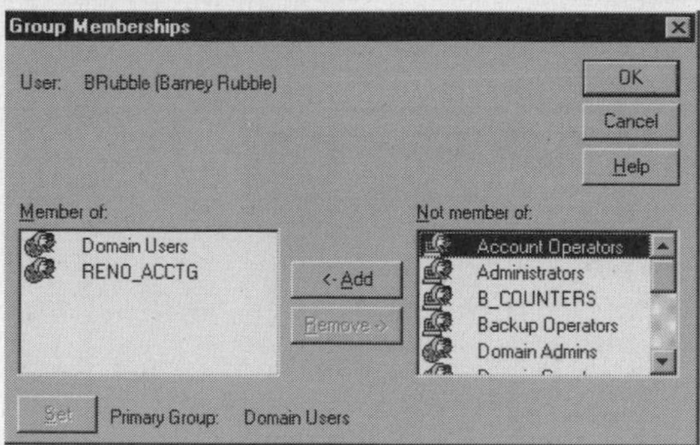

FIGURE 7.3: Group Memberships

Although the Group Memberships screen shows you where you add a user to a group, you still don't know how and why groups interact.

Managing Windows NT Groups

Windows NT uses a very sophisticated group model that consists of local groups and global groups. At its simplest, in a multiple-domain environment you create users and global groups in the domain. Users get placed in global groups. Local groups are created on individual NT computers to give access to resources of that server or workstation. Global groups are made a part of local groups, and the users can access the resources.

Global Groups

Global groups are users from the same domain grouped together. Global groups can contain only user accounts from their domain–they cannot contain other groups. While a global group can contain only users in its domain, it is not limited to receiving permissions from only that domain. Global groups can be granted permissions to access resources in other domains. Global groups are created only on NT servers functioning as domain controllers using User Manager for Domains.

Local Groups

Unlike global groups, which can receive authentications from outside their domain boundaries, local groups can receive permissions only on the computer in which they were created. Local groups are created to grant permission to resources or allow users to perform specific tasks. Local groups can be made up of local user accounts, users from within their domain, users from trusted domains, and global group accounts both from their domain and from any trusted domains.

Default Groups

The types of groups described above are those that you can create. NT has taken some of the work out of planning for groups by creating some default groups to do various management tasks:

Domain Users Global group containing all domain users except the user Guest.

Domain Guests Global group giving limited access and containing the user Guest.

Domain Admins Global group that allows administrator permissions to the entire domain.

Guests Local group for server guests containing the global group Domain Guests.

Print Operators Local group for the members that are assigned to administer domain printers.

Replicator Local group for the accounts that support directory and file replication in the domain.

Server Operators Local group for the members that can administer domain servers.

Users Local group for ordinary users. Contains the global group Domain Users by logging on locally and conducts sharing, hard drive, and backup operations.

Backup Operators Local group for backing up and restoring the server regardless of directory and file permissions.

Administrators Local group that has full control over the server. Includes the Administrator local user account and the Domain Admins global group.

Account Operators Local group that can access both the server's local SAM and domain SAM (if the server is a domain controller).

NOTE

Always remember that in the Microsoft-selected model of group management, users are always put in global groups. Global groups are added to local groups. Local groups are always assigned access permissions. Users are never put in local groups.

Administering Account Policies

There are other ways of improving the security settings of a user account. One way is to alter the default account policies. *Account policies* are the defaults that the administrator sets to handle various security issues. Account policies are handled through User Manager for Domains. System policies are administered through the System Policy Editor.

Account Policies

Account policies set broad policies for all the users of your domain. To access the Account Policies page, start User Manager for Domains and choose Policies ➢ Account (see Figure 7.4).

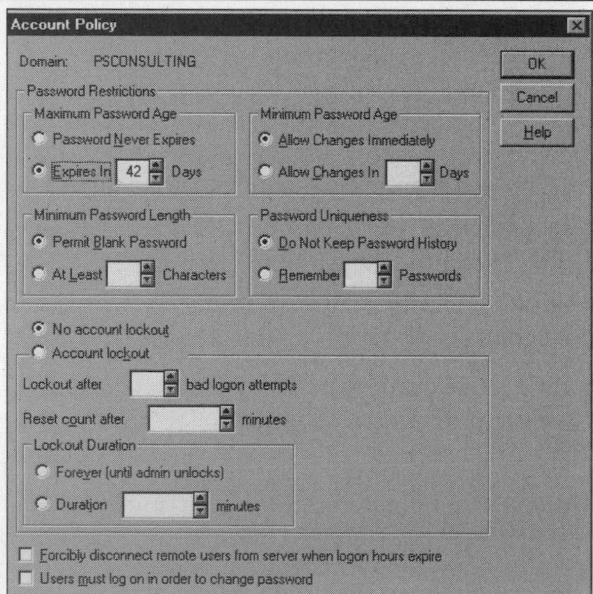

FIGURE 7.4: Account Policy options

Setting default user security is key to this utility. However, setting user security is a two-edged sword. The network and data are more secure, but your end users will probably whine about the changes. The Account Policy page offers the following selections:

Maximum Password Age For password restrictions, the administrator can set the Maximum Password Age. If you work in an environment where security is not an issue, you may choose Password Never Expires. If security is an issue, there is a setting that forces passwords to be changed every so many days. Keep in mind as you view this figure that the default is set to 42 days. While decreasing the amount of time a password is active may make great sense from a security point of view, the chances that your users will understand why they have to change their passwords so often are slim to none.

Minimum Password Age This forces a user to keep a password for at least a certain period of time. By default, users can change their passwords immediately.

Minimum Password Length How long must a password be? If no changes are made, blank passwords are permitted. If you increase the minimum password length, your users will have to start thinking before typing. Most experts say that six to eight characters is about the right length, but Microsoft doesn't have a particular policy.

Password Uniqueness You have heard the stories of the user who kept the same password for years and years. By the time the user left the company, everyone knew his or her password. This is almost as bad as having no password at all. Password Uniqueness, which is turned off by default, will remember a number of passwords, forcing the user to come up with something new every time the password must be changed, even if changing only capitalization (recall that passwords are case sensitive). You get to choose the length of the history list.

Account Lockout This is an attempt to prevent hackers from attempting to access your network over and over again. If Account Lockout is enabled and someone tries to log onto a valid user account unsuccessfully so many times, the account will be locked and the user will not be able to log onto the system. You can set the number of bad logon attempts, reset the count after so many minutes, and set the lockout duration. Once the account is locked, the hacker doesn't know if it is locked for 10 minutes or an hour and 10 minutes. At that point, there are probably easier networks to attack.

Forcibly Disconnect Remote Users from Server When Logon Hours Expire If you select this checkbox, it will cause users who are working when the allowed time expires to be kicked off the system. If this option is not selected, the remote server user can continue to use the system, but cannot open any new sessions.

Users Must Log On in Order to Change Password This selection makes your users change their passwords before they expire. If the password expires, the end user will have to contact the administrator, and the administrator will have to reset the password.

Auditing Changes to the User Account Database

NT allows you to audit what is happening to user accounts and who is making changes or performing certain tasks. Don't get bogged down with auditing, but if you know how to use it, it can come in handy. It can certainly help answer an exam question or two. Setting an audit policy can help spot security breaches. By default, auditing is turned off. You can change the audit policy through User Manager for Domains by choosing Policies ➢ Auditing. Take a good, close look at Figure 7.5.

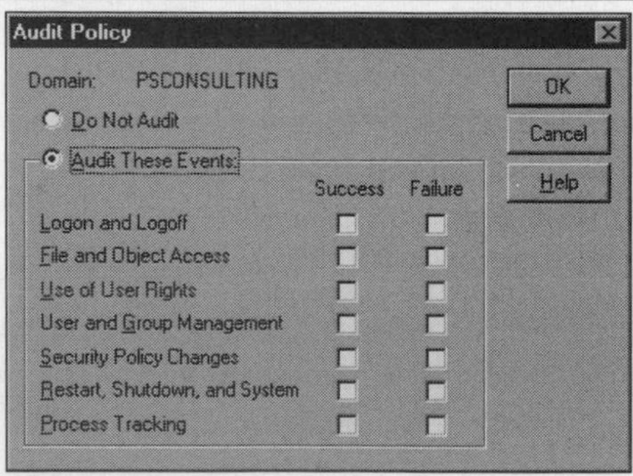

FIGURE 7.5: Audit Policy screen

You have a limited amount of options for auditing. Remember that if you turn on auditing, it may help you track down a security breach. However, it will also put a serious load on your server, perhaps slowing response time. As you can see from the options on the Audit Policy screen, you can audit the success or failure of seven common network events. The information is stored in a security log. You can view the log by using the Event Viewer.

Routine Management Procedures

This section explains the procedures for performing several routine management tasks.

Creating a Global User Account

To create a global user account, fire up User Manager for Domains and open the New User dialog box:

1. Click Start.
2. Select Programs.
3. Select Administrative Tools.
4. Click User Manager for Domains. The New User dialog box appears. (See Figure 7.1 earlier in the chapter.)

NOTE

You can also create a new user by using the Administrative Wizard, or by starting User Manager for Domains and choosing User ➢ New User.

Using the New User dialog box, you can enter the basics to create a new user. Start with a unique user name. In many cases, Username will differ from the next field–Full Name. Depending on corporate standards, the user name might be GGovanus and the full name might be Gary Govanus.

Description An optional field for location, title, or any indentifying information.

Password Can be up to 14 characters and is case sensitive. You can force the new user to change the password at the next logon.

TIP

Some applications or services require a special account to start the service. If this is the case, enable the checkboxes for User Cannot Change Password and Password Never Expires.

Account Disabled Disables the user account. If you want an account to be available when a user returns from a short leave, you can disable the account. The account will be inactive until the user returns from leave. This is also a good way to store user accounts that may be set up as templates without them being illegally used.

Groups button Gives the administrator the ability to add users to global and/or local groups.

Profile button Activates the User Environment Profile screen, specifying where the user profile is stored, the name of the login script, and where the user's home directory is located. (See Figure 7.2 earlier in the chapter.)

Hours button You can force your users off your network by setting the hours during which they can access the network.

TIP

Using the Hours button is an especially handy trick when you are trying to get a clean backup with as few open files as possible.

Logon To button Specifies which workstations a user may log onto. The default is All. If this is selected, a maximum of eight workstations can be assigned.

Account button Allows you to expire an account and specify the account type. The account types are Global Account for a regular user in the domain and Local Account for a user from an untrusted domain. (See Figure 7.1 earlier in the chapter.)

Dialin button Allows the user to access the server using remote access service (RAS).

NOTE

Remote access service will be discussed further in Chapter 8.

Creating a User Template

One of the ways to create a large number of users with the same requirements is to create a user template or model user. The user template is configured exactly the way you want your new users configured, except this account has the Account Disabled field enabled. When it is time to create the new account, you simply copy the model and provide the information necessary to make the account unique.

The fields that can be copied include: Description, Groups, Profiles, Hours, Logon To, Account, and Dialin.

The mandatory fields include: Username and Full Name, The Account Disabled checkbox is always cleared when an account is created by copying a template. The User Must Change Password at Next Logon checkbox is set.

To create and use a template:

1. If you are logged on as an administrator, go into User Manager for Domains and create a model user with all the properties that will be the defaults for the new group of users. Be sure to select the Account Disabled checkbox. Consider using an account name that represents the fact that this account is a template, such as Finance Template. Add the user.
2. Highlight the user you have just created and press F8 to copy the user. Notice that the Username and Full Name fields are blank, and that the Account Disabled checkbox has been cleared.

Deleting User Accounts

To delete a user account:

1. Log on as an administrator.
2. Start User Manager for Domains.
3. Select the user account to be deleted.
4. Either choose User and Delete or simply press the delete key.
5. Agree to the screen asking if you really want to delete the user.
6. Choose Yes to actually delete the user.
7. Close User Manager for Domains.

Renaming Users

When you change the name of the account, nothing else about the account changes. To change the user name of an account:

1. Log on as an administrator or a similar superior being.
2. Start User Manager for Domains.
3. Select the user to be renamed from the User account list.
4. Choose User ➢ Rename.
5. Change the Username and click OK.

Create and manage policies and profiles for various situations.

Policies and profiles include:

- Local user profiles
- Roaming user profiles
- System policies

NT provides you with tools called policies and profiles that allow you to maintain some semblance of order and control over the workstations on your network. As you can see from the objective, there are local user profiles, roaming user profiles, and system policies–which entail control over the local user, control over the user who roams from system to system, and control over hardware profiles.

Local User Profiles

Local user profiles store information on how a user has configured their computing environment. This isn't really flashy stuff; it is more everyday information such as:

- Have you ever wondered where the information is stored that lets 32-bit applications know the last few documents you accessed? It's in the profile.
- How does the computer know to reattach all those connections to all those shares and printers? It's in the profile.

- How does the computer remember where you put all the bookmarks in Help? It's in the profile.

The subdirectory on every Windows NT machine that contains the user profile information is \WINNT\Profiles. Under that folder, there is a subfolder named for each user. Those subfolders contain a file called NTUSER.DAT. This file contains all the registry entries. There are also folders for Application Data, the Desktop, Favorites, Personal, Start Menu, and other information that pertains to a specific user.

When a user logs onto a system for the first time, the system knows there is no local user profile, so it goes out to the network to look for a roaming user profile. If there is no roaming user profile, NT creates a local user profile subdirectory for the user in the \WINNT\Profiles directory. NT then needs to provide the user with some of the basics, so it gets the information from the \WINNT\Profiles\Default user directory.

At this point, the user has the default profile settings. Any changes that the user makes will be stored in the local user profile for the new user. The next time the user logs onto the local machine, the user is presented with the system just the way it was left.

To keep a user from being able to change the desktop, configure the system the way you want it for the tech-weenie-wannabe and save the settings by logging out. Go back into the system as another user and change the name of the NTUSER.DAT file to NTUSER.MAN. When you add that little extension—.MAN—it changes the file to a mandatory profile. The user can change the desktop in a variety of fashions, but none of the changes will be retained.

Roaming User Profiles

With a roaming user profile, a profile is created and centrally stored. When a user logs onto a workstation on the network, the workstation checks for a roaming user profile, finds it, and the desktop looks just the same, no matter where the user logs on from.

If there is a local user profile and a roaming user profile, and the local one is more recent, then NT will ask which profile you want to use. When the user logs off, the new profile is saved (if it is not mandatory or the user has not logged on as guest), and any changes that have been made are saved for posterity.

TIP

The path to the roaming user profile is specified using User Manager for Domains.

System Policies

System policies are created with the System Policy Editor. Using system policies, you will be able to maintain both machine configurations and user policies from one machine. The System Policy Editor operates in either Registry mode or System Policy mode. Since the objective mentions system policies rather than Registry mode, apparently the exam writers think system policies are more significant.

Registry mode allows you to edit all sorts of interesting things. Take a look at Figure 7.6.

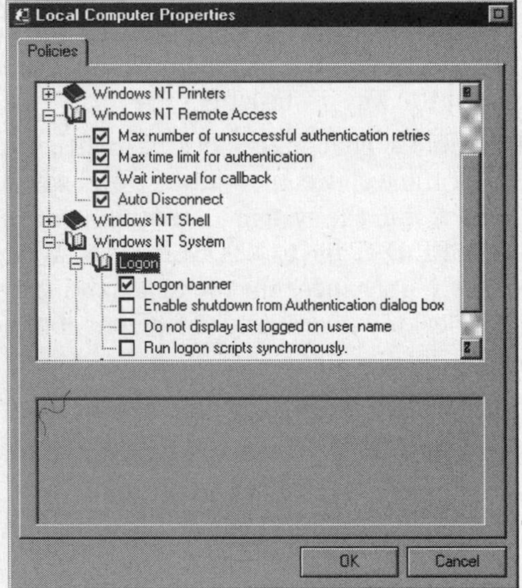

FIGURE 7.6: Local Computer Properties

Several things jump out at you while looking at this screen:

- You can specify which applications to run at startup.
- You can create hidden drive shares for workstations or servers.

- From the Windows NT Remote Access section, you can set the maximum number of unsuccessful authentication attempts and for the system to automatically disconnect.
- From the Windows NT System\Logon section, you can specify a specific logon banner or make sure the name of the last user who logged on is not displayed.

System Policy vs. Registry Mode

System Policy mode is like Registry mode, but with an *attitude*. If there is a setting in the registry and a system policy conflicts with the registry, the system policy takes precedence. You can find the system policy file. For NT systems, the file is named NTCONFIG.POL. Suppose you want to impose a set of restrictions on machines that the user cannot change. How is that accomplished?

Use the System Policy Editor to make the changes you want replicated across the network. Save the file as NTCONFIG.POL in the \WINNT\System32\Repl\Import\Scripts folder on the boot partition of the domain controllers.

When a computer attempts to log onto the network, it will check for the system policy. When the computer finds the NTCONFIG.POL file that affects the user or the computer, it brings this information into the registry and configures the workstation accordingly.

NOTE

If the changes are made in System Policy mode rather than Registry mode, the changes will overwrite the local registry.

Creating and Changing Profiles

The previous section examined the different types of profiles, but did not address how to create or change the settings. For a local user profile, there is not much to do, because it is automatically created and administered by NT. The configuration and dissemination of the roaming user profile are more challenging.

Creating a Local User Profile and a Mandatory User Profile

Local user profiles are created when the user logs on and makes changes to the computer. When the user logs off, these changes are saved in the file \WINNT\Profiles\UserName\NTUSER.DAT. To change this profile to a mandatory profile, change the extension from .DAT to .MAN. This changes the file to read only. Remember that with a mandatory user profile, if the NT domain controllers fail, the user will not be able to log onto the domain.

Creating a Roaming User Profile

Roaming user profiles are created from User Manager for Domains, which is accessed as follows:

1. Choose Programs ➢ Administrative Tools ➢ User Manager for Domains.
2. Double-click Administrator.
3. Select Profile. (See Figure 7.2 earlier in the chapter.)
4. In the User Profile Path, enter a universal naming convention (UNC) path to the \WINNT\Profiles directory. The syntax for a UNC path is *Servername**Foldername**Subfoldername*\WINNT\Profiles.
5. Close the User Enivironment Profile box by clicking OK.
6. Close the User window by clicking OK.
7. Close User Manager for Domains.

You may think nothing has changed. However, go to a different machine and log on as administrator. Your new profile will follow you.

Copying a User Profile to Make It a Remote User Profile

Create a central repository for user profiles on a server attached to the network, such as *Servername**Profile**Username*, and share the directory. Then, do as follows:

1. Start Control Panel.
2. Double-click System.
3. Choose the User Profiles tab.

4. Select the profile for the user you want to copy and click Copy To. You will be prompted to enter a path to the location of the share: *Server Name**Profile**Username*.
5. Under Permitted to Use, make sure the appropriate user name is selected.

Creating and Implementing a System Policy

There are many ways and reasons to set system policies. In this example, a system policy will be created to ensure that the name of the last user to log onto a system is not displayed. This policy will be replicated throughout the network to all NT systems.

Log on as administrator and do as follows:

1. Choose Programs ➢ Administrative Tools ➢ System Policy Editor.
2. Choose File ➢ New Policy.
3. Click Default Computer.
4. Click Windows NT System.
5. Click Logon.
6. Check the box next to Do Not Display Last Logged On User Name.
7. Select OK.
8. Choose Save As and save the file as NTCONFIG.POL on the domain controller in the \WINNT\System32\REPL\Import\Scripts folder.

Administer remote servers from various types of client computers.

Client computer types include:

- Windows 95
- Window NT Workstation

It is much more convenient to be able to perform routine tasks, such as checking the event log or starting User Manager for Domains, directly from your desktop workstation. If your desktop workstation is running Windows 95 or Windows NT Workstation, your system can access the tools necessary to administer a network remotely. When Microsoft designed the remote administration tools, it considered the usual administration mindset. If you can run Windows NT Workstation, you will have more flexibility than if you have a Windows 95 computer.

Windows 95

If your workstation is running Windows 95, has an extra 3MB of disk space, and runs the Client for Microsoft networks, you can configure the system to access the following items:

Event Viewer Viewer used to view the system log.

Server Manager Powerful utility that allows you to monitor and manage all aspects of your network, including active users, shares, replications, alerts, and services.

User Manager for Domains Utility that allows you to create and manage users and groups. This utility allows the administrator to set account policies, user rights, and audit accounts, as well as manage trust relationships with other domains.

File Security The ability to set rights and permissions for files.

Print Security The ability to set rights and permissions for various print objects.

You can also configure some utilities to help you manage NetWare services.

NOTE

The system must be at least a 486DX/33.

Windows NT Workstation

If, on the other hand, your workstation is running Windows NT Workstation and is a 486DX/33 with at least 2.5MB of disk space, you can access the following items:

DHCP Manager Gives you the ability to configure a dynamic host control protocol (DHCP) manager on a network segment. A DHCP host will pass out IP addresses to workstations on the network segment.

Remote Access Administrator Utility that allows you to administer RAS connections to the system.

Remote Boot Manager Utility for the administration of images for diskless workstations.

Services for Macintosh Administration tools for the Macintosh environment.

Server Manager Powerful utility that allows you to manage all aspects of your network, including users, shares, replications, alerts, and services.

System Policy Editor Utility that allows you to edit system policies. In Registry mode, you can edit any computer on the network.

User Manager for Domains Utility that allows you to create and manage user and group accounts.

WINS Manager Utility that allows you to manage Windows Internet name service (WINS). WINS is the Microsoft method of resolving Internet protocol (IP) addresses to Microsoft networking names.

Copying Client-Based Administration Tools

Installing client-based administration tools is a two-step process. First, you prepare the server. Second, you install the tools on the workstation.

1. Start Network Client Administrator by selecting Start ➢ Programs ➢ Administrative Tools ➢ Network Client Administration.

2. Select the Copy Client-based Network Administration Tools radio button and click OK.

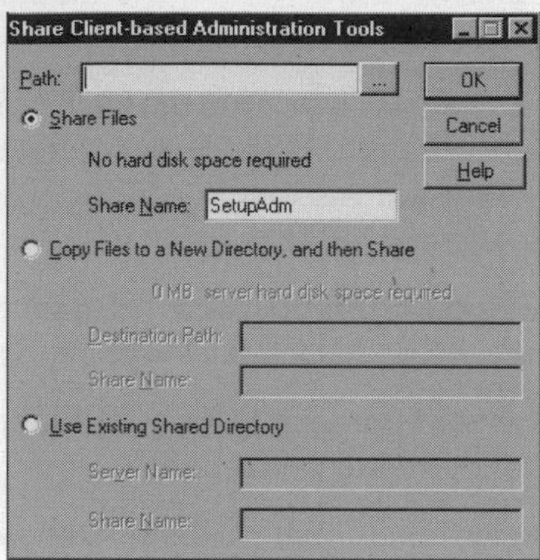

3. You can share files by providing a path name to the files, you can copy files to a new directory and then share, or you can use an existing shared directory. At the top of the dialog box, enter the path to the NT installation CD. Then, select the second option. You are given a destination path of C:\Clients\Srvtools by default and a share name of SetupAdm. At this point, the files will be copied and the share will be created automatically.

Now that the share has been created, you can go back to your workstation and use NT Explorer to attach to the share you have just created. Once you have attached to the share, go into the \WINNT folder and execute SETUP.BAT by highlighting the filename and double-clicking it. When the installation is finished, the remote tools will be available.

Manage disk resources.

Tasks include:

- Copying and moving files between file systems
- Creating and sharing resources
- Implementing permissions and security
- Establishing file auditing

This objective starts out with a discussion of the effects on a file when that file is moved or copied from one file system to another. You know from the discussion of file systems in Chapter 5 that the NT file system (NTFS) has some capabilities that plain, old FAT doesn't have, such as local directory- and file-level security and compression. If you can copy or move a file from one drive to another, you must be able to access that file. Access to a file is provided through a combination of things, but foremost is the ability to find the location of that file. Users access remote files, directories, or entire drives through share points, which the administrator creates.

Once the user has access to an area using a share point, some restrictions may need to be placed on what a user can do in a particular share. This is where folder- and file-level security come into play. NT has several levels of share access security. In addition, if the share is located on an NTFS partition, additional local security can be applied to the folder or file. Each of these levels of security is applied in a specific order with predictable results.

NOTE

For a complete discussion of the differences between NTFS and FAT, see the section in Chapter 5 on file systems. The current section will assume that you understand the differences between the two file systems.

Copying and Moving Files between File Systems

NTFS offers several advantages over the FAT file system. Security, obviously, is one of the biggest advantages. Another advantage that NT offers is the ability to maximize your investment in disk subsystems by implementing file compression. The level of compression may not be as extreme as in programs such as Stacker or even DOS 6.22, but compression is still available—every little bit helps.

Compression and local-level security are only available on NTFS partitions. You made the call on whether to use NTFS or FAT back in Chapter 6 when you installed the operating system. If you chose the FAT file system and now want to change to NTFS, you can do that. Conversion is a relatively painless process using the CONVERT.EXE command-line utility.

NOTE

Conversion works only from FAT to NTFS.

Copying a file, by definition, is creating a mirror image of that file. Moving a file, by definition, is picking that little sucker up and putting it somewhere else, and then deleting the original. This issue arises when you cross compression boundaries.

> Instance one: A file called C:\Data\Docs\RESUME.DOC is copied from an uncompressed partition to D:\Data\Docs\RESUME.DOC, which is on a compressed partition.
>
> Result one: The original RESUME.DOC maintains its attributes. It stays the same (uncompressed). The copy of RESUME.DOC takes on the attributes of the partition it is placed in, so in this case it becomes compressed.

This is common sense. The original stays the same, the new file takes on attributes of its new home. What about when a file is *moved* from one location to another? The same thing occurs. The file takes on the attributes of the new home.

> Instance two: RESUME.DOC is moved from a folder on an uncompressed partition to a folder on a compressed partition.
>
> Result two: The only copy of the document becomes compressed.

NTFS compression can be handled at the drive level, the directory level, and the file level. Once compression has been implemented, compression of new files happens automatically. It is a completely transparent process that the application or user will not see.

In general, if files are copied, they will inherit the attributes of their new homes. If files are moved, the attributes of the files will stay the same, unless the files are moved across partitions. In this case, the file takes the attributes of its new home.

Creating and Sharing Resources

In this case, sharing resources means sharing folders. Folders are shared so that other people on the network can use the information or applications in the folder. You create a share so users can put their stuff on your network, in the *Servername*\Users*Username* subfolder. You also put shares on the network so users can access the network version of Excel, from *Servername*\Apps\Excel. Another share might point to the *Servername*\Shared\Data\Budgets area.

Just because you have created a folder called Data with a subfolder called Budgets, it does not mean that anyone else can see the folders. On the contrary, nothing is visible by default. For users to see a directory, the administrator must make the concerted effort to share the directory.

The administrator can share any directory on the network if the administrator has been given the LIST permission. If a user on a remote computer has blocked the administrator from having the LIST permission, chances are the user does not want the information spread across the network, so the administrator cannot create a share.

Look closely at Figure 7.7. To access this dialog box, open My Computer, browse to the folder and highlight it, right-click, and choose Sharing. Once the Sharing tab is displayed, choose Shared As and enter the share name–in this case, Applications. You can also add a comment so users will know what the share is for. You will notice that you can set a limit of users who can hack away on this share. You can allow the Maximum Allowed for the server or set a number of users with which you feel comfortable.

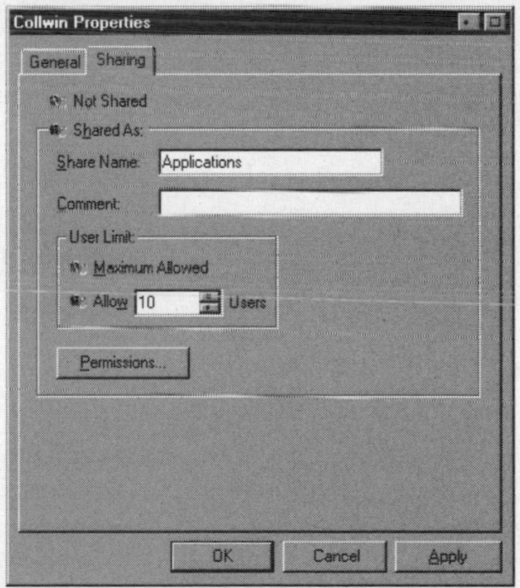

FIGURE 7.7: Sharing a drive using My Computer

Using NT Explorer or My Computer to create a share is not the only way of doing it–it is just one of the most convenient. You can also create a share using File Manager (if you still use File Manager). If you happen to work in Server Manager, you can also create a share while doing normal management tasks. For the GUI-challenged or those of us who still feel most comfortable at a command prompt, you can use the Net Share utility.

In addition to the shares that the administrator creates, if you are using an NT-based system that has a hard-coded access control list (ACL), you will find that there are at least two hidden shares. These hidden shares are the C$ share, which shares the root computer's C: drive, and the ADMIN$ share, which shares the root of the NT installation. These shares give administrators a path to the \WINNT directory or the operating system directory. Remember that a share name ending in *$* results in a hidden or nonvisible share.

Implementing Permissions and Security

Shares have been created. It is time to start thinking about what kinds of permissions you want to grant users or groups of users for each one of the shares. By default all shares are granted Full Control to the Everyone group. If the share you are looking at is a data directory, your users will need to be able to see the filenames, open the files, write to the files, and even delete the files. If the directory you are looking at is a folder that houses an application, your users may just need to read the filenames and execute the files.

Permissions are applied at various levels by various processes. For example, there is a share-level permission. If the share points to a folder on an NTFS partition, then local computer permissions can point to the folder or directory.

Share-Level Permissions

When you create a share using NT Explorer, you open NT Explorer, track to the folder you want to share, highlight the folder, and right-click. Click Share to open the Properties page for the folder. If you look closely at the Share tab of the Properties page, you will notice a button marked Permissions. Click the Permissions button to bring up the Access Through Share Permissions (or ATS permissions) screen (see Figure 7.8).

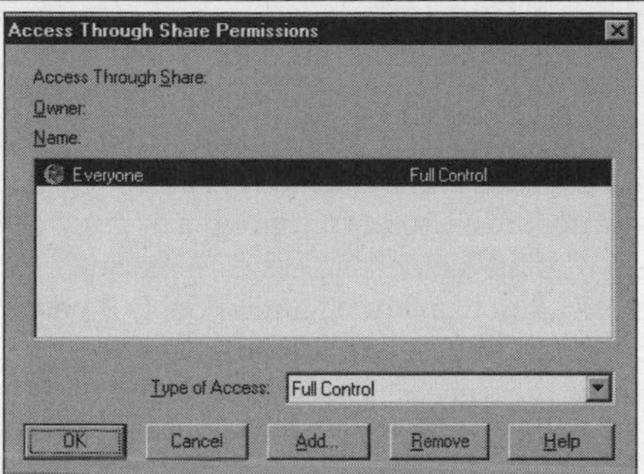

FIGURE 7.8: Access Through Share Permissions

By default, the ATS share allows the group Everyone to have Full Control access to the share. If you use the Type of Access drop-down menu, you will see four types of share permissions you can control: Full Control, Change, Read, and No Access.

These ATS share-level permissions grant the following rights:

Full Control The user can read or see a folder, subfolder, or file; execute an application; write to a closed file; and delete a folder or file. If the share resides on an NTFS partition, the user can also take ownership of the resource and change permissions.

Change The user can read or see a folder, subfolder, or file; execute an application; write to a closed file; and delete a folder or file.

Read The user can read and execute permissions to the share, folders, subfolders, and files.

No Access The user can connect to the share, but will not be able to access any resources.

Share permissions deal with shares, and shares can point to folders regardless of the file system on which the folder resides. So, you can have a share that points to a folder on a FAT file system partition. If the share is on a FAT partition, once you assign the ATS permissions to the share, you are done. If there is a subfolder or file that needs more or less restrictive access, you are out of luck. Folder level is as deep as security gets on a FAT partition. If deeper security is necessary, the folder or file should reside on a drive that is based in NTFS.

If the share resides on an NTFS partition, another set of permissions can be granted to the local file or folder. When determining what a user can really do, you must consider the share permissions granted to the share and the NTFS permissions granted to the folder or file. This is called the user's effective permissions to a folder. A user may get conflicting permissions from a variety of sources. One group may grant Full Access, another group may grant Limited Access, and the end user may have been given No Access as an individual permission. Is it possible to sort it all out? Yes, if share and NTFS permissions are applied, the most restrictive permissions take precedence. This is especially true of the No Access permission. If you have been given the No Access permission, either as an individual user or as a member of a group, you have no access, regardless of any other permissions you may have been assigned by other group memberships. You can attach to the share, but you cannot see anything.

To do anything, each permission is made up of one or more actions. There are six basic actions, four of which apply to both share and NTFS permissions:

Read (R) Users can read or see a file. Usually used in conjunction with Execute.

Write (W) Users can add data to a file.

Execute (X) Users can execute a file. Usually used in conjunction with Read.

Delete (D) Users can delete a file.

Change Permissions (P) NTFS permission–users can change the access level of other users on this file or folder. Granted as part of Full Control if the share is on an NTFS partition.

Take Ownership (O) NTFS partition–users can claim ownership of a file. Granted as part of Full Control if the share is on an NTFS partition.

Directory-Level Permissions

NTFS permissions are permissions granted to *local* files and directories on a host computer. These permissions can be granted by the owner of the directory. Separate permissions can be granted at the directory and file levels.

Directory-level permissions enable the following:

No Access Users cannot access the directory at all.

List Users cannot access the directory, but can see the c tents of the directory.

Read Users can read data files and execute application fil

Add Users cannot read any information from the directory even see the files that are stored in the directory, but they car add data to the directory.

Add and Read Users can see information in the directory and add information (new files) to the directory. Users cannot modify existing files in the directory.

Change Users can see files in the directory, add files to the directory, modify files within the directory, and delete files from the directory (or even delete the whole directory). Users can also change the attributes of the directory.

Full Control Users can do everything they can do with Change, but they can also make changes to resources they do not own.

Permissions given to a directory flow down into the directory. If you have given the group EXCEL_Users the Read permission to the folder D:\Applications\Excel, a member of that group can execute the file EXCEL.EXE.

File-Level Permissions

There are times when security needs to be taken one step further, down to the individual file level. When you make the change to just one file, all the other files are not affected.

File-level permissions enable the following:

No Access Users cannot access the file at all.

Read Users can read a data file or execute it if it is an application file.

Change Users can read, execute, modify, or delete the file.

Full Control Users can read, execute, write to, or delete the file, as well as change permissions or take ownership away from the owner of the file.

To set NTFS permissions for a folder or file, highlight the folder or file, right-click, and select Properties. From the Properties page, select the Security tab and then choose Permissions.

Establishing File Auditing

One way to check the security of ultra-sensitive documents or folders is to enable auditing. Auditing will not allow you to choose which folders, subfolders, and files you want to audit, but it will provide you with a way of determining who is accessing the files.

You can audit the success or failure of the following actions by any user or group of users: Read, Write, Execute, Delete, Change Permission, and Take Ownership. After you enable auditing, the results of the audit are written to the event log.

Performing Disk Management Tasks

Converting a Drive from FAT to NTFS

There is a one-time-only conversion of drive partitions from FAT to NTFS. This is done using a command line, CONVERT.EXE. To convert a partition:

1. Log on as administrator.
2. Select Start ➢ Programs ➢ Command Prompt.
3. The convert syntax is shown below. To convert the D: drive from FAT to NTFS, the command-line syntax would be as follows:

```
CONVERT D: /FS:NTFS
```

NOTE

You can access the following information by going to the command prompt and typing Convert /?.

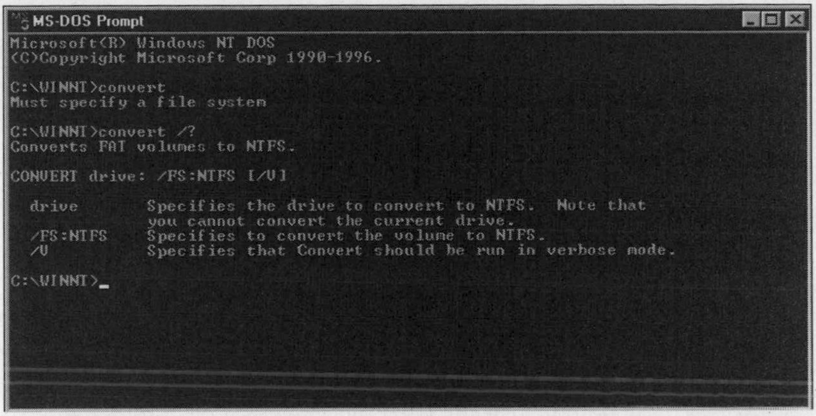

```
MS-DOS Prompt
Microsoft(R) Windows NT DOS
(C)Copyright Microsoft Corp 1990-1996.

C:\WINNT>convert
Must specify a file system

C:\WINNT>convert /?
Converts FAT volumes to NTFS.

CONVERT drive: /FS:NTFS [/V]

  drive       Specifies the drive to convert to NTFS.  Note that
              you cannot convert the current drive.
  /FS:NTFS    Specifies to convert the volume to NTFS.
  /V          Specifies that Convert should be run in verbose mode.

C:\WINNT>_
```

4. The /V parameter can be used if you want to use Verbose mode. Verbose mode can be output to a file so that you can keep a record of what the utility accomplished. The syntax for that would be as follows:

   ```
   CONVERT D: /FS:NTFS /V > FILENAME.TXT
   ```


Compressing a File, Folder, or Drive

You can set compression at the file level, the folder level, or the drive level. There are several ways to accomplish compression. This section will demonstrate the use of NT Explorer and the command-line utility COMPACT.EXE.

To compress a file or multiple files using NT Explorer:

1. Open NT Explorer and locate the files to be compressed.
2. Highlight the files to be compressed. You can select multiple files by using the Shift+click or Ctrl+click method. Shift+click allows you to select multiple individual files; Ctrl+click allows you to select a block of files.
3. Right-click to bring up the Properties page.
4. Enable the Compressed checkbox.
5. Click OK.

To compress a folder or multiple folders using NT Explorer:

1. Open NT Explorer and locate the folders to be compressed.

2. Highlight the folders to be compressed. You can select multiple folders by using the Shift+click or Ctrl+click method. Shift+click allows you to select multiple individual folders; Ctrl+click allows you to select a block of folders.
3. Right-click to bring up the Properties page.
4. Enable the Compressed checkbox.
5. Click OK.

When you compress a folder, all the files in that folder take the compressed attribute. Subfolders will *not* be compressed unless you enable the Also Compress Subfolders checkbox on the NT Explorer warning screen. You will receive the warning screen for each folder you select.

To compress a drive or multiple drives using NT Explorer:

1. Open NT Explorer and locate the drive to be compressed.
2. Highlight the drive to be compressed. You can select multiple drives by using the Shift+click or Ctrl+click method. Shift+click allows you to select multiple individual drives; Ctrl+click allows you to select blocks of drives.
3. Right-click to bring up the Properties page.
4. Enable the Compress *Drive Letter*:\ checkbox.
5. Click OK.

When you compress a drive, all the files in the root folder take the compressed attribute. Subfolders will *not* be compressed unless you enable the Also Compress Subfolders checkbox on the NT Explorer warning screen. In this case, you are not prompted for each subfolder.

NOTE

If a folder, subfolder, or drive is compressed, files that are created in these areas in the future will be compressed.

TIP

You can uncompress drives, folders, subfolders, and files by using NT Explorer to highlight the appropriate selections, right-clicking, and clearing the Compressed checkbox.

To use COMPACT.EXE:

1. Open a command prompt by selecting Start ➢ Programs ➢ Command Prompt.
2. The syntax for COMPACT.EXE is as follows:

```
COMPACT [/C : /U] [/S[:DIR]] [/A] [/I][/F][/Q][FILENAME]
```

The following COMPACT.EXE command-line switches perform these functions:

/C Compresses

/U Uncompresses

/S Compresses an entire subfolder tree. [:DIR] allows you to specify the subfolders to compress (if it is not the current folder).

/A Compresses hidden and system files. The only file that cannot be compressed is the NTLDR hidden system file.

/I Ignores error messages and keeps compressing

/F Forces compression

/Q Quiet mode

filelist Lists individual files to be compressed, separated by a space

Part II

Creating a Share

There are several ways to create a share—by using NT Explorer, My Computer, Server Manager, or the Net Share utility.

To create a share using NT Explorer:

1. Open NT Explorer.
2. Open directories until you locate the folder that you want to share.
3. Highlight the directory name and right-click.
4. Select Sharing from the drop-down menu. This will open the Sharing tab of the Properties dialog box.
5. When you reach the Sharing tab, you will notice that the default share name is the name of the directory. Some users

are not excited about having a share name such as APPS_EXCEL. So, you can enter a new name for the share–one that is more user friendly. When you change the name of the share, it does not change the name of the directory–it just presents users with a name that makes sense to real people rather than computer people.

There is an opportunity to change the path, but if you have to do that, why did you choose this folder in the first place?

You will notice there is also a spot for comments. Comments are optional, and be careful, because what you enter will show up next to the share in NT Explorer.

To create a share using My Computer:

1. Open My Computer.
2. Click the drive letter on which the target folder resides.
3. Open directories until you locate the folder that you want to share.
4. Highlight the directory name and right-click.
5. Select Sharing from the drop-down menu. This will open the Sharing tab of the Properties dialog box.
6. When you reach the Sharing tab, you will notice that the default for the directory is Not Shared. Click the Shared As radio button. The usual share name is the name of the directory. Some users are not excited about having a share name such as APPS_EXCEL. So, you can enter a new name for the share that is more user friendly. When you change the name of the share, it does not change the name of the directory–it just presents users with a more user-friendly name.

To create a share using Server Manager:

1. Log on to the computer as administrator.
2. Start Server Manager by choosing Start ➢ Programs ➢ Administration Tools ➢ Server Manager.
3. Highlight the server name.
4. Choose Computer from the top menu; then select Shared Directories.

5. In the Shared Directory menu, click New Share.
6. Fill in the information on the New Share page, including Share Name, Path, and a comment.
7. Finally, you can add the maximum number of users allowed or choose to allow a specific number of users.

Net Share is a command-line utility. As such, you start the process by opening a command prompt. To create a share using Net Share, choose Start ➢ Programs ➢ Command Prompt. The syntax for the Net Share utility is shown below.

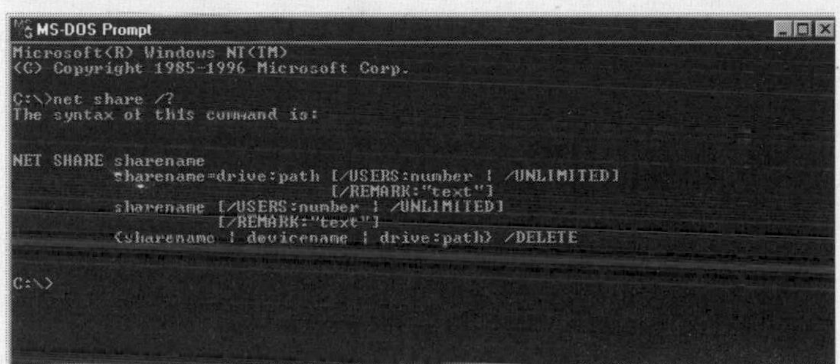

As an example, suppose you need a temporary share to point to D:\Applications\Excel. You want to call the share Excel and allow 10 users to access the share.

From the command prompt, the syntax would be as follows:

```
Net Share Excel=d:\applications\excel /users:10
```

To delete the share, the syntax would be as follows:

```
Net Share Excel /delete
```

Setting Share Permissions

You can set share permissions only on network shares. ATS permissions are usually assigned to a group, rather than an individual.

NOTE

There are several ways of accessing the Properties page for a share, folder, or file. In the examples that follow, NT Explorer is the utility of choice.

To set ATS permissions:

1. Log onto the network as administrator or a user with Full Control over the share.
2. Start NT Explorer by selecting Start ➢ Programs ➢ Windows NT Explorer.
3. Browse to the share where the permissions will be applied. Highlight the share and right-click.
4. Click Sharing.
5. Click Permissions.
6. With the Access Through Share Permissions screen showing, click Add, which brings up the Add Users and Groups window.
7. Select the group that will receive the permissions, highlight the group, and click Add.
8. In the lower half of the Add Users and Groups window, use the Type of Access drop-down menu to choose No Access, Read, Change, or Full Access.
9. Click the appropriate choice. This will bring you back to the Add Users and Groups window.
10. Click OK to return to the ATS Permissions screen.
11. Click OK to return to the share's Properties window.
12. Click OK to return to NT Explorer.

Setting NTFS Folder- and File-Level Permissions

To set lower-level (folder or file) permissions, you must use NTFS permissions. NTFS permissions are not available for FAT partitions.

NOTE

NTFS permissions are usually assigned to a group, rather than an individual.

To set NTFS permissions:

1. Log onto the network as someone who has ownership over the folder or file.

2. Start NT Explorer by selecting Start ➢ Programs ➢ Windows NT Explorer.
3. Browse to the folder or file where the permissions will be applied. Highlight the folder or file and right-click.
4. Click Sharing.
5. Click Security.
6. Click Permissions. This brings up the Directory Permissions window.
7. With the Directory Permissions window showing, click Add, which brings up the Add Users and Groups window.
8. Select the group or user that will receive the permissions, highlight the group or user, and click Add.
9. In the lower half of the Add Users and Groups window, use the Type of Access drop-down menu to choose No Access, List, Read, Add, Add and Read, Change, or Full Access.
10. Click the appropriate choice. This will bring you back to the Add Users and Groups window.
11. Click OK to return to the Directory Permissions window.
12. At the top of the Directory Permissions window, there are two radio buttons.
    - If you select Replace Permissions on Subdirectories, it will push the changes down to any subdirectories.
    - If you select Replace Permissions on Existing Files, it will push the changes down to any files.
13. Click OK to return to the folder's Security tab.
14. Click OK to return to NT Explorer.

Establishing File Auditing

Before you can configure auditing, you must turn it on. Auditing is turned off by default. To enable auditing:

1. Start User Manager for Domains by selecting Start ➢ Programs ➢ Administrative Tools ➢ User Manager for Domains.
2. Click Policies.

3. Click Audit.
4. Select the Audit These Events button.
5. Enable the checkboxes for the events you want to audit. Your choices involve the success or failure of the following items:
   - Logon and logoff
   - File and object access
   - Use of user rights
   - User and group management
   - Security policy changes
   - Restart, shutdown, and system
   - Process tracking
6. Click OK. Auditing is now enabled for the domain.

To start auditing activities of a specific folder or file, access the Auditing tab by choosing Properties ➢ Security ➢ Auditing. To select auditing:

1. Log on as an administrator or equivalent user.
2. Start NT Explorer by selecting Start ➢ Programs ➢ Windows NT Explorer.
3. Browse to the folder or file you want to audit. Highlight the folder or file and right-click.
4. Select Properties.
5. Click the Security tab.
6. Click Auditing.
7. At the top of the Directory Auditing window, you can select Replace Auditing on Subdirectories or Replace Auditing on Existing Files.
   - Replace Auditing on Subdirectories will start the audit process for all current and new subfolders.
   - Replace Auditing on Existing Files will start the audit process for all current and new files.
8. Click Add.

9. Select the users or groups you want to audit. Click Add after each selection.
10. When the selection of users and groups is complete, click OK.
11. Enable the appropriate checkboxes for the actions you want to audit.
12. After you have selected the actions to audit, click OK to begin auditing.

Auditing writes the information to the event log. This is a processor-intensive task and should be undertaken with great care.

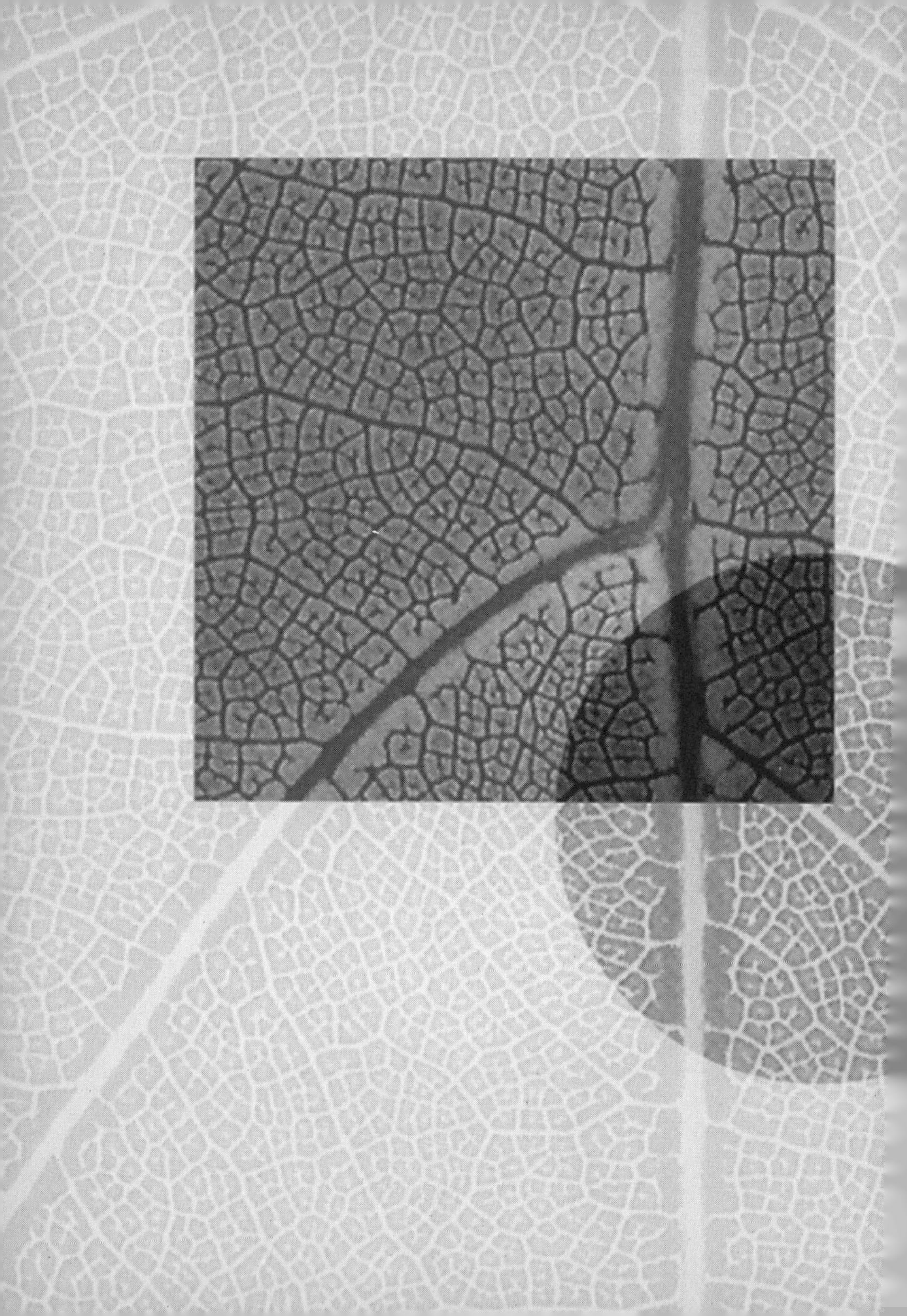

Chapter 8

Connectivity

Given the state of many networks, one of the most important criteria for new systems is interoperability. When you add to this the ability to grow with technology, you have only a handful of potential operating systems worthy of consideration. Microsoft Windows NT has a few design features that make it the perfect choice for today's networks. One of these features is NT's modular design. Every function that an NT server can perform is designed as a separate subsystem of the operating system. This modular design means that NT can be updated to meet the needs of future technologies. It also means that third-party developers can add functionality to the base operating system.

Adapted from *MCSE Exam Notes: NT Server 4* by Gary Govanus and Robert King

ISBN 0-7821-2289-2 360 pages $19.99

Configure Windows NT Server for interoperability with NetWare servers by using various tools.

Tools include:

- Gateway Service for NetWare
- Migration Tool for NetWare

One of the features of Windows NT is its ability to coexist with a NetWare environment. This means companies can ease into an NT network, while maintaining the NetWare services that they currently use. Because of the number of Novell networks in existence, Microsoft tests heavily on the skills necessary to add an NT server to a Novell NetWare environment. You will find NetWare-related questions on many of the MCSE examinations.

Gateway Service for NetWare

There are two ways to configure your network so that your clients can access NetWare servers:

- Install Client Service for NetWare (CSNW) on each NT workstation that might need to access a NetWare server.
- Install Gateway Service for NetWare (GSNW) on an NT server and use it as a gateway to the NetWare environment.

CSNW is not listed in the exam objectives, but you should know what it is and when to use it. CNSW is software loaded on the *client* computers. This software allows them to directly connect to and communicate with NetWare servers. (The clients will also have to have the NWLink IPX/SPX-compatible network protocol installed and configured as one of their protocols.) CSNW should be used if your clients extensively use the NetWare servers or if you have a lot of users who will use the NetWare servers simultaneously.

Another option is to install GSNW on an NT server. GSNW acts as a gateway to the NetWare environment. When clients need to access services on a NetWare server, they send the request to the GSNW service on the NT server. It, in turn, passes the request to the NetWare server. GSNW offers two benefits to the network administrator. First, only one computer (the NT server) has to have special software installed (GSNW). Second, the gateway server is the only computer that has to have NWLink installed and configured. Anytime you can bring management of a service to your server, rather than your workstations, you save time and effort. In addition, the GSNW connection uses only one NetWare connection regardless of the number of clients connected through it, while each CSNW connection uses an individual, which can be limited by the number of access licenses held.

The downside to this configuration is that all of your clients that need to access NetWare services must share this one connection. If you have a large number of users or your users access the NetWare server continuously, you will get better performance by using CSNW on your clients.

When configuring GSNW, you need to configure the NT side and the NetWare side. On the NetWare side, you must:

1. Create a user account with the same name and password configuration as on the gateway account on the NT server.
2. Assign to the NetWare user account created in step 1 all necessary trustee rights to NetWare network resources.
3. Create a group account named NTGATEWAY.
4. Make the user (from step 1) a member of this group.

WARNING

Since all users share this one account to access the NetWare server, the account must include all permissions that any GSNW user might need. This might be a security issue in your environment.

Migration Tool for NetWare

There are many reasons to migrate from a NetWare to an NT environment. Whatever the reason, Microsoft has provided a tool to make the migration process smooth and painless. The Migration Tool for NetWare (MTFN) can be found on your NT server in the *Windows root*\System32 directory. The executable file named NWCONV.EXE. MTFN allows you to easily transfer information from a NetWare server to an NT server. MTFN performs the following tasks:

- Preserves user account information, including logon and station restrictions.
- Preserves user login scripts. Microsoft Windows NT supports network login script commands.
- Offers control over how user and group names are transferred.
- Offers control over passwords on the transferred accounts. NT cannot read network passwords, so all passwords must change.
- Offers control over how account restrictions are transferred.
- Offers control over how administrative privileges are transferred.
- Creates a volume for network users.
- Selects which files and directories to transfer.
- Selects the directories to which transferred files will be copied.
- Preserves effective rights on files and directories (only if copied to an NTFS volume).

This tool transfers user information and data from one server (NetWare) to another (NT), but it does not upgrade an existing NetWare server to Windows NT. This is actually the best form of migration. If, at any time, you are not happy with the results, you can reformat the new NT server to get back to where you started.

TIP

If you are migrating multiple NetWare servers, you do not have to replace each computer. Migrate each one in turn, testing the results before moving on. After you have confirmed that the migration was successful, you can take down the NetWare server. At this point, if the hardware supports NT, you have the computer for your next NT server.

Configuring Gateway Service for NetWare

GSNW is installed like any other NT service. In the Services tab of NT Server's Network applet, click Add. There are no configuration options during the installation, but as in all network service changes, you will be asked to restart your server. After this restart, you will be presented with a window that asks for your preferred NetWare server or Tree and Context. The former is used in bindery-based NetWare 3.*x* environments, the latter in NetWare 4.*x* NDS (Novell directory service) environments.

1. In Control Panel, you will find a new applet, GSNW, which is used to manage your NetWare gateway. The opening screen of GSNW allows you to change the default server, set some default print parameters, and determine whether clients should run a login script when they connect to the NetWare server.

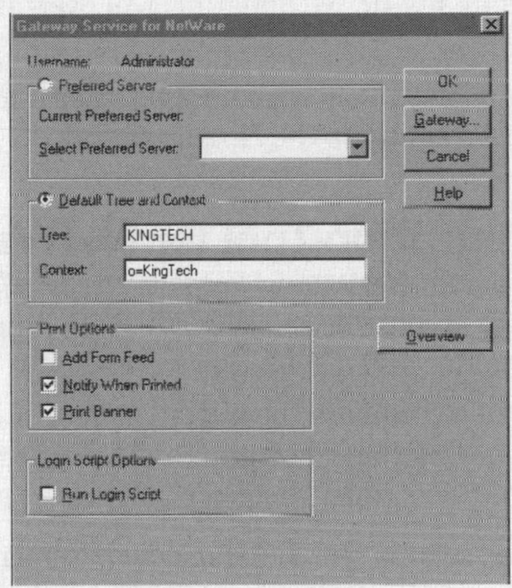

2. Click the Gateway button. Enable the gateway and enter the NetWare gateway account and password defined earlier.

3. You are ready to allow your clients access to resources on the NetWare server. Create shares that point to those resources. In the Configure Gateway dialog box, click Add to get the New Share dialog box.

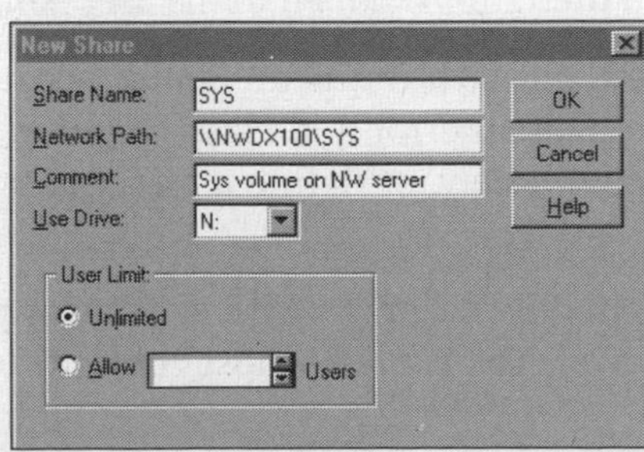

4. Give the share a name and define the UNC path to the resource. Define the mapped drive letter if desired. You can also limit the number of users that can simultaneously access the resource, although the default is Unlimited.
5. Once the share is configured, you can set permissions like on any NT share. Click the Permissions button in the Configure Gateway dialog box.

Remember that the Novell permissions set on the gateway account, which are more restrictive in nature, will overrule any permissions you set here.

From the client, the new share appears as if it is located on the NT server, which is acting as the Novell gateway.

Using Migration Tool for NetWare

Migration Tool for NetWare is found in the *Windows root*\System32 directory. The executable is NWCONV.EXE. When you run it, it will ask you for the source and destination servers.

You can then configure the migration itself. Click the User Options button in the next dialog box and configure the migration parameters for user and group accounts. You can configure:

- How passwords should be handled. Remember that NT cannot read the NetWare password. You have three options: Users will have no password, password will be the same as the user name, or users will have a default password. You can also force users to change their new password the first time they log onto the NT domain.
- How Migration Tool should deal with duplicate user names. You have four options: Log an error but do nothing, ignore the problem and skip the user, overwrite the existing NT account, or define a prefix to be added to the user name.
- How to deal with duplicate group accounts. You have three options: Log an error and skip the group, ignore the duplicate group completely, or define a prefix to be added to the group name.
- How to handle accounts with supervisor privileges on the NetWare server. You can add those accounts to the domain admins

group. (By default, they do not inherit any administrative privileges in the NT domain.)

The next step is to configure the file transfer between the two servers. On the MTFN main screen, click the File Options button. Here, you can decide which files and directories should be transferred and where they should be copied. By default, everything is copied to the NT server–remember to change the default settings so that the Novell management directories are not copied (you won't need NetWare management tools on an NT server).

This utility has a great function that can save you hours of time and prevent a catastrophic failure–the ability to run a trial migration. The trial migration attempts the migration without actually transferring any information. This allows you to determine any problems you will run into and correct them before they occur. The trial migration creates a series of three log files:

LOGFILE.LOG Describes the setting you configured for the migration.

SUMMARY.LOG Summarizes the activity, reporting which servers were involved, how much disk space was required, how many user accounts were migrated, and how many files and directories were migrated.

ERROR.LOG This is probably the most useful log file during a trial migration. It lists areas where the utility encountered a problem. It lists duplicate user names, duplicate group names, etc. This provides you with a list of problems that you can correct before performing the actual migration.

Once you're ready to go, click the Migrate button. Remember that this process will take quite a bit longer than the trial migration and places a huge system load on the servers. Schedule this to be done during low usage times. This time, the files actually have to be copied from server to server.

Install and configure remote access service (RAS).

Configuration options include:

- Configuring RAS communications
- Configuring RAS protocols
- Configuring RAS security
- Configuring dial-up networking clients

RAS (remote access service) allows a workstation computer running NT to connect to remote systems using just the POTS (plain old telephone system). When the client connects, the workstation is treated just like any other client. The user can access the network, check e-mail, get documents, and do just about anything they would do from their desk, except that now they are using a laptop. The purpose of RAS is to allow for communications between a local host and hosts that operate from remote locations, utilizing just telephone lines. RAS can, however, be configured to work with ISDN and X.25 connections, as well as some WAN implementations such as asynchronous transfer mode (ATM).

Configuring RAS Communications

If you are going to configure a system to which your workstations can call in and get information, something should be there to answer the phone. In this case, it will be your NT server. In an earlier chapter, communication products that allow you up to 256 dial-up connections from a single multiport expansion modem card were mentioned. RAS will take advantage of systems like that, as well as just a plain old modem hooked up to a COM port.

The first question to ask yourself is, What is the main goal of this communication channel? In some cases, your main goal may be to provide dial-up service to all those sales people and executives out there traveling around the country. If your company is small, you may not have a lot of sales people or high-powered executives traveling all over the country selling your company's wares. You may, however, have a remote site that needs to communicate with the home office and doesn't need all the power of a T-1 line. In that case, an ISDN line may be just the ticket.

ISDN stands for Integrated Services Digital Network. ISDN is a faster, better version of what you normally think of as a modem connection. However, an ISDN does not use a modem. In fact, it is a purely digital data path from start to finish. It does require an adapter, which most people casually call a modem, but no modulation or demodulation actually occurs. A modem, on the other hand, requires an analog connection provided by the public switched telephone network (PSTN), generally referred to as the phone company.

NOTE

Anytime you want faster and better, that usually translates into *more expensive*. Costs vary on ISDN service around the world, but it is more expensive than a standard dial-up line.

Modems modulate and demodulate the signals between two computers, sending the signal over the phone line. Your computer speaks digital. The phone company speaks analog. A modem turns a digital signal into an analog signal on the sending end, and turns the same signal from analog to digital at the receiving end.

The key word in the definition of ISDN is digital. With ISDN, you are now using a phone line that speaks digital, so there is no translation necessary. The ISDN modem or router just sends digital signals over a line that understands how to deal with ones and zeros. You have a cleaner, faster communication link. If you are planning on connecting two sites, you may look at installing ISDN service. However, in some places, it may not even be available. In others, the cost may be prohibitive. In some areas, it may be just the solution you're looking for. When judging cost, keep in mind that ISDN service is like having two phone lines. Therefore, you would expect it to cost twice as much as a single phone line. Because there are two channels, you get twice the speed. Because it is digital, and analog modems rarely give you their rated speed, it is usually more than twice as fast.

If you are going to use the dial-up capabilities of the phone company, the phone line has to be dedicated to RAS communications. RAS is *very* selfish—it doesn't want to share. So, if your system is configured to dial out and notify you when the power goes out, or if you are running a fax-server solution using a modem and phone line, you need to add more hardware. RAS requires its own line with its own modem.

If you are installing an ISDN device, follow the manufacturer's directions. The ISDN device is slightly more challenging to install than a modem. Make sure you have somewhere to connect to (another ISDN connection) and make sure you have all the paperwork the phone company left for you when they installed the ISDN line. There are some interesting parameters that you will need to configure, such as SPIDs (service profile IDs). SPIDs identify which services the ISDN line is providing. The SPID looks like a normal 10-digit phone number, except that there are two of them.

Since RAS is a networking service, it is installed through the Network applet in Control Panel. It is just a matter of NT copying some files off the installation CD and linking the RAS with the modem or communication device you already have configured. Partway through the installation process, the system will begin asking you questions about protocols, which is a great segue into the next section of this objective.

Configuring RAS Protocols

RAS supports the big three protocols–TCP/IP, NWLink, and NetBEUI.

TDI

Transport driver interface is an interface specification to which all Windows NT transport protocols must be written so that they can be used by higher-level services such as RAS. In other words, you will read that all of the dial-up protocols must be TDI-compliant.

PPP and SLIP

The next two acronyms deal with communication-framing protocols–the set of rules that allows communication devices to negotiate how information will be framed or blocked as it is sent over the network. The two framing protocols that RAS can use are point-to-point protocol (PPP) and serial line Internet protocol (SLIP). Since SLIP is the granddaddy of framing protocols, it is just an implementation of Internet protocol (IP) over a serial line. Developed for use by UNIX computers, SLIP has been improved on and replaced by PPP. PPP is a data-link-layer transport that performs over point-to-point network connections such as serial or modem lines. PPP can negotiate with any TDI-compliant protocol used by both systems involved in the link and can automatically assign IP, domain name service (DNS), and gateway addresses when used with transmission control protocol/Internet protocol (TCP/IP).

When a dial-up client accesses a RAS server, it will use PPP as its network-layer protocol. Think of PPP as the Ethernet or token ring of the dial-up world. Once a modem is connected to a RAS server, it can support TCP/IP, NWLink, and/or NetBEUI. Each protocol can be bound to a modem, and a modem may have more than one protocol bound to it. Each of the three protocols have advantages and disadvantages, depending on the job you are configuring the system to do.

TCP/IP

TCP/IP is the standard protocol suite of the Internet. TCP/IP is a mature, stable, robust protocol suite that brings a lot to the table, including routing capabilities and the ability to handle less-than-perfect phone connections. However, while it is robust, it is not necessarily the fastest protocol out of the gate. RAS using TCP/IP will allow the administrator to configure whether the client computer can access just the RAS server or the entire NT network. In addition, the RAS server controls how the client receives its TCP/IP address.

NWLink

NWLink is an Internet packet exchange/sequenced packet exchange (IPX/SPX) wanna-be. It is fast and efficient, and works well with interconnecting NetWare clients and servers. If you have a mixed environment with NetWare servers and NT servers, you are probably already aware of the advantages of NWLink. If you configure your RAS to use the NWLink protocol, you will not have to add a second protocol to those dial-up clients. Like TCP/IP, NWLink can be configured to allow a RAS connection access only to the server or the entire network. You can also specify network-addressing and node-addressing selections through RAS protocol configurations.

NetBEUI

NetBEUI is an efficient, simple protocol that protects against overuse of the network bandwidth. If you don't need to use TCP/IP or NWLink, NetBEUI is the protocol of choice. NetBEUI configuration allows the administrator to determine only whether a user can access just the server or the entire network from the RAS connection.

Configuring RAS Security

RAS has some built-in security features. You can configure the RAS connection security using permissions, encrypted passwords, point-to-point tunneling protocol (PPTP), and call back. If you look at the Administrative Tools menu, you will see a new utility listed, Remote Access Admin.

Permissions

When a user dials in and authenticates to a RAS, permissions are the first line of defense for the network. If a user has been granted Remote Access Permission, the user can log onto the RAS server. Using the Remote Access Admin utility, RAS permissions can be granted to all users of the server, revoked for all users of the server, or granted to individual users. Notice that permissions cannot be granted to global groups or local groups. Basic RAS permissions can also be granted through the User Manager utility. The Remote Access Permissions screen is shown in Figure 8.1.

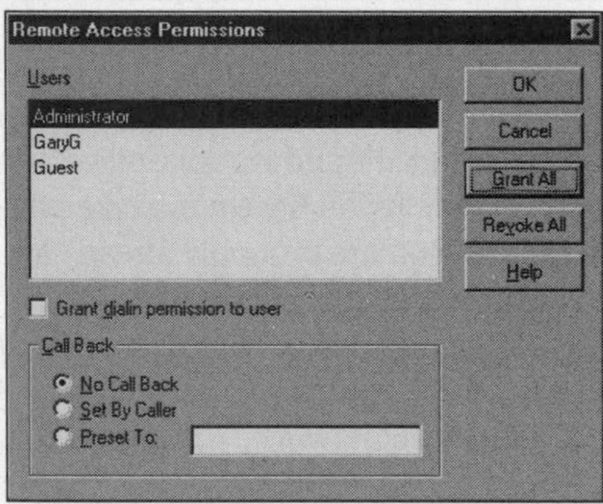

FIGURE 8.1: Remote Access Permissions

Call Back

One of the ways RAS enforces security is to call back the initiating client system to reestablish communication. This way, RAS is sure that the system calling is really what it says it is and can record the number it called to validate the user and minimize long-distance charges borne by the client. Call-back features can be set for each user with dial-up access. Notice in Figure 8.1 that you can configure three choices per user: No Call Back, which disables the call-back feature; Set by Caller, which prompts the caller for a number; and Preset to, which calls back a user at a predefined phone number. The server will call back this number only for the user. You cannot set call back authentication for groups of users or a particular modem.

Passwords and Data Encryption

There are several ways of protecting information sent over phone lines—the most common is encryption. When the client and the server begin to communicate, they use point-to-point protocol (PPP). To authenticate over PPP, RAS supports three authentication protocols: Password authentication protocol (PAP); Challenge handshake authentication protocol (CHAP); and Microsoft extensions of CHAP (MS-CHAP). You might anticipate that protocol selection is done through the Remote Access Admin tool, but your anticipation would be misguided. The protocol selection is done from the Network Configuration window of Remote Access Setup (see Figure 8.2).

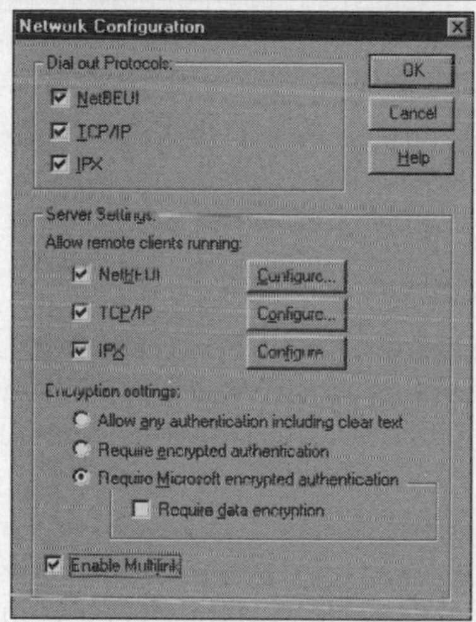

FIGURE 8.2: Network Configuration of RAS

As you can see from Figure 8.2, the three settings show up under the heading Encryption Settings. The default selection is MS-CHAP, although that does not appear to be an option. It is just camouflaged by calling it Require Microsoft Encrypted Authentication. When you configure a client to call the RAS, it will encrypt its password via MS-CHAP. Using MS-CHAP ensures that the system on the other end of the phone is at least using Windows 95 or above for an operating system.

If the Require Data Encryption button is selected, not only is MS-CHAP used, but the data that are sent over the phone lines are also encrypted.

Suppose that you have a diverse environment that is not Microsoft-centric. That is the politically correct way of saying that you have some bit-head who wants to dial in from a UNIX box. Since that system cannot use MS-CHAP, something else needs to be provided. You can require encrypted authentication. This option sets up the system to run CHAP as well as MS-CHAP.

The final selection you can make involves those systems that do not support encrypted password authentication. In that case, you can check Allow Any Authentication Including Clear Text. This is the free-for-all method of system access.

Another security feature mentioned above is point-to-point tunneling protocol (PPTP). PPTP is a new NT 4 feature. It is Internet centered and uses a two-step approach to connecting the client to the server: Connect the client to the Internet, then use the Internet to create an encrypted link to the RAS server. In some areas, this is called creating a virtual private network (VPN).

Multilink

By filling the Enable Multilink checkbox in Figure 8.2, you are allowing RAS to combine multiple serial signals into one. This is especially helpful when dealing with the two channels of ISDN, because now you can take full advantage of both channels. Multilink will also allow you to link regular modems together.

There is a catch—to use multilink, both computers have to be running NT and both must have multilink enabled. Furthermore, it is important to remember that multilinking is not possible with the call-back option enabled.

Configuring Dial-Up Networking Clients

At this point, you have configured the server, but now the server needs something to talk to. So, you need to configure the client workstation to call into the RAS server. From a Windows NT workstation client, you may need to install RAS services to provide for dial-up networking capabilities. For a Windows 95 client, dial-up networking needs to be installed.

NOTE

For more information about how to install and configure RAS services on a Windows NT workstation machine, see *Windows NT Workstation 4 Study Guide*, by Gary Govanus and Bob King (Sybex, 1998).

When the fundamental services, such as RAS services, are in place, it is time to get specific–configuring the client to dial into a particular RAS server. Before beginning, you need to know the ground rules for that server, such as what is the phone number, what protocols does it use, and what kind of security does it offer.

Once that information is in place, you create a new dial-up connection in the RAS phone book. Create one entry for each server the system needs to access. If the network's dial-up requirements are complicated, you can even create login scripts to automate much of the process, such as what would be needed for a SLIP-based UNIX server.

The final step in the process is to test the new service. Dial into the RAS server, connect, and make sure you have access to the resources on the remote server. Once you have disconnected, your remote access system is in place.

RAS Configuration Procedures

This section is where the meat of the process lies–actually doing the work.

Configuring RAS Communications

RAS is a network service and is installed like most of the other network services–from the Network applet in Control Panel. Before beginning to install RAS or any network service, be sure to have the NT installation CD handy, or at least have access to the files it contains. To install and configure RAS:

1. Log onto the computer as administrator.
2. Choose Start ➢ Settings ➢ Control Panel.
3. Double-click the Network icon.
4. Open the Services tab by clicking it. Since RAS is not installed, click Add. This will open the Select Network Service window, which is a selection of all the services available but not currently installed on your server.

5. Scroll down to Remote Access Service, highlight it with a single click, and then click OK. This will open the Windows NT setup screen. This window asks for the location of the NT setup files. Provide the appropriate location and click the Continue button. At this point, the Installation Wizard copies the files it needs to the places it needs to put them.

6. The next window you are presented lists all the RAS-capable devices attached to the server. If you have more than one modem attached to the server, the drop-down menu will allow you to select the device for RAS communications. If you haven't installed a modem, you can choose Install Modem or Install X.25 from this screen. Once you have chosen your RAS-capable device, click OK.

7. At this juncture, you should see the Remote Access Setup screen. Instead of continuing at this time, click Configure.

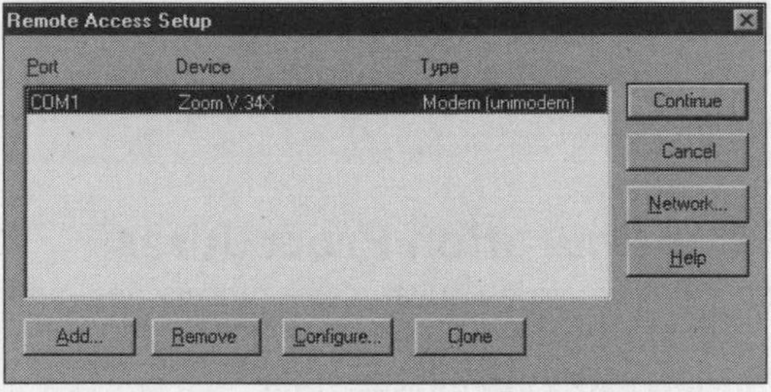

8. When you click Configure, it opens the Configure Port Usage screen, which allows you to specify how you want the port used. Make your selection from the choices below and click OK to return to the Remote Access Setup screen.

   Dial Out Only If you are configuring this server to dial into another RAS connection and you want this machine only to dial out, this is the appropriate selection.

   Receive Calls Only If your RAS connection will not be going out looking for work and dialing into other servers, this is the appropriate selection. It is also the default selection.

   Dial Out and Receive Calls This selection provides two-way communication.

9. You should now be back at the Remote Access Setup screen. Click Continue to open the RAS Server NetBEUI Configuration window.

Configuring RAS Protocols

The first protocol that is configured is the simplest, most basic network protocol–NetBEUI. You will also be prompted to provide information about TCP/IP and NWLink.

1. The RAS Server NetBEUI Configuration window allows you to choose how far your NetBEUI clients can go. Do you want them to access the entire network or just this particular computer? Make your choice by selecting the appropriate radio button and then click OK.

2. The next screen is the RAS Server TCP/IP Configuration screen. This screen is a little more complicated than the NetBEUI screen. There are several decisions to make before continuing.

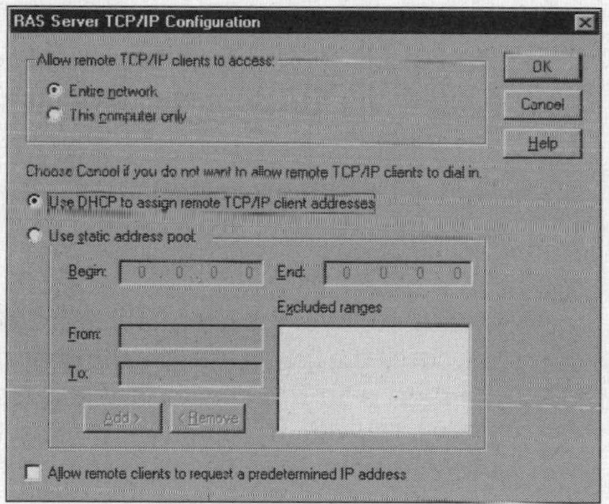

- The first set of radio buttons will allow you to decide how far the TCP/IP client will be allowed to go. Again, as with NetBEUI, the choices are Entire Network or This Computer Only.
- Now, things begin to get interesting. You will have to make some decisions about TCP/IP addressing.

- The first radio button is a "cop out" button. By selecting Use DHCP to Assign Remote TCP/IP Client Addresses, the server will pass the buck to a DHCP server to provide the IP address.
- If you choose Use Static Address Pool, it will let this service decide which of the IP addresses to assign to each connecting device.
- You can also check the box at the bottom of the screen that allows the remote client to request a predetermined IP address from either the DHCP server or the static pool. After making the appropriate selections, click OK.

NOTE

For a more complete discussion of TCP/IP addressing, read *MCSE: TCP/IP for NT SErver 4 Study Guide* (Sybex, 1998).

3. When you click OK, it brings up the next (and last) protocol to configure–IPX. There are several decisions to make here.
   - The top selection of radio buttons allows you to choose whether the IPX client uses the entire network or just this computer.
   - The next selection of radio buttons allows you to choose whether network numbers are allocated automatically or within the range you provide.
   - In the bottom of the screen, there are two checkboxes. If you check the first, it will give the same network segment number to all IPX clients. If you check the second, it allows the client computer to select its own node address.
4. Click OK and close the RAS Installation Wizard.
5. Agree to allow NetBIOS broadcasts for IPX clients.
6. Click OK to close the Network Configuration window.
7. Finally, select Yes to restart the computer.

Configuring RAS Security

RAS security is configured using both the Remote Access Admin utility and the Network Configuration window from the Remote Access Setup screen. The security settings involved with the Admin tool revolve around granting dial-up access rights to the server and call-back selections.

Encryption information and selections are made through the Network Configuration tool.

To provide dial-up access:

1. Start the Remote Access Admin utility by selecting Start ➢ Programs ➢ Administrative Tools (Common) ➢ Remote Access Admin.
2. From the Remote Access Admin screen, click Users to show users with access to this server. To provide access to users from another domain or another server, even if it is across a slow link, choose Server ➢ Select Domain or Server, and then choose the domain you would like to administer. To actually select the domain, double-click the domain name in the Select Domain window. Once this has been accomplished, the users in the other domain will show up in the Remote Access Admin screen.
3. Click Permissions to show the Remote Access Permissions screen.
4. The Remote Access Permissions screen will show you the users associated with this system. By using the selection buttons to the right, you can Grant All access to dial-up networking or Revoke All access from dial-up networking. To grant individual users the right to dial up, highlight the user account and select the Grant Dialin Permission to User checkbox at the bottom of the screen. (Remember that RAS permission can also be granted in the User Manager utility.)
5. You can also use this screen to provide three levels of Call Back support:
   - No Call Back–Disables the call-back feature.
   - Set by Caller–Prompts the caller for a number.
   - Preset to–Calls back a user at a predefined phone number. The server will call back this number only for the user.

To change the default encryption scheme for passwords and data:

1. From the NT Server desktop, highlight Network Neighborhood and right-click.
2. Click Properties.
3. Click the Services tab and highlight Remote Access Services.
4. Click the Properties button to bring up the Remote Access Setup screen.
5. Click the Network button. This brings up the Network Configuration window.
6. The default encryption setting is Require Microsoft Encrypted Authentication. This provides for MS-CHAP. If you fill the Require Data Encryption checkbox, it will encrypt not only the password, but any data flowing between the RAS server and the client.
    - Select Require Encrypted Authentication if you are providing access to non-Microsoft-based operating systems, such as UNIX. This provides for CHAP-based encryption in addition to MS-CHAP.
    - Select Allow Any Authentication Including Clear Text, which allows all three methods, including no encryption.

Configuring Dial-Up Networking Clients

On a Windows NT computer, before you can connect to the RAS server, you must have RAS services installed. If you are using an NT Server, refer to the first section to install RAS. Once installed, you must configure a dial-up connection in the RAS phone book. To configure the dial-up connection:

1. Double-click the My Computer icon on the desktop.
2. Double-click the Dial-Up Networking icon.
3. If this is the first entry in your phone book, you will get a nagging screen that tells you the phone book is empty. Click OK. After you pass the annoying screen, click New to start the New Phonebook Entry Wizard.
4. Type in the name of the phone-book entry and then click the Finish button.

5. You need to enter a name for the dial-up entry you are creating. The receiving server name seems appropriate, don't you think?
6. Did you notice the Dial Using box? Select the modem to use.
7. Click the Use Telephony Dialing Properties option.
8. Enter the area code and phone number of your RAS server in the Phone Number input lines.
9. Does your RAS server have more than one phone number? If so, you can check the Alternate button and add any other phone numbers to call.
10. Click the Server tab. Select the protocol that your RAS server uses. The protocols must match between the client and the server for communication to take place.
11. The security must also be the same on the server and the host, so click the Security tab. Since this is a nonsecure network, check Allow Any Encryption Including Clear Text.
12. Click OK to save the settings and then click Close. You may be prompted to restart your computer, but in this case, it is not necessary.

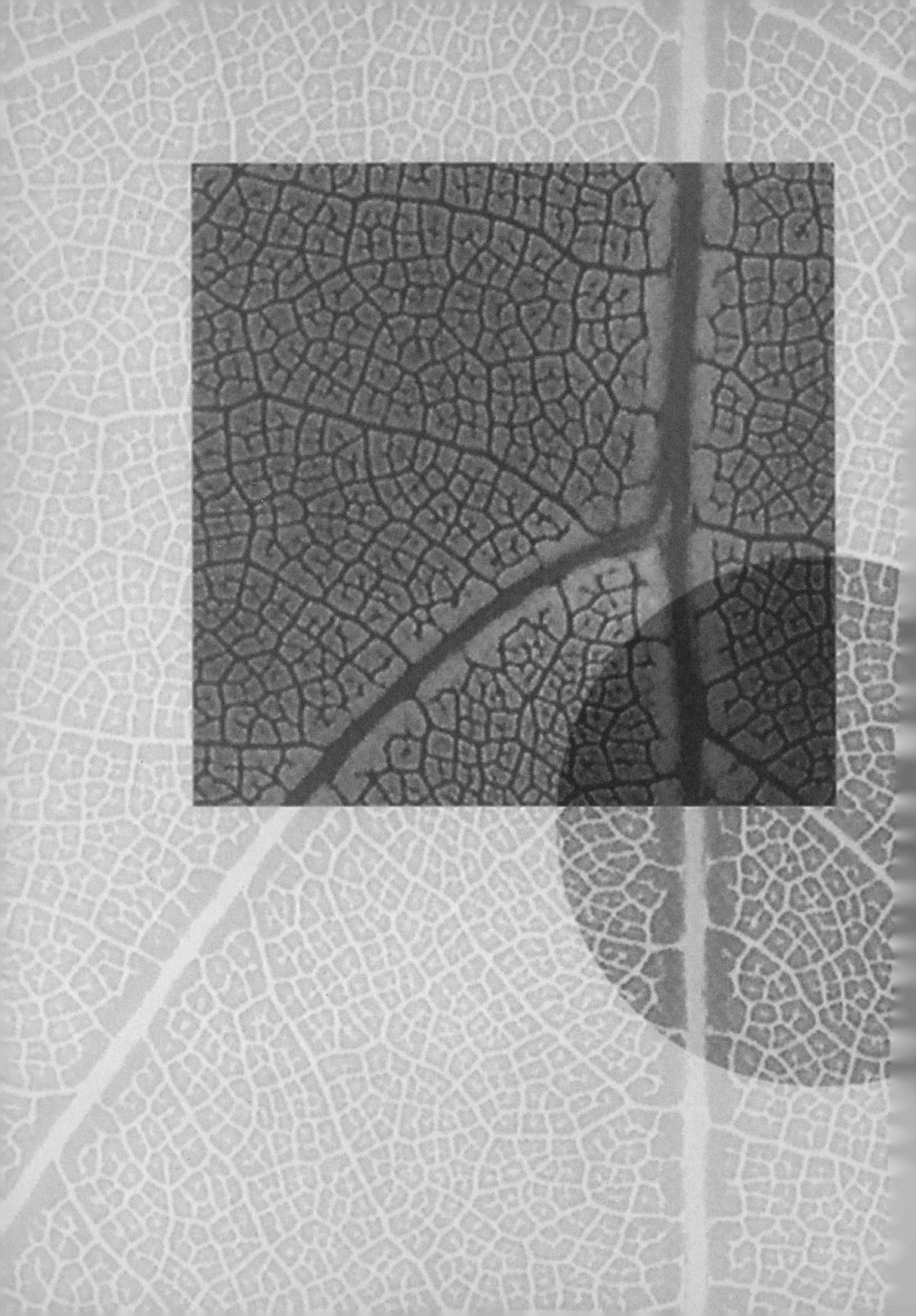

Chapter 9

Monitoring and Optimization

The objectives for this portion of the exam cover your ability to use tools to gather information about your network and to analyze the data gathered. To manage your network, rather than react to it, you need a set of tools that allow you to measure the impact of each service on both an individual server and the network as a whole. Once you have this information, you can manage your resources to optimize performance and efficiency.

Adapted from *MCSE Exam Notes: NT Server 4*
by Gary Govanus and Robert King

ISBN 0-7821-2289-2 360 pages $19.99

Monitor performance of various functions by using performance monitor.

Functions Include:

- Processor
- Memory
- Disk
- Network

When you troubleshoot any kind of complex system, one of the most important skills is knowing what to look for–the questions you ask and how you interpret the answers are critical to both problem solving and optimizing your network. In this section, the Performance Monitor counters that track each of the major subsystems of an NT server will be discussed. While any given environment might stress other particular components, there are four main physical components to any NT server: processor, memory, disk, and network. These four areas are good indicators of the health of your system.

Performance Monitor

Performance Monitor is the tool provided by NT to gather statistics at the server. Performance Monitor uses objects and counters to describe the statistics that can be gathered. An object is a subsystem, while a counter is a specific statistic of an object. Performance Monitor has a list of 12 objects that can be monitored. Some software creates its own counters when you install it. Each of the four main subsystems has an associated object with counters that you should track.

When creating your baseline, you will often want to gather statistics while a specific process happens. Backups, for instance, often strain both the servers involved and the network. Unfortunately, most companies do their backups during nonpeak hours or, in other words, during your personal time. You can use the AT command to start Performance Monitor automatically. The AT command allows you to schedule a start time for any process or application. Using the AT command, you can make Performance Monitor load and begin collecting data automatically. Once you've collected your data, you'll want to analyze it. Performance Monitor can save data in a format that many commercial applications can read. When you dump the statistics into a database or spreadsheet, it is called *creating a measurement database.*

When gathering information, you will often track a lot of counters and check those counters frequently. How often Performance Monitor checks the values of counters you are tracking is called the *interval.* If your interval is set low, NT will gather the values often, which can result in huge data files. Microsoft suggests that after you have analyzed the data, you relog the information with a larger interval. This will reduce the size of the log file, but still leave you information for trend analysis and comparison.

Performance Monitor offers many ways to view the statistics that it gathers. You will need to be familiar with each of them for the exam.

Chart View

Chart view provides a real-time chart showing the values of the counters you have chosen. The first step is to add the counters to your view, as shown in Figure 9.1. Highlight the appropriate object and then pick a counter from the list.

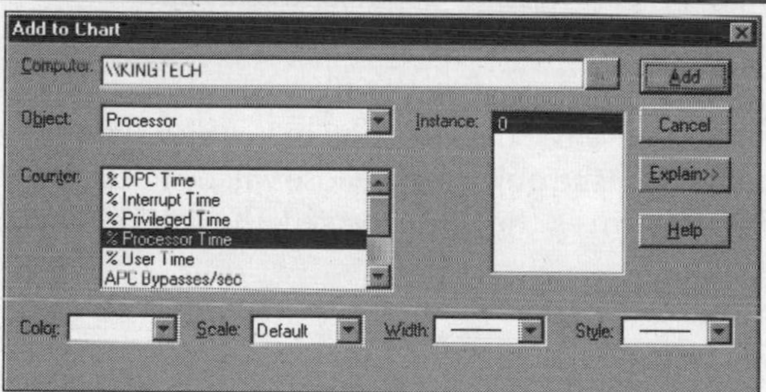

FIGURE 9.1: Add to Chart

When you have added all of the counters you want to chart, click Cancel. The chart will show the value of those counters in real time, as shown in Figure 9.2.

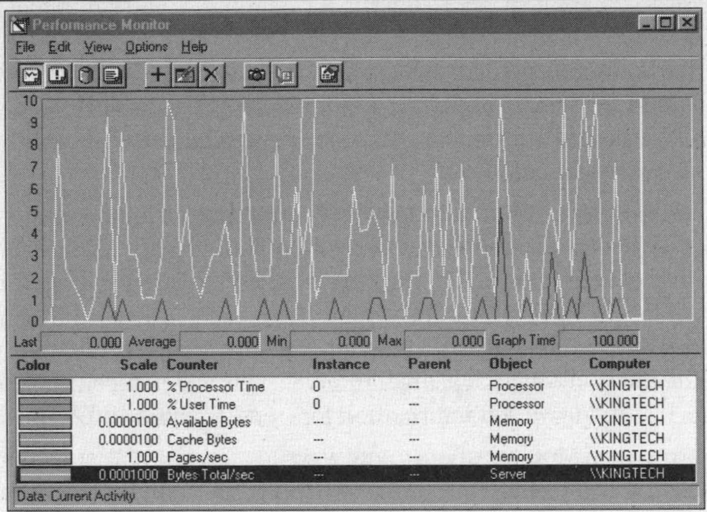

FIGURE 9.2: A real-time Performance Monitor chart

Report View

Report view shows the same information as Chart view. However, with Report view, the values are shown in the form of a text-based report. As in Chart view, the report data are updated in real time.

Log View

Log view allows you to save the data to a file. In Log view, you do not pick counters—all counters for the objects you chose will be tracked. Rather than the data being shown as they are collected, the data are saved to a file for later analysis.

Alert View

Alert view is different from the other three views. With Alert view, you set a threshold for a counter. When this threshold is reached, you can make Performance Monitor run an application that pages you, for instance.

Processor

To determine whether the processor is the bottleneck, monitor the counters listed in Table 9.1.

TABLE 9.1: Processor-Related Counters in Performance Monitor

COUNTER	ACCEPTABLE VALUE	DESCRIPTION
%Processor Time	Under 80 percent	If the processor is busy more than 80 percent of the time, it is likely that the processor is the bottleneck.
%Privileged Time	Under 80 percent	This is the amount of time that the processor is busy performing operating-system tasks.
%User Time	Under 80 percent	This is the amount of time that the processor is busy performing user tasks, such as running a program.
Interrupts/sec	Varies	This is the number of hardware interrupts generated each second. Each type of processor can handle a different number. On a 486/66, this number should be under 1,000; on a Pentium 90 system, this number could run as high as 3,500. If this number is consistently high, the system probably has an IRQ conflict or a piece of hardware that is going bad.
System: Processor Queue Length	Less than 2	This represents the number of threads that are ready to execute, but are waiting for the processor.
Server Work Queues: Queue Length	Less than 2	This represents the number of threads in the queue for a given processor.

If the bottleneck is your processor, you can: add a faster processor; add another processor; or move processing to another server.

Memory

Memory in an NT system can be divided into two classifications: paged and nonpaged. Paged memory is used by most applications. It can be made up of either physical RAM or virtual memory (hard disk space). Nonpaged memory is used by programs that cannot be "paged" to the hard disk. The operating system and its components use nonpaged memory.

NT uses a virtual memory model. In this model, applications that can use paged RAM are given a full set of memory addresses with which to work. The operating system keeps track of actual physical memory. When memory is full, the OS will move "pages" of memory to a file on the hard drive (PAGEFILE.SYS). If that code is needed later, it will be moved back to physical memory. By using a virtual memory model, your applications can use more memory than is physically available (up to the limits of your hard drive).

Whenever the data that a program needs are not in RAM, they must be acquired from the hard drive. This process is called a *hard page fault*. If you have a consistently high number of hard page faults (over five per second), it could indicate that performance is being significantly degraded since there is not enough memory available on the server. The goal on an NT server is to have enough memory in the server so that most data requested are found in memory. (Obviously, the first time the data are used, they will have to come from the disk. But after that, if you have enough memory for file caching, it can greatly increase performance.)

Monitor the counters listed in Table 9.2 to determine whether memory is your bottleneck.

TABLE 9.2: Memory-Related Counters in Performance Monitor

Counter	Acceptable Value	Description
Pages/sec	0–20	The number of pages that were either not in RAM when requested or needed to be moved to virtual memory to free up space in RAM. This is really a measurement of disk activity related to memory management.
Available Bytes	Minimum of 4MB	The amount of available physical RAM at any point in time. This number will usually be fairly low, because NT will utilize memory that is available and free it up as needed.
Committed Bytes	Should be less than the physical amount of RAM in the computer	This indicates the amount of memory in use. If the number is greater than the amount of physical RAM in the machine, you need more memory.
Pool Non-Paged Bytes	Should remain steady	This is the memory used by non-paged processes (i.e., the operating system). If this number fluctuates, it could indicate that a process is not using memory correctly.

If memory is the bottleneck on your server, the fix is simple–add more RAM.

Disk

The disk is usually the slowest component on your computer. NT compensates for this by using file caching and memory management to reduce the number of disk accesses. Often, what appears to be a disk problem is really just a lack of memory, so be sure to watch both subsystems–disk and memory. Before you can track disk counters in Performance Monitor, you must turn on those counters. The disk counters are not activated by default, because tracking physical-disk access used to add measurable overhead to the workstations and servers that ran older Intel processors. Today's CPUs aren't affected to nearly the same degree, but the counters still must be turned on and off.

To activate the disk counters, type **diskperf –y** at a command prompt. If your disks are configured as a RAID set, type **diskperf –ye**.

NOTE

The added overhead of tracking disk counters is constant once they are activated—not just when you are monitoring them. You should turn them off when you are not actively watching them. To turn them off, type diskperf–n at a command prompt.

Once you have activated them, you can monitor the counters listed in Table 9.3.

TABLE 9.3: Disk-Related Counters in Performance Monitor

Counter	Acceptable Value	Description
%Disk Time	Under 90 percent	This is the amount of time that the disk drive is busy. If this number is consistently high, you should monitor specific processes to find out exactly what is using the disk. If you can, move some of the disk-intensive processes to another server.
Disk Queue Length	0–2	This value represents the number of waiting disk I/O requests. A high number indicates that I/O requests are waiting for access.

TABLE 9.3 continued: Disk-Related Counters in Performance Monitor

Counter	Acceptable Value	Description
Avg. Disk Bytes/Transfer	Depends on use and type of subsystem	The larger this number is, the more efficiently your disk subsystem is working. This value depends on the type of access—are your users saving many small files or a few large ones? It also depends on the types of disks and controllers.
Disk Bytes/sec	Depends on use and type of subsystem	The larger this number is, the more efficiently your disk subsystem is working. This value depends on the types of disks and controllers.

If you find that the disk subsystem is the bottleneck, you can do the following things: add a faster controller and disk drive; if using RAID, add more disks to the set to spread the work across more physical devices; or move disk-intensive processes to another server to spread the workload.

WARNING

None of these solutions is really a simple fix. If you add a faster controller, it will help only if your disks are compliant with the controller type. If they are not, you will have to replace the disks as well to gain any benefit.

Network

Due to the complexity of today's networks, monitoring the network portion of your environment can be a difficult task. The network doesn't end at your NIC card–the network includes the entire infrastructure that makes up your enterprise. Everything attached to your network could be a potential problem. Don't try to fix the entire network, try to find out which component is causing the problem and fix that.

Performance Monitor has a few counters, listed in Table 9.4, that can help you determine where the problem lies. A few of the counters analyze the overhead on the server itself, while others give an overview of what is happening on the wire.

TABLE 9.4: Network-Related Counters in Performance Monitor

Counter	Acceptable Value	Description
Server: Bytes Total/sec	Varies	This counter shows the number of bytes sent and received through this server. It is a good indicator of how busy the server is.
Server: Login/sec	Varies	Use this value to determine the authentication overhead being placed on the server. If this number is high and other services are slow, it might indicate the need for another domain controller.
Server: Login Total	Varies	This is the number of login attempts this server has serviced since the last time the server was started. It can be used to justify another domain controller.
Network Interface: Bytes Sent/sec	Varies	Used to determine whether a particular network interface card is being overused.
Network Interface: Bytes Total/sec	Varies	This is the total number of bytes sent and received through a particular NIC.
Network Segment: %Network Utilization	Usually lower than 30 percent	This shows the percentage of network bandwidth in use. This number should be lower than 30 percent for most networks. Some network technologies can sustain a higher rate.

The Network Segment object is not available until you install the Network Monitor Agent as a service on the server. Once this service is installed, Performance Monitor will put the NICs in promiscuous mode when you are monitoring Network Segment counters. When in promiscuous mode, a NIC processes *all* network traffic, not just those packets destined for the server. This can add a tremendous amount of overhead to the server.

Each protocol that you add to your server also has its own counters. These counters allow you to determine the overhead being placed on your server by each protocol. Most of these counters have no acceptable range of values. The values will depend upon the hardware, topology, and other protocols used on your network.

NetBEUI and NWLink

These two protocols have similar counters, listed in Table 9.5.

TABLE 9.5: NetBEUI- and NWLink-Related Counters in Performance Monitor

Counter	Acceptable Value	Description
Bytes Total/sec	Varies	This is the total number of bytes sent and received using this protocol. This counter is an excellent way to compare network overhead created by various protocols.
Datagrams/sec	Varies	This is the total number of nonguaranteed datagrams (usually broadcasts) sent and received.
Frames Sent/sec	Varies	This is the number of data packets sent and received.

TCP/IP

The counters listed in Table 9.6 will not be available unless both the TCP/IP protocol and the SNMP service are installed on the server.

TABLE 9.6: TCP/IP-Related Counters in Performance Monitor

Counter	Acceptable Value	Description
TCP Segments/sec	Varies	This is the total number of TCP frames sent and received.
TCP Segments Re-translated/sec	Varies	This is the total number of segments retranslated on the network.
UDP Datagrams/sec	Varies	This is the number of UDP-based datagrams (usually broadcasts) sent and received.
Network Interface: Output Queue Length	Less than 2	This is the number of packets waiting to be transmitted through a particular NIC. A high number can indicate a card that is too busy.

The following strategies are potential fixes if the network is your bottleneck:

- Upgrade the hardware at the server. Add a faster NIC, add RAM, or upgrade the processor.
- Upgrade the physical components of your network, such as routers and bridges. Shift to higher-speed network protocols such as 100BaseT Ethernet.
- Decrease the number of protocols used on your network.
- Segment your network to split the traffic between segments.
- Add servers to split the workload.

Performance Monitoring Procedures

This objective primarily concerns your ability to use Performance Monitor.

Creating a Baseline Using Performance Monitor

To build a baseline, use the Log view in Performance Monitor. First, pick the objects that you want to track. Remember to start with the four main subsystems. At a minimum, you will want to track processor, memory, disk, and whatever objects are available for protocols in use on your network. Save this log to a file. You will use this file–the baseline–as a basis for comparison. Performance Monitor can use this file later as the input material for graphs or reports.

Relogging Your Data at a Longer Interval

Use the Log view in Performance Monitor.

1. Choose Options ➢ Data From.
2. Choose Log File and browse to your baseline log file.
3. Build the log again, using the same steps as before–only this time, change the interval.
4. When you start the log, it will save information at the new interval, reducing the size of the log file.

WARNING

Although this method is great for archiving trends, the resulting log file contains less-accurate data. Since you have reduced the sampling rate, the resulting information will be less detailed in terms of time.

Exporting Information to Another Program

Build a chart using your log file. Choose File ➢ Export Chart. Save the chart in a format your application can import.

Identify performance bottlenecks.

NT servers are used for a lot of different tasks. Microsoft defines three main server environments–File and Print, Application, and Domain. Each of these environments will stress different components of a server. In this section, each of these environments will be defined; and which components utilized most heavily, and the specific objects and counters tracked to analyze each environment, will be discussed.

WARNING

Microsoft assumes that the server is used to provide only one service. In most networks, servers perform multiple services. In a real-world network, you will have to analyze how each function affects all other functions that the server performs.

File and Print Server

A file and print server is used to acquire and save data, to load server-based software, and as a print server. A breakdown of this type of server is given in Table 9.7.

NOTE

The values in the following tables represent relative importance. Some components may have equal values.

TABLE 9.7: File and Print Server

SUBSYSTEM	IMPORTANCE TO ENVIRONMENT*	CRITICAL INFORMATION
Memory	1	Servers use memory to cache the files that users request. Caching a frequently used file can increase process performance by over 100 percent.
Processor	2	Each network connection uses processor time at the server.
Disk	3	Since most connections are used to save or retrieve data, the disks can have an impact on performance. However, since servers use file caching, memory will have a bigger impact.
Network	3	Every transaction will add to the traffic on the network, but this is usually not the bottleneck on a file and print server.

***1= highest; 4=lowest**

Application Server

An application server is a client/server environment. In a client/server environment, the actual processing happens at the server, not the client computer. A good example is a database server. The client runs a small piece of software called a front-end, which is used to formulate a query of the database. The server runs the actual database software. When the front-end sends a query, the server looks through the database and returns only the results of the query. Notice that most of the processing happens at the server. The details of this environment are listed in Table 9.8.

TABLE 9.8: Application Server

Subsystem	Importance to Environment*	Critical Information
Memory	2	Each application or service you add to a server will use memory. Most client/server-based applications use a lot of memory. Make sure the server has sufficient memory for both the operating system and the application.
Processor	1	As discussed above, most of the actual processing occurs at the server.
Disk	3	This is a tough one to categorize. If the application is disk intensive (a database, for instance), the disk could be a potential bottleneck. In most cases, though, its impact will be negligible compared to the processor and memory.
Network	4	Client/server-based applications put very little traffic on the network. Instead of transferring a large amount of data to be processed by the client, only the pertinent information is transferred.

***1= highest; 4=lowest**

Domain Server

A domain server is a server that is involved in providing network management services. This server will be a domain controller, a DHCP server, a WINS server, etc. Most communication will be server to server, rather than client to server. The components of a domain server are listed in Table 9.9.

TABLE 9.9: Domain Server

Subsystem	Importance to Environment*	Critical Information
Memory	1	Each service the server provides will use memory.
Processor	2	Each network connection will use processing time. Domain controllers need to synchronize the SAM and act as login servers for users.
Disk	3	Domain servers are usually not disk intensive.
Network	1	All transactions will involve the network. Limited connection speed will slow down the overall operation of the workstations while waiting for server processes such as security authentication.

***1= highest; 4=lowest**

Now that you know the different kinds of servers that might be found in your environment and which subsystem(s) is most important to each, you can use this information to choose what to include in your baseline. For each of the "big four" subsystems, you will need to know which counters to watch and what ranges of values are acceptable for each environment.

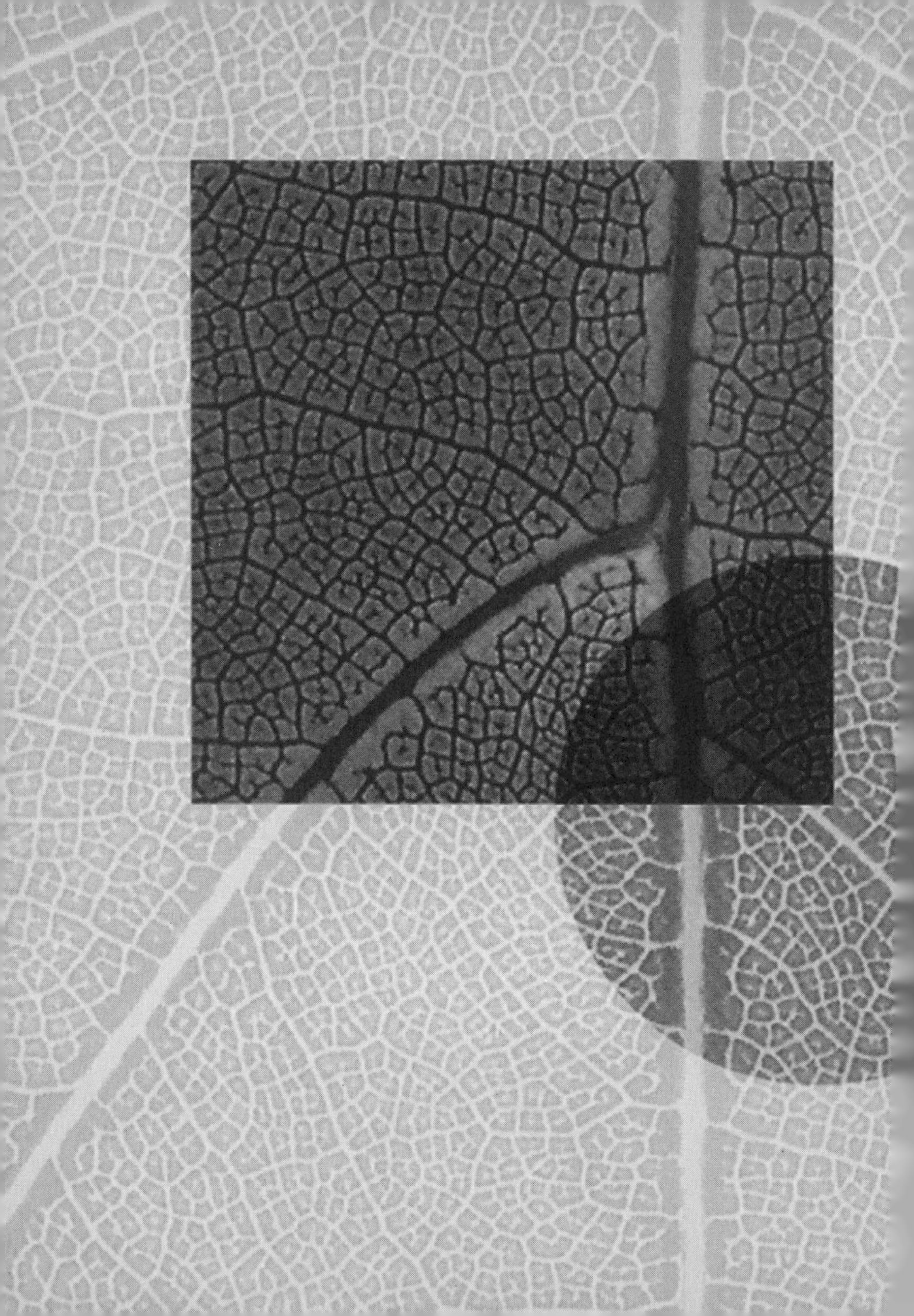

Chapter 10

Troubleshooting

The objectives for this chapter cover the actions you should take to correct a specific set of problems. Some of these problems occur often in the workplace, while others occur rarely. Whether the problems are common or rare, knowing how to correct them is a very big part of being a network administrator. Learning to troubleshoot technical problems is a lifelong process. You can pick up some useful tips by reading books or taking classes, but you can never know everything—experience plays a big role in developing troubleshooting skills. However, this book can act as a starting place to help you build a "troubleshooting database" in your head.

Adapted from *MCSE Exam Notes: NT Server 4*
by Gary Govanus and Robert King
ISBN 0-7821-2289-2 360 pages $19.99

Choose the appropriate course of action to take to resolve installation failures.

In the real world, installation failures can be fairly common. They are also the most fortunate type of problem, because they manifest before the server has been placed in production. While you are usually under a deadline during installation, there is usually less pressure to fix the problem immediately.

An NT installation might fail for many reasons. The easiest way to avoid installation problems is to purchase equipment that has been tested to be compatible with Microsoft Windows NT. Microsoft provides a tool–the NT hardware qualifier (NTHQ) utility–that will help you determine whether your equipment is on the tested list. Always download the latest version of NTHQ from the Microsoft Web site, and make it a policy to specify *NT 4.0 certified* when you talk to vendors.

Media Errors

If you get an error message that indicates that a particular file cannot be copied or is corrupt during an installation of NT, it could indicate a media error. Try using another CD-ROM if you have one. If not, try using another method of installation. For example, copy the I386 directory to the C: drive (assuming it is a FAT partition) and try the installation from there. Another option is to copy the I386 directory to another server, sharing the directory, and then install from that share point.

Nonsupported SCSI Adapter

If your CD-ROM is attached to a SCSI adapter that is not supported by NT, you can lose the ability to read from it halfway through the installation process, after the server has been restarted under NT. Unfortunately, even if the CD-ROM manufacturer provides an NT SCSI driver, you cannot use it until after NT is fully installed. If you run into this problem, you will have to use the techniques listed in the "Media Errors" section. Try installing from a share point on another server. Or, boot to DOS, copy the I386 directory to the C: drive, and install from there.

Insufficient Disk Space

Know the minimum requirements before you start the installation, and make sure your hardware meets or exceeds them. The only fix for insufficient disk space is to provide NT with enough disk space either by deleting an existing partition or by adding another drive.

Failure of Dependency Service to Start

When the dependency service fails to start, it is usually a configuration error. Most of these errors result from network interface card (NIC) problems, requiring you to go back to the network setup section of the installation and ensure that the protocols are configured correctly, that you have chosen a unique computer name, and that the NIC settings are correct.

Inability to Connect to the PDC

Ensure that you have entered the domain name correctly, that the NIC settings are correct, and that you have chosen the correct network protocols. This problem is quite common—it usually occurs when you try to install a BDC on a computer that has a nonsupported NIC. If NT doesn't provide a NIC driver, the card cannot initialize and you cannot communicate with the server.

Error in Assigning a Domain Name

When you install a PDC, ensure that the domain name is not already in use on your network. The domain name cannot be the same as any other domain or computer name.

Failure of NT to Install or Start

When NT fails to install or start, it usually indicates that a piece of hardware is not compatible with NT. Run NTHQ to determine which component is not on the hardware-compatibility list and replace the component.

▶ Choose the appropriate course of action to take to resolve boot failures.

NT goes through four distinct phases during the boot process. For the MCSE examination, you will need to know what happens in each phase. After the stages have been examined, specific errors and possible solutions will be examined.

NT Boot Phases

The four boot phases are initial, boot loader, kernel, and logon.

Initial Phase

During the initial phase, the computer performs a power on self test (POST), during which it determines how much memory is installed and whether the required hardware is available. During this process, the computer executes the BIOS and reads the information stored in CMOS to determine what storage devices are available, the date and time, and other parameters specific to the hardware.

In CMOS, the computer will read the type and configuration of possible boot devices. Based upon this information, it will determine which device it should examine to find operating system boot information. If your computer is configured to boot from the hard drive, your computer will read the first sector in an attempt to find the master boot record (MBR). The MBR contains critical information for the boot process—a list of partitions defined on the disk, their starting and ending sectors, and which partitions are active. (The active partition is the one that the computer will attempt to boot from.) If there is no MBR on the disk, the computer cannot boot to an operating system. This is why many computer viruses attack the MBR.

Once the computer has determined which partition it should look to for boot information, it will access that partition and read the partition boot sector (PBS). The PBS contains operating system–specific information. In the case of Windows NT, it directs the computer to load a file called NTLDR (NT loader), which is found in the partition root folder. If the PBS is missing or corrupted, you may see an error message that implies that no operating system was found, a nonsystem disk is being used, or a disk error has occurred. This is what happens when you restart your computer with a nonsystem floppy disk in the A: drive. There is no boot information on it, so the server doesn't know where to find the operating system.

Boot Loader Phase

Once NTLDR has been found and starts to load, the boot loader phase begins. During this phase, NT uses various programs to gather information about the hardware and drivers needed to boot. The following files will be utilized during this phase:

NTLDR This is the operating system loader. It must be in the root directory of the active partition. NTLDR remains the overall conductor of the NT startup process.

BOOT.INI This is an important text file that controls which operating system will be loaded. The user will see a menu offering various operating system choices. NTLDR expects to find this file in the root directory. The BOOT.INI file will be discussed in more detail later in this section.

BOOTSEC.DOS If the computer is configured to dual boot between NT and another operating system, the NT installation program will gather all of the information needed to boot the other OS and place it in this file. When the user chooses to boot to another OS, NT will call this file.

NTBOOTDD.SYS This is a device driver used to access a SCSI hard drive when the SCSI controller is not using its own BIOS.

NTDETECT.COM This is a program that attempts to analyze the hardware on the computer; it passes this information to the operating system for inclusion in the registry later in the boot process. NTDETECT.COM can detect the following components: computer ID; bus/adapter type; video, keyboard, and communication ports; parallel ports; floppy disks; and mouse/pointing device. While NTDETECT.COM performs its function, it displays the following message on the screen:

```
NTDETECT V1.0 Checking Hardware…
```

NTLDR controls the initial startup of NT on the hardware. It also changes the processor from real-time to 32-bit flat memory mode, starts the appropriate miniature file system (NTLDR has code that enables it to read FAT and NTFS partitions), and reads the BOOT.INI file to display the menu of operating system choices.

Once NT has been selected and NTDETECT.COM has run its course, NTLDR will display the following message:

```
OS Loader V4.0
Press SPACEBAR now to invoke Hardware Profile/Last Known Good
menu.
```

Part II

If the spacebar is not pressed and there is only one hardware profile, NTLDR will load the default control set. If the spacebar is pressed, NTLDR will display a screen offering hardware profile choices and the option to use the last known good configuration. This is an important method to restore driver and configuration settings from the registry following changes that caused an operating system failure. The old settings are called from the registry's saved control sets and used in place of the erroneous settings.

Once the hardware configuration has been chosen, NTLDR will load the NT kernel–NTOSKRNL.EXE. NTLDR loads this kernel into memory, but does not initialize it at this point. Next, the boot loader loads the registry key–HKEY_LOCAL_MACHINE\SYSTEM. NTLDR scans all of the subkeys in CurrentControlSet\Services for device drivers with a start value of zero. These drivers are usually low-level hardware drivers, such as hard disk drivers, needed to continue the boot.

Kernel Phase

The boot loader phase ends when NTLDR passes control to NTOSKRNL .EXE. At this point, the kernel-initialization phase begins. The screen will turn blue, and you will see a message similar to the following one:

```
Microsoft®  Windows NT™ Version 4.0 (Build 1381)
1 System Processor (16MB Memory)
```

The kernel then creates the HKEY_LOCAL_MACHINE\HARDWARE registry key using information passed to it by the boot loader (gathered by NTDETECT.COM).

The next step is to load the device drivers. NTOSKRNL.EXE looks in the registry for drivers that need to be loaded, checks through their DependOnService and DependOnGroup values for dependencies, and determines the order in which drivers should be loaded. It then loads the services, reads and implements the specified parameters, and initializes the various services and drivers that are needed.

Logon Phase

An NT boot is not considered successful until a user successfully logs on. The Windows subsystem automatically starts WINLOGON.EXE. The Begin Logon box now appears on the screen. The user can press Ctrl+Alt+Delete to log on even though other services might still be initializing in the background.

The service controller performs one last sweep through the registry to locate any remaining services that need to be loaded. At this point, NT has just about finished the boot process.

When a user logs on, NT considers the boot to have been successful. Only then will it take the CurrentControlSet and copy it to create the last known good configuration (for use in the next boot of this computer).

BOOT.INI File

The BOOT.INI file is a text file located in the root of the boot partition. Here is an example of a BOOT.INI file for an NT server that is set up to dual boot with the Windows 95 operating system:

```
[boot loader]
timeout=30
default=multi(0)disk(0)rdisk(0)paritition(1)\WINNT
[operating systems]
multi(0)disk(0)rdisk(0)paritition(1)\WINNT="Windows NT Server
Version 4.0"
multi(0)disk(0)rdisk(0)paritition(1)\WINNT="Windows NT Server
Version 4.0 [VGA mode]" /basevideo /sos
C:\="Windows 95"
```

A BOOT.INI file has two sections. In the [boot loader] section, you will find settings that control the defaults—how long the menu should be on the screen before a default is selected and which operating system should load if the user makes no selection. In the [operating systems] section, you will find the various choices that are presented to the user, and the path and switches for each of the operating system files. The ARC path conventions were discussed earlier. Now you see where that information is put to use. If there is no BOOT.INI file, the system will attempt to boot from the location where the NT installation program places boot files by default—the \WINNT directory on the active partition. If you have placed the operating system files in another location, the BOOT.INI file is critical to the boot process.

BOOT.INI Switches

You can use numerous switches within the BOOT.INI file to help control the way that NT boots. These switches are placed at the end of the line that describes the location of the operating system.

/basevideo This switch forces NT to boot using a standard VGA driver, which allows an administrator to recover from installing an incorrect or corrupted video driver that disables video output. The NT installation program creates an operating system choice, annotated [VGA mode], in the BOOT.INI file that implements this switch. This allows you to fix a video driver problem by rebooting, choosing the VGA option, and replacing the bad driver.

/maxmem:n This switch allows the administrator to specify how much physical memory NT can use. You can use this switch to troubleshoot various memory problems such as parity errors, bad SIMMs, etc.

/noserialmice=[COM x or COM x,y,z] NT will occasionally detect a device on a communication port and assume that it is a mouse–even if it is another type of device. When this happens, that device will be unusable in Windows NT because a mouse driver will be loaded that uses that port. This switch disables detection on the communication port(s) specified. This can be used to prevent NT from issuing shutdown signals to a UPS during the boot process.

/sos This switch will cause NT to display the names of drivers as they are loaded rather than the default progress dots.

/crashdebug This switch enables the automatic recovery and restart capability in the event of a stop screen. This parameter can also be set in the System applet in the Control Panel.

A number of switches relate to advanced troubleshooting techniques that will be covered later in this chapter. These switches configure NT to "dump" its memory contents into a file for analysis. You can configure where this memory dump file will be placed. Often, a problem will be so severe that the computer is inaccessible. With this type of error, you will want to configure the system to dump its memory to another computer's hard drive. The following switches control this transfer:

/baudrate=nnnn This switch is used to configure the communication port if you are going to dump memory to another computer.

/debugport=comx This switch sets the communication port to be used.

BOOT.INI Error Messages

Various error messages are commonly seen when there is a problem with the BOOT.INI file. If the BOOT.INI file is missing or the operating system line does not point to the NT operating system files, you will see the following message.

```
Windows NT could not start because the following file is
missing or corrupt:
    <winnt root>\system32\NTOSKRNL.EXE
Please reinstall a copy of the above file.
```

If the ARC path points to a nonexistent or inaccessible disk or partition, you will see the following error message:

```
OS Loader V4.0
Windows NT could not start because of a computer disk hard-
   ware configuration problem. Could not read from the
   selected boot disk. Check boot path and disk hardware.
Please check the Windows NT documentation about hardware disk
   configuration and your hardware reference manuals for
   additional information.
```

In either event, you can either edit the BOOT.INI file to correct the problem or restore the BOOT.INI file off of your emergency repair disk.

Part II

Last Known Good Configuration

If your Windows NT server refuses to boot after you have added new hardware or software, you can attempt to boot using the last known good configuration. The *last known good configuration* is the hardware configuration used during the last successful boot. Remember, though, that when you successfully log onto the computer, you will overwrite the last known good configuration with the current control set.

If one of the files used during the boot process has become corrupted, you can attempt to replace it with a good copy. You can accomplish this task in a couple of ways. If you boot to a FAT partition, you can boot to a DOS disk and copy the new file over the suspect file. The only file that is unique to the server's hardware is the BOOT.INI file. All of the other files are generic, so you can grab a copy from any other NT server. You can also expand a copy from the NT Server CD-ROM using the Expand –r utility.

Another way to replace suspect boot files is to use your emergency repair disk (ERD). You create the ERD by running the RDISK.EXE utility. This utility creates a disk with the following files on it:

SETUP.LOG An information file that is used for verifying the system files

SYSTEM._ A copy of the system registry hive

SAM._ A copy of the security accounts manager database

SECURITY._ A copy of the security hive

SOFTWARE._ A copy of the software hive

DEFAULT._ A copy of the default hive

CONFIG.NT The Windows NT version of the CONFIG.SYS file used to configure an NT virtual DOS machine

AUTOEXEC.NT The Windows NT version of the AUTOEXEC .BAT file used to configure an NT virtual DOS machine

NTUSER.DA_ A copy of the *System Root*\Profiles\Default-User\Ntuser.DAT file

Files with an underscore (_) in their extensions are in compressed form and can be decompressed using the expand utility. By default, the repair disk utility will *not* back up the entire SAM or security files. Use the /s switch when running this tool to get a complete backup. If you do not use this switch, your repair disk will have a default user accounts database. If you have a problem with the registry and need to restore from the ERD, you will lose all of your user account information.

To restore from the ERD, you must boot from the setup disks provided with Windows NT Server (or create a set by using the CD-ROM). On the screen that asks whether you want to install NT or repair files, type **R** to select the repair option. After that, just follow the instructions.

The repair process can do the following things:

- Inspect the registry files—Replaces existing registry files with those on the ERD. Remember that you will lose any changes that have occurred since the last time you updated the ERD.
- Inspect startup environment—Attempts to repair a BOOT.INI file that does not list NT as an option in the user boot menu.
- Verify Windows NT system files—Verifies each file in the installation against the file that was installed originally (this is what the SETUP.LOG file is used for). If it finds a file that does not match the original, it will identify the file and ask whether it should be replaced.
- Inspect boot sector—Copies a new boot sector to the disk.

Choose the appropriate course of action to take to resolve configuration errors.

Almost everything you do on an NT-based computer will access the registry. The registry contains information about your hardware settings, the drivers needed to access that hardware, your user profiles, the software you have installed, etc. Each time you boot, the registry is read from and written to in order to determine what should happen. When you run a program such as Microsoft Word, the registry is read to determine where the program is located. When you log onto the system, the registry is read to build your security context. In other words, the registry is critical to the health of your server's operating system. Both Windows NT and Windows 95 have registry files, but the keys are not identical; this is one of the principal reasons that you cannot upgrade from Window 95 to NT.

Windows NT Registry

The *registry* is a database that contains NT configuration information. This database is organized in a hierarchical structure that consists of subtrees and their keys, hives, and values. The NT registry is made up of five subtrees, each of which holds specific types of configuration information. Each subtree holds keys that contain the computer or user databases. Each key can have specific parameters and additional subkeys. The term *hive* refers to a distinct subset of a key. You can back up a hive as a single file.

It is important that you know the five main subtrees and understand the type of information that is found in each one.

HKEY_LOCAL_MACHINE Contains hardware and operating system configuration parameters for the local computer, such as bus type, processor, device drivers, and startup information. This is the subtree that is most commonly used in the troubleshooting process for operating system errors or crashes.

HKEY_CLASSES_ROOT Defines file associations and configuration data for COM and DCOM objects.

HKEY_CURRENT_USER Contains the user profile for the user that is currently logged in. You will find parameters for the user's desktop, network connections, printers, and application preferences.

HKEY_USERS Contains all actively loaded user profiles, including a copy of HKEY_CURRENT_USER.

HKEY_CURRENT_CONFIG Contains the current hardware configuration.

Backing up and Restoring the Registry

You can back up the registry in four ways:

- Choose Save Registry in the NT Backup utility found in the Administrative Tools (Common) group. This is the preferred method if you have a tape backup unit. This method can back up and restore the registry while Windows NT is running.
- Use the two command-line tools that can also back up and restore the registry while NT is running–REGBACK.EXE and REGREST .EXE. These tools are included in the Windows NT Resource Kit.
- On the Registry menu within the registry editor, click Save Key. This process saves a single key, and everything below it, to a file. Online restorations using this method are not guaranteed, so use the backup utility whenever possible.
- Create or update your emergency repair disk. Remember to use the /s switch to ensure a complete backup.

Editing the Registry

Most of the time, you will avoid editing the registry directly–you will use various tools to adjust the configuration of your environment, and these tools will write to the registry for you. There are, however, many optimization and troubleshooting techniques that will require you to use the registry editor. You use two modes when working with the registry–backup and read-only mode.

Backing up is a simple form of protection against a moment of clumsiness. Everyone makes mistakes; the trick is to be prepared for them. The best protection is a good backup.

An option in the registry editor allows you to use read-only mode. In this mode, you can look at parameters, do your research, and know that, at the very least, you didn't inadvertently make a problem worse. After careful consideration of your options, you can then go back into the editor and make changes to the registry (after making a good backup).

Many of the troubleshooting and performance optimization techniques that have been discussed required you to make changes to the registry. By default, only members of the administrator group can change the registry; normal users are limited to read-only access. NT ships with two tools designed for manual editing of the registry database–the Windows NT registry editor (REGEDT32.EXE) and the Windows 95 registry editor (REGEDIT.EXE). While both tools allow you to edit the registry, certain keys can only be edited using the NT version.

When you edit the registry, certain changes may take effect immediately, while others might require some action on your part. In general, when you edit values in the CurrentControlSet subtree, the computer must be restarted before changes will take effect. When editing values in HKEY_CURRENT_USER, the user will often be required to log off before changes take effect.

Using the Registry Editor to Back Up a Key

Both the NT and Windows 95 versions of the registry editor allow you to back up the registry. They accomplish this goal in different ways–the NT version, shown below, will save each subkey as a separate file, so you have to save each of the five main hives individually.

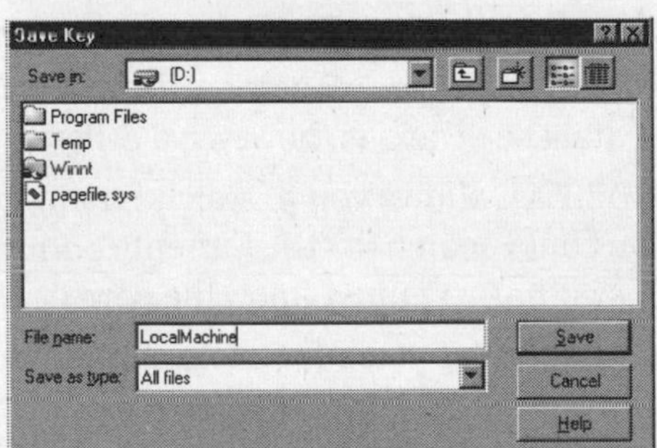

The Windows 95 version, shown below, will allow you to save the entire registry as a single file.

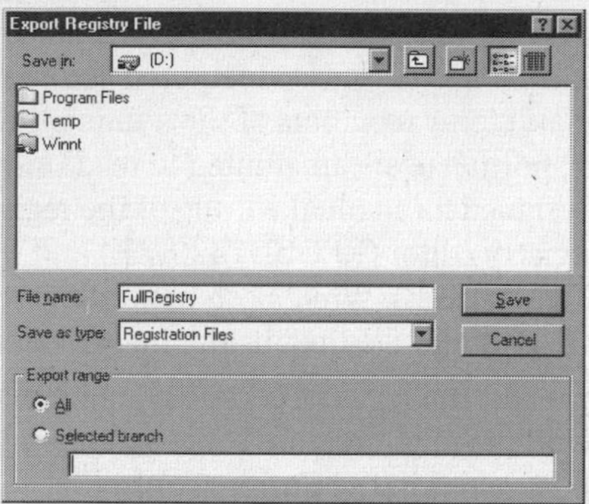

Creating or Updating an Emergency Repair Disk

The emergency repair disk creation utility, RDISK, allows you to create and update a repair disk as registry changes on your NT server. Run RDISK.EXE from a command prompt. The program will ask you for a floppy disk to copy the information to. Remember to use the /s switch when running RDISK .EXE so that you get a complete backup of the registry.

Using the Registry Editor to Search the Database

Both the NT and Windows 95 version of the registry editor allow you to search the database–there is, however, a difference in functionality.

REGEDT32.EXE allows you to search for any key by name; for instance, you could search for the CurrentControlSet key. The only problem with this is that you must know the correct name of the key.

REGEDIT.EXE gives you a few more choices as to what you can search for. You can search for the actual value or data within a key. This will come in handy if you are looking for information, but don't know which subkey it is in. For example, suppose that you have a problem with a device set to interrupt 5. In the NT version, you would have to know the name of the key in which this value was stored; in the Windows 95 version, you could search for the number 5.

Using the Registry Editor to Add or Edit the Value of a Key

To add or edit the value of a key:

1. Open REGEDT32.EXE.
2. Choose Edit ➢ Add Value.
3. You will have to determine what type of data will be entered. There are five types of data:

   REG_BINARY Represents data as a string of binary numbers

   REG_SZ Represents data as a string

   REG_EXPAND_SZ Represents data as an expandable string

   REG_DWORD Represents data as a hexadecimal value with a maximum size of 4 bytes

   REG_MULTI_SZ Represents data as multiple strings

Unless you are a software developer, you probably will not have to determine the type of data—just the value. You will choose the type based upon information found in a manual or reference material.

Using the Registry Editor to Troubleshoot a Remote Computer

You can use the registry editor to access the registry of a remote computer. You are allowed to access the HKEY_LOCAL_MACHINE and HKEY_USERS subkeys of the remote machine. Choose Registry ➢ Select Computer.

Choose the appropriate course of action to take to resolve printer problems.

Printing problems are easy to resolve if you understand the printing process. Experience has shown that printing problems fall into two basic categories—SEU (stupid end user) problems and system problems. The SEU problems are easy to solve:

- Plug in the printer.

Part II

- Turn the printer back on.
- Put paper in the printer.
- Clear the paper jam in the printer.
- Put the printer back online.
- Redirect the user to the proper printer.

Troubleshooting printing subsystem problems can be more difficult. One technique to use when troubleshooting printing problems is to generate a mental flowchart of where the print job goes. If you can figure out which step along the way is causing the problem, you can usually understand how to solve the problem.

Printing from the workstation starts when an application sends output to the software-based printer at the workstation.

NOTE

Remember that an HP LaserJet 5P is not a *printer*, it is a *print device*. The printer is the software that runs at the workstation to prepare the print job.

At this point, NT checks whether the workstation has the most up-to-date version of the printer driver. If it does, all is well. If it doesn't, NT downloads a copy of the print driver from the print server to the client.

The printer sends the job to the print spooler. The client (workstation) spooler writes the data to a file and sends a remote procedure call (RPC) to the server spooler. Then, the data are transferred from the workstation to the server spooler on the print server machine.

The print server machine sends the print job to the local print provider, which translates the information into something the printer can understand, and if necessary, adds a separator page to the print job. Separator pages are used, in some cases, to signal to the printer that a change in printer languages is coming–it needs to switch from Hewlett-Packard's printer control language (HP PCL) to PostScript or back again.

When the local print provider is done with the job, it sends the job to the print monitor, which sends it to the appropriate printer port and printing device.

If you remember the process, you can check each step along the way. When you find out where the print job stops, you can reset the application that should handle the next step. If the job comes out garbled, make sure the printer driver is up to date or determine whether there is a SEU problem.

Print troubleshooting can be divided into the following key areas:

- SEU (stupid end user) problems
- Applications (non-Windows)
- Print drivers
- Spooling
- Printing speed

Troubleshooting with SEU Tricks

When a group of end users has a printing problem, you usually find out about it when your pager goes off. Here is a list of SEU tricks:

1. Is the print device plugged in? The cleaning staff chooses the most creative places to plug in vacuum cleaners.
2. Is the printer cable attached at both ends?
3. Is the print device turned on? The end user may have told you that it is turned on, but is it really?
4. Does the print device have paper in it?
5. Does the print device need toner, ink, or a ribbon?
6. Is there a paper jam?
7. Is the paper the right size for the job the user wants to print?
8. Has someone replaced the letter-size input tray with the legal-size input tray?
9. Is the print device trying to tell you something? Check the control panel for messages or flashing lights. Read the manual to find out how to solve the problem.
10. Is there really something wrong with the print device, or is the SEU just confused? If the SEU is confused, straighten them out, politely.
11. Is the print device online? Did someone try to troubleshoot it themselves by taking the print device off-line and then forget to reset it?

Troubleshooting Non-Windows-Based Applications

Non-Windows–based applications can be tricky to troubleshoot, because they change the normal print routine. Here are some things to check:

1. Each non-Windows–based application needs to have its own set of print drivers. Does this application have the right drivers?
2. Each non-Windows–based application needs to be told where to go to print. Is this application network aware? Do you have to use the NET USE LPT1: command or some other method of setting up the printer port? Read the manual.

Troubleshooting Print Drivers

Print driver problems manifest in strange ways—print jobs suddenly take on odd appearances. Here are some common print driver problems:

1. A print job is submitted for a small document. Instead of receiving their document, the user receives page after page of smiley faces or other strange characters. Make sure that the user has a PCL print driver selected in the application. This is a classic case of a print job using a PostScript driver to print to a PCL printer.
2. A print job is submitted for a document. You can trace the print job all the way to the printer, but nothing comes out. Other than with this job, the printer works fine. Check the print driver. The user may be sending a job formatted with a PCL driver to a PostScript printer. PostScript will not act on a job that is not formatted with the appropriate driver.
3. A print job comes out with garbage embedded in the document, especially in graphics. Check to make sure that tabs and form feeds are turned off for the job. This is primarily applicable to jobs going to PostScript printers and is a workstation setting.
4. When you find a print driver update, the update needs to be made only at the print server. Drivers need to be updated only at the print server—the print server will distribute the job to the clients.

Troubleshooting Spooling

Spooling is the act of copying a file from one spot to another. Spoolers must be running at both the print server and the workstation.

1. If print jobs get stuck in a print spooler, stop and restart the spooler. Choose Start ➢ Settings ➢ Control Panel ➢ Services ➢ Spooler.
2. You can also stop and start the spooler using the NET START SPOOLER and NET STOP SPOOLER commands from the command line.
3. By default, print spoolers are stored in the \WINNT\System32\Spool\Printers folder. Be sure the disk that contains this folder has plenty of free disk space. Bad things happen when you try to print a 100MB file to a print spooler that resides on a drive with only 50MB free. Change the location of the print spooler from the Advanced tab of the Server Properties dialog box.
4. You can assign a separate spooler for each printer. Enter a path for the new spooler directory in the registry. The path will act as the data for the value SpoolDirectory . The printer name is also needed. The registry entry is HKEY_LOCAL_MACHINE\System\CurrentControlSet\Control\Print\Printers*Printer*. Be sure to stop and start the spooler so that this will take effect.
5. If the computer that houses the print spooler suffers an unexpected shutdown, the jobs that are in the spooler should print when the print spooler is restarted.

NOTE

Print jobs in the spooler are made up of two files, *.SPL and *.SHD. The file with the .SPL extension is the actual spool file—the .SHD file is a shadow file. Check the spooler directory occasionally to clean out the old, corrupted files. You can tell which ones they are by the date and time stamp.

Troubleshooting Printing Speed

A *very* common complaint of end users is the speed of the network. Here are some things you can do to remedy this situation:

1. Print spooling is a background process. NT Workstation assigns it a process priority of seven. NT Server, on the other hand, gives it a higher priority of nine, which means that it is as important as a foreground application. If your NT workstation is just a print server, increase the priority. To change the priority, add a value called PriorityClass of type REG_DWORD to HKEY_LOCAL_MACHINE\System\CurrentControlSet\Control\Print and set it with the priority class you desire.
2. Many times, third-party print servers are faster than NT-based print servers. Printers that have a built-in network card are usually the fastest providers.

NOTE

Hewlett-Packard requires that the dynamic link control (DLC) protocol is installed so that a network interface can communicate with the rest of the system.

Choose the appropriate course of action to take to resolve RAS problems.

When you troubleshoot remote access service problems, there are always two sides to the issue. You may know that your side is correct, but if the other side isn't configured exactly the same as your side, you are simply not going to talk. As a network administrator, the task is even more frustrating, because you are working with end users who are working with configurable software, cables, IRQs, internal or external modems, etc.—the list of things that can screw up is practically endless. Some common troubleshooting tools for RAS connections will be examined in the next section.

Troubleshooting Dialing Problems

Before you can establish modem communications, you have to be able to dial the phone. Here are some simple things to look for:

1. Does the phone line actually work? Is there an analog telephone you can plug into the line to make sure that there is a dial tone?
2. Now that you know there is a real phone line on the other side of the jack, are you sure the cable is good? Often, you use a different cable for your modem than you do for the phone. Replace the phone cable with your cable, if possible, and retest for a dial tone.
3. So, there is a real phone line running through your phone cable—plug the cable into your modem and try again.
4. If you still don't have a connection, start checking modem connections. If it is an internal modem, is it firmly in the slot? Did you screw it down? If so, unscrew it and reseat the card. Is it an external modem? Are the cables tight to the modem and the PC? Does the modem have power? Is the modem turned on? Is the modem working properly? Is it installed properly?
5. Is RAS installed properly? Have you selected Receive Calls Only? Have you selected Dial Out Only? Can you dial out with another simple terminal program such as HyperDialer?

Troubleshooting Connection Problems

Troubleshooting connection problems can be frustrating. Many different settings can change and mess up the works.

1. Are you dialing the right phone number?
2. Are both computers using the same type of authentication?
3. Are both sides of the conversation using the same protocols from within RAS?
4. Does the user account have dial-in privileges and is the callback feature properly set?
5. Did you verify the user name, password, and domain name when dialing in?

6. If your user can dial in, appears to connect, and then gets disconnected after authentication, did you try to enable RAS logging? When in doubt, check the log file, DEVICE.LOG.

Choose the appropriate course of action to take to resolve connectivity problems.

In reality, before you start troubleshooting your NT configuration, you should ensure that the network is functioning properly. If two computers are having problems communicating, the first step is to see if *any* computers can communicate. Pick a computer on the same physical network and try to connect from there. If you can successfully attach, the problem is probably a configuration issue. If you cannot connect, you should begin by troubleshooting your network components, such as the wiring, routers, and other physical aspects of your network. Determine whether your outage is system wide or just located on a network segment.

Once you have determined that the problem is confined to a particular computer, you can begin the process of troubleshooting its configuration. To do this, you must understand the networking architecture of Microsoft Windows NT.

Both user-mode and kernel-mode network components are in the NT architecture. Like the rest of the operating system, the network components are modular–distinct components perform each network function. If you understand the architecture, it makes troubleshooting easier. Once you have analyzed the symptoms of the problem, you can usually determine which components are involved. The overall structure of the NT networking architecture is shown in Figure 10.1.

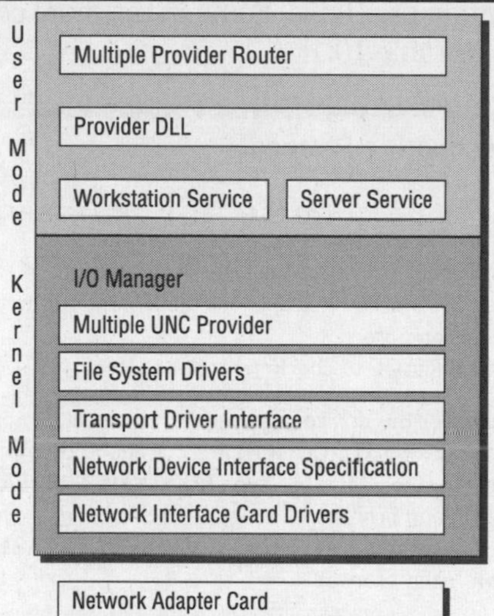

FIGURE 10.1: NT architecture

Network Interface Card (NIC) Drivers

Each type of NIC installed in your server will have a specific driver associated with it. The driver should be NDIS (network device interface specification) 4 compliant. (NDIS 3 compatible drivers will still work on an NT 4 server, but it is recommended that newer drivers be used.)

NDIS is a specification that defines how a NIC driver should communicate with the adapter, the protocols, and the operating system. Specifically, NDIS is a library of network functions that are predefined for NIC driver developers. NDIS acts as an interface layer between the driver and card, submits requests to the operating system, and allows the network drivers to receive and send packets independent of the operating system.

Typical problems at this layer of the architecture include corrupt, out-of-date, or missing drivers. Microsoft certifies all of the drivers found on the NT CD-ROM and those available for download from their Web sites. If you are using a card that is not on the hardware compatibility list, you should contact the manufacturer to determine whether they have an NT 4 driver.

Transport Protocols

The various protocols that can be used on an NT network were discussed earlier. Each of these protocols has its own tools and techniques for troubleshooting communication problems. Some of the more commonly used tools are described in Table 10.1.

TABLE 10.1: Tools for Troubleshooting Protocols

PROTOCOL	TROUBLESHOOTING TOOL OR TECHNIQUE
TCP/IP	PING the address of the remote computer. Use IPCONFIG /ALL to check the IP configuration of the local computer. Use IPROUTE to check the routing table.
NWLink	To check the IPX configuration of the local computer, type **IPXROUTE CONFIG** at a command prompt. To view the SAP table, type **IPXROUTE SERVERS** at a command prompt. To view the routing table, type **IPXROUTE TABLE** at a command prompt.
NetBIOS and AppleTalk	Neither of these protocols has a set of configuration tools. To troubleshoot these protocols, use Network Monitor to capture and analyze traffic.

Transport Driver Interface (TDI)

The TDI acts as the interpreter between the protocols and redirectors, and services above them. From a developer's perspective, the TDI acts as a common interface between these two layers. This makes writing NT networking modules easier, since the APIs (application programming interfaces) are well documented.

The server has a specific set of services that it can provide, but each protocol will ask for those services in a different way. The TDI is the interpreter because each transport protocol knows how to talk to it, and it knows how to talk to each of the services.

File System Drivers

The file system drivers are above the TDI. NT supports peer-to-peer networking, so NT Server and NT Workstation provide server services. All of the network server and redirector modules are written as file system drivers. From a developer's perspective, this makes writing networked applications easier–if the program needs to open a file, it can make the same sort of call whether the file is local or remote.

Redirectors

Redirectors provide the ability to access remote computer resources. The Windows NT system redirector allows access to Windows NT, Windows for Workgroups, LAN Manager, LAN Server, and a few other types of servers. When you design the redirector as file system drivers, it allows applications to make the same sort of call for local and remote files. The redirector runs in kernel mode, so it can take advantage of other kernel-mode modules (such as the cache manager) to increase performance; it can be dynamically loaded and unloaded; and it can coexist with other redirectors.

In addition to the NT redirector, some redirectors are used to connect to other operating systems, such as Novell NetWare and Banyan Vines. This is the true benefit of using a modular design—you can add functionality as needed.

Server Service

The server service also acts as a file-system driver. It handles incoming requests for files from the network. It is composed of the following components: SRV.SYS and LanmanServer.

Multiple UNC (Universal Naming Convention) Provider (MUP)

The MUP handles requests for files that have names following the UNC standard. In the UNC standard, names begin with a double backslash (\\), which indicates that the resource exists on the network. The MUP receives these requests and recognizes that the requested resource is remote. It then passes the request to each registered redirector until one recognizes the requested name.

Multiple Provider Router (MPR)

One of the registered redirectors that the MUP will hand requests to is the MPR. The MPR is specifically designed to handle requests that do not follow the UNC standard. It is made up of a series of provider .DLLs that provide the ability to communicate with a foreign system, such as NetWare or Banyan Vines.

Resolving Connectivity Problems

Now that the various components that make up the networking environment of the NT operating system have been examined, the objective for this section—how to resolve connectivity problems—can be discussed. Actually, given all of the discussion that led up to this, the resolution process is fairly straightforward.

Most communication problems will revolve around configuration errors rather than problems with specific software modules. The only two software components that might cause problems are the NIC driver and the third-party-provider .DLL files. The solution for either type of problem is simple—install a new copy, preferably the latest available version.

Troubleshooting configuration issues relies upon your knowledge of the various protocols in use on your network. The steps are simple, though:

1. Determine whether the problem is the transport protocol—for instance, if you are using TCP/IP, try using the PING utility to communicate. If this works, you can move up the OSI layers to the next step.
2. Test the NetBIOS connection by using a NET command. At a command line, type **NET VIEW *Server Name***. This should return a list of all shared resources on that server. If it does, the problem is probably application related.

Choose the appropriate course of action to take to resolve resource access and permission problems.

In the case of resource access or permission problems, it is simple to locate the problem. Finding the solution can be more difficult. For example, the problem may be that people cannot access a resource because they cannot log on. Is this a hardware, software, network, or, most likely, an SEU (stupid end user) problem?

Troubleshooting Resource Access and Permission Problems

When a user calls and says that they cannot access the system or a resource:

1. Ask questions. Is it just one person, or is there more than one person involved? What resource is it? Is it a hardware problem; is the printer shut off?
2. If the user cannot log on, make sure that the user is attached to the right domain, is using the right logon name, has the caps-lock key set properly to on or off (*PASSWORD* is not the same as *password*), and is supposed to be on during that time.
3. If the user cannot access a resource, can you access the resource using a different account? If so, you now have a permission problem.
4. When you have determined that the access problem is due to a permission rather than a hardware problem, the next step is to determine how the user was *supposed* to be able to access the account. Were the permissions to be assigned to a group? Can the rest of the group access the resource? If the rest of the group can access the resource, the problem lies with the individual and the group or user memberships they have been given.

TIP

Be very suspicious of the no-access permission. If a user belongs to a group that is given no access to a resource, that user will not gain access to the resource, no matter what other group membership they enjoy.

5. Make sure that the user is spelling the name of the resource correctly. You would be surprised how fast fingered some users can be, and it is amazing how long you can look at **www.micorsoft.com** before realizing that it is not the same as **www.microsoft.com**.
6. If no one can log on, has the NetLogon service stopped? Check it by going to Start ➢ Settings ➢ Control Panel ➢ Services. While you are there, check the Server and Workstation service.

7. If this is a new server and has never been brought online before, it may not be communicating with the outside world. Check the protocol bindings and make sure you are talking the same language as everyone else. You can check bindings by choosing Start ➢ Settings ➢ Control Panel ➢ Network.
8. Rights and permissions will take effect the next time the user logs on. If it is a new assignment, have the user log off and then on again.
9. The last place to look is the system policy editor. Is there a new system policy for the user or the user's computer?
10. Is the resource a directory subject to both NTFS and share permissions?

Choose the appropriate course of action to take to resolve fault-tolerance failures.

Fault-Tolerance Methods Include:

- Tape backup
- Mirroring
- Stripe set with parity
- Disk duplexing

Fault tolerance is defined as a system designed so that the failure of one component will not affect functionality. Of the three subobjectives, only two really deal with fault tolerance. A tape backup is not fault tolerant in the sense that server functionality is not affected by a failure. When you are forced to use your tape backup to recover from a critical failure, there will be a lapse in network services. Tape backups just allow you to re-create your system from archived data. Those data are only as fresh as the last time you backed them up–any data saved since that time will have to be re-created.

Tape Backup

No matter what business you are in, you need a way to archive your data to protect against loss due to hardware failure, user error, and acts of nature. The most cost-effective technology available today is tape backups. While the intent is different, tape backups offer a few advantages over the disk-based fault-tolerance technologies discussed in earlier chapters:

- The hardware and media are fairly inexpensive.
- Tapes can be stored off-site to protect against theft, fire, or flood.
- Tapes can be used for long-term archival of data. Disk-based technology is usually too expensive for long-term storage.
- A backup freezes data at a specific point. If you want an earlier version of a file, retrieve it from one of your older tapes.
- Tapes can be used to protect against mistakes when making changes to your environment. With a disk-based solution, your data are vulnerable when you are working on the server.

Most companies have a tape backup process in place. Many of those companies, however, have no plan of action in the event of a critical failure. The LAN administrators can retrieve files from the tape, but have no idea of the steps involved in recovering a complete server.

This exam objective requires you to understand the basics of server recovery from a tape backup.

1. Fix whatever physical problem is forcing the recovery. This is the step that is ignored most often when administrators put together a disaster recovery plan. If the problem is a hard drive failure, you should know which vendors to call for a replacement part and what the average turnaround time is on delivery. If your local vendor cannot deliver replacement parts within an acceptable amount of time, consider a contract with a company that guarantees their turnaround time. You should have a plan for the replacement of every critical piece of hardware on your network.

2. The next step will depend upon what piece of hardware has failed. If the disk that died is your boot device, you will have to reinstall the operating system and the partitions that existed before the disaster.

3. After the operating system is up and running, recover the registry from your backup set. Remember that any changes that were made since the backup was created will be lost. Be sure to re-create those changes before continuing with the recovery process.

4. Restore the data from your tape. Remember to check the option that restores file permissions. Once again, the tape will not contain any data created since the backup was done. Have someone from each department verify which data will have to be reentered.

The steps involved in the restoration of your data will depend upon the type of backups that you are doing. There are three main techniques for data backup:

Full backup Each time a backup is performed, the entire server is backed up. While this method of backing up your server will take the longest amount of time, it is the easiest to use for recovery. To restore you server, just use the latest available backup tape.

Incremental backup When using the incremental method of backup, first perform a full backup. Each evening after that, you back up only the data that have changed since the day before. This form of backup takes the least time to perform each evening, but can be the most confusing and time-consuming method of backup from which to recover. To recover, you must first restore the full backup, and then each tape, in order, since the full backup was performed.

Differential backup Once again, start by performing a full backup. Each evening, back up all data that have changed since that full backup. The length of time that it takes to accomplish this will increase each evening until it makes sense to do another full backup and start the process again. Recovery is fairly straight-forward–first, restore the full backup, and then restore the last differential tape.

Mirroring

As discussed in Chapter 5, disk mirroring is a software-controlled fault-tolerance system that results in two disks containing the same data. If one disk fails, the other will continue to function and users will not experience any downtime. A subset of mirroring, called duplexing, provides even more redundancy by physically connecting the two disks to two different controller boards. Duplexing not only protects against a disk-drive failure, it also provides redundant cabling and controllers.

Since NT's boot and system partitions can be mirrored, this process is used extensively in today's business environments. For this exam objective, you need to know how to reinstate the mirrored state if one of the disks fails.

Correct this problem in the Disk Administration utility found in the Administrative Tools (Common) group. It is a three-step process:

1. Break the mirror set.
2. Install the replacement hard drive.
3. Reboot and re-create the mirrored set.

The operating system will then copy the data from the existing drive to the new one. However, if the primary drive of the mirror set is the one that failed, it requires the extra step of rebooting the computer with a floppy disk containing a modified BOOT.INI file.

Stripe Set with Parity

As discussed in Chapter 5, a stripe set with parity is a software-controlled fault-tolerance disk system in which a series of disks are seen as one logical drive. Each time data are written to this logical drive, the operating system calculates parity information, which is stored on another physical disk in the set. You can use the parity information to re-create the data if one of the disks in the set fails.

When one of the disks in the set dies, the system will automatically begin using the parity information. In this way, the data are still available to users, although there is a performance cost–the data must be rebuilt from the parity information. The process of rebuilding the data can take a large amount of processor time and will usually decrease performance.

The steps to rebuild the stripe set with parity are as follows:

1. Replace the dead drive. On some of the more advanced servers, you can do this while the server is still running; otherwise, you will have to shut down your server for the installation of the new drive.

2. In the Disk Administrator utility, select the stripe set with parity. Control+click an area of free space (on your new drive), and then choose Fault Tolerance ➢ Regenerate. The regeneration process will not begin until you restart your server.

NOTE

If you have a system with hot-swappable drives (a system that allows the installation of new drives while the server is running), you should be aware of two things. First, your system probably has hardware-controlled RAID technology. Since hardware-controlled RAID is faster than software-controlled RAID, you should implement the manufacturer's version and read the manual for your server to learn about the recovery process. Second, if for some reason you do use NT's stripe set with parity technology, be aware that when you install the new drive and finish the recovery process, the system will not begin rebuilding the data on the new drive until you restart the server. This process will add a tremendous amount of overhead to your server.

Disk Duplexing

Disk duplexing is a subset of mirroring. The only difference is that in a duplexed system, the two drives are attached to different disk controllers. On a mirrored system, if one disk dies, the other takes over with no interruption of service. If the controller fails, however, there is no way to get to the data on either disk. In a duplexed system, if a controller fails, the other hard drive in the mirrored set is still active. The second controller can still access the redundant disk. Basically, you have extended the fault tolerance to the next piece of hardware—the controller.

Another advantage of duplexing is performance. In a mirrored system, each time data are written to disk, the operating system must first write to one drive and then the other. This is often referred to as a serial procedure. In a duplexed system, the operating system can write to both disks simultaneously, reducing the overall time it takes to write data to disk. This is often referred to as a parallel process.

To create a duplexed system, set up a mirrored set using Disk Administrator. A mirrored set is automatically considered to be duplexed if the two disks are attached to separate controllers. You will not see the term *duplex* in any of the menu choices. To recover from a disk failure in the duplexed set, follow the same procedure for recovering from a failure in a mirrored set—break the mirror, install the new hardware, and re-create the mirror.

Breaking the Mirrored Set

To break the mirrored set:

1. Highlight the mirrored partitions in the Disk Administrator utility.
2. Choose Fault Tolerance ➢ Break Mirror.

Re-creating the Mirrored Set

To re-create the mirrored set:

1. In Disk Administrator, Ctrl+click the two partitions of equal size.
2. Choose Fault Tolerance ➢ Establish Mirror.

Regenerating a Stripe Set with Parity

To regenerate a stripe set with parity:

1. Install the new hard disk.
2. In Disk Administrator, Ctrl+click the stripe set and an area of free space.
3. Choose Fault Tolerance ➢ Regenerate.
4. Restart the server.

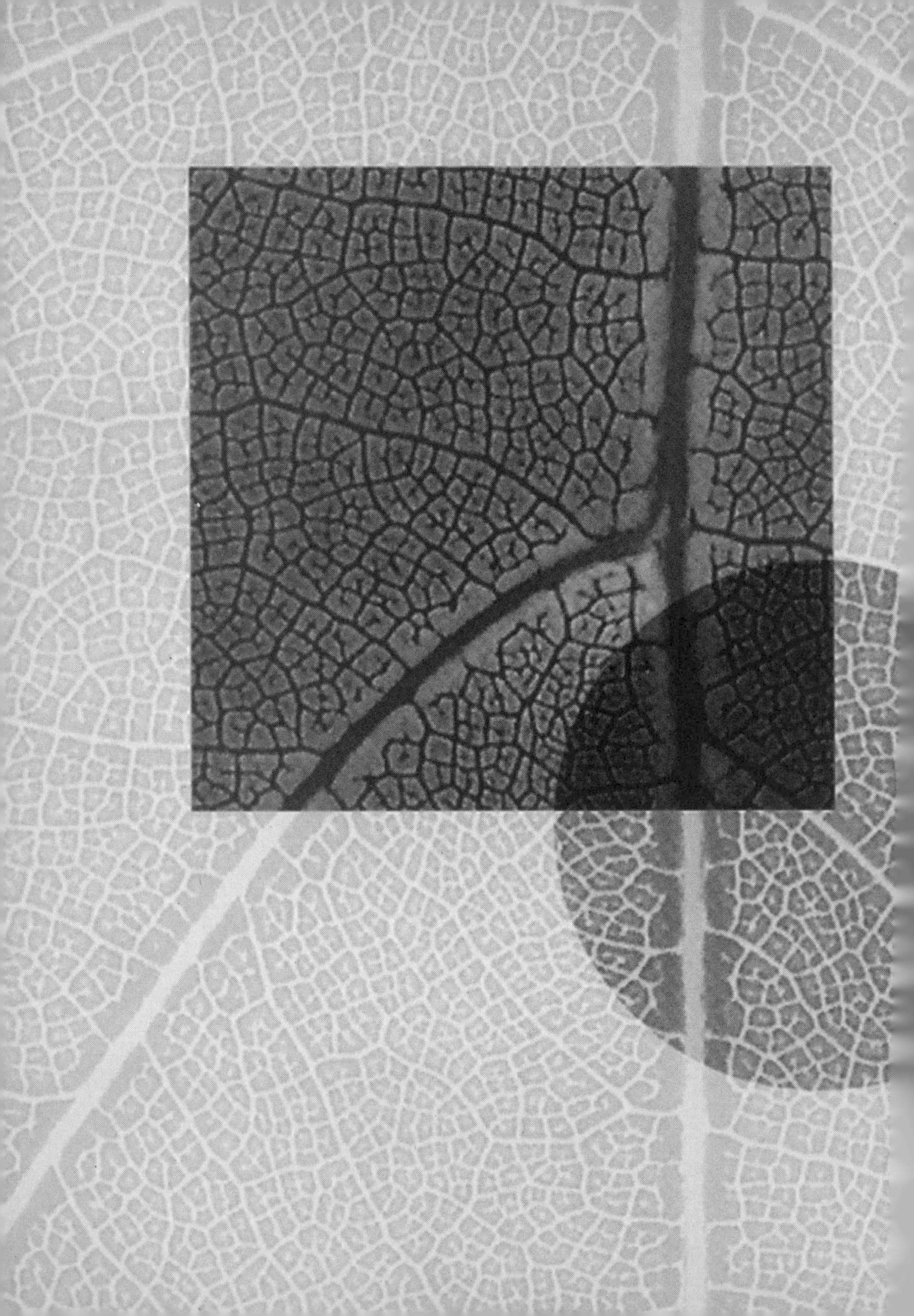

Part II

NT Server 4 Practice Exam

1. Which of the following selections is a valid disk configuration?

   A. Three primary partitions—two set active

   B. Three primary partitions—one set active, one extended partition

   C. Two primary partitions—one set active, one extended partition

2. When assigning drive letters, in what order does NT perform the following actions?

   A. Starting with drive 0, assign letters to logical drives

   B. Starting with drive 0, assign letters to primary partitions

   C. Starting with drive 0, assign letters to the first primary drive on each disk

3. A network administrator has noticed that network performance has decreased since 20 new workstations were added to the network. Which of the following services might help correct this problem?

   A. DHCP

   B. WINS

   C. RAS

   D. IIS

4. Suppose that your network consists of an NT 4 primary domain controller. It is configured with 50 CALs and set to use Per Server licensing. Your users continue to access the resources provided by your network, and it has become necessary to add a second server to provide BDC capabilities. Your client workstations include 35 NT 4 workstations, 5 Windows 95 workstations, and 5 Windows for Workgroups workstations. What would be the most cost-effective way to license the servers?

5. When the change log fills up, which of the following things will occur?

   A. A new log will be created

   B. Records will be overwritten

C. A complete update will occur in the next pulse

D. An administrative alert will be sent to members of the administrators group

6. The /OX switch, when used in conjunction with the WINNT.EXE file, will do what?

A. Start an unattended installation

B. Point to the unattended installation file

C. Run the installation without creating three startup diskettes

D. Create three startup diskettes

7. Suppose that you are charged with creating a distribution server. Which two subdirectories do you need to XCOPY from the NT installation CD to the distribution server?

A. Windows

B. i386

C. Tools

D. DRVLIB

8. Which of the following parameters should be configured for the IPX/SPX protocol?

A. Frame type

B. Packet size

C. Network number

D. NetWare server name

9. When you install a network interface card, if you are using a 16-bit AT bus slot, what must the interrupt setting on the card be?

A. Unique

B. Shared

C. Assigned to the slot

D. The same for every card

10. Which types of licenses will License Manager track?

    A. NT Server client access licenses

    B. Number of licenses purchased for Microsoft Office

    C. Number of licenses purchased for Microsoft Word

    D. Any license for any product

11. Configuring a modem in NT can be done through:

    A. Control Panel

    B. Rocker switches on the bottom of the modem

    C. Buttons on the front of the modem

    D. User Manager for Domains

12. Which of the following items are true for a volume set?

    A. Adds together multiple sections of free space.

    B. Data are written to each partition until that partition is full before moving to the next partition.

    C. Data are written to each partition in sequence so that all are used equally.

    D. Can hold the system and boot partition for Windows NT.

13. The basic Microsoft understanding of groups is as follows:

    A. Local groups can be placed in global groups.

    B. Global groups should be placed in local groups.

    C. Never use local groups; always use global groups.

    D. Never use global groups; always use local groups.

14. Suppose that your boss is a control freak. He wants to make sure that each NT workstation has exactly the same system policies. Each workstation is attached to the network, and the users must always log onto the domain before starting work. How can you keep your boss happy?

    A. Create a system policy file and export it to each workstation the first time it logs on.

    B. Create a system policy file for each end user and copy it to the user profiles directory on the domain controller.

C. Create a system policy file and copy it to each workstation's WINNT folder.

D. Create a system policy file that will affect all end users and copy it to the NETLOGON folder of the PDC.

15. After you created a system policy and stored it in the NETLOGON directory so that people can access it, you find that the policy is virtually ignored by several systems on your network. What is a possible cause?

A. The computers may have a local policy that conflicts with the system policy.

B. The user on the computer is logging onto the domain as administrator, nullifying any policy changes.

C. The user on the computer is logging onto the domain as guest, nullifying any policy changes.

D. You screwed up.

16. Given the default permissions assigned to groups, which groups would you need to belong in to create a share?

A. Administrators

B. Backup users

C. Guests

D. Users

17. Suppose that a user is a member of three groups—Administrators, MIS, and Apps_Acctg. There is a share created called Accounting. The Administrators group has Full Control permissions to the Accounting share. The MIS group has been assigned No Access permissions, and the Apps_Acctg group has been given the Change permission. What can the user do with the share?

A. The user has full rights to the share, granted to them through their membership in the Administrators group.

B. The user can read or see a folder, subfolder, or file; execute an application; write to a closed file; and delete a folder or file. These are inherent in the Change permission the user received through their membership in Apps_Acctg.

C. The user can attach to the share, but cannot see or do anything. This is a result of the No Access permission given to the MIS group.

18. Which of the following items is loaded on client computers to allow direct access to Novell NetWare servers?

A. CSNW (Client Service for NetWare)

B. GSNW (Gateway Service for NetWare)

C. NCS (Novell connection software)

D. Novell TCP/IP services

E. NWLink IPX/SPX Compatible Transport

19. What is multilink?

A. The ability to have two or more modems handling different calls at the same time

B. The ability to have two or more modems call out at the same time

C. The ability to use more than one communication channel for the same connection

D. The ability to have two network interface cards in the same system at the same time

20. Which of the Performance Monitor views allows you to save data for later analysis?

A. Chart

B. Report

C. Log

D. Alert

21. On a file and print server, which of the four main components is most likely to be the bottleneck?

A. Memory

B. Processor

C. Disk

D. Network

22. On an application server, which of the four main components is most likely to be the bottleneck?

A. Memory

B. Processor

C. Disk

D. Network

23. What are the four phases of an NT boot (in the correct order)?

A. Initial, Boot loader, Kernel, Logon

B. Boot loader, Initial, Kernel, Logon

C. Boot loader, Kernel, Initial, Logon

D. Logon, Initial, Boot loader, Kernel

24. A user is given the chance to use the last known good configuration in which phase of the NT startup?

A. Initial

B. Boot loader

C. Kernel

D. Logon

25. Which of the five main registry subtrees holds file association information?

A. HKEY_LOCAL_MACHINE

B. HKEY_CLASSES_ROOT

C. HKEY_CURRENT_USER

D. HKEY_USERS

E. HKEY_CURRENT_CONFIG

26. Suppose that a user has a big report due in the morning. They are trying to print that report to an HP printer that has an onboard network interface card using the DLC protocol. DLC is currently installed and working on their computer. Even after the user resets the printer, they still cannot print to it. What is the most likely cause of the problem?

    A. The user isn't sending their print job to the HP printer; they are using a printer on a different floor.

    B. The printer is out of paper.

    C. Somewhere on the network, there is another computer hooked to the printer using DLC in continuous-connection mode.

    D. The print device is currently servicing an Apple computer and will come back online when it is finished with the Apple print job.

27. All else has failed–it is time to read the log. Where are entries made for RAS logging?

    A. WINNT\DEVICE.LOG

    B. WINNT\System32\RAS.LOG

    C. WINNT\System32\RAS\DEVICE.LOG

    D. WINNT\System32\RAS\Ras.LOG

28. How do you view the RAS log?

    A. Use Event Viewer

    B. Use a text editor

    C. Only through Word

    D. Only through WordPerfect

29. Which of the following items accepts and handles network requests that use UNC names?

    A. MUP

B. MPR

C. TDI

30. Which of the following items accepts and handles requests not formatted using a UNC name?

A. MUP

B. MPR

C. TDI

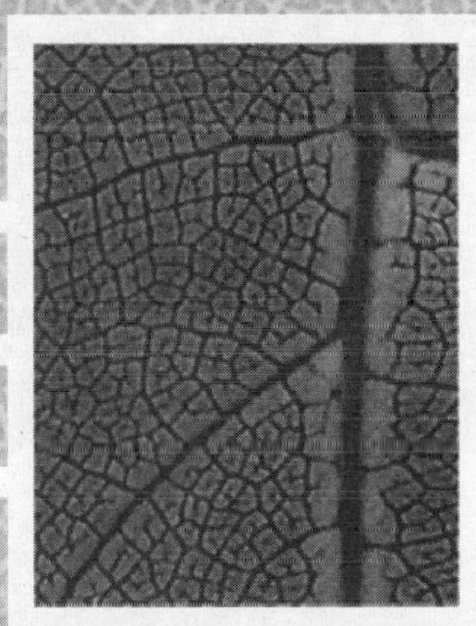

PART iii
NT Workstation 4

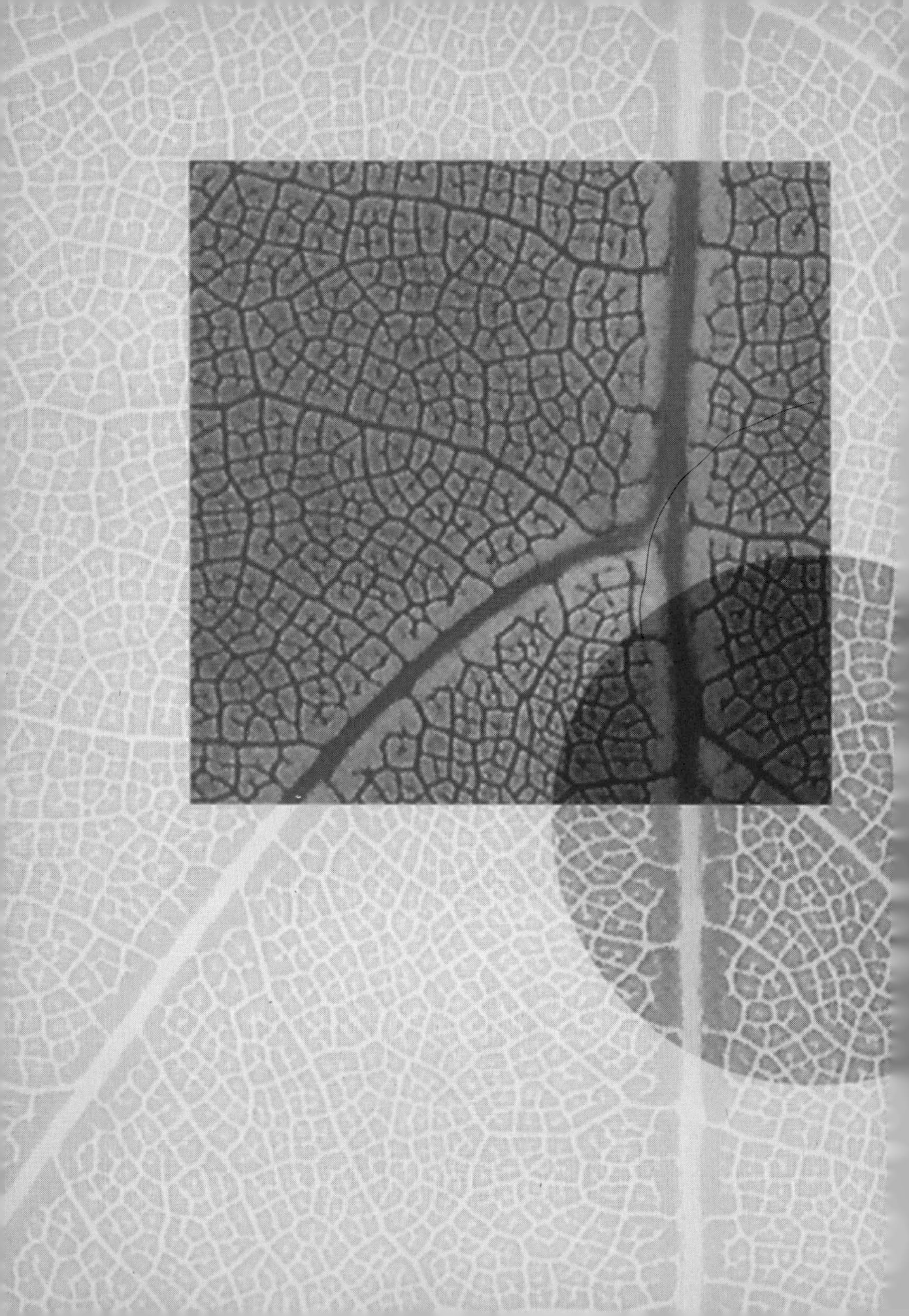

Chapter 11

Planning

Implementing a new desktop operating system is not an easy process. It has major implications, even if you are discussing changing the operating system of just your desktop computer, not to mention an entire organization. Sometimes, the reasons for the change are irrefutable, and once the final decision has been made, it is up to you to implement the decision. Mastering the objectives covered in this chapter will make the projected rollout run smoother with much less work.

Adapted from *MCSE Exam Notes: NT Workstation 4* by Gary Govanus and Robert King

ISBN 0-7821-2290-6 352 pages $19.99

Once you have NT deployed to the desktop, you need to understand the whole reason behind networks: the sharing of resources and information. If a user is sharing the information on their computer with others, they are going to want some reassurance that the data will be safe from unauthorized access. The same is true with the hardware resources on your network. The chances that the Human Resources department will want every Tom, Dick, and Harriet printing to the printer that is loaded with payroll checks are slim to none.

If you decide that security is an issue, implementing it is part of a multi-tiered process. An important factor in that process is the way your disk drives access information, that is, the basic file system the computer will use. NT is capable of using the New Technology File System (NTFS), the File Allocations Tables (FAT), and the CD File System (CDFS). Each of these file systems has advantages and disadvantages.

Create unattended installation files.

An unattended installation can be the next best thing to sliced bread for an administrator who is rolling out a large number of desktops. For the administrator who has to do five or ten workstations, the work involved in setting up and configuring an unattended install may not be worth it. Besides, there are more and more third-party utilities that make this a really easy process without all the grunt work. While this may or may not be something you will use, it will be something you will be tested on, so read on, my friend.

Before you have visions of walking into your boss's office one afternoon to say that in the last four hours you configured 2,000 workstations, remember that there is some groundwork that needs to be laid. Actually, there are several steps to take. You can use an *unattended answer file* to handle the routine questions that NT asks, plus you can use a uniqueness database file (UDF) to handle the not-so-routine questions. Finally, after NT has been configured as the operating system of choice, you can complete the installation by using the SYSDIFF utility to download a complete application suite to the desktop.

Here is how it works. You should start by looking at the computers you are going to configure and making some notes about how you are going to configure them. You may want to look at the NT Workstation installation CD and find the file named UNATTEND.TXT, located in the \i386 folder. This is a sample of the file you will be customizing to provide you with the starting point of your "simple" install.

TIP

At first glance, preparing an unattended installation may not look all that easy, but if you are configuring lots of workstations, the time invested is well worth it.

Looking at the UNATTEND.TXT file, you will see some generic questions. For instance, in the first section, you will be asked if this is an OEM (Original Equipment Manufacturer) installation, if you want to confirm hardware, if it is an NT upgrade, whether you are upgrading from Windows 3.1, and where to put the root folder. The next section provides some unique information on the user: the user name, the organization name, and a computer name. You get the idea—all the generic information that you would be entering time after time after time if you did this without the unattended files. You will also be prompted for information on the Display setting, time zones, network installation, protocols, and DHCP.

Since this is such routine information, there must be some way to automate the creation of the UNATTEND.TXT file. Actually, there is, but it is going to cost you some bucks. The Setup Manager is a graphical utility that comes on the Windows NT Resource Kit CD, which is pricey.

NOTE

The UNATTEND.TXT file on the NT Workstation installation CD shows a small number of the options you can configure. For more information, refer to the Microsoft TechNet CD.

But, you ask, keen of eye and all-knowing in the ways of installations, that is all fine and good for some of the information, but what about all that stuff that is unique to the computer? For that, you can create a uniqueness database file, or UDF.

The UDF contains information that is unique to each system. You can create the UDF with any text editor, and it will contain information that must be unique per computer: things like the user's full name, the organization name, and the computer name. These instructions are contained in sections defined as UniqueIDs. Once the UDF file is completed, you can use these two pieces—the UNATTEND.TXT file and the UDF file—to do an unattended install.

Here's a scenario to illustrate the point. You have to install 10 machines that contain exactly the same hardware. You have invested in the resource kit, so you fire up Setup Manager and create a generic unattended installation file called UNATTEND.TXT. In addition, you have brushed up on your typing skills and created a uniqueness database file that contains information on all 10 new owners of these machines. This work of art is named UDF10.TXT. Each user has its own UniqueID, numbered 1 to 10. The unattended answer file and the uniqueness database file have been installed out to a network share that is assigned a drive letter of J:. In addition to the two text files, you have also copied the \i386 folder from the Windows NT Workstation installation CD. When you are ready to install your first workstation, you boot the workstation, configure the share to point to J:, and then from a command prompt, type in the following syntax:

```
winnt /s:f:\ /u:UNATTEND.TXT /UDF:id1,udf10.txt
```

As NT begins to install, all information will be taken from the source subdirectory (`/s:f:\`). Information will be filtered in from the UNATTEND .TXT file (`/u:UNATTEND.TXT`) and unique information will come for user 1 from the UDF10.TXT file (`/UDF:id1,udf10.txt`).

The NT operating system will now be installed using all the parameters you passed to it from the two files. The workstation configuration is far from completed, however. After all, you have to configure it to run Microsoft Office, along with several proprietary applications that may take you an additional four or five hours to install on each machine. SYSDIFF to the rescue!

The SYSDIFF Utility

SYSDIFF is a utility that is used to take a snapshot of the machine after the installation of the operating system, but before the installation of any applications. Once the snapshot has been taken, all the applications are installed and configured on the model machine. After that configuration is completed, then SYSDIFF is run again, this time in *difference mode*. SYSDIFF looks at the machine and finds and records the differences between the state of preliminary NT installation and the current state of the computer. This information is then saved to a *differences file*. When SYSDIFF is run on the next machine, it will apply the data from the difference file to another Windows NT installation, completing the automated installation of the workstation.

WARNING

SYSDIFF will work only on computers of the same hardware configuration.

SYSDIFF can also be used to create an INF file and installation data from the difference file. This information can be saved to the server-based installation share, and these changes can be applied to any installations done from this share.

Requirements for Unattended Process

Three components are necessary to the unattended process:

- The UNATTEND.TXT file
- The UDF file
- The SYSDIFF utility

The UNATTEND.TXT File

This sample file is taken directly from the Windows NT 4.0 Workstation CD. It is in the \i386 folder.

NOTE

The UNATTEND.TXT file can be edited using any text editor to provide for generic input specific to your site.

Let's see how you may need to configure this file. You are going to be installing Windows NT on a workstation, but you do not want to hang around while the files are being copied. You know it will be a clean installation with no upgrades, but you will be changing the default location of the root directory to \WIN instead of \WINNT; after all, old habits die hard. In addition, the workstation has a VGA card in it, and the display will be 800 × 600 instead of the default 640 × 480. You want the system to detect the network cards and install the TCP/IP protocol. Finally, you want the computer to join the PSMain domain to accept DHCP.

What needs to be changed from the boilerplate file? Let's take a quick look at it section by section.

[Unattended]

```
OemPreinstall = no
ConfirmHardware = no
NtUpgrade = no
Win31Upgrade = no
TargetPath = WINNT
OverwriteOemFilesOnUpgrade = no
```

Part III

From this section, in looking at the instructions, the only section that will have to be edited is the `TargetPath`:. WINNT should be changed to WIN.

[UserData]

```
FullName = "Your User Name"
OrgName = "Your Organization Name"
ComputerName = COMPUTER_NAME
```

Here a number of changes need to be made. In this case, the installing user and organization name will have to be replaced with the corporate standards. In place of `"Your User Name"`, enter something descriptive like Dilbert. For the `OrgName` line, put in the name of your organization—let's say it's ACME Blasting Co. The `ComputerName` needs to be a unique entry in the Domain. Let's say Wally.

NOTE

Since you weren't told to change the time zone, the [GUIUnattended] section will stay the same.

[Display]

```
ConfigureAtLogon = 0
BitsPerPel = 16
XResolution = 640
YResolution = 480
VRefresh = 70
AutoConfirm = 1
```

Get out the user manual for the display and see if you have to change bits per pixel or VRefresh. Otherwise, just change the `XResolution` to 800 and the `YResolution` to 600, and the [Display] section is finished.

[Network]

```
Attend = yes
DetectAdapters = ""
InstallProtocols = ProtocolsSection
JoinDomain = Domain_To_Join
```

This section is not very self-explanatory. The first choice—`Attend = yes`—means that the system will slip back into interactive mode (you get to push buttons) when it hits the section on installing the Network adapter card. If you change this to `no` you will have to add sections to the file that will allow the installation to configure the installed network adapter card.

`DetectAdapters` and `InstallProtocols` can be changed to point to a user-defined section name. If you are installing multiple 3Com 575 cards in each machine, you may create a section called [3C575]. If `DetectAdapters` is left at `""`, the system will attempt to detect and install the first network adapter card it finds. If you are installing multiple protocols, you would configure a section for the protocols.

WARNING

Make sure that there is no space between the two quotation marks ("") in the `DetectAdapters` section. Also, if the `InstallProtocols` and the `DetectAdapter` keys are not present, the system will default to interactive mode.

Here is an example of the section after you have customized it.

```
[Network]
Attend = no
DetectAdapters = 3c575
InstallProtocols = TCPIPSection
JoinDomain = PSMAIN
CreateComputerAccount=BrandiceC, DeniseB

[3C575]
DetectCount=1
IRQ=3
IOBaseAddress=0x300
IOChannel=auto
Transceiver=auto

[TCPIPSection]
TC=TCPIPParams

[TCPIPParams]
DHCP=Yes
DNSServer=192.1.1.2, 192.1.1.3, 192.1.1.4
WINSPrimary=111.2.2.2
DNSName=PSCONSULTING.COM
```

When the unattended installation is completed using the UNATTEND .TXT file, the system files will be installed in the WIN folder instead of the WINNT folder. The user who installed the system is named Dilbert, and he works for the ACME Blasting Co. The computer is named Wally. Since you did not mess with the default time zone, it is set for the Pacific

Part III

time zone. The display will be an 800 × 600 VGA display. There will be a 3Com 575 Ethernet adapter installed with an IRQ of 3 and a base I/O address of 300. The IO Channel and the transceiver will be automatically selected. The system will have TCP/IP configured to use Dynamic Host Control Protocol. It will receive the Domain Name Service from the host at address 192.1.1.2, 192.1.1.3, or 192.1.1.4. The Windows Internet Name Service or WINS will be handled by the host at 111.2.2.2. The computer will be added to the Domain Name Service of PSCONSULTING.COM.

NOTE

For more complete coverage of all the sections available in the unattended answer file, refer to the *MCSE: NT Workstation 4 Study Guide* by Charles Perkins, Matthew Strebe, and James Chellis (Sybex, 1998).

The Uniqueness Database File (UDF)

The following is a sample to create five different computers. This file is created using a text editor and saved in plain text format. In the case above, there was still some information on user data that needed to be added to the UNATTEND.TXT file. You can configure the UDF file to provide that information, as shown below.

In the section above, the example showed you entering information into the [UserData] section. You could choose to use a UDF file that lays out the information for multiple users, and this information would be used in order during the installations. For example, the first installation would use the information from the UNATTEND.TXT file until it came to the [UserData] section. At that point it would jump to the UDF file and grab the information about the first user. When it had input Gary Govanus at Paradigm Shift using a computer name of PS1, it would go back and get more information from the UNATTEND.TXT file. Here is the layout of a customized UDF file.

```
;UDF file to complete installation of 5 new computers
;
;
[UniqueIds]
u1 = UserData
u2 = UserData
u3 = UserData
u4 = UserData
u5 = UserData
```

```
[u1:UserData]
FullName = "Gary Govanus"
OrgName = "Paradigm Shift"
ComputerName = PS1
[u2:UserData]
FullName = "Bob King"
OrgName = "Royal Technologies"
ComputerName = RT1
[u3:UserData]
FullName = "Bobbi Govanus"
OrgName = "For Your Instructors"
ComputerName = FYI1
[u4:UserData]
FullName = "Susan King"
OrgName = "Nursing Specialities"
ComputerName = NS1
[u5:UserData]
FullName = "Brandice Carpenter"
OrgName = "Paradigm Shift"
ComputerName = PS2
```

The SYSDIFF Utility

The System Difference, or SYSDIFF, utility is found on the Windows NT Workstation 4.0 CD. To install the tool, simply copy *<driveletter>*:`\support\deptools\i386\SYSDIFF.EXE` and SYSDIFF.INF to a directory on your hard drive.

The syntax of a SYSDIFF command line is as follows:

```
SYSDIFF.EXE [/snap | /diff | /apply | /dump | /inf]
[/log:log_file]
```

The individual components of this line are explained below:

/snap When you run SYSDIFF the first time, it takes a snapshot of the Windows Registry, the file systems, and the directories. The information is stored in a snapshot file.

/diff Once the model machine has been completely configured, SYSDIFF is run again. This time the utility records any changes made to the file system, the directories and the registry. This information is stored in a difference file.

/apply On the next computer that is installed, SYSDIFF applies the differences, simplifying the application installation process.

Part III

/dump Generates a file that allows you to look at the details of the difference file.

/inf SYSDIFF can automatically create an INF file and installation data based on the differences file. This can be applied to a server-based share and the differences will be applied to any further Windows NT installations made from that share.

/log Location of the log file.

Plan strategies for sharing and securing resources.

Before planning your data structure, you will need to gather two critical lists. The first should be a list of system users, and the second should be a list of the data and applications that will be stored on your network. The process of gathering this information can be difficult–you will have to talk to representatives of each department, and possibly even do a series of interviews with key employees. Some of the questions you should ask are:

- What information is critical to your function?
- Who should have access to this data?
- What applications do you use?
- Are there any special hardware or licensing issues with that software?

Based upon the answers to these questions, you can begin to build a list of resources that will be shared across the network, and who will need access to those resources. After gathering this data, build a table that lists the data and applications across the top and the users down the side. You can then document what resources each user will need. Figure 11.1 shows a spreadsheet from a recent installation.

Users	Win3.1	Win95	WinNT	Word	Excl	Access	Accounting	Research	Sales
	Applications						**Data**		
Bking			X	X	X	X		X	
Sking		X		X	X		X		
Kking	X			X	X				X
Ggovanus			X	X	X	X		X	
Bmalone			X		X	X		X	
Jgibson			X	X	X	X		X	
Dkarpinski		X		X	X				X
Ekarpinski		X		X	X			X	
Danderson	X			X	X	X	X		

FIGURE 11.1: Planning resources

Once your data is gathered and you've organized it, the next step is to look for logical groupings of users. Be aware that it is usually easier to manage a system where most permissions are managed through groups rather than through individual assignments.

Once you've decided how to group your users, you can add these groups to your overview, as shown in Figure 11.2.

Users	Win3.1	Win95	WinNT	Word	Excl	Access	Accounting	Research	Sales
	Applications						**Data**		
Word users				X					
Excel users					X				
Access users						X			
Accounting							X		
Research								X	
Sales									X
Bking			X	X	X	X		X	
Sking		X		X	X		X		
Kking	X			X	X				X
Ggovanus			X	X	X	X		X	
Bmalone			X		X	X		X	
Jgibson			X	X	X	X		X	
Dkarpinski		X		X	X				X
Ekarpinski		X		X	X			X	
Danderson	X			X	X	X	X		

FIGURE 11.2: Planning resources using logical groupings

Now you are ready to start planning rules for resource access. While each environment will be different, there are a few general guidelines that you should consider. In general, there are two types of files that users will need to access–application and data. Each type has its own set of guidelines.

Part III

Network Applications

Microsoft suggests that applications not be stored on the same volume as your operating system and boot files. If you keep them separate, in the event that you have to reinstall NT, there is a good chance that the application volume will not have to be restored. Some other guidelines include:

- Make any permission assignments *before* you share the resource. This prevents unauthorized access during the period between sharing and securing.
- Make executable files read-only for all users.
- Create and share a common applications folder. Within that folder, create a folder for each application. This allows you to set permissions on the upper folder that can be applied to each of the lower folders automatically.
- If licensing issues require it, you can then remove permissions from selected lower-level application folders on a case-by-case basis—allowing only the appropriate users access to the applications.
- If your software is licensed on a simultaneous users basis, meaning that access is limited to a certain number of users at one time, share the appropriate folder and limit the number of users who can connect to it.
- Remember to assign the Administrators group full control to the application directory, and remove the Full Control permission from the Everyone group.
- Remember to assign the Change permission to whomever will be responsible for maintaining each application.

Network Data Folders

Microsoft suggests that data folders also be kept on a separate volume from your operating system and boot files. This allows you to easily configure your backup software to back up only data, since the operating system and applications rarely change. Some other guidelines include:

- Make any permission assignments *before* you share the resource. This prevents unauthorized access during the time between sharing and securing.

- Analyze the type of access the users will need. If users need to edit the data, make sure they have the appropriate permissions.
- Organize your data for ease of access and management. Create a main folder to store all shared data folders.
- Assign permissions to each subfolder as appropriate.

WARNING

Remember human nature—it is much easier to give higher permissions later than it is to take away rights that someone has grown used to!

Choose the appropriate file system to use in a given situation.

File Systems and Situations Include:

- NTFS
- FAT
- HPFS
- Security
- Dual-Boot systems

The file system controls the mechanics of how a file is written to, or read from, the physical hard drive. Microsoft Windows NT supports multiple file systems—each of which has strengths and weaknesses. As an MCSE you will be required to choose the file systems that will be used on your NT computers based upon the needs of your business.

NT supports four different file systems:

- NTFS (New Technology File System)
- FAT (File Allocation Table)
- HPFS (High Performance File System)

NOTE

Although you cannot create or manage an HPFS partition on NT 4, you can still mount it. This comes in handy during an upgrade.

- CDFS (CD-ROM file system)

NOTE

Since CDFS is a specialized file system used for CD-ROMs, it will not be discussed here.

NTFS

NTFS is the file system specifically designed to be used on a Windows NT–based computer. It offers many advantages over the older FAT file system. NTFS offers the following:

- File and directory-level security
- Support of larger file and partition sizes. Theoretically, both the maximum file and partition size is 16 exabytes. Functionally, with today's hardware, the limit is 2 terabytes.
- Support for file compression
- A recoverable file system. It uses a transaction log for disk activity. The log file can be used to redo or undo operations that failed.
- Bad-cluster remapping. If a write error occurs, the file system will move the data to another sector of the disk.
- Support for Macintosh files. (You must install Services for Macintosh.)
- Support for POSIX.1-compliant software
- Reduced file fragmentation

There are only two small drawbacks to NTFS: Since it has a fairly high overhead (about 50MB), floppy disks cannot be formatted with NTFS; also, NTFS does not support removable media. When using removable media formatted with NTFS, you must restart the computer to change disks.

FAT

The FAT file system has been in use since the earliest days of DOS computers. FAT has minimal overhead (less than 1MB) and is the most efficient file system for partitions smaller than 400MB. Since it is the only file system that both DOS (or Windows 95) and Windows NT have in common, the system partition must be a FAT partition on dual-boot machines. RISC-based computers will only boot from a FAT partition, so all RISC systems must have a small FAT partition to hold boot files.

On the down side, performance decreases as the number of files in a partition increases due to the way files are tracked. Another drawback is that the FAT file system has no features to prevent file fragmentation, another problem that can affect performance. Lastly, as a security feature, Windows NT prevents a deleted file from being undeleted, but on a FAT partition (if the computer is booted to DOS) undelete tools might be able to recover deleted files. There is also no file or directory-level security available on a FAT partition. The only security would be that available through directory-level sharing. We'll discuss security issues in more detail later in this section.

The version of the FAT file system included with Windows NT has been enhanced to support long filenames. Filenames adhere to the following criteria:

- Names can be up to 255 characters (including the full path).
- Names must start with a letter or number and can include any characters except: "/\[];:=,^*?.
- Names can include multiple spaces.
- Names can include multiple periods.
- Names preserve case but are not case sensitive.

TIP

As an aid to troubleshooting, many administrators will create a FAT partition and place the NT boot files there. In the event of a problem they can then boot to DOS, and access the files on the partition—replacing corrupt files or using DOS based disk diagnostic tools.

HPFS

HPFS is the native file system used by OS/2. Earlier versions of Microsoft Windows NT allowed the management of HPFS partitions on an NT server. This capability was provided primarily to ease the migration from OS/2 to NT. NT version 4.0 no longer supports the ability to manage HPFS partitions.

TIP

HPFS was covered in the MSCE exams for earlier versions of NT, but is not being heavily covered in the NT 4.0 exams. This objective may actually be a holdover from earlier exams.

The key features of the HPFS environment follow:

- Long filenames are supported–up to 254 characters.
- Names preserve case but are not case sensitive.
- Any characters can be used except the following: ?"/*|:.
- HPFS does not create a "short" or DOS-compatible filename for each file. This could impact accessibility from some applications.
- HPFS partitions cannot be protected by local file or directory-level security.
- Performance might suffer on drives larger than 400MB.

Security

First, let's define *local file and directory-level security*. On an NT system, this phrase can only be applied to an NTFS partition. It implies that security will be applied to file access of a user sitting at the computer upon which the files are stored. This differs from *share security*, which can be used on all file systems. Share security applies only to users who are accessing a directory over the network.

The following three items should give you enough detail to make an informed decision.

HPFS Will never be the file system of choice unless you are in the process of upgrading an OS/2 computer to Windows NT. HPFS on NT provides no mechanism for local file or directory level security.

FAT Does not provide local or file level security. Anyone who successfully logs in at a computer can access any file stored on a FAT partition. Share security still applies at the directory level. About the only benefit to FAT over NTFS is the fact that a FAT partition can be accessed by DOS. In the event of problems, you can boot to a DOS disk and access any data on the partition.

WARNING

Of course, this also means that anyone can do the same thing; in other words, a FAT partition is an open door for data thieves.

NTFS Provides security at the local file and directory level. NTFS also has various tools that protect data from disaster–bad-cluster remapping and a log file to recover from interrupted transactions.

Dual-Boot Systems

Microsoft is very specific in recommending that you do not dual-boot your Windows NT computer with another operating system. Since this is not a supported configuration, you are pretty much on your own as far as troubleshooting any problems.

With that said, there will be times where you are forced to dual-boot between NT and either DOS or Windows 95. You might have a legacy software package that won't work with NT, or you might need to set up a machine in your testing lab to serve multiple functions. The setup process will be discussed in Chapter 12. For now you should know that there is only one file system that creates partitions that can be read by DOS, Windows 95, *and* Windows NT–the FAT file system. If you intend to dual-boot your computer you will have to boot to a FAT partition.

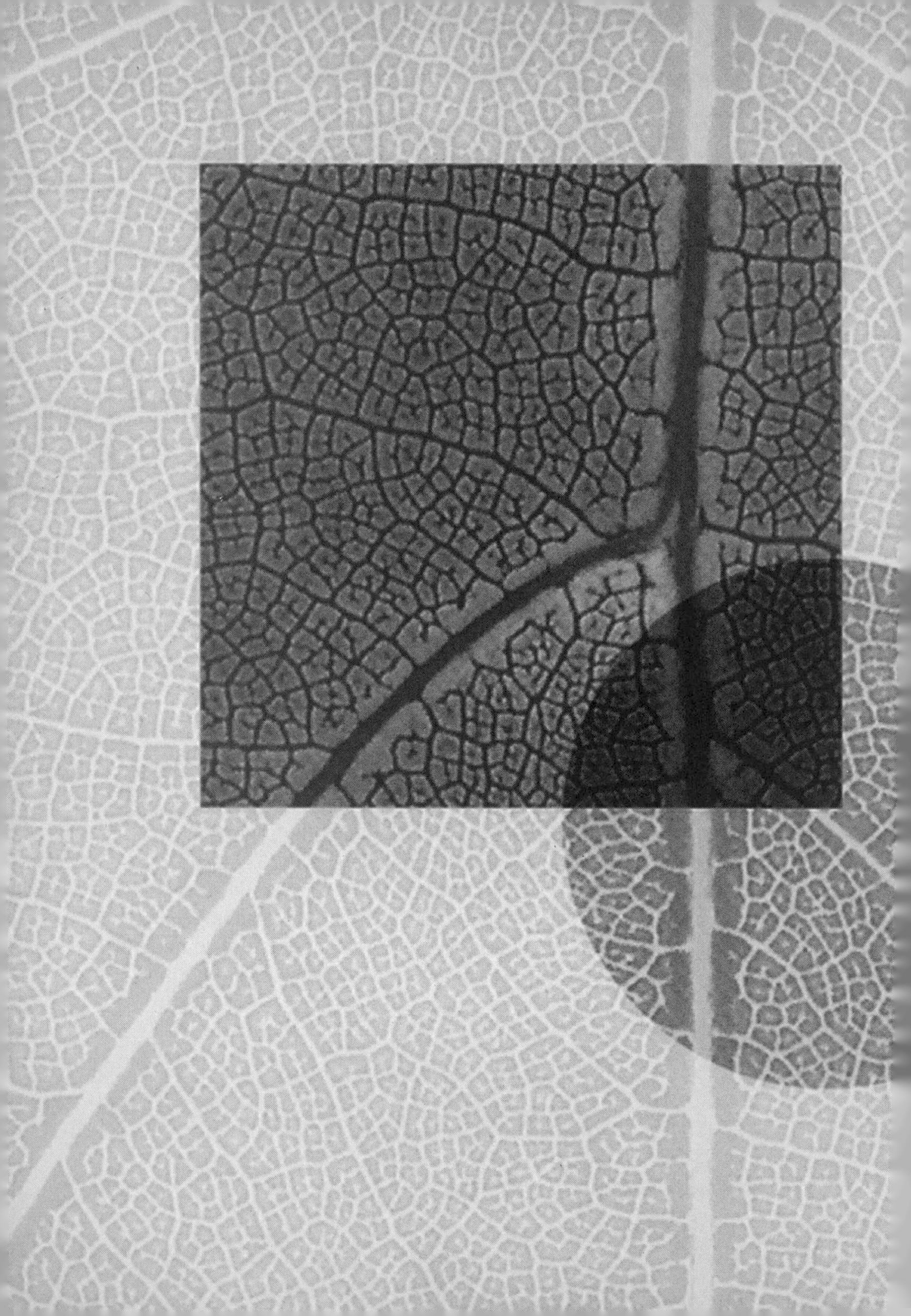

Chapter 12

Installation and Configuration

These objectives cover the procedures necessary to install and configure NT Workstation, not only on one system, but on a large number of computers. As you scan this list, you can see there's a lot of work that needs to be done. For a computer to be useful, it must provide services to its customers in an easy-to-use format. The company's newest employee should be able to sit down and be productive *immediately*. Using the information in this chapter will help you reach that goal and will make your life much less stressful. Some administrators have anxiety attacks at the mere thought of taking the top off of a computer to add a new component. This chapter will help relieve that anxiety.

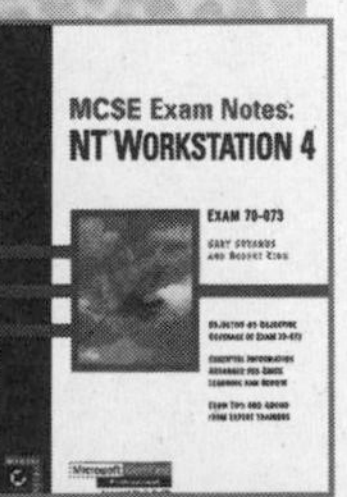

Adapted from *MCSE Exam Notes: NT Workstation 4*
by Gary Govanus and Robert King
ISBN 0-7821-2290-6 352 pages $19.99

In the first chapter, you developed a task list of things to do to configure each workstation that will be running NT Workstation. By the end of this chapter, you will see how you can change and adapt that configuration to meet the demands of everyday life. Each workstation has to meet the end user's individual needs.

NOTE

Microsoft's testing philosophy has revolved around testing "real world" tasks and concepts. The objectives in this section epitomize that philosophy.

Install Windows NT Workstation on an Intel-based platform in a given situation.

NT Workstation 4 can be installed on a variety of platforms, including the Intel *x*86 or Pentium-based platforms and RISC-based computers. As a matter of fact, NT 4 will run on the MIPS R4x00-based micro-processor or higher, as well as the Digital Alpha AXP-based microprocessor. This book (and the exam) concentrates on the Intel platform.

There are some minimal hardware requirements for NT Workstation 4 that must be met before the installation begins. These are:

- 12MB of RAM
- VGA-level video support
- Keyboard
- IDE, EIDE, SCSI, or ESDI hard disk
- 486/33 processor or better
- CD-ROM drive, 1.44MB or 1.2MB floppy disk drive, or active network connection
- Mouse or Pointing Device

Microsoft's "suggested minimum" list is:

- 486DX2/50 processor or better
- 32MB of RAM
- 28.8 v.34 external modem, for remote debugging and troubleshooting

- Windows NT–compatible CD-ROM drive

Again, this machine will never be described as one that is really fast, but it will at least come up and the services will start. The folks from Redmond also forgot to mention a Network Interface Card (NIC). If your workstation is going to attach to the network, you must have one of those, and it must be on the Microsoft NT Hardware Compatibility List (HCL). You can find the HCL on Microsoft's Web page.

How much disk space will an NT Workstation and Server installation take? That will depend on the accessories that you install, but you should start with the following:

- Standard Installation: 124MB of free disk space
- WINNT /b: 124MB of free disk space
- Copying i386 folder to hard disk: 223MB of free disk space

NOTE

Don't worry if you are not familiar with the WINNT /b command. The command line switches for the NT Installation Wizard will be covered later in this chapter.

These disk space requirements assume a standard hard disk controller, not an Enhanced IDE (EIDE) hard disk controller. If you are using a hard disk controller that uses a translation mode for addressing the hard disk drive, increase the above sizes by 80MB.

NOTE

Some 486 computers have an idea that Integrated Device Electronics (IDE) drives can be a maximum of 504MB in size. It wasn't that long ago that 504MB was a LARGE drive. Translation mode means you are faking out the system. The inner workings of the computer may think that the new Extended Integrated Device Electronics (EIDE) drive is only 504MB in size when in reality it might be 5 gigabytes in size.

Make sure the disk is partitioned and formatted. Here are the recommendations from Microsoft on the disk configurations:

- The root folder (the folder where you are going to install NT 4) should be on a disk formatted with either the FAT translation or NTFS from NT version 3.51 or NT 4. If you are using NTFS, the drive can be compressed. NT will not install on a hard drive that has been compressed with any other utility.

TIP

If you are using an IDE drive, do not format it using Windows 95 FAT32 file system. NT 4 does not recognize FAT32 and will not install on a FAT32 partition.

- If your target drive does use address translation, it should use one of the following:
  - Logical Block Addressing (LBA)
  - ONTrack Disk Manager
  - EZDrive
  - Extended Cylinder Head Sector

These are the translations methods supported by NT 4. If you make sure your BIOS and your hard drive support these, you should be in good shape.

NOTE

If you are unsure of the translation method used for your drive, try to find the manual for the disk. If you are unsuccessful, check the Internet and the drive maker's Web site. As a last resort, do an Internet search on the make and model number. The appropriate specifications are out there somewhere.

Now that you know what NT demands in the way of hardware, it is time to examine what is going to happen during the installation process. If you have installed NT Workstation, you know that there are several ways you can install the operating system. Microsoft has three pre-configured setup scenarios for you, as well as the Custom option. Selecting the Custom option gives you the right to make all the decisions necessary to install NT just the way you want it. The three pre-configured options give you access to different features of NT.

Table 12.1 lays out what components are available with which option. The Compact option is designed to save disk space, so it does not give you any optional components. Portable is used for laptops; it is not as spartan as Compact, but you can choose to leave just about everything off. If you want messaging or games, the only way to get them is to choose Custom.

TABLE 12.1: Characteristics of Setup Options

	TYPICAL	PORTABLE	COMPACT	CUSTOM
Accessibility Options	Yes	Yes	None	All options
Accessories	Yes	Yes	None	All options
Communication	Yes	Yes	None	All options
Games	No	No	None	All options
Multimedia	Yes	Yes	None	All options
Windows Messaging	No	No	None	All options

Windows NT Setup Stages

There are seven stages in the setup:

- Text Mode
- Disk Configuration
- Graphic Mode
- Virtual Memory Configuration
- Printer Configuration
- Network Configuration
- Final Stages

Text Mode

Let's assume that you have booted the target computer to the WINNT Setup Boot Disks that came with the operating system. Booting to these setup floppies will load SETUPLDR, the Windows NT setup utility. SETUPLDR needs to know more about your system, so it kicks off NTDETECT.COM, which goes out and looks at the hardware installed in the computer. Once NTDETECT has finished its work, SETUPLDR shuts it down and starts SETUPAPP.EXE.

SETUPAPP is nosy, it wants to know what you want to do. Are you going to specify what needs to be installed, or is the setup program? This is where you get to choose which of the hardware detection routines you will use.

Are there any SCSI devices in the system? If there are, does NT already have the driver for the disk drive or CD-ROM, or do you have to provide it from a manufacturer's disk? Once the SCSI issue is resolved, there are other devices to discover. NT will look at machine type, display adapter, mouse, and keyboard information.

NOTE

Much of the information that NT discovers here can be updated or changed later. See the objective on installing, configuring, and removing hardware components, later in this chapter.

Once hardware discovery has been completed, NT loads all the drivers it needs to run the computer in an installation mode. Now it is time to find out where you want to put NT, so the system checks the hard drive to see if this will be a Windows 3.1 upgrade. NT looks for WIN.COM, and, if it finds it, the installation program will ask if you want to use the `<drive letter>:Windows\System 32` directory. Otherwise, it will prompt you for the location where you want the system files copied. The default is the WINNT folder.

Disk Configuration

If no installation of Windows 3.1 is found, the installation process needs to find out about the hard disks in the computer. You will be shown a list of available partitions and free space. Here, you can create, delete, format, or determine file systems for any given area of disk space.

NOTE

If the drive is formatted with the IBM OS/2 high performance file system (HPFS) you will be prompted at this point to convert the drive to either NTFS or FAT.

Now that NT knows where and how to install the files, it wants to check and make sure the hard drive is physically capable of handling the installation. It will run CHKDSK to check the drive. When CHKDSK has been completed, NT begins copying files to the directory specified (default: C:\WINNT.) Once the file copy has been completed, NT is ready to come up on its own, so you are told to remove the floppy and the CD (if present) and restart the computer.

Graphic Mode

The graphics portion of the installation gathers information about how the computer will be identified. It wants things like a user name and company, the name of the computer, and where it will be located. Location is important, because this is how NT knows how to format date, time, and currency information.

If you chose to use a Custom setup, this is the section that deals with all the "extras" you may want to install–accessories, NT messaging, games–the really important stuff. You can also choose whether or not you want network support, setup printers, and setup system applications on the hard drive.

Virtual Memory Configuration

While all the installation is going on, one of the things happening in the background is the determination of how much Virtual Memory the system will be provided. By default, NT creates a page file that is RAM plus 12MB. If your system has 64MB of RAM, the recommended size for the page file would be 76MB.

TIP

Be sure to know the recommended size of page files. The formula is RAM plus 12MB.

NOTE

To change the size or location of a page file after installation, click Start ➢ Settings ➢ Control Panel. Double-click System, then select the Performance tab, and click Change.

Network Configuration

At this stage of the process, NT is ready to configure the system to talk to the outside world. If you are using Custom mode, NT will now begin to look for any installed network interface cards (NICs). If you know what kind of NIC is installed in the system and if you have the appropriate drivers, you can choose to do a manual installation. If you are using a Typical installation, NT will automatically start the search for the network card.

Once the card has been discovered, you will be presented with a dialog box showing the input/output port address (I/O) and the interrupt request

(IRQ) settings. After you approve the settings, NT will install the files necessary to drive the NIC, and the Network Control Panel applet will start. If you click OK, the installation utility will bind the appropriate protocols to the card. The system will start the network services, and you will be given the opportunity to have the workstation join a workgroup or a domain.

Final Stages of Setup

Setup will create the Emergency Repair disk. Setup prompts for a blank disk, or one that can be reformatted, and then checks to be sure that it has not been given the Boot Floppy, by checking for TXTSETUP.INF. Setup will then format the disk and then save the default configuration information (necessary to restore Windows NT) on the Emergency Repair disk. Finally, Setup will ask for the system's time zone setting. Unless the system happens to be in the Greenwich mean time zone, the correct time zone must be selected.

The system reboots again and the process is completed by having you choose the video display type and the time zone the workstation will reside in.

Procedures for Installing Windows NT

The NT installation program works fastest from an NT environment. This presents an interesting dilemma: how do you install from an NT environment without having NT installed? Microsoft has provided a simple solution. There are three 3 1/2" disks in the box. These disks are used to boot the target computer and start the installation. As part of the boot process, the system hardware is analyzed and the CD-ROM is recognized, providing the medium for the installation program.

NOTE

There are several methods for installing NT Workstation, including attaching to a share and doing an unattended install (see Chapter 11). This section will assume you are installing for the Windows Workstation CD-ROM.

You may be installing NT for the second, third, or fourth time, and you have the licenses, you have the CD, but the disks seem to have been misplaced. No sweat. These disks, which can make the installation process run much smoother, can be re-created. To re-create the disks:

1. Put the NT Installation CD in a CD-ROM drive and open a command prompt. The operating system of the computer you

are using for this procedure does not matter. You need only to have a computer that has a working CD-ROM and a working 3 1/2-inch drive.

2. Change to whatever drive contains the CD. For example, D:.
3. Change into the i386 directory. You will see a file called WINNT.EXE.
4. Type **WINNT /?** at the command prompt. Press Enter.

When you press Enter, you will be presented with a list of all the command lines switches for the NT installation program. The proper syntax for utilizing these switches is:

```
Drive:\i386\WINNT.EXE [/S[:]sourcepath] [/T[:]tempdrive]
[/I[:]inffile] [/X | [/F] [/C] [/D[:]winntpath]]
```

Table 12.2 provides a list of the functionality the command line switches provide.

TABLE 12.2: Command-Line Switches and Their Functionality

Switch	Functionality
/S[:] source path	Specifies where the NT files are located
/T[:] temp drive	Specifies where NT stores temp files during the install
/I[:]inf file	Tells NT where the information files are located
/OX	Create boot floppies for CD ROM installation.
/X	Don't create the boot floppies, you already have them.
/F	You will create the boot floppies, but you will not verify the files that are being copied to those floppies.
/C	Skip the free space check on those floppies; you know they are empty and formatted.
/B	Floppyless operation, requires the /S parameter
/U:script file	Unattended operation, requires the /S parameter
/R:directory	Specifies optional directory to be installed
/RX:directory	Specifies optional directory to be copied
/E:command	Specifies command to run at the end of the GUI setup

TIP

To create a set of installation disks, your command line syntax would be WINNT /OX.

If you have created the disks or have the originals from Microsoft, put the first disk in the A: drive of the target computer. Turn the machine on, and the system will boot making use of at least two of the disks you just created. The Installation Wizard will also load the drivers to access the target system's CD-ROM drive. You must have the NT Workstation CD in that drive. You are on your way!

Here is the step-by-step process:

1. Put the first disk in the floppy drive. Make sure the NT Workstation CD is in the CD-ROM drive. Turn the target computer on. The boot process loads the Windows NT Executive. After the NT Executive has been loaded, the system will load the Hardware Abstraction Layer (HAL).
2. You will be prompted to put the disk labeled Setup Disk #2 into drive A: and press Enter. The computer now loads the NT Setup Wizard from the floppy. The Setup Wizard will load PCMCIA support and video support. Once video support has been loaded, the system loads floppy drive support.
3. With disk #2 still in the floppy driver, you will see the "Welcome to Setup" screen. You have three options: continue the installation (press Enter), repair a damaged installation (press R), or quit (press F3). Press Enter to continue.
4. The Setup Wizard now starts to search for drive controllers. You can press Enter to have the system do it, or press S to have the system skip the search. Press Enter to have the Installation Wizard search the system.
5. You are prompted to insert disk #3. Disk #3 loads CD-ROM support, SCSI Disk Driver support, and any other drivers that NT finds necessary. You are given a Workstation Setup screen that asks if you need to find any additional devices or drivers. If there is nothing else to find, press Enter to continue.
6. Once you have provided the source path, the lawyers get involved: You will see the license agreement. Page down and press F8 to agree.

7. You will now see the Workstation setup screen. Check it to make sure that everything agrees with your system, and press Enter to continue.
8. You will be asked which partition and drive you want to install the system files on. Make your choice and press Enter. From this screen you can also format the partition using either of the default file systems (NTFS or FAT). If a partition does not already exist, you can also create a partition from this menu.
9. Make your choice and choose to format the partition with FAT, format with NTFS, convert it to NTFS, or leave it alone. The selections you see may vary, depending if you are upgrading the computer or doing a new installation to an unformatted partition.
10. Choose which partition you will install NT onto and also which folder will be the root. To install NT into the default folder, choose C:\WINNT.
11. Setup now examines your hard disk for corruption. You are given a choice: Press Enter for an exhaustive search, or press Esc to skip the exhaustive search altogether.
12. Since you pressed Enter, the setup wizard examines the target disk and starts copying files. This is one section that may take some time.
13. After the file copying is completed, NT is ready to move on to the next phase of the installation process. You will be told to remove the CD from the CD-ROM drive and remove the floppy disk. Once this has been done, you can press Enter to restart the computer.
14. As the computer reboots, setup initializes and begins asking questions. It will also prompt you to re-insert the installation CD-ROM. Press Enter to continue the process.
15. The Setup Wizard will now set about gathering information about the computer, and this leads to the Preparing to Install screen. This screen has that little blue bar that moves slowly across the screen. Click Next.

16. Now you can choose which setup option you want to use. The choices are Typical, Portable, Compact, or Custom. For the purposes of this exercise, Choose Typical. Click Next.

17. You will be prompted to enter your name and your organization.

18. On the next screen, enter the CD key found on the back of the CD case. Click Next to continue.

19. Enter a unique computer name. Click Next to continue.

20. The next screen has you enter a password for the administrator. You will also have to confirm the password before clicking Next to continue.

21. The Wizard now wants to know if you would like to create an emergency repair disk. If you choose yes, you will be asked for the diskette at the end of the installation process.

22. The next step asks which Windows NT components you would like to install. You can choose to install the most common options or you can see a list of things to install. The list has accessibility options, accessories, communications, games, multimedia, and windows messaging. Make your selections and click Next to continue. This will take you to the Windows NT Setup progress screen.

23. To install Windows networking, from the NT Setup screen, click Next.

24. Since you chose to install networking on the computer, you need to tell NT which kind of networking you want to install. You are presented with options to not connect the computer to a network, to connect to a network via an ISDN line, via a LAN line, or via remote access to network through dial in. Make your selection and click Next.

NOTE

If you have parts of networking that you want to install, but you do not want to install the network adapter at this time, you can choose to install the Microsoft LoopBack Adapter. This will give you the opportunity to install network components without having a physical adapter installed.

25. The Wizard now starts its search for network adapters. Click Start Search to begin the search, or select from a list. We will install another network driver later, so make your choice and click Next to continue. This will let you choose the protocols to install. Choose carefully. You don't want your workstation flooding the network with unwanted packets!

NOTE

One of the tweaks you may want to make after the installation is the binding order of the protocols. The client determines which protocol will be used and the decision is made through binding order. The most used protocol should be at the top of this list. If you are unsure how to change binding order, see the section on installing a network adapter driver.

26. When you have selected the protocols to install, click Next. That will return you to an informational screen that lets you know NT is about to install all the stuff you told it to install. Click Next to get rid of the informational screen.

27. If you selected TCP/IP as a protocol, you will be prompted to use DHCP. If your system has a DHCP server on it, this is a great way to minimize addressing headings. Choose Yes or No and the Installation system is off to the races. Once it has finished, click Next to start the network.

28. Once the network is started, you will be presented with a screen to make your computer part of a Workgroup or part of a Domain. Add the appropriate information. If you choose to make the computer a member of the domain, you can have your workstation create a computer account in the domain by filling the checkbox and giving the system the Administrator's user name and password.

29. Click Finish and setup will configure your computer.

30. To finish the installation, choose the time zone the workstation will be used in, and check the Date and Time tab before clicking Close.

31. The system will now find the video display type. Choose OK for the adapter type, usually some form of VGA. You need to test the selection before leaving this screen; click OK to start the test. You will be asked if you saw the test screen. Select

Yes or No, and then save settings if the bitmap displayed properly. To continue with setup, click OK.

32. Click OK to close Display Properties.
33. NT now starts the configuration process.
34. If you chose to create an emergency repair disk, now is the time. Place a blank, formatted diskette in drive A:. You will be told that everything on the disk will be erased; press OK to continue.
35. Install copies more files, sets security, deletes all those unnecessary temporary installation files, and then prompts you to restart the computer.

When the system restarts, you will have a computer running NT Workstation.

Set up a dual-boot system in a given situation.

There will be times where you will want to configure one computer for multiple operating systems—maybe you'll be faced with a critical application that cannot run under NT, or maybe you will need a test bed computer to serve multiple functions. In any event, this objective is concerned with the steps involved in this type of configuration.

As discussed in Chapter 11, there are only two pieces of critical information in this objective:

- While dual-booting is possible, it is not a supported configuration.
- The only file system that will support a dual-boot configuration is the FAT file system.

Non-Supported Configuration

The bottom line here is that Microsoft does not expect you to rely upon a dual-boot configuration as a long-term solution. If you have legacy software that demands either DOS/Windows 3.*x* or Windows 95, you should be in the process of upgrading it to NT compatibility. This may sometimes seem an unreasonable expectation, but that's the way it is.

FAT Considerations

The FAT file system is required on a dual-boot system. Be aware that this means that there will be no local file or directory level security. Another consideration is that files on a FAT partition are accessible—even without any login authentication—if the machine is booted to a DOS disk. Fat partitions are also vulnerable to DOS utilities that can read deleted files from the disk.

Do not store confidential or critical data on a FAT partition. This might mean that you have to create a NTFS partition that will be inaccessible when the computer is booted to DOS or Windows 95.

WARNING

Windows 95 includes the option to use FAT32—a new and improved version of the Fat file system. Windows NT cannot access a FAT32 partition. Do not use the FAT32 file system when installing Windows 95 on a dual-boot computer.

Rather than give two different procedures—one for DOS/NT and another for WINDOW95/NT—this section will detail the process for creating a multi-boot computer (DOS, Windows 95, and NT). If you don't need all three operating systems, just skip the appropriate steps. The most important thing is to install them in the order listed.

NOTE

The only dual-boot configuration that Microsoft discusses is that of Windows 95 and Windows NT. If you need to dual boot NT with some other operating system (OS/2 for instance), you will need to research the process.

Setting Up a Multi-Boot Computer

1. Install DOS. Use the setup program for whichever version you have available. Make sure that DOS is working correctly with any programs that will require it before continuing.
2. Install Windows 95. Windows 95 will automatically include the option to boot back to your original version of DOS, if desired. (Press the F8 key during the boot to bring up a menu.)
3. Install Windows NT. NT will automatically include your old operating system in its boot menu choices.

When the computer boots, you will be presented with the NT boot menu. If you want either Windows 95 or DOS, make the appropriate selection. If you want DOS, press the F8 key when you see the "Loading Windows 95" message on the screen.

WARNING

Remember, Windows 95 and NT have different structures to their registry files. You must install each application that will be used while booted to each operating system it will be used under. In other words, if you are going to use Excel while booted to both NT and 95, you must install two copies of Excel in different directories.

Remove Windows NT Workstation in a given situation.

In most cases you will find NT to be so stable, reliable, and easily managed that you would never go want to remove it from a computer. (Okay, thus ends the Microsoft sales pitch.) There are occasions, however, when it will be necessary to remove it. Knowing the proper procedure will prevent unnecessary work.

Removing NT from a System That Boots from a FAT Partition

1. First, boot the computer from a DOS or Windows 95 floppy that contains a copy of SYS.COM.
2. From your A: drive, type **SYS C:**. This will transfer the appropriate system files to your hard drive.
3. Restart your system, booting from the hard drive.
4. Other than deleting a few NT files to save disk space, you are finished.
5. The following files can be deleted:
    - All paging files—PAGEFILE.SYS (Remember that you might have created more than one in an effort to optimize your computer.)
    - C:\BOOT.INI

- C:\NT*.*
- C:\BOOTSECT.DOS
- The <*Winnt_root*> directory
- Program files\Windows NT

NOTE

The BOOT.INI, NT*.*, and BOOTSECT.DOS files are marked as System, hidden, read-only files; you will have to change these attributes before you can delete them.

Removing NT from a Computer That Boots from an NTFS Partition

Unfortunately, the only operating system that can read and write to an NTFS partition is Windows NT. This means that if your system boots to an HTFS partition you will have to delete it. There are a couple of ways to accomplish this:

- Use FDISK.COM from DOS 6.0 or later.
- Use the OS/2 installation disk to remove all partitions from the first physical disk.
- Boot to the first floppy of the NT setup disks. When prompted for a partition upon which to install NT, select the NTFS partition and press **D** to delete. Then press F3 to exit the setup program.

Install, configure, and remove hardware components for a given situation.

Hardware components include:

- Network Adapter Drivers
- SCSI Device Drivers
- Tape Device Drivers
- UPS
- Multimedia devices

- Display Drivers
- Keyboard Drivers
- Mouse Drivers

Installing hardware components isn't as complicated as it sounds, if you know some of the basics. Generally, you locate resources you have available in the computer. You read the documentation that comes with the hardware to find out how to configure the component to take advantage of the available resources. You physically install the component, configure the driver to use the new device, reboot the workstation, and the new component will be available. In this section, the assumption will be made that the hardware is already installed on the workstation, and it is up to you to configure or install new drivers.

Removing resources is even easier, since there is no search for resources. Usually, you remove the driver or service, shut down the PC and physically remove the device. Reboot the PC and things should work. (He says with an all-knowing grin.)

Understanding Hardware Drivers

This is a great section to read, especially when you are trying to install something that isn't installing just right. You may learn some tips or tricks. It is also a good section to read before testing, because this material is covered extensively on the exam.

Network Adapter Drivers

Windows NT Workstation has the ability to handle multiple network adapters in the same computer. While NT *can* do that, the question is why would it? A workstation rarely would need a second network card. A more likely scenario would be that a network card currently installed in a workstation has had its network adapter driver updated and you would like to remove the old driver and install a new driver. This is done from the Network icon in the Control Panel.

NOTE

One of the fundamental laws of computing states that there is ALWAYS more than one way to do something; you should use the method you prefer. An example is the network adapter driver settings. These can be accessed through the Network icon in Control Panel, or by highlighting Network Neighborhood, and right-clicking and then selecting Properties.

Configuring the network adapter driver is something you will probably do on each workstation. Depending on the driver, the choices you have available to tweak may differ.

To access this window, open Control Panel, double-click Network, click the Adapters tab, and select Properties. Notice that you can use this screen to determine the hardware configuration of the card, the physical address of the card, the cable type, and the line speed. Which of these might have to be configured after installation? Possibly cable detect and line speed. Cable detect determines if you are using (in this case) a 10-Base T connection or Coax connection. Line Speed will vary between 10MB per second and 100MB per second.

NOTE

The Network Settings page for each Network Adapter will be different, depending on the driver installed.

If you click OK on the Properties page, you will return to the Network Window. Earlier in this chapter, we discussed the binding order of protocols. The workstation controls which protocol the workstation and the server will use to communicate. Clicking the Bindings tab will open the bindings window. You can make your choices by opening the workstation NetBios Interface, the Server Interface, and the Workstation interface. You can change the binding order so the most frequently used protocol is the first listed.

TIP

Don't bind (or install) more protocols than you actually need. Each protocol will generate traffic on your network. If there is nothing to answer, you are generating unnecessary traffic.

SCSI Device Drivers

This section of the Exam Objective is covered in Part 2: NT Server 4, Chapter 6 "Installation and Configuration." The Practice Exam at the end of Part 4 will test you on this material.

Tape Device Drivers

This section of the Exam Objective is covered in Part 2: NT Server 4, Chapter 6 "Installation and Configuration." The Practice Exam at the end of Part 4 will test you on this material.

UPS Devices and UPS Service

This section of the Exam Objective is covered in Part 2: NT Server 4, Chapter 6 "Installation and Configuration." The Practice Exam at the end of Part 4 will test you on this material.

Multimedia Devices

Multimedia devices include such things as:

- An audio driver for playback and for recording of voice or music
- A video setting that allows you to choose how you want to view your movie–full screen or in a window
- The Musical Instrument Digital Interface (MIDI), that lets you control several devices, instruments, or computers that can send and receive messages and create music, sound, or control lighting
- A CD music setting (on some machines) that lets you listen to a CD through headphones while the computer is shut off
- Miscellaneous drivers like mixer devices that control the volume of various input channels, video capturing devices, and even a joystick

Display Drivers

This section of the Exam Objective is covered in Part 2: NT Server 4, Chapter 6 "Installation and Configuration." The Practice Exam at the end of Part 4 will test you on this material.

Keyboard Drivers

This section of the Exam Objective is covered in Part 2: NT Server 4, Chapter 6 "Installation and Configuration." The Practice Exam at the end of Part 4 will test you on this material.

Mouse Drivers

This section of the Exam Objective is covered in Part 2: NT Server 4, Chapter 6 "Installation and Configuration." The Practice Exam at the end of Part 4 will test you on this material.

Network Adapter Driver Procedures

Each of the drivers that will be discussed is accessed through the Control Panel folder. To access Control Panel, click Start ➢ Control Panel.

Installing a Network Adapter Driver

If you are installing multiple cards as part of the installation process, once NT finds the first card, there is a button that tells it to go out and look for more. NT will continue looking for cards until it doesn't find any more, or until you run out of manufacturer's diskettes. If you are installing a new PCI card into an available slot:

1. Install the card per manufacturer's directions. When you reboot the computer, open the Network window in the Control Panel.
2. Click the Adapters tab.
3. Click Add.
4. From the Select Network Adapter window, select the appropriate network card and click OK or click Have Disk. If you chose Have Disk, insert the disk in drive A:\ or provide the appropriate path, and click OK.
5. If you chose a network card, you will be prompted for the path to Windows NT system files, either from the CD or from the location that the files have been copied to. After providing the path, click Continue. The files will be copied and a default binding provided.
6. Close the dialog boxes and restart the system when prompted.

If you do not have an open PCI slot, you will have to install an ISA-compatible card. Each card has its own installation routine, so before beginning any installation be sure to RTFM (Read The Fine Manual). For example, if you were installing a plug-and-play compatible LinkSys 16-bit ISA-compatible Ethernet card, you would take the following steps.

NOTE

Since each installation will be a little different, this is just for demonstration purposes only; the steps you follow may be different.

1. Turn the PC off.
2. Remove the cover.
3. Physically install the card.
4. Cable the card to the concentrator.
5. Turn the computer back on and log on as Administrator.

The card is now physically installed. The next step is to configure the card to work in your server. Because the demonstration card went into an ISA slot, you have to run the setup utility. Boot the server to DOS and run setup, which shows the default parameters of an IRQ setting of 3 and a memory address of 300. The final IRQ and memory address will be Plug-and-Play Compatible, meaning that the operating system should handle the actual settings.

To install the new card and driver for NT:

1. From the Network window, click the Adapters tab.
2. Next, click Add, which will bring up the Select Network Adapter dialog box.
3. Choose Have Disk.
4. As part of the Insert Disk window, add the path to the software drivers; in this case, A:\WINNT.
5. Select the card by highlighting the card name, then click OK.
6. Enter in an open I/O port or choose Auto, depending on the capabilities of the card.
7. Enter in an open IRQ number or choose Auto, depending on the capabilities of the card.
8. Enter in a network address, if necessary.
9. Click OK.

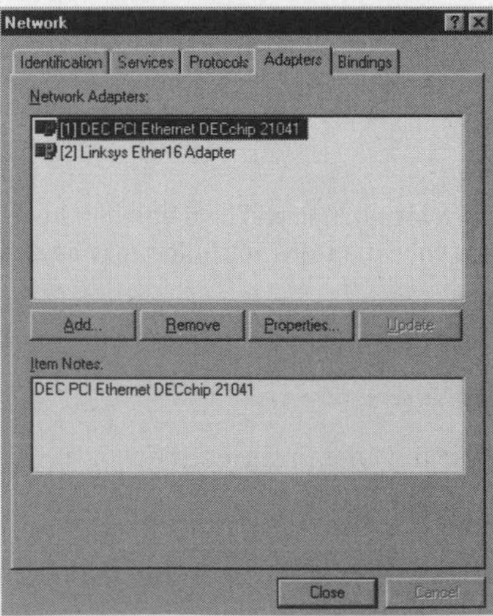

This graphic shows that both network cards have been installed. When Close is clicked, the system begins to examine the network subsystem and checks to make sure everything is just the way it is supposed to be.

10. Since IP is loaded by default, the first "glitch" the system found was that the new card did not have a working IP address. The Microsoft TCP/IP Properties box opens, from which you can choose to receive your IP address from a DHCP server or from a static address.

11. Enter in DNS information and WINS information, if necessary. Click OK to close.

12. Restart the computer.

Configuring the Network Adapter Driver

From the Network window with the Adapters tab selected and an adapter highlighted:

1. Click Properties to access the Network Settings window.

2. Depending on the type of network adapter card you have installed, the Network Settings screen will display a variety of configuration options. Some common Ethernet options include:

   I/O Port The I/O port address is the hexadecimal designation of the address the adapter is using. This must be unique.

   Memory Address The memory address is the hexadecimal designation of the memory location that the card will use to access information.

   Interrupt Also known as IRQ. This is the channel that the card will use to gain the CPU's attention.

   Cable type This option will allow you to choose between twisted-pair cable and coax cable.

   Line Speed This option will let the card auto-detect the line speed; choose 10MB per second or 100MB per second.

3. Make the appropriate choices and click OK when you are finished.

4. Click Close to close the Network window. Click Yes when prompted to shut down and restart your computer to have the changes take effect.

Removing a Network Adapter Driver

To remove a Network Adapter driver, start from the Network window with the Adapter tab selected.

1. Highlight the network adapter driver that you would like to remove.
2. Click Remove.
3. Click Yes to close the window telling you that you are about to permanently remove the component from the system.
4. Restart the computer to allow the changes to take effect.

SCSI Driver Procedures

Before the computer can access the wonderful world of SCSI devices, a controller must be installed.

Installing and Configuring a SCSI Device Driver

This section of the Exam Objective is covered in Part 2: NT Server 4, Chapter 6 "Installation and Configuration." The Practice Exam at the end of Part 4 will test you on this material.

Removing a SCSI Device Driver

SCSI adapter drivers are accessed through the SCSI Adapters icon in Control Panel. You can open the SCSI page by double-clicking the SCSI Adapters icon and then clicking the Drivers tab.

1. From the Drivers tab, highlight the driver you would like to remove.
2. Click the Remove button.
3. Click Yes or No when asked if you are sure you want to remove this driver.
4. Restart the computer when prompted by clicking Yes.

Tape Device Driver Procedures

Configuring a tape drive is a two-step process: First you configure the driver and then have NT discover the tape device.

Installing and Configuring the Tape Device Driver

This section of the Exam Objective is covered in Part 2: NT Server 4, Chapter 6 "Installation and Configuration." The Practice Exam at the end of Part 4 will test you on this material.

Removing a Tape Device Driver

From Control Panel, double-click the Tape Device icon to open the Tape Devices window.

1. Click the Drivers tab.
2. Highlight the driver that you would like to remove and click the Remove button.
3. Answer Yes to the screen that tells you the driver will be removed.
4. Restart the computer after the process has been completed.

UPS Procedures

UPS devices usually come with a program that allows for a more robust configuration than the standard NT installation. For the purpose of this book, we'll use the standard configuration.

Installing and Configuring a UPS

This section of the Exam Objective is covered in Part 2: NT Server 4, Chapter 6 "Installation and Configuration." The Practice Exam at the end of Part 4 will test you on this material.

Removing the UPS

To remove the UPS, double-click the UPS icon in Control Panel and clear the "Uninterruptible Power Supply is installed on:" box.

Multimedia Device Procedures

See the instructions below for installing and configuring a multimedia device.

Installing and Configuring a Multimedia Device

1. Install the hardware (for example, a sound card) per manufacturer's instructions. Keep documentation on any hardware settings for the card.
2. To install the driver for the new device, select the Devices tab from the Multimedia Properties window. Click Add.
3. Choose from the list of available drivers to selected Unlisted or Updated driver. Click OK.
4. You will be presented with a window asking for the details of the hardware install. This may include things like the following:
    - **Direct Memory Access (DMA) channel** The DMA channel provides the component direct access to system memory. You may specify the DMA Channel buffer size by selecting Advanced Settings.
    - **I/O Address** The hexadecimal address of the Input/Output port the component will be using
    - **Interrupt (IRQ)** The channel the component will use to get the CPU's attention
5. Once the Driver window has been filled out, click OK to close the dialog box. Windows NT will go out and look for the device and tell you if it found it at the settings you provided.
6. Close the dialog box and restart the system when prompted by the operating system.

Multimedia devices can be configured by selecting the type of the device from the Multimedia Properties window. Again, the exact settings will vary with the card and system, but you may have Audio, Video, and MIDI.

1. Audio devices can be configured by selecting the Audio tab from the Multimedia Properties screen.

A. Under Playback:

- You can use the slide bar to set the volume for device playback and also for recording.
- You can choose to show the volume control on the Taskbar by filling in the checkbox.
- You can choose your preferred device.

B. Under Recording:

- You can use the slide bar to set the volume for recording.
- You can select the preferred device.
- You can select the preferred quality, including Radio Quality, CD Quality, or Telephone Quality.

2. Video devices can be configured by selecting the Video tab from the Multimedia Properties window. You can choose to show videos in a window by selecting Full screen.
3. MIDI drivers can be configured by selecting the MIDI tab from the Multimedia Properties window. MIDI output can use either a single instrument or a custom configuration.

Removing a Multimedia Device

From Control Panel, select the Devices tab from the Multimedia Properties window.

1. Highlight the device you wish to remove, and click Remove. Click Yes to tell the system you really know what you are doing.
2. After the device has been removed, restart the computer as prompted by the operating system.

Display Driver Procedures

See the instructions below for installing, configuring and removing a display driver.

Installing and Configuring a Display Driver

This section of the Exam Objective is covered in Part 2: NT Server 4, Chapter 6 "Installation and Configuration." The Practice Exam at the end of Part 4 will test you on this material.

Removing a Display Driver

Since all computers must have some sort of display, there is no way to remove the display driver other than overwriting it with a new driver. To install the new driver, see the section above.

Keyboard Driver Procedures

Keyboard drivers are like video drivers–every system has to have one.

Installing and Configuring Keyboard Drivers

This section of the Exam Objective is covered in Part 2: NT Server 4, Chapter 6 "Installation and Configuration." The Practice Exam at the end of Part 4 will test you on this material.

Removing the Keyboard Driver

Keyboard drivers are like video drivers–every system has to have one. To remove a keyboard driver, you must overwrite it with another driver. See the section above for installation of new keyboard drivers.

Mouse Driver Procedures

See the following instructions to change or update a mouse driver.

Installing and Configuring Mouse Drivers

This section of the Exam Objective is covered in Part 2: NT Server 4, Chapter 6 "Installation and Configuration." The Practice Exam at the end of Part 4 will test you on this material.

Removing the Mouse Driver

Mouse drivers are also like video drivers–every system has to have one. To remove a mouse driver, you must overwrite it with another driver. See the section above for installation of new mouse drivers.

▶ Use Control Panel applications to configure a Windows NT Workstation computer in a given situation.

In the preceeding objective we discussed many of the tools used to configure the hardware components of your NT computer. This objective is concerned with the process of configuring the NT operating system itself.

Within Control Panel, you will find the System applet. This applet has three main functions:

- Startup and Shutdown properties

- Virtual memory configuration
- Set environmental variables

You can also use the Add/Remove Programs applet to change installation software or change the options you chose when installing the NT operating system.

Control Panel Functions

See the instructions below for Control Panel functions.

Startup and Shutdown Properties

This is really two different sets of parameters: Startup and Shutdown. The system startup options allow you to configure which operating system the computer should boot to by default and how long the boot menu should stay on the screen before accepting that default.

The shutdown parameters allow you to decide what actions NT should take in the event of a critical error, otherwise known as a *stop screen*. While critical errors are rare, they do bring your server to a crashing halt (hence the name stop screen). You have various choices concerning the actions to be taken by NT when it encounters a critical error, as listed in Table 12.3.

TABLE 12.3: Recovery Options

Option	Explanation
Write an event to the system log	The system will write an event message to the system event log. These messages can be used to troubleshoot the cause of the error.
Send an administrative alert	The system will send an alert to any members of the administrators group who are currently logged in.
Write debugging information to:	
<path>	The operating system will attempt to write the contents of memory into a file for later analysis.
Overwrite any existing file	If you have chosen to write debugging information to a file, this option lets you decide whether or not to overwrite the last debugging information. Be aware that there is no compression—if you have 128MB of memory, this file will be 128MB.
Automatically reboot	If this option is chosen, the operating system will reboot itself if it encounters a stop screen.

Virtual Memory Configuration

Microsoft Windows NT has a mechanism that allows it to use hard disk space as if it were RAM. This allows the operating system to give applications more memory than is physically available on the computer—up to the limits of empty disk space. This is called *virtual memory*. The process of exchanging data between RAM and the hard disk is called *demand paging*. Whenever a process needs more memory, it is the responsibility of the operating system to allocate it. NT will look through the memory to see if any is available. If not, it will copy a section of memory into this virtual memory space on a hard disk. The system creates a file named PAGEFILE.SYS to act as repository for this virtual memory (by default, this file is placed on the disk with the most free space).

Moving the paging file to a less busy disk or splitting it into pieces scattered across multiple disks are some of the more common optimization techniques used in NT. They are also topics that are tested upon in multiple MCSE exams. Moving the paging file can have a great impact on performance. Microsoft suggests that the paging file not be on the same physical disk as the operating system files, since that disk will be busy handling other processes.

While the paging file will grow as needed, there is a delay built in to prevent wasted space (the file will never decrease in size on its own). Setting the initial size to the optimum can also increase performance.

Set Environmental Variables

Variables are just strings of data that can be used by a process for configuration information. Some variables are used by multiple applications, while others are specific to an application or process. Many applications, for instance, know to look for a TEMP variable for the path to the directory where they should place their temporary files.

There are two basic types of variables in an NT environment: system and user. The administrator usually sets system variables and they apply to all users of the system. User variables, on the other hand, are specific to a particular user, and are usually set by that user. Both of these types of variables can be set in the Environment tab of the System Properties dialog box, as we'll see later. NT variables can also be set in an AUTOEXEC.BAT file. As an NT computer boots, it looks for an AUTOEXEC.BAT file and sets any variables it describes.

The value of a variable is not protected by the operating system. That is, the value can be dynamically changed while the system is running. NT sets the values of variables in the following order:

1. Those found in the AUTOEXEC.BAT file
2. System variables
3. User variables

Since the value of a variable is not protected, you could create a system variable that would pertain to all users, and then reset it on a user-by-user basis for exceptions. A good example would be the default location of files. For most users, you might want documents stored locally, so you would set a system variable to point to a local directory. For a few users, you might want documents to be placed on a server so that you could create a user variable for those users. Since NT reads the values in the order listed above, the user variable value would overwrite the system value.

You can prevent NT from looking for an AUTOEXEC.BAT file by editing the Registry. Add the registry parameter `ParseAutoexec: REG_SZ = 0` to the `\HKEY_CURRENT_USER\SOFTWARE\Microsoft\WindowsNT\CurrentVersion\Winlogon` key.

NOTE

For more information on editing the Registry, see Chapter 16.

Configuring Windows NT

See below for Windows NT configuration instructions.

Customizing the NT Installation

If you need to change any of the choices you made (add or remove options) during the NT installation process, you can do so within the Add/Remove Programs window.

You can also add or remove any programs that use a SETUP.EXE or INSTALL.EXE program for installation. Just run the EXE to install or highlight the software in the list, and choose Remove.

Now that we've discussed the options available, we can look at the procedures involved in configuring your Windows NT workstation.

Setting Startup/Shutdown Parameters

1. From within Control Panel, open the System Properties window.
2. Choose the Startup/Shutdown tab.

From here you can set which operating system will be chosen by default and how long the boot menu will remain on the screen. You can also decide what actions NT should take to recover from a critical error.

Configuring Virtual Memory

1. Once again, within the System Properties window, choose the Performance tab.
2. Click the Change button to configure virtual memory.

Here you can determine which drive or drives should hold the paging file and the initial and maximum sizes of that file.

Setting System and User Variables

Within the System Properties window, choose the Environment tab.

Here you can change, add, or delete system and user variables.

Changing the Options Installed on Your NT Workstation

1. Within Control Panel, open the Add/Remove Programs Properties window.
2. To install a new program, click the Install button.
3. To remove an installed application, highlight it in the list and click the Add/Remove button.

Changing the NT Options Installed

1. Within the Add/Remove Programs Properties window, choose the Windows NT Setup tab.
2. Check those items that you wish to install or uncheck those you wish to remove.
3. If you wish to be more specific, highlight a component and click Details. You will then be shown all of the specific components of that choice. Within the Details dialog box, check

those items you want to install or uncheck those you wish to remove.

Configure server-based installation for wide-scale deployment in a given situation.

A server-based installation is simply providing a central point for the storage of the NT Installation files. To do an over-the-network installation, you access files normally stored on the NT 4.0 CD from the potential NT Workstation and start the installation. Before you can access files stored on the distribution server, there is some work to be done.

There are two ways to provide access to the files from the NT 4.0 CD. First, you can put the NT Installation CD into a CD Tower or a shared CD-ROM and share various folders. An optional method, if you have the available hard disk space, is to XCOPY the NT Installation CD to a drive and share the various folders. If you opt for this method, be sure to use the /S parameter to the XCOPY command to get all the subfolders copied. In reality, you don't even have to copy over the whole CD, just the \i386 folder and probably the \DRVLIB folder.

TIP

You can also use NT Explorer to copy the folders to the disk. Be sure the default settings are changed to allow files with extensions like .DLL, .SYS, and .VXD to be displayed and copied. Default settings for Explorer are changed by selecting View ➢ Options, and then, in the Hidden files list, clicking Show all files.

TIP

If you are using a RISC-based computer, the over-the-network method can only be used for upgrades or reinstalls. Original installs must be done from the CD.

Creating Network Client Disks

Once your original NT server is installed, you can create a set of network client disks. This will provide the basic communications to the network. In order to create this set of disks, you can access the client administration tools from the Administrative Tools menu, located on the NT server.

Entering into the Administrative Tools menu, you will see the Network Client Administrator utility. Selecting this brings up the menu shown below.

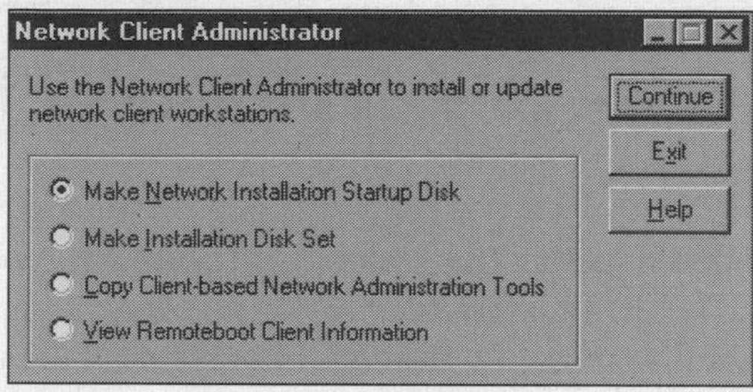

If you check Make Network Installation Startup Disk, you will create a DOS disk that can be used to connect to a network share and install the Windows 95 or Microsoft Network client for DOS and Windows.

To create the disk:

1. Select the Make Network Installations Startup Disk radio button, and click Continue. This brings up the Share Network Client Installation Files dialog box.
2. Enter the path to the client files. If you are using the CD, the path will point to the \CLIENTS directory. This is where the system will copy files *from*.
3. Now you have to make a decision. Are you going to leave the CD on the server and share the CD, are you going to copy the client files to a folder on the server hard drive and then create a share pointing to the folder, or do you already have a folder set up? The client folder on the target server will be located at c:\clients. There is going to be a share name created called clients, and it will take up to 64MB of disk space to accomplish this task. After you have made your decision, select OK.
4. Now the server is configured to work with the clients, but you need a disk to carry around and use on the all workstations. After all the information is copied to your servers folder in step 3, you will get a message that tells you 254 directories were just added and 1141 files had been copied. Memorize this piece of minutia to use at your next cocktail party, and click OK to continue.

5. The Target Workstation Configuration dialog box comes up. Here, choose the size of the disk (Does anyone really still use 5.25- inch disks anymore?) and the network client to install—either Network client 3.0 for DOS/Windows or the Windows 95 client. The final section asks about the NIC that is installed in your workstations. There is a drop-down menu with a large selection. Once you have made your choices, select OK to continue.

NOTE

A quick perusal of the list of NICs failed to turn up any selection for PCMCIA cards for laptops. Also, there is no Browse feature to supply your own driver.

6. Next, a dialog box appears with the Network Startup Disk Configuration selections. This allows you to enter a computer name, along with the User's Name, the Domain, and the Network Protocol. You can specify whether this computer will be using DHCP to acquire an IP address or if it will have a static IP address. You also select where the destination for the new disk is located. After filling in the appropriate selections, again, click OK.

7. The confirmation screen comes up, reiterating all the information you have just entered. Before clicking OK, make sure the disk in the A:\ drive has been formatted with the appropriate version of DOS and is a system disk. If all the above criteria are met, click OK to continue. This will create the Startup Disk.

Now, it might just be easier to create a set of disks to carry around with you, especially if you only have need of one or two clients. In that case, you can select Make Installation Disk Set from the Network Client Administrator screen. You will be prompted for the client or service and the drive to create the disks in. Once that information has been provided, you will be told how many disks you really need. Click OK to continue.

Upgrade to Windows NT Workstation 4.0 in a given situation.

One of the most demanding tasks that an administrator will face is that of keeping up-to-date. Hardware changes on an almost daily rate. Upgrades are a major source of income for software companies, so we face new versions every time we turn around. There are numerous variables to keep in mind when upgrading to Windows NT 4. This objective concerns each of the possible scenarios that you might encounter.

Upgrading Windows 95 to Windows NT 4

Because the registries of the two operating systems are completely different, there is no upgrade path from Windows 95 to Windows NT. If you are faced with the task of moving an environment from Windows 95 to Windows NT, you will have to completely install NT and then reinstall any applications so that they can register themselves with the NT registry. You should also be aware that NT cannot read from a FAT32 partition–if you have taken advantage of the benefits of FAT32 in your environment, you will have to completely back up your data, destroy the partition, and start from scratch.

Upgrading from Windows NT 3.51

There are a lot of variables involved with this upgrade:

- Was the original computer an NT Workstation or Server?
- Will the new operating system be Workstation or Server?
- If Server, will it be a domain controller?

We'll look at each of these possibilities in this section. Microsoft has written a utility specifically designed to upgrade from earlier versions of NT: WINNT32.EXE. This program was specifically written to run under the NT operating system, taking full advantage of the 32-bit architecture. It is fast and runs as a background process. This means that it could conceivably upgrade a production server with very little impact on the users attached at the time.

WARNING

While Microsoft implies that WINNT32.EXE could be run on a server while it was in production, it could be dangerous. While it *should* be safe, you are making some major changes to the operating system. Upgrade your servers during non-business hours to ensure minimum impact on your users.

When a Windows NT computer is upgraded, the process preserves the following:

- User and group accounts
- Network configuration
- Desktop
- Preferences set for administrative tools

Upgrading from NT Workstation 3.51

Table 12.4 lists the options available when upgrading from version 3.51 to 4.0.

TABLE 12.4: NT Workstation 3.51 Upgrade

Upgrade To	Can Be Done?	Bottom Line
Windows NT Workstation 4.0	Yes	Easy, simple process—basically moving to same type of environment
Windows NT Server Member Server	Yes	Changing someone's desktop to a server is not done very often, but it can be accomplished.
Windows NT Server Domain Controller	No	If it wasn't a domain controller to begin with, it can't be one when you are done.

Upgrading from NT Server 3.51 Member Server

Table 12.5 lists the options available when upgrading an NT 3.51 Member Server to NT 4.0.

TABLE 12.5: NT Server 3.51 Member Server Upgrade

Upgrade To	Can Be Done?	Bottom Line
Windows NT Workstation 4.0	No	If it wasn't a workstation before the upgrade, it can't be one after.
Windows NT Server Member Server	Yes	Basically upgrading to the same type of server
Windows NT Server Domain Controller	No	If it wasn't a domain controller to begin with, it can't be one when you are done.

Upgrading from NT Server 3.51 Domain Controller

Table 12.6 lists the options available when upgrading an NT 3.51 Domain Controller.

TABLE 12.6: NT Server 3.51 Domain Controller Upgrade

Upgrade To	Can Be Done?	Bottom Line
Windows NT Workstation 4.0	No	If it wasn't a workstation before the upgrade, it can't be one after.
Windows NT Server Member Server	No	If it wasn't a member server before the upgrade, it can't be one after.
Windows NT Server Domain Controller	Yes	Basically upgrading to the same type of server

On the Windows NT 4.0 CD-ROM, in the directory appropriate for your hardware (i386 for Intel-based computers), run the WINNT32.EXE application. It will automatically sense that there is an earlier version of NT on the computer and ask if you would like to upgrade. Answer Yes, and follow the instructions.

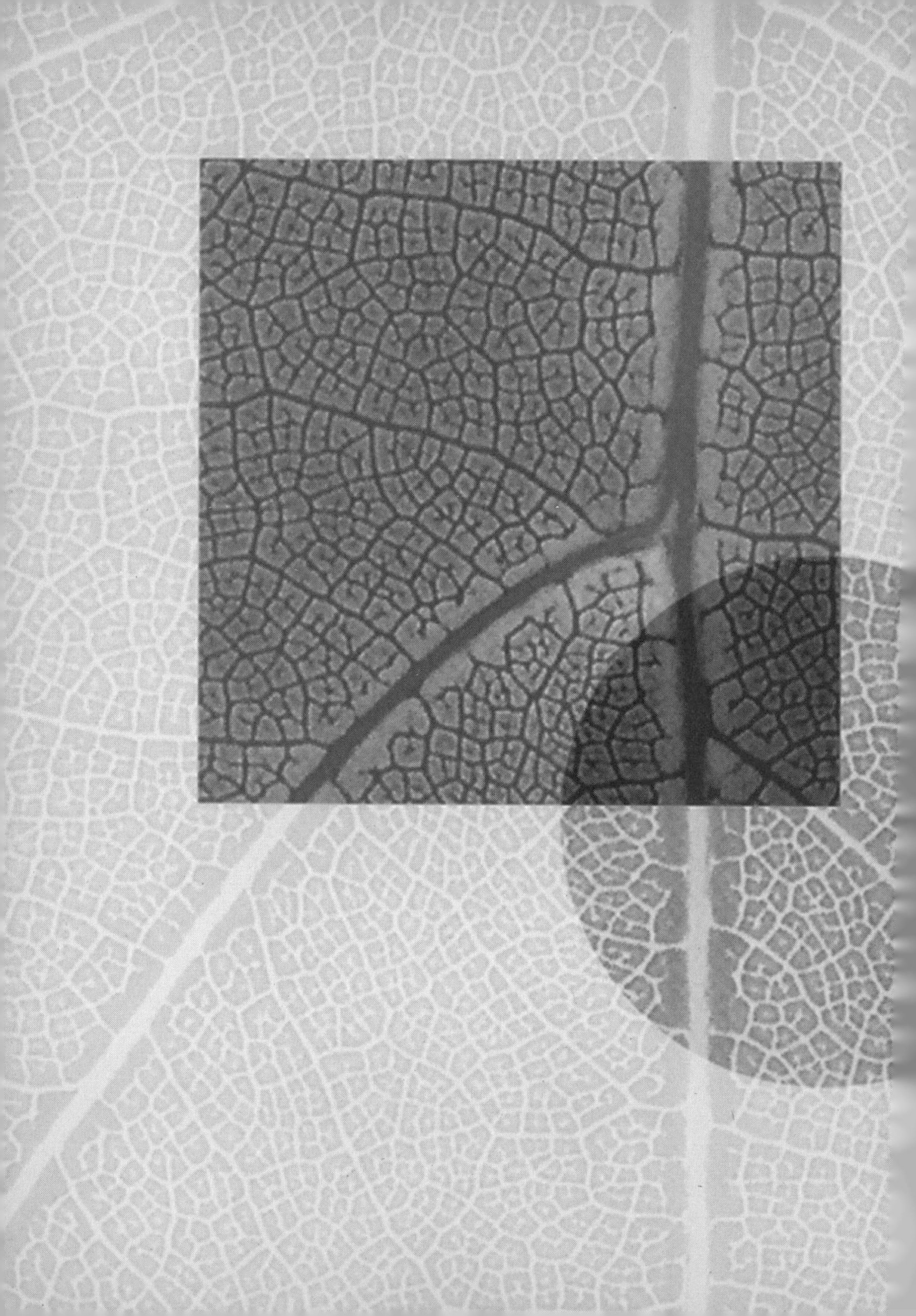

Chapter 13

Managing Resources

One of the things that sets Windows NT Workstation apart from all the other operating systems out there is sharing. More than one person can share a workstation and the data on that workstation can be shared or secured, depending on the owner's preference. There are other desktop operating systems that provide some sort of security, but NT is the most robust.

Adapted from *MCSE Exam Notes: NT Workstation 4*
by Gary Govanus and Robert King

ISBN 0-7821-2290-6 352 pages $19.99

What exactly does managing resources mean? In Chapter 12, hardware resources were discussed. You learned how to get the most out of your disk drive subsystem, your communication devices, SCSI devices, and tape backup units. Those resources are all *things*. How do you manage the resources that are living, breathing parts of your network—your end users?

Create and manage local user accounts and local group accounts to meet given requirements.

With Windows NT Workstation, every user that logs on to the computer must have a user name and a password to access the account. Giving the user a user name gives NT the opportunity to store certain information about the user for retrieval at a later time. In addition, assignments can be made for the user—they can have things like their own user home directory and profile path.

Security of the system starts with the user. A user account is created and a password is assigned for the user using the User Manager utility. The information on the user account is stored in the Security Account Manager database, or SAM.

NOTE

For the purposes of this book, a user account is one created on a particular computer. For the user to attach to a domain, they will also need to have a user account created for that domain. For more information on user accounts in a networked environment, see *MCSE: NT Server 4 Study Guide, Second Edition* by Matthew Strebe and Charles Perkins, with James Chellis (Sybex, 1998).

In addition to user accounts, you can also use the User Manager utility to create Local Group accounts. A local group is simply a group of users brought together for a specific purpose. For example, the NT Workstation has the company accounting software stored on it. Over the course of a week, five different people may access the computer, but only three of these will need to access the accounting software. In this case, the local administrator can create an accounting group, and give the accounting group permission to use the accounting software and see information stored in the accounting data directory. The computer can be configured so that others using the computer can be excluded from even knowing that the accounting software or data is stored on this computer. If you are a network administrator, think of this workstation as a mini-server.

To ease the burden of trying to figure out when and how to create users and groups, NT has provided you with some defaults. These are shown in Table 13.1.

TABLE 13.1: Default Account Types

	Type	Description
Administrator	User	Built-in account for administering the computer
Guest	User	Built-in account for guest access to the computer
Administrators	Group	Members of this local group can administer the computer
Backup Operators	Group	Members can bypass file security to backup files
Guests	Group	Users granted guest access to the computer or domain
Power Users	Group	Members can share directories or printers
Replicator	Group	Supports file replication in a domain
Users	Group	Ordinary Users

In addition to setting security preferences for each user, you can make some global settings using System Policies.

To complete this objective, it is necessary to know how to create a user or group and how to add users to the group. Each of these tasks is completed from the User Manager utility. The User Manager utility is accessed through Programs ➢ Administrative Tools (Common) ➢ User Manager.

Creating a New User

To create a new user, start User Manager while you are logged on as an administrative user.

1. From the User Manager screen, select the top menu option of User ➢ New User. This will bring up the New User screen shown below.

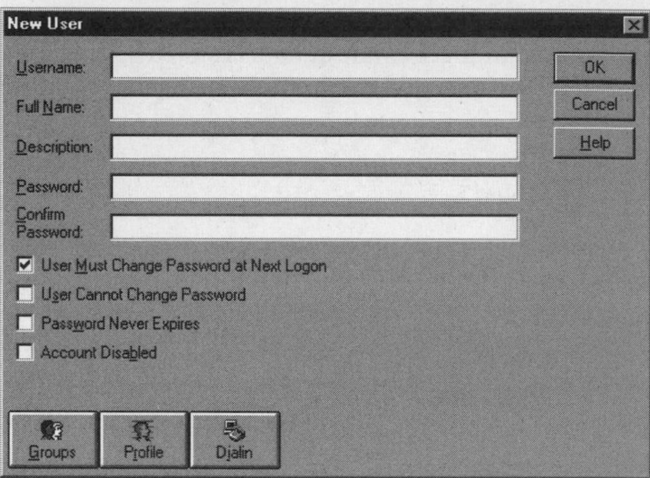

2. There are text boxes for providing the Username and Full Name, a description of the user, and assigning and confirming a password.
3. The box User Must Change Password at Next Logon is checked by default. This forces the user to come up with a different password.
4. If you are creating a "system" user–a user that will be used by a program or service–you may not want the user to be able to change the password. The same may be true of a generic user you are creating. In either case, check the box and the user cannot change the password.
5. Checking the box Password Never Expires gives the user the right to keep the same password forever. This would be a wise idea for the "system" user discussed in step 4.

WARNING

Checking the Password Never Expires box for an individual user will override any system-wide settings an administrator may attempt to enforce.

6. Checking the box Account Disabled temporarily disables an account. You may want to disable an account if the person is leaving for an extended time. You want the account to be

available when they get back, but you do not want anyone using it while they are gone.

7. Clicking the Groups button brings up the Group Memberships screen shown below. You will notice that you can add or remove this user from the groups created on the computer.

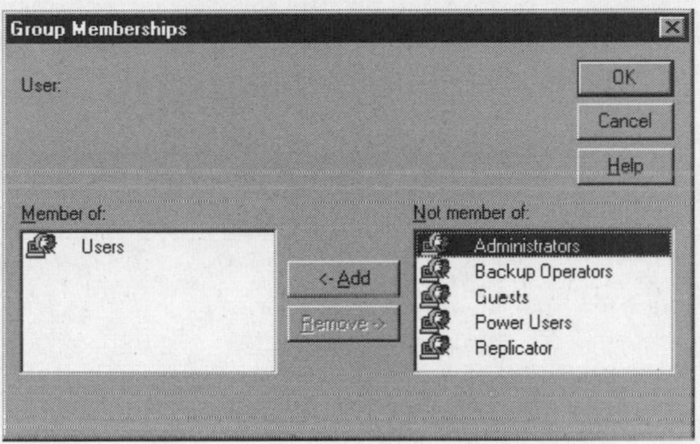

NOTE

The user may not be removed from membership in the Users default group.

8. Clicking the Profile button brings up the User Environment Profile screen shown below. Here you can specify where the user profile is stored, where the logon script can be found, and where the user's home directory is located. You can also connect a drive letter to the home directory.

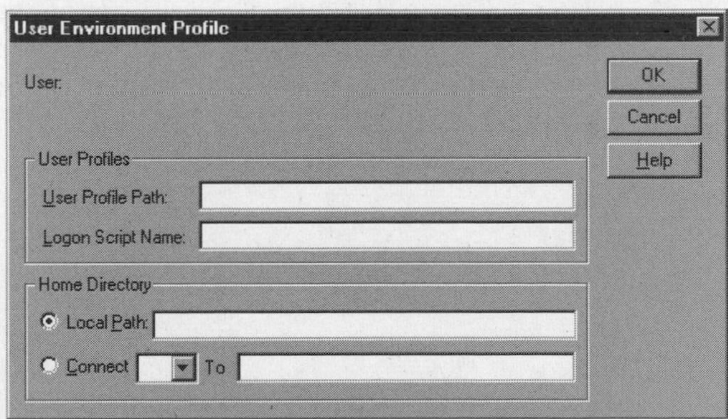

9. Clicking the Dialin button from the New User dialog box brings up the Dialin Information window shown below. This screen will let you grant this user dial-in privileges to a Remote Access Service Server (RAS) and specify how much security is needed. If No Call Back is selected, the user can connect without any verification. Selecting the Set By Caller radio button will prompt the user for a phone number where they can be called back, and the Preset To radio button means the user will be called back at that preset number.

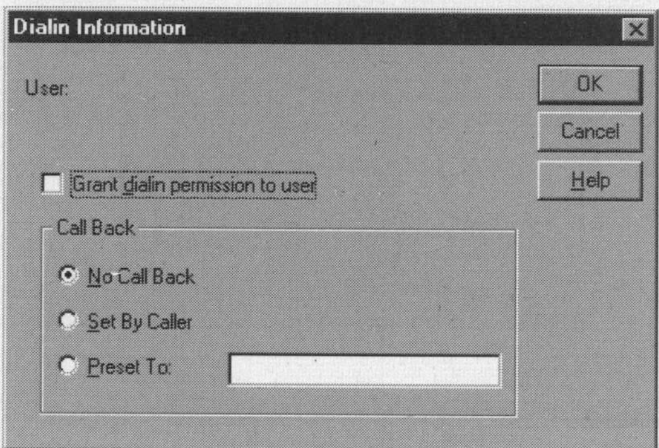

Creating a New Group

To create a new group:

1. Start User Manager while you are logged on as an administrative user.

2. From the User Manager screen, select the top menu option of User ➢ New Local Group. This will bring up the New Local Group dialog box shown below. From here, you can create a new group, give it a name and a description, and add users to the group.

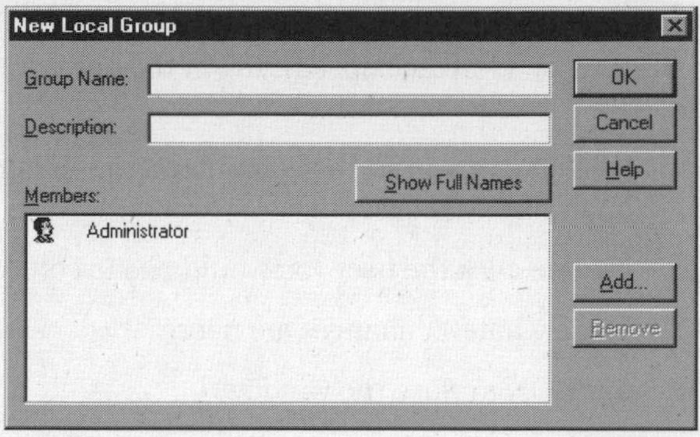

Copying a User

While not specifically covered in the objectives, you may get a test question on what it takes to copy a user or when you would do it. Copying a user is effective if you have a new person coming into the organization replacing or working with another person. The new person would need exactly the same rights and permissions as the current user, so rather than reinventing the wheel, you can just copy the current user, change the user name and password, and the account is finished.

To copy a user:

1. Log on to the computer as a user with administrative rights.
2. Start User Manager.
3. Highlight the user to be copied.
4. From the User menu on the top of the screen, choose copy or press F8.
5. You are now presented with the Copy of UserX screen. Fill out the Username, Full Name, Password, and Confirm Password, make any changes to Groups, Profile, or Dialin and click OK. The user will be created with the same attributes as the template user.

Editing a Current User

Again, this is not addressed specifically in the objective, but there may be questions on it.

1. While logged on to the computer as an administrative user, open User Manager.
2. Double-click the user you would like to edit.
3. Make whatever changes are necessary.
4. Click OK to close the window.

Editing a Current Group

You will frequently have to add or remove users to/from an existing group.

1. While logged on to the computer as an administrative user, open User Manager.
2. Double-click the Group you would like to edit.
3. Make whatever changes are necessary.
4. Click OK to close the window.

WARNING

If you add or remove a user to a group, the change will not take place until the user logs off and logs back on again.

Set up and modify user profiles.

Wouldn't it be nice to be able to make some universal settings for all users? Things like making sure they use the corporate logo as wallpaper, or making sure the network hookup is just the way you want it. It would also be nice to be able to control some universal settings, things that deal with all the users of a specific computer. This is the flexibility that you gain when you understand user profiles and system policies. If you understand these two tools you can take control of your user's desktops and configure them the same way for each user in a given situation.

TIP

Paying close attention to this section will not only help you take control of the desktop, it will also help you on the exam. This area is one of the exam writers' favorites!

A *user profile* is configuration information that is saved on a user-by-user basis. This includes *all* the user settings of the Windows NT environment, such as the desktop arrangement, personal program groups and the program items in those groups, screen colors, screen savers, network connections, printer connections, mouse settings, window size and position, and more. When a user logs on, the user's profile is loaded and the user's Windows NT environment is configured according to that profile. In addition to each user having a profile, you can create and save a mandatory user profile, so an individual user or all users have to have certain things on their desktop, just the way you want it.

User profiles contain those settings and configuration options specific to the individual user–such as installed applications, desktop icons, color options, and so forth. This profile is built in part from System Policy information (for example, those things that a user has access to and those things that the user can and cannot change) and in part from permitted, saved changes that a user makes to customize his or her desktop.

User *profiles* deal with a specific user. User *policies* deal with all users of a computer. User policies are set to configure the following settings:

Maximum Password Age If you work in an environment where security is not an issue, you may choose to have system passwords never expire. If security is an issue, there is a setting that forces passwords to be changed every so many days. Keep in mind that the default is set to 42 days. While decreasing the amount of time a password is active may make great sense from a security point of view, the chances of your users understanding why they have to change their passwords so often are slim to none.

Minimum Password Age This forces a user to keep a password at least a certain period of time. By default, users can change their passwords immediately.

Minimum Password Length How long must a password be? If no changes are made, blank passwords are permitted. If you increase the minimum password length, your users will have to start thinking before typing.

Password Uniqueness We have all heard the stories of the user who kept the same password for years and years. By the time the user left the company, everyone knew his/her password. This is almost as bad as no password at all. Password Uniqueness, which is turned off by default, will remember a number of passwords, forcing the user to come up with something new every so often. You get to choose the history list.

Account Lockout This is an attempt to prevent hackers from attempting to access your network over and over again. If Account Lockout is enabled and someone tries to log on unsuccessfully so many times, the account will be locked and the user will not be able to log on to the system. You can set the number of bad logon attempts, reset the count after so many minutes, and set the lockout duration. Once the account is locked, the hacker doesn't know if it is locked for 10 minutes or an hour and 10 minutes. At that point, there are probably easier networks to attack.

Forcibly disconnect remote users from server when logon hours expire Selecting this button will cause users who are working when the allowed time expires to be kicked off the system. If this is not selected, the remote server user can continue to use the system, but just cannot open any new sessions.

Users must log on in order to change password This selection means that your users must change their password before it expires. If it expires, then the end user will have to contact the Administrator, and the Administrator will have to reset the password.

NOTE

While user policies are not covered in the exam objectives, the topic dovetails so closely with user profiles that it requires at least a brief mention.

Profile Types

See the following for local and roaming user profiles.

Local User Profiles

This section of the Exam Objective is covered in Part 2: NT Server 4, Chapter 7 "Managing Resources." The Practice Exam at the end of Part 4 will test you on this material.

Roaming User Profiles

This section of the Exam Objective is covered in Part 2: NT Server 4, Chapter 7 "Managing Resources." The Practice Exam at the end of Part 4 will test you on this material.

System Policies

This section of the Exam Objective is covered in Part 2: NT Server 4, Chapter 7 "Managing Resources." The Practice Exam at the end of Part 4 will test you on this material.

Creating and Modifying Profiles

Since creating a local user profile is done by the user that logs on, the only profiles the administrator may have to worry about is a mandatory user profile or a roaming user profile.

Creating a User Profile and a Mandatory User Profile

This section of the Exam Objective is covered in Part 2: NT Server 4, Chapter 7 "Managing Resources." The Practice Exam at the end of Part 4 will test you on this material.

Modifying a User Profile

If a user is not subject to a mandatory user profile, any time the user logs on and makes any changes to the desktop and logs out, the user profile will be modified.

Creating a Roaming User Profile

This section of the Exam Objective is covered in Part 2: NT Server 4, Chapter 7 "Managing Resources." The Practice Exam at the end of Part 4 will test you on this material.

Copying a User Profile to Make It a Remote User Profile

This section of the Exam Objective is covered in Part 2: NT Server 4, Chapter 7 "Managing Resources." The Practice Exam at the end of Part 4 will test you on this material.

Set up shared folders and permissions.

This Exam Objective is covered in Part 2: NT Server 4, Chapter 7 "Managing Resources," under the Manage Disk Resources objective. The Practice Exam at the end of Part 4 will test you on this material.

Set permissions on NTFS partitions, folders, and files.

This Exam Objective is covered in Part 2: NT Server 4, Chapter 7 "Managing Resources," under the Manage Disk Resources objective. The Practice Exam at the end of Part 4 will test you on this material.

Install and configure printers in a given environment.

What is the name of the device that actually puts the ink/toner to paper? You go out and buy an XYZ Laser Printer. In MicroSpeak, the object you load paper into is called a *printing device*. A *printer* is the software interface that takes the information from your application and redirects it to a printing device. A *print driver* is the piece of software that translates application information into the printer-specific commands that are passed on to the actual printer.

In the NT print architecture, the application that you are using to generate the output does not care what kind of printer you are using. It just sends the job off to the printer and somehow, magically, the print job appears. The magic is made up of many processes working together to give your users the desired results.

There are two ways that you can add a printer to a Windows NT Workstation: You can add a local printer or add a network printer. A local printer is a printer that is hooked directly to your workstation, a network printer is a printer somewhere in the office that someone has graciously decided to share. Connecting to either is a painless process utilizing either My Computer or the Printers icon from Control Panel.

Configuring a printer takes on many faces, depending on the driver that is supplied with the printer. Usually, you will be able to configure paper size, input trays, duplexing, fonts, and paper layout. You can also specify default settings for specialty printers.

Installing a Printer

A local printer is defined as a printer that is physically connected to your workstation, either by a parallel cable or serial cable. To begin the process, open My Computer by double-clicking the desktop icon.

1. Once My Computer has opened, choose the Add Printer icon from the Printers folders. This will start the Add Printer Wizard.
2. Once the Add Printer Wizard has started you will be presented with a choice. You can choose to install a printer attached to My Computer or you can choose to connect to a Network print server. Connecting to a network print server means you will be printing to a printer not hooked directly to your computer.
3. If you choose My Computer and click Next, you can designate the port the printer is attached to, usually LPT1. From this screen you can add a port or configure the transmission retry count for an existing port. You can also choose to enable printer pooling, which allows several similar devices to share printing responsibilities. Make your choices and click Next.
    - Choose the printer manufacturer and model if you are using a printer that NT already has drivers for, or select Have Disk if it is a "non-standard" printer. Click Next.
    - Enter a printer name and decide if this will be the default printer. Click Next.
    - Decide if the printer will be shared with others on the network. If the printer will be shared with others, you will need to specify the operating systems the other users have installed on their computers. The workstation that controls the printer also controls the printer drivers. The drivers will be passed to the requesting clients when there is a printing request. Click Next.

- You are prompted to print a test page. Make your choice and click Finish.
- At this point the system will prompt you for the CD-ROM or a location where the files are stored. Provide the information and the drivers will be copied.

4. If you choose to connect to a Network Print Server and click Next, you will be presented with the Connect to Printer box. You will be shown a list of shared printers or you can enter in the path to the printer. Click OK. When you choose to print to that printer, a print driver will be downloaded to your computer.

Configuring Printer Properties

There are times in the world of computing when you just have to say, "It depends." This is one of those times. The properties you can configure depend on the printer and depend on the driver that is supplied with the printer. To configure a printer, open the Printers folder, right-click, and select properties. There are six tabs to explore.

General Tab

This tab is mostly informational, allowing you to comment on the printer or show the location. The driver is listed and there is a button marked New Driver to allow you to change or update the present software.

The Separator Page is known in the Novell world as a Banner Page. It comes out before the print job and gives information about who sent the print job. It can also be used to switch printers between the two printer control languages, PCL and PostScript.

The Print Processor button lets you choose how you want the print jobs to be processed. The default is Winprint.

The Print Test Page button allows you to test the printer at your discretion.

Ports

The Ports tab show which ports are utilized for which printers, and lets you add a port, delete a port, or configure a port. This is a repeat screen from the Printer Installation Wizard. You can also define and configure Printer pooling.

Scheduling

Choosing the Scheduling tab allows you to pick when the printer will be available for general use and which priority the printer will have. Lowest is the default priority.

You can also spool documents so the program finishes printing faster, returning control of the desktop to the end user. Printing can either start immediately or after the last page has been spooled. If you decide not to spool, there is a radio button to print directly to the printer. Finally, the system will allow you to hold mismatched documents, print spooled documents first, or keep documents after they have printed. Usually, when a print job has finished printing, the job is deleted. If you opt to keep the job, the job will be saved.

Sharing

Again, a repeat from the Add Printer Wizard. You can choose to keep the printer private or share it. If you share it, you can assign a share name and determine which operating systems will need drivers.

Security

The Permissions tab lets you give users or groups of users the rights to print to the printer.

Auditing allows you to choose which events you want to audit. The event choice is made by user or group. You could decide to audit the success of all print jobs by the group Management. Before you can audit printers you must enable auditing of File and Object auditing in User Manager.

Ownership lets you decide who will "own" the printer.

Device Settings

This is the setting where you get to pick things like how tray assignments will be handled and what the default paper size will be.

NOTE

For more information on Printing, check out the *MCSE: NT Server 4 Study Guide, Second Edition* by Matthew Strebe and Charles Perkins with James Chellis (Sybex, 1998).

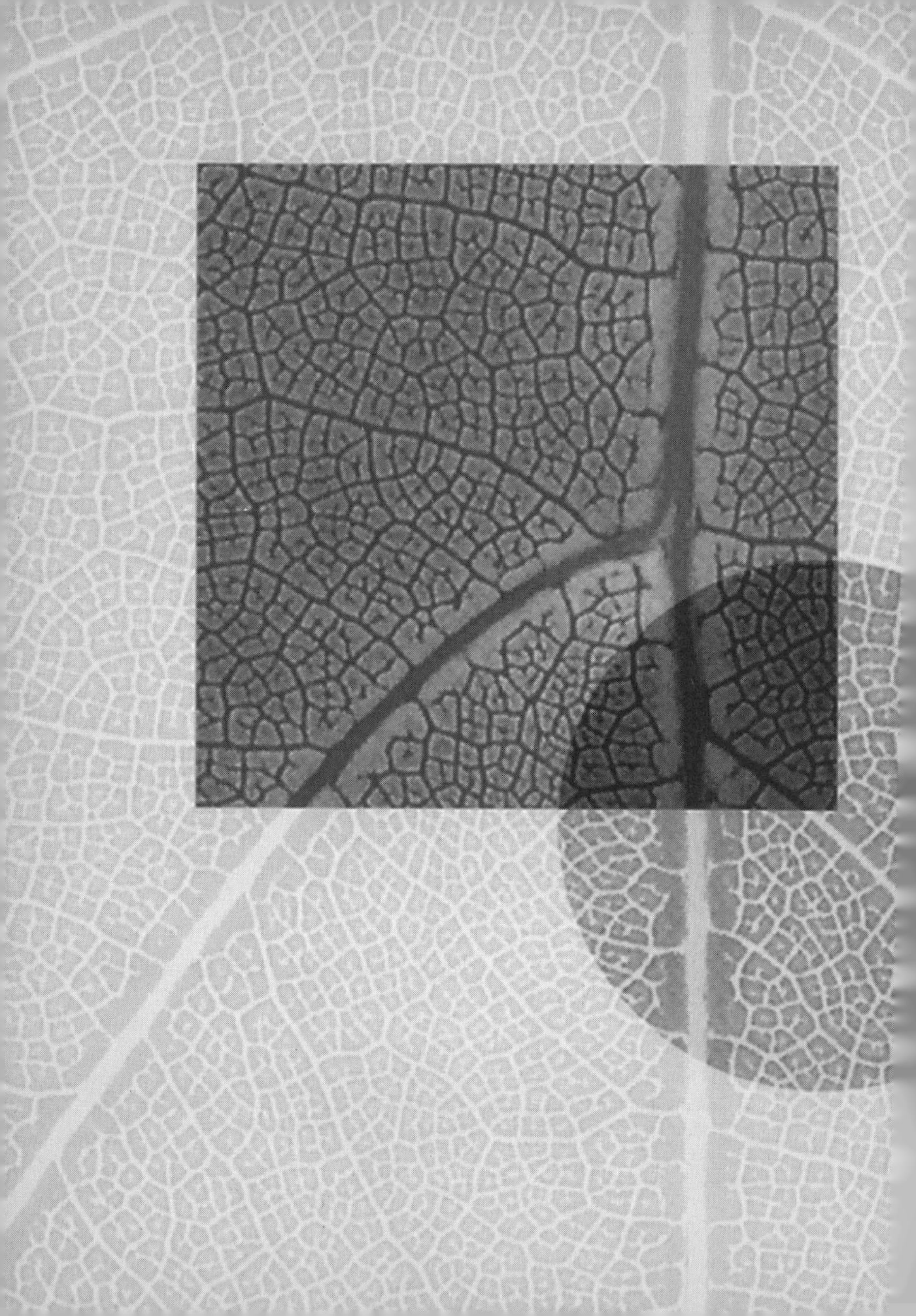

Chapter 14

Connectivity

The objectives in this chapter are concerned with connecting your Windows NT Workstation to a network. These topics are not only important for this exam, they are topics which are touched upon in just about every MCSE test. Microsoft places a lot of emphasis on the networking abilities of the NT operating system.

Adapted from *MCSE Exam Notes: NT Workstation 4*
by Gary Govanus and Robert King
ISBN 0-7821-2290-6   352 pages $19.99

Add and configure the network components of a Windows NT Workstation.

This entire chapter revolves around the various options available to connect Windows NT to your network. The first step is to cover the basic NT tools used to configure your workstation as part of a network.

Windows NT Network Components

This is a *hands-on* objective. That is, there are not many theoretical or design issues. You must have a good overall feel for what options are available, and what tools are used, before you can begin to discuss any specific networking scenarios involving an NT Workstation.

NetBIOS Names

Each computer in an NT network needs a unique identifier called a NetBIOS name. This name is one of the tools used to differentiate computers on the network. When you install an NT Workstation on the network you will be asked to provide this name. You can change the NetBIOS name after the installation by accessing the Network applet in Control Panel.

The NetBIOS name is a 15-character user-friendly name usually assigned during the installation of NT. This is not, however, the end of the story. This name has a sixteenth character that is used to identify each service provided by the computer. Let's say, for instance, that a user had named a computer "Endeavor200." Each time the computer starts, one of the first things it will do is announce itself to the network, using this name combined with a sixteenth character for each service. This is how communication is routed to each of the services on a particular computer.

NOTE

For more information on the initialization process of an NT-based computer see *MCSE: NT Server 4 in the Enterprise Study Guide*, Second Edition, by Lisa Donald and James Chellis (Sybex, 1998).

Computer Accounts for Windows NT Workstations

While this exam concerns NT Workstation, you will have to know a little about NT Servers to fully configure any NT Workstation on a network. In an NT domain, certain NT Servers hold a master list of user, computer, and group accounts that are valid on computers in the domain. This list, or database, is called the SAM (Security Accounts Manager database).

When an NT Workstation joins a domain, an account must be created for the workstation in the domain's SAM. This can be done in one of two ways.

One way is for the LAN administrator to create the account, using the Server Manager tool, before attempting to add the workstation to the domain. In Server Manager, the administrator chooses Add to Domain from the Computer menu and specifies the NetBIOS name of the workstation. The other way is to give an administrative user account and password while joining the domain. This will result in the account being created as the workstation joins the domain.

In either event, the domain SAM must have a record for the workstation if it is to join the domain.

Network Redirectors

The NT operating system is made up of various modules, each of which provides a specific function. When an NT computer tries to access a resource on the network, the process of connecting to that resource is handled by a Network Redirector. There are redirectors that know how to communicate to other NT-based computers, to Novell NetWare networks, Banyan Vines networks, and to just about every other type of network found in the business world. Each redirector understands the naming conventions, access rules, and other pertinent communication facets of a particular network operating system.

When an NT Workstation attempts to connect to a network resource it consults a "Network Access Order List" to determine which network it should try first. One of the more common performance optimization techniques is to order this list so that the most commonly used network is tried first.

Protocols Supported

The Microsoft Windows NT operating system can use many different protocols to communicate on the network. We'll discuss each exam-pertinent protocol later in this book, but for now you should be aware of the more commonly installed protocols. The most commonly used network protocols are NetBEUI, TCP/IP, and NWLink IPX/SPX Compatible Transport. Each protocol represents a different set of rules used to communicate on a network. Each has strengths and weaknesses; these will be discussed later.

Network Interface Card (NIC) Drivers

A NIC is a physical device placed in a computer that connects the PC to the network. There are numerous makes and models of NICs on the market. Before NT can communicate with a NIC installed in your workstation, a driver must be loaded. The NIC driver is software that acts as an interpreter between the operating system and the physical device. NT ships with drivers for most of the more common NICs on the market. If the driver for your NIC is not on the NT CD-ROM, you can install a driver provided by the manufacturer.

Binding Order

In the simplest case, to bind is to join together. In an operating system, to bind is to join together two software components. When you install a NIC in an NT computer, the NIC driver must be bound to the various protocols that it will support. In most cases this will be done for you automatically as part of the installation process for the NIC driver software. There are, however, a few specific cases where you would need to configure this manually.

The order in which the protocols are bound to the driver determines the order in which NT will use those protocols for communication. For instance, if TCP/IP was bound first and NWLink second, NT would always try to use TCP/IP first whenever it was trying to communicate. This would be a great configuration if TCP/IP was the primary protocol used on your network. If, however, your primary (or most used) protocol was NWLink, this would cause a delay for any communication using NWLink. You can change the binding order to optimize for performance.

You might also use the protocol bindings as a sort of firewall. If a protocol is not bound to a NIC, then that NIC cannot use the protocol. One configuration seen fairly often is using protocol bindings to provide security on a server attached to the Internet. The administrator might use only NetBEUI on the company network and TCP/IP for communication to the Internet. In this case, you would unbind TCP/IP from the NIC attached to the company network. This would stop any traffic from the Internet from reaching your company network.

Configuring Windows NT Components

All of the procedures discussed for this section begin with the Network applet found in Control Panel.

We'll discuss options available within each of the five tabs across the opening window: Identification, Services, Protocols, Adapters, and Bindings.

Identification Tab

The Identification tab allows you to confirm the NetBIOS name or workgroup/domain information for an NT Workstation. Clicking the Change button allows you to change these settings.

Here you can either change the NetBIOS name or workgroup/domain membership. In this case, the NetBIOS name option is grayed out, as the workgroup/domain membership section is active.

If you elect to change the domain membership information, remember that an NT workstation account must be configured in the Domain Security Account Manager database (SAM.) This can either be done before the computer attempts to join the domain using the Server Manager tool or by entering the name of a domain administrator.

Services Tab

Many optional services can be added to an NT Workstation to provide added network functionality. Most of these services will be added by accessing the Services tab and clicking the Add button. We'll discuss each of the exam-pertinent services as necessary for each objective.

If you have multiple network redirectors (software used to connect to various networking environments) installed, you can also change the order in which your NT Workstation attempts to connect to the network. Clicking the Network Access Order button will display a dialog box that lists the various networks that your computer will attempt to attach to; highlight one, and you can move it up or down the list as appropriate.

Protocols Tab

We'll discuss each of the protocols for other objectives, but, for now, we'll concentrate on how protocols are installed and configured on an NT computer. Basically, on the Protocols tab, click Add and choose the protocol off the list. Each protocol will have a different set of parameters that you might have to configure during the installation.

Adapters Tab

The Adapters tab allows you to add, remove, configure, or update the Network Interface Card (NIC) information on your NT Workstation.

Clicking the Add button will bring up a dialog box with a list of the NIC drivers that ship with NT. You will also have the opportunity to click the Have Disk button for drivers not shown on the list.

Each NIC driver will have its own parameters that you may have to configure. Common parameters include the IRQ, port address, and memory address. Before installing a NIC in your computer you should have a firm understanding of your PC and how it is configured.

Bindings Tab

The Bindings tab allows you to disable or enable protocols in use on your workstation and change the order in which they are used to communicate. Changing the binding order so that the most commonly used protocols are used first is a very common performance optimization technique.

Use various methods to access network resources.

Once you've added networking to your workstation, the next step is to access network resources. As with most functions in NT, there are numerous ways to accomplish this task. For this objective, we'll discuss the various methods available to access resources on the network.

Universal Naming Convention (UNC) Paths

The UNC naming standard is a standardized way of naming resources on a network. In a UNC path you must identify both the computer (using its NetBIOS name) and the shared resource on that computer. The format is as follows:

```
\\<server_name>\<share_name>\<directory>
```

Where `<server_name>` is the NetBIOS name of the device which hosts the resource, `<share_name>` is the assigned name for that resource, and `<directory>` is the path to a directory on that resource.

NOTE

Since this book is expressly written for experienced administrators or as a supplemental study aid, it is safe to assume that you are comfortable with UNC names. If this is not the case, see *MCSE: NT Workstation 4 Study Guide, Second Edition*, by Charles Perkins, Matthew Strebe, and James Chellis (Sybex, 1998).

Accessing Network Resources

As with the preceeding objective, the information presented here is considered part of the basic skill set necessary to work with NT. The procedures presented here are not heavily tested upon, but they are considered prerequisite knowledge in many of the questions that you will see on your exam.

Using Network Neighborhood to Access Network Resources

There are two ways to use Network Neighborhood to gain access to a shared resource on your network. The first way is to keep opening resources, starting with the "Entire Network" option until you find the computer that the resource resides upon. Then open that computer to see a list of shared resources. Click the resource you wish to access. This method allows you to find the desired resource without knowing its complete UNC path–you just "walk the network" until you find what you are looking for.

Once you've found the appropriate share point, choose Map Network Drive from the file menu. Notice that you are given the opportunity to connect using a different user account in the event that your current account does not have the necessary permissions.

Using the Net Command Line Utility

Microsoft Windows NT's networking components are based upon the LanManager network operating system. Many of the commands that are available in LanManager are available in NT. One such command is the Net command line utility. While this tool can be used to perform many useful administrative functions, we are concerned with only two of its options: VIEW and USE.

The Net command is a command prompt tool. Typing **Net View \\\\<*server_name*>** will display the shared resource on a given server.

Typing **Net Use <d>: \\\\<unc_path_to_resource>** where <d> is a drive letter will map that drive to the shared resource.

Implement Windows NT Workstation as a client in a NetWare environment.

No discussion of networking is complete without talking about Novell's NetWare. At one time, not so long ago, Novell owned over 90 percent of the worldwide networking market. Even today, that number is probably still over 50 percent. Given this, the odds are you will have to connect to a NetWare server at some point in your career. One of the features of Windows NT is its ability to coexist with a NetWare environment. This means companies can ease into an NT network, while maintaining the network services that they are currently using.

Windows NT-NetWare Connection Methods

There are two ways that a Windows NT environment can connect to a Novell NetWare system: one server-based solution and one workstation-based solution. On the server side, NT ships with a tool called Gateway Services for NetWare (GSNW.) This tool allows an NT-based server to connect to a NetWare server and share its resources as if they were part of the NT environment. With this solution, no special configuration is necessary at the client, since they see the NetWare resources as if they were a shared resource at the NT server. This solution is great in a small network, or in an environment where the NetWare resources are used infrequently.

For our purposes, that is all you need to know about GSNW. It is covered in more detail in the NT Core Technologies and NT Enterprise Technologies examinations.

This objective is really concerned with configuring an NT Workstation as a NetWare client. This is a two-step process.

1. Configure your NT Workstation with a protocol that NetWare can use to communicate.
2. Add the NetWare client, Client Services for NetWare, to your workstation.

To access resources on a NetWare server, your workstation has to be configured to use the NWLink IPX/SPX Compatible Protocol. This is Microsoft's implementation of the IPX/SPX protocol used in NetWare environments.

There are two configuration parameters associated with this protocol—Frame Type and Network Number.

Frame Type Frame type refers to an industry standard set of rules for organizing packets in an IPX/SPX network. When you send a request to another computer on the network, that request is passed through various layers of software before it is ready to be transmitted. Each layer adds information to the request, building what is known as a *packet* for transmission. The definition of how this management information is organized is known as the Frame Type. If both computers (the originator and the recipient) are configured to use the same frame type, then each computer will know how to interpret the information in the packet. If not, then communication cannot occur.

Network Number In an IPX/SPX environment, each network segment is given a unique identifier. This identifier is used to deliver the packet to the proper destination. The network number is this unique identifier. To confuse the issue, each network segment has a unique identifier for each frame type. If you are using multiple frame types, you will have multiple network numbers for each segment.

Addressing in an IPX/SPX environment can be a confusing topic. There are three types of addresses used to route information, only two of which we need to discuss here. The two addresses are the node or MAC (Media Access Control) address and the Network Number. The MAC address is the physical address burned into the NIC (Network Interface Card). The Network Number represents a network segment.

In most cases, you will not have to worry about configuring the NWLink protocol. It can automatically sense the frame type and network number in use and will configure itself appropriately. It does this by grabbing one IPX/SPX packet off the network and analyzing its content. If you are configured with multiple frame types, it will not configure all of them and you will have to do this manually.

Once the NWLink IPX/SPX Compatible Protocol is installed and configured, you must add the appropriate client software to your computer. NT ships with NetWare client software known as Client Services for NetWare (CSNW). CSNW is best described as the NetWare *redirector*. A redirector is a software component that passes requests to a particular network operating system—in this case, NetWare.

A computer configured with both the NWLink protocol and CSNW can access a NetWare server using the NetWare Core Protocol (NCP), the internal language of NetWare. CSNW also supports the following:

- Large Internet Protocol (LIP), which determines the optimum packet size to be used for communication
- Long filenames, if the NetWare server is configured to accept them
- NetWare Directory Services (NDS), which is Novell's X.500-compliant directory service used to organize network resources

Connection Procedures

Windows NT Workstation must be able to connect to these networks or administrators will think twice about implementing the Microsoft solution. You will probably see questions on your exam that concern the implementation of the NetWare client software.

Installing NWLink IPX/SPX Compatible Protocol

This protocol is installed like any other–Use the Network applet in Control Panel. On the Protocols tab, choose Add.

Configuring the Frame Type and Network Number

As mentioned earlier, if you are using only one frame type on your network, you can leave these parameters at the default setting of Auto Detect. If you are using more than one frame type, however, you will have to manually configure this protocol.

1. In Control Panel, open the Network applet.
2. On the Protocols tab, highlight NWLink IPX/SPX Compatible Transport and click the Properties button.
3. To configure the frame type and network number, choose the frame type from the drop-down list and then enter in the network number.

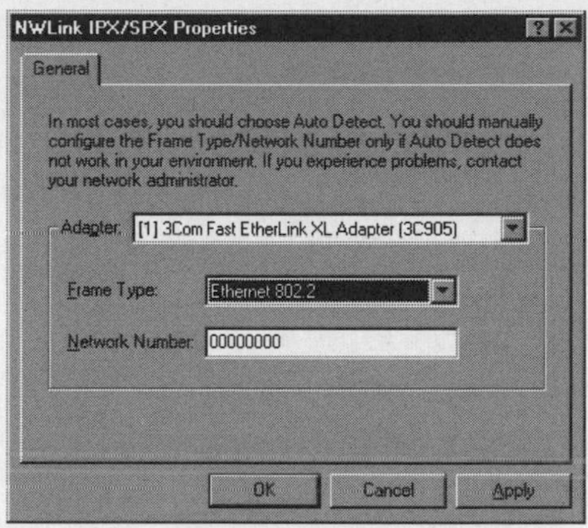

Installing Client Services for NetWare

CSNW is installed like any other service in the NT operating system.

1. From Control Panel, open the Network applet.
2. On the Services tab, choose Add.
3. From the list, highlight Client Service for NetWare and click OK.
4. After the process completes you must restart your computer.

At the first restart of your computer, a dialog box will appear asking for your preferred server or, in a NetWare 4.*x* network, your preferred tree and name context. You can either enter this information at that point or choose the CSNW applet in Control Panel, shown below. The CSNW applet will include a few more options.

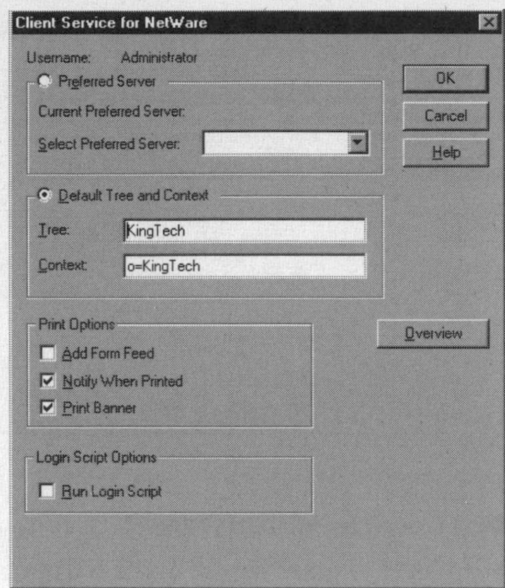

Use various configurations to install Windows NT Workstation as a TCP/IP client.

While this is a fairly short objective, it is critical to Microsoft's positioning of Windows NT as an Internet-ready operating system. When you install the networking components of NT Workstation, TCP/IP is chosen as the default protocol. The information covered for this objective is critical to both the Enterprise exam as well as most of the other tests in the MCSE program.

NOTE

For a more detailed discussion of TCP/IP, see *MCSE: TCP/IP for NT Server 4 Study Guide*, by Todd Lammle with Monica Lammle and James Chellis (Sybex, 1997).

Understanding TCP/IP

You cannot finish the MCSE program without at least a rudimentary understanding of the TCP/IP protocol suite. While a full discussion is beyond the realm of this objective, you will need to understand a little bit about why TCP/IP is chosen and how it works.

Why TCP/IP?

TCP/IP was specifically designed to allow dissimilar devices to communicate. This is key to understanding why TCP/IP is so popular in today's networking environments. Most networks are a combination of old and new—legacy systems that would cost too much to replace, and new systems that have been purchased over the years. There are very few networks made up of only one type of hardware running only one operating system.

Many of the early *connected systems* (before the term *network* was coined) were proprietary in nature—that is, they could only communicate with like systems. At the time this was no problem because Wide Area Networks (WAN) did not exist. As companies started to connect their offices together, a need for a common method of communication was perceived. TCP/IP was designed to fulfill that need.

How Does TCP/IP Work?

TCP/IP is based upon a common set of rules that define how communication should occur and how each device is located on the network. For our purposes, we will need to understand how each TCP/IP device, or *host*, is configured.

Each host on a TCP/IP network needs to be assigned a unique identifier, known as its IP address. This address must be unique against all other devices on the networks to which this host can connect.

TIP

To put the IP address in perspective, think about the millions of computers attached to the Internet. Each has its own unique IP address that is different from all other computers connected.

This IP address is made up of four octets—each octet is made up of eight bits; an IP address follows this syntax: 206.100.11.179. For this exam you won't really need to understand how those addresses are decided upon—just how they are physically assigned to each workstation.

Of the IP address, a certain number of bits will represent the network to which the device is connected and the rest will represent that device on the network. In other words, the IP address is really made up of two parts—network and host. Unfortunately, it is rarely obvious from the address where the network address ends and the host address begins. To make this distinction, each host must be configured with a subnet mask. The subnet mask is used by the network to determine which part of a computer's IP address is network and which part is host.

One last important configuration parameter must be set at each host—the Default Gateway. When a computer attempts to communicate with another host, the local networking software must determine if that host is local or remote (on the same network or a different one). If the destination host is remote, the computer must pass its communication to a device that can route the packets to the destination—a router. Each device on a routed network (an environment made up of multiple networks) must be configured with the IP address of the router it should send remote communication to. This is known as the Default Gateway.

To recap—each Windows NT computer on your network will need to be configured with three parameters: IP Address, Subnet Mask, and Default Gateway.

The focus of this objective is the procedures used to configure these parameters. There are two methods: manual and dynamic.

NOTE

For testing purposes, Microsoft really pushes the use of the dynamic method, so be sure to study it carefully.

Manual Configuration of a TCP/IP Host

When using the manual configuration method, you will have to set parameters at each computer by hand. While this method has been used to configure TCP/IP hosts for quite a while, it does have its drawbacks. Since each computer needs to be configured, you will have to travel to each computer, sit down, and manually enter the data. This method is fine in a small environment, but in a large company it can consume hours.

The manual method also invites mistakes. Mistakes in the TCP/IP configuration can mean that no communication will be possible. Overall, the manual method is fine for small environments but is not recommended for larger networks.

Dynamic Configuration of TCP/IP Clients

The TCP/IP protocol suite includes a protocol specifically designed to configure clients automatically as they connect to the network. The Dynamic Host Configuration Protocol (DHCP) is implemented as a service on an NT Server. The administrator configures the parameters that should be configured for clients at that server. When those clients attach to the network, they find the DHCP server and request an IP address and any other configuration parameters that they might need.

DHCP allows the administrator to configure the TCP/IP environment from a central location. This reduces the time, effort, and potential mistakes that the manual method would entail.

Configuring the DHCP service is beyond the scope of this exam, but you will need to know how to configure an NT Workstation to take advantage of dynamic TCP/IP configuration.

Installing Windows NT Workstation as a TCP/IP Client

The procedures that follow are the main focus of this objective, so spend some time getting comfortable with the differences. No matter which method you choose to use to configure your clients, the first step will be installing the TCP/IP protocol.

Installing TCP/IP

1. In Control Panel, open the Network applet.
2. On the Protocols tab, click Add.
3. Highlight TCP/IP Protocol, and click OK. After NT copies in the appropriate files, you will be prompted to restart your computer.

Manually Configuring a TCP/IP Client

1. In Control Panel, open the Network applet.
2. On the Protocols tab, highlight TCP/IP Protocol and click Properties.

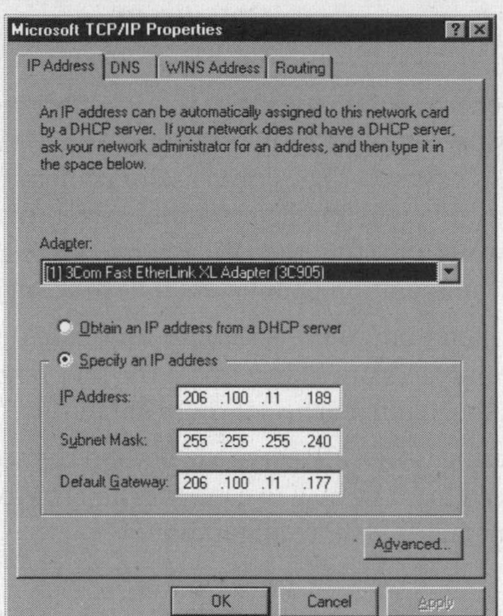

3. For our purposes, enter the IP address that the computer has been assigned, the subnet mask, and the IP address of the default gateway. Notice that there are other tabs that contain configuration options. While they are beyond the scope of this exam, in real life you would need to configure numerous other parameters.

Setting up a DHCP Client

There is very little involved in configuring a workstation as a DHCP client. The whole point, after all, is to avoid configuring each client individually.

1. In Control Panel, open the Network applet.
2. On the Protocols tab, highlight the TCP/IP Protocol and click the Properties button.
3. On the opening screen, you will see the option "Obtain an IP address from a DHCP server." Make sure it is selected.

Configure and install Dial-Up Networking in a given situation.

Windows NT Workstation supports two of the most common telephone line protocols: Serial Line Internet Protocol (SLIP) and Point-to-Point Protocol (PPP). Each of these line protocols takes the standard LAN protocols of TCP/IP, NetBEUI, and NWLink and hides them (the actual word is encapsulates, but hides makes more sense) within the telephone protocol. SLIP is the older of the two protocols and is rarely used anymore. PPP is the most popular because it supports things like Dynamic Host Control Protocol (DHCP) as well as static IP addressing.

Windows NT Workstation also supports a procedure called multilink. With multilink, you can have multiple lines calling the same destination at the same time for faster throughput. In addition to the standard line protocols, NT supports Point-to-Point Tunneling protocol. This protocol allows you to "steal" a part of the Internet to create a Virtual Private Network between your remote location and the office.

Remote Access Service (RAS) and Dial-Up Networking (DUN) can be installed together or separately. They can be installed either at the time of initial NT Workstation installation or later. This section will cover how to install Dial-Up Networking after the initial installation of NT Workstation.

Install Dial-Up Networking

Start the installation of Dial-Up Networking by double-clicking the My Computer icon on the desktop, and then click the Dial Up Networking icon. This will start the Installation Wizard.

1. The first screen you see tells you how you can use either a modem or an ISDN line to use dial-up networking. Microsoft marketing invades the Installation Wizard arena. Click Install to get to work.

2. Once you click Install, NT goes out and starts to copy files. It will locate the Remote Access Service device installed in your computer (your modem or ISDN adapter). If you don't like the modem it found, there are choices to Install a Modem or Install an X.25 pad. Click OK to add the RAS device we installed back in Chapter 11.

3. This brings up the Remote Access Setup screen. The RAS setup screen shows the modem installed and allows you to add or remove components, configure or clone (copy) a component, or click Continue. Click Continue.

4. Windows NT Workstation installs RAS and binds the appropriate protocols. You finally get a message that says DUN has been installed and you need to restart your computer for the changes to take effect. Click Restart.

Configure Dial-Up Networking

The configuration of the Dial-Up Networking client really begins with the configuration of Remote Access Services and the modem. To access the modem configuration options, go into Control Panel, then double-click Modems, highlight the modem, and click Properties.

Depending on the modem, there may not be much to configure. You can configure default line speed, the volume of the modem speaker, and the way the modem connects.

From the modem General page, you can configure your dialing properties. This specifies how your calls are to be dialed.

- You can set your location depending on the area you are calling from.
- You can specify if you need to dial an access code to get an outside line for either local or long distance.
- You can set the system up to use a calling card.
- You can disable call waiting.
- You can tell the system to use tone or pulse dialing.

Once modem configuration has been completed, you can configure RAS. To start the RAS configuration, from Control Panel, double-click the Network icon.

1. Click the Services tab.

2. Click Remote Access Service, then click Properties. This returns us to the Remote Access Setup screen. Click Configure. Configure gives you the opportunity to specify how the port the modem is attached to is used. You can tell the system to use the port for Dial out only, Receive calls only, or

Dial out and receive calls. The default is Dial out only. Make your selection and click OK.

3. Click Network. The network selection lets you choose which network protocols will be used on dial out. Your choices are NetBEUI, TCP/IP, and IPX. TCP/IP and IPX are selected by default. Make your selections and click OK. If you made changes to the RAS configuration, you must restart the computer.

At this point, DUN is configured and RAS is configured; we just don't have anywhere to call. Now, we must create a phone book entry. Phone book entries are important, not just because they give us somewhere to call, but because this is where RAS security is configured. Phone book entries, by the way, are part of the configuration information for the user, so the other people who use your NT Workstation won't know where you are calling.

To create a new phone book entry, double-click My Computer on your desktop, double-click Dial-Up networking and click New. This starts the New Phonebook Entry Wizard.

1. You will be asked to name the new phone book entry. Provide a name and click Next.

2. You now receive a Server screen, and you can check any or all of the three options:

   - I am calling the Internet.
   - Send a plain text password if that's the only way to connect.
   - The non-Windows NT server I am calling expects me to type login information after connecting or to know TCP/IP addresses before dialing.

   Make any and all choices and click next.

3. Enter in the phone number and choose to use telephony dialing properties. You can add alternate phone numbers, so if your ISP has three local access numbers, NT will try each number. Click Next.

4. Now you can choose your serial line protocol. When in doubt, stay with PPP. It's newer and more widely accepted. Click Next.

5. You are now prompted to enter a login script to follow the connection. If in doubt, go with the default of None. Again, click Next.
6. Now you are prompted to enter a static IP address. If you are planning on using a DHCP-assigned address, leave the entry set to all zeros. Click Next. Again, you are asked for some IP addresses, this time for Domain Name Service servers or Windows Internet Name Service servers. When in doubt, leave it at zeros. Click Next.
7. Click Finish.
8. To test the connection, click Dial. This brings up the Connect screen. Here you can add your user name, password, domain (if required), and check the box to save your password. Click OK to dial.

Configure Microsoft Peer Web Services in a given situation.

Peer Web Services (PWS) is basically a Web server designed for departmental-sized environments. While it is not robust enough to handle the amount of traffic an Internet Web server would be subjected to (that's what Internet Information Server is for), it is more than enough for most small networks.

The beauty of using a Web server to disseminate information is in the fact that most business users will already be comfortable with the technology used to access it. Almost everyone will have used a Web browser at some point or another. The interface is fairly intuitive, it is easy to keep the data current, and you can control who has access to the information. All in all, using Internet technologies makes a lot of sense.

Installing PWS

The physical requirements for PWS are fairly straightforward. You will need the following:

- A computer running Windows NT Server 4.0 and TCP/IP
- The NT Workstation CD-ROM and some way to access it (either a local CD-ROM drive or across the network)

- Enough disk space to store the information you wish to publish

PWS is installed through the Network applet in Control Panel—just like any other service you wish to add to your NT Workstation.

PWS Services

PWS performs three services:

WWW A service that allows you to make data available to Web browsers.

Gopher A service that allows you to index information, create links to other servers, and create custom menus.

FTP A service that allows you to set up your NT Workstation as an FTP server. FTP provides the ability to copy files between the client and the server.

During its installation, PWS will add a new group to your Start menu—Microsoft Peer Web Services (Common). Within this group you will find a utility named Internet Service Manager. PWS is managed through this tool.

That's really as deep as you need to get for this exam.

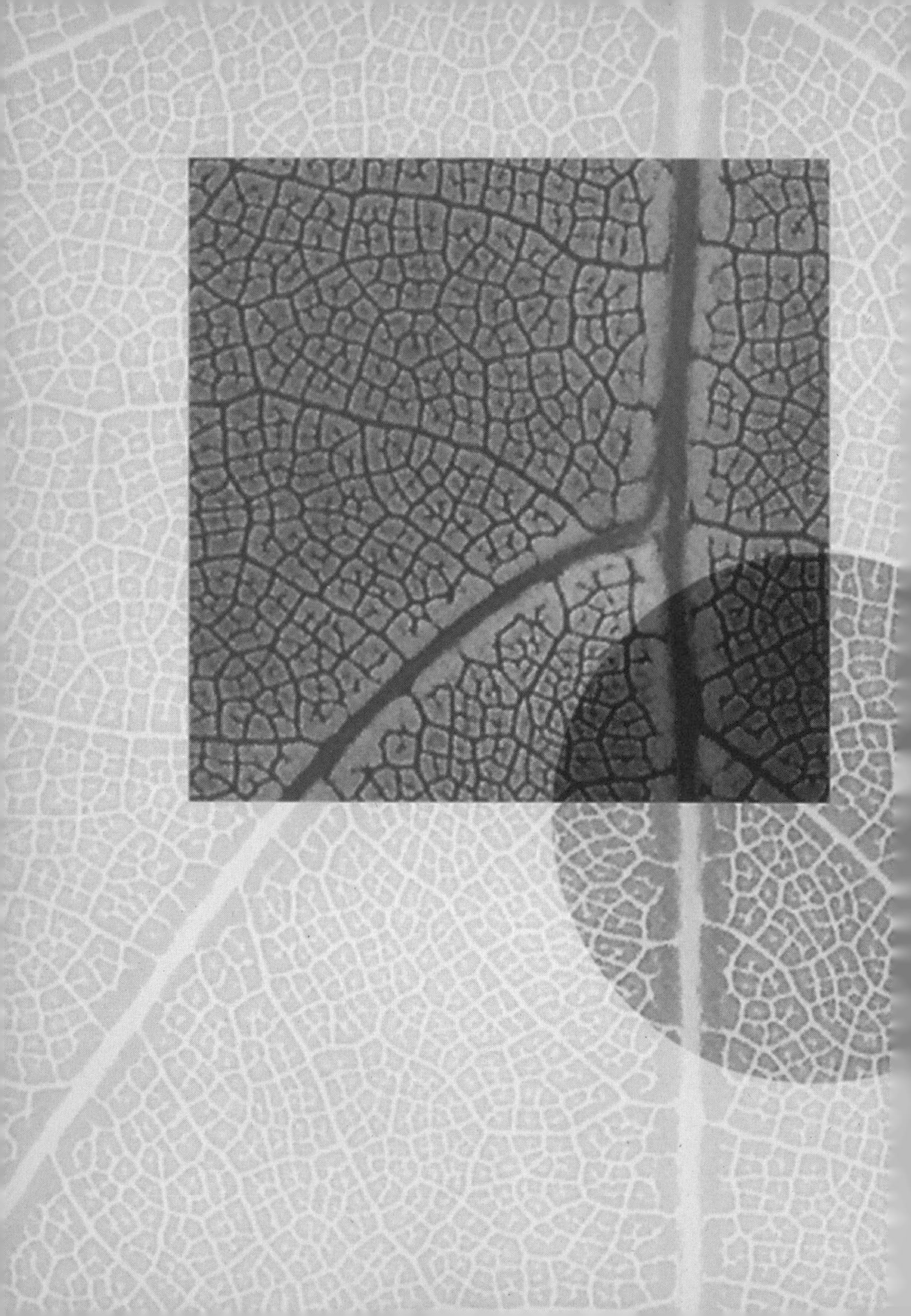

Chapter 15
Running Applications

When the new breed of 32-bit operating systems began to appear, there were few applications written to take advantage of the new features and benefits. That has changed, as Windows 95 and Windows NT have increased in popularity. But there are still many OS/2, 16-bit Windows, and even DOS-based applications being run in the workplace. Windows NT Workstation had to be backward-compatible to make allowances for these legacy applications, as well as provide support for POSIX- or RISC-based applications.

Adapted from *MCSE Exam Notes: NT Workstation 4*
by Gary Govanus and Robert King
ISBN 0-7821-2290-6 352 pages $19.99

NT handles this diversity through Executive Services, which has the application support that Windows, OS/2, and POSIX applications require. When an application is started, the API can work with the Executive Services layer rather than the system hardware. The Executive Services layer translates requests when a subsystem needs hardware services and passes these requests on to the hardware.

Start applications on Intel and RISC platforms in various operating system environments.

Application problems are always a challenge to solve. Knowing how the operating system is interfacing with the application will give you a headstart in the troubleshooting area. It may even help during testing, too. Window NT provides support for several different layers of application support. It supports:

Win32 32-bit Windows support for applications written for Windows 95 and Windows NT.

Virtual DOS Machine (VDM) Support for some legacy DOS applications.

Win16 16-bit Windows application support for applications from the Windows 3.1 environment.

OS/2 Provides support for IBM's OS/2 operating system, in both OS/2 and DOS mode.

POSIX Windows NT does not "run" POSIX programs, it provides easy access to compile the POSIX program so it will run in an NT environment.

Win32 Subsystem

The Win32 application subsystem is a *big* player in running applications. It lets programmers write 32-bit applications that utilize multiple threads. Each application that uses the Win32 subsystem is given a 2GB address space to work in, and has memory protection built in. The Win32 subsystem is where the 2-D and 3-D graphics operations come from using the industry standard OpenGL interface. This subsystem also supports ActiveX, DirectX, and OLE support.

32-Bit Processor

A 32-bit processor can work with larger numbers, so it handles instruction sets more quickly than the old 16-bit processor. The Win32 subsystem is written to take advantage of the Intel 32-bit processors, which is everything after the 386. If another manufacturer makes a 32-bit processor, NT supports it. This includes the MIPS, PowerPC, and even the 64-bit–capable Alpha chip.

Multiple Threads

A thread is the lowest form of work that a processor can do. In older environments, a program was executed a line at a time, and the instruction was completed. With multiple threads, more than one instruction can be carried out at the same time.

2GB Address Space

This is a programmer's tool that allows programs to be written in larger chunks and to take advantage of larger data sets. This provides better performance. The NT Virtual Memory Manager utilizes disk space, and RAM comes up with the address space each application needs.

Memory Protection

Memory protection keeps work stoppages to a minimum. Since each application runs in its own memory space, it does not have to worry about infringing on the rights of other applications.

Application Interface

Each application running on an NT Workstation creates an input queue for instructions. You may have five applications running on the workstation, but when you move the mouse, or enter information from the keyboard, it goes into the queue for just that application. By keeping this information separate, NT is eliminating the problem of conflicting instruction sets.

Virtual DOS Machine

While not all DOS applications will run on a Windows NT computer, many of them will, thanks to something called the VDM or Virtual DOS machine.

Software Components of the VDM

To run a DOS application, the NT system needs to trick the application into thinking it's not as powerful as it really is. The software pieces that make this work include the NTVDM.EXE, which runs in protected mode, just like the old 8088 machines. NTVDM translates the DOS application calls into the Win32 calls, and then forwards those calls onto the Win32 subsystem.

NTIO.SYS and NTDOS.SYS replace the IO.SYS and MSDOS.SYS pieces of the DOS environment. NTDOS.SYS runs in real mode, just like a 386 computer.

The last software piece is the VDMREDIR.DLL. This dynamic link library redirects file system calls and input/output calls to the Win32 subsystem.

Virtual Device Drivers

NT uses a group of files called virtual device drivers, or VDDs, to create the hardware environment that the DOS applications require. DOS applications usually talk directly to the hardware. NT has two or three layers between the application and the actual hardware component. The VDDs make the application "think" the hardware is really there.

Configuration Files

DOS applications don't use registry entries or INI files, they use the AUTOEXEC.BAT and CONFIG.SYS files. With the VDM, it reads from the AUTOEXEC.NT file and the CONFIG.NT file to start the application.

Win16-Bit Applications

16-bit applications–legacy applications that were written to run on earlier versions of Windows, but were never upgraded to Windows 95 or Windows NT–run because of WOW, or Windows on Windows. Just like when Windows runs on a DOS machine, the Win16 subsystem makes use of the default VDM.

In the Win16 subsystem, when you start multiple 16-bit Windows applications they all run in the default VDM. If you run any other Win16 applications, they run in a separate VDM. No matter how many 16-bit applications you have running in the VDM, it just appears as one application to the Win32 subsystem.

Software Components of WOW

WOW makes use of all the components of the Virtual DOS Machine. In addition, WOW uses:

- **KRNL386.EXE** Windows 3.1 modified to run under NT.
- **USER.EXE** Modified version of Windows 3.1 USER.EXE. This one passes calls on to the Win32 subsystem.
- **GDI.EXE** Translates graphics calls to the Win32 subsystem.
- **WOWEXEC.EXE** Windows emulation for the VDM.

Input Queue

WOW uses the single input queue. All applications running under WOW will use the same instruction queue.

Scheduling

WOW scheduling is handled in the same way as Windows scheduling. Each application gets its shot at the microprocessor in turn. You can have multiple applications open at the same time, but the processor is paying attention to only one application at a time. WOW applications can be started from the command prompt, from the Start menu, or from NT Explorer.

OS/2 Subsystem

Native NT will not support any application written for OS/2 version 2.0 or greater. In order to provide for OS/2 support for applications greater than 2.0, you need to install an add-on Presentation Manager subsystem.

Software Components of the OS/2 Subsystem

Like most things IBM, OS/2 works in a world all its own. This is not a knock on OS/2, just a statement of fact. After all, who makes personal computers that are not IBM-PC compatible? IBM.

OS2SS.EXE and OS2SRV.EXE These provide the environment the OS/2 applications expect. If you have multiple copies of OS/2-based applications running, only one version of OS2SRV will be loaded.

OS2.EXE For each OS/2 application running, there is a separate version of OS2.EXE running. It handles all the program-specific management tasks.

NETAPI.DLL and DOSCALLS.DLL These contain the NT versions of the application programming interfaces that OS/2 programs are looking for.

POSIX

The Portable Open System Interface or POSIX is a programming specification that is independent of any operating system. NT support for POSIX is not for applications. Rather, it is designed to provide a friendly environment for POSIX applications to be compiled in, so they will run successfully under NT.

POSIX offers several challenges. Like UNIX, it uses case-sensitive naming. That means that RESUME, Resume, and resume are not the same file. POSIX also has hard link support. Hard link support means that one file can have two different names. NT supports this process. Any application written to be POSIX-compliant must be written using a library of C routines that are POSIX.1-compliant.

Software Components of POSIX

PSXSS.EXE Main POSIX component. It is loaded when the first POSIX application is run and remains in memory until the user unloads it. Only one instance will be loaded, no matter how many POSIX applications are running.

POSIX.EXE Handles communication between POSIX and Executive services.

PSXDLL.DLL Contains the library routines that POSIX says must be present.

Viewing Processes

Applications for each of the supported subsystems are started by using the Start menu, Explorer, or the command line. While there are several ways to start the application, you can view the processes it kicks off by doing the following:

1. Log on to the NT Workstation as Administrator.
2. Run NT Task Manager by right-clicking an empty space in the taskbar and selecting Task Manager.
3. Click the Process tab and view the processes that are currently running to establish a base line.

4. Start an application from one of the supported operating systems.
5. Review Task Manager to see the changes that have taken place.
6. Close Task Manager.

Start Command

You can start 16-bit Windows applications from the NT command line using the Start command.

The Start command uses the following switches: `["title"] [/Dpath] [/I] [/MIN] [/MAX] [/LOW | /NORMAL | /HIGH | /REALTIME] [/B] [command/program] [parameters]`.

"title" The title displayed in the Windows title bar.

Dpath The directory where the application is started from.

I The new environment will be the original environment passed to the command interpreter and not the current environment.

MIN Start minimized.

MAX Start in a maximized window.

LOW Start application in the IDLE priority class.

NORMAL Start application in the NORMAL priority class.

HIGH Start application in the HIGH priority class.

REALTIME Start application in the REALTIME priority class.

B Start application without creating a new window.

parameters These are the parameters passed to the command/program.

Suppose you wanted to start an application called TESTME.EXE. The program resides in the C:\APPS\TEST folder, and you wanted it maximized in its own memory space, and run at high priority with I PASS as the Windows title. The command would be:

```
start "I Pass" /C:\apps\test /max /HIGH TESTME.EXE
```

Part III

Start applications at various priorities.

Since Windows NT Workstation allows you to run multiple applications simultaneously, it only makes sense that you be allowed to prioritize which applications should get the most processor time. Suppose your workstation also served as a performance monitor for the network. You would want applications that you were using to do "real" work to get more of the processor time than the background-information gathering tools.

Processor Priorities

Processors have a finite number of cycles that can be devoted to any application. By using a multitasking operating system like Windows NT, multiple applications can be run simultaneously, each getting a piece of the processor pie. NT allows you to set the priority to processor time. This can be done when the application starts (from the command line) or can be accomplished from Task Manager after the application is running.

Even if you don't take any action on the priority of an application, NT changes things around for you without any user input. When you start an application, it is given a base priority rating of 8. Base priority ratings go from 1 (basically comatose) to 31 (real time). Base priority ratings from 0 to 15 are to be used for dynamic applications, and ratings from 16 to 31 are reserved for real-time applications that cannot be written to the NT pagefile.

NT will increase the priority of the application if it is running in the foreground. It will also boost the priority for lower-priority applications on a random basis. This prevents the higher priority application from hogging the processor or resource.

One of the switches for the Start command allows you to set one of four priority levels. You can start an application at Low Priority, Normal Priority, High Priority, or Real-Time Priority.

Boosting Priority

As mentioned above, there are two ways of boosting the priority rating of an application. The priority can be altered as the application starts by using the Start command or by increasing the priority of an application that is already running by using Task Manager.

Start Command

The Start command uses the following switches: `["title"] [/Dpath] [/I] [/MIN] [/MAX] [/LOW | /NORMAL | /HIGH | /REALTIME] [/B] [command/program] [parameters]`.

"title" The title displayed in the Windows title bar

Dpath The directory where the application is started from

I The new environment will be the original environment passed to the command interpreter and not the current environment.

MIN Start minimized.

MAX Start in a maximized window.

LOW Start application in the IDLE priority class.

NORMAL Start application in the NORMAL priority class.

HIGH Start application in the HIGH priority class.

REALTIME Start application in the REALTIME priority class.

B Start application without creating a new window.

parameters These are the parameters passed to the command/program.

Suppose you wanted to start and application called TESTME.EXE. The program resides in the C:\APPS\TEST folder, and you wanted it maximized in its own memory space, and run at high priority with I PASS as the Windows title. From the command line, the command would be:

```
start "I Pass" /C:\apps\test /max /HIGH TESTME.EXE
```

Task Manager

To access Task Manager after the application is running:

1. Press Ctrl+Alt+Del, and click Task Manager.
2. Click the Processes tab.
3. If the Base Priority column is not showing up, choose View ➢ Select Columns ➢ Check the Base Priority column and click OK.

4. In the Process list, right-click the application you want to change.
5. Highlight Set Priority and click the new priority.
6. Click Yes to the Task Manager warning.

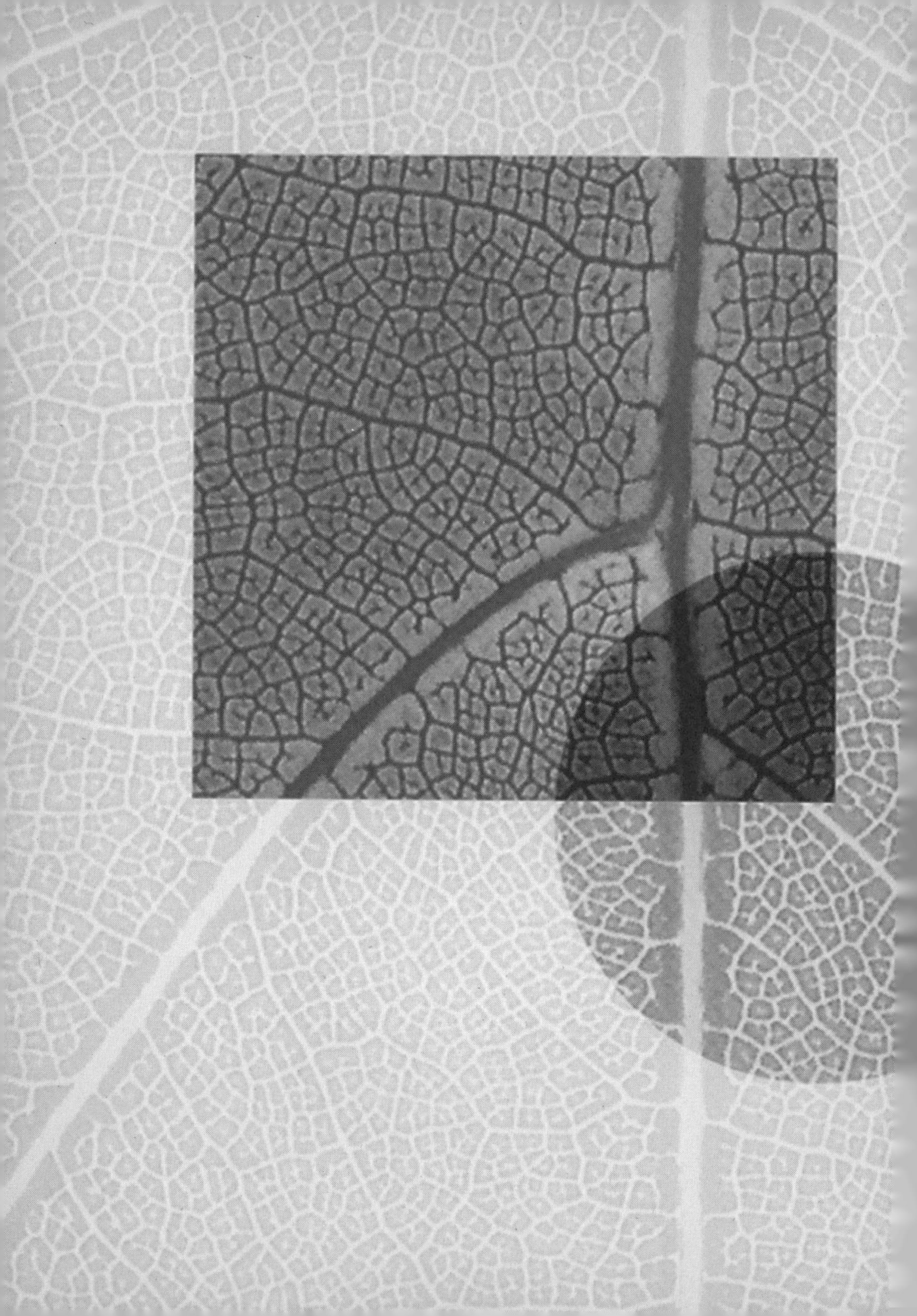

Chapter 16

Monitoring and Optimization

This chapter will act as an introduction to the tools used to monitor the performance of your workstation, detect and correct problems, and optimize your environment. The NT operating system can be a complicated beast. Knowing the tools available to tame it can be extremely valuable in the workplace. NT includes tools that allow you to monitor and optimize just about every facet of your workstation.

Adapted from *MCSE Exam Notes: NT Workstation 4*
by Gary Govanus and Robert King
ISBN 0-7821-2290-6 352 pages $19.99

Monitor system performance by using various tools.

Before we can begin our discussion of optimization, you will have to be familiar with the tools available to monitor your computer.

System Performance Monitor Tools

There are three tools with which you will need to be comfortable for this objective:

- Server Manager
- Windows NT Diagnostics
- Performance Monitor

Server Manager

Server Manager is found in the Administrative Tools group. It is basically used to monitor network-related information for an NT computer. It can be used to manage both your local machine and other computers on the network. With Server Manager you can view a list of connected users, open resources, and shared resources. Server Manager also allows you to send messages to connected users, administrate shared resources, and create a list of users who should receive Windows NT system alerts.

Windows NT Diagnostics

Windows NT Diagnostics is used to gather information about the hardware and software settings of an NT computer. It is used to help troubleshoot hardware- and memory-based problems.

Performance Monitor

Of the three tools discussed in this objective, Performance Monitor is covered most extensively on the test. You can use Performance Monitor to gather very specific information about the various components (both hardware and software) of your computer.

Within Performance Monitor you will find *objects* that can be monitored. An object is a major sub-component of your environment–things like the processor, disk subsystem, memory, or network. Each object has specific *Counters* that represent items that can be tracked–memory, for instance, includes counters like % Committed bytes in use, Available bytes, and Cache bytes.

TIP

If you are pursuing the MCSE, it would be prudent to take the time to understand the objects and counters in Performance Monitor. For more information, see *MCSE: NT Server 4 in the Enterprise, Second Edition*, by Lisa Donald and James Chellis (Sybex, 1998).

Monitoring System Performance

This objective concerns your ability to use the various tools. For this reason, most of your critical information will be found here.

Using Server Manager

Server Manager can be broken down into two types of functions–passive and active. The passive functions allow you to view information, while the active functions allow you to make changes to the configuration of the system.

Passive functions include viewing a list of connected users, viewing a list of shared resources, and viewing a list of open resources. Active functions include sending a message to users connected to a server, administering shared directories, and creating a list of users who should receive administrative alerts.

Viewing a List of Connected Users To view a list of users attached to your computer, open Server Manager. Double-click the computer you wish to check. The dialog box shown below will appear, in this case, in reference to a computer named END200. We'll be referencing this graphic a number of times as we look at some of the other options available.

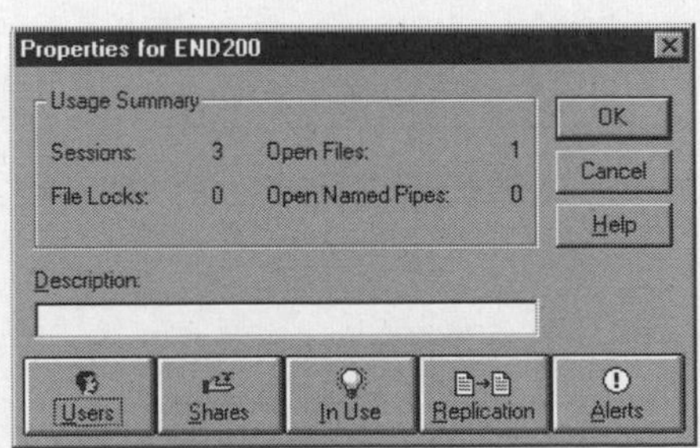

Notice the options across the bottom of the dialog box. We'll be looking at each of the choices available. For now, click the Users button and you will see a list of users connected to the chosen computer.

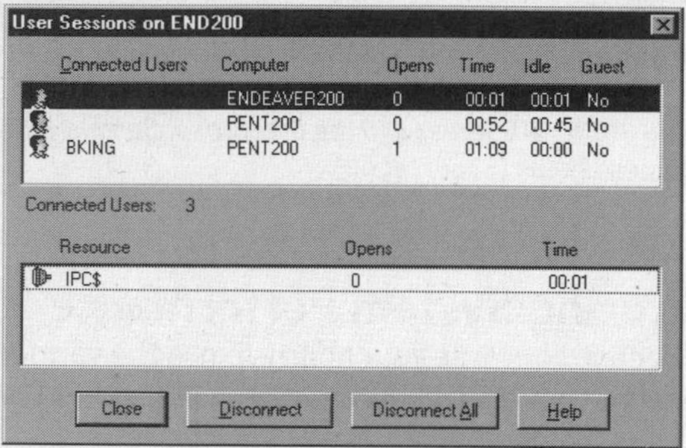

From here you can see who is connected to the computer and which shared resources they are using. You can also disconnect any or all users from this screen.

Viewing a List of Shared Resources From the Shared Resources dialog box, click the Shares button. From here you can see all of the various shares that have been created. You can also highlight any share and see a list of who is connected to it.

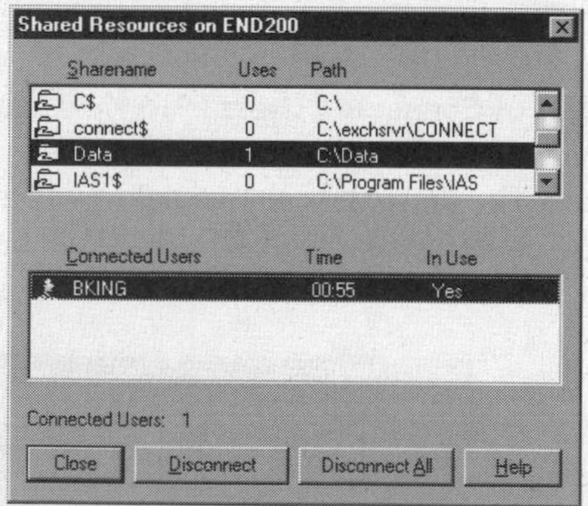

Viewing a List of Open Resources Click the In Use button and you will see a list of the resources currently open.

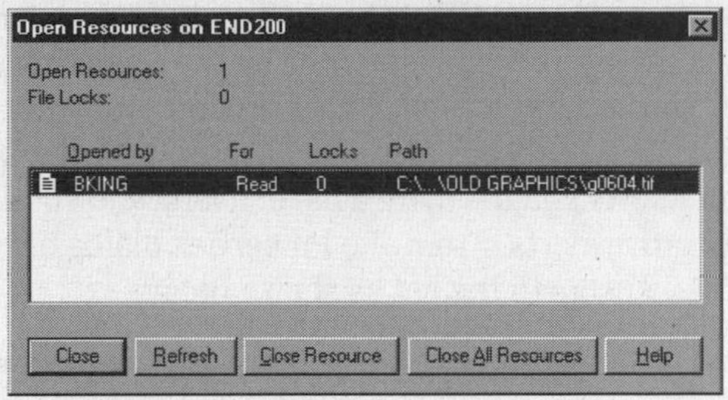

Sending a Message to Users Connected to a Server Server Manager provides an easy way to send a message to all users connected to a server before shutting the server down. From the main screen, highlight the server you are going to shut down and choose Send Message on the Computer menu. As shown here, you then just type in your message and click OK.

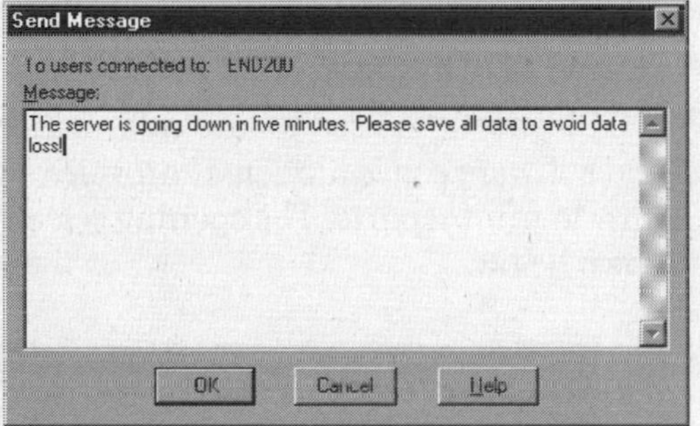

Administering Shared Directories Server Manager also allows you to create new shares or manage existing shares on the target computer. Highlight the chosen computer and chose Shared Directories from the Computer menu. You will see a list of shared directories and actions that you can take.

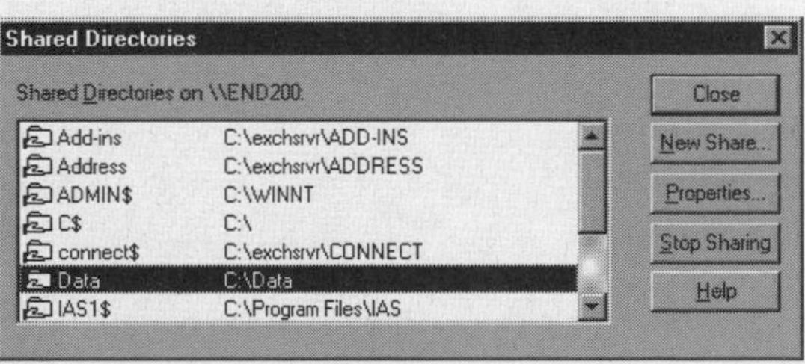

Create a List of Users Who Should Receive Administrative Alerts

Administrative alerts are generated by the operating system to warn of security and access problems, user session problems, power problems (when the UPS service is also running), and printer problems. Server Manager allows you to create a list of users who should receive these administrative alerts. From the Properties dialog box, choose the Alerts button. Add users to the list as shown below.

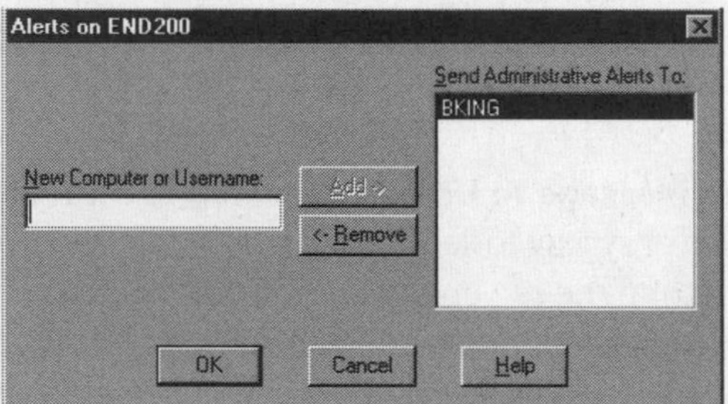

Using Windows NT Diagnostic

Windows NT Diagnostic is used to view information about a computer's hardware and software configuration. It provides a graphical interface and the ability to print reports. The opening screen of Windows NT Diagnostic is shown below.

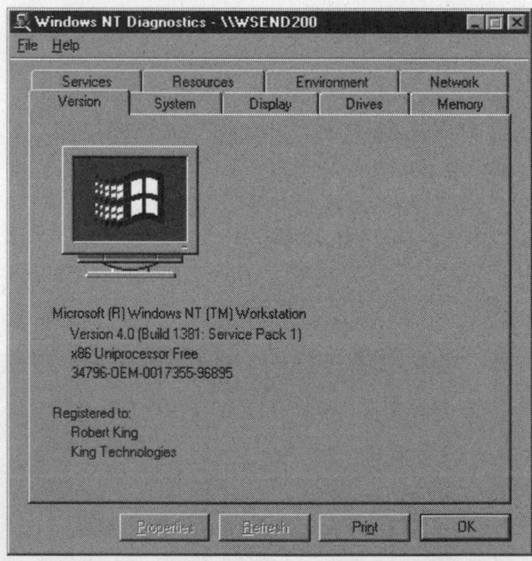

Table 16.1 lists each of the options available and what type of information they provide.

TABLE 16.1: Using Windows NT Diagnostic

Tab	Usage
Version	Operating system information
System	ROM BIOS and CPU information
Display	Video driver and adapter information
Drives	Information about the drives on your system, including file system and drivers
Memory	Physical and virtual memory information
Services	A list of the services in the CurrentControlSet and their status
Resources	Device information including physical configuration (Memory addresses, IRQ, DMA, and port addresses)
Environment	Shows a list of environmental variables
Network	Network related information, including current statistics

Using Performance Monitor

Performance Monitor offers many ways to view the statistics that it gathers. You will need to be familiar with each of them for the exam.

Chart View The chart view provides a real time graph showing the values of the counters you have chosen. The first step is to add the counters to your view. Highlight the appropriate object and then pick a counter from the list.

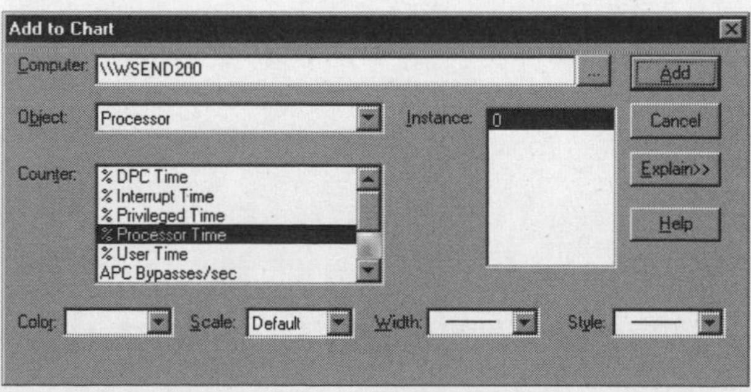

When you have added all of the counters you want to graph, click Done. The graph will show the value of those counters in real time.

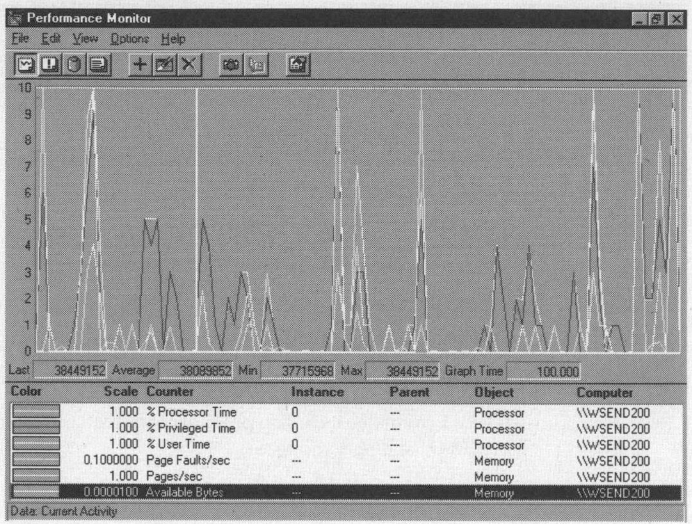

Report View The report view shows the same information as the chart view. With the report view, the values are shown in the form of a report, rather than as a graph.

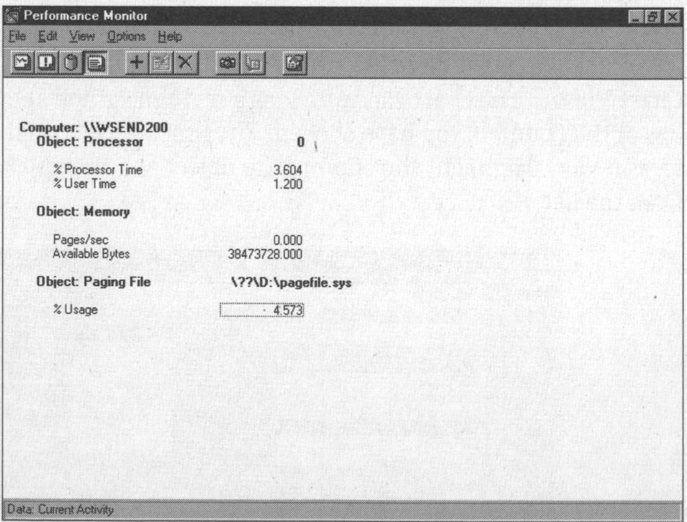

Log View The log view allows you to save the data to a file. In the chart view you do not pick counters—all counters for the objects you choose will be tracked. Choose your objects, and pick a destination directory and filename.

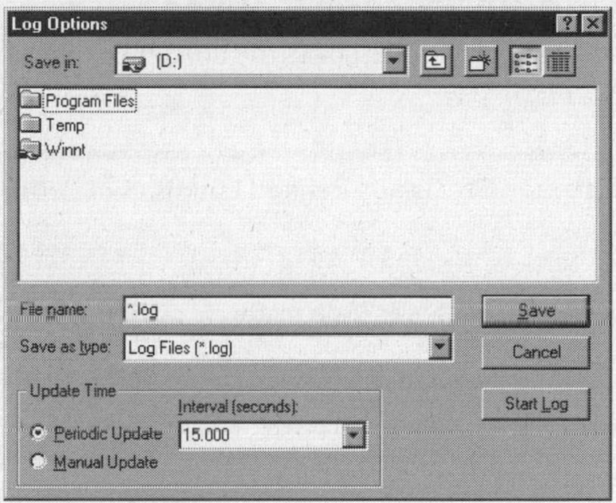

Alert View The alert view is different from the other three views. With the alert view, you set a threshold for a counter. When this threshold is reached, you can have Performance Monitor run an application.

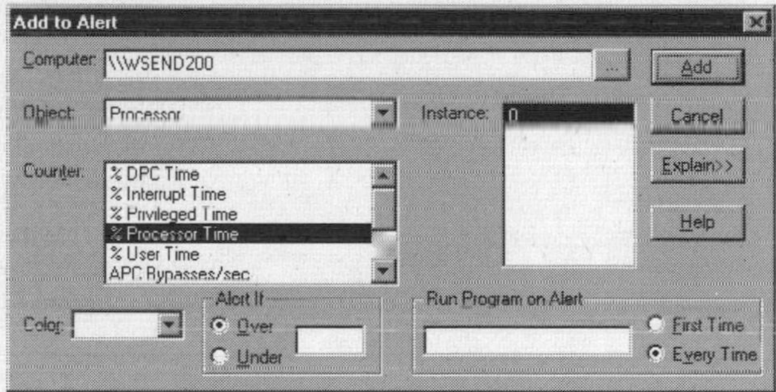

Identify and resolve a given performance problem.

While any given environment might stress particular areas, there are four main physical components to any NT server—Processor, Memory, Disk, and Network. These four areas are a good indicator of the "health" of your system. When monitoring any NT server, always start with these four components and then add any additional counters that might be appropriate in your environment.

Tracking Processor Counters

To determine if the processor is the bottleneck, monitor the counters listed in Table 16.2:

TABLE 16.2: Processor-Related Counters in Performance Monitor

Counter	Acceptable Value	Description
% Processor time	Under 75 percent	If the processor is consistently busy more than 75 percent of the time, it is likely that the processor is the bottleneck.
%Privileged Time	Under 75 percent	This is the amount of time that the processor is busy performing operating system tasks.
%User Time	Under 75 percent	This is the amount of time the processor is busy performing user tasks, such as running a program.
Interrupts/sec	Varies	This is the number of hardware interrupts generated each second. Each type of processor can handle a different number. On a 486/66 this number should be under 1000, while on a Pentium 90 system, this number could run as high as 3500. If this number is consistently high, the system probably has an IRQ conflict, or a piece of hardware is going bad.
System: Processor Queue Length	Less than 2	This represents the number of threads that are ready to execute, but are waiting for the processor.
Server Work Queues: Queue Length	Less than 2	This is the number of threads in the queue for a given processor.

Tracking Memory Counters

Before we discuss the counters to monitor to determine if memory is your system bottleneck, we need to review how NT uses memory. Memory in an NT system can be divided into two classifications: Paged and Non-Paged. Paged memory is used by most applications. It can be made up of either physical RAM or virtual memory (hard disk space). Non-Paged memory is used by programs which cannot be "paged" to the hard disk. The operating system and its components use Non-Paged memory.

NT uses a virtual memory model. In this model, applications that can use paged RAM are given a full set of memory addresses to work with. The operating system keeps track of actual physical memory. When memory is full, the OS will move "pages" of memory to a file on the hard drive (PAGEFILE.SYS). If that code is needed later, it will be moved back to physical memory. By using a virtual memory model, your applications can use more memory than is physically available (up to the limits of your hard drive).

Whenever the data a program needs is not in RAM, it must be acquired from the hard drive. This process is called a "hard page fault." A consistently high number of hard page faults—over five per second—could indicate that there is not enough memory available on the server. The goal on an NT Server is to have enough memory in the server so that most data requested is found in memory. (Obviously, the first time it is used it will have to come from the disk, but after that, having enough memory for file caching can greatly increase performance.)

Monitor the counters listed in Table 16.3 to determine if memory is your bottleneck.

TABLE 16.3: Memory-Related Counters in Performance Monitor

Counter	Acceptable Value	Description
Pages/sec	0–20	Total of the number of pages that were either not in RAM when requested, or needed to be moved to virtual memory to free up space in RAM. This is really a measure of disk activity related to memory management.
Available Bytes	Minimum of 4MB	The amount of available physical RAM at any point in time. This number will usually be fairly low, as NT will utilize memory that is available and free it up as needed.
Committed Bytes	Should be less than the physical amount of RAM in the computer	This indicates the amount of memory in use. If the number is greater than the amount of physical RAM in the machine, it indicates a need for more memory.

TABLE 16.3 continued: Memory-Related Counters in Performance Monitor

Counter	Acceptable Value	Description
Pool Non-Paged Bytes	Should remain steady	This is the memory used by non-paged processes (i.e. the operating system). If this number fluctuates, it could indicate a process that is not using memory correctly.

Tracking Disk Counters

The disk is usually the slowest component on your computer. NT compensates for this by using file caching and memory management to reduce the number of disk accesses. Often what appears to be a disk problem is really just a lack of memory, so be sure to watch both subsystems.

Before you can track disk counters in Performance Monitor, you must turn on those counters. The disk counters are not activated by default because tracking physical disk access adds measurable overhead to the server. To activate the disk counters, type **diskperf –y** at a command prompt. If your disks are configured as a RAID set, type **diskperf –ye**.

NOTE

The added overhead of tracking disk counters is constant once they are activated—not just when you are monitoring them. It is a good idea to turn them off when you are not actively watching them. To turn them off type diskperf –n at a command prompt.

Once activated, monitor the counters listed in Table 16.4.

TABLE 16.4: Disk-Related Counters in Performance Monitor

Counter	Acceptable Value	Description
%Disk Time	Under 50 percent	This is the amount of time that the disk drive is busy. If this number is consistently high, you should monitor specific processes to find out exactly what is using the disk. If you can, move some of the disk-intensive processes to another server.

TABLE 16.4 continued: Disk-Related Counters in Performance Monitor

Counter	Acceptable Value	Description
Disk Queue Length	0-2	This value represents the number of waiting disk I/O requests. A high number indicates that I/O requests are waiting for access.
Avg. Disk Bytes/Transfer	Depends on use and type of subsystem	The larger this number, the more efficient your disk subsystem is working. This value will depend on the type of access; are your users saving many small files or a few large ones? It is also dependent on the type of disks and controllers.
Disk Bytes/sec	Depends on use and type of subsystem	The larger this number, the more efficient your disk subsystem is working. This value is dependent on the disk and controller type.

Tracking Network Counters

To monitor a network, you have to have a little familiarity with all components on that network, the routers, the wiring, the protocols, the operating systems—this list goes on. The list can be intimidating. The first task in troubleshooting is to limit your view. Don't try to fix the entire network—try to find out which component is causing the problem and fix it.

Performance Monitor has a few counters, listed in Table 16.5, which can help you determine where the problem lies. A few analyze the overhead on the server itself, while others give an overview of what is happening on the wire.

TABLE 16.5: Network-Related Counters in Performance Monitor

Counter	Acceptable Value	Description
Server: Bytes Total/sec	Varies	This counter shows the number of bytes sent and received through this server. It is a good indicator of how busy the server is.

TABLE 16.5 continued: Network-Related Counters in Performance Monitor

Counter	Acceptable Value	Description
Server: Logon/sec	Varies	Use this value to determine the authentication overhead being placed on the server. If this number is high and other services are slow, it might indicate the need for another domain controller.
Server: Login Total	Varies	This is the number of logon attempts the server has serviced since the last time the server was started. Can be used to justify another domain controller.
Network Interface: Bytes sent/sec	Varies	Used to determine if a particular Network Interface Card is being overused.
Network Interface: Bytes total./sec	Varies	Total number of bytes sent and received through a particular NIC.
Network Segment: %Network Utilization	Usually lower than 30 percent	Shows the percentage of network bandwidth in use. This number should be lower than 30 percent for most networks. Some network technologies can sustain a higher rate.

The Network Segment object is not available until you install the Network Monitor Agent as a service on the server. Once installed, Performance Monitor will put the NICs in promiscuous mode when you are monitoring Network Segment counters. When in promiscuous mode, a NIC processes *all* network traffic, not just those packets destined for the server. This can add a tremendous amount of overhead to the server.

Each protocol that you add to your server will also have its own counters. These counters allow you to determine the overhead being placed on your server by each protocol. Most of these counters have no "acceptable" range of values. The values will be dependent upon the hardware, topology, and other protocols in use on your network.

NetBEUI and NWLink Counters

These two protocols have similar counters, listed in Table 16.6.

TABLE 16.6: NetBEUI- and NWLink-Related Counters in Performance Monitor

Counter	Acceptable Value	Description
Bytes Total/Sec	N/A	The total number of bytes sent and received using this protocol. This counter is an excellent way to compare network overhead created by various protocols.
Datagrams/sec	N/A	The total number of non-guaranteed datagrams (usually broadcasts) sent and received
Frames sent/sec	N/A	The number of data packets sent and received

TCP/IP Counters

The counters list in Table 16.7 will not be available unless both the TCP/IP protocol and the SNMP service are installed on the server.

TABLE 16.7: TCP/IP-Related Counters in Performance Monitor

Counter	Acceptable Value	Description
TCP Segments/sec	N/A	The total number of TCP frames sent and received
TCP Segments re-translated/sec	N/A	The total number of segments re-translated on the network
UDP datagrams/sec	N/A	The number of UDP-based datagrams (usually broadcasts) sent and received
Network Interface: Output Queue Length	Less than 2	The number of packets waiting to be transmitted through a particular NIC. A high number can indicate a card that is too busy.

Optimize system performance in various areas.

Now that we've taken a close look at how to use Performance Monitor to track resources at your computer, we can stop and analyze the results. Based upon this we can then make suggestions with the goal of optimizing system performance. In the preceding objective we talked about the various Performance Monitor counters that you might want to track, and gave some suggested values for those counters on a healthy computer. Based upon that information, you should be able to analyze the data and determine which component is the bottleneck on your system.

We'll look at the four main components of an NT environment and offer suggested actions for optimizing each of them.

Processor

If the bottleneck is your processor you can:

- Add a faster processor.
- Add another processor.
- Move processing to another server.

WARNING

These are the Microsoft answers. In reality you very seldom have the option of the first two choices.

Memory

If memory is the bottleneck on your server, add more RAM. In the interim, move users to another server or unload services.

Disk

If you find that the disk subsystem is the bottleneck you can do the following:

- Add a faster controller.

- If you are using RAID, add more disks to the set. This spreads the work across more physical devices.
- Move disk-intensive processes to another server to spread the workload.

WARNING

None of these solutions is really a simple fix. Adding a faster controller will only help if your disks are compliant with the controller type. If they are not, you will have to replace the disks as well to see any benefit. As for the RAID solution, adding a disk is dependent upon you having a slot open and the funding for more hardware. As for moving the process to another server, this depends on you having a server that is not too busy to accept the extra workload. The proper solution to this problem is to have prevented it in the first place. Proper capacity planning (projecting throughput needs, comparing technologies, and implementing the best solution) is the best "fix."

Network

The following are potential fixes if the network is your bottleneck:

- Upgrade the hardware at the server. Add an additional or faster NIC, add RAM, or upgrade the processor.
- Upgrade the physical components of your network, such as routers and bridges.
- Decrease the number of protocols in use on your network.
- Segment your network to split the traffic between segments.
- Add servers to split the workload.

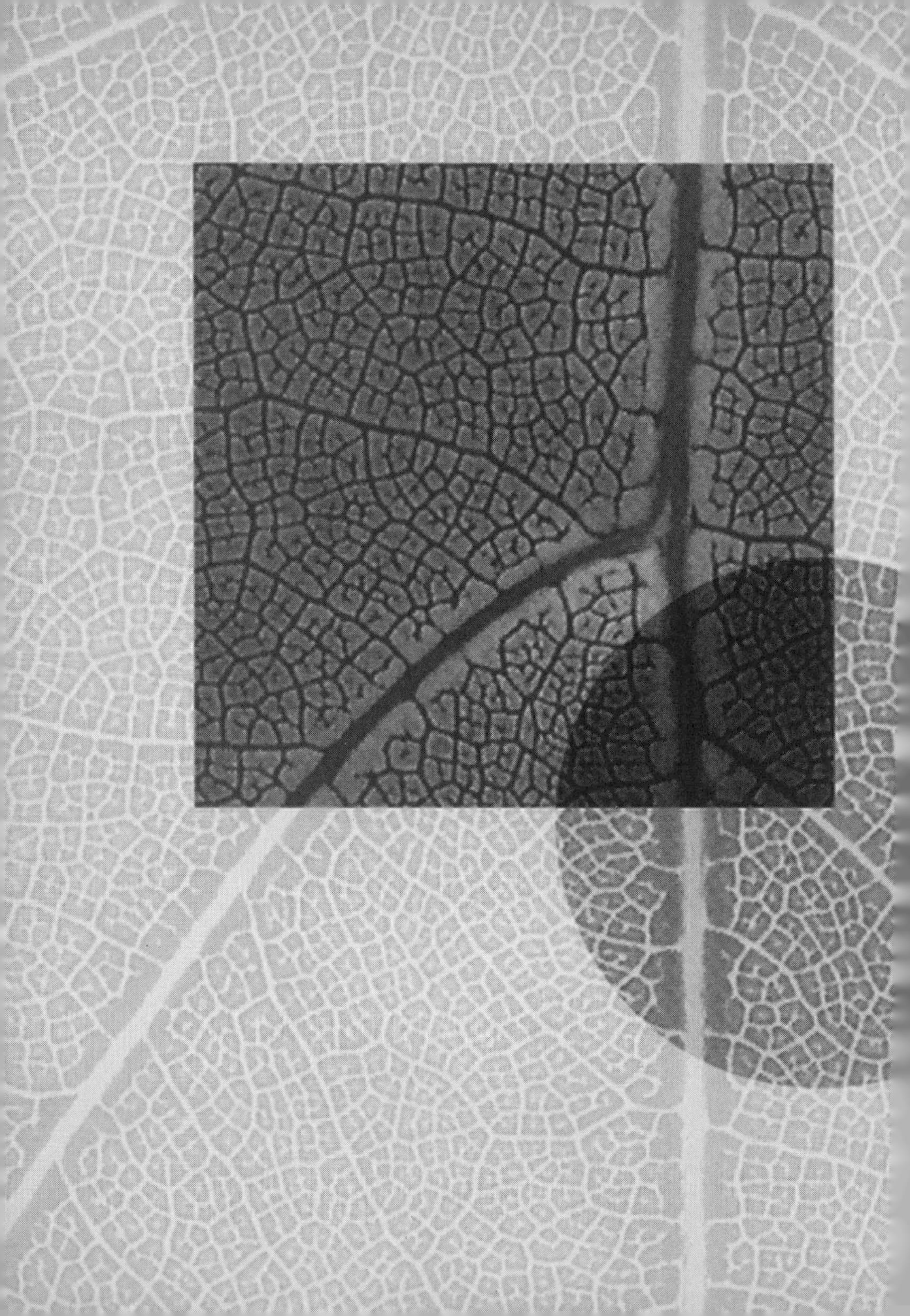

Chapter 17

Troubleshooting

The test objectives for this chapter cover the actions you should take to correct a specific set of problems. Some of these problems are very common in the workplace, while others rarely occur. Whether common or rare, knowing how to correct them is a very big part of being a network administrator.

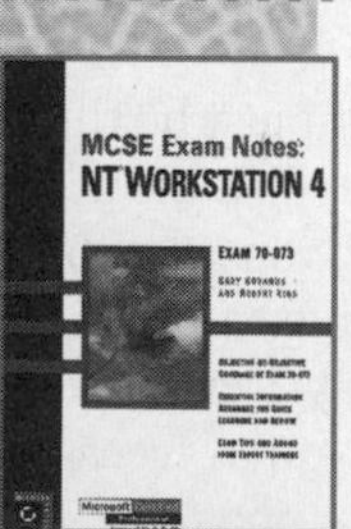

Adapted from *MCSE Exam Notes: NT Workstation 4* by Gary Govanus and Robert King
ISBN 0-7821-2290-6 352 pages $19.99

Choose the appropriate course of action to take when the boot process fails.

This Exam Objective is covered in Part 2: NT Server 4, Chapter 10 "Troubleshooting." The Practice Exam at the end of Part 4 will test you on this material.

Choose the appropriate course of action to take when a print job fails.

This Exam Objective is covered in Part 2: NT Server 4, Chapter 10 "Troubleshooting." The Practice Exam at the end of Part 4 will test you on this material.

Choose the appropriate course of action to take when the installation process fails.

This Exam Objective is covered in Part 2: NT Server 4, Chapter 10 "Troubleshooting." The Practice Exam at the end of Part 4 will test you on this material.

Choose the appropriate course of action to take when an application fails.

Applications fail for a variety of reasons. Sometimes it might just be that the application is having a bad day: applications tend to act just like petulant people, they simply stop working. When this happens, you have to figure out how to close the application that is not responding to any of your best computer-geek tricks. When in doubt, try Ctrl+Alt+Del. This "three-finger salute" will open a dialog box that will allow you to access Task Manager. From Task Manager, it is a simple process to open the

Applications tab, select the application, and choose Close. Problem solved.

Sometimes the cause of failure is easy to spot, like you are running a DOS application on an NT machine. Sometimes the application helps you out by giving you an error message. Rarely, but sometimes, the application helps you out by giving you an error message that makes sense. Most of the time these things just happen. You close them out, restart the application, and everything goes along just fine.

Some applications have error logs. If the offending application has a log, check it, and the manual. For consistent errors, refer to the application's Web site and check for patches. When in doubt, call the application's tech support hotline.

Closing a Failed Application

To close an application that has stopped functioning:

1. Press Ctrl+Alt+Del to open the Windows NT Security dialog box.
2. Click the Task Manager button.
3. Click the Applications tab.
4. Select the application (it will say Not Responding) and click the End Task button.
5. Close Task Manager.

Choose the appropriate course of action to take when a user cannot access a resource.

This Exam Objective is covered in Part 2: NT Server 4, Chapter 10 "Troubleshooting." The Practice Exam at the end of Part 4 will test you on this material.

Modify the registry using the appropriate tool in a given situation.

This Exam Objective is covered in Part 2: NT Server 4, Chapter 10 "Troubleshooting." The Practice Exam at the end of Part 4 will test you on this material.

Implement advanced techniques to resolve various problems.

When a workstation crashes, it is often a complex set of circumstances that has caused the problem. This objective covers some of the actions you can take to analyze the situation.

Diagnosing and Interpreting a Blue Screen

When the Microsoft NT operating system encounters a fatal error it will display a stop screen, often called a "blue screen" (more often called the "blue screen of death"). The stop screen contains debugging information useful in interpreting exactly what was happening at the time of failure. If the system recovery options are turned on, NT will also generate a file with this debug information. At first glance, the blue screen can seem intimidating, but there is actually a small amount of data that you will use to determine the cause of the error. With some errors, the cause of the problem is immediately apparent from this information. With others, you might have to rely upon Microsoft Technical Support for assistance.

There are five distinct areas on a stop screen. Each area provides specific information regarding the error or recovery options.

Area 1: Debug Port Status Indicators

Later in the chapter we will look at a process that allows you to dump the debug information out the serial port to another computer. This connection is seen much like a modem connection. In the upper-right corner of a stop screen, you will see a series of indicators that display the status of this connection. The various indicators are listed in Table 17.1.

TABLE 17.1: Connection Status Indicators

Status Indicator	Description
MDM	Modem controls are in use
CD	Carrier detected
RI	Ring indicator
DSR	Data set ready
CTS	Clear to send
SND	Byte being sent
RCV	Byte received
FRM	Framing error
OVL	Overflow
PRT	Parity error

Area 2: BugCheck Information

This area starts with `*** Stop`, after which is the error code. There are also up to four developer-defined parameters in parentheses, followed by an interpretation of the error. Don't get your hopes up on the interpretation—while there are occasions where it leads you to the solution of your problem, it is more likely to be some obscure message.

Area 3: Driver Information

This area lists information about the drivers loaded at the time of the error. The three columns list the preferred load address, the creation date (also known as the link-time stamp), and the name of the driver. This can be useful because many stop screens list the address of the instruction that caused the problem. You can compare that information with the preferred load address to determine which driver might have caused the problem.

Area 4: Kernel Build Number and Stack Dump

This area shows two things—the build number of the operating system kernel (it will not indicate the presence of any service packs); and a range of addresses that *may* indicate the failed code.

Area 5: Debug Port Information

This area confirms the configuration of the communication port used to dump information to another computer (if configured), and it indicates whether a dump file was created.

Each stop screen will have a unique stop code. For information on a particular stop screen, search the Microsoft TechNet for the code found in area 1.

Configuring a Memory Dump

When an NT server displays a blue screen, you will have to correct the problem as soon as possible to minimize server downtime. Sometimes the solution will be obvious from the data displayed. You might also have a good idea of what caused the problem by looking through the server change log and noting recent changes to its configuration. On those occasions where the solution is not obvious, you might have to take more drastic measures–you might have to have the memory contents at the time of the stop screen analyzed. There are three ways to accomplish this:

Local Debugging On-site analysis of memory. Two computers are attached using a null modem cable, the target (the server with the problem), and the host. The host runs debugging software designed to analyze problems in NT.

Remote Debugging Once again, the target and host are connected with a null modem. The difference is that Microsoft Technical Support uses RAS to dial into your system and they analyze the memory contents remotely.

CrashDump By far, the most common method is to configure NT to dump the contents of memory into a file when the fatal error occurs. You can then send this file to Microsoft Technical Support for analysis.

To set up the target and host computers, you must have two computers each running the same version of NT, including any service packs you have installed. They should be connected by a null modem cable (or you can set up a dial-in connection from the host). The host computer must have the proper symbols file installed. The symbols file contains code used in the debug process. You must have the symbols file that matches the build, including service packs, of the target computer.

Once you have met the prerequisites, you modify the BOOT.INI file on the target server. Add the /debug switch to the appropriate operating system choice line. On the host computer you must configure the communication port by setting some environmental variables. Next, restart the target computer. When the stop screen is generated you will be able to debug the problem from the host computer.

It is unlikely that you will actually debug a stop screen. Most administrators do not have the technical knowledge necessary to accomplish this type of task. It is far more likely that you will generate a memory dump file to be sent to Microsoft Technical Support.

In the Control Panel, System applet, you will find a Startup/Shutdown tab. On this tab you can configure NT to perform certain functions when a fatal error is encountered. You can have NT write a message to the system event log, send an administrative alert, write the contents of memory to a file, and automatically reboot the system.

If you choose to have the contents of memory written to a file, the system dumps the contents of RAM into the PAGEFILE.SYS file. When the system restarts, this information is written to a file named MEMORY.DMP. You can then send this file to Microsoft for analysis. Be aware that there is no compression involved in this process so the dump file will be at least as large as your memory.

NT ships with three tools for processing memory dump files–DUMPFLOP, DUMPCHK, and DUMPEXAM. For the exam we only have to concern ourselves with the latter two.

DUMPCHK.EXE Verifies the contents of a dump file to ensure that it will be readable by a debugger. Running this program can help to ensure that you don't waste time uploading a corrupt dump file to Microsoft.

DUMPEXAM.EXE Analyzes the contents of the dump file and extracts any useful information. This information is placed into a text file that can be considerably smaller than the dump file itself.

Using the Event Log Service

The two main skills necessary to troubleshooting are gathering pertinent information and correlating that information into a plan of action to correct the problem. A common mistake is to address the symptoms without understanding the underlying cause. This is true of troubleshooting anything—not just computer systems.

NT ships with a great tool for gathering information about errors on your server—the Event Log. The Event Log service tracks certain activities on your server and logs information about those events into a series of log files. There are three distinct log files: System, Security, and Application.

Each log file is responsible for tracking different types of events. Many events will not be tracked unless the system is configured to audit those types of events. The application log tracks application-related events, such as the starting and stopping of application-related services. The security log tracks NT security events, such as the logons. The system log tracks events that affect the operating system.

There are also different levels of event messages. Some are purely informational; others are generated when an error is encountered. Still others are indicative of the failure of a service. For troubleshooting, the fatal error messages can be extremely informative. Figure 17.1 shows the contents of a typical system event log. The circle icons with an "I" in them indicate informative messages. The stop sign icons indicate failure messages.

Event Viewer - System Log on \\KINGTECH

Log View Options Help

Date	Time	Source	Category	Event
4/20/98	3:35:53 PM	El90x	None	3
4/20/98	3:35:47 PM	EventLog	None	6005
4/20/98	3:35:53 PM	El90x	None	0
4/19/98	7:39:11 PM	BROWSER	None	8033
4/19/98	7:39:11 PM	BROWSER	None	8033
4/19/98	6:22:40 PM	W3SVC	None	14
4/19/98	6:19:00 PM	W3SVC	None	14
4/19/98	6:18:24 PM	W3SVC	None	14
4/19/98	5:39:57 PM	W3SVC	None	14
4/19/98	7:28:44 AM	BROWSER	None	8015
4/19/98	7:28:44 AM	BROWSER	None	8015
4/19/98	7:28:42 AM	BROWSER	None	8021
4/19/98	7:27:28 AM	El90x	None	3
4/19/98	7:27:28 AM	El90x	None	3
4/19/98	7:27:28 AM	El90x	None	3
4/19/98	7:27:21 AM	EventLog	None	6005
4/19/98	7:27:28 AM	El90x	None	0

FIGURE 17.1: Event Viewer

Each message will contain the data and time that the event occurred, an Event ID, the service that generated the message, and a short message, as shown in Figure 17.2.

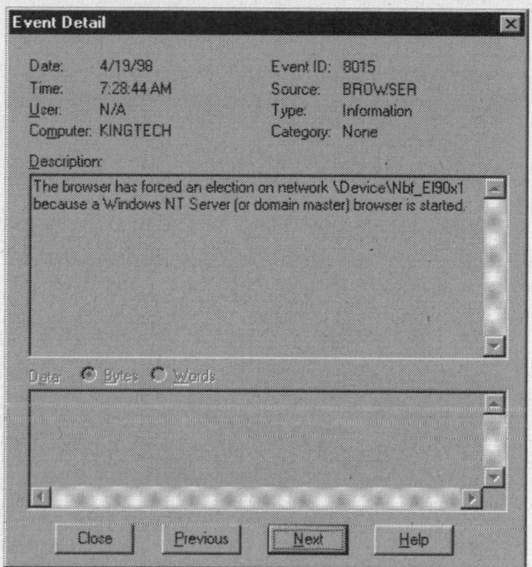

FIGURE 17.2: Event Detail

You can often use this information to determine the cause of a problem. Make sure to look through all of the fatal messages though, because many services are dependent upon other services. The last message listed might only be a symptom of the real problem.

Sometimes the information in the event messages will give you enough information to determine the cause of your problem. In these cases you can write down the Event ID, and research that particular error in TechNet. Microsoft Technical Support will often request the Event ID of any errors when you call for support.

The only real procedure for this objective concerns dumping memory into a file for later analysis (usually by someone at Microsoft Technical Support).

1. In Control Panel, open the System applet.
2. Access the Startup/Shutdown tab and make your choices of the options available.

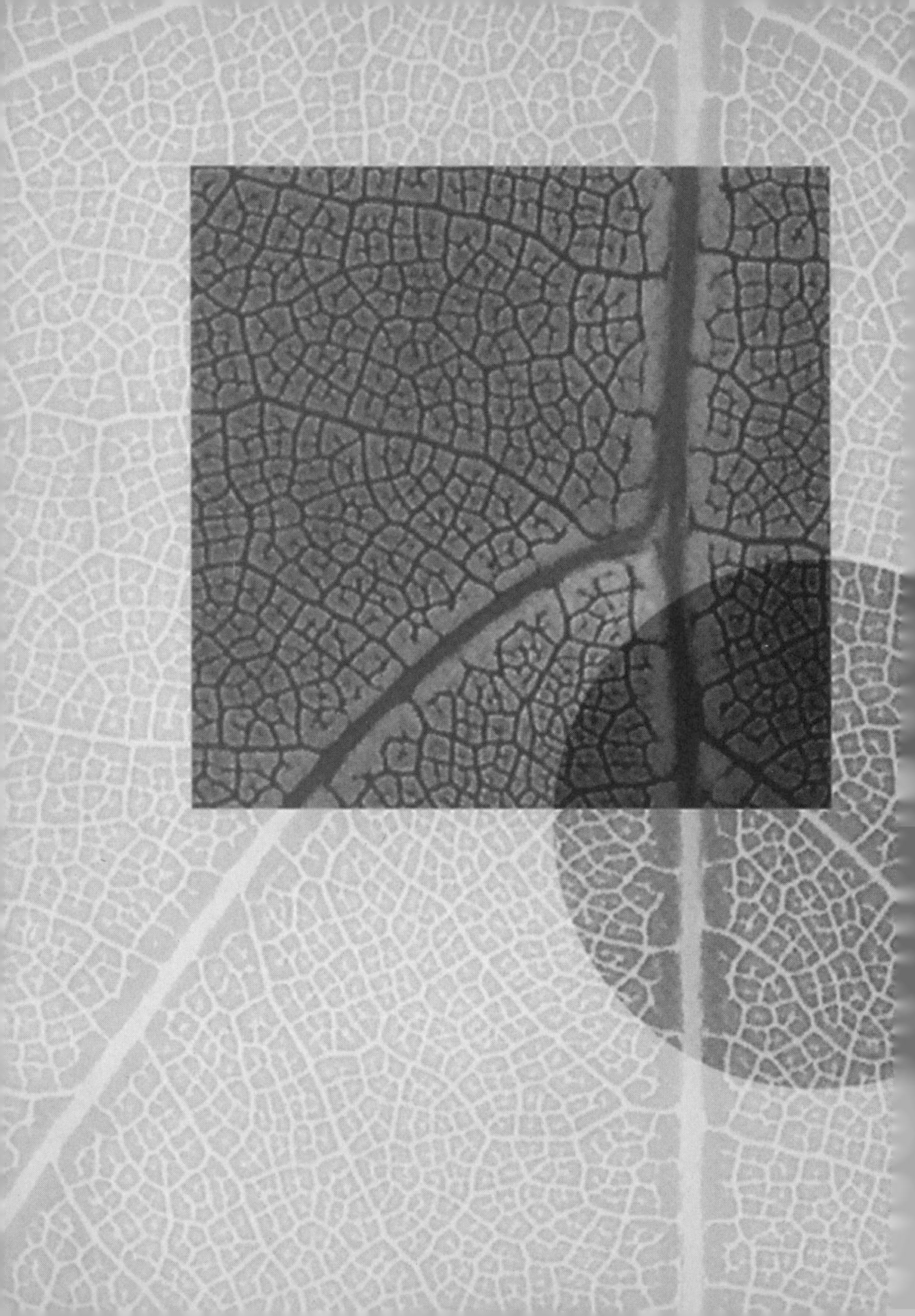

Part III

NT Workstation 4 Practice Exam

1. What is an unattended answer file used for during automated installations?

   A. It provides specific information about that particular computer, including things like the system serial number.

   B. It answers some or all user-supplied information during an NT Workstation setup.

   C. It installs and configures software application suites.

   D. It provides a way to automate hardware installation.

2. What is the function of the SYSDIFF utility during an automated installation?

   A. It provides specific information about that particular computer, including things like the system serial number.

   B. It answers some or all user-supplied information during NT Workstation setup.

   C. It installs and configures software application suites.

   D. It provides a way to automate hardware installation.

3. Which of the following file systems offer local file and directory level security?

   A. NTFS

   B. FAT

   C. HPFS

   D. CDFS

4. Workstation performance and network access seem to be slow. What is one way of improving performance?

   A. Change the protocol binding order on the client machine. Move the most widely used protocols to the bottom.

   B. Change the protocol binding order on the server. Move the most widely used protocols to the bottom.

   C. Change the protocol binding order on the workstation. Move the most widely used protocols to the top.

   D. Change the protocol binding order on the server. Move the most widely used protocols to the top.

5. You are installing NT Workstation on a computer that is currently configured to run NT 3.51. The workstation makes use of the High Performance File System (HPFS). How can you complete the installation?

   A. NT 4 supports HPFS, so there will be no problem.

   B. Convert the HPFS file system to NTFS before the upgrade.

   C. Back up all the data, reformat the hard drive, install NT, reinstall the applications, and then restore the data.

   D. NT 4 will convert HPFS to NTFS as part of the normal installation process.

6. Which of the following methods can be used to delete an NTFS system partition?

   A. FDISK

   B. The OS/2 boot disks

   C. The NT boot disks

   D. The disk administration utility

7. Which of the following are recommendations for optimizing the virtual memory system?

   A. Place your paging file on the same disk as your operating system files.

   B. Do not place your paging file on the same disk as your operating system files.

   C. Split the paging file across multiple hard drives.

   D. Make one big paging file and place it on a key disk.

8. Which GUI-based utility can you use to copy the \i386 and the \DRVLIB folders to the distribution server?

   A. Administration Manager

   B. User Manager for Domains

   C. User Manager

   D. Microsoft NT Explorer

   E. XCOPY

9. Which of the following tools is used to upgrade from Windows 95 to Windows NT 4?

   A. UPGRADE.EXE

   B. The Upgrade applet in Control Panel.

   C. Winnt /u:95

   D. There is no upgrade path from Windows 95 to Windows NT.

10. Bobbi has an account created on an NT Workstation that is a part of a network that has two separate domains. When the user account is created on the computer, how many domain user accounts are created?

    A. None

    B. One

    C. Two

    D. Three accounts are created, one for the workstation and one for each domain.

11. Your boss is a control freak. She wants to make sure that each NT Workstation has exactly the same system policies. Each workstation is attached to the network and the users must always log on to the domain before starting work. How can you keep your boss happy?

    A. Create a system policy file and export it to each workstation the first time it logs on.

    B. Create a system policy file for each end user and copy it to the user profiles directory on the domain controller.

    C. Create a system policy file and copy it to each workstation's \WINNT folder.

    D. Create a system policy file that will affect all end users and copy it to the NETLOGON folder of the PDC.

12. Given the default permissions assigned to groups, which groups would you need to belong to in order to create a share?

    A. Administrators

B. Backup Users

C. Guests

D. Power Users

E. Users

13. Denise is a member of three groups: Administrators, MIS, and Apps_Acctg. There is a share created called ACCOUNTING. The Administrators group has full control permissions to the Accounting share, the MIS group has been assigned No Access permissions, and the Apps_Acctg Group has been given the Change permission. What can Denise do with the share?

A. Denise has full rights to the share, granted to her through her membership in the Administrators group.

B. Denise can read or see a folder, subfolder, or file, execute an application, write to a closed file, and delete a folder or file. These are inherent in the Change permission Denise received through her membership in Apps_Acctg.

C. Denise can attach to the share but cannot see or do anything. This is a result of the No Access permission given to the MIS group.

D. Denise cannot see the share.

14. Jack just started to work for your firm today as a temporary programmer. When you set up his account you made him a member of the following groups, each with permissions given to the share \NewApps: Everyone - List, Users - List, Developers - Full Control, and Temps - No Access. What will Jack's rights be to the \NewApps share?

A. Full Control

B. List

C. No Access

D. Not enough information has been given.

15. The Windows NT Workstation that you are configuring contains a shared folder that resides on an NTFS partition. How is access to the folder determined?

   A. A user accessing the folder remotely has the same or more rights than a user accessing the folder locally.

   B. A user accessing the folder remotely has the same or more restrictive access permissions than if he were a local user.

   C. A user accessing the system remotely has the same rights as the user who accesses the system locally.

   D. The user who accesses the system locally is not bound by NTFS permissions.

16. The chief executive officer of your company comes to you and tells you that she has a problem. It seems that she and all the executive vice presidents print to the same printer, and quite frankly she is tired of waiting for their stuff to print. How can you handle this situation?

   A. Create two printers printing to the same print device. Call the first one Boss and the second one NotBoss. Set the priority on Boss to 99 and the priority to NotBoss to 1. Connect the CEO to Boss and everyone else to NotBoss.

   B. Create two printers printing to the same print device. Call the first one Boss and the second one NotBoss. Set the priority on Boss to 1 and the priority to NotBoss to 99. Connect the CEO to Boss and everyone else to NotBoss.

   C. Get her a printer of her own.

   D. Tell her to work and play well with others and deal with the delay.

17. Which of the following describe ways to add a computer account to the domain SAM for an NT Workstation computer?

   A. Use Server Manager before installing the Workstation.

   B. Use the ADDCOMP.EXE command line utility.

   C. It will happen automatically during the installation of the networking portion of NT Workstation.

D. Choose the option to add the computer to the domain during the installation and provide an account/password for a domain administrator.

18. Client Service for NetWare should be loaded on which of the following computers?

A. The NetWare servers that any NT client will attach to

B. Any NT client that will need to connect directly to a NetWare server

C. Each router between a client and a NetWare server

D. All computers in your network

19. Which of the following parameters must be configured on each TCP/IP client in a routed network?

A. IP address

B. DNS server address

C. Subnet mask

D. Dcfault Gateway

20. What is multilink?

A. The ability to have two or more modems handling different calls at the same time

B. The ability of two or more modems to call out at the same time

C. The ability to use more than one communication channel for the same connection

D. The ability to have two network interface cards in the same system at the same time

21. PWS provides which of the following services?

A. WWW

B. DHCP

C. FTP

D. WINS

E. Gopher

22. Windows NT Workstation assigns how much address space to each application?

    A. 2K

    B. 2MB

    C. RAM+2MB

    D. 2GB

    E. 2TB

23. You are running a Windows 3.1 application that is performing slowly. How can you increase performance?

    A. Go into Control Panel ➢ System ➢ Processor and assign a higher priority.

    B. Right-click the application icon and edit the PIF file.

    C. The next time you start the application, use the Start command with the /HIGH option.

    D. Upgrade to a 32-bit application.

24. Which of the following memory counters represents the number of pages that were not in RAM when requested?

    A. Pages/Sec

    B. Available bytes

    C. Committed bytes

    D. Pool non-Paged bytes

25. Which of the following would be an appropriate fix for a system in which the network is the bottleneck?

    A. Add another NIC card to segment your LAN.

    B. Upgrade the NIC card to a faster type.

    C. Upgrade the bridges, routers, and other network devices involved in communication.

    D. Add another processor to your server.

26. The Current configuration becomes the Last Known Good configuration at which point in the boot process?

A. After all services have successfully loaded in the kernel phase

B. After a user successfully logs on

C. After the BOOT.INI file has executed

D. When the user chooses Save Configuration on the Startup/Shutdown tab of the System applet

27. Which of the following actions should you take if you encounter a media error when installing NT?

A. Try another NT CD-ROM.

B. Try another method of installation: across the network, copy the i386 to the local drive first, etc.

C. Give up and try another operating system.

D. Clean your CD-ROM drive.

28. What permissions can be granted to a folder on a FAT partition?

A. Full Control

B. No Access

C. Read, Write, and Supervisor

D. Folders on FAT permissions cannot receive permissions.

29. Which of the following are methods used to back up the registry?

A. Use any Windows-based backup software.

B. Use the Save Registry option in the NT backup utility.

C. Use REGBACK.EXE from a command prompt.

D. Update your Emergency Repair Disk.

30. In the driver information section of a stop screen, which of the following are included in the data shown?

A. The IRQ of the offending device

B. Preferred load address

C. Creation date

D. Name of the driver

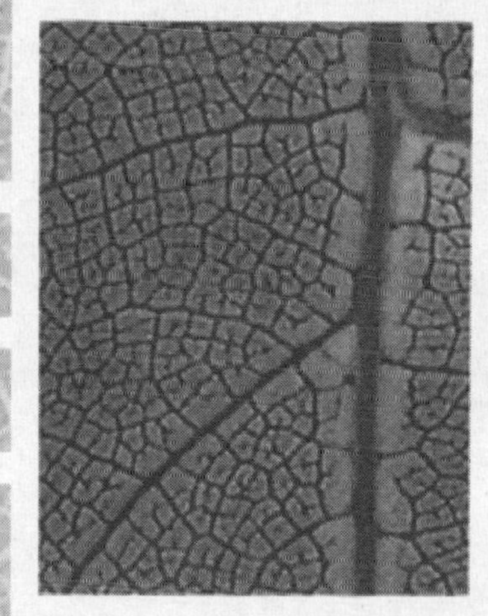

PART IV
NT SERVER 4 IN THE ENTERPRISE

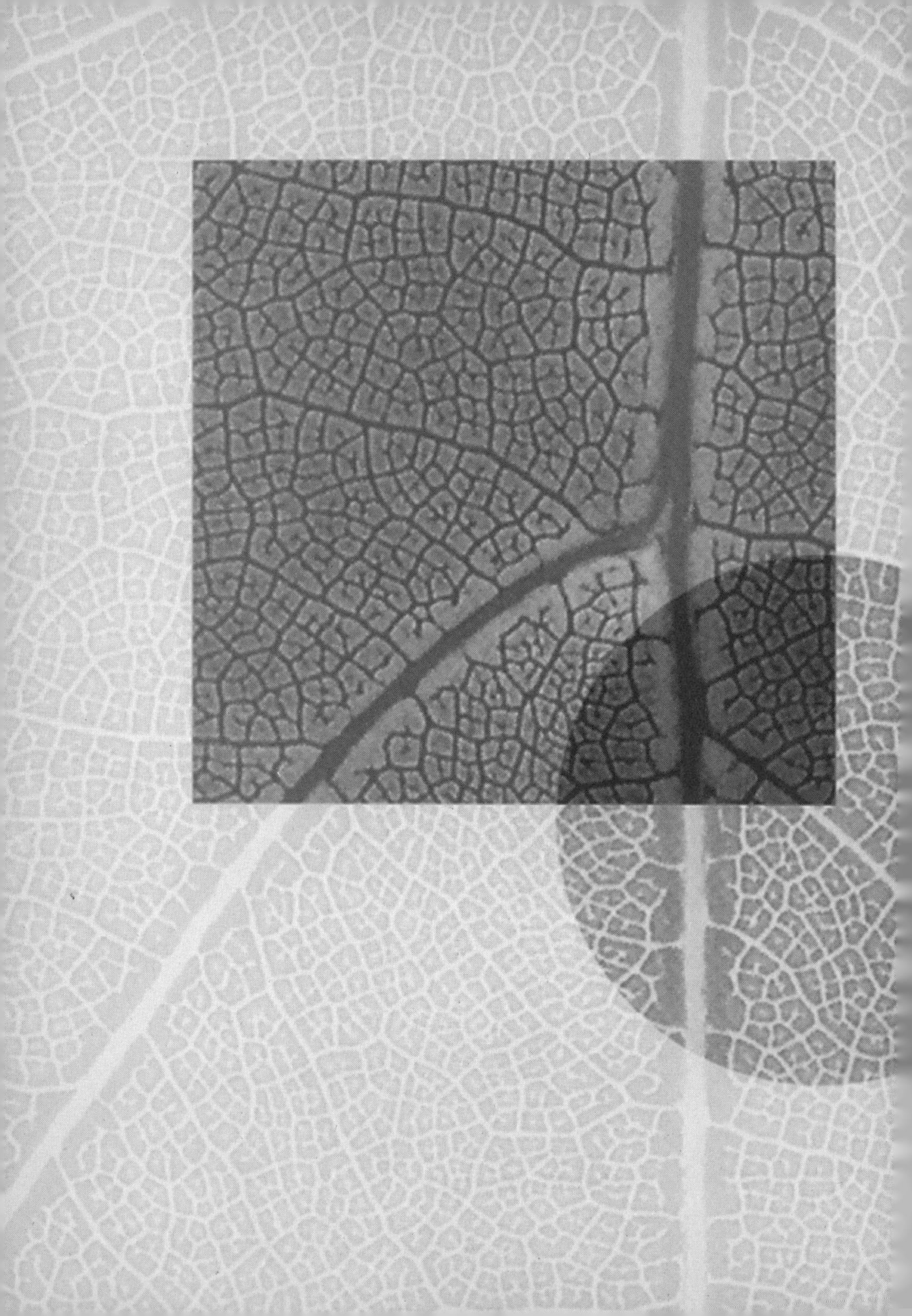

Chapter 18

Planning

The information covered in this chapter revolves around decisions that you need to make *before* the physical implementation of Windows NT or a migration from another operating system. Much of this information is theoretical, which is the hardest material to study because it is always open to interpretation. Before you can start installing servers, you need to define what services the network will be required to provide. In addition to the requirements, you will probably have a list of desired services. Some services will not be feasible given your budget and will be potential future plans.

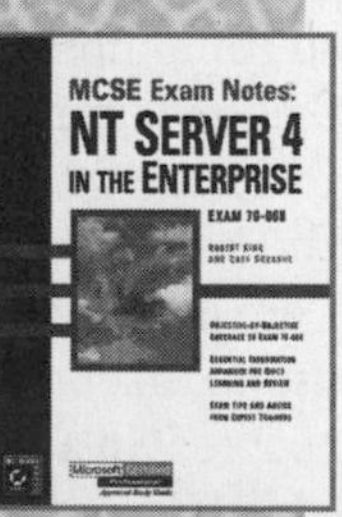

Adapted from *MCSE Exam Notes: NT Server 4 in the Enterprise* by Robert King and Gary Govanus

ISBN 0-7821-2292-2 416 pages $19.99

Each of the objectives covered in this chapter concerns specific sets of decisions that you must make when planning a network. If you make the right decisions, you end up with a network that is efficient, fault tolerant, and easy to administrate. If you make the wrong decisions, you end up with a network that is none of these things. Remember that proper planning will save a tremendous amount of time and effort in the future—and given the mission-critical importance of modern information technology systems, proper planning can save the business.

Plan the implementation of a directory services architecture.

Considerations include:

- Selecting the appropriate domain model
- Supporting a single logon account
- Allowing users to access resources in different domains

When designing an NT environment, the system administrator has two goals: simplify administration, and simplify access for the users. As an administrator, you would like to be able to manage your entire network from a single location, have a single account for each user, provide fault tolerance for your account information, integrate the other network operating systems into your NT structure, and ease the administration of the critical applications on which your users depend.

At the same time, you want to allow users to log on at any machine, have only one account and password to remember, and be able to access appropriate resources no matter where they are located in your environment.

Domain Models

Microsoft defines a *domain* as a "logical grouping of users and computers organized for administrative purposes," (*Microsoft Student Guide Course 689*, p. 23). Unfortunately, Microsoft also uses this phrase to define the term *workgroup*, (*Microsoft Student Guide Course 922*, p. 35). The major difference between a workgroup and a domain is where users are authenticated for the resources they are trying to access. In a workgroup, user accounts are defined locally on the machine that holds the resource. In a domain, user accounts are defined and managed in a central database—this database, called the security accounts manager (SAM), is managed by NT's directory services. So, a more accurate definition of an NT domain would be *an administrative grouping of users and computers, defined and managed through a single database.*

The SAM is a secure database that contains information about the users, computers, global groups, and local groups defined in a domain. Each of these items is called an *object* in the database. The maximum number of objects that can be organized in a single SAM is 40,000. The SAM is stored on an NT server, which plays the role of domain controller for your network. A *domain controller* is an NT server that contains the domain SAM or accounts database. Domain controllers are responsible for the authentication of users–in other words, the logon process. There are two types of domain controllers–primary domain controllers (PDCs) and backup domain controllers (BDCs). The differences between the two types will be defined in Chapter 19, "Installation and Configuration."

Although the accounts database can support up to 40,000 objects, a system might be designed with multiple domains (accounts databases) for various reasons. These reasons include: having more than 40,000 users, computers, and groups; wanting to group users or resources for management purposes; and wanting to reduce the number of objects viewed in management tools.

The act of splitting the users and resources into multiple domains is called *partitioning the database.* There are two main benefits to this type of design. First, you can delegate administration for each domain so that each department or location can manage its own resources. Second, you reduce the length of the list you have to scroll through to find a given object.

By default, each domain is a separate entity–domains do not share information, and resources from one domain are not made available to users defined in another domain. To allow users to access resources in another domain, you must establish a trust between the two domains. A *trust* can be defined as a one-way communications link between two domains. There are two domains involved in a trust–one that contains the user accounts that should have access to resources and another that contains those resources. The domain with the user accounts is called the *trusted* domain; the domain with the resources is called the *trusting* domain.

When you document your system, you should represent trusts with arrows. The arrows should point to the trusted domain. When one domain trusts another, this is known as a *one-way trust* (see Figure 18.1).

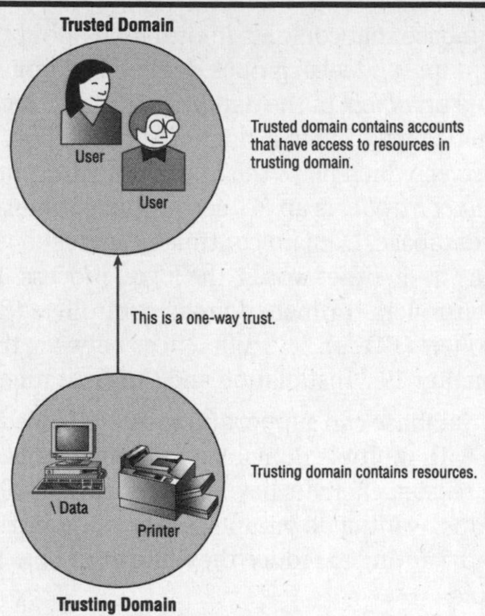
Trusted Domain
User
User
Trusted domain contains accounts that have access to resources in trusting domain.
This is a one-way trust.
Trusting domain contains resources.
\ Data
Printer
Trusting Domain

FIGURE 18.1: One-way trust

When both domains have users that need to access resources in the other domain, you will create a two-way trust. A *two-way trust* is just two one-way trusts set up in each direction (see Figure 18.2).

NT trusts are *nontransitive*—they are never inherited from one domain to another. If domain A trusts domain B, and domain B trusts domain C, this does not imply that domain A trusts domain C. You would have to create this trust manually. (This is a key point about trusts.)

AGLP is an acronym that describes the fundamental process for granting permissions to resources across trusts—*A*ccounts go into *G*lobal groups, which go into *L*ocal groups, which are granted *P*ermissions.

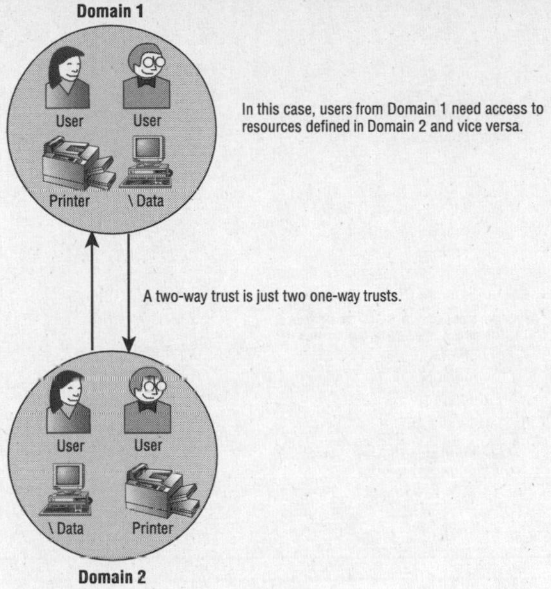

Domain 1

User User

Printer \Data

In this case, users from Domain 1 need access to resources defined in Domain 2 and vice versa.

A two-way trust is just two one-way trusts.

User User

\Data Printer

Domain 2

FIGURE 18.2: Two-way trust

The steps for granting these permissions are shown in Figure 18.3.

1. In the domain where the users are defined (Domain 1), either use an existing global group or create a new one, and make the appropriate users members of this group.
2. In the domain that contains the resource (Domain 2), create a local group with the necessary permissions.
3. Make the global group from Domain 1 a member of the local group in Domain 2.

This AGLP process is tested often on all of the Microsoft exams. You need to know it and be comfortable using it to succeed.

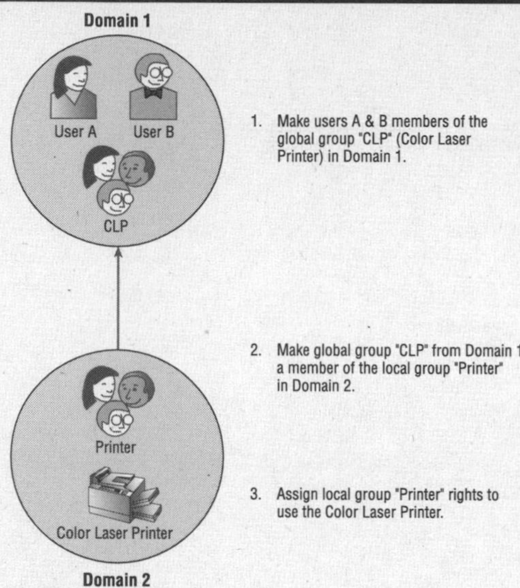

FIGURE 18.3: AGLP

Selecting the Appropriate Domain Model

The way you design your NT environment can have a big impact on its performance. Microsoft emphasizes an understanding of the variables involved in planning, implementing, and maintaining an NT domain structure.

A *domain model* is a definition of how you will use directory services in your environment. There are four basic domain models–single, single master, multiple master, and complete trust – each has some definite advantages and disadvantages.

Single Domain Model The single domain model is the easiest to implement of the four models. All users and computers are defined in a single NT domain, as shown in Figure 18.4. This domain model is most appropriate when there are less than 40,000 users in close proximity to each other (no significant remote locations) and there is a need for central administration of the environment.

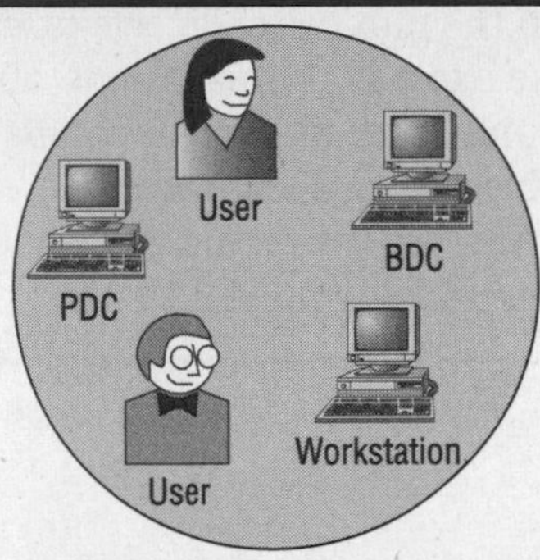

FIGURE 18.4: Single domain model

Since all resources are defined in a single domain SAM database, no trusts need to be established. Users have access to all resources to which they have been granted permissions. The advantages and disadvantages associated with the single domain model are listed in Table 18.1.

TABLE 18.1: Advantages and Disadvantages of the Single Domain Model

Advantages	Disadvantages
Simple to implement and manage	Performance can degrade as the number of resources increases because the load on Security Manager increases
Central control of user accounts	All users are defined in the same database—no grouping by location or function
Central control of all resources	All resources are defined in the same database—no grouping by location or function
No trusts are necessary	Performance of browser service (not Web browser) will slow with large numbers of servers

Single Master Domain Model A single master domain model consists of at least two domains. All user accounts are defined in a *master* domain. The other domains are used to manage physical resources, as shown in Figure 18.5. This design is most appropriate when you desire central control of user accounts, but departmental or geographic control of physical resources is the responsibility of a local administrator. Thi domain model is also appropriate when the number of objects (users and resources) defined in the SAM database exceeds the maximum (40,000). In this case, if you move the computer and other resource accounts to another domain, it would spread the object records over multiple domains. (Although, in a company of this size, you would probably start with the next model–the multiple master domain model.)

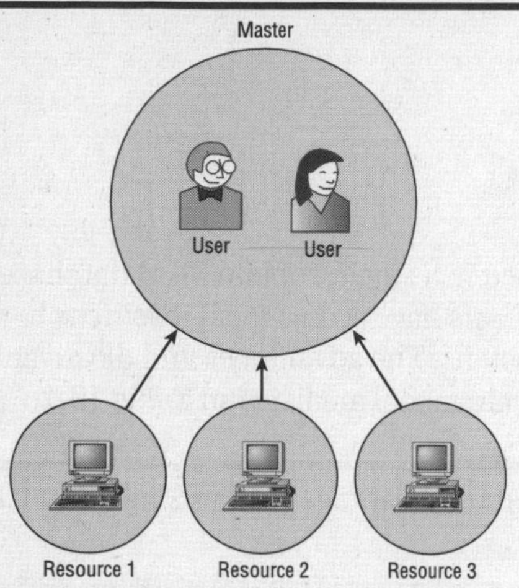

FIGURE 18.5: Single master domain model

NOTE

Each resource domain establishes a one-way trust with the master domain.

You use the AGLP process to assign users in the master domain permissions to the resources defined in the resource domains, as shown in Figure 18.6. Create a global group in the master domain with the appropriate members, then create a local group in the resource domain and assign it the necessary permissions. Next, make the global group a member of the local group.

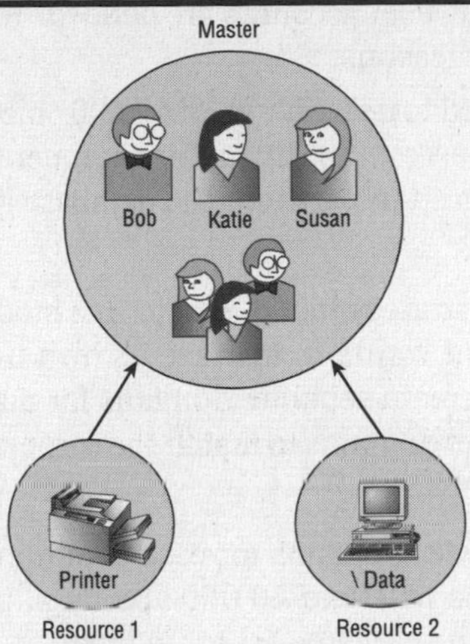

FIGURE 18.6: Groups in a single master domain model

The advantages and disadvantages associated with the single master domain model are listed in Table 18.2.

TABLE 18.2: Advantages and Disadvantages of the Single Master Domain Model

ADVANTAGES	DISADVANTAGES
Best choice if resources need to be managed by different groups	As in a single domain, performance can degrade as the number of users defined in the master domain increases.
User accounts are centrally located	Local groups must be defined in each resource domain.
Resources are grouped logically (either by department or by geographic location)	The administrator of resource domains must trust the administrator of the master domain to set up global groups correctly.
Global groups need to be created in only one domain	

Multiple Master Domain Model The multiple master domain model is shown in Figure 18.7. This domain model is the most scalable of the four models. It looks much like the single master domain model, except that there is more than one domain where user accounts are defined. You might choose this model for various reasons:

- The accounts database is limited to a maximum of 40,000 objects (users, groups, and computer accounts). If your environment is large enough, you might be forced to partition the database just to stay within the limits.
- Your company's management strategy might lead to this model. If each location or department wants to manage its own user accounts, you might want to create separate domains for management purposes or divide user domains to match the corporate departmental structure.
- You might create multiple master domains for ease of administration–the accounts database *will* hold 40,000 accounts, but you will not like paging through that large list to find items.
- In a WAN (wide area network) environment, you might make multiple domains to reduce the amount of network traffic that crosses the wide area links.

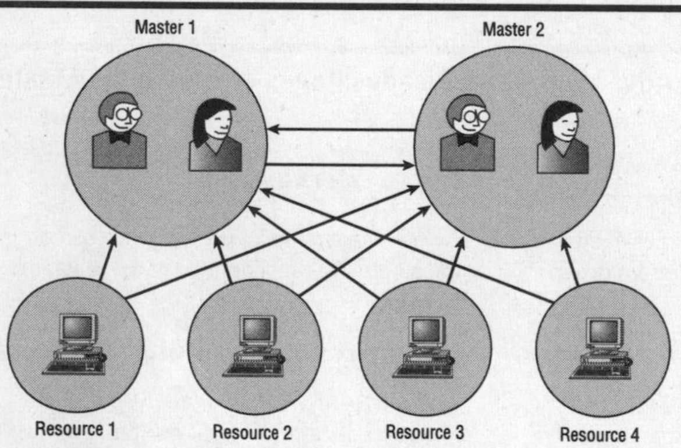

FIGURE 18.7: Multiple master domain model

Master domains have two-way trusts between them; resource domains have a one-way trust to each master that contains users who might have to access their resources. You can determine the number of trusts in a multiple master structure by using the following formula: M*(M–1) + (R*M), in which *M* is the number of master domains and *R* is the number of resource domains. (This formula assumes that each resource domain will have to trust each master domain.)

Assigning rights in a multiple master environment is a bit more confusing than in the preceding models. You still use the AGLP method, but you might have to create the global groups in each of the master domains, as shown in Figure 18.8.

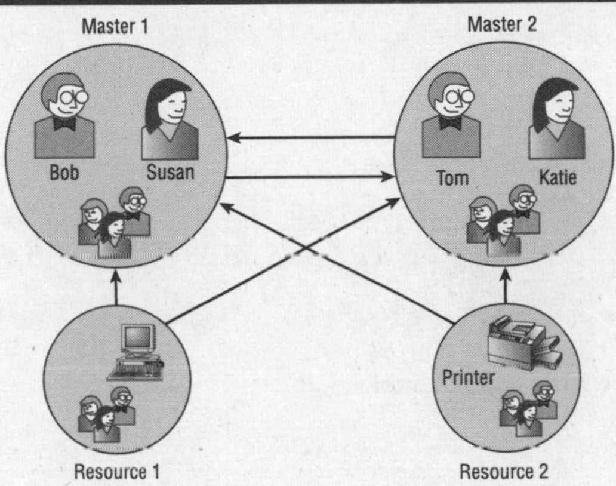

FIGURE 18.8: Groups in a multiple master domain model

The advantages and disadvantages of the multiple master domain model are listed in Table 18.3.

TABLE 18.3: Advantages and Disadvantages of the Multiple Master Domain Model

ADVANTAGES	DISADVANTAGES
Best model for a large environment with a central MIS department	Both local groups and global groups might have to be defined in multiple domains
Scalable to a network of any size	Large number of trusts to manage
Each domain can have a separate administrator	User accounts are not all in one domain database

Complete Trust Domain Model The complete trust domain model takes full advantage of directory services. In this model, each domain has both user accounts and resources, and each domain must trust all other domains. This model, as shown in Figure 18.9, is perfect for a company in which each department or geographic location wants to control both its physical resources and its user accounts.

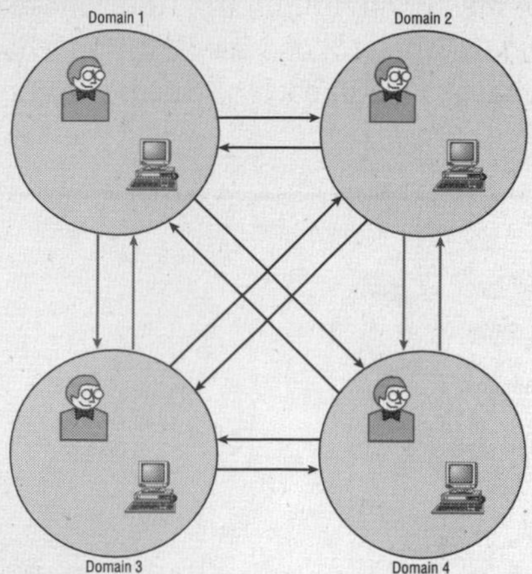

FIGURE 18.9: Complete trust domain model

TIP

In a complete trust domain model, all domains trust all other domains. You can determine the number of trusts by using the following formula: D*(D–1), in which D is the number of domains in the network.

Assigning rights in a complete trust environment can be extremely confusing. In this model, you must create both local groups and global groups in every domain, as shown in Figure 18.10.

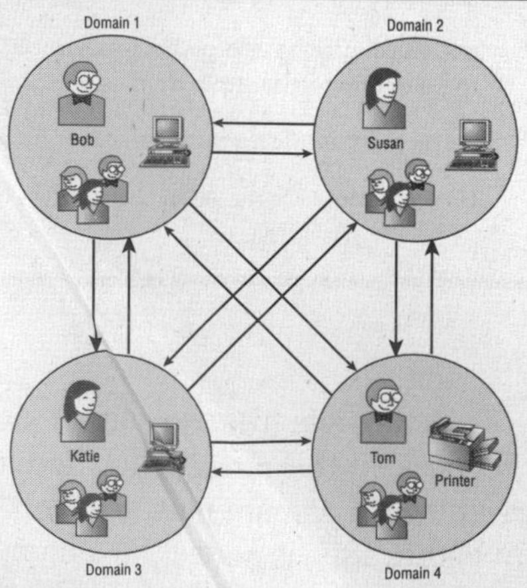

FIGURE 18.10: Groups in a complete trust domain model

The advantages and disadvantages of the complete trust domain model are listed in Table 18.4.

TABLE 18.4: Advantages and Disadvantages of the Complete Trust Domain Model

ADVANTAGES	DISADVANTAGES
Works well for companies with decentralized MIS functions	Large number of trusts to manage
Scalable to any number of users	With more domains, there are more points of management
Each domain can have its own administrator	Each administrator must assume that all other administrators know what they are doing
Resources and user accounts are grouped into management units	

Supporting a Single Logon Account

In a traditional server-based network, each server maintains its own list of users who can access its resources. Since there are multiple lists of users (one for each server), users often have to remember multiple user account names and passwords, which is often confusing for the users. From an administrative perspective, defining users in multiple places adds complexity and redundant management.

Microsoft Windows NT allows a user to use a single user account to access resources on the entire network. A process called pass-through authentication makes it possible for users to log on from computers or domains in which they have no account. When a user sits down at a computer defined in a domain that trusts their home domain, they can choose their domain from a drop-down list.

The NT server in the computer's domain will then use the trust relationship to pass the authentication request in the user's home domain. If user Bob from DOMAIN 1 attempts to log on at a machine in DOMAIN 2, the logon process will use the procedure shown in Figure 18.11 and listed below.

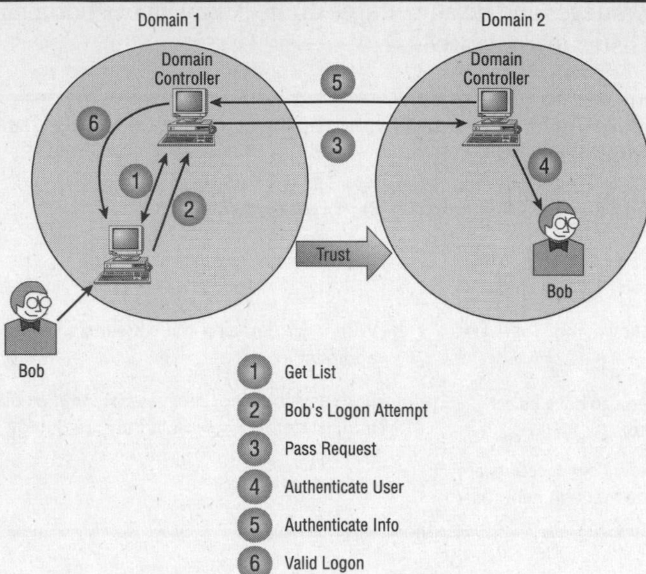

FIGURE 18.11: Pass-through authentication

1. When the Windows NT Workstation machine boots, its NETLOGON service locates the primary domain controller in DOMAIN 1. As part of this process, the computer receives a list of all trusted domains to present on the logon screen.
2. When the user identifies himself as Bob from DOMAIN 2, the NETLOGON process passes the request to a domain controller in DOMAIN 1.
3. The domain controller in DOMAIN 1 recognizes that the request is for a user defined in a trusted domain, so it passes the request to a domain controller in DOMAIN 2.
4. The domain controller in DOMAIN 2 checks its accounts database to ensure that the user name is valid and the right password has been entered.
5. If the request to log on is valid, the domain controller in DOMAIN 2 passes the user's SID and group information to the domain controller in DOMAIN 1.

6. The domain controller in DOMAIN 1 trusts that the authentication was done properly, so it passes the information about user Bob back to the NT machine where Bob is trying to log on, completing the logon process.

Allowing Users to Access Resources in Different Domains

To grant a user rights to a resource in a trusting domain, create a global group in the user's home domain, which must be the trusted domain. Then, create a local group in the trusting domain. Grant the local group permission to the appropriate resource, and make the global group a member of the local group.

Creating a Trust

Use the User Manager for Domains utility to create a trust between two domains. This is basically a two-step process—you must define the trust at both the trusted and the trusting domains. To set up the trust, you must be logged on as an administrative account in the domain. Although you can create either side of the trust first, it is better to establish the trusting relationship first and then move to the trusting domain to establish the trusted side of the relationship—the trust relationship will be established immediately. If you start at the trusted domain, there will be a 15-minute delay in establishing the trust relationship. Although 15 minutes is not excessive, it can seem like forever when you are staring at a computer screen.

1. In both domains, start the User Manager for Domains utility.
2. Choose Policies ➢ Trust Relationships.
3. At the trusted domain, add the name of the trusting domain to the Trusting Domains box.
4. At the trusting domain, add the name of the trusted domain to the Trusted Domains box. At the trusting domain, you should see a message telling you that the trust relationship was successfully established.

Plan the disk drive configuration for various requirements.

Requirements include:

- Choosing a fault-tolerance method

This Exam Objective is covered in Part 2: NT Server 4, Chapter 5 "Planning." The Practice Exam at the end of Part 4 will test you on this material.

Choose a protocol for various situations.

Protocols include:

- TCP/IP
- TCP/IP with DHCP and WINS
- NWLink IPX/SPX Compatible Transport
- Data Link Control (DLC)
- AppleTalk

In its simplest sense, *protocol* can be defined as a set of rules that govern behavior. Protocols govern the communication between computers. If you understand how communication protocols work, it will help you choose the protocols you want to implement in your environment.

Implementing too many protocols on the network is probably the most common cause of slow performance. As a systems engineer, you need to understand when each protocol is appropriate and when it is not. You need to know how you can use a single protocol to provide as many services as possible, and you need to know how to choose that protocol for a given environment. Also, you need to know how to configure each protocol and implement it in the most efficient manner.

TCP/IP

This section of the Exam Objective is covered in Part 2: NT Server 4, Chapter 5 "Planning." The Practice Exam at the end of Part 4 will test you on this material.

TCP/IP with DHCP and WINS

As mentioned earlier, numerous tools are available to help manage the TCP/IP protocols. Two of the most commonly implemented tools are DHCP and WINS. Each of these tools is designed to alleviate some of the more common headaches encountered in a TCP/IP network.

DHCP (Dynamic Host Configuration Protocol)

To really appreciate the value of DHCP, you must understand a little more about how TCP/IP works. In an IP network, each host has a unique identifier called an IP address. This address must be unique when compared to all other hosts that are attached to any network with which the local host can communicate. (Stop and think about this–if you are connected to the Internet, your computer must have an address that is different from the addresses of millions of other hosts that can attach to the Internet.)

A discussion of IP addressing is beyond the scope of this book. You do need to know that a unique IP address must be configured on every device that communicates (using TCP/IP) on your network. Along with the IP address, numerous other parameters might also need to be configured. The traditional method for configuring an IP host was to walk to the device, sit down, and start typing. While this was OK for small companies, it had some big drawbacks on most networks.

TRADITIONAL IP HEADACHES

- Configuration by hand means mistakes! It does not matter how well you type—if you are configuring 500 machines, you are bound to make at least a couple of mistakes. At best, duplicate or invalid addresses will affect only the host where the mistake was made; at worst, they can affect communication across your network.

CONTINUED →

- Change is problematic. There is a very strict and complicated set of rules for addressing in an IP network. Networks will grow, and sometimes you have to change your addressing scheme. This means changing the configuration at all hosts.
- If you add a new IP-based service, you may need to add or change a configuration parameter at each host.
- If you physically move a device within your environment, you may need to change its IP configuration. Usually, when you move a machine, the last thing on your mind is its configuration (you are thinking about what a pain users are, you are griping about a management team that can't leave well enough alone, or you have a list of more important things that you should be doing). Even worse—users occasionally take it upon themselves to move a device without letting you know. In this case, you have addressing problems and don't even know what has changed.

Why DHCP? Using traditional methods to manage an IP network was a hassle, but it was necessary. DHCP was designed to overcome some of these hassles. The theory behind DHCP is fairly simple–DHCP is a protocol specifically designed to configure IP hosts as they attach to the network. DHCP runs as a service on an NT server. This service manages a pool of IP addresses and configuration parameters. When a DHCP client boots, one of the first things it does is try to find a DHCP server. If it finds one, the DHCP sends it all of the TCP/IP configuration information necessary to function on the network. From a management perspective, this means you have only one place to manage your TCP/IP environment. You assign addresses appropriately, make changes, and add configuration parameters to the "pool"–these changes are reflected every time a client boots on your network.

WINS (Windows Internet Name Service) Another tool designed to ease the management of a Windows-based network that uses the TCP/IP protocol is WINS. Once again, to really appreciate WINS, you have to delve a little deeper into how IP and NetBIOS work. (NetBIOS is the upper-level protocol that Windows-based networks use to communicate.) WINS adds two basic services to your network—NetBIOS name registration and name resolution.

Name Registration In a NetBIOS-based network (any Windows network), each computer is given a unique name—the NetBIOS name. Since NetBIOS uses this name to communicate between machines, these names *must* be unique. In a traditional NetBIOS network, each machine sends a NetBIOS broadcast that announces its name as it boots. If another host already exists with that name, it will send a message to the new client saying that the name is in use. If it doesn't get a message back, the client assumes that the name is available.

This process works OK on a single-segment network. Unfortunately, most routers do not pass NetBIOS broadcast traffic. This means that there is no mechanism to prevent two computers from having the same name if they are on different network segments. Duplicate names *will* cause communication errors somewhere down the line!

While routers can be set up to pass these broadcasts, there is a more elegant and effective solution—the Windows Internet naming service (WINS). In a WINS environment, each client is configured with the IP address of the WINS server. When the client boots, it sends a message to this server—a request to use a name. The WINS server keeps a database of all the NetBIOS names that are in use—if the name is *not* already in use, it returns an acknowledgement; if the name *is* already in use, it returns a denial. If the name is approved, the WINS server places a record for that client (made up of its NetBIOS name and IP address) in its database.

WINS clients send a name release to the WINS server when they are properly turned off. This allows the WINS server to update its database so that it contains only names for computers that are currently available on the network.

Name Resolution Users shouldn't be forced to remember complicated IP addresses for all of the machines with which they need to communicate. Unfortunately, acquiring this address is mandatory before communication can happen. You should give your computers names that are easy to remember so that users can use a "friendly" name to represent a computer.

First, the NetBIOS name (the name you gave the computer when you installed NT) must be resolved into an IP address. Traditionally, this is done by broadcasting a request on the network. Basically, the computer shouts on the wire, "Hey, I'm looking for a computer named XYZ." If computer XYZ receives the request, it will send a message back that contains its IP address. There are two problems with this technique. First, broadcast traffic must be analyzed by *every* computer on the network, adding overhead to machines that are not involved in the communication. Second, most routers are configured *not* to pass broadcast traffic, so your request will be fulfilled only if you are attempting to communicate with a device on your own network segment.

To get around the broadcast problem, you could create a text file named LMHOSTS on every computer. This text file would contain the NetBIOS name and IP address of every computer with which you are going to communicate. What a hassle! Every time you add a new computer to your network, you will have to update the LMHOSTS file on all other computers in your network.

If you have implemented WINS, though, you already have a database that contains the names and IP addresses of all computers available on the network. In a WINS environment, when your computer wants to communicate with another computer, it sends a name-resolution request to the WINS server. This request contains the NetBIOS name of the machine to which you wish to connect. The WINS server looks through its database. If it finds a matching NetBIOS name, it returns the IP address of that machine.

Why WINS? WINS saves time and traffic on your network, therefore helping to keep it efficient. Without WINS, many of the procedures for establishing a connection with another machine are based upon broadcast traffic. Broadcast traffic is the bane of systems engineers. When a packet is broadcast, all computers that receive it must stop what they are doing and waste time reading the packet to determine if they should respond. In a WINS environment, all of this traffic is directed to the WINS server. It is the only computer that will analyze these packets, while all other computers continue processing without interruption.

NWLink IPX/SPX Compatible Transport

This section of the Exam Objective is covered in Part 2: NT Server 4, Chapter 5 "Planning." The Practice Exam at the end of Part 4 will test you on this material.

Data Link Control (DLC)

You need to know even less about DLC than about NWLink. The DLC protocol is mostly used to communicate with printers that are directly attached to the network, or to access SNA (system network architecture)-based mainframes. It can also be used to communicate with some Hewlett-Packard network printers, but those are usually legacy hardware installations.

AppleTalk

AppleTalk is the transport protocol developed by Apple for Macintosh networks. The NT implementation is designed to allow your Macintosh clients to access your NT servers for file and print services. Since NT servers are fully AppleShare compliant, they need to be able to communicate with Macintosh clients. Most modern Macintosh clients have TCP/IP connectivity, so that is preferentially used to ensure maximum access to network resources.

NOTE

Although AppleTalk allows your Macs to connect, Services for Macintosh must be installed and configured on your server to allow any real functionality.

All Macintosh computers can use AppleTalk to communicate on a network. However, only Macintosh computers can use AppleTalk to communicate. You will still have to configure another protocol for your Windows 95 and NT clients.

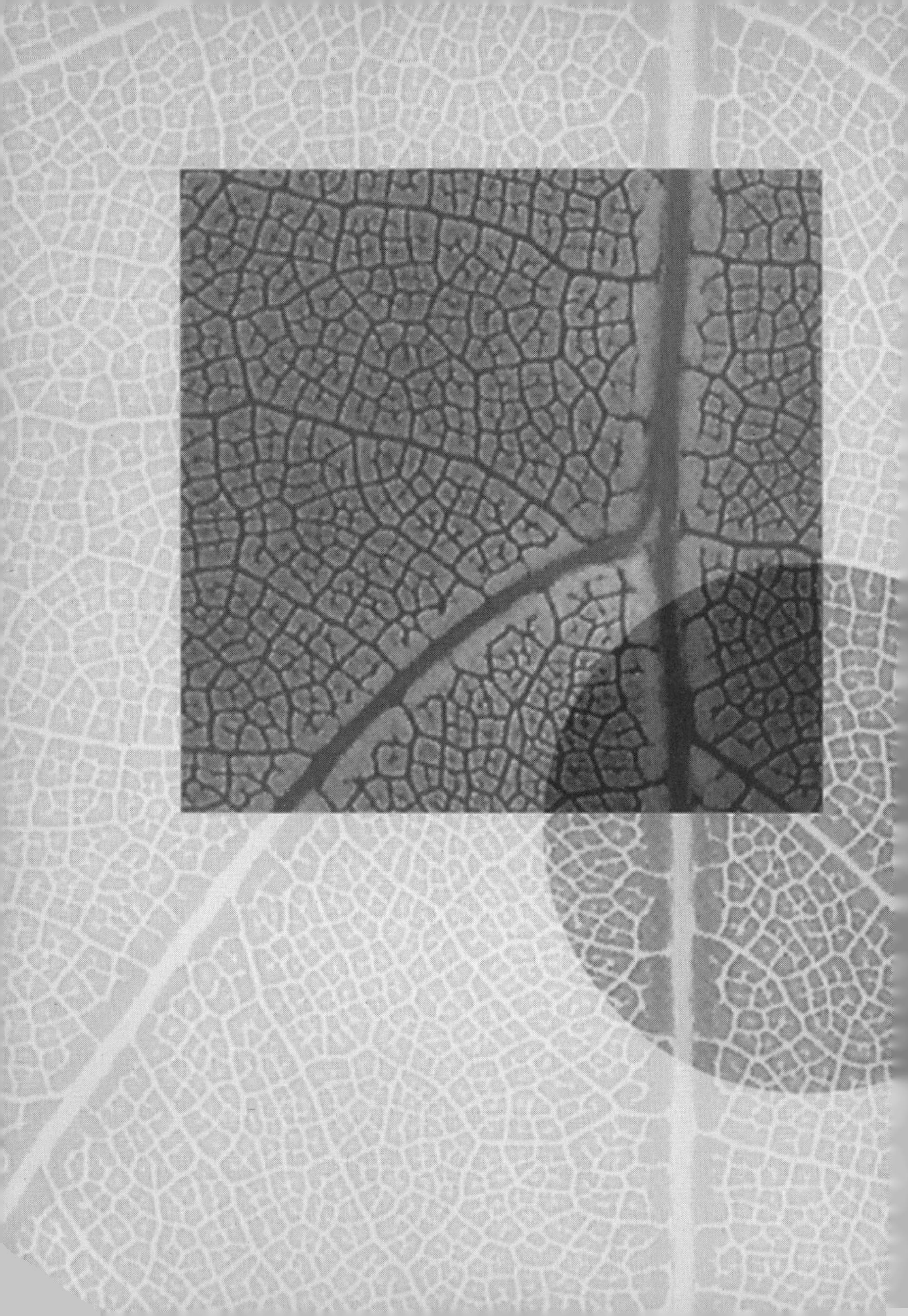

Chapter 19

Installation and Configuration

Now that you have planned your network—chosen the domain model, designed a disk subsystem, and chosen a protocol—the next step is to implement your plan. In this chapter, the installation and configuration of an NT server in a multiple server or domain environment will be thoroughly discussed. If you make the proper choices during the installation of NT, it will make working with that server easier in the future. At best, if you make a wrong choice, you will have to work a few extra hours. At worst, you will have to reinstall the operating system.

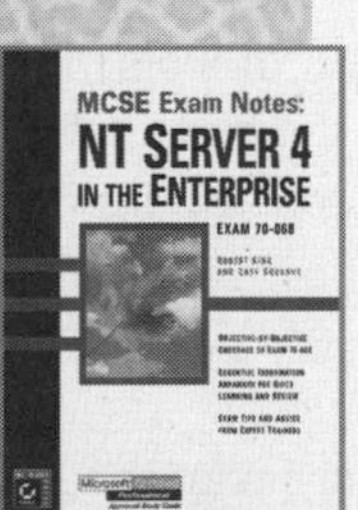

Adapted from *MCSE Exam Notes: NT Server 4 in the Enterprise* by Robert King and Gary Govanus
ISBN 0-7821-2292-2 416 pages $19.99

Install Windows NT Server to perform various server roles.

Server roles include:

- Primary domain controller
- Backup domain controller
- Member server

NOTE

All exam objectives in this chapter are covered in Part 2: NT Server 4, Chapter 6 "Installation and Configuration." The Practice Exam at the end of Part 4 will test you on this material.

Configure protocols and protocol binding.

Protocols include:

- TCP/IP
- TCP/IP with DHCP and WINS
- NWLink IPX/SPX Compatible Transport
- DLC
- AppleTalk

In this section, the installation and configuration of the protocols discussed in Chapter 18 will be examined. For each protocol, the tools used for installation and the configuration parameters available will be discussed.

TCP/IP with DHCP and WINS

The configuration of DHCP and WINS clients was previously examined. Now, setting up the DHCP and WINS server services will be discussed.

DHCP Once you have added the DHCP service to a server, you will find a new tool in the Administrative Tools group–DHCP Manager. Although a complete discussion of the configuration of a DHCP server is beyond the scope of this exam, you will need to know a couple of the basics, which are discussed later in this section.

WINS WINS is also installed as a service on your server. Once it is installed, you will find a new menu item in your Administrative Tools group–WINS Manager. There isn't a lot to configure at a WINS server. If the service is turned on and your clients are configured with the correct IP address, WINS builds the database without much trouble.

WINS provides two basic services to your network–name registration and name resolution. When a WINS client initializes, it contacts that WINS server, announcing itself and its name. The WINS server checks its database to ensure that the name is unique on the network. If not, the WINS server will send back a negative acknowledgment–the client will display a message saying that the name is already in use on the network. If the name is not already in use, WINS will add the name and IP address of the client to its database.

When a WINS client needs to access another computer on the network, it will contact the WINS server, asking for the IP address of the destination computer. The WINS server will search its database for a computer with the name requested and return the IP address if available.

The only configuration information that you need to be aware of is the partner relationship between multiple WINS servers. If a company has multiple sites, it won't want its clients to have to cross the WAN link every time they need to communicate with a local host. In this case, you would set up a WINS server on each side of the link. Each WINS server would build a database of the local computers. You can then configure the two WINS servers to trade their databases back and forth so that each has a complete list of the computers in your network. The process of trading the databases is called WINS replication.

There are two kinds of partnerships–push and pull. In a push relationship, the WINS server waits until a certain number of changes have been made to the database. When this number has been reached, the WINS server will alert all of its partners that replication needs to occur. In a pull relationship, each server asks its partners for changes at scheduled intervals.

NOTE

This has been a very quick discussion of configuring DHCP and WINS on an NT server. While it should be enough for the Enterprise Exam, it is not the entire story. For more information, check out *Mastering TCP/IP for NT Server 4*, by Todd Lammle and Mark Minasi (Sybex, 1997).

NWLink IPX/SPX Compatible Transport

This section of the Exam Objective is covered in Part 2: NT Server 4, Chapter 6 "Installation and Configuration." The Practice Exam at the end of Part 4 will test you on this material.

DLC

There are no configuration options available with this protocol. To install this protocol, open the Network control panel and select the Protocols tab. Click the Add button.

AppleTalk

The AppleTalk protocol is installed as part of the Services for Macintosh service. The configuration of this environment will be discussed later in this chapter.

Protocol Bindings

In the most generic sense, to *bind* is to link components at different levels to enable communication. The architecture of NT is made up of various layers–each layer provides a certain type of service. Some of these services will need to communicate with the services on another layer. The process of binding enables this communication. In the discussion of protocols, binding referred to establishing a communication channel between the network adapter card driver and a protocol.

Increasing Security Binding enables communication between the adapter's driver and a protocol. If you do *not* bind a protocol to an adapter, that card cannot communicate using that protocol. You can use binding to control traffic on your network and provide increased security.

To increase security, first consider your environment. Which protocols are needed, and where are they needed? After analyzing your needs, you determine that you really don't need TCP/IP on your internal network. You will use NetBEUI instead, because it is fast and easy to configure. Your server will have two network adapters installed–one attached to the internal network, one with access to the Internet. You can use the protocol bindings to ensure security by disabling the TCP/IP binding to the adapter attached to your internal network. This configuration would ensure that no TCP/IP traffic can be routed from the Internet to your internal network.

Increasing Performance In the Network applet on the Binding tab, you can manage the protocol bindings. The protocols are bound to both server and workstation services. The order in the list of bindings affects the efficiency of network communication. When an NT-based computer attempts to communicate with another device on the network, it will try to communicate using the protocols in the binding list–in the order that they are listed. If you have multiple protocols in the list, make sure that the most commonly used protocol is listed first.

Configuring DHCP as a Server

There are two main configuration tasks associated with setting up the DHCP server. Both are accomplished through DHCP Manager. The first task is to create a scope. The scope is the pool (or pools) of IP addresses that this server will hand out to clients. For each subnet on which this server might provide addresses, you will need to create a different scope if a DHCP relay agent is not available to pass broadcast DHCP messages across the subnet boundary.

When configuring the scope, you will need to provide the information listed in Table 19.1.

TABLE 19.1: DHCP Scope Parameters

Parameter	Description
Start and end address	The contiguous range of IP addresses that this scope hands out to clients.
Subnet mask	Identifies which portion of the IP addresses represents the network address. Subnet masking is often considered the most confusing part of configuring an IP network.
Exclusion range (start, end)	If some addresses within the defined range should not be given to clients, you can exclude those addresses here.
Lease duration	DHCP clients "lease" an IP address from the DHCP server for a defined period of time. When a client is given an IP address, the DHCP marks that address as in use. If the client machine is removed from the network, the address will be marked as available when the lease time runs out.
Name	A descriptive name for administrative purposes.

The second task in configuring DHCP services is to decide which additional TCP/IP configuration parameters should be associated with each scope. In addition to the minimum IP address and subnet mask, you might need to set many parameters on your clients—everything from a default gateway to the address of your WINS servers.

To add a parameter to a scope, scroll down the list on the left, pick the parameter, and click the Add button. Then, with that parameter highlighted in the Active Options list, click the Value button and set the value(s).

Configuring a DHCP Relay Agent

You will need to be aware of one more DHCP for this exam—the DHCP relay agent. When a DHCP client asks for and receives its IP configuration, all traffic in the process is broadcast based. As you'll remember from Chapter 18, most routers are configured to block broadcast traffic. This presents a problem when using DHCP on a routed network—the clients are not able to reach the DHCP server if it is not on their own subnet. To overcome this limitation, you can configure an NT server as a DHCP relay agent. The agent is configured with the IP address of your DHCP server.

The DHCP relay agent "listens" for the broadcast traffic generated when a client tries to find a DHCP server. The agent passes this request along to the DHCP server. Because the agent is on another subnet, it must have a static IP address (you must manually configure the address). Since it has been manually configured *and* knows the IP address of a DHCP server, it can use directed calls to cross the router.

▶ Configure Windows NT Server core services.

Services include:

- Directory Replicator
- Computer Browser

Configure hard disks to meet various requirements.

Requirements include:

- Providing redundancy
- Improving performance

Configure printers.

Tasks include:

- Adding and configuring a printer
- Implementing a printer pool
- Setting print priorities

Configure a Windows NT Server computer for various types of client computers.

Client computer types include:

- Windows NT Workstation
- Windows 95
- Macintosh

These exam objectives are covered in Part II: NT Server 4, Chapter 6 "Installation and Configuration." The practice exam at the end of Part IV will test you on this material.

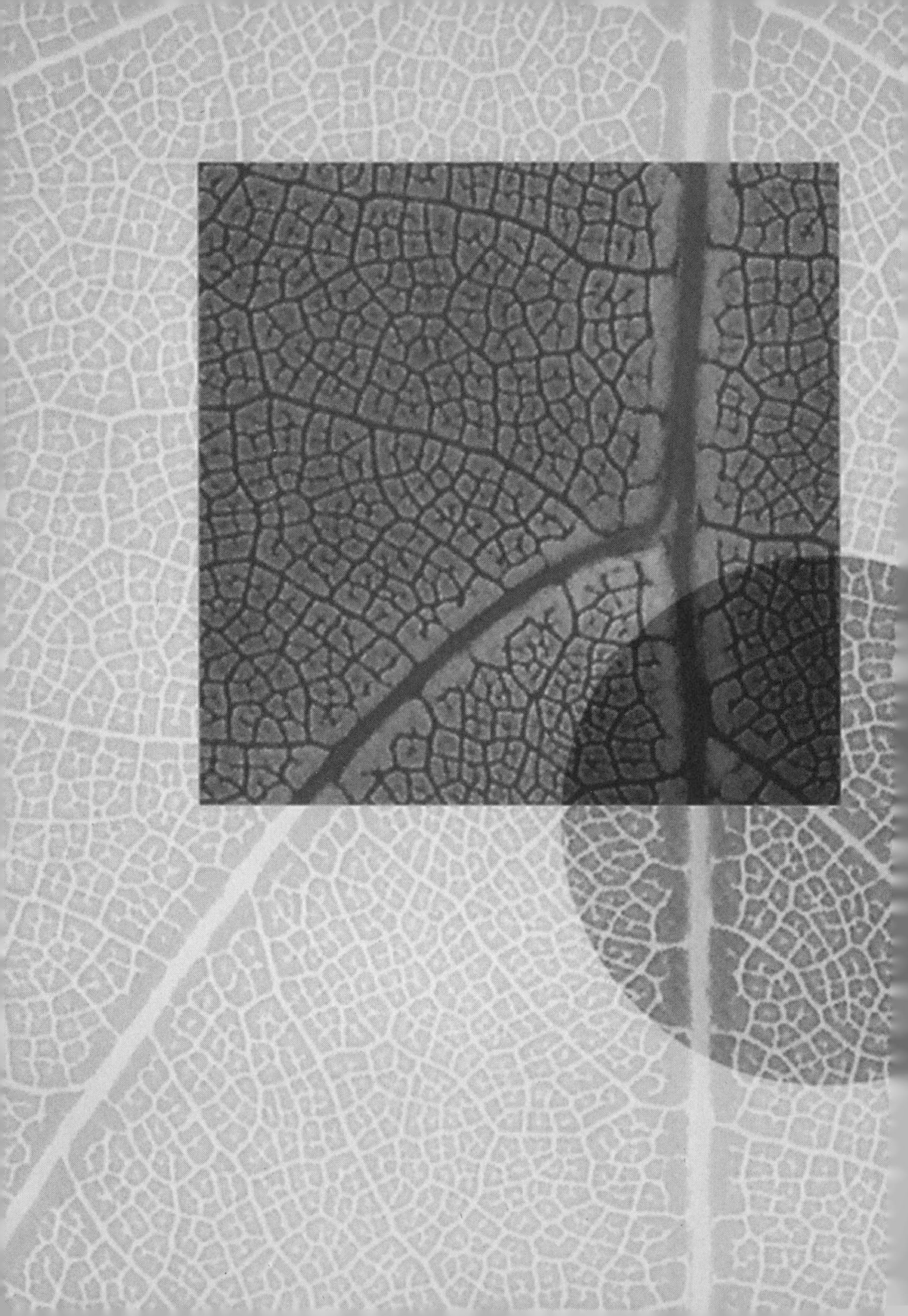

Chapter 20

Managing Resources

One of the best definitions of a network is having two or more people with information to share, a communication medium to send the information, and rules to govern the communication. The whole reason for having a computer network is sharing–sharing information, sharing resources, and sharing applications. That very broad overview is great for discussions over your favorite frosty, cold beverage, but it tends to get complicated really quickly when the amount of people with something to share grows to 50, 100, 1,000, or more. It is especially complicated when *you* have to provide others with the opportunity to share files and peripherals throughout the entire company. It can be a daunting task. However, it doesn't have to be that way. As you study these objectives, you will find ways to cut that task down to size.

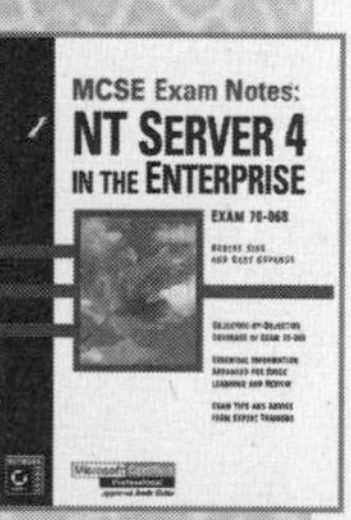

Adapted from *MCSE Exam Notes: NT Server 4 in the Enterprise* by Robert King and Gary Govanus

ISBN 0-7821-2292-2 416 pages $19.99

Manage user and group accounts.

Considerations include:

- Managing Windows NT user accounts
- Managing Windows NT user rights
- Managing Windows NT groups
- Administering account policies
- Auditing changes to the user account database

Create and manage policies and profiles for various situations.

Policies and profiles include:

- Local user profiles
- Roaming user profiles
- System policies

Administer remote servers from various types of client computers.

Client computer types include:

- Windows 95
- Windows NT Workstation

Manage disk resources.

Tasks include:

- Creating and sharing resources
- Implementing permissions and security
- Establishing file auditing

All of these Exam Objectives are covered in Part 2: NT Server 4, Chapter 7 "Managing Resources." The Practice Exam at the end of Part 4 will test you on this material.

Chapter 21

Connectivity

There are very few "pure" networks in the world. Most networks are a combination of a legacy system purchased over the years. Given the state of many networks, one of the most important criteria for new systems is interoperability. When you add to this the ability to grow with technology, you have only a handful of potential operating systems worthy of consideration.

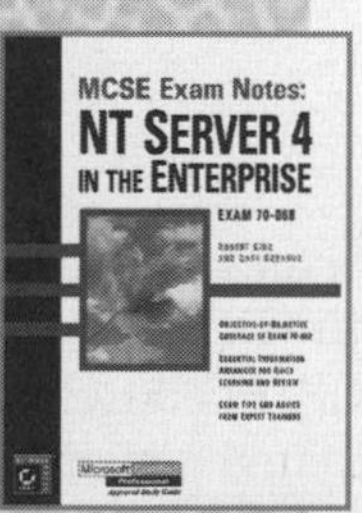

Adapted from *MCSE Exam Notes: NT Server 4 in the Enterprise* by Robert King and Gary Govanus

ISBN 0-7821-2292-2 416 pages $19.99

Microsoft Windows NT has a few design features that make it the perfect choice for today's networks. One of these features is NT's modular design. Every function that an NT server can perform is designed as a separate subsystem of the operating system. This modular design means that NT can be updated to meet the needs of future technologies. It also means that third-party developers can add functionality to the base operating system. These are important features in a business world that can't decide what the power tie of the week should be, let alone standardize a set of services for the network.

Configure Windows NT Server for interoperability with NetWare servers by using various tools.

Tools include:

- Gateway Service for NetWare
- Migration Tool for NetWare

This Exam Objective is covered in Part 2: NT Server 4, Chapter 8 "Connectivity." The Practice Exam at the end of Part 4 will test you on this material.

Install and configure multiprotocol routing to serve various functions.

Functions include:

- Internet router
- BOOTP/DHCP Relay Agent
- IPX router

This section discusses routing–how to set up your server as a router in both an IP and an IPX network. A few more details about the DHCP Relay Agent will be provided–the process of acquiring a TCP/IP address from a DHCP server and how this process is affected by a routed network.

Microsoft expects that you not only know how to implement routing, but that you understand it.

Multiprotocol Routing Options

Without the ability to route the TCP/IP protocol, an operating system is unable to connect to the Internet or any other networks outside of its own subnet. Of all the protocols available to NT, TPC/IP is the protocol chosen by default during the installation process. Know it inside and out!

Internet Router

The phrase *Internet router* is really a marketing invention. An Internet router is just a router that can route the TCP/IP protocol suite. Understanding the process of routing TPC/IP traffic has become very important as more and more businesses connect to the Internet.

Routing *Routing* is the process of finding a path between networks. Routers are devices that perform the routing function. The process of how a router decides the best path to a given network segment differs with the protocol in use–each protocol has its own procedure for building a list of networks, called a routing table. The router uses its routing table to determine the path that a packet should take to reach its destination.

NT servers can be configured to act as routers. Physically this entails putting more than one NIC (network interface card) in a server and configuring it appropriately for each protocol that it will route. Microsoft calls a computer with more than one NIC a multi-homed computer. After you have determined the proper physical settings for the additional card(s) and installed them in the server, you add the driver in the Network applet, within the Adapters tab.

The routing table on an IP router contains information on where a packet should be sent to reach a given network segment. In Figure 21.1, there are three networks. Each router knows about the segments that it is physically attached to, but not any other segments.

The IP addressing has been simplified by giving each interface a two-digit identifier–IP addressing is a complex subject that is beyond the scope of this exam. The description of the processes used to route traffic has also been simplified. For the Enterprise exam, you just need to understand the theory.

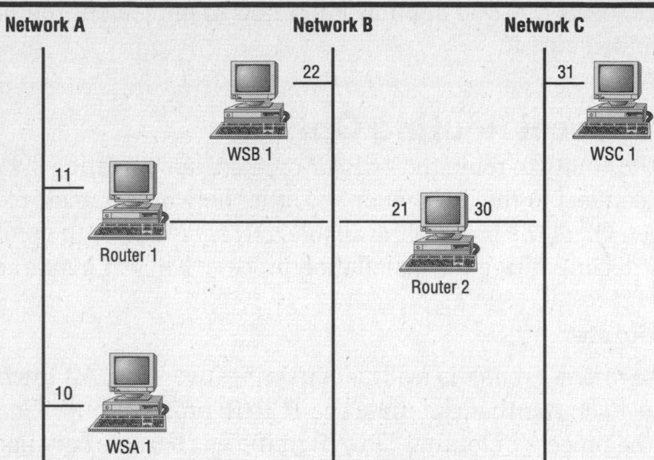

FIGURE 21.1: Three networks with two routers

When a device needs to communicate with another device, it must first resolve the host name into an IP address. This can be done in a number of ways, but the Microsoft solution is to have a WINS server perform this function. Once the device has the IP address, it performs a calculation on the address to determine whether the destination is local or remote (on its network or another network). If the host is remote, the device will send the communication to its default gateway or router. The router is responsible for picking the next hop in the path to the destination.

In Figure 21.1, if WSA 1 needs to communicate with WSB 1, it would first determine whether WSB 1 is a local or remote host. Since WSB 1 is on another network segment, it would be a remote host. WSA 1 would then check its default gateway address and pass the packets of information to that address–WSA 1 *should* be configured with Router 1 as its default gateway.

Router 1 would then perform the same calculation to determine whether the destination is on a local network (one to which it is physically attached). If local, it would then pass the packets to the appropriate network segment.

Easy, right? Now, let's look at WSA 1 attempting to communicate with WSC 1. Everything would be the same, until the router determines that the destination is not on a network to which it is attached. At this point, the router would have to have a reference to look up the path to the destination network. This reference is the routing table.

The routing table contains a list of all known networks. This list contains information about which of the router's NIC cards should be used to send packets to a particular network and the address of the next router in the path.

The routing tables for each router in the example are shown in Tables 21.1 and 21.2.

TABLE 21.1: Routing Table for Router 1

Destination Network	Local NIC Card	IP Address of Next Router
Network A	11	Local
Network B	20	Local
Network C	20	21

TABLE 21.2: Routing Table for Router 2

Destination Network	Local NIC Card	IP Address of Next Router
Network A	21	20
Network B	21	Local
Network C	30	Local

When WSA 1 tries to communicate with WSC 1, it determines that the destination is remote. It then sends the packets to its default gateway—Router 1. Router 1 determines that the destination network is not local, so it checks its routing table. It discovers that to reach Network C, it must send the packets to the next router—out its own interface 20, addressed to IP address 21. Router 2 will then make the same calculations and discover that it is physically attached to the destination network.

There are two types of routing tables: static and dynamic.

Static routing As an administrator, you can manually build the routing tables at your routers. This would involve typing in the appropriate information at each router in your network. This method is not favored by many administrators—it's a lot of work and can lead to mistakes. If you build static routing tables, you must update the tables every time you change your network.

Dynamic routing The TCP/IP protocol suite has a protocol specifically designed to pass this routing information between routers. Each router can then incorporate this information into its routing table. The protocol used to pass this information is RIP (routing information protocol). You must install RIP on your NT server as a separate service. Once RIP is installed, your NT server-based routers will begin exchanging route information.

RIP is a broadcast-based protocol. Every 30 seconds, RIP-enabled routers broadcast the contents of their routing table on each network to which they are attached. Since it is a broadcast, all routers on those segments will analyze the content of the broadcast and add any information to their own routing table. In Figure 21.1, if RIP is enabled on our routers, every 30 seconds both Router 1 and Router 2 will broadcast their routing tables on all of the networks to which they are attached. Each router's table begins with information about the networks to which they are attached. In this way, Router 1 will inform Router 2 about Network A and Router 2 will inform Router 1 about Network C. Note that both routers then know about the entire network, and the administrator does not have to configure the routing tables manually. RIP also has a mechanism built in to remove routes that have become unavailable, so the routing table will be a current representation of the network.

NOTE

RIP was first made available on NT server in version 4. For older servers, you have to create static routes.

BOOTP/DHCP Relay Agent

DHCP is a great administrative tool—it saves time and effort, and reduces mistakes. It does, however, have one small drawback—the way communication occurs. All DHCP communication is accomplished with broadcast traffic using the BOOTP protocol, which is a protocol specifically designed to configure network clients.

When a client accesses a DHCP server, all traffic is maintained as broadcast-based traffic. Four packets are generated every time a client attempts to acquire an IP address.

- Request–In this packet, the client asks for an IP address. It has to be a broadcast because, at this point, the client has no IP configuration–in other words, it has no IP address and cannot communicate using IP in any other way. The request packet is sent to all DHCP servers on the network.
- Offer–All DHCP servers that receive the request will respond with an offer. This is also done as a broadcast packet. It has to be a broadcast because the recipient has no IP address. All DHCP servers that send an offer mark the address as "offered" in their scope.
- Selection–The client receives the offers from the DHCP servers. Whichever offer is received first will be chosen. This packet is sent out as a broadcast for two reasons. First, the client still does not officially have an IP address. Second, it lets all other DHCP servers know that it has made a choice (they can now unmark the address they offered so that they can offer it to another client).
- Acknowledgment–The DHCP server sends another broadcast acknowledging the selection by the client. The server then marks the IP address as "in use" and begins the lease time. The client now has an IP address and default mask (and often, information such as the default gateway) to use.

In most environments, a client is given an IP address for a specific amount of time, known as the lease period. The client will reestablish the lease on the IP address when the time has expired. The protocol used for these broadcasts is BOOTP. In the TCP/IP protocol suite, BOOTP is defined as both a service and a protocol used to deliver this service. It was designed for use by diskless workstations when booting from files stored on a server. Windows NT DHCP services take advantage of the fact that BOOTP is a fast and efficient protocol designed to pass configuration information to clients. NT does not, however, implement the BOOTP service to facilitate booting diskless workstations from a central server.

Because BOOTP was designed with a very specific purpose, most routers are not configured to pass BOOTP packets. (Actually, by default, most routers do not pass broadcast packets at all.) This leads to a problem in a DHCP environment–users can contact the DHCP server only if it is located on the same network. In other words, the DHCP server cannot, by default, service any clients located on the other side of a router. You can overcome this problem by configuring your router to pass BOOTP packets, but most system engineers would agree that this is not a good idea. You don't want to flood your network with broadcast packets every time a client boots. A better solution is to implement a DHCP Relay Agent on each network.

A DHCP Relay Agent is an NT server configured to pick up the clients' DHCP packets and forward them to the DHCP server. The Relay Agent must have a manually configured IP address and be configured with the IP address of the DHCP server. Since it has an address, it can use directed packets to reach the server. The bottom line is that the Relay Agent makes it possible for clients to receive their IP addresses from a DHCP server located on the other side of a router.

IPX Router

IPX has its own mechanism for building a routing table. It works much like IP in that it uses a protocol named RIP (routing information protocol) to pass information about the network from router to router.

To implement IPX routing on an NT server, you must first install RIP for NWLink IPX/SPX Compatible Transport. This service is installed from the Services tab of the Network applet. After the installation, you must restart your NT server.

As in IP, IPX routers use RIP to pass network information. An IPX routing table holds the network addresses of known networks and the number of networks that have to be crossed to reach each destination. Each network that has to be crossed is known as a *hop*. The RIP packets in Figure 21.2 would contain the information listed in Table 21.3.

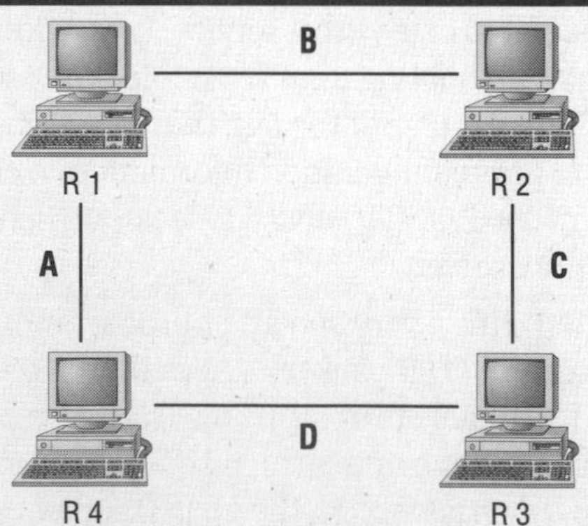

FIGURE 21.2: IPX network

TABLE 21.3: RIP Packets from Router 1 (R 1)

Destination Network	Number of Hops	Send To Router ID
Network A	0	Local
Network A	3	Router 2 (R 2)
Network B	0	Local
Network B	3	Router 4 (R 4)
Network C	1	Router 2
Network C	2	Router 4
Network D	1	Router 4
Network D	2	Router 2

Each router will have a similar routing table. Note that in this example, the router keeps track of all possible routes to each destination. If communication fails on a given route, the router will automatically switch to another route to the destination.

RIP for IPX is a broadcast-based protocol. As such, since every router announces every route it knows, the amount of traffic can be prohibitive. Many companies refuse to allow IPX routing information across slow (and costly) WAN links. Full implementations of the IPX/SPX protocol suite allow filtering of this traffic. They usually have other tools to decrease the amount and frequency of traffic. NWLink and Microsoft's implementation of RIP for IPX do not include these tools. When you need to be able to control IPX traffic, it is better to purchase a dedicated router with these tools.

Installing and Configuring Internet Routing

Installing and configuring the Internet routing components is simply a matter of knowing where to look and then reading the screen. Remember that the Internet routing pieces are managed through the Network applet found in Control Panel.

Installing RIP for Internet

Select Control Panel ➢ Network ➢ Services ➢ Add ➢ RIP for Internet. There are no configurable options.

Enabling IP Routing

Select Control Panel ➢ Network ➢ Protocols ➢ TCP/IP Properties ➢ Routing. Check Enable IP Forwarding.

Configuring a DHCP Relay Agent

Select Control Panel ➢ Network ➢ Protocols ➢ TCP/IP Properties ➢ DHCP Relay. Add the IP address(es) of your DHCP server(s).

Installing RIP for IPX

Select Control Panel ➢ Network ➢ Services ➢ Add ➢ RIP for IPX. There are no configurable options.

Enabling IPX Forwarding

Select Control Panel ➢ Network ➢ Protocols ➢ NWLink Properties ➢ Routing. Check Enable RIP Routing.

WARNING

RIP for IPX must be installed before IPX forwarding becomes available. This option is checked by default when you install RIP for IPX.

Install and configure Internet Information Server.

Over the past few years, Microsoft has tried to change its focus from the desktop to the network. An important part of that change is the inclusion of tools for connecting a Microsoft network to the world at large–mainly through the Internet. Internet Information Server (IIS) is one of the main pieces of this philosophy. By default, IIS 2 is installed when you install NT server. If you don't want to install it, you must clear the checkbox on the appropriate page. If you didn't install IIS 2 and want to install it at a later time, you can start the process in one of three ways:

- If IIS 2 is not installed, the NT installation program will put an icon on your desktop. This icon will start the installation of IIS.
- If you removed the icon from your desktop, you will also find it in Control Panel.

- If all else fails, you can access the installation program on your NT Server CD-ROM. It is in the \I386\Inetsrv directory. The executable is named INETSTP.EXE.

TIP

The NT Server CD-ROM includes IIS version 2. You should apply the latest NT service pack to upgrade IIS to the latest version. At the time of this writing, the latest version is 4. You can find the NT service packs at `www.microsoft.com`.

Installing IIS 2

Here are the steps for installing IIS 2:

1. Start the installation program and work through the opening screen that warns you to close all programs before continuing. The first dialog box allows you to configure the options you will install on your server. (The various options that are relevant to the exam will be described in the next section.)
2. After making your choices, click OK. The next window allows you to configure where the various services will store their published material. These default directories for WWW, FTP, and Gopher services should be used and placed on a partition formatted with NTFS so that you can use NT security to protect these data. Based on the decisions you made in these windows, the installation program will then copy files to various locations. For this exam, you will not need to know what is copied or where these files are placed.
3. Your next decision is which OBDC drivers, if any, you wish to install on your server. These drivers allow IIS to access data stored in files created by various database programs. Highlight the appropriate drivers and click OK. The drivers will be copied to your system.

 Install and configure Internet services.

Services include:

- World Wide Web
- DNS
- Intranet

Once a company decides to move forward with Internet technologies, quite a few more services can (or must) be added to the network. Configuring these services is critical to an efficient and secure network. In this section, tips and techniques for configuring three of the most common services will be examined.

Identifying Internet Technologies

Microsoft has placed a lot of emphasis on the various Internet technologies available within an NT environment. The MCSE examination reflects this emphasis. While you are not expected to be an expert in any of the following technologies, you are expected to understand what they are, how they are used, and how to configure them.

World Wide Web

A Web server is nothing more than a server that provides file-retrieval privileges using a specific set of protocols, namely HTTP. Configuring a Web server concerns more than just creating content. In many ways, content is secondary to the major concern–security. One of the best features of IIS is that it integrates very well with NT. When using IIS as your Web server, you can protect files using the same tools and techniques that you use in NT, such as the SAM database and the NT security model. When you install IIS, it creates a user account that is used to define the security assigned to anonymous users. That user account, named IUSER_*SERVER NAME*, can be granted limited permissions–just like any other NT account.

WARNING

The Internet anonymous-access account is a normal user account in all respects. Any resource that the group Everyone has permissions to is accessible to this account. Some administrators remove the group Everyone from the access control list (ACL) of *all* shares when they create anonymous-access accounts, thereby avoiding any potential problems.

The IIS environment is managed using the Microsoft Internet Service Manager, which is accessible by choosing Start ➢ Programs ➢ Microsoft Internet Server. In addition, the Web-based version of this utility is also available. This utility allows you to accomplish the following tasks: connect to IIS servers and view their properties; start, stop, and pause a service; and configure services.

The three services provided by IIS are as follows:

WWW service—This service allows users to connect to and view your Web site. You can configure a default page so that users do not have to specify a particular file when they connect.

Gopher service—This service was primarily designed to allow administrators to index files and directories.

FTP service—This service allows users to use FTP (file transfer protocol) to view, upload, and download files on a server FTP site.

DNS

DNS (domain name service) is the service used on the Internet to resolve user-friendly, fully qualified domain names (more commonly called domain names) into IP addresses. Basically, DNS is just a giant database. Its basic function is to hold records that have a host name and the IP address of that host. The DNS database is divided into domains (also known as zones). The piece of the DNS database that a DNS server holds—a domain—contains records that define the host name and IP address of resources.

NOTE

Other types of records are defined in the DNS specification. DNS can store everything from simple host/IP address records to records that define how e-mail should be handled.

When a user wants to find a resource, they send a request to their DNS server. The DNS server performs a search for the associated record. It will first compare the request against its domain. If the domain holds that piece of the DNS database, it will return the IP address of the WWW server to the client. On the Internet, each DNS server is configured with a list of root servers. These root servers contain the IP addresses of all registered domain names.

If the local DNS server cannot resolve the domain name, it will query a root server for the IP address of the DNS server. Your DNS server will then query that DNS server for the IP address of a server named WWW.

NOTE

DNS includes the ability to use aliases for hosts. Most companies do not name their Web server WWW. They create a record that acts as a pointer to the actual host-name record.

NOTE

A full discussion of DNS is outside the scope of this examination. For more information, check out *Mastering TCP/IP for NT Server* by Mark Minasi and Todd Lammle (Sybex, 1997).

DNS is installed as a service on your NT server. Once DNS is installed, you manage the DNS service using the DNS Manager utility found in your Administrative Tools group.

Intranet

The term *intranet* refers to an internal network that utilizes the tools and techniques of the Internet to provide services limited to local network users. For the examination, this objective revolves around a series of tips for securing an intranet or connection to the Internet.

- Remember that if you are going to allow anonymous access, the anonymous user (IUSR_ *SERVER NAME*) is made a member of the domain guests group. Be aware of this fact when assigning permissions to this group.

- Configure both the WWW and the FTP services to require a valid user name and password for access. Two types of authentication are available:

  Basic—Transmissions are not encrypted, so the user name and password are sent as clear text. FTP supports only Basic authentication.

  Windows NT Challenge/Response—Supported by Microsoft Internet Explorer 2 and above, and provides a secure login over the network.

- Require passwords on all user accounts; require a minimum length of six or more characters and frequent changes.
- Lock out accounts after multiple failed logon attempts and require an administrator to unlock locked-out accounts.
- Use time restrictions and automatically disconnect users whose time has expired.

Configuring Internet Services

You are not expected to be an expert in the following subjects for this examination. However, you are expected to be able to install and configure them for basic services.

Configuring the WWW Service

IIS and its services are configured using the Internet Service Manager utility (the normal or HTML version) found in the Microsoft Internet Server (Common) group. The opening screen displays the IIS services running on your NT server. You can connect to another NT server by choosing Properties ➢ Connect to Server. If you right-click on any service, it will bring up a menu with options that allow you to start, stop, or pause the service, or access its Properties page for more advanced configuration options.

Numerous configuration options are available for the WWW service:

1. On the Service tab, you can configure various TCP connection parameters, decide whether you will allow anonymous access, and if so, which account should be used, and configure which levels of password authentication your Web server will use. It is recommended that you leave the default settings unless the Web server is on an intranet where all users

are using Internet Explorer 2 or a later version; in that case, the Allow Anonymous checkbox should be cleared.

2. On the Directories tab, you can configure which directories will be made available to the WWW service and which HTML page should be shown by default if the user does not request a particular document.

3. The Logging tab allows you to configure the logging of WWW activity to a log file. Several file types are available, including SQL formats. Note that you can make the system add the log files to a SQL database.

4. Finally, the Advanced tab allows you to control which computers can access the WWW service. You can allow access to only selected IP addresses or domain names, or you can exclude all computers except certain IPs or domains.

Installing the DNS Service

The DNS service is installed like any other service on an NT server:

1. Open the Network applet in Control Panel.
2. Choose the Service tab.
3. Click Add.
4. Choose DNS from the list.

Configuring DNS

A full discussion of configuring DNS is outside of the scope of this examination. You should, however, be familiar with the DNS Manager tool found in the Administrative Tools (Common) group.

1. Add your server's IP address as a member of DNS by choosing New Server from the DNS menu. You will be asked for the IP address of the new DNS server.

2. Create the domain information by choosing New Zone from the DNS menu. You will be asked whether this is to be a primary or secondary DNS server. A primary DNS server holds the master copy of the domain database. A secondary DNS server holds a copy and helps the primary server resolve domain names. If you choose Primary, you will be asked for the domain name.

3. Once you have set up your zone, you are ready to start creating DNS records for the resources in your environment. Choose New Record from the DNS menu (the New Resource Record dialog box is shown below) and start building your DNS database.

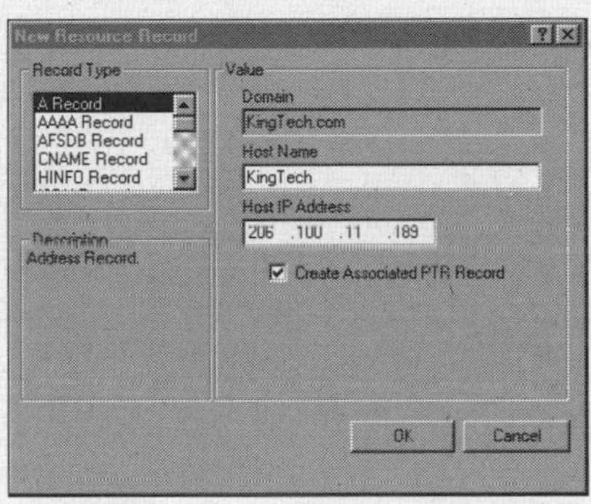

NOTE

For this examination, you will not be required to know the details of configuring DNS—just the tools used.

Install and configure remote access service (RAS).

Configuration options include:

- Configuring RAS communications
- Configuring RAS protocols
- Configuring RAS security

This Exam Objective is covered in Part 2: NT Server 4, Chapter 8 "Connectivity." The Practice Exam at the end of Part 4 will test you on this material.

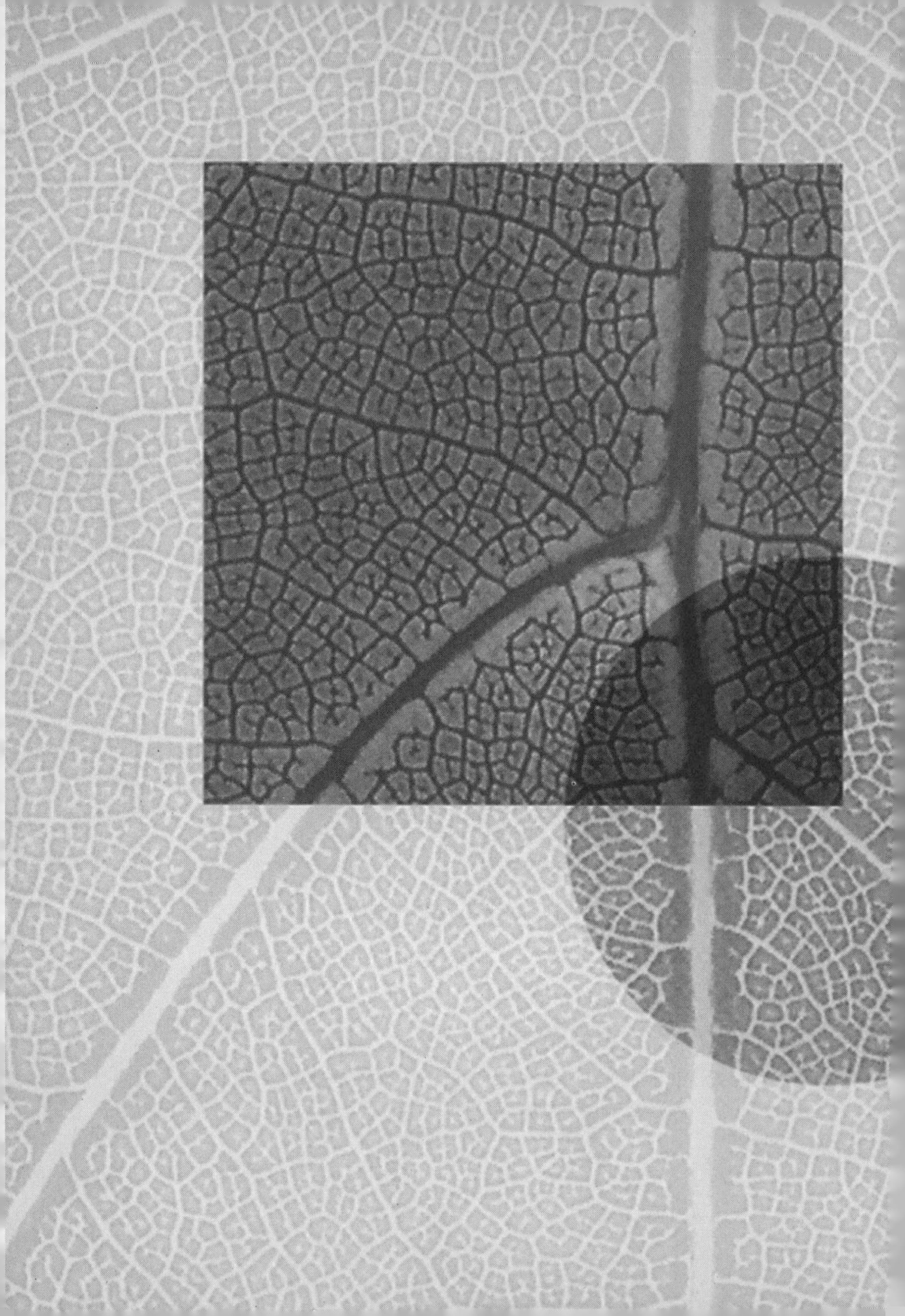

Chapter 22

Monitoring and Optimization

The objectives for this portion of the exam cover your ability to use tools to gather information about your network and analyze the data gathered. Your server has a limited amount of resources—just so much memory, hard disk, and CPU with which to play. With those resources, you have to provide certain services to your users—e-mail, shared data, print services, and backups. Once again, the act of managing the environment involves balancing needs against resources.

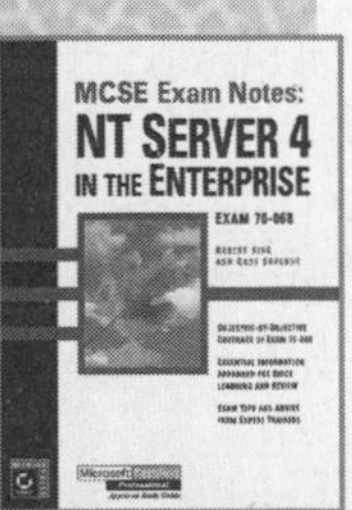

Adapted from *MCSE Exam Notes: NT Server 4 in the Enterprise* by Robert King and Gary Govanus

ISBN 0-7821-2292-2 416 pages $19.99

Establish a baseline for measuring system performance.

Tasks include:

- Creating a database of measurement data

A *baseline* is a set of statistics that can be used for comparison. You should gather a standard set of statistics from your network and servers on a regular basis. This information should be saved so that it can be used to provide trend analyses and plan for future growth over time.

In any given environment, there are four major subsystems—processor, memory, disk, and network. When creating a baseline, you should always start with these subsystems. Then, analyze the other resources that are critical on your server and add them to the list.

Performance Monitor

Performance Monitor is the tool provided by NT to gather statistics at the server. Performance Monitor uses objects and counters to describe the statistics that can be gathered. An object is a subsystem, while a counter is a specific statistic of an object. Performance Monitor has a list of 12 objects that can be monitored. Some software creates its own counters when you install it. Specific objects and counters will be examined later in this chapter. Each of the four main subsystems has an associated object with counters that you should track.

When creating your baseline, you will often want to gather statistics while a specific process happens. Backups, for instance, often strain both the servers involved and the network. Unfortunately, most companies do their backups during nonpeak hours or, in other words, during your personal time. You can use the AT command to start Performance Monitor automatically. The AT command allows you to schedule a start time for any process or application. Using the AT command, you can make Performance Monitor load and begin collecting data automatically. This can come in handy when you want to gather information on a regular basis or you are not available to start the process manually.

Once you've collected your data, you'll want to analyze it. Performance Monitor can save data in a format that many commercial applications can read. When you dump the statistics into a database or spreadsheet, it is called *creating a measurement database.* If you use a database or spreadsheet, it allows you to track information over time. Performance Monitor does not have this innate ability–it shows either current information or statistics since the server was booted. You can easily export Performance Monitor data in a format that a program such as Microsoft Excel can import.

When gathering information, you will often track a lot of counters and check those counters frequently. How often Performance Monitor checks the values of counters you are tracking is called the *interval.* If your interval is set low, NT will gather the values often, which can result in huge data files. Microsoft suggests that after you have analyzed the data, you relog the information with a larger interval. This will reduce the size of the log file, but still leave you information for trend analysis and comparison.

Performance Monitor offers many ways to view the statistics that it gathers.

Chart View

Chart view provides a real-time chart showing the values of the counters you have chosen. The first step is to add the counters to your view, as shown in Figure 22.1. Highlight the appropriate object and then pick a counter from the list.

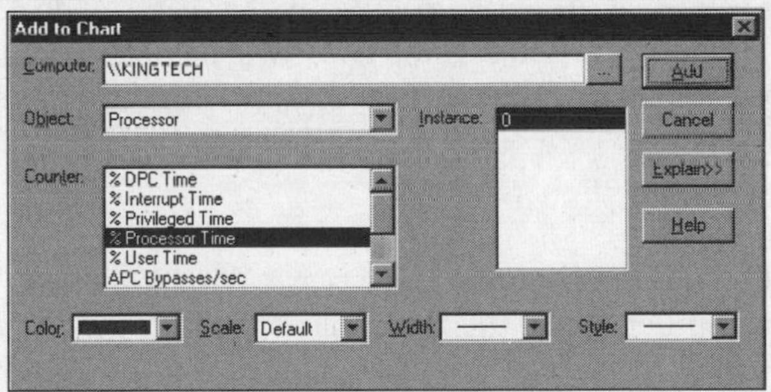

FIGURE 22.1: Add to Chart

When you have added all of the counters you want to chart, click Cancel. The chart will show the value of those counters in real time, as shown in Figure 22.2.

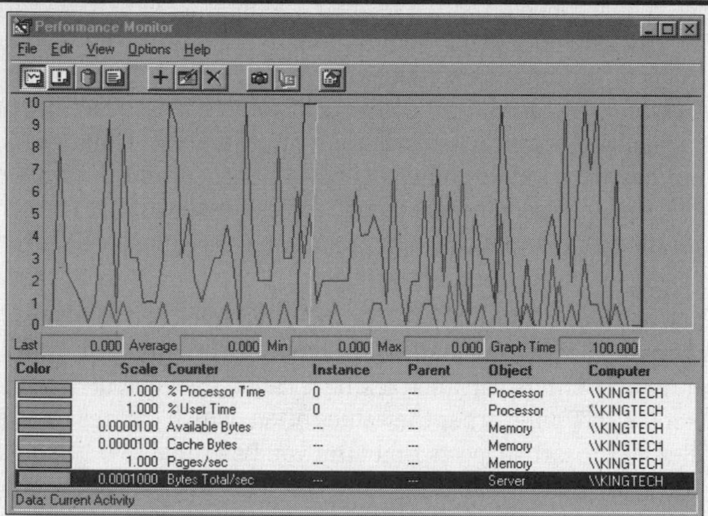

FIGURE 22.2: A real-time Performance Monitor chart

Report View

Report view shows the same information as Chart view. However, with Report view, the values are shown in the form of a text-based report. As in Chart view, the report data are updated in real time.

Log View

Log view allows you to save the data to a file. In Log view, you do not pick counters—all counters for the objects you chose will be tracked. Rather than the data being shown as they are collected, the data are saved to a file for later analysis.

Alert View

Alert view is different from the other three views. With Alert view, you set a threshold for a counter. When this threshold is reached, you can make Performance Monitor run an application that pages you, for instance.

This objective primarily concerns your ability to use Performance Monitor. You must understand the available options before taking the exam.

Creating a Baseline Using Performance Monitor

To build a baseline, you use the Log view in Performance Monitor. First, pick the objects that you want to track. Remember to start with the four main subsystems. At a minimum, you will want to track processor, memory, disk, and whatever objects are available for protocols in use on your network. Save this log to a file. You will use this file–the baseline–as a basis for comparison. Performance Monitor can use this file later as the input material for graphs or reports.

Relogging Your Data at a Longer Interval

Use the Log view in Performance Monitor.

1. Choose Options ➢ Data from.
2. Choose Log File and browse to your baseline log file.
3. Build the log again, using the same steps as before–only this time, change the interval.
4. When you start the log, it will save information at the new interval, reducing the size of the log file.

WARNING

Although this method is great for archiving trends, the resulting log file contains less accurate data. Since you have reduced the sampling rate, the resulting information will be less detailed in terms of time.

Exporting Information to Another Program

Build a chart using your log file. Choose File ➢ Export Chart. Save the chart in a format your application can import.

Monitor performance of various functions by using Performance Monitor.

Functions include:

- Processor
- Memory
- Disk
- Network

This Exam Objective is covered in Part 2: NT Server 4, Chapter 9 "Monitoring and Optimization." The Practice Exam at the end of Part 4 will test you on this material.

Monitor network traffic by using Network Monitor.

Tasks include:

- Collecting data
- Presenting data
- Filtering data

Network Monitor allows you to capture and analyze the packets flowing through your network. Unlike Performance Monitor, which shows you only the numbers of packets, Network Monitor allows you to page through the captured information to find specific types of communication and even look into the packets to see exactly what's happening on your network.

Network Monitor

The opening screen of Network Monitor, shown in Figure 22.3, is divided into four panes. Each pane provides a specific type of information.

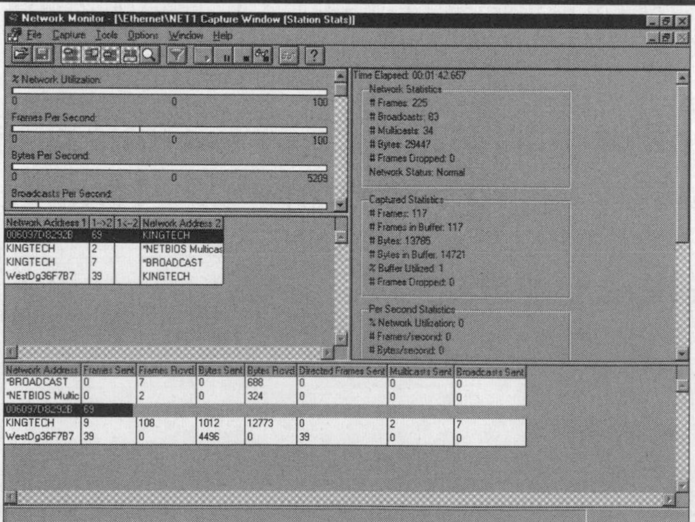

FIGURE 22.3: Network Monitor

- Graph pane–Displays current activity.
- Session Statistics pane–Displays summary information about communication between two machines.
- Summary Statistics pane–Displays information about the data capture in progress.
- Station Statistics pane–Displays a summary of the traffic generated by each host.

This is another section in which the objective concerns your ability to use a particular tool.

Collecting Data

Network Monitor can capture the traffic on your network. To start this process, choose Capture ➢ Start. When the desired sampling interval has passed, choose Capture ➢ Stop.

Presenting Data

Oncc traffic has been captured, you can analyze its content. Choose Capture ➢ Display Captured Data. The data will be displayed in the order in which it was captured. When you double-click any packet, it will bring up three additional panes in the view.

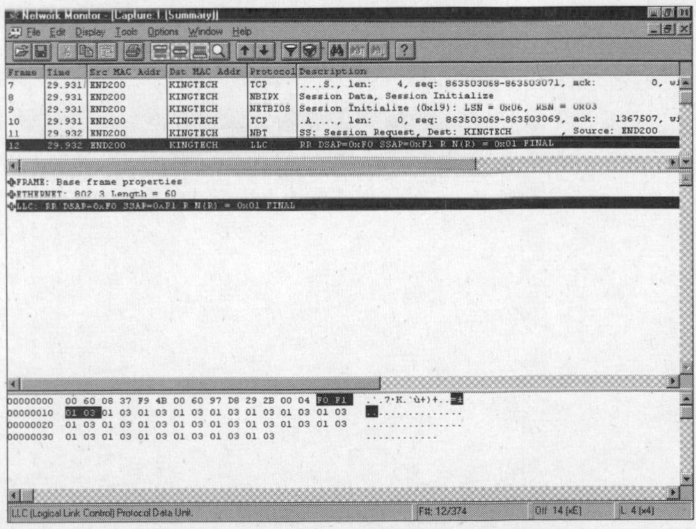

Part IV

- The Summary (top) pane gives a summary of the traffic generated, including the protocol used, the sender and destination addresses, and a short description of the purpose.
- The Detail (middle) pane displays the contents of the highlighted packet in a text format. This is where you can analyze the contents of each packet.
- The Hex (bottom) pane shows the contents of the packet in hex and ASCII format.

Filtering Data

When you do a generic capture of the data on your network, it can create a large amount of data. Often, the amount of data presented can make it difficult to find whatever you are looking for. Network Monitor can filter the data as they are collected or as presented from the captured packets.

Filtering Data as They Are Collected

To specify the types of data to be included in your capture, choose Capture ➢ Filter. You will then be able to filter the packets collected by either address or protocol.

Filtering Data as Presented

View the captured data and choose Display ➢ Filter. You will be presented with the Display Filter dialog box, which will allow you to reduce the captured database using a number of options.

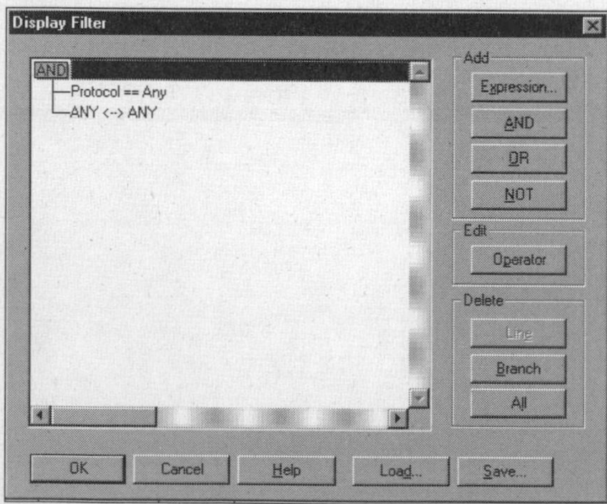

When you're done, you have the fastest network money can buy. Unfortunately, this network has as much in common with a normal business environment as an Indy 500 race car has with your family minivan.

The first step in optimization is to purchase hardware and software that are designed for the functions that they will perform in *your* network. The second step is to determine the minimum acceptable level of performance mandated by your environment. If your network will be used to do real-time reservations for a large airline company, you would need high bandwidth and redundancy. If your network will be used to do nightly updates of plant inventory, you could probably get by with less bandwidth and slower hardware.

Controlling Network Traffic

There are three main ways to optimize network traffic:

- Reduce the amount of traffic by removing an unnecessary service.
- Add services that reduce the amount of time it takes for users to accomplish a task. (Note that this might actually increase the amount of traffic generated.)
- Reduce or control the frequency of the traffic that is generated.

For each type of traffic, the methods that can be used to optimize your network will be discussed. For the examination, you will be required to understand the purpose of the traffic, the number of packets generated, and the frequency with which the traffic is generated. At the end of this section, you will find a table that summarizes this information.

Client-Initialization Traffic

The first type of traffic that will be discussed is the traffic that might be generated when a client attaches to the network or attempts to connect to another workstation or server computer. There are two things to remember about this type of traffic: it is usually not a significant percentage of your overall network load and it is necessary if your clients are going to use your network. Because of this, in the real world, most administrators do not spend a lot of time analyzing this type of burst, high-volume traffic that occurs infrequently for short periods of time—the reduction in traffic is usually not worth the amount of time that would be spent in optimization.

You can then choose to limit either the computers involved i munication or the protocols that will be displayed. If you double Protocol == Any line, you will be presented with the expression-b windows shown below.

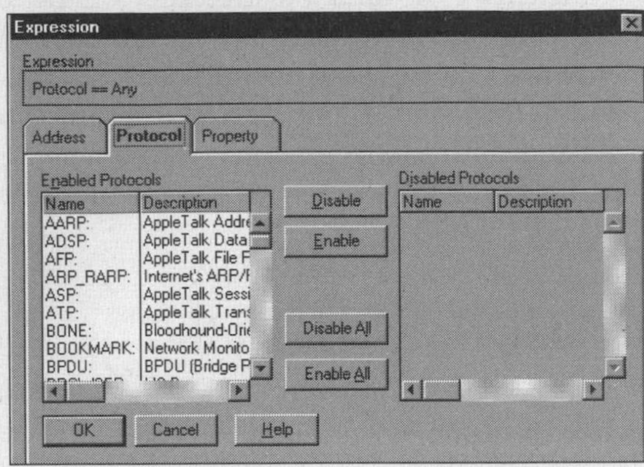

In these windows, you can enable or disable the presentation of any protocol.

Identify performance bottlenecks.

This Exam Objective is covered in Part 2: NT Server 4, Chapter 9 "Monitoring and Optimization." The Practice Exam at the end of Part 4 will test you on this material.

Optimize performance for various results.

Results include:

- Controlling network traffic
- Controlling server load

Most administrators would define *optimization* as the act of configuring a component for maximum performance. The problem is that this is not a complete definition of the term. You throw high-end components into your environment and spend hours tweaking configuration parameters.

DHCP Traffic

Dynamic host configuration protocol (DHCP) is both a protocol and a service. It is an industry standard way to configure clients with TCP/IP configuration data such as IP addresses and subnet masks from a central server. There are two major types of traffic associated with DHCP: lease acquisition and lease renewal. Neither of these two types of traffic generates enough packets on the wire to be considered significant.

Each time a DHCP client initializes, it must contact the DHCP server to acquire its IP configuration. This process generates four packets on the network.

All DHCP acquisition traffic is accomplished through broadcast packets. There are two reasons for this. First, until the acknowledgment is received, the client does not have an IP address, so packets cannot be addressed directly to it. Second, all DHCP servers respond to the discovery packet if they receive it, which means that each DHCP server has earmarked an IP address for the client. When they receive the broadcast acknowledgment packet, they know that the client has accepted an address. If it is not theirs, the DHCP server can free up that address for another client.

If you use Network Monitor to view the contents of the DHCP packets, you will notice the following things:

- The Ethernet destination is set to FFFFFFFF. This denotes a broadcast packet.
- The IP source address is set to 0.0.0.0, and the IP destination address is set to 255.255.255.255. This combination alerts the DHCP server that it should process the packet.
- The UDP source and destination ports are listed as the BOOTP port.

Two frames will be generated to renew the lease. This will happen each time the client starts up or when half of the lease duration has been reached.

DHCP traffic has such a small impact on the network—four packets to acquire an address and then two packets to renew—that most administrators do not exert a lot of effort to optimize this service. There are, however, a couple of techniques to optimize this service of which you should be aware:

- Reduce the renewal traffic by increasing the lease duration.

- If your router is configured to pass BOOTP packets, you can usually configure the router with a retry count. This parameter configures the router to pass the packet only if the request has been outstanding for a specified period of time. This gives all local DHCP servers the chance to answer the client request before that request is passed to another subnet.

WINS Client Traffic

Windows Internet network server (WINS) is a service loaded at an NT server. It provides two very important functions for your network: It acts as a registration agent for NetBIOS names, effectively preventing duplicate names on your network, and it builds a database of NetBIOS names and IP addresses that can be used to resolve a computer name into its IP address. By using a WINS server, you reduce the amount of broadcast traffic on your network and allow browsing across a routed network.

There are four types of WINS traffic generated: registration, renewal, resolution, and release.

Registration During the initialization of a WINS client, it will contact the WINS server to register its NetBIOS name. The WINS server will search its database to confirm that the requested name is not already in use on the network. If the name is in use, the WINS server will return a negative response to the client.

The importance of this becomes apparent when you compare it to the process used in a non-WINS environment. Without a WINS server, the client will announce itself on the local subnet by broadcasting a packet. This packet announces the computer to the network. If another computer on the local subnet is using the name being announced, the local subnet will respond with a negative acknowledgment, telling the client that it cannot use the name with which it was configured. There are two major problems with this procedure. First, it adds broadcast traffic on the local subnet—traffic that all other computers must process. Second, since it is a broadcast packet, most routers will not pass it to other subnets. This results in an environment where duplicate names can exist on the network.

Renewal When a client registers its name with a WINS server, the server returns a lease duration. Like DHCP, this lease must be renewed on a regular basis to ensure that the WINS server's database of names is up to date. The client will begin the renewal process when half of the lease duration has passed. This is a two-packet process.

Resolution The WINS server also acts as a name-resolution database. When one NetBIOS computer needs to communicate with another, it sends a request to the WINS server. The server looks through its database to find the record for the requested computer. If it finds a record, it returns the IP address to the requesting computer. This process generates two packets on the network—a request and an answer.

Release The WINS database is supposed to contain records for computers that are online and available. Unlike DHCP, though, when a WINS client is properly shut down, one of the last things it does is send a packet to the WINS server releasing its lease on its registered NetBIOS names. This alerts the WINS server to remove those records from its database. This process consists of two packets for each name the computer has registered.

Since WINS generates such a small amount of traffic on the network, you probably won't spend a lot of time optimizing your clients. There are, however, a few steps you can take should the need arise:

- Remember that each client must register a unique name for each service that it provides. One way to reduce the amount of WINS traffic is to disable unnecessary services at your clients. This has the added benefit of reducing the size of the WINS database—which will help reduce the server-to-server traffic. That traffic will be discussed later in this section.
- You can also increase the NetBIOS name-cache parameter. Each time a name is resolved, the client will put it in its NetBIOS name cache. By default, this information is stored for 10 minutes. After 10 minutes have passed, the client will have to resolve the IP address again. Unfortunately, you must edit the registry to change this parameter. The registry setting is as follows:

  ```
  HKEY_LOCAL_MACHINE\SYSTEM\CurrentControlSet\Services\
  NetBT\Parameters\CacheTimeOut
  ```

- You can also configure a text file at each client, called the LMHOSTS file, that contains the NetBIOS name and IP addresses of computers the client is likely to communicate with. You can have these entries preload during initialization. Preloaded entries are placed in cache permanently, foregoing the need to use the WINS server to resolve the name.

- You can also increase the lease time for registered names. However, this choice doesn't make a lot of sense. By default, the lease duration is three days. This means that renewal traffic is two packets every one-and-a-half days. If you increase the duration, it will reduce the frequency of this action—but it will also take the WINS server longer to remove records from its database if a machine is not shut down correctly.

File-Session Traffic

Except when using broadcast-based services, computers must establish a "session" before communication can occur. The amount of traffic generated is not significant, but if you understand the process, it can help when you are analyzing other types of traffic. File-session traffic can be divided into the following six areas: address resolution, TCP session establishment, NetBIOS session establishment, SMB protocol negotiation, connection sequence, and session termination.

The six types of file-session traffic are used to manage the connection between two computers for data transfer. Because of this, the amount of network bandwidth utilized is usually negligible when compared to the overall transaction. The size of the actual files transferred will determine the amount of traffic generated for the process.

Address Resolution Once the host or NetBIOS name has been resolved to an IP address, using one of the methods discussed earlier, the IP address must be resolved to a hardware or MAC (media access control) address. This process is called address resolution, and it utilizes ARP (address resolution protocol) to accomplish the task. Basically, the computer sends a request to the destination computer asking for its hardware address. The destination computer replies with the requested information. Both computers then move this information into their respective ARP caches so that address resolution will not have to occur for every packet. This is a two-packet process, which occurs the first time the computers attempt to communicate.

TCP Session Establishment Once the MAC address has been acquired, a TCP session must be established. This is known as the TCP *three-way handshake.* Three packets are involved—a request to communicate, an acknowledgment of the request, and an acknowledgment of the acknowledgment. This process occurs only once between the client and the server. Multiple file connections can be established over the same TCP session.

NetBIOS Session Establishment Once the TCP session has been built, a NetBIOS session must be established. Basically, you are working your way up the OSI model, ensuring that communication can occur. As in the TCP session, this process occurs only once, because multiple file sessions can be established of the same NetBIOS session. This is a two-packet process.

SMB (Server Message Block) Protocol Negotiation The next step is for the two computers to agree upon an SMB version to use in communication. SMB is the language spoken internally by the operating system. Like any other piece of mature software, SMB has gone through numerous revisions and updates. The client sends a list of all SMB versions or dialects that it understands. The server looks through the list and returns a packet identifying the highest revision that both computers can utilize. This will be the SMB dialect that is used in communication between the two machines. This process occurs once, while the file session is being established. It generates two packets on the network.

Connection Sequence The last step in the file-session establishment is for the client to connect to the shared resource on the server. This process will generate a varying amount of traffic depending upon the length of the names of share points and the SMB options that are used.

Session Termination When the data have been transferred, the client will disconnect from the server's resource. This generates two packets of traffic. When the client disconnects from the last resource on the server, the TCP session will be terminated. The termination involves another three-way handshake and generates three packets of network traffic.

Optimizing File-Session Traffic There are two main methods of optimizing file-session traffic. First, remove all unnecessary protocols. Session requests are sent over all protocols simultaneously, so if you remove unused protocols, it can significantly reduce the amount of file-session traffic on the network. Second, ensure that the data users' access is located on a server near them (on the same TCP/IP subnet). While this does not reduce the amount of traffic generated, it does reduce the amount of traffic that must be routed across multiple network segments.

Logon-Validation Traffic

Before a user can take advantage of the resources on the network, they must log onto the network. This process is called logon-validation. The domain controllers in your NT domain handle this process. The relative impact of validation traffic on your network depends upon many variables. When designing your network, you will have to determine the number of domain controllers needed and the appropriate placement of those servers on your network. You will also have to think about when this traffic occurs—do all users log on at 8:00 A.M. every morning, or will logon traffic be randomly generated throughout the day?

Logon-validation traffic can be divided into four categories: finding a logon server, preparation, validation, and session termination.

Finding a Logon Server Before the logon process can begin, the client must find a logon server (domain controller). There are two ways that this can be accomplished—through a broadcast request or through a query of a WINS server. The preferred method is, of course, using a Microsoft WINS server.

Preparation The next step in the process is the establishment of a session between the client and the server. This is the same process used for establishing a file session.

Validation Once the session is established, validation can proceed. On a Windows 95 client, this will entail approximately four packets. On a Windows NT client, more traffic will be generated because the server must return a list of trusted domains to the client.

Session Termination Upon completion of the logon process, the session must be terminated. This will generate approximately five frames of network traffic.

Numerous techniques can be used to optimize logon-validation traffic:

- Determine the number of domain controllers needed for your network. Microsoft estimates that one domain controller should be available for every 2,000 users. This should ensure that no domain controller is overwhelmed by the validation traffic. A couple of Performance Monitor counters can help determine the logon workload being placed on a server. *Server: logons/sec* monitors the number of logon attempts, both successful and unsuccessful, each second; *Server: logons total* monitors the total number of logon requests handled by a server since the last start-up.

- By default, NT servers are configured to maximize throughput for file sharing. While this is appropriate for a file and print server, it is not necessarily the best configuration for a domain controller. In the Network applet in Control Panel, you can change this configuration to maximize throughput for network applications. This should increase the number of logon requests the server can handle from 6 to 7 per second to around 20.
- Place domain controllers so that they are near users. This reduces the amount of logon traffic that must be routed across multiple subnets or slow WAN links.
- Ensure that your server meets the hardware requirements for the task. Use your knowledge of Performance Monitor to ensure that no bottlenecks slow down the validation process.

Client-Server Traffic Now that the client has initialized and logon-validation has occurred, the other client-to-server traffic that will be generated on your network can be examined. Three types of traffic generate a predictable amount of traffic between the server and the client: browser, domain name system (DNS), and intranet.

Browser Traffic Browser traffic is generated by a server when announcing itself to the network and by clients when retrieving the browse list. The entire process will be examined later in this section.

There are various ways to optimize the browser traffic on your network:

- Disable unnecessary server service components. Remember that every computer that can act as a server must announce itself to the network every 12 minutes. These computers are also added to the browse list, increasing its size. Every server adds at least 27 bytes to the browse list.
- Control the number of potential browsers on your network. The number of backup browsers is determined automatically by the browser service on the master browser. When the master browser determines that an additional backup browser is needed, it will choose from the list of potential browsers. You can control which computers will be considered for this function, thus ensuring that only computers with the necessary bandwidth will be chosen. By

default, all Microsoft computers on the network are potential browsers. You change this default setting in different ways depending upon the operating system in use. In NT you edit the registry, changing the value of `HKEY_LOCAL_MACHINE\SYSTEM\CurrentControlSet\Services\Browser\Parameters\MaintainServerList` to No. On a Windows 95-based computer, use the Network applet in Control Panel to disable the master browser parameter. On a Microsoft Windows for Workgroups computer, edit the SYSTEM.INI file and add MaintainServerList = NO to the [network] section.

- Eliminate all unnecessary network protocols. All browser traffic is initiated on all protocols. Reducing the number of protocols in use can greatly reduce the amount of traffic generated.

DNS Traffic DNS traffic is generated by using a domain name server to resolve host names. When users try to access a resource using TCP/IP commands, such as PING or a Web browser, the host name must be resolved to an IP address. This process, called host name resolution, can be accomplished using DNS.

DNS is a database that contains the host name and IP address of all hosts that can be resolved using the DNS process. Unlike WINS, the DNS database is static in nature–the administrator must manually create records in the DNS database for each host, and these records are available whether or not the host is online.

Three types of DNS traffic will affect your network:

Lookups–In the best of worlds, a DNS lookup consists of two packets: a request from the client and an answer from the DNS server. Since the client is configured with the IP address of the DNS server, all traffic is handled using directed, rather than broadcast, packets. After obtaining the IP address from the server, the client can then initiate communication with the destination host.

DNS recursion–If the DNS server does not contain the requested IP address, it must pass the request to another DNS server. This process is called a *recursive query.* The DNS server will act on behalf of the client, asking another DNS server for the requested information. If it receives an answer, it will return the IP address to the client.

Integration with WINS—Keeping the DNS database can be a hassle on a busy network. Every time you add a computer, move a computer, change an IP address, or make any other changes to your IP network, you must manually enter these changes into the DNS database. Another drawback to DNS is that the database does not indicate which computers are currently available on the network. A client could conceivably go through the process of host name resolution only to receive an error while trying to communicate with a machine that is not currently available. To avoid these drawbacks, Microsoft allows you to configure DNS to query the WINS database. Remember that the WINS database has a record for each computer currently available that includes the NetBIOS name and IP address of each machine. When the DNS server receives a request for a host that is not found in its database, it will convert the host name into a NetBIOS name and submit it to the WINS server. The WINS server will check its database for a corresponding IP address.

To optimize DNS traffic, you can do the following things:

- Do not configure your DNS servers for recursive lookups. While configuring your DNS servers for recursive lookups would reduce the amount of traffic, it severely curtails the effectiveness of DNS. If a DNS server does not contain the requested information, it will return an error to the client rather than attempting to find the information on another DNS server.
- Configure your clients so that the DNS server they use is most likely to have the information they need. Basically, this reduces the need for recursive lookups.
- Increase the TTL (time to live) setting on your DNS server. Each time a name is resolved, the DNS server moves the host name and IP address into cache. When a client makes a request, the first place DNS looks is in this cache. If the information is available, the DNS server will not need to look any further. If you increase the TTL from the default 60 minutes, it will reduce the number of recursive lookups.

Intranet Browsing Traffic Intranet browsing traffic is generated by a Web browser when downloading information from a Web server. Browsing a Web server can generate a lot of traffic on your network. Unfortunately, there is no way to characterize the traffic generated while downloading each page. However, certain aspects of the traffic will be the same no matter what the content is of the Web pages accessed.

Connecting to a Web site—Before you can download the content of a Web page, you must establish a TCP session to the Web server. This session is established in the same way as any other TCP session—the three-way handshake.

Requesting a Web page—Once the TCP session has been established, the user can begin the process of requesting information, usually in the form of pages. Web pages are requested using the HTTP protocol. Using HTTP, the browser must issue a "get" command for a page and another get command for each image or graphic that is part of that page. Each get command constitutes a separate packet of communication.

Browsing security—Most Web server software, including Microsoft's Internet Information Server (IIS), can be configured to use some sort of authentication process to control access to information. While this will add overhead to your network, both in network traffic and in processing, the type of information stored on the Web server might mandate it.

Web browsing, even on an intranet, can add a significant amount of traffic to your network. There are a few common-sense rules that you should follow to control the impact of this technology:

- Keep Web pages small. Good Web design takes advantage of linking in HTML documents. Users will download only the pages they request—a small opening page with well-defined links to other pages will reduce the amount of information that a user will have to download.
- Limit the number and size of images. While the graphical interface of Web technologies is what has made them so popular, images make up a large percentage of the download on many pages. Many sites mandate both a text- and a graphics-based page so that users can determine the type of information that they will see.
- Increase the size of the local cache at the client. Each time a client accesses a Web page, the browser looks in its cache to see if it already has the page available. The larger this cache is, the more

likely it is that the user will receive a page from the local cache rather than having to access the Web server.

- Think about security. If your information is intended to be public, allow anonymous connections. If you have information that is not intended to be public, implement Web security, but be aware of the access costs.

Server-to-Server Traffic

Another type of traffic that will be generated on your network is traffic between servers as they carry out network maintenance tasks. While these functions do not usually generate a significant amount of traffic, you should be aware of each type of traffic, its function on the network, and its frequency. Six types of server-to-server traffic will be discussed: account synchronization, trust relationships, server browsing, WINS replication, directory replication, and DNS server.

Account Synchronization In a Microsoft Windows NT network, a domain controller—either the primary (PDC) or a backup (BDC)—authenticates user logon attempts. All changes to the accounts database must occur on the PDC. The PDC will, in turn, update the information stored on the BDCs. The process of updating the account database on a BDC is called account synchronization.

The traffic involved in account synchronization can be divided into five types:

Find PDC—Each time a BDC is started, it must find the name of the PDC for its network. This information is placed in cache, so this process occurs only once. Four packets are generated on the network.

Session establishment—Once the NetBIOS name and IP address of the PDC are found, the BDC will establish both TCP and NetBIOS sessions with the PDC. This process is the same as discussed earlier.

Secure-channel establishment—Next, the BDC must establish a secure channel to the PDC. This process generates approximately eight packets of network traffic and is done only once. This channel is held open until one machine or another goes offline.

Verify database—The BDC sends the version ID for each of the SAM databases to the PDC. The PDC compares this value with its own version of those files. If the BDC is out of date, the PDC will initiate the synchronization process.

Announcement of change—Every five minutes, the PDC looks for changes to any of the three databases that make up the SAM. When a change is noted, the PDC sends a message to each BDC notifying them that a change has occurred. Each BDC will then request the updated information from the NETLOGON service of the PDC.

Two types of updates can occur—partial and full. In a partial update, only the changed information is sent to the BDC. In a full update, the entire SAM database is sent to the BDC. In most cases, it is preferable to do a partial update because this reduces the amount of traffic involved in the process.

The PDC keeps a log of all changes to the SAM. This log is of a fixed size (by default, it is 64KB) and will hold approximately 2,000 changes, depending on the size of the changes. Each change is given a version ID—think of this as a counter. The PDC keeps track of the highest version ID sent to each BDC. When it notes a change to the SAM, it compares the version ID of the change with the version ID of the last change sent to each BDC. If the version ID is higher than the last one sent, the PDC will notify the BDC of the change and a partial update will occur.

Occasionally, there will be more than 2,000 changes between updates. When this occurs, the change log will "wrap" or begin overwriting change information. When the PDC checks version IDs, it will notice that wrapping has occurred and institute a full update to the BDC.

You can change various registry parameters to optimize this traffic (see Table 22.1).

Each of these parameters will be found in the following area of the registry:

```
HKEY_LOCAL_MACHINE\CurrentControlSet\Services\Netlogon\
Parameters
```

TABLE 22.1: Synchronization Parameters in the Registry

Registry Parameter	Description
Pulse	Determines how often the PDC checks for changes in the SAM databases. The default value is 5 minutes. It can be set as high as 48 hours. Be very careful when increasing this value because a long interval could result in BDCs not being updated in a timely manner.
Pulse-Maximum	Determines how often the PDC will send a message to each BDC even if no changes have occurred to the SAM database. The default is every 2 hours. This parameter can be set as high as every 48 hours.
Change Log-Size	Controls the number of changes to the SAM that can be stored. By default, this log has a maximum size of 64KB, or enough room to store approximately 2,000 changes. If you increase the size of the change log, it will reduce the number of full updates to the BDCs.
Pulse-Concurrency	By default, the PDC can send out change notifications to only 10 BDCs simultaneously. If you increase this number, the BDCs will be updated faster, but the process will use more network bandwidth. If you decrease this value, it spreads the synchronization process over a longer period of time.
Replication Governor	Controls two aspects of the synchronization process—the amount of bandwidth that it can utilize and the amount of data that can be transferred. The default value is 100. This means that the synchronization process can use 100 percent of the available bandwidth and each transfer can be up to 128KB of data. If you set this number to 50, it would indicate that the NETLOGON service can use only 50 percent of the available bandwidth and can transfer only 64KB of data in a single synchronization process. If you set this value too low, it can result in the BDCs never fully synchronizing with the PDC.

Trust Relationships There really isn't a lot of traffic generated to maintain an existing trust relationship. Most of the traffic will be generated when you access resources across the trust. Three types of traffic are specific to the trust relationship: establish trust, import accounts, and pass-through authentication.

Establish trust–There are three steps to establishing a trust relationship between two domains. First, the trusted domain must permit the trusting domain to trust it. This will generate synchronization traffic as the PDC lets the BDCs know that the trust has been permitted. The trust is added as a hidden user in the SAM database, and this record must be synchronized to all BDCs. Second, the trusting domain must add the first domain as a trusted domain. It must find the name and address of the trusted PDC, establish TCP and NetBIOS sessions with that PDC, attempt to connect to the PDC (this first attempt will fail because the trust account is not yet valid, but it validates the creation of an account in the trusted domain), and then retrieve a list of all backup browsers and servers in the trusted domain. Finally, the trusting PDC will query WINS for a list of all domain controllers in the trusted domain. This traffic is generated only once during the establishment of the trust relationship. Once the relationship is established, very little traffic is generated to maintain the relationship. Basically, every time the trusting PDC is restarted, it must query WINS for a list of domain controllers in the trusted domain. Additionally, every seven days, the two domains change the password assigned to the trust relationship.

Import accounts–One of the main reasons to establish a trust relationship between two domains is to allow users from the trusted account access to resources in the trusting account. In User Manager for Domains, the administrator of the trusting domain can see a list of users and groups from the trusted domain. Every time this list is viewed, the list must be retrieved from a domain controller in the trusted domain. This can generate a lot of network traffic depending upon the number of user and group accounts defined in the trusted domain.

Pass-through authentication–The most frequent form of traffic generated across a trust relationship is pass-through authentication. If a user from the trusted domain sits down at an NT-based machine defined in the trusting domain and attempts to log in, the following things will occur:

1. The NETLOGON service will query a domain controller for a list of trusted domains.

2. The user picks their home domain from the drop-down list.

3. The NETLOGON service passes the logon request to a domain controller for its own domain.
4. That domain controller recognizes that the user's account exists in a trusted domain and passes the request to a domain controller in the trusted domain.
5. That domain controller authenticates the user and passes the security information for the user back to the domain controller in the trusting domain.
6. The domain controller in the trusting domain passes the security information to the NT computer from which the user is attempting to log on.

NOTE

Notice that the domain controller from the trusting domain "trusts" the authentication information from the trusted domain. This is known as pass-through authentication.

Another type of pass-through authentication occurs when a user tries to access a resource in a trusting domain. Since the trusting domain does not contain the user's account information, the same process will take place.

There are two main ways to optimize the traffic generated by trust relationships–reduce the number of trusts and assign permissions to groups rather than individuals.

Server Browsing For the MCSE examination, you will need to know what types of traffic are generated to maintain the browse list. Browser traffic can have a great impact on your network. Microsoft estimates that server browser traffic makes up approximately 51 percent of the "maintenance" traffic on your network. Because of this large percentage, it is imperative that you understand how the browser service operates.

Five types of browser traffic are generated in a Microsoft Windows NT network:

- Host announcements
- Local master announcements
- Workgroup announcements

- Elections
- Browse list exchanges

Before the individual types of traffic can be discussed, how the browser service works needs to be reviewed. First, a single domain environment will be discussed.

Each computer that has a server component configured will announce itself at boot and every 12 minutes thereafter. This announcement is made using a broadcast packet. The computer expects to receive a response from the segment's master browser. If no master browser responds, the computer will force the election of one.

There is a master browser on each network segment. The master browser collects and answers each computer announcement. It places the information contained in the announcement into a database. There are a few rules about which machines will become the master browser on a network segment. First, the PDC will always be the master browser for the segment to which it is attached. If there is no PDC on a segment, a list of election criteria will determine which machine will become the master browser. These criteria work their way down from NT Server to Windows for Workgroups–with the latest operating system having the highest criterion.

The master browser will then appoint a certain number of machines to act as backup browsers. These computers get a copy of the browse list from the master browser. This list is updated every 12 minutes.

The PDC is not only the master browser for its segment; it may also be the domain master browser–receiving the browse list of all master browsers in the network. It correlates this information into a domain browser list and then sends the domain list to all of the master browsers. The master browsers contact the domain master browser every 12 minutes to update their information.

Stop and analyze this arrangement. Basically, you have a computer on each network segment funneling information about the computers on its segment to a central location (the domain master browser). This machine, in turn, correlates the information from all over the network into a master list and sends it back to a computer on each segment. This is how the browse list is kept current. Now, think about the timing involved–these lists are exchanged every 12 minutes. This explains why a machine booted on a segment might not appear in the browse list for quite some time.

To make this even more complicated, there is a master browser on each segment for every domain that has machines on that segment. In other words, a particular network segment might have multiple master browsers—one for each domain represented by a computer. These master browsers announce their presence to each other with a broadcast packet every 12 minutes.

Now that you understand how the browse list is maintained, you need to understand how it is used by a client. When a user clicks Network Neighborhood, they see a list of all computers that have a server component configured. First, they must find out which computer is the master browser on their segment. They can either broadcast this request or query a WINS server. Once they have this information, they will ask the master browser for a list of backup browsers on their network segment. They will then ask a backup browser for the current list.

All in all, the traffic generated can have a pretty big impact on your network. You will probably look for ways to optimize this process. There are three methods of which you need to be aware:

- Reduce the number of protocols in use on your network. All browser traffic is generated on *all* protocols.
- Reduce the number of entries in the browse list. Disable the server service on computers that do not need to share resources.
- You can configure a couple of registry parameters. Both are found in the `HKEY_LOCAL_MACHINE\SYSTEM\CurrentControlSet\Services\Browser\Parameters` subkey. The first parameter is the MasterPeriodicity parameter. This parameter specifies how often a master browser contacts the domain master browser. The default is 720 seconds (12 minutes). The second parameter is the BackupPeriodicity parameter. This parameter specifies how often a backup browser contacts the master browser for a fresh copy of the browse list.

WINS Replication The WINS server serves two functions—name registration and name resolution. Computers use the WINS server to ensure that their NetBIOS names are unique on the network and to resolve their NetBIOS names into IP addresses. A single WINS server is sufficient in most LAN environments, but think about how this would work on a WAN. Every time a computer starts, it has to cross the WAN link to register its name. It also has to cross the WAN link to resolve the IP addresses of local hosts. This slows response times, and the ability to communicate with local hosts depends upon the WAN link being up and available. Having a single WINS server on a WAN is clearly not acceptable.

Most companies will configure a WINS server for each physical location. This keeps registration and resolution traffic off their expensive WAN links. However, clients will have no way to resolve the IP addresses of hosts in another physical location. This is where WINS replication comes into play. As an administrator, you can configure the WINS servers to replicate their local information to other WINS servers. In this way, each WINS server can have information about computers across your entire network. This replication process will generate traffic between the WINS servers.

There is no way to quantify the amount of traffic that will be generated by the WINS replication process. The amount depends upon the size of the network, the number of services each computer needs to register, and the number of changes to the WINS database. You will, however, want to optimize this service as much as possible.

The WINS partnership is configured as either a push or a pull relationship. Choosing the correct configuration is the best way to optimize this service.

In a push relationship, each WINS server will notify its partners when a certain number of changes have occurred to its database. Each partner will then request these changes when convenient. In this type of configuration, you have no control over when the replication of data will occur—when the threshold number of changes has been reached, the replication process will begin.

In a pull relationship, you configure each WINS server to request changes from its partner at a specific time interval. With this configuration, you can configure replication so that it occurs during off-peak hours on your network.

Microsoft suggests that you configure WINS servers as push partners within a physical site and pull partners across wide-area links.

Directory Replication The directory replication service allows you to store a master copy of data and automatically update copies of the data on other servers. This service was designed to allow the replication of logon scripts so that users will run the same logon script no matter which domain controller they have attached to for authentication. The amount of traffic generated by this process is fairly slight since logon scripts are usually small files that don't change very often. The process can also be used to replicate other types of data. In this case, the amount of network traffic generated depends upon the amount of data and the frequency with which it is changed.

The replication process is fairly straightforward. The computer that has the master copy is known as the export server. The computer that will receive a copy of the data is known as the import server. The export server checks its data for changes on an interval known as a pulse. By default, the pulse is five minutes. If there are no changes, the export server will send a packet out to the import servers letting them know that it is still up and running as an export server. If there are changes, it will notify the import computers of this fact.

The import computers will then request the changed information from the export server. Each import computer will establish a session with the export server. One of the first things the import computer will request is the NetRemoteTOD (the time of day) of the export server. The import server does this because replication cannot occur if the two servers' clocks are off by more than 10 minutes. The next step is to check various replication parameters and, if all conditions are met, request the changes.

In a normal environment, where replication is used only to replicate logon scripts, you should not need to spend a lot of time optimizing this service. If you are replicating a large amount of data, however, you can do a few things to make the process more efficient.

It is best to have a flat, shallow directory structure for the data being replicated. The replication process checks to see if any file in a directory or its subdirectories has changed. If *any* file has changed, the entire subdirectory will be replicated—not just the file that has changed.

You can change a couple of registry settings to control the frequency of communication between the export and import computers. These registry entries will be found in the `HKEY_LOCAL_MACHINE\SYSTEM\CurrentControlSet\Services\Replicator\Parameters` subkey. The first registry setting is the Interval parameter. This parameter controls how often the export server checks for changes to its data. The second parameter is the pulse. This parameter controls how often the import computer contacts the export server if no communication has occurred. If an import computer has not heard from an export server in *Interval*Pulse* minutes, it will contact the export server and request changes.

Part IV

DNS Server Large companies might have multiple DNS servers on their network. This can provide some fault tolerance to the DNS database and split the DNS workload between servers in a busy environment. With this configuration, one DNS server will be the primary one. It will contain the master copy of DNS. The other servers will be configured as secondary

DNS servers. They will receive a copy of the DNS database from the primary server. The process of replicating the DNS database from the primary to a secondary is called a *zone transfer.*

The overall amount of traffic will vary depending upon the size of the DNS database, but a certain amount of traffic will be generated just managing the zone transfer process. First, the secondary server will query the primary server for changes, generating two packets on the network (query and response). If the response indicates that changes have occurred, the secondary server will then establish a TCP session with the primary DNS server. There is no process for determining which records have changed, so the entire DNS database will be sent to the secondary server.

Three parameters can be set in the DNS Manager tool to optimize the zone transfer process:

Refresh interval–The amount of time the secondary server will wait before querying the primary server to see if changes have occurred. The default is 60 minutes.

Retry interval–The amount of time the secondary server will wait to try the zone transfer in the event of failure. The default is 10 minutes.

Expire time–The amount of time the secondary server will continue to respond to name-resolution queries after it has lost contact with the primary server.

Controlling Server Load

Although Microsoft NT Server is optimized for an average workload, it does not mean that the generic configuration is best for all networks. Luckily, NT offers many ways to optimize its performance for varying network conditions. NT can be optimized for various uses by accessing the properties of the server service. These properties can be found in the Services tab of the Network control panel. Each of the optimization parameters is designed for a different type of server environment:

Minimize Memory Used–Choose this option for servers that will support 10 connections or fewer.

Balance–Optimizes the server for up to 64 simultaneous connections.

Maximize Throughput for File Sharing—Allocates the maximum amount of memory for file-sharing applications. This option should be chosen for servers on a large network.

Maximize Throughput for Network Applications—Optimizes server memory for client/server applications that manage their own memory, such as SQL Server or Exchange Server. This option should be used on servers that support large networks.

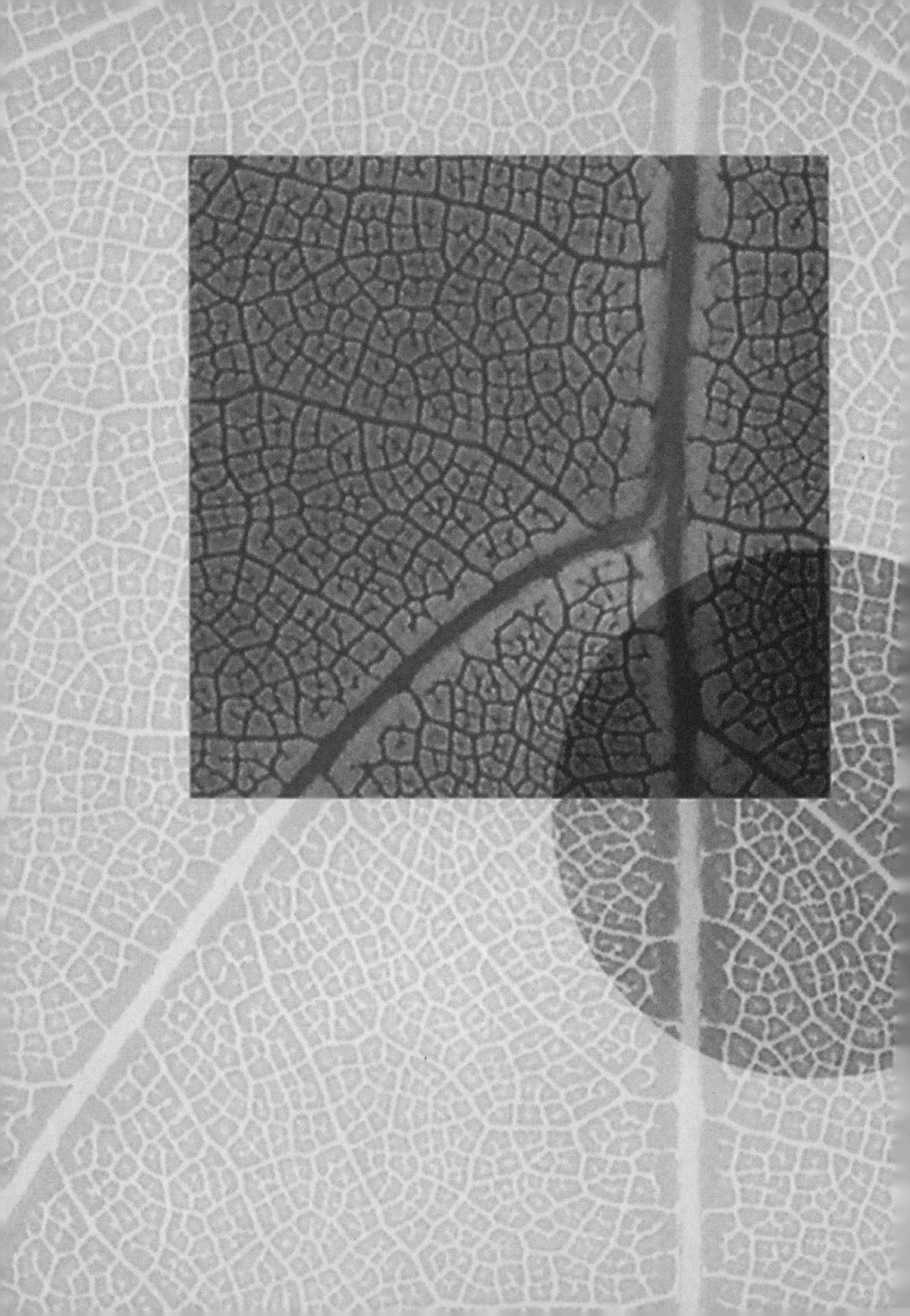

Chapter 23

Troubleshooting

The objectives for this chapter cover the actions you should take to correct a specific set of problems. Some of these problems occur often in the workplace, while others occur rarely. Whether the problems are common or rare, knowing how to correct them is a very big part of being a network administrator. Learning to troubleshoot technical problems is a lifelong process. You can pick up some useful tips by reading books or taking classes, but you can never know everything—experience plays a big role in developing troubleshooting skills. However, this book can act as a starting place to help you build a "troubleshooting database" in your head.

Adapted from *MCSE Exam Notes: NT Server 4 in the Enterprise* by Robert King and Gary Govanus

ISBN 0-7821-2292-2 416 pages $19.99

Choose the appropriate course of action to take to resolve installation failures.

This Exam Objective is covered in Part 2: NT Server 4, Chapter 10 "Troubleshooting." The Practice Exam at the end of Part 4 will test you on this material.

Choose the appropriate course of action to take to resolve boot failures.

This Exam Objective is covered in Part 2: NT Server 4, Chapter 10 "Troubleshooting." The Practice Exam at the end of Part 4 will test you on this material.

Choose the appropriate course of action to take to resolve configuration errors.

Tasks include:

- Backing up and restoring the registry
- Editing the registry

This Exam Objective is covered in Part 2: NT Server 4, Chapter 10 "Troubleshooting." The Practice Exam at the end of Part 4 will test you on this material.

Choose the appropriate course of action to take to resolve printer problems.

This Exam Objective is covered in Part 2: NT Server 4, Chapter 10 "Troubleshooting." The Practice Exam at the end of Part 4 will test you on this material.

Choose the appropriate course of action to take to resolve RAS problems.

This Exam Objective is covered in Part 2: NT Server 4, Chapter 10 "Troubleshooting." The Practice Exam at the end of Part 4 will test you on this material.

Choose the appropriate course of action to take to resolve connectivity problems.

This Exam Objective is covered in Part 2: NT Server 4, Chapter 10 "Troubleshooting." The Practice Exam at the end of Part 4 will test you on this material.

Choose the appropriate course of action to take to resolve resource access and permission problems.

This Exam Objective is covered in Part 2: NT Server 4, Chapter 10 "Troubleshooting." The Practice Exam at the end of Part 4 will test you on this material.

Choose the appropriate course of action to take to resolve fault-tolerance failures.

Fault-tolerance methods include:

- Tape backup
- Mirroring
- Stripe set with parity

This Exam Objective is covered in Part 2: NT Server 4, Chapter 10 "Troubleshooting." The Practice Exam at the end of Part 4 will test you on this material.

Perform advanced problem resolution.

Tasks include:

- Diagnosing and interpreting a blue screen
- Configuring a memory dump
- Using the Event Log service

There is no such thing as a crash-proof server—there are only servers that have yet to meet the set of circumstances necessary to bring them to their knees. When a server crashes, a complex set of circumstances have usually caused the problem. This objective set covers the actions you can take to analyze the situation.

Diagnosing and Interpreting a Blue Screen

When the Microsoft NT operating system encounters a fatal error, it displays a stop screen, often called a blue screen. The blue screen contains debugging information useful in interpreting exactly what was happening at the time of failure. If the system recovery options are turned on, NT will also generate a file with this debugging information.

There are five distinct areas on a blue screen. Each area provides specific information regarding the error or recovery options.

Area One: Debug Port Status Indicators

Later in this section, a process that allows you to dump the debugging information out the serial port to another computer will be examined. This connection is similar to a modem connection. In the upper-right corner of a blue screen, you will see a series of indicators that display the status of this connection (see Table 23.1).

TABLE 23.1: Connection Status Indicators

Status Indicator	Description
MDM	Modem controls are in use
CD	Carrier detected
RI	Ring indicator
DSR	Data set ready
CTS	Clear to send
SND	Byte being sent
RCV	Byte received
FRM	Framing error
OVL	Overflow
PRT	Parity error

Area Two: Bug-Check Information

This area starts with *** Stop. The error code follows *Stop.* There are also up to four developer-defined parameters in parentheses, followed by an interpretation of the error. However, don't get your hopes up on the interpretation. Sometimes, it leads you to the solution of your problem, but more likely it is an obscure message.

Area Three: Driver Information

This area lists information about the drivers loaded at the time of the error. The three columns list the preferred load address, creation date (also known as the link time stamp), and name of the driver. This area can be useful because many blue screens list the address of the instruction that caused the problem. You can compare that information with the preferred load address to determine which driver might have caused the problem.

Area Four: Kernel Build Number and Stack Dump

This area shows two things—the build number of the operating system kernel (the presence of any service packs is not indicated) and a range of addresses that *may* indicate the failed code.

Area Five: Debug Port Information

This area confirms the configuration of the communication port used to dump information to another computer (if configured), and it indicates whether a dump file was created.

Each blue screen has a unique stop code. For information on a particular blue screen, search Microsoft TechNet for the code found in area one.

Configuring a Memory Dump

When an NT server displays a blue screen, it is your responsibility to correct the problem as soon as possible to minimize server downtime. Sometimes, the solution will be obvious from the data displayed. You might also have a good idea of what caused the problem by looking through the server change log and noting recent changes to the server's configuration. When the solution is not obvious, you might have to take more drastic measures—analyzing the memory contents at the time of the blue screen. There are three ways to accomplish this:

Local debugging—In other words, onsite analysis of memory. Two computers—the target (the server with the problem) and the host—are attached using a null modem cable. The host runs debugging software designed to analyze problems in NT.

Remote debugging—Once again, the target and host are connected with a null modem cable. The difference is that Microsoft technical support uses RAS to dial into your system and then analyze the memory contents remotely.

Crash dump—By far, the most common method is to configure NT to dump the contents of memory into a file when the fatal error occurs. You can then send this file to Microsoft technical support for analysis.

To set up the target and host computers, you must have two computers running the same version of NT, including any service packs you have installed. They should be connected by a null modem cable (or you can set up a dial-in connection from the host). The host computer must have the proper symbols files installed. The symbols file contains code used in the debug process. The symbols file must match the build, including service packs, of the target computer.

Once you have met the prerequisites, modify the BOOT.INI file on the target server. Add the /debug switch to the appropriate operating system choice. On the host computer, configure the communication port by setting environmental variables. Next, restart the target computer. When the blue screen is generated, you will be able to debug the problem from the host computer.

It is unlikely that you will actually debug a blue screen. Most administrators do not have the technical knowledge necessary to accomplish this type of task. It is far more likely that you will generate a memory dump file to be sent to Microsoft technical support.

In the System control panel, you will find a Startup/Shutdown tab. On this tab, you can configure NT to perform certain functions when a fatal error is encountered. You can have NT write a message to the system event log, send an administrative alert, write the contents of memory to a file, and automatically reboot the system.

If you choose to have the contents of memory written to a file, the system dumps the contents of RAM into the PAGEFILE.SYS file. When the system restarts, this information is written to a file named MEMORY.DMP. You can then send this file to Microsoft for analysis. Be aware that there is no compression involved in this process, so the dump file will be at least as large as your memory.

NT ships with three tools for processing memory dump files–DUMPFLOP, DUMPCHK, and DUMPEXAM. For the exam, you have to be concerned only with the latter two.

DUMPCHK.EXE–Verifies the contents of a dump file to ensure that it will be readable by a debugger. When you run this program, it can help ensure that you don't waste time uploading a corrupt dump file to Microsoft.

DUMPEXAM.EXE–Analyzes the contents of the dump file and extracts any useful information. This information is placed into a text file that can be considerably smaller than the dump file itself.

Using the Event Log Service

The two main steps in troubleshooting are gathering pertinent information and correlating that information into a plan of actions to correct the problem. A common mistake is to address the symptoms without understanding the underlying cause. NT ships with a great tool—the Event Log—for gathering information about errors on your server.

The Event Log service tracks certain activities on your server and logs information about those events into a series of log files. There are three distinct log files: system, security, and application.

Each log file is responsible for tracking different types of events. Many events will not be tracked unless the system is configured to audit those types of events. The application log tracks application-related events, such as the starting and stopping of application-related services. The security log tracks NT security events, such as logons. The system log tracks events that affect the operating system.

There are also different levels of event messages. Some are purely informational; for instance, an application might generate an event message when it is started. Others are generated when an error is encountered. Still others indicate the failure of a service. For the purpose of troubleshooting, the fatal error messages can be extremely informative.

Figure 23.1 shows the contents of a typical system log. The circle icons with an *i* in them indicate informative messages. The stop-sign icons indicate failure messages.

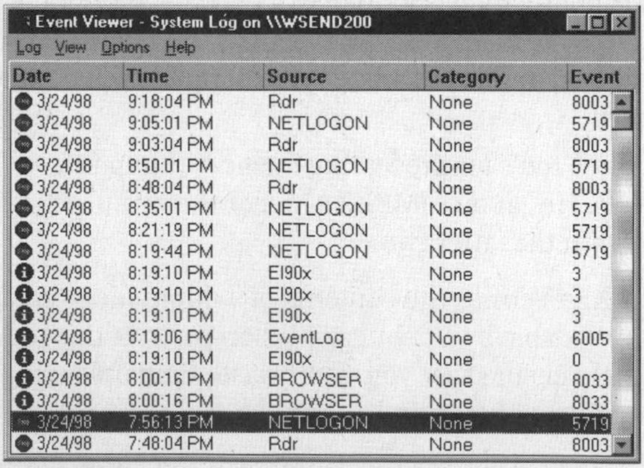

Event Viewer - System Log on \\WSEND200

Log View Options Help

Date	Time	Source	Category	Event
3/24/98	9:18:04 PM	Rdr	None	8003
3/24/98	9:05:01 PM	NETLOGON	None	5719
3/24/98	9:03:04 PM	Rdr	None	8003
3/24/98	8:50:01 PM	NETLOGON	None	5719
3/24/98	8:48:04 PM	Rdr	None	8003
3/24/98	8:35:01 PM	NETLOGON	None	5719
3/24/98	8:21:19 PM	NETLOGON	None	5719
3/24/98	8:19:44 PM	NETLOGON	None	5719
3/24/98	8:19:10 PM	El90x	None	3
3/24/98	8:19:10 PM	El90x	None	3
3/24/98	8:19:10 PM	El90x	None	3
3/24/98	8:19:06 PM	EventLog	None	6005
3/24/98	8:19:10 PM	El90x	None	0
3/24/98	8:00:16 PM	BROWSER	None	8033
3/24/98	8:00:16 PM	BROWSER	None	8033
3/24/98	7:56:13 PM	NETLOGON	None	5719
3/24/98	7:48:04 PM	Rdr	None	8003

FIGURE 23.1: A typical system log

Each message will contain the date and time that the event occurred (an event ID), the service that generated the message, and a short message. You can often use this information to determine the cause of a problem. Make sure that you look through all of the fatal messages, though, because many services depend upon other services. The last message listed might only be a symptom of the real problem.

Sometimes, the information in the event messages will give you enough information to determine the cause of your problem. In these cases, you can write down the event ID and research that particular error in TechNet. Microsoft technical support will often request the event ID of any errors when you call for support.

Configuring NT to Dump Memory into a File When a Fatal Error Is Encountered

To configure NT to dump memory into a file when a fatal error is encountered:

1. Open the System control panel.
2. Access the Startup/Shutdown tab and choose from the options listed below:

   Write an Event to the System Log.

   Send an Administrative Alert–Unless the system is unable to do so, a message will be sent to all members of the administrator group.

   Write Debugging Information to–The contents of memory will be written to the file specified.

   Overwrite Any Existing File–If a debugging file already exists, this option will instruct the system to overwrite it with the new memory dump.

   Automatically Reboot–Since most critical errors are the result of a certain set of circumstances, if you make the system restart, it will often allow processing to continue.

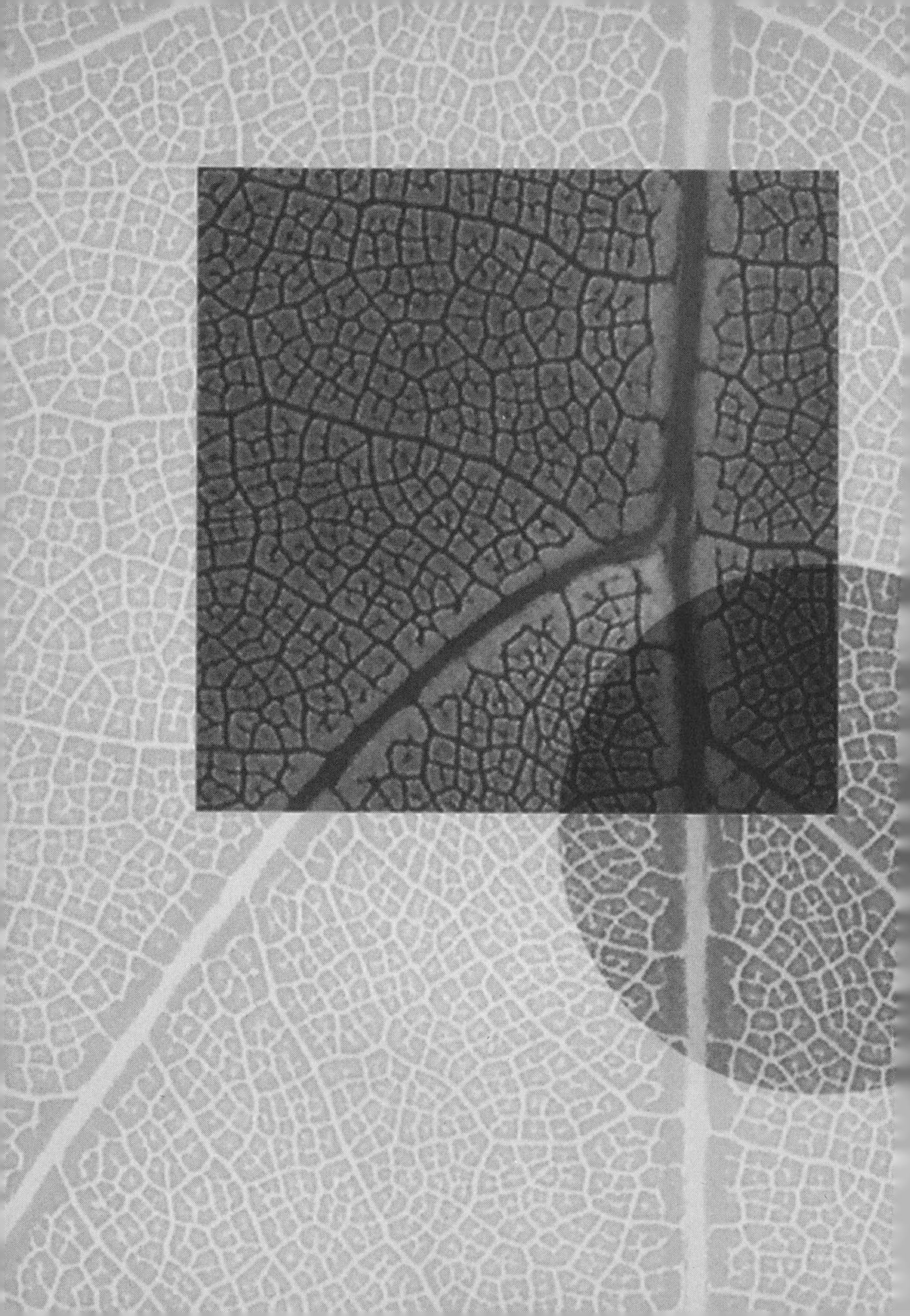

Part IV

NT Server in the Enterprise Practice Exam

1. If users in Domain 1 need access to resources in Domain 2, which of the following trust relationships should be created?

   A. Domain 1 should trust Domain 2.

   B. Domain 2 should trust Domain 1.

   C. Both domains should trust each other.

2. When a disk fails in a stripe set with parity, you can expect which of the following things?

   A. Users will no longer have access to the data stored on the stripe set with parity.

   B. Users can continue to access the data stored on the stripe set with parity.

   C. Performance will not change.

   D. Performance will degrade.

3. Which of the following protocols must be used to communicate with a Novell NetWare server?

   A. TCP/IP

   B. NWLink IPX/SPX Compatible Transport

   C. Data Link Control

   D. NetBEUI

   E. AppleTalk

4. DHCP is used to perform which of the following tasks?

   A. Assign IP addresses to clients

   B. Dynamically upgrade client software

   C. Configure NetBEUI parameters

5. If you are placing domain controllers to facilitate the logon process, which of the following statements would be correct?

   A. Place all domain controllers on the same side of a WAN link.

   B. Place domain controllers near the users that will need them.

   C. The placement of domain controllers will have no effect on the logon process.

6. Which of the following items describes the purpose of a subnet mask?

   A. To mask out unwanted hosts from your Network Neighborhood

   B. To prevent communication between a list of hosts

   C. To define which portion of the IP address represents a network and which represents a host

   D. To define a NetBIOS scope ID

7. Which of the following parameters should be configured for the IPX/SPX protocol?

   A. Frame type

   B. Packet size

   C. Network number

   D. NetWare server name

8. The types of browser computers include:

   A. Domain master browser

   B. Backup browser

   C. Potential browser

   D. BDC browser

9. How many partitions can exist on a hard disk?

   A. 1

   B. 2

   C. 4

   D. There is no limit.

10. Which of the following ARC paths would point to the second partition of drive 1 in the question above? (Assuming IDE disks.)

    A. multi(0)disk(0)rdisk(2)partition(2)

    B. multi(0)disk(1)rdisk(0)partition(2)

    C. scsi(0)disk(1)rdisk(0)partition(2)

D. multi(0)disk(1)rdisk(0)partition(1)

11. In the world of NT, what is an HP Laserjet 5P?

A. A printer

B. A print device

C. A print server

D. A print spooler

12. You notice that the NT workstation you are using communicates slowly on the network. What can you do to speed up communications?

A. Change the Ethernet card to a Token Ring card

B. Change the Token Ring card to an Ethernet card

C. Change the binding order of the protocols

D. Add another network card to the workstation

13. Which of the following statements is true?

A. Global groups can contain members from multiple domains.

B. Global groups must contain members from multiple domains.

C. Local groups can contain members from multiple domains.

D. Local groups must contain members from multiple domains.

14. How do you change a user profile to a mandatory user profile?

A. Change the extension in the NTUSER.MAN file to NTUSER.DAT.

B. Change the extension in the NTUSER.DAT file to NTUSER.MAN.

C. That is covered in the rights and permissions section of this book, and you haven't gotten that far yet.

D. Store the profile in the \NETLOGON directory of the PDC with the filename NETUSER.DAT.

15. Remote administration is accomplished by:

A. Dialing in and using a RAS connection

B. Using RCONSOLE and an SPX connection

C. Using a workstation running Windows for Workgroups

D. Using a workstation running Windows NT Workstation

16. Given the default permissions assigned to groups, which groups would you need to belong in to create a share?

A. Administrators

B. Backup users

C. Guests

D. Users

17. Which of the following features are benefits of GSNW?

A. Only the server needs to load NWLink.

B. NetWare resources look like NT shares to your clients.

C. Each user can have their own set of permissions on the NetWare server.

D. Since only one session is created to the NetWare server, performance is enhanced.

18. When creating an NT Server-based TCP/IP router, in what order are the following actions taken?

A. Select Enable IP Forwarding.

B. Configure the NIC cards.

C. Install TCP/IP.

D. Install the NIC driver.

E. Assign each NIC an IP address.

19. What are the three RAS call-back options?

A. No Call Back

B. Preset

C. Set by User

D. Only if asked

20. Which dial-up line protocols does RAS support?

A. PPP

B. TCP

C. SLIP

D. IPX/SPX

E. UDP

21. If the parameter %User Time is consistently over 80 percent, which of the following subsystems is most likely the bottleneck?

A. Processor

B. Memory

C. Disk

D. Network

22. Which of the following tactics would be used to reduce the amount of information presented in a Network Monitor capture?

A. Filtering the data collected by computers involved

B. Filtering the data collected by protocol

C. Filtering the data after the capture has occurred

D. Saving the data for later import into Performance Monitor

23. On a domain server, which of the four main components is most likely to be the bottleneck?

A. Memory

B. Processor

C. Disk

D. Network

24. Which of the following actions should you take if you encounter a media error when installing NT?

A. Try another NT CD-ROM.

B. Try another method of installation—across the network, copy the I386 to the local drive first, etc.

C. Give up and try another operating system.

25. The current configuration becomes the last known good configuration at which point in the boot process?

A. After all services have successfully loaded in the kernel phase

B. After a user successfully logs on

C. After the BOOT.INI file has executed

26. Which of the five main registry subtrees holds file association information?

A. HKEY_LOCAL_MACHINE

B. HKEY_CLASSES_ROOT

C. HKEY_CURRENT_USER

D. HKEY_USERS

E. HKEY_CURRENT_CONFIG

27. Your RAS connection is using call back with multilink over a regular phone line. How many numbers can you configure RAS to call back per call?

A. Unlimited

B. 1

C. 3

D. 5

E. 7

28. Which of the following items accepts and handles network requests that use UNC names?

A. MUP

B. MPR

C. TDI

29. Which of the following items accepts and handles requests not formatted using a UNC name?

    A. MUP

    B. MPR

    C. TDI

30. Which of the following parameters must you add to the BOOT.INI file to implement a memory dump?

    A. Com:x

    B. Crashdebug

    C. Mem:xx

    D. Basevideo

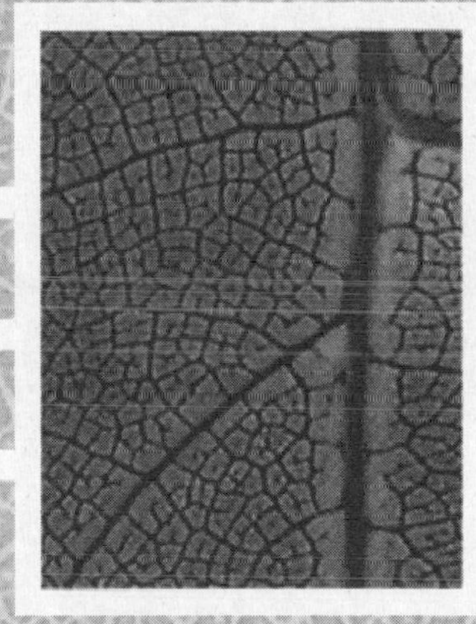

PART V

WINDOWS 98

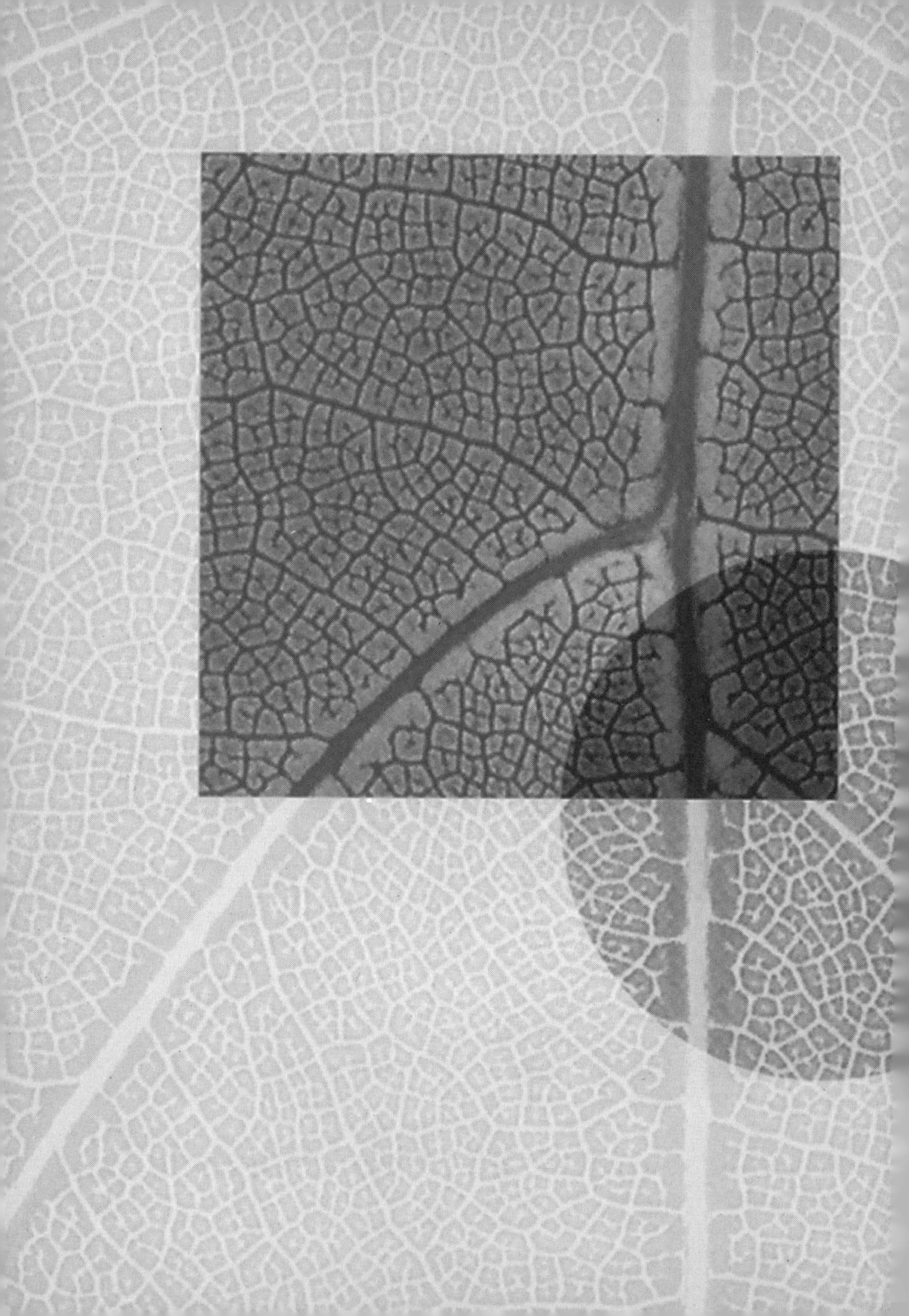

Chapter 24

Planning

The objectives for this portion of the exam are intended to test your ability to determine which file system to choose for Windows 98, when a workgroup or a domain should be used as the networking environment for Windows 98, and the advantages and disadvantages of each. You will also need to know how to configure the Windows 98 computer so that it can participate in, and browse, the appropriate workgroup or domain. Although the exam objectives discuss Microsoft and NetWare network environments, for all intents and purposes there are no differences between the two for this chapter.

Adapted from *MCSE Exam Notes: Windows 98* by Rick Sawtell and Lance Mortensen

ISBN 0-7821-2421-6 416 pages $19.99

Develop an appropriate implementation model for specific requirements in a Microsoft environment or a mixed Microsoft and NetWare environment.

Considerations include:

- Choosing the appropriate file system
- Planning a workgroup

Windows 98 includes a new file system that brings many needed benefits, including the ability to create large partitions, use space more efficiently, and increase speed. Microsoft expects you to know how to configure various networking parameters of Windows 98, including how to change your workgroup or join a domain. What follows is a discussion of workgroups and domains to help prepare you for questions dealing with selecting one over another. Many situations will have specific requirements that will dictate which model you should implement while other situations may not be so clear.

File Systems

Before you can format a hard drive, it must be partitioned. There are two types of partitions supported under Windows 98: *FAT16* and *FAT32* partitions.

- FAT16: The original partitioning scheme for MS-DOS and Windows 95 partitions, and limited to 2GB in size.
- FAT32: A new partitioning scheme that allows for much larger partitions at the expense of some lost backward compatibility.

NOTE

FAT stands for file allocation table. It is the file system used by MS-DOS and available to other operating systems (such as Windows) to track data clusters.

FAT16 versus FAT32

Hard drives are organized by sectors and clusters (groups of sectors). A *cluster* is the smallest unit of disk space that a file uses when it is saved; clusters can't be subdivided between files. The FAT file system that is used to format floppy disks and hard drives first appeared with DOS 1.0. It was never intended for huge partitions such as those occurring today. Because DOS and Windows 98 must remain backward-compatible with older versions of DOS, newer operating systems (including Windows 98) must find ways to extend the operating system while adhering to the restrictions of previous DOS versions. DOS and Windows 98 overcome the FAT's partition size limitations by increasing each cluster size as the partition grows bigger. This older way of partitioning drives is referred to as *FAT16*.

Size of Partition	Size of Clusters in FAT16
1–15MB*	4KB
16–127MB	2KB
128–255MB	4KB
256–511MB	8KB
512–1023MB	16KB
1024–2047MB	32KB

***The FAT for 1-15MB partitions is a 12-bit FAT. All others are 16-bits.**

When partitions become bigger, the cluster size also becomes bigger. Anytime a file is saved, it uses at least one cluster, so files saved on large partitions have more wasted space than those on smaller partitions.

NOTE

Windows NT can create 4GB partitions using FAT16. Dual-booting such a system with Windows 98 should work fine, but is not recommended because of various, non-critical compatibility issues (such as programs reporting zero bytes free, etc.).

The FAT32 Solution

Microsoft's response to the problem of large cluster sizes has been to release a partitioning scheme that supports partitions up to 8GB with a cluster size of only 4KB and a maximum volume size of 2TB (terabytes). This new FAT scheme is called *FAT32*.

NOTE

FAT32 first appeared with Windows 95B, also known as OSR2. No Microsoft conversion tool was available for FAT16 volumes until Windows 98.

Size of Partition	Size of Clusters in FAT32
1–512MB	FAT16 is used
512MB–8GB	4KB
8GB–16GB	8KB
16GB–32GB	16KB
32GB–2TB	32KB

The only problem is that FAT32, which comes with Windows 98, is no longer backward-compatible with DOS and some third-party utilities that were compatible with the original version of Windows 95.

WARNING

FAT32 partitions are not visible to Windows NT 4.0 or MS-DOS without special utilities, but will be visible to Windows NT 5.0. A utility that allows Windows NT 4.0 to read/write to FAT32 partitions is available at `www.sysinternals.com`.

There are several issues that must be taken into consideration before converting a FAT16 partition to FAT32.

- The name of the protected-mode Drive Converter program is CVT1.EXE, and the name of the real-mode program is CVT.EXE. Normally you would use the protected-mode program.
- Windows 98 comes with a one-way conversion program. If you want to convert a FAT32 partition back to a FAT16 partition, you will need to use a third-party utility such as Partition Magic from Power Quest.
- Most third-party compression programs are incompatible with FAT32, and if you are using such a program you will be unable to convert to FAT32.
- If you convert a removable media drive, such as a Zip or Jaz drive, that drive can only be used by Windows 98 or by Windows 95B (OSR2).

- You cannot uninstall Windows 98 after converting to FAT32 (unless you use a third-party utility to first go back to FAT16).
- You cannot dual-boot with MS-DOS or Windows NT 4.0 (or earlier) after converting to FAT32.
- FAT32 is considerably slower than FAT16 when running in MS-DOS mode or Safe mode.
- Many older third-party disk utilities are not compatible with FAT32 and may need to be upgraded.
- Many programs (such as setup programs for various applications) will not show available space over 2GB in size on a FAT32 volume. This is a cosmetic bug and should not affect the operation of the program.
- Many laptops will have "hibernate" software installed, which may cause the Drive Converter program to either suggest not converting the drive or automatically cancel the conversion process. To override the defaults, run the CVT.EXE with the `/HIB` switch on to delete any hibernation programs it finds.

The conversion program may take an hour or more. After the conversion, you should run the Disk Defragmenter, which may take more than two hours to run.

Workgroups and Networks

There are three general ways to integrate Windows 98 into an environment: as a stand-alone computer; as a member of a workgroup; or as a member of a Windows NT domain or other type of server-based network. Placing Windows 98 in either a workgroup or domain will also affect the way Network Neighborhood acts, as your particular workgroup or domain is the first level shown in Network Neighborhood. To see other workgroups or domains you must choose Entire Network.

NOTE

Just because the computer belongs to a certain workgroup or domain doesn't mean the user has to log in to that particular workgroup or domain. A Windows 98 computer can be a member of a particular workgroup while the user account resides on the domain. In this case, whenever Network Neighborhood is started, the workgroup of the computer will be shown.

Stand-Alone Installations

The easiest way to install Windows 98 is as a *stand-alone installation.* Most home computers are installed this way, as are many laptop computers. The major advantage of a stand-alone installation is that it doesn't rely on other computers, which means that any problems you encounter originate with the computer in question.

The major disadvantage of a stand-alone installation is the lack of connectivity. Without a connection to other computers you are dependent on the old "sneaker net," which means you must resort to copying data to floppies and then physically running the floppies around by foot—or in sneakers. (At my university in the late 1980s we had a slightly more advanced version called "Frisbee net," where we distributed floppies by throwing them back and forth, but it still left a lot to be desired.)

Workgroups

A *workgroup*, in its strictest sense, is a peer-to-peer network, in that no single computer is in charge of user names, passwords, and security. Windows 98 can participate in a workgroup without any additional software or servers required. A workgroup is typically encountered only in very small networks (six to nine computers, maximum) before a dedicated server is installed.

- Advantages of a workgroup: No dedicated server is required, it's inexpensive to set up and maintain, and all necessary software is provided with Windows 98.
- Disadvantages of a workgroup: Because there is no dedicated server, someone with a computer that shares a folder or printer can interrupt the network by turning off their computer. Also, because there is no central database of users and passwords, you may have to memorize 10 different usernames and passwords in order to connect to 10 different computers.

WARNING

Workgroup security models are based on passwords, which means that anyone who knows the password can gain access to shared resources. This is called *share-level security* and is inherently insecure, as you *cannot* limit access to certain users.

Domains

A *domain* exists when one or more Windows NT servers are responsible for a central database of usernames and passwords, and authenticate users at logon. The first Windows NT server that helps control the domain is called the *primary domain controller*, or *PDC*. Subsequent Windows NT servers that are installed as controllers in the domain are called *backup domain controllers*, or *BDCs*. A Windows NT server can also be installed into a domain where it won't act as a controller. It is referred to as a *member*, *application*, or plain *server*, in that it relies on the controllers in the domain for authentication purposes.

- Advantages of a domain: One central database of users and passwords means that you only have to log on once each session to access all the servers and resources in the domain.
- Disadvantages of a domain: You need to have a separate computer running Windows NT server to act as a PDC. For small companies, this could be cost prohibitive.

NOTE

Because the security model of a domain is based upon users and groups, you can limit access to people based on their user account or group membership. This is called *user-level security* and is the best form of security available for Windows 98.

Develop a security strategy in a Microsoft environment or a mixed Microsoft and NetWare environment.

Strategies include:

- System policies
- User profiles
- File and printer sharing
- Share-level access control or user-level access control

Windows 98 includes a powerful tool in the System Policy Editor that affords a high level of system control over what users can and cannot do. You need to know how to create and use system policies for the Microsoft exam. System policies work by selectively modifying the Registry when a user logs in. Policies can be based on specific users, groups, and computers, or more generic policies can be created that affect all users or computers.

You create policies with the System Policy Editor by loading a template, making the desired changes, and then saving the template as a policy file. Policies are flexible enough to do almost anything that you want, with respect to restrictions that may be required for your network. Windows 98 can track individual preferences and settings separately for each person who logs in to a computer and store them in a user profile. Profiles can track such user preferences as wallpaper, Desktop design, persistent network connections, and shortcuts, among others.

System settings are held in the SYSTEM.DAT file and user settings are held in the USER.DAT file located in the Windows 98 system folder. Windows 98 creates user profiles by making a unique USER.DAT file and personal folder for each system user.

System Policies and Windows 98

System policies are no more than an automated way to enforce certain restrictions on certain users or computers. System policies work by selectively modifying the Registry when a user logs in. You can set policies that not only restrict the user when he or she logs in, but that also restrict the user from making changes during his or her session by prohibiting access to the Registry Editor.

Two types of files are used in creating system policies:

Template (.ADM) files ASCII files that are filled in and modified

Policy (.POL) files Template files that are saved as policy files and read by Windows 98

Template files can be thought of as source code (which can be modified and added to), and *policy files* can be seen as compiled code (which is loaded and executed on a computer). When the policies are read and applied by Windows 98, they modify the Registry to enforce one or more restrictions. Figure 24.1 shows how the two types of policy files are used, and Figure 24.2 illustrates how Windows 98 processes policy files.

Template
*. ADM
Policy
*. POL
Registry
USER.DAT
SYSTEM.DAT

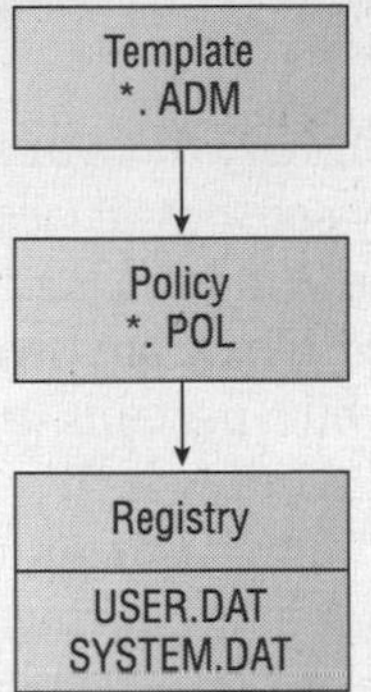

FIGURE 24.1: Templates, policies, and the Registry

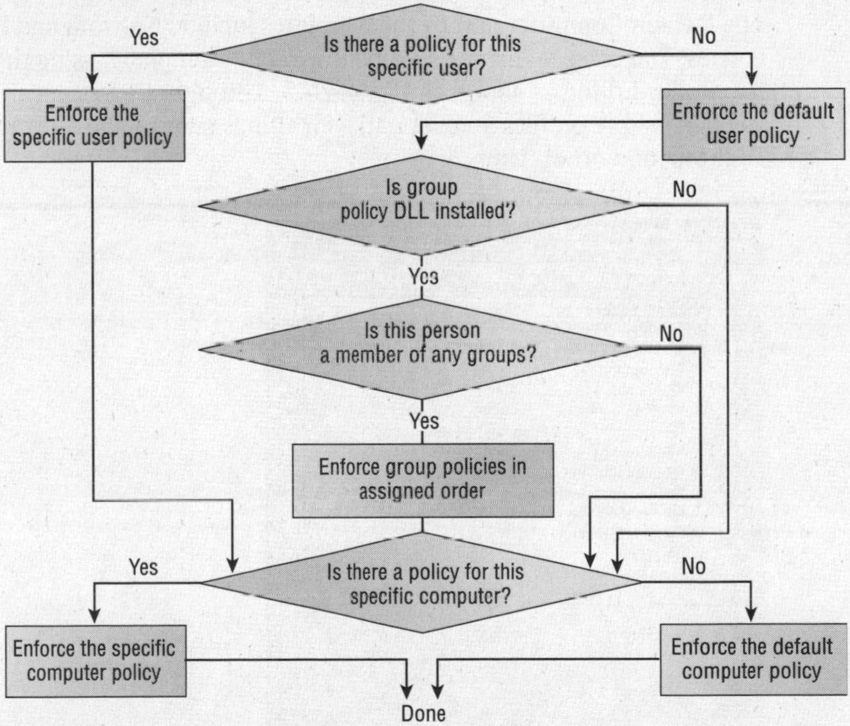

Is there a policy for this specific user?
Yes
No
Enforce the specific user policy
Enforce the default user policy
Is group policy DLL installed?
No
Yes
Is this person a member of any groups?
No
Yes
Enforce group policies in assigned order
Is there a policy for this specific computer?
Yes
No
Enforce the specific computer policy
Enforce the default computer policy
Done

FIGURE 24.2: How Windows 98 processes policies

Policies can be based on group membership. Groups can come from either an NT server or a NetWare server. Support for group policies is not installed by default; you must install this support for every computer that is expected to load group policies.

Microsoft supplies default templates called COMMON.ADM and WINDOWS.ADM, which contain many popular Registry settings. These files are located in the (hidden) INF folder located in the Windows installation folder after the System Policy Editor is installed. There are two major sections to the templates: the Default Computer (which pertains to the Hkey_Local_Machine Registry key) and the Default User (which pertains to the Hkey_Users Registry key). You can view the Default Computer and Default User entries in the System Policy Editor by double-clicking their icons in the System Policy Editor window. These parts of the templates are described in the following sections.

Default Computer Settings

The Default Computer part of the templates include Network and System entries. You can see this by opening the default templates using the System Policy Editor, as shown in Figure 24.3. Through the System entry, you can enable profiles and set paths for things such as the Start menu, Desktop, and other items.

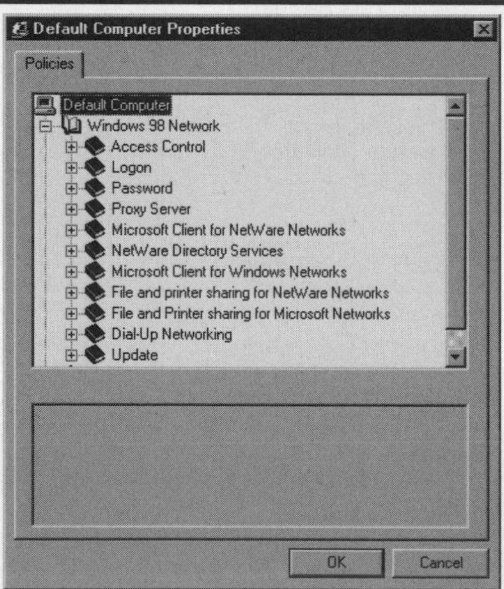

FIGURE 24.3: The Default Computer Windows 98 Network settings

The Windows 98 Network entry is divided into the following elements (the Proxy Server, NetWare Directory Services, and File and Printer Sharing for Microsoft Networks elements will be discussed in subsequent chapters):

Access Control Allows you to assign user-level security and enter the server name or domain name to base security on.

Logon Allows you to include a logon banner and require a valid logon before Windows 98 will let the user into the system. Selecting this option will also restrict access for users who try to bypass the login security by clicking Cancel on the login screen.

Password Allows you to set a minimum length for the Windows password, disable password caching, and set other password options.

Proxy Server Allows you to disable the automatic search for a proxy server.

Microsoft Client for NetWare Networks Allows you to set the preferred server and other various options for a NetWare client machine.

NetWare Directory Services Allows you to set configurations for the MS-NDS client, including the Preferred Tree, default Context, and advanced login options.

Microsoft Client for Windows Networks Allows you to assign the workgroup name or enter the NT domain the user will log on to.

File and Printer Sharing for NetWare Networks Allows you to set whether or not SAP (Service Advertising Protocol) will be sent out.

File and Printer Sharing for Microsoft Networks Allows you to disable file and/or printer sharing.

Dial-Up Networking Allows you to disable the dial-in client.

Update Allows you to set the path for future system policy updates.

The Windows 98 System settings allow you to change the way Windows 98 works and upgrades itself. (See Figure 24.4.)

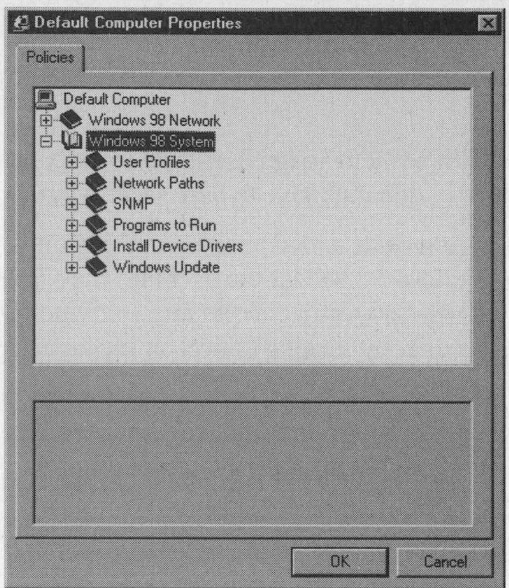

FIGURE 24.4: The Default Computer Windows 98 System setting

The various Windows 98 System settings include:

User Profiles: Allows you to enable profiles.

Network Paths Allows you to set the path to Windows 98 installation and tour files.

SNMP Allows you to set where the SNMP (Simple Network Management Protocol) error codes will go.

Programs to Run Allows you to specify programs to run a single time at the next startup or to run every time the system starts up.

Install Device Drivers Allows you to specify if non-Microsoft drivers will generate a prompt before installation or will not be allowed.

Windows Update Allows you to specify the URL from which Windows 98 gets its updates.

Default User Settings

The Default User part of the COMMON.ADM and WINDOWS.ADM templates are shown in Figure 24.5.

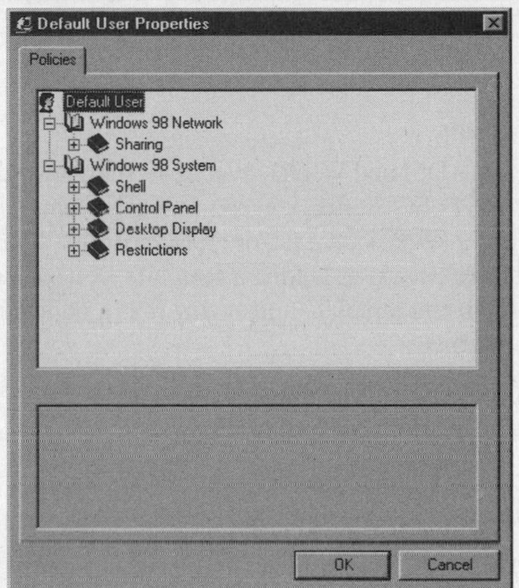

FIGURE 24.5: The Default User Properties window

The Default User has the following entries:

Windows 98 Network Through the Sharing subentry, you can restrict the user from changing any of the current shares or creating new shares.

Windows 98 System Through the Restrictions subentry, you can disable MS-DOS mode, disable the Registry Editor, and create a list of approved programs so that Windows 98 will run only those programs.

Shell Through the Custom Folders subentry, you can set various parts of Windows 98 (such as the Start menu or Desktop) to reside on places other than the local hard drive. Through the Restrictions subentry, you can shut down most of the functionality of Windows 98. For example, you could disable the Run command or hide the drives in My Computer and Network Neighborhood.

Control Panel Each one of these entries allows you to restrict various tabs within the Control Panel applet's dialog box—Display, Network, Passwords, Printers, and System.

Desktop Display This entry allows you to set various items pertaining to the Desktop, including the wallpaper and color scheme.

Setting Policy Restrictions

Along with the COMMON.ADM and WINDOWS.ADM templates that are loaded with the System Policy Editor, you can find other templates and policies in the *Windows 98 Resource Kit* or on Microsoft's Web site (`www.microsoft.com`). After you've loaded a template, you can set various restrictions by filling in the template and saving it as a policy file. You generally have three choices:

- A *gray* setting is the default. No change is made to the Registry by the policy—the restrictions are left as they were.
- A *checked* setting means that the policy is enforced—the restrictions are put in place.
- A *blank*, or white, setting means that the policy is reset—the restrictions are removed.

Some policy settings are enabled or disabled by default. Clearing or checking a box could restrict or unrestrict, depending on the setting. When you leave a policy gray (which is the default), Windows 98 doesn't change the policy currently recorded in the Registry. Although leaving boxes gray is faster to process (because nothing is being changed), Windows 98 will not reset a restriction to an earlier version. For example, if you had a restriction set (checked) for a low-security person, that restriction is in place on the computer until someone who has the restriction reset (set to white) logs in.

User Profiles and Windows 98

There are two types of user profiles: local profiles and roaming profiles.

Local Profiles These profiles are stored only on the local computer. If a user logs on to one computer, makes changes to the environment, and then logs on to another computer, the changes from the first computer are not reflected on the second computer.

Roaming Profiles These profiles are stored on either a NetWare or Microsoft (NT) server. When a user logs on to the server, that user's profile is downloaded to his or her computer. When the user logs off, changes to the profile are saved back to the copy on the server. When the user logs on to a different computer, the profile (and any changes) are downloaded to the local computer again.

User profiles are not enabled by default. All users share the same settings on a computer until profiles are enabled. Once profiles are enabled, users on that computer will be asked to log in, so that Windows 98 will know who the user is and can load the appropriate profile.

The user will be prompted the first time he or she logs in and a profile is not found. If the user chooses not to create a profile, the default profile will be used.

You can enable user profiles from the User Profiles tab of the Passwords Properties dialog box, shown in Figure 24.6.

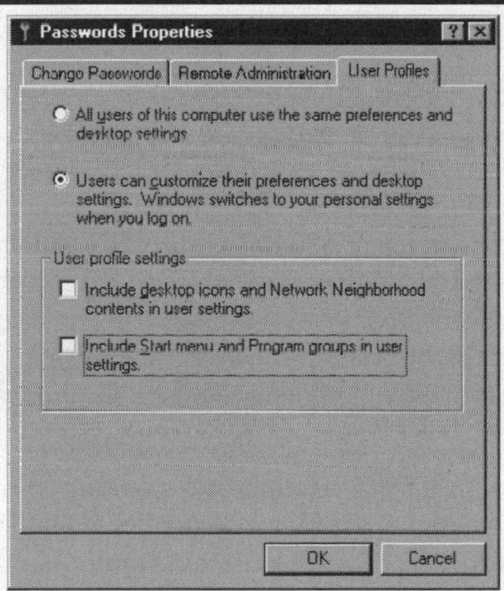

FIGURE 24.6: The User Profiles tab of the Passwords Properties dialog box

The first two options disable or enable profiles:

All users of this computer use the same preferences and desktop settings. This is the default option. Windows 98 uses the same settings for everyone. Choose this option to turn off profiles.

Users can customize their preferences and desktop settings. Windows switches to your personal settings when you log on. Choose this option to enable profiles. You need to restart Windows 98 after you select this option to have profiles take effect.

Profiles always contain the USER.DAT file, with unique user Registry settings. In addition to those settings, you can choose the following options in the User Profile Settings section of the User Profiles tab:

Include desktop icons and Network Neighborhood contents in user settings. Choose this setting to create folders called Desktop, Recent, and NetHood under the user profile folder. The Desktop folder contains shortcuts from the common Desktop, and changes the common Desktop to a unique one for each user. The Recent folder keeps track of the documents that the user has recently opened. The NetHood folder contains any network shortcuts. Folders and files stored on the Desktop are not included in profiles; just the shortcuts are included.

Include Start menu and Program groups in user settings. Choose this setting to create a folder called Start Menu under the user profile folder. This folder is used as the Start menu for the user, instead of the common one found under <*Windows Root*>\Start Menu. Note that applications installed when saving the Start menu in profiles will be available to only the user who installed the program, because that user is the only one who will have the Program group and icon in his or her unique Start menu folder.

Before you enable profiles, user configurations are stored in the USER.DAT file, and in the Desktop, Start Menu, Recent, and NetHood folders located in the root of the Windows installation folder. User settings in the Registry are held in the USER.DAT file, which makes up the Hkey_Current_User key.

After you enable profiles, Windows 98 will create a Profiles folder and store settings for each user in a folder named after that user. A unique copy of USER.DAT will be saved in each user's folder as well.

Sharing Resources with Windows 98

Windows 98 computers can have an additional service installed that allows them to share resources and act like Windows NT file and print servers. Allowing users to share their resources does make sharing information more convenient, but it also makes more work for those who maintain and administer the network and is a lot less secure. You now have many administrators to train and supervise instead of just a few. Problems can arise if users share their drives incorrectly and sensitive information gets out, or if users have too many rights and delete the wrong files.

Many smaller companies love the fact that they don't need a dedicated, expensive computer in order to share a few files and printers. Larger companies tend to have more resources for both hardware and administrators, and usually don't allow users to share their local resources on the network. Restrictions can be enforced with system policies.

Follow these steps to set up and manage shared resources:

1. Choose a security model (share-level versus user-level).
2. Install File and Printer Sharing for Microsoft Networks.
3. Configure File and Printer Sharing.
4. Create shared resources.
5. Modify shared resources.

Share-Level Security

Share-level security is the same as it is in Windows for Workgroups; that is, a password is assigned to a shared resource when the shared resource is created. This is the default level of security. With share-level security, if a user knows the passwords, he or she can access the resources, even if the original owner did not intend for that particular user to have access to those shared resources.

Using share-level security has the advantages of being easy and fast. However, it has the following disadvantages:

- It is not secure.
- Specific users cannot be blocked.
- The passwords can be discovered.
- There is no centralized control (central Information Systems is no longer in charge).

- Changing passwords requires informing all intended users.
- There are only two access permissions: Read-Only and Full.

NOTE

Share-level security is the default security setting for the sharing service for Microsoft networks.

User-Level Security

Because of the limitations of share-level security, Microsoft added a more advanced option in Windows 98 that is much more secure. The *user-level* access control bases its security on an existing server called a security provider: either a Windows NT server (NT Workstation, NT Server, or a domain controller) or a NetWare server. After a new share is made, existing users or groups are then given rights to the share. This means that you must have some kind of server in place before you can switch to user-level security.

User-level security has the following advantages:

- Rights can be assigned to users or groups.
- It allows centralized control of users and groups.
- It's more flexible than share-level (custom rights can be assigned).

There are a few disadvantages to using user-level security, however:

- Some kind of server must be in place.
- It's more complex than share-level.
- A live network connection to the server must be maintained when assigning rights and shares.

Changing the Security Model

If you change from share-level security to user-level security, or vice versa, all currently shared resources will have to be shared again. As explained earlier, the default security model is share-level, which allows you to assign passwords to shared resources. User-level is more secure, and thus preferable if users are to share resources. Before you can change to user-level, however, you need a server (either NetWare or NT) in place.

You switch to user-level security through the Access Control tab of the Network Control Panel, as shown in Figure 24.7. If you set user-level to an NT server that is not a domain controller, you will need to provide the server name. If you set user-level to an NT domain, you will need to provide the domain name.

Once File and Printer Sharing for NetWare Networks is installed, you can share files and printers so that NetWare clients can connect to your resources. NetWare servers have no support for share-level security. Thus, if a Windows 98 computer wants to share its resources on a NetWare network, it must be configured for user-level access, with the list of users pulled from an existing NetWare server. When a client connects to the Windows 98 machine and tries to log on to it, Windows 98 doesn't actually authenticate the request–it passes it to the server assigned to support user-level security. You also need to enable SAP (Service Advertising Protocol) support so that non-Windows 98 clients can see the Windows 98 machines.

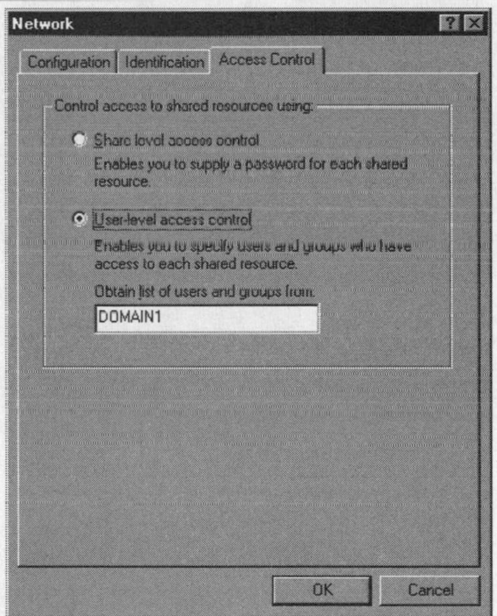

FIGURE 24.7: Changing to user-level security

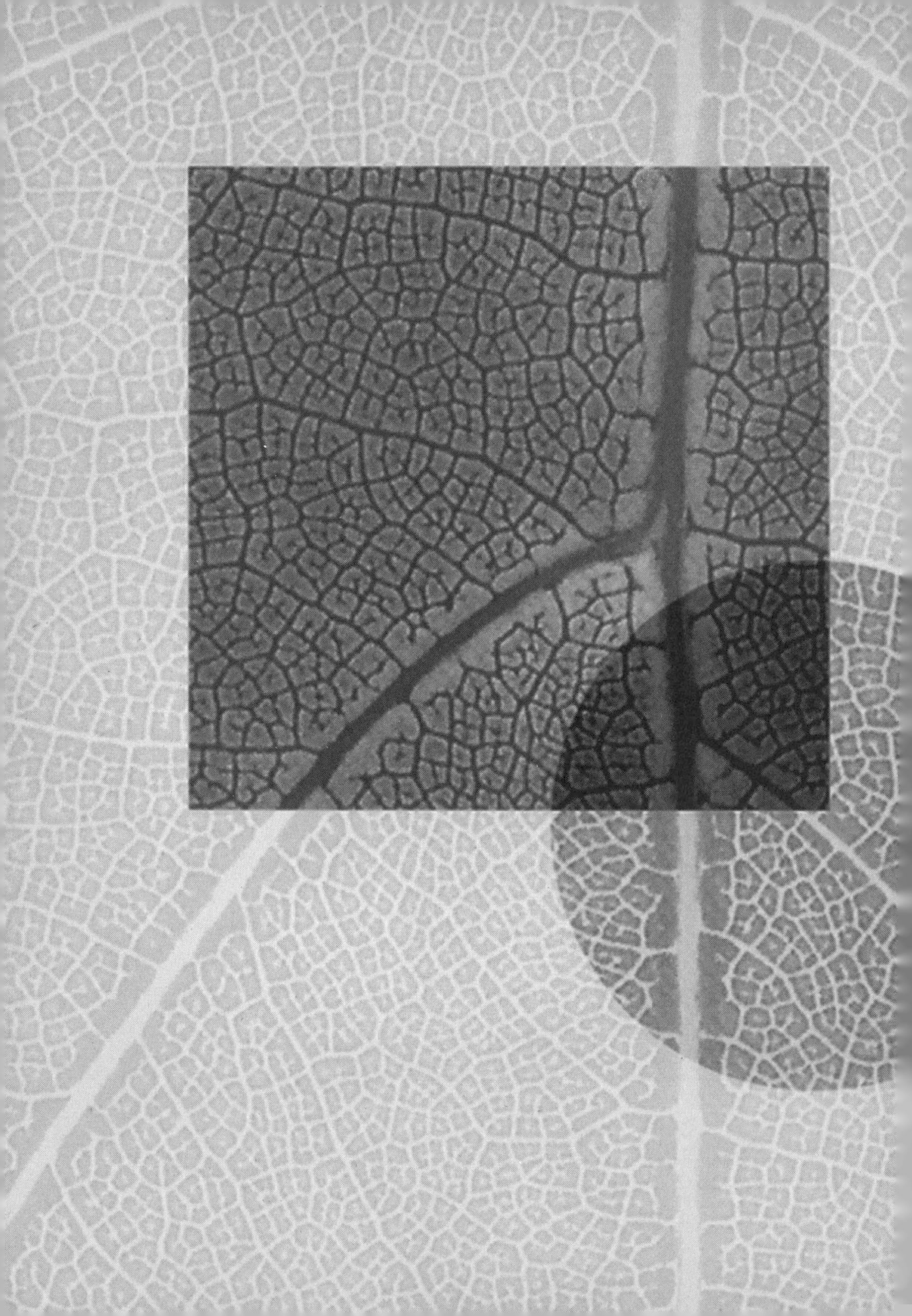

Chapter 25

Installation and Configuration

This chapter provides an overview of the Windows 98 installation process, including how to prepare for installation and how to install Windows 98 in a stand-alone or networked environment. It also discusses how to automate the installation process. Windows 98 is intended to operate singularly on a computer system; it can, however, coexist with Microsoft DOS, Caldera's Digital Research DOS (DR-DOS), IBM OS/2, Windows 3.*x*, Windows NT 3.5*x*, or Windows NT 4.0.

Adapted from *MCSE Exam Notes: Windows 98*
by Rick Sawtell and Lance Mortensen
ISBN 0-7821-2421-6 416 pages $19.99

Install Windows 98.

Installation options include:

- Automated Windows setup
- New
- Upgrade
- Uninstall
- Dual-boot combination with Microsoft Window NT 4

This objectve is heavily covered on the test.

Installation Requirements

Windows 98 comes in two media forms: floppy disks and CD-ROMs. The Windows 98 installation files come in the form of CAB files. (A *CAB file*, or *cabinet file*, is actually a container file of several compressed files.) Both of these mediums can be used to upgrade your system to Windows 98. When using Windows 95 with networked systems, most administrators either copied the CAB files to a directory on the server or used the Windows 95 utility NetSetup to create an Administration installation source.

Hardware Requirements

Before you install Windows 98, you must ensure that your system meets the minimum hardware requirements as set forth by Microsoft. Table 25.1 identifies the minimum and recommended hardware requirements for installing Windows 98.

TABLE 25.1: Windows 98 Hardware Requirements

Hardware	Minimum	Recommended
Disk space to upgrade Windows 95	120MB	295MB
Disk space to upgrade Windows 3.*x*	120MB	295MB
Disk space for new install of FAT16	225MB	355MB
Disk space for new install of FAT32	175MB*	225MB
Floppy disk drive	One 3.5-inch high-density	One 3.5-inch high-density

TABLE 25.1 continued: Windows 98 Hardware Requirements

HARDWARE	MINIMUM	RECOMMENDED
Memory	8MB; 16MB for Internet Explorer and Messaging	32MB is the de facto standard (64MB or more is even better)
Monitor	VGA (16-color)	Super VGA 16- or 24-bit color
Processor	486DX-66MHz	Pentium 133 or higher
OPTIONAL COMPONENTS		
ATI All-in-Wonder card or compatible device	N/A	Required to watch TV using WebTV for Windows
Audio card and speakers	Sound Blaster or Sound Blaster-compatible device	Full-duplex sound card
CD-ROM	1x speed or faster	8x speed or faster
Modem	14.4 baud modem	28.8 baud modem or faster
Mouse	Windows 98-compatible device	Whatever works best for you
Network adapter card	NDIS 2.0 or MAC Driver Support	NDIS 4.0 or 5.0 with OnNow power management support

*** A new installation could require up to 355MB. You also need to plan for a certain amount of disk space for the swap file, which is usually 25MB to 35MB but can go higher than 75MB. If you plan to save the previous file system, you will need between 50MB to 75MB to save your current system to the uninstall files.**

The Windows 98 CD-ROM comes with many, but not all, hardware drivers. Most hardware vendors provide Web site posts of the files that are needed to support Windows 98. Keep in mind that a specific driver may not be available for your older hardware devices; if this is the case, you must use the existing real-mode drivers. Microsoft suggests that you choose hardware components that carry their "Designed for Microsoft Windows" logo to ensure optimal performance.

NOTE

Real-mode drivers are MS-DOS-based, 16-bit drivers that are loaded in the CONFIG.SYS and AUTOEXEC.BAT files. Protected-mode drivers are 32-bit drivers that are loaded during the protected-mode boot phase. Windows *9x* replaces 16-bit drivers with 32-bit drivers whenever possible.

WARNING

Windows 98 does not support every CD-ROM drive. Keep your existing AUTOEXEC.BAT and CONFIG.SYS files (as well as the necessary drivers) to ensure you always have CD-ROM access and the real-mode network connection drivers.

Software Requirements

According to Microsoft, your system must have MS-DOS version 5.0 or later to install Windows 98. Because of the various OEM (Original Equipment Manufacturer) versions of DOS, installing Windows 98 using MS-DOS 5.0 or higher is strongly recommended.

Windows 98 can be installed onto a system that is using disk compression drivers. Microsoft has many compression engines. When you install Windows 98 on a system that has a compressed drive, you will need at least 3MB of free, uncompressed hard disk space on the host drive. If you are using a third-party compression utility, you should contact the product's support team to see what steps need to be taken to ensure compatibility with Windows 98 and the compression product.

WARNING

Do not erase DRVSPACE.BIN or DBLSPACE.BIN if you have compressed your drive. Windows 98 uses D*XX*SPACE.BIN files to mount old volume files compressed with either DoubleSpace or DriveSpace.

Windows 98 Installation Features

Windows 98 can be installed on any drive that has enough available disk space and is FAT16 partitioned. If you plan to dual-boot Windows 98 with another operating system, the boot partition must be FAT16. Windows 98 cannot be installed on an NTFS (Windows NT File System) partition.

Likewise, Windows 98 cannot be installed on an HPFS (OS/2 File System) partition. Dual-boot configurations will be discussed later in this chapter.

New Features

The Windows 98 setup process includes many new features and is now down to five phases. The new Setup utility makes the installation process faster and minimizes unnecessary user input. When you upgrade from Windows 95, the Windows 98 setup is optimized such that current Windows 95 system configurations and settings are used. This results in the overall improvement of the setup process by requiring the least amount of user input. Here are some of the key changes and enhancements:

- Legacy settings are verified and maintained; undetected legacy or undetermined legacy components require full hardware detection.
- Generic CD-ROMs are supported on the Startup disk.
- CAB files are grouped by function; only the files required by your specific setup are copied.
- Enumeration is performed before detection, thereby reducing errors.
- An option is available to run antivirus programs.

WARNING

Setup will not detect protected-mode drivers until after the first restart (when hardware detection and device enumeration take place), so keep real-mode drivers available throughout the installation process.

Setup Switches

To install Windows 98, go to the Windows 95 Explorer, or the File Manager for Windows 3.*x*, and double-click the SETUP.EXE file in the root directory on the Windows 98 CD-ROM. Microsoft employs Setup command-line switches to control tasks. In these cases, you can either run Setup from a DOS prompt, from the Start ➢ Run command of Windows 95, or from the File ➢ Run command for Windows 3.*x*. The following list explains some of the key Setup command-line switches that can be employed when installing Windows 98.

Switch	End Result
/?	Provides a list of Setup switches and the syntax to use.
/c	Prevents SmartDrive from loading and creating a cache.
/d	Prevents Setup from detecting or using any existing version of Windows (typically used in the DOS Setup on a Windows NT system).
/ic	Ignore Configuration Files. Performs a clean boot.
/id	Ignore Disk. Does not check for the minimum disk space.
/ie	Ignore Emergency Disk Option. Skips the Startup disk screen.
/ih	Ignore ScanDisk in the Background. Runs ScanDisk in the foreground.
/im	Ignore Memory. Does not check for low conventional memory.
/in	Ignore Network. Does not install the networking software. Does not use the Networking Wizard.
/iq	Ignore Crosslinked Files. Doesn't check for crosslinked files.
/is	Ignore ScanDisk. Runs Setup without running ScanDisk first.
/iv	Ignore Verbose Ads. Advertisement graphics will not be displayed as Setup proceeds.
/IW	Ignore Windows Agreement. Option must be uppercase. Skips the Windows licensing screen.

Switch	End Result
`/nf`	No Floppy. Skips prompt to remove floppy drive A:. Use this option when installing from a bootable CD.
`/nr`	No Registry Check. Skips the Registry check and analysis.
`Script filename`	Scripted file (MSBATCH.INF) will be used to automate installation process.
`/s filename`	Specifies the SETUP.INF file when starting Setup.
`/SRCDir`	Specifies the source directory in which the Windows 98 source files are located.
`/t:TempDir`	Specifies the directory to which Windows 98 will copy the temporary Setup files. The directory must exist, and any preexisting files in this directory will be deleted during the setup process.

Typically, only advanced users or situations require the use of the Windows 98 Setup switches.

Setup Log Files Used by Windows 98

Windows 98 utilizes several key logs during the installation process. Table 25.2 details the log files and their role in the setup process.

TABLE 25.2: Setup Log Files for Windows 98

Log Filename	Role during the Setup Process
DETLOG.TXT	This file keeps a record of devices found during the setup process. It records the start of a detection test and then the test outcome, i.e., the information about this particular piece of hardware. This file will be located on the root of the C: drive as a hidden file once Windows 98 is installed.

TABLE 25.2 continued: Setup Log Files for Windows 98

Log Filename	Role during the Setup Process
DETCRASH.LOG	This file keeps information about which components of the setup process loaded successfully or failed. If the component fails and you must restart the setup process, DETCRASH.LOG tells the Setup Wizard where the previous failure occurred and instructs the Wizard to skip that procedure during installation. Even though this file contains the .LOG extension (which suggests that this is a log file that can be viewed), it is not a log file and cannot be viewed. This is a binary file stored in the root of the C: drive and is a hidden file.
SETUPLOG.TXT	This file actually identifies what took place during the setup process. This is the file that Safe Recovery uses to determine where it will resume the setup process. This is a regular read/write file located in the root of the C: drive.
BOOTLOG.TXT	This file contains a record of the current start-up processes involved in starting Windows 98. When you install Windows 98 for the first time, this file is created automatically. This file shows the components and the drivers that have been loaded and initialized, as well as the current state of said items. This file is located in the root of the C: drive, is a normal read/write file and can be used after Windows 98 is installed to identify startup problems.

Automated Installs

This section deals with the issues surrounding automated setups and three specific tools that assist the setup process: Microsoft Batch 98 (BATCH.EXE), INFINST.EXE, and DBSET.EXE. To upgrade multiple systems, the installation medium that is most frequently used is the network. Copy the Win98 folder from the CD-ROM to a location on the file server, then share this location so that you can access it. The Windows 98 files are still in a compressed format in the CAB files, but they can easily be accessed from computers on the company server.

A *push installation* can also be performed on a network. In a push installation, the server sends an automated upgrade of Windows 98 to client workstations. Windows 98 does not include the software for this method. A Microsoft BackOffice product called Systems Management Server (SMS) can perform a push installation from an NT server.

Microsoft Batch 98

With Windows 98, you can use the scripted file if you are upgrading from the CD-ROM or are upgrading multiple systems on a company network. A setup script file allows you to include all the components that you want installed during the upgrade process. In Windows 95, a setup script file called MSBATCH.INF contains predefined settings for all the options to be selected. In Windows 98, the MSBATCH.INF file is used during a System Recovery situation. However, you can easily create a script file using the Microsoft Batch 98 tool.

The Microsoft Batch 98 utility is a Windows-based program that makes it easy to create installation script files. You customize the Setup Wizard to accept the EULA (End User License Agreement), to inhibit display of the Product Key, and to control all user input (including user, company, computer, and workgroup names). Batch 98 can also be used to install printers and network components, select the optional components you desire, and customize the Internet Explorer 4.*x* setup. In addition, Batch 98 can scan your computer's Registry to see what components you have installed, create an .INF file, and store your settings in the .INF file.

Microsoft Batch 98 offers a more intuitive interface and improved functionality, as shown in Figure 25.1.

When you use the Batch 98 utility, you work with seven key options:

Gather Now allows you to scan the local system for current settings.

General Setup Options allows you to customize most Windows 98 general settings.

Network Options allows you to customize network settings.

Optional Components allows you to choose which Windows 98 components to install.

Internet Explorer Options allows you to customize the Internet Browser and Shell options.

Advanced Options allows you to choose Registry, Policy, and Windows Update options.

Save Settings to INF allows you to save local settings or new MSBATCH.INF type files to an .INF file.

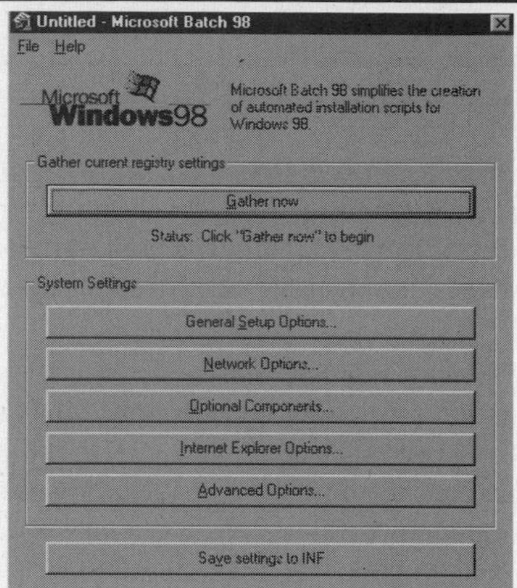

FIGURE 25.1: The Microsoft Batch 98 utility

With the newly created setup script, you can run the Windows 98 Setup utility with the command-line parameter that uses the script filename (D:\Win98\SETUP.EXE C:\Temp:\MYBATCH.INF, for example). The D:\ is the CD-ROM drive letter with the setup executable specified. C:\Temp is the location of the script file MYBATCH.INF. You can use any name you like, just make sure you use the .INF extension.

NOTE

When you use Microsoft Batch 98, the .INF file you create will contain a single computer name. Each computer on your network must have a unique name. The Multiple Machine-Name Save utility allows you to create and incorporate a text file that contains unique machine names for use during the Windows 98 setup.

INF Installer for Windows 98

Even though you can automate the Windows 98 installation process, some files and drivers cannot be controlled by the Microsoft Batch 98 program. The INF Installer program, INFINST.EXE, allows you to add device drivers, network drivers, and other third-party software (see Figure 25.2). INFINST.EXE allows you to install all of the drivers just as if they were part of the Windows 98 Setup program.

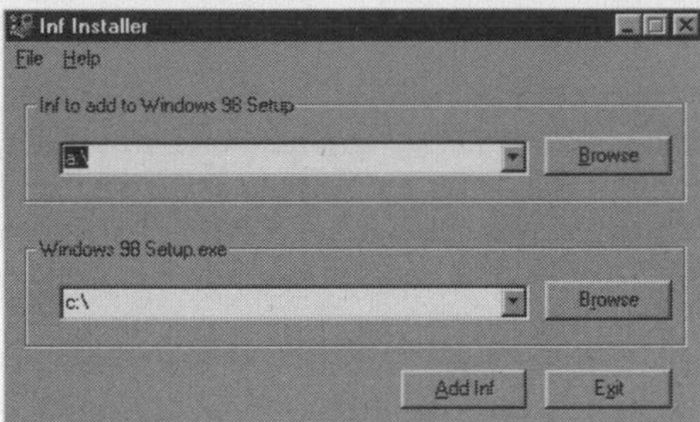

FIGURE 25.2: The INF Installer window

DBSET.EXE for Windows 98

DBSET.EXE is another new utility in the Windows 98 suite of tools. It allows you to personalize the setup process by creating a database. The information in this database can be used to change information on a system or systems when installed from a server. One of the options available in DBSET is illustrated in Figure 25.3.

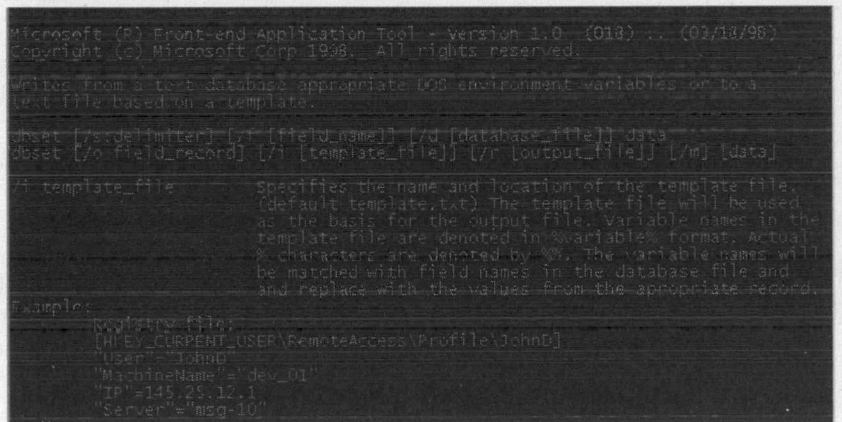

FIGURE 25.3: A DBSET example

With this tool, you can individualize setup scripts by creating a database file containing specific data for each user. DBSET.EXE can also be used to customize Registry files and write environment variables.

TIP

Other files can be modified to enhance the setup process. NETDET.INI is used to detect NetWare components and TSRs (terminate-and-stay-resident programs) during the Windows 98 installation. You can use a file named WRKGRP.INI to specify a list of workgroups in which users can participate. APPS.INI lets you define information that permits users to upgrade from Windows 95 to Windows 98 with a one-click installation.

Installation Options

Multiple installations require more work than single, stand-alone installations. Automated tools (like Microsoft Batch 98's INFINST and DBSET) make the installation process easier.

New Installations

You can also install Windows 98 from the MS-DOS prompt. This installation method is preferred in two main circumstances:

- You are installing Windows 98 on a new or recently formatted hard disk drive.
- You want to dual-boot your system with another operating system, such as Windows NT or a DOS 6.2*x*/Windows 3.*x* combination.

WARNING

When running the Windows 98 Setup Wizard from MS-DOS, you must have the real-mode network drivers and the real-mode CD-ROM drivers available and loaded. Otherwise, you will lose your network connection or the use of your CD-ROM. Make sure the appropriate drivers are on the local hard disk. The driver settings can most likely be found in the CONFIG.SYS and AUTOEXEC.BAT files.

TIP

If you have an OEM version of Windows 98, you can use it to update a DOS computer. If you have Microsoft's version, you will need to verify previous versions of a Windows operating system.

Upgrading to Windows 98

The setup process is not as complicated as it may seem. Microsoft invested a great deal of time and testing to ensure that the setup and installation processes are simple and straightforward. Most Windows 98 Setup dialog boxes contain Next and Back command buttons that allow you to easily progress or move back to review your selections. You can cancel the setup process at any time. Setup prepares the Windows 98 Setup Wizard, which in turn guides you through a simple five-phase process:

1. Preparing to run Windows 98 Setup
2. Collecting information about your computer
3. Copying Windows 98 files to your computer
4. Restarting your computer
5. Setting up hardware and finalizing settings

Using the Uninstall Feature

Installing a new operating system can be a one-way street unless a good uninstall component is present. Because your software needs may change, Microsoft created the Uninstall feature so you can remove unwanted software (including Windows 98 itself).

To uninstall Windows 98, you must meet the following conditions:

- The system files must have been saved when you were prompted to save them; this operation produces two files: WINUNDO.DAT and WINUNDO.INI.
- The hard disk where Windows 98 is located cannot be compressed.
- The current Windows 98 file system partitions cannot be FAT32.

If the previous conditions are met, you should be able to successfully uninstall Windows 98. Please keep in mind that this process does not always work and is not fail-safe.

Dual-Booting with Windows 98

There may be times when you or someone on your administration team requires two operating systems on the same machine. If you are currently running IBM OS/2, Microsoft Windows NT, or Caldera's DR-DOS on your system, you can install Windows 98 to coexist with any one of these operating systems. Here are a few points to consider:

- Typically, Windows 98 is going to be used to upgrade an existing Windows 95 or Windows 3.*x* system. Windows 98 is not intended to dual-boot. Windows 98 Plug-and-Play drivers can conflict with Windows NT drivers. You might be better off with two separate machines.
- To dual-boot, the boot partition must be FAT16. Windows NT is not compatible with FAT32. Windows 98 is not compatible with NT's NTFS or OS/2's HPFS.
- To dual-boot, you need to install Windows 98 into a folder other than C:\Windows.
- You must be using MS-DOS 5.0 or later to dual-boot.
- You must install your applications twice, once for each system.

Dual-Booting Windows 98 with Windows NT The Windows NT Boot Loader tool will direct the flow of the boot process. When you boot your system, the Windows NT Boot Loader appears and allows you to choose between Windows NT and Microsoft DOS. Choose the MS-DOS option to install Windows 98. Once the Setup Wizard runs and your system has rebooted, you will need to select the MS-DOS option once again to finalize the Windows 98 setup.

Dual-Booting Windows 98 with OS/2 Like Windows NT, the IBM OS/2 operating system has a boot loading tool, the Boot Manager. OS/2 must be set up to dual-boot to MS-DOS. You must run the Windows 98 Setup from the MS-DOS prompt. Go to the folder location of the Windows 98 source files and type **Setup** to start the Setup Wizard. Install Windows 98 as previously discussed, but make sure to install Windows 98 into a separate directory and do not delete the partition on which OS/2 is installed.

Upon completion, you may need to re-enable the OS/2 Boot Manager by running the OS/2 command FDISK from the OS/2 boot disk. With the OS/2 Boot Manager re-enabled, reboot the system. The Multiboot Option window will appear. Once you make your selection, you are ready to go.

WARNING

Microsoft does not advise, nor support, a dual-boot environment with IBM's OS/2 or DR-DOS.

Dual-Booting Windows 98 with DR-DOS Installing Windows 98 onto a computer that already has Caldera's DR-DOS installed is very similar to the MS-DOS installation procedure. Make sure that you REM any programs or TSRs in the CONFIG.SYS and AUTOEXEC.BAT files that could conflict with the Windows 98 setup process. For example, if you have enabled the DR-DOS Volume Protection option, you must disable it before you start the setup process.

At the DR-DOS prompt, switch to the directory that contains the Windows 98 source files, and install as usual. When Setup is complete, you are ready to go.

Installation Procedures

Using various Windows 98 utilities to perform installations is heavily covered on the test. Major test sections include automating the installation and installing a dual-boot computer.

Automating Installations

Windows 98 comes with various tools that allow you to automate the installation. The most frequently used tool is Microsoft Batch 98.

Using Microsoft Batch 98 To fully appreciate the Microsoft Batch 98 tool, you must use it. The following steps show you just how easy it is to create an MSBATCH.INF file and use the Batch 98 program.

1. Make sure your Windows 98 CD-ROM is in the CD-ROM drive.
2. Right-click the Start button. Select Explore ➢ CD-ROM drive ➢ \Tools\ResKit\Batch.
3. Double-click SETUP.EXE.
4. Select and accept all of the defaults. Batch 98 is now installed on your system.
5. Your system does not need to restart. Select Start ➢ Programs ➢ Microsoft Batch 98.
6. The Batch 98 program is started. Click Gather Now. Windows 98 will peruse the current Registry settings and collect all of the current Windows 98 settings and data.
7. Click through each of the five Batch 98 options: General Setup Options, Network Options, Optional Components,

Internet Explorer Options, and Advanced options. You should see information about your personal settings and your current Windows 98 installation.

8. Click Save Settings to INF.
9. Name the file C:\Temp\MYBATCH.INF.
10. Select File ➢ Exit.
11. Select Start ➢ Programs ➢ Accessories ➢ Notepad.
12. Select File ➢ Open ➢ C:\Temp\MYBATCH.INF. Click Open.
13. Review the file and identify the various sections.
14. Select File ➢ Print. The script file will print.
15. Select File ➢ Exit.

Creating New Installations

This section identifies the steps that the Setup Wizard will follow during the installation of a new, or recently formatted, hard disk.

Phase 0: Start at Ground Level When you install from the MS-DOS prompt, Setup performs a routine check on your system to ensure that a Windows 98 environment can exist. You can think of this procedure as Phase 0. Setup runs the real-mode version of ScanDisk, which checks the directory structure, file allocation table (FAT), and the file system. It does not check for physical errors, nor does it correct long filename errors. The MINI.CAB file is expanded and a run-time version of Windows is loaded. If needed, a special Extended Memory Manager is loaded to run Windows during the setup process. The mini-Windows program is loaded with the necessary files to run Windows, and the Setup Wizard can be started.

Phase 1: Preparing to Run Windows 98 Setup Installing Windows 98 to a new or recently formatted disk is very similar to the Windows 95 and the Windows 3.*x* installation. After typing **Setup** and pressing Enter to activate the Setup Wizard, you begin Phase 1. The following tasks are performed:

- The Windows 98 Setup dialog box is displayed.
- SETUPLOG.TXT is created in the root of drive C:.

- The target drive (the drive you are installing to) and the source drive (the drive you are installing from) are identified. (This step is unique to this setup process.)
- The Wininst0.400 directory is created for temporary files.
- The MINI.CAB FILE, PRECOPY1.CAB, and PRECOPY2.CAB files are extracted. The files required to run the Windows 98 Setup Wizard are loaded.

Phase 2: Collecting Information about Your Computer This phase asks the user questions in order to customize the installation. The general steps are given here, with more details provided under the "Upgrading Using Windows 98" section.

- You are asked to complete the EULA.
- You are asked to input the Product Key.
- You are asked to select the directory into which you prefer Windows 98 installed.
- You are asked to choose the type of installation: Typical or Custom.
- You are prompted for user information (name and company).
- You are asked to install the window components. You can select "Show me the list of components so I can choose." You are then taken to the Select Components window.
- You are asked to provide computer information for the network.
- You are asked to provide hardware component information about the keyboard and region.
- You are asked to choose the channel source.
- You are asked to create a Startup disk.

Phase 3: Copying Windows 98 Files to Your Computer Phase 3 consists of copying Windows 98 files to your computer. Since files are copied as the process begins, avoid interruptions—otherwise, you will most likely have to restart the entire setup process.

Phase 4: Restarting Your Computer Windows 98 needs to restart in order to correctly initialize device drivers. After 15 seconds, the computer is restarted and the message "Getting ready to start Windows 98 for the first time" is displayed.

Phase 5: Setting Up Hardware and Finalizing Settings In this final phase, Windows 98 performs a complete hardware detection of Plug-and-Play components and attempts to correctly identify and install the legacy devices. If Windows 98 does not find a particular device, you will have to install it manually by selecting Control Panel ➢ Add New Hardware.

After the hardware devices are identified, the Setup Wizard continues. The Control Panel entries are added. Programs on the Start menu are created and the Help file is set up. Support for MS-DOS programs is installed. You are prompted for time zone and date verification. The driver database is built, and the core system configuration file is initialized and ready to roll.

Upgrading Using Windows 98

While upgrading to Windows 98 is similar to initiating a new installation, there are several additional steps that include saving old system files and settings.

Phase 1: Preparing to Run Windows 98 Setup When you start the Windows 98 CD-ROM, you will be presented with the Introduction screen shown below. This is where your installation process will begin.

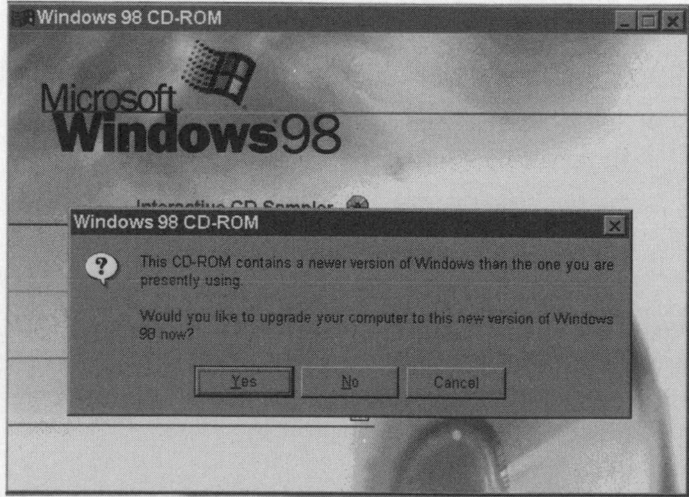

When you select the Yes button, you are taken to the Windows 98 Setup screen. If any applications are still running, you will first see the warning screen.

As noted in the Preinstallation Checklist, you should close all open applications. After you close them, click the OK button to continue. Then you will see the Windows 98 Setup Welcome screen.

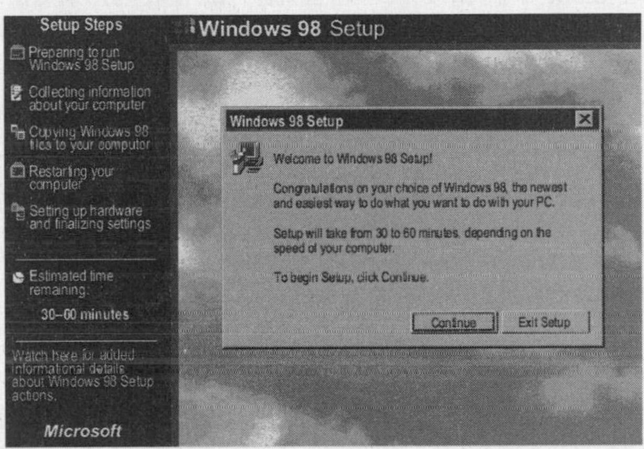

This new Setup Wizard provides much more information about the setup process than did prcvious installation Wizards. The information on the left side of the screen identifies which of the five Setup phases you arc at, givcs thc timc rcmaining to complete the setup process, and describes the current Setup activity.

NOTE

The "Estimated time remaining" information is usually incorrect.

During this preparation phase, a temporary directory called Wininst0.400 is created on drive C:. Windows 98 uses this directory to expand and copy the files required to run the Setup Wizard. MINI.CAB, PRECOPY1.CAB, and PRECOPY2.CAB assist in the initial launch of the setup process.

A file called SETUPLOG.TXT is created in the root directory of drive C:. The SETUPLOG.TXT file is an ASCII text file that contains information about the setup process. Entries in this file document the installation steps and identify whether or not they were successful. During a recovery, Setup uses this file to avoid repeated failure at the same location and/or problem and determine where Setup should resume.

During the first phase, Windows 98 also checks for antivirus software and systems that may contain a CMOS-enabled virus checker. An activated antivirus program will prevent Windows 98 from changing the Master Boot Record. If an antivirus program is detected, Windows 98 will ask you to restart the system and disable the software or CMOS setting. Windows 98 also adds an entry to the AUTOEXEC.BAT file, warning you that you need to disable all antivirus software.

NOTE

If you see the \Wininst1.400 or \Wininst2.400 directories, this means the setup process has failed and the Recovery feature was not selected when the prompt appeared. If, however, Windows 98 has installed and is functioning, you can delete these directories.

Phase 2: Collecting Information about Your Computer After the Setup Wizard is loaded, the temporary directory is created, and the SETUPLOG.TXT file is enabled, Setup collects information about your system and prepares to copy the Windows 98 files. During this phase, the EULA screen appears.

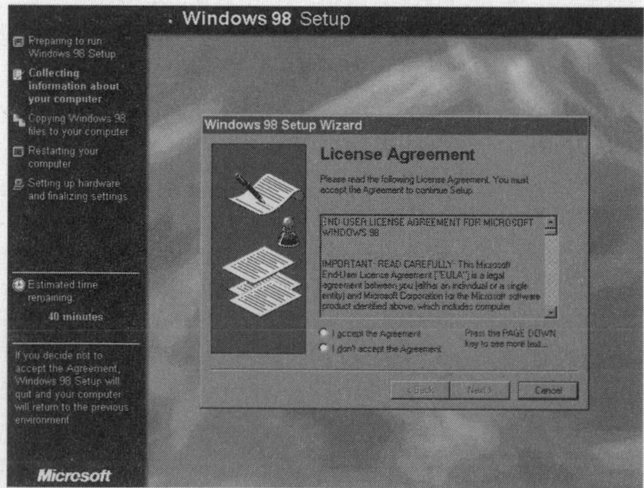

You must accept the terms of the license agreement to continue the setup process.

You will next be prompted to enter the Product Key (a 25-character alphanumeric code) as shown below. This code is located either on the Certificate of Authenticity that shipped with your documentation or on the back cover of your CD case.

TIP

The Product Key is case sensitive.

TIP

The Product Key dialog box may not appear if you are installing Windows 98 from a network and/or are using a script and/or command-line switches.

By default, Windows 98 will install to the directory where the Windows 95 files are located; typically C:\Windows. If you are prompted with a window that asks for a directory, accept the default directory of C:\Windows. However, if you plan to dual-boot Windows 98 with another operating system, install Windows 98 to a different directory (e.g., C:\Win98).

The Checking Your System dialog screen will appear next.

Setup checks your system at this point. ScanDisk runs in protected mode. If ScanDisk finds a problem, it will stop and allow you to run ScanDisk manually. Upon completion of the ScanDisk operation, Setup checks to see that the Registry settings have not been corrupted. To do this, the Setup Wizard runs the ScanRegW utility, which checks the integrity of the Registry files. ScanRegW does not fix corrupted Registries; it only detects Registry status (either Okay or Not Okay). If there is a problem, you can run the ScanReg program from the command line. ScanReg will attempt to replace the corrupted Registry with a known valid backup. If ScanReg cannot do this, it will attempt to fix the source of corruption.

NOTE

When ScanDisk runs in protected mode, it does not check for physical errors or perform a surface scan. This is why it is preferable to complete the ScanDisk task on the Preinstallation Checklist.

When your system checks out okay, Windows 98 verifies that the required disk space is available. You will see a Preparing Directory dialog box where Setup checks for installed components based on the current

Windows 95 system. Setup then creates the Windows 98 directory structure; typically in C:\Windows and C:\Program Files folders.

The next step in the Collection phase is determining whether or not you want to save your existing MS-DOS and Windows system files. The Save System Files dialog box will appear.

When you choose to save your existing files, two files will be created: WINUNDO.DAT and WINUNDO.INI.

The WINUNDO.DAT file contains all the files required to restore your old system. This file ranges in size from 35MB to 75MB. The WINUNDO.INI file contains the information necessary to restore the files contained in the WINUNDO.DAT file. Typically, these files are located in the root of drive C: and are marked as read-only and hidden. (If you have more than one local hard disk drive, you will be prompted to select the drive to which information should be saved.)

WARNING

If you are using a compressed drive or FAT32, you might be prompted to save the system files during the installation. Windows 98 cannot be uninstalled from either of these environments, even if you are able to save your system files.

If you are unsure of the Windows 98 setup process, select the Save System Files option. The two WINUNDO files are then created, and you can choose to uninstall Windows 98. (If you skip this section, you can always use the data you backed up per the Preinstallation Checklist.)

When all is said and done, Setup saves the current system files in the root directory. When you go to the Control Panel ➢ Add/Remove Programs applet, "Uninstall Windows 98" will be listed.

As you complete the Collection Phase process, you need to address a few items:

- The type of setup to be performed
- User information
- What medium to use to receive information
- The Startup disk

Once the Save System Files procedure is complete, you will be asked to specify the location where you prefer to receive information from Internet channels. Internet channels allow you to receive information from Web sites that are designed to deliver content from their site to you via the Internet. The Establishing Your Location dialog box will appear, giving you the option of choosing your channel information source.

After you have established your channel location, Setup prompts you to create a Startup disk (often referred to as the Emergency Startup Disk). Because the Windows 98 and Windows 95 Startup disks are not compatible, you should create a new Startup disk. The Startup Disk Wizard simplifies the task of creating a new Startup disk.

The Windows 98 Startup disk will enable you to effectively troubleshoot problems should the system fail to boot.

When you boot from the Windows 98 Startup disk, a menu will appear asking you if you want CD-ROM support. This is a new addition to the Startup disk. Support for generic CD-ROM drivers is based on the IDE and SCSI technologies. Keep in mind that these drivers will not work with all CD-ROMs; you may still need the real-mode drivers for your hardware devices. From the menu, make your decision to install support for the CD-ROM drive if you need it. The Startup disk will then create a RAM drive and expand a series of needed utilities.

Included with Windows 98 is a new batch file called BOOTDISK.BAT that will create a Windows 98 Startup disk. This utility was created for laptop users who must exchange CD-ROM and floppy devices (i.e., physically remove their CD-ROM drive and replace it with their floppy drive). Simply type **Bootdisk** and a Startup disk can be created. You can also use the Add/Remove Programs applet in the Control Panel to create a new Startup disk. Start the applet and choose the Startup Disk tab. From there, click the Create Startup Disk button.

WARNING

The CD-ROM that you use must be connected to the motherboard or a controller card. A CD-ROM connected to a sound card will have problems and probably won't be recognized at startup. Keep a backup copy of your MS-DOS drivers for your sound card and CD-ROM. Also keep a backup copy of the original CONFIG.SYS and AUTOEXEC.BAT files, as well as the 16-bit drivers listed there.

Whether or not you load the CD-ROM real-mode drivers is up to you. After you make your menu selection as to whether or not you need CD-ROM access, the Startup disk creates a 2MB RAM drive. In order to place multiple drivers on one disk, Microsoft elected to compress several files.

A new file entitled EBD.CAB contains most of the MS-DOS diagnostic tools found on the Windows 95 Startup disk. Once the RAM drive is installed, the contents of the EBD.CAB file are extracted and placed on the RAM drive.

After the files are copied and the Startup disk is created, you will be prompted to remove the disk and continue the setup process.

TIP

You are free to add additional files and tools to the EBD.CAB file using a utility called CABARC.EXE. This tool is available from the Microsoft Web site (`www.microsoft.com`).

NOTE

The files on the Startup disk are not copied to the \Windows\Command folder as part of the copy process. They are copied to the \Windows\Command folder when you create a Startup disk during setup. Make sure this occurs when you set up Windows 98 for the first time.

Phase 3: Copying Windows 98 Files to Your Computer After the Setup Wizard finishes with the Startup disk, you enter the third phase of the setup process. Setup has all the necessary information to proceed; no input is required during this phase. The Start Copying Files window is the last screen you will see.

WARNING

Do *not* interrupt the copy process.

Phase 4: Restarting Your Computer Now that the Windows 98 files have been copied to your computer, Setup prompts you to restart the computer. You can select the Restart Now button, or you can just watch and wait. After 15 seconds, the system will reboot automatically.

After Setup has restarted your computer, the following message appears briefly on your screen: "Getting ready to start Windows 98 for the first time."

The computer system starts as a Windows 98 operating system with the following modifications:

- The WIN.INI and SYSTEM.INI files are modified to add Windows 98-specific settings.
- The Registry files are modified to add Windows 98-specific settings.
- The AUTOEXEC.BAT and CONFIG.SYS files are modified to reflect the Windows 98 environment.

Once these files are adjusted to Windows 98, it is time to move to the final phase of the installation process.

NOTE

During this phase, Windows 98 may REM (remark out) items in any of the mentioned files. Some programs require specific entry information in the CONFIG.SYS and AUTOEXEC.BAT files. After the Windows 98 Setup is complete, check these files to see that your requisite device drivers still exist. If a problem exists, delete the REM statement or manually add the entry to ensure that you have full access to all of your resources. Under normal conditions, Windows 98 will only REM the drivers for which it has a 32-bit version. Test your system before you "unremark" drivers. With newer computers, you may not even need your CONFIG.SYS and AUTOEXEC.BAT files.

Phase 5: Setting Up Hardware and Finalizing Settings Unlike Windows 95, Windows 98 waits until this final phase to "talk" to your specific hardware devices. Because hardware detection is now placed at the end of the copy process, the setup process is more reliable and less problematic.

Setup attempts to retain and verify the settings used by Windows 98. If a problem or failure occurs, Setup will perform a full hardware detection. Once the hardware information has been internalized for the legacy devices and the Plug-and-Play devices have enumerated themselves, Windows 98 is ready to conclude with the final settings. Enumeration refers to the process by which Plug-and-Play devices notify the system of their resource requirements and are then assigned the requested resources.

The following items are configured in the final Setup phase:

- Control Panel entries are added and updated.
- Program items on the Start menu are created.
- The Windows Help file is established.
- Support for MS-DOS programs is installed.
- WALIGN (the Tuning Up application) is started.
- Time zone and date may be changed, if necessary.
- The core system configuration files are modified and upgraded to reflect the Windows 98 operating system.

When Setup has finished setting up the hardware and finalizing the configuration settings, Windows 98 is restarted for the second time. When Windows 98 returns, you are asked to log on. If you have installed network software, you will be asked to log on to the network. When you log on, Setup builds the information driver database, updates the system settings, and displays any personalized settings you might have selected during the setup process (e.g., viewing channels).

When all of these phases are completed and you have successfully upgraded to Windows 98, Setup displays the Welcome to Windows 98 dialog box.

Upgrading from Windows 3.*x* to Windows 98

The migration path for Windows 3.*x* users is very similar to the procedure for Windows 95 users. The main difference is that Windows 3.*x* still depends on real-mode drivers and does not have a Registry from which Windows 98 can glean and access data. The points discussed in the previous section on deployment strategies, the Preinstallation Checklist, and whether any Setup switches are required still apply; decisions must be made regarding these salient issues.

Uninstalling Windows 98

Windows 98 makes it relatively easy to uninstall itself, as long as the prerequisites have been met. From the Add/Remove Programs item, locate the two uninstall components in the list of items on the Install/Uninstall tab.

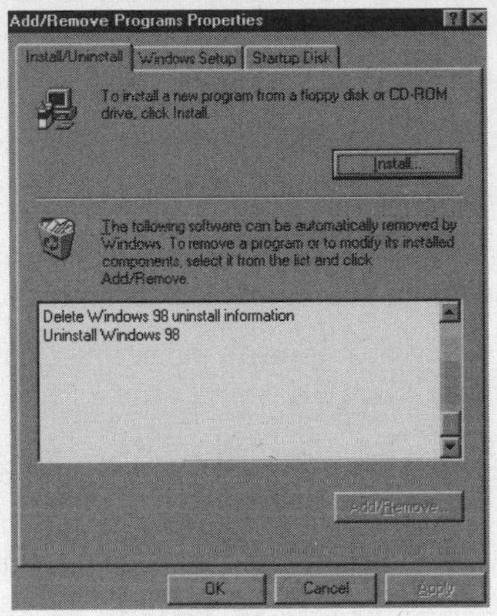

Follow these steps to uninstall Windows 98:

1. Go to the Control Panel.
2. Select Add/Remove Programs.
3. Select the Install/Uninstall tab (default view).
4. Select the Uninstall Windows 98 option.
5. Select Add/Remove.
6. A dialog box appears indicating status. Click Yes to continue.
7. Another dialog box appears indicating that your disk will be checked for errors. Click Yes to continue.
8. The ScanDisk program runs, and yet another dialog box appears asking if you want to continue. Click Yes to continue.
9. The system restarts.
10. You should return to Windows 95.

If you choose to keep Windows 98 as your installed operating system, you should remove the Windows 95 file system. You can manually delete the WINUNDO.DAT and the WINUNDO.INI files or follow these steps to remove them automatically:

1. Go to the Control Panel.

2. Select Add/Remove Programs.
3. Select the Install/Uninstall tab (default view).
4. Select Remove Windows 95 System Files.
5. Select Add/Remove.
6. A dialog box appears indicating that you will not be able to go back to the Windows 95 environment. Click Yes to continue.
7. A dialog box appears indicating that the files have been deleted. Click OK.

Configuring Dual-Booting with Windows 98

If Windows 98 is already installed on your system, you can follow these steps to install Windows NT so that you have a dual-boot system:

1. After you have booted into Windows 98, select Start ➢ Programs ➢ MS-DOS Prompt.
2. The MS-DOS prompt will appear. Switch to the directory that contains the Windows NT source files. (This directory will usually appear as a folder entitled \I386 on the Windows NT CD-ROM or as a share installation source on your network.)
3. At the source folder location, type **winnt /b /w**. WINNT is the Windows NT Setup program. The NT files will be copied from the source to your local system. The /b option prevents the Setup program from creating the floppy disks. The /w option allows you to run WINNT in a Windows environment.
4. Follow and accept the prompts of the WINNT Setup Wizard. Windows NT will load the files that it needs, including the Boot Loader tool.
5. After the installation is complete, your system will boot to the Windows NT Loader window. Make your selection from the various options. Now you can choose to go to the operating system you need.

If Windows NT is already installed on your system and does not allow you to boot to MS-DOS so that you can install Windows 98, you can follow these steps to install Windows 98 to support a dual-boot situation.

1. Start the computer with an MS-DOS floppy disk—a Windows 95 or 98 Startup disk should work fine. The disk should contain the MS-DOS utility SYS.COM.
2. Once the system has booted successfully and you are at the command prompt, enter **A:SYS C:**. This operation will transfer the MS-DOS files needed to dual-boot with Windows NT. You should then see the message "System transferred."
3. Remove the floppy disk and reboot the system. You should be at an MS-DOS prompt once the system starts.
4. Go to the folder location of the Windows 98 source files and type **Setup**. The Windows 98 Setup Wizard will appear. Make sure you install Windows 98 into a separate directory and do not delete the partition on which Windows NT is installed.
5. After all of the Windows 98 installation reboots are complete and Windows 98 appears to be working, reboot the system using the Windows NT Setup disks. Boot the system with the NT Setup disk in drive A:. The Windows NT Setup utility will start, and a list of menu options will appear.
6. At the Windows NT Setup options window, select R to repair Windows NT. This process repairs only the Windows NT boot sector. Do not choose to inspect the Registry, the system files, or the boot environment. Repair only the boot sector.
7. Reboot the system one more time and you should see the Windows NT Multiboot Option screen.
8. Edit the Windows NT BOOT.INI file. To allow changes, you may need to use the MS-DOS ATTRIB command to change the file's attributes. Once in the BOOT.INI file, add the following line to the [OPERATING SYSTEMS] section: **c:\=Windows 98**.
9. Save the file, restore the attribute, and restart the system.
10. After you reboot the system, you will see the Windows NT boot-loader menu. MS-DOS is one of the options from which the Windows 98 program will load.

Configure Windows 98 server components.

Server components include:

- Microsoft Personal Web Server 4.0
- Dial-Up Networking Server

This objective covers adding functionality to Windows 98 with the Personal Web Server and the Dial-Up Networking Server software. Configuring the services is also covered.

Personal Web Server for Windows 98

Using Personal Web Server (PWS) is an alternative to paying someone to create your page for you. With a copy of PWS and Microsoft FrontPage or Microsoft Publisher, Windows 98 allows you to create your own professional-looking Web page documents and share them as an HTTP server.

Although Windows 98 can operate as an HTTP server using PWS, it was not designed for heavy-use, mission-critical production environments. For a heavy-use informational HTTP server, you should use a Windows NT server coupled with an Internet Information Server (IIS). For a mission-critical, electronic-commerce HTTP server, Site Server for Windows NT should be used. Note that IIS is available for Windows NT at no additional charge, while Site Server is an add-on product for Windows NT.

TIP

Details about IIS and Site Server can be found in *MCSE: IIS 4.0 Study Guide* (Sybex, 1998).

Windows 98 as a Dial-Up Networking Server

Windows 98 can also install software that allows it to become a Dial-Up Networking server. When used as a dial-up server, Windows 98 permits a single connection to its resources. Windows 98 supports other Windows 98 machines, LAN Manager, Windows for Workgroups 3.11, Windows NT, and any PPP-based remote client.

Installation Procedures

While installing both PWS and Dial-Up Networking Server is relatively easy, you will also need to know how to configure these services for a given situation.

Installing PWS

Installing PWS into Windows 98 is quick and simple. Go to Control Panel ➢ Network, choose Add, highlight Service, pick Microsoft, and highlight Personal Web Server. Then click OK. You can also install PWS by running \add-ons\pws\SETUP.EXE from the CD.

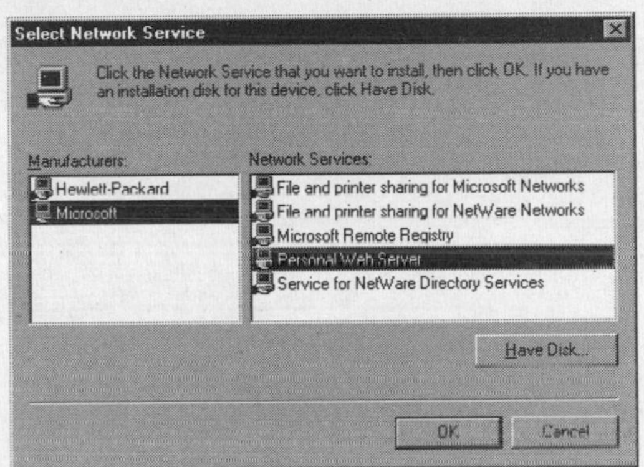

NOTE

PWS version 4.0 has been released and can be downloaded for no charge from `www.microsoft.com`. PWS 4.0 also comes as part of the Windows NT 4.0 Option Pack CD-ROM.

If you install Microsoft FrontPage, PWS will be installed automatically as one of the add-on items. Whichever way you install it, with PWS your Windows 98 machine will turn into a fully operational Web server.

Configuring PWS

You configure PWS by clicking the PWS icon that is added to your Control Panel or by going to Start ➢ Programs ➢ Internet Explorer ➢ Personal Web Server ➢ Personal Web Manager (for version 4.0). This brings up the Personal Web Server Properties dialog box (for older versions) or the Personal Web Manager (for 4.0). Either program allows you to start, configure, and stop the HTTP and FTP services—the Personal Web Server Properties dialog box is shown below.

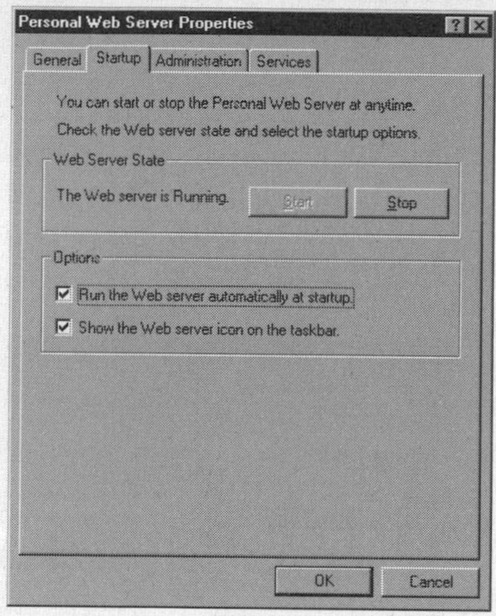

Installing and Configuring the Dial-Up Server

Dial-Up Networking Server is installed using the Add/Remove Programs applet of the Control Panel and is listed in the Communication section. To set up a dial-up server, you need to enable caller access by opening the Dial-Up Networking window and going to Connections ➢ Dial-Up Server.

You can also choose the server type and set password encryption and software compression options.

Follow these steps to turn your Windows 98 machine into a Dial-Up Networking server:

1. Install the Dial-Up Networking Server software (if it isn't already installed) by going to Control Panel ➢ Add/Remove Programs and selecting Dial-Up Server from the Communications section. Close the applet.
2. From the Dial-Up Networking folder, select Connections ➢ Dial-Up Server to bring up the Dial-Up Server dialog box.
3. To make your Windows 98 machine a dial-up server, click the "Allow caller access" option.

4. If you want to create a password that a client must use to access your dial-up server, click the Change Password button.
5. Click the Server Type button to bring up the Server Types dialog box. Choose a server type from the drop-down list and click the Enable Software Compression and/or Require Encrypted Password checkboxes if you want to use these options. Then choose OK.
6. In the Dial-Up Server dialog box, click OK to complete the setup. Your Windows 98 machine is now ready to accept calls from clients.

Install and configure the network components of Windows 98 in a Microsoft environment or a mixed NetWare and Microsoft environment.

Network components include:

- Client for Microsoft Networks
- Client for NetWare Networks
- Network adapters
- File and Printer Sharing for Microsoft Networks
- File and Printer Sharing for NetWare Networks
- Service for NetWare Directory Services (NDS)
- Asynchronous transfer mode (ATM) components
- Virtual private networking and PPTP
- Browse Master

Windows 98 excels as a networking client. In order to understand your options when installing client software for Windows 98, it is important to know how networking works for both Novell and Microsoft networks. Table 25.3 lists the possible choices for Windows 98.

TABLE 25.3: Clients That Windows 98 Can Use

Manufacturer	Name	Server Support	Server Versions
Microsoft	Client for Microsoft	Microsoft (SMB)	All
Microsoft	Client for NetWare	NetWare (NCP)	2.*x*, 3.*x*, bindery modes in 4.*x* or 5.*x*
Microsoft	Service for NDS	NetWare (NCP)	4.*x*, 5.*x* (NDS)
NetWare	NETX, VLM*	NetWare (NCP)	2.*x*, 3.*x*, 4.*x*, 5.*x*
NetWare	Client for Windows 95**	NetWare (NCP)	All

***These are real-mode clients and are not recommended for use with Windows 98.**
****This client can be downloaded from `www.novell.com`.**

Novell NetWare servers communicate using a language called *NCP* (NetWare Core Protocol). This language is spoken by both the NetWare clients and servers. When you install the Client for NetWare Networks, you are enabling Windows 98 to communicate (using NCP) with NetWare servers, as illustrated in Figure 25.4.

Microsoft servers communicate using a language called *SMB* (Server Message Blocks). By installing the Client for Microsoft Networks, you enable Windows 98 to communicate with Microsoft (Windows NT) servers. Windows 98 is flexible enough to have both client languages (NCP and SMB) installed at the same time. This allows Windows 98 to simultaneously communicate with both NetWare and Microsoft servers, as illustrated in Figure 25.4.

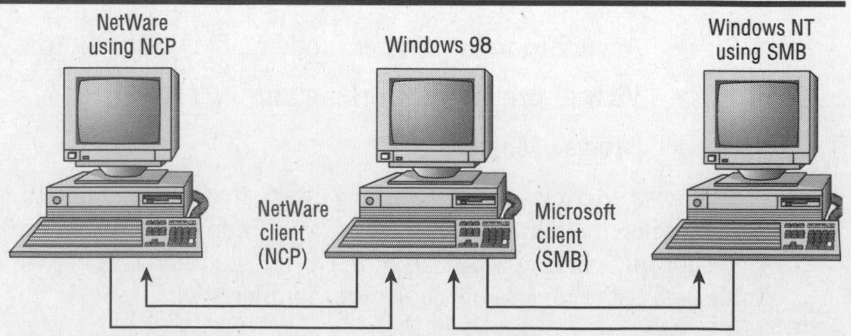

FIGURE 25.4: Windows 98 and simultaneous connections to NetWare and Windows NT

Using SMB or NCP is independent of which network protocol is in use. SMB and NCP are used at a higher level of the OSI model (the Application layer); protocols are used at a lower level (the Data Link).

Besides functioning as a client, Windows 98 can also function as a server, allowing others to connect to shared drives or shared printers. Such an arrangement is commonly called a *peer-to-peer network*. Windows 98 can perform both client and server functions simultaneously, but larger networks tend to have dedicated servers for security and performance reasons. However, small offices may have neither the budget nor the need for a dedicated server.

Client for Microsoft Networks

Connecting a Windows 98 computer to a Windows NT network is fairly straightforward. All of the software needed to connect Windows 98 to an NT computer is included on the Windows 98 CD-ROM, and is relatively easy to install. The major decision that must be made is whether to allow each Windows 98 computer to share its resources (act like a server) in addition to being a client on the network.

There are several steps involved in installing the client software for Windows NT:

1. Check the licensing agreements to ensure legality.
2. Install the network card and drivers.
3. Configure the network card.
4. Install the client software.
5. Configure the protocols.
6. Configure the client software.

Client for NetWare Networks

Before you begin client installation, you should check to make sure that you have enough NetWare client licenses for all of your clients. NetWare will not allow more than the licensed number of clients to connect to a server. In order for Windows 98 clients to save files on NetWare servers using long filenames (LFNs), you need to install NetWare's OS2 or LONG support for the server volumes. See your NetWare documentation for instructions. To set up the client software for NetWare on a Windows 98 machine, you need to install and configure the network card and drivers, the client software, and the protocols.

Network Card Drivers and NetWare Clients

When installing the network card, you have two basic choices for the drivers you can use: ODI real-mode drivers, or NDIS 3.1/5.0 protected-mode drivers.

WARNING

The 32-bit client for NetWare and MS-NDS clients both require that NDIS drivers be used.

If you choose to use NDIS 3.1/5.0 protected-mode drivers, you follow the same procedures for installing a network card and drivers as you use for a Microsoft client. All of the protected-mode clients mentioned in this chapter can use the NDIS drivers for the network card.

If you choose to use the older ODI drivers, which are necessary for NETX or VLM (real-mode) client software, you load the drivers from the AUTOEXEC.BAT file. One way of doing this is by adding the following commands to your AUTOEXEC.BAT:

LSL	The supporting driver.
NE2000	This is the driver for a NE2000-compatible card. Other cards would have a differently named driver.
IPXODI	The protocol driver.
VLM or NETX	The client software.

Windows 98 reads your AUTOEXEC.BAT file during the boot process, and opens an MS-DOS window to load the drivers. You are then prompted to log in at the MS-DOS screen. After you log in, Windows 98 continues loading.

Sharing Resources with Windows 98

Windows 98 operates as a peer-to-peer server when it uses share-level security (the default) as shown in Figure 25.5. Windows 98 can also act like a dedicated server when it uses user-level security.

Windows 98 can be installed as either a Microsoft or a NetWare server—not both. Only Windows NT can simultaneously be both a Microsoft and NetWare server (by using File and Print Services for NetWare to provide NCP support).

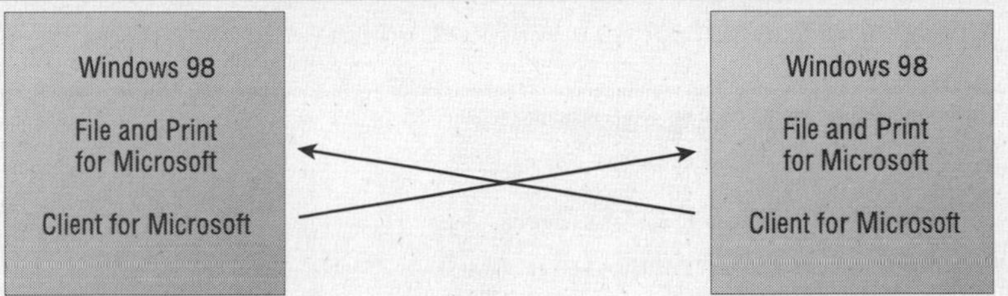

FIGURE 25.5: A peer-to-peer network

Sharing Resources on a Microsoft Network

You can have Windows 98 share its resources as a Microsoft server by installing File and Printer Sharing for Microsoft Networks, as illustrated in Figure 25.6. This allows both folders and printers to be shared.

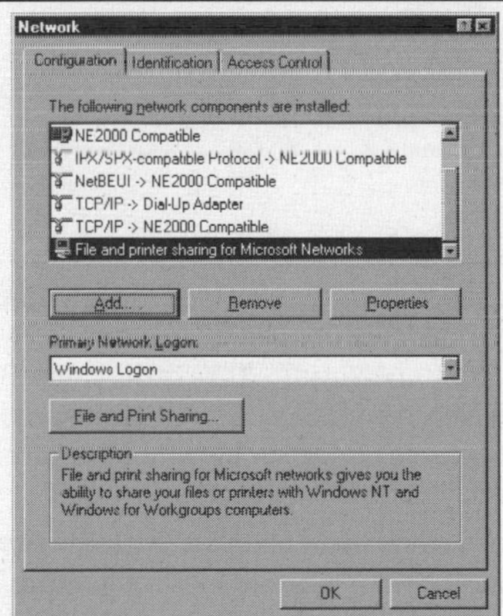

FIGURE 25.6: File and Printer Sharing installed for Microsoft networks

Sharing Resources on a NetWare Network

For Windows 98 to act like a NetWare server, you need to install File and Printer Sharing for NetWare Networks, as shown in Figure 25.7. This allows NetWare clients to use the server's folders and printers. The major restriction is that a NetWare server must already be in place on the network before you can set up a Windows 98 server.

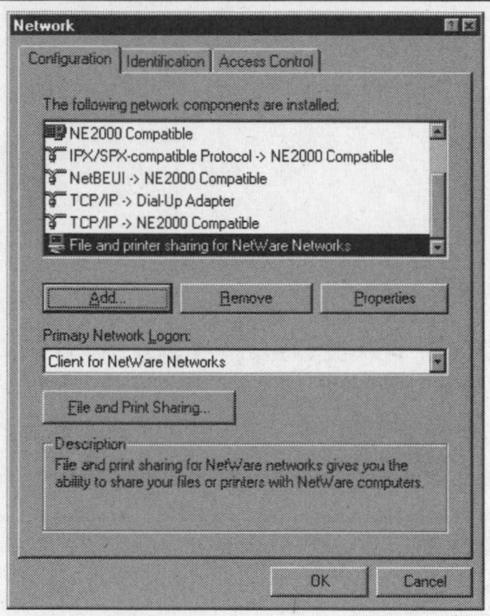

FIGURE 25.7: File and Printer Sharing installed for NetWare networks

Asynchronous Transfer Mode (ATM)

ATM is a technology that has resulted from the efforts of the International Telecommunication Union Telecommunication Standardization Sector (ITU-T) Study Group XVIII (formerly known as CCITT) to develop a Broadband Integrated Services Digital Network (BISDN) for the high-speed transfer of data, images, video, text, and audio through public networks. ATM is the transfer mode of choice for BISDN networks.

An ATM *cell* (packet) is always made up of 53 bytes, with the first five bytes comprising the header and the remaining 48 bytes constituting the payload. By using a fixed-length cell, ATM can easily be routed and multiplexed on a network and the bandwidth usage of its various services can be tightly controlled. Microsoft ATM services support LAN emulation so that protocols such as TCP/IP or IPX/SPX can be used across an ATM connection.

Virtual Private Networking (VPN)/Point-to-Point Tunneling Protocol (PPTP)

PPTP is used to make a secured, encrypted connection (a virtual private network, or VPN) via the Internet. In other words, the Internet can function as a WAN link for a secured, virtual connection. It is virtual in the sense that if you reestablish the connection, it may follow a different path through the Internet–it is not limited to a single physical connection.

PPTP support is enabled by installing the PPTP software and then configuring a connection to use the PPTP adapter instead of a standard modem.

The Browser Service

The network browsing service is designed to allow clients to access a complete list of available servers, shared folders, and shared printers, without needing to keep their own copy of the list. When a computer browses the network, it downloads a list of available servers and shares from a central computer that maintains the list. As the number of clients increases, Windows (both NT and 98) will increase the number of servers keeping lists.

The default number of browse servers is one server for every 32 clients. If Windows 98 is part of a domain, the primary domain controller (PDC) of the domain will be the browse master for the entire domain, and will have helper servers (backup browsers) provide lists to clients. When a browse master or backup browser is turned off, there will be an "election" to pick a new browse master. The order of precedence is as follows:

- Windows NT Server
- Windows NT Workstation
- Windows 98
- Windows for Workgroups

You can "stuff the ballot box" by changing the properties of the sharing service to make one server a preferred browse master over another. For example, you may have two Windows 98 computers–a 486 with 8MB of RAM and a Pentium 200 with 64MB of RAM. Obviously, the Pentium computer would make the faster browse master.

Browsing on a NetWare Network

Every 60 seconds, NetWare servers broadcast a SAP packet, which contains the server name and the shared resources it contains.

Installation and Configuration Procedures

You will need to know how to install and configure the various network clients and sharing services. You will also need to know how to configure the browser services for a given situation.

Installing and Configuring the Client for Microsoft Networks

All network configurations are established and modified from the Network applet of the Control Panel. Highlight the service, card, or protocol that you want to adjust, and then choose Properties.

Licensing the Client By purchasing Windows 98, you have license to use it on a single computer, but not necessarily on a network. If you connect the Windows 98 computer to an NT server, you will need to make sure you have a Client Access License (CAL) for each client attached.

Installing a Network Card and Driver The first step in installing network support in Windows 98 is to install the physical card in the computer. If the card is an older legacy card (its settings are made by jumpers and/or switches), you should make a note of its settings. If the card is of the Plug-and-Play variety, Windows 98 should be able to automatically detect and configure the card to the correct settings.

If Windows 98 can auto-detect the card, it may install the driver automatically. You can force Windows 98 to search for new hardware by starting the Add New Hardware Wizard from the Control Panel.

Configuring the Network Card Windows 98 should detect and install the correct drivers for your network card. Every device connected to your computer needs to be assigned a unique IRQ, I/O port, and memory address (if used). If more than one device is assigned a particular setting, you will need to resolve the conflict before Windows 98 will work properly.

How you change the settings of your network card depends on whether it is a Plug-and-Play card or a legacy (jumpered or set by software) card. If it is a Plug-and-Play card, you should be able to change its settings in Device Manager by going to the property sheet for the card and choosing Change

Setting from the Resources tab. After you reboot, the card should reflect the new settings.

If your card is a legacy card, you will need to power off the computer and then change the jumpers or switches on your card or use a software setup program (sometimes called *softset*) to change the settings. When you are finished, turn on your computer, start Windows 98, and then make the changes in Device Manager. Reboot for the changes to take effect.

Installing the Client Software

By installing the client software, you allow Windows 98 to see and connect to Windows NT servers.

1. Go to Control Panel ➢ Network and choose Add.
2. Highlight Client and choose Add.
3. Highlight Microsoft in the Manufacturers list.
4. Highlight Client for Microsoft Networks in the Network Clients list.
5. Click OK twice.
6. Reboot Windows 98.

Installing the Microsoft Client for NetWare Networks

You install the Microsoft Client for NetWare Networks by adding a client using the Network applet of the Control Panel. Follow these steps to install this client.

1. Go to Control Panel ➢ Network and choose Add.
2. Highlight Client and choose Add.
3. Highlight Microsoft in the Manufacturers list.
4. Highlight Client for NetWare Networks in the Network Clients list.
5. Click OK twice.
6. Reboot Windows 98.

Installing the Microsoft Service for NDS Client

You install the Microsoft Service for NetWare Directory Services (MS-NDS) client software by adding it as a service using the Network Control Panel.

Follow these steps to install this client:

1. Go to Control Panel ➢ Network and choose Add.
2. Highlight Service and choose Add.
3. Select Microsoft in the Manufacturers list.
4. Select Service for NetWare Directory Services.
5. Choose OK. The Service for NetWare Directory Services should load. You may be prompted for the Windows 98 CD-ROM.
6. Choose OK in the Network Control Panel to save your changes.
7. Reboot Windows 98.

Installing and Configuring ATM Support

Support for ATM services is easy to install with Windows 98. After installing the ATM support services, you will also need to install and configure the protocol (TCP/IP or IPX/SPX) you will use across the ATM connection. There are three separate protocols that must be individually installed for ATM support. To install ATM support, do the following:

1. Go to Control Panel ➢ Network, choose Add, highlight Protocol, choose Add, highlight Microsoft, and choose ATM Call Manager.
2. Select OK to add the protocol.
3. Repeat step 1, highlighting ATM Emulated LAN.
4. Select OK to add the protocol.
5. Repeat step 1, highlighting ATM LAN Emulation Client.
6. Select OK to add the protocol.
7. Install any protocols you need that are not already installed (TCP/IP, IPX/SPX).

8. Select OK from the main Network Properties screen to save your changes.
9. Reboot Windows 98.

Once the ATM services are installed, you will need to specify the name of the emulated LAN. To configure the ATM services, do the following:

1. Go to Control Panel ➢ Network.
2. Highlight the ATM LAN Emulation Client.
3. Select Properties.
4. Enter the name of the emulated LAN in the Value box.
5. Select OK to save your changes.

Installing File and Printer Sharing for Microsoft Networks

A Windows 98 computer can have many different client pieces installed simultaneously, but it can have only one sharing service installed at a time. Installing File and Printer Sharing is quite easy. This is a network service that you can install from the Network Control Panel.

Another way to access the network configuration dialog box is by right-clicking Network Neighborhood and selecting Properties.

Installing and Configuring VPN/PPTP

Support for VPN/PPTP is installed using the Add/Remove Programs applet of the Control Panel. Virtual private networking (VPN) is found in the Communication section. Simply check the box, insert the Windows 98 CD-ROM if prompted, and support for VPN/PPTP connections will be installed.

NOTE

Your dial-up server must also be configured for VPN/PPTP support in order for VPN/PPTP to work correctly.

Once you have installed Dial-Up Networking and support for VPN, you can create a VPN/PPTP connection by specifying the VPN adapter instead of your regular modem when defining a Dial-Up Networking connection.

Configuring the Browse Master

Browse Master is a property of File and Printer Sharing for Microsoft Networks.

There are three settings for this property:

Automatic This is the default and means that the computer can be elected to become a browse master, if necessary.

Enabled This means that the computer will always be a browse master.

Disabled This means the computer will never become a browse master.

Configuring an SAP Server SAP advertising is a property of the File and Printer Sharing for NetWare Networks service. If File and Printer Sharing for NetWare is installed on all of your Windows 98 computers and SAP support is enabled, a large amount of background traffic will be generated by the SAP broadcasts alone.

Install and configure network protocols in a Microsoft environment or a mixed Microsoft and NetWare environment.

Protocols include:

- NetBEUI
- IPX/SPX-compatible protocol
- TCP/IP
- Microsoft DLC
- Fast Infrared

Installing and configuring protocols is one of the key components in getting Windows 98 to successfully participate on a network. There are many different protocols to choose from. Each has its advantages and disadvantages. You need to know when to choose a certain protocol for a given situation, and how to configure the major settings of TCP/IP and IPX/SPX.

The Protocols—A Quick Overview

Networks must use some kind of protocol to communicate. The three major protocols that Windows 98 supports are TCP/IP (Transmission Control Protocol/Internet Protocol), IPX/SPX (Internet Packet Exchange/ Sequenced Packet Exchange), and NetBEUI (NetBIOS Enhanced User Interface). Support for DLC (Data Link Control) and NetBIOS (Network Basic Input/Output System) is also available. Here is a brief overview of these and other protocols, which are each discussed in more detail in later chapters.

TCP/IP This protocol is popular for many reasons, including its open design, its nonproprietary heterogeneous support, and its use for the Internet. Suffice it to say that every network administrator needs to be at least familiar with, if not an expert in, TCP/IP.

IPX/SPX This is a proprietary protocol that Novell developed for use in its NetWare networks. In the past, Microsoft called its compatible protocol NWLink; now it is called by the very inventive name "IPX/SPX-compatible protocol." Almost every application that works with, and expects, NetWare's IPX/SPX will also work with Microsoft's IPX/SPX-compatible protocol. In order to communicate with NetWare servers, the IPX/SPX-compatible protocol must be installed. Installing and configuring IPX/SPX is covered later.

NetBEUI This protocol was developed by IBM for small interoffice networks. NetBEUI has severe limitations because it was designed for no more than 254 nodes and can't be routed. Interoffice mail may be a good analogy for NetBEUI: Inter-office mail is quick and cheap inside your company, but if an envelope is put in the regular mail bin, there is no way of delivering it since it has no address (other than the person's name) on it. This protocol is almost never used as a regular protocol, but can be useful as a dial-up protocol.

Microsoft DLC This protocol must be used in conjunction with another protocol–TCP/IP, IPX/SPX, or NetBEUI. DLC is used to communicate with IBM mainframe computers and Hewlett-Packard (HP) JetDirect adapters. Windows 98 includes a new 32-bit version of DLC.

NetBIOS This is not a protocol per se, but is a specification that protocols and applications can be designed to support.

IPX/SPX adds support for NetBIOS via TSRs (terminate-and-stay-resident programs), but Microsoft's IPX/SPX-compatible protocol, TCP/IP, and NetBEUI come with native NetBIOS support. Microsoft's networking, as well as many applications, requires NetBIOS support in order to function correctly.

Fast Infrared This is a relatively new protocol designed for communication between devices that have infrared ports (like laptops, digital cameras, and certain printers).

IP Addresses

Unlike IPX or NetBEUI, TCP/IP requires each node or host to be assigned a unique address to participate on the network. This can require much more administrative work than other protocols, because each host (which includes desktop computers, printers, routers, and any other device that needs to communicate on the network) needs to have an address assigned to it. The address, commonly referred to as an *IP address*, looks similar to this:

```
131.107.2.200
```

An IP address is a 32-bit address, where each of the four numbers presented is actually an octet, or contains eight bits of data. For example, the above address is actually:

```
10000011.01101011.00000010.11001000
```

or four 8-bit numbers (octets). Because this binary format is not easily read by humans, it is converted into decimal format as first shown.

In determining IP addresses, there are several factors to consider: address class, address uniqueness, and address restrictions.

IP Address Classes

The address class, along with the subnet mask (explained later in the chapter), determines which part of the IP address is used for network identification (net ID) and which part is used for host identification (host ID). Although there are five address classes defined, only three can be used for host addressing: Class A, Class B, and Class C.

NOTE

The first octet in the address determines whether an address is a Class A, B, or C address.

Table 25.4 provides a summary of the properties for each address class. They are discussed in more detail in the following sections.

TABLE 25.4: IP Address Class Summary

Address Class	Range of Network IDs	Number of Networks	Hosts per Network
Class A	1–126	126	16,777,214
Class B	128–191	16,384	65,534
Class C	192–223	2,097,152	254

This separation between net ID and host ID in an IP address helps define the subnet mask. In this example of a Class A address, because the first octet is taken to identify the network, it is "masked out" from being used for host IDs. The default subnet mask with a Class A address is 255.0.0.0, signifying that the first octet is unavailable for host IDs. The default subnet mask for a Class B address is 255.255.0.0 since the first two octets are masked out from being used as host IDs. The default subnet mask for a Class C address is 255.255.255.0 because these octets are used for the net ID and are unavailable for use as host IDs.

IP Address Uniqueness and Restrictions

IP addresses must be unique for every host on the network. This means that there must be a unique combination of net ID and host ID for every host. Also, every host on the same network segment must have the same net ID. This is because local communication is established through a series of broadcasts that are for that network only. These broadcasts will not cross a router (which connects the different networks). So, if a host with the same net ID is across a router, it will never be reached. (In TCP/IP terminology, *router* and *gateway* mean the same thing.)

Subnets and Subnet Masks

Before studying subnet masks, it is important to understand what a subnet is. Simply put, a *subnet* is a network segment. However, from an IP perspective, it is a segment in a multiple-segmented network that has been given a net ID derived from a "parent" net ID. For example, in Figure 25.8, a Class B parent net ID of 131.107.0.0 is the assigned address and has been subnetted into smaller networks.

In this diagram, there are three subnets connected by routers:

- 131.107.8.0
- 131.107.16.0
- 131.107.24.0

Since the parent address has been subnetted, it is no longer used as a single network, but all the subnets together are the network of 131.107.0.0.

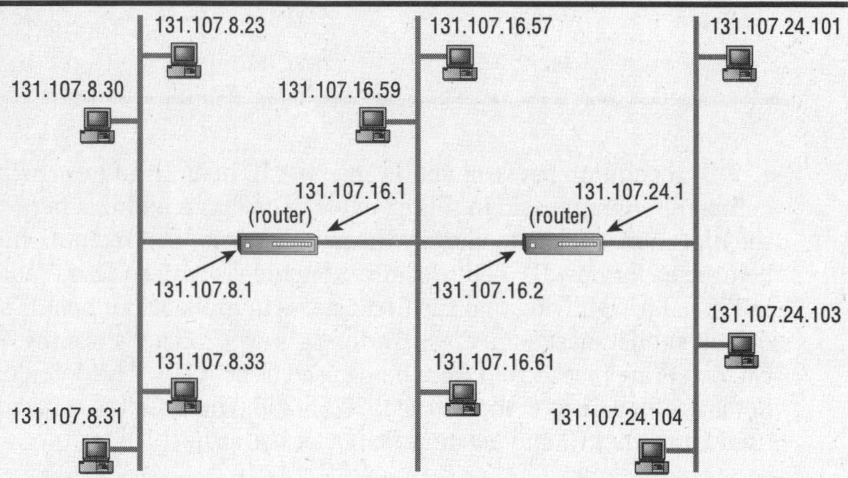

FIGURE 25.8: Subnets are segments of multiple-segmented networks.

The subnet mask used determines how many subnets have been created. Whatever the subnet mask is, it must be the same for all the subnets created, even though they will each have their own unique net IDs. The subnet mask not only determines what part of the IP address belongs to the host (host ID) and what part belongs to the network (net ID), it also determines what is local or remote to a subnet.

NOTE

Each subnet must be connected by a *router* (or *gateway*) to the other subnets in order to communicate.

The Default Gateway

The *default gateway* is the way out of a subnet. It is the router that connects one subnet to another so that hosts can communicate with hosts on other interconnected networks. The default gateway has its own IP address, which the hosts on its subnet must know to use.

When a host determines that a destination host is not local, it sends its data to its configured default gateway. The router then refers to its route table to determine if it has a direct connection to the destination network or if it must send the data on to another router that can deliver the data to the destination host.

DHCP and TCP/IP

Microsoft bundles a service called DHCP (Dynamic Host Configuration Protocol) with Windows NT Server that allows you to preconfigure TCP/IP addresses, subnet masks, and default gateway settings (as well as other settings), so that clients can ask for and automatically receive their settings.

Your configuration choices are whether to use DHCP to dynamically assign addresses and subnet masks or to manually assign addresses and subnet masks. The addresses of DNS servers, WINS servers, and default gateways can also be assigned manually or by DHCP.

Installing and Configuring Protocols

Installing protocols is relatively straightforward.

1. Start the Network applet from the Control Panel, choose Add, and then Protocol.
2. Select Microsoft from the list of protocol providers and then select the protocol you wish to install.

Although the default settings for the protocols work almost all of the time, you can change many of the settings for each of the protocols. If you have more than one protocol installed, you should designate the protocol you use the most often as the default protocol.

Installing and Configuring NetBEUI

NetBEUI parameters will rarely, if ever, need to be changed. Changing these settings affects only real-mode NetBEUI. Windows 98 dynamically adjusts the protected-mode NetBEUI parameters.

NOTE

Remember, NetBEUI cannot handle more than 254 nodes, and NetBEUI packets cannot cross a router. Although NetBEUI is rarely used as a standard protocol, it can be useful as a dial-up protocol.

Installing and Configuring IPX/SPX

Installing IPX/SPX is relatively straightforward. Simply select IPX/SPX from the list of protocols provided by Microsoft. There are only a couple of settings you may need to change on a regular basis when using the IPX/SPX protocol: selecting the frame type and enabling NetBIOS support. The most important setting to check when using the IPX/SPX protocol on an Ethernet network is the frame type. There are four basic frames that can be run under Ethernet:

- Ethernet 802.2
- Ethernet 802.3
- Ethernet_II
- Ethernet_Snap

Microsoft's IPX/SPX default frame selection is Automatic, which means that Windows 98 will try to determine the frame type being used and match itself to the first frame type it finds. If a frame cannot be determined, it will default to 802.2 (which is the default for NetWare 3.12 and higher).

NOTE

For best performance, you should run the same frame type on all your computers.

The Automatic setting will bind to only the first frame it finds. If you have multiple frames on your network, Windows 98 may bind to the wrong one. If you have servers with various frame types, you should specify the frame for the client software so it will see the correct servers. The Frame Type setting is on the Advanced tab of the IPX/SPX-Compatible Protocol Properties dialog box.

Another parameter you may need to set is whether to support NetBIOS over IPX/SPX. NetBIOS is a specification that some programs require to work on a network. The documentation for the network application should specify which protocol(s) are supported, and if NetBIOS support is required. (Older network applications often require NetBIOS support.) This setting is on the NetBIOS tab of the IPX/SPX-Compatible Protocol Properties dialog box.

Installing and Configuring TCP/IP

TCP/IP has become one of the most widely used protocols in today's computing environments. There are three major configuration items that must be set for TCP/IP.

IP Address This is the address of the computer. Addresses must be unique.

Subnet Mask This shows which part of the address connotes the network vs. the client.

Default Gateway This tells the computer how to reach an outside network.

The TCP/IP settings are configured by going to the properties of the TCP/IP protocol by using the Network applet of the Control Panel. The following screen shows the IP Address tab where you can choose to manually assign an address and subnet mask, or have DHCP automatically do the assignment. The default gateway is set using the Gateway tab.

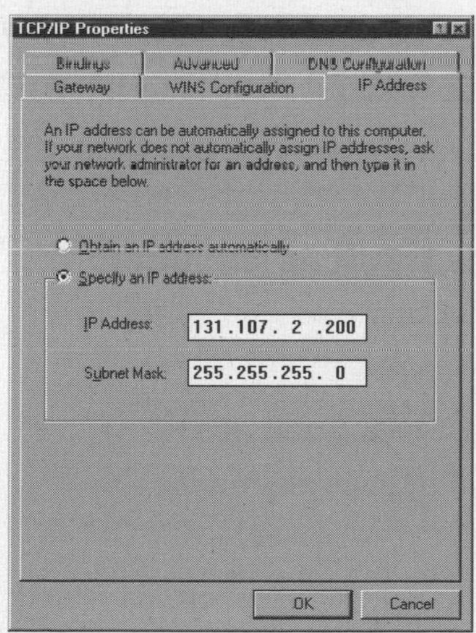

Installing and Configuring the DLC Protocol

The DLC protocol can be used for direct communication and connection with mainframe computers that support DLC, as well as PC-based peripherals like Hewlett-Packard printers that have an HP JetDirect network card installed. The JetDirect card allows you to connect your printer directly to the network rather than to a printer port on a PC.

To use an HP printer with an HP JetDirect card on your network, you must have the following configuration: an HP printer with an HP JetDirect card installed and connected to the network; Microsoft DLC installed and running on the PC that is to be the print server; and a network printer in the Printers folder on the print server.

NOTE

Only the print server needs to have the DLC protocol installed.

To use the HP JetAdmin program, you must first install the DLC protocol and then you must install the HP JetAdmin Network Service. To do this, follow the steps outlined above, but select the HP JetAdmin service instead of a protocol. Once you have rebooted, the JetAdmin icon will appear in your Control Panel.

Install and configure hardware devices in a Microsoft environment and a mixed Microsoft and NetWare environment.

Hardware devices include:

- Modems
- Printers
- Universal Serial Bus (USB)
- Multiple display support
- IEEE 1394 FireWire
- Infrared Data Association (IrDA)
- Multilink
- Power management scheme

One of the major advantages of Windows 98 is its ability to support a large variety of hardware devices. Successfully installing and configuring hardware devices is critical in using Windows 98 to its fullest.

Hardware Options

You will need to know how to install various hardware devices and how to configure those devices for various scenarios.

Modems

Windows 98 supports a wide variety of modems. The best way to add a new modem is to have Windows 98 automatically detect it using the Add New Hardware applet from the Control Panel. Modems can be tested and configured from the Modem applet of the Control Panel once they are installed. Procedures for installing and configuring modems are discussed later in this chapter.

Printing Features and Drivers

Windows 98 supports several enhanced printing features.

Printing Features in Windows 98

Here are 10 printing features:

Plug and Play If your motherboard is Plug-and-Play–compliant, all you need to do to install a printer is plug it in. Windows 98 should recognize the printer and install the appropriate drivers.

Drag-and-drop You can place printer shortcuts, to both local and network printers, on your Desktop and then drag files to be printed onto the printer icon. Your print jobs will be sent to that printer.

Extended Capabilities Port (ECP) ECP allows you to add printer cards to your PC. The additional cards will become ECPs and can be used to attach a printer.

Improved color management Windows 98 supports Image Color Matching (ICM) version 2.0 standards. This allows you to maintain an image's original color from its source (scanner, digital camera, Internet, etc.), through your editing tools, and at output. In other words, you get device-independent, WYSIWYG color.

Point-and-Print setup Windows 98 uses a special Point-and-Print setup feature for installing networked printers. To install a printer, you only need to navigate to the printer or print queue and double-click its icon. Windows 98 will then begin the printer installation.

Microsoft Print Server for NetWare Windows 98 can be configured to act as a NetWare print server and despool (remove) print jobs from a NetWare print queue.

Working offline Windows 98 can print documents to a temporary queue while your computer is not hooked up to any printer. When Windows 98 detects that a printer has been attached, it will print the queued documents.

Font loading Unlike Windows 3.*x*, Windows 98 will load font files only as it needs them, thus saving valuable memory space.

HP JetAdmin 2.54 utility This is an updated version of the Hewlett Packard JetAdmin utility which comes on the Windows 98 CD-ROM. HP JetAdmin allows you to manage HP-compatible printers that are connected to your enterprise through a network cable.

DLC support Windows 98 can use the DLC protocol to connect directly to some network printers.

Print Drivers Windows 98 uses a set of universal drivers and minidrivers to handle the complex tasks of rendering and printing. *Minidrivers* are printer-specific chunks of code that can speak directly with the printer and also speak the common universal driver language.

There are currently three types of printers and, therefore, three different universal drivers:

Regular This is used for all black-and-white printers that do not use PostScript. (Some Hewlett-Packard inkjet printers will not use this driver either.) Regular universal drivers use a printer-specific minidriver.

PostScript This is used for all black-and-white PostScript printers. PostScript drivers will use PostScript minidrivers that adhere to the Adobe PPD (PostScript Printer Description) and SPD (Standard Printer Description) formats.

HP Color Inkjet This is used for inkjet printers and nearly all color printers. This special case uses a monolithic driver, which means that the minidriver code that would normally be in the minidriver is part of the universal driver itself.

These minidriver/universal driver combinations allow for device independence. In other words, you can have any program send output to any printer, and Windows 98 will be able to print it.

TIP

Printer drivers are stored in the \Windows\System directory on your hard drive. Printer Registry entries are stored in the Hkey_Local_Machine\System\CurrentControlSet\Control\Print folder.

Windows Metafiles

Windows *metafiles* (*.WMF) are files that contain the Windows internal graphics language. Windows 98 supports both the old WMF format and an enhanced metafile format (EMF). These metafiles are basically a collection of internal commands that Windows 98 uses to render graphics to the screen. Metafiles are generally not device-specific, which makes it easy to send them to other computers for printing. When a metafile is converted for output to a specific printer, it becomes a *raw* file. The raw file contains printer-specific codes that tell the printer how to print the images in the file.

Another advantage of using EMF files for printing is that they can be spooled to a hard disk location rather than being printed directly. Spooled print jobs are located in the \Windows\Spool\Printers directory.

USB (Universal Serial Bus)

Universal Serial Bus is an external bus standard for computers. Its main advantage is that it takes the Plug-and-Play functionality of hardware devices outside of the computer. When you attach a USB-compliant device, it can be automatically configured as soon as it is attached to the PC. In most cases, this can be done without rebooting the PC, or running through the setup sequence.

USB supports the following devices: audio devices; data gloves; digital still cameras; digitizers; ISDN and digital PBX systems; joysticks, keyboards, and mice; low bandwidth video; modems; monitor controls; printers and scanners; and telephones.

USB supports the following features:

Hot Plug and Play You can plug a USB device into your system at any time. It will be automatically configured and the operating system will be notified that it is present and available.

Power Management Support With a USB device, you can take advantage of three different power modes: Off, On, and Suspend. A beneficial feature of the Suspend mode is that the device has the ability to wake itself up and then wake up the system. For example, a USB modem might wake up when an incoming phone call is received. The modem might then determine that the call is a fax and then wake up the PC so that the fax software can receive the incoming fax.

USB also specifies a new standard for connectors, sockets, and the cables that a USB-compliant device may use. Through standardization, hardware manufacturers can create a single device that will run on any computer that supports USB without making modifications to these three parts.

USB supports the following transfer rates based upon the device's data requirements:

1.5Mbps This transfer rate is used for devices that do not require a large amount of data transfer. These include devices like the mouse, keyboard, and joystick.

12Mbps This transfer rate is used for devices that require a guaranteed level of data transfer and a large amount of bandwidth. This includes devices like scanners, telephones, speakers, and printers.

Multiple Display Support

A really cool new feature of Windows 98 is the ability to gain more screen "real estate" by adding additional monitors and "enlarging" the Desktop to cover them. This larger virtual Desktop can be spread across as many as nine different monitors. The screen space on each monitor butts up against the screen space displayed by every other monitor. When your mouse moves to the edge of the Desktop display on one monitor, it instantly appears at the appropriate location on the next monitor. This provides the appearance of a seamless Desktop as shown in Figure 25.9.

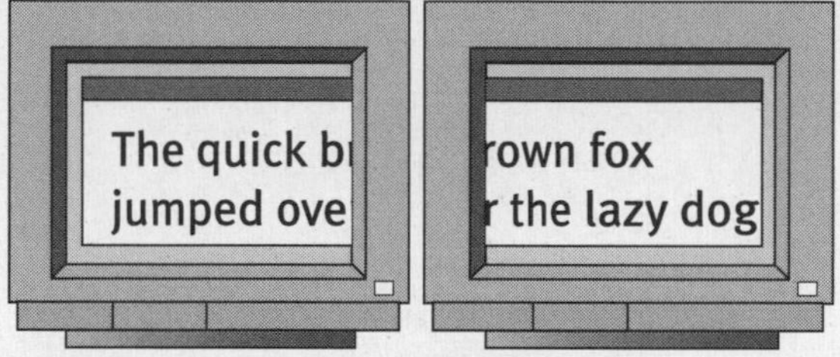

FIGURE 25.9: Multiple displays are supported by Windows 98.

For this multidisplay screen to work, the BIOS picks one of the monitors to be the primary display based upon the PCI slot order; all other monitors are secondary monitors. The primary monitor has a coordinate system starting with 0,0 for the upper-left corner. The lower-right corner is specified by the screen resolution on the primary monitor (for example 800,600). You can specify the additional monitors based on this coordinate system. For example, in Figure 25.9, let's say that the right monitor is the primary monitor with a resolution of 800 × 600. The monitor on the left would then have an upper-left coordinate of -800,0 and a lower-right coordinate of -1,600.

You are not restricted by the resolution constraints of the primary monitor. For example, if the primary monitor had a resolution of 1024 × 768 and the secondary monitor had a resolution of 800 × 600, you would still be able to use multidisplay capabilities. The virtual Desktop is defined by the monitor coordinates. It is possible to have some portion of the screen real estate that is not displayed on a monitor as shown in Figure 25.10. You can still use that screen real estate by moving portions of open windows into it, but you just can't view it unless you change the resolution on your monitor or you adjust the coordinates of the secondary monitors.

There are a couple of rules regarding the secondary monitor that you must adhere to if you wish to take advantage of this new multiscreen display technology:

- It must be a PCI or AGP device.
- It must be able to run in GUI (graphical) mode or support GUI mode without the use of VGA resources.
- There must be a Windows 98 driver that supports it as a secondary device.

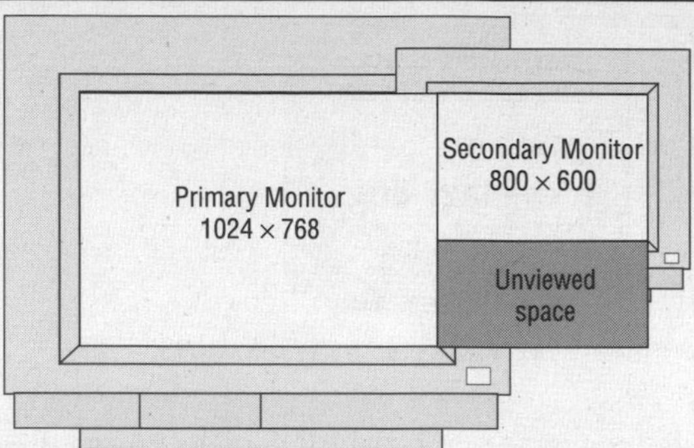

FIGURE 25.10: The virtual Desktop is defined by the coordinates of the monitors.

IEEE 1394 FireWire

Windows 98 now supports the IEEE 1394 standard. Because of its extremely high bandwidth, it is sometimes called FireWire. It is used to support devices like cameras, videodisc players, and digital camcorders. FireWire is also supported by the new WDM (Windows Driver Model).

IEEE 1394 can support up to 63 devices on each bus. You can interconnect busses to support up to 1,023 additional busses, each of which can support up to 63 devices. In other words, you can create a network with nearly 64,500 devices attached to it. The bus also allows each device to address up to 256 terabytes of memory. This might seem overwhelming at first, but the topology of IEEE 1394 was designed to be scalable. Every device will have equal access to the bus itself.

IEEE 1394 is still in development. Proposals are on the table to standardize FireWire over OpenHCI, SBP-2 (a general-purpose command transport protocol), power management schemes, and hot Plug-and-Play interoperability.

Infrared Data Association (IrDA)

Windows 98 supports all types of infrared devices. You can wirelessly connect a laptop to PCs, printers, and other devices like infrared cameras. Infrared supports File and Printer Sharing as well as other utilities like Direct Cable Connection. Windows 98 does this through the Microsoft Infrared 3.0 drivers. These drivers support two formats: IrDA 1.0 for serial interfaces (SIR), and IrDA 1.1 for fast infrared devices (FIR).

Using infrared technology, SIR can support transfer speeds of 115Kbps; FIR can support transfer speeds of 4Mbps; and Microsoft utilities can support file transfer. Infrared has high transfer rates, is a well-understood technology, and is, therefore, the most widely accepted form of wireless communication currently available to the PC world.

Multilink

Multilink is a new, multichannel support technology that allows you to combine multiple dial-up adapters for a single session. To use multilink, you must have the PPP Multilink Protocol installed on both the client and the server. In essence, multilink combines multiple physical links and aggregates them into a single "bundle." This increases your bandwidth and therefore your throughput. Bundling occurs most often over ISDN channels, but multilinking is also supported for modems, or modem/ISDN combinations.

NOTE

Although multilink supports mixing ISDN and analog, use devices that connect at the same speeds for best compatibility.

Power Management Schemes

Power management is a part of Microsoft's SIPC (Simply Interactive Personal Computer) initiative. Windows 98 uses the OnNow power management initiative in much the same way. With OnNow power management, you will be able to put not only your PC, but all peripherals into low power modes when they are not in use. These power policies are called *power schemes* and can be manipulated through the Power Management icon in the Control Panel.

There are three main Power Management Schemes:

Home/Office Desk This is ideal for desktop computers and is automatically installed when you install Windows 98.

Portable/Laptop This scheme is optimized for laptop users. It has additional settings for computers that sometimes run on battery power.

Always On This scheme is used primarily for personal servers. It is similar to the Home/Office Desk scheme, but the standby timer is not available and the hard disk timer is significantly increased. This is the default power scheme.

You can create as many additional schemes as you feel are necessary. Simply set your timer values and then choose Save As.

If you activate the Power Management icon in the Control Panel, you should see something similar to Figure 25.11. If you are using a laptop computer, you will have the Alarms and Power Meter tabs in addition to the Power Schemes and Advanced tabs.

There are options to put the computer in standby mode, turn off the monitor after a predetermined amount of time, and turn off the hard disks after a predetermined amount of time. Because Figure 25.11 is from a laptop computer, there are additional values specified for shutdown times on battery power.

The Alarms tab allows you to set an alarm (both audio and textual) that will notify you when the batteries become low, as well as critically low (see Figure 25.12).

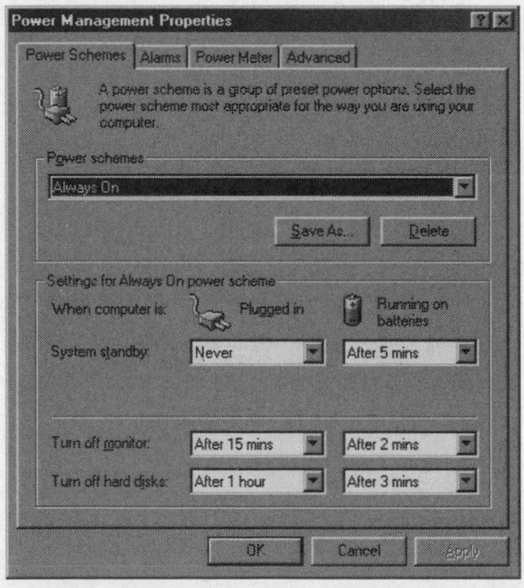

FIGURE 25.11: The Power Management Properties dialog box

The Power Meter tab allows you to determine whether or not you wish to display a power meter in the system tray of your Taskbar and, if so, what form it will take. The Advanced tab is used to determine whether or not you wish to show your power meter, and if you would like to password-protect your computer when it comes out of standby or sleep mode.

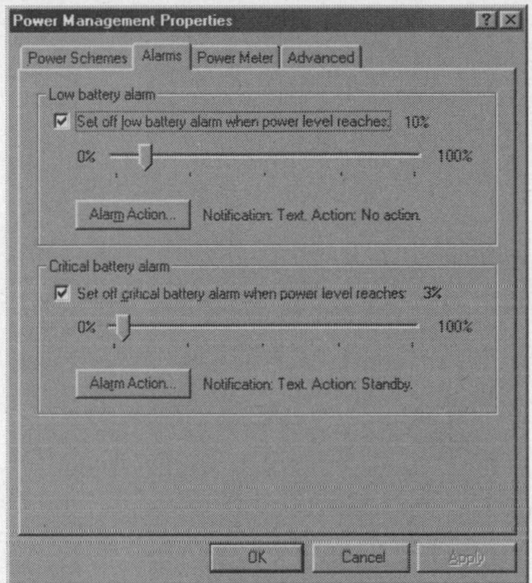

FIGURE 25.12: The Alarms tab

Hardware Configuration

You will need to know how to configure various hardware devices, such as modems and printers, and create power management schemes.

Using the Device Manager to Configure Devices

The Device Manager provides a graphical representation of devices connected to the system. From here, you can check the properties of different devices to determine whether they are functioning properly. You can also discover what may be wrong with devices that are not working. You can configure many devices with their Control Panel applets, but there are many other devices that you must configure using the Device Manager. To access the Device Manager, right-click the My Computer icon on the Desktop and select Properties, Device Manager, or go to the System/Control Panel applet.

When you start up the Device Manager on a system with no hardware problems and select the View Devices By Type button it looks like the following box.

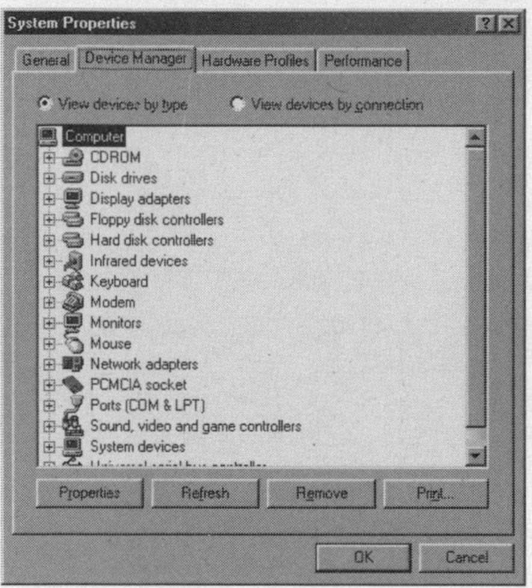

To look at specific devices listed under each main category, click the plus sign (+) to the left of the heading. Each main category heading now lists the individual devices below it. By double-clicking any specific device, or highlighting it and pressing the Enter key, you can see the properties for that device. The following screen shows an example of the property sheet for a Yamaha OPL3 sound card.

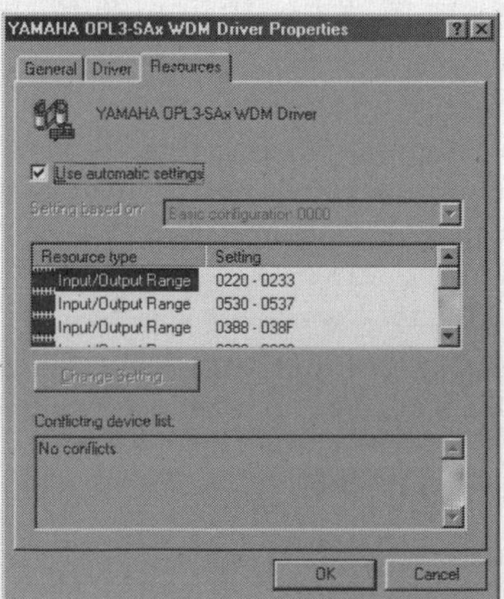

You can obtain the following information from a device's property sheet: device type; manufacturer; hardware version; supporting drivers installed; whether the installed drivers are configured properly; and resources used by the device, including any conflicts that might be present.

Clicking the View Devices By Connection option on the main Device Manager screen changes the view to show items listed according to their connection. For example, your CD-ROM will be listed under your sound card if it is using the sound card for its connection to the motherboard.

When you boot your system in Safe mode (press F5 after the "Starting Windows 98" message, or press F8 and choose Safe Mode from the Startup menu), you may see devices listed more than once. This is fairly common but can cause problems. When you are working in Device Manager after a Safe mode boot, you should check for and remove multiple instances of any device.

NOTE

Safe mode is a way of booting Windows 98 without the Registry, CONFIG.SYS, AUTOEXEC.BAT, and any protected-mode drivers.

Installing and Configuring Modems

Modem is short for *modulate/demodulate*. Modems work by converting binary electrical signals into acoustic signals for transmission over telephone lines (called *modulation*), and then converting these acoustic signals back into binary form at the receiving end (*demodulation*).

Installing Modems If you have a Plug-and-Play-compliant computer and a Plug-and-Play-compliant modem, Windows 98 should auto-detect the modem when your system is booted. Windows 98 will then install the appropriate drivers. If you don't have a Plug-and-Play system, you can easily install a modem (or, more accurately, install a modem minidriver) through the Modems applet of the Control Panel.

When you click the Add button, the Install New Modem Wizard takes you through a series of steps for installing the modem.

Configuring Modems You can make changes to your modem's default settings through its Properties dialog box. You can also change the speaker volume and connection settings.

To begin, go to the modem's Properties page (double-click the Modems icon in the Control Panel), select the modem that you want to configure, and then click the Properties button. The modem's Properties dialog box has two tabs: General and Connection. The following sections describe the options available for most modems.

Adjusting General Modem Settings The General tab of the modem's Properties dialog box, shown below, allows you to modify the general features that are part of all modems.

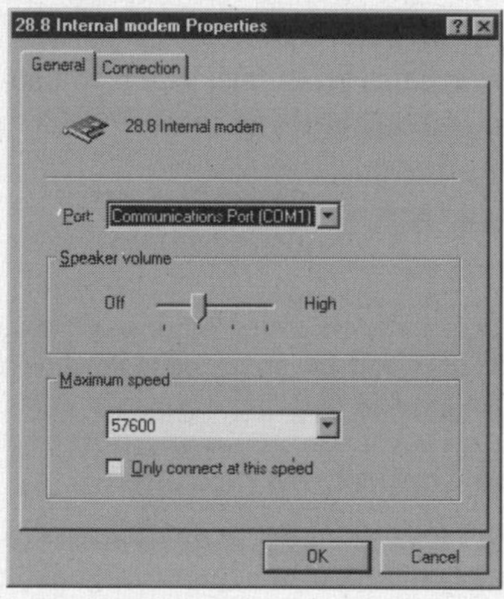

This tab includes the following settings:

Port Allows you to change to a different communications port.

Speaker volume Allows you to change the setting for the speaker volume. Normally, you will hear your modem dialing out, which sounds like a normal telephone call. Once the other modem answers, there will be a "handshake" period in which the modems try to synchronize themselves and let each other know how fast they want to communicate. This will sound like a high-pitched whine that may change in tone several times. Once the modems have synchronized, you will be connected, and the speakers will shut themselves off.

Maximum speed Allows you to specify the maximum speed at which your modems will communicate. In the past, some manufacturers' modems were not compatible with other manufacturers' modems at high speeds. To avoid this problem, you could connect at a slower speed. If you have purchased a new modem since mid-1994, you should not have this problem. Set your maximum speed to the speed that is greater than or equal to your modem's speed. For example, if you have a 28,800bps modem, you should choose 28,800 or 38,400.

Modifying Connection Settings The Connection tab of the modem's Properties dialog box, shown below, allows you to modify your connection and call preferences.

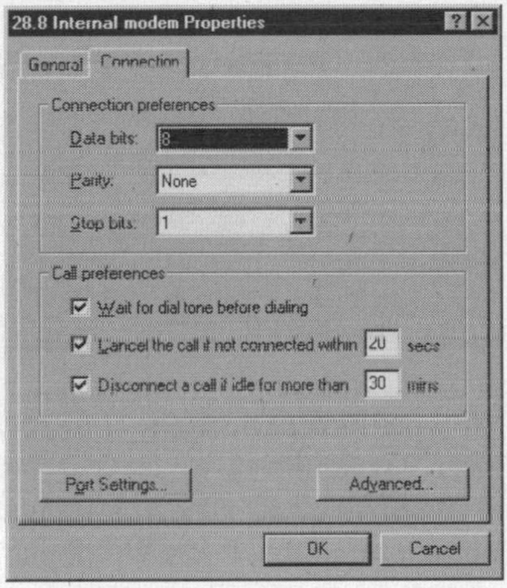

Connection Preferences The Connection Preferences options allow you to modify how the packets of data are configured and sent across the telephone line:

Data bits The data bits are normally either 7 or 8; 8 has become the default setting for most modems (in the past, 7 data bits were the norm). This setting means that 7 or 8 bits of packet information will be sent across the wire at a time.

Parity In the past, parity was used to make sure that the information sent across the wire was received properly.

Stop bits The stop bits are normally always set to 1. Occasionally, you might encounter an older network that uses 2. The stop bits are used to identify the end of a packet.

Call Preferences The Call Preferences options allow you to determine how your modem will behave. You can set the modem to wait for a dial tone before dialing, cancel the call if it's not connected within the specified number of seconds, and disconnect if the connection is idle for more than the specified number of seconds.

Port Settings Clicking the Port Settings button in the Connection tab brings up the Advanced Port Settings dialog box, shown below. These settings allow you to decide how your FIFO (First In-First Out) buffers are used. These buffers are temporary storage areas for transmitting and receiving packet information through your modems. You should set them to their maximum levels for the best throughput of information.

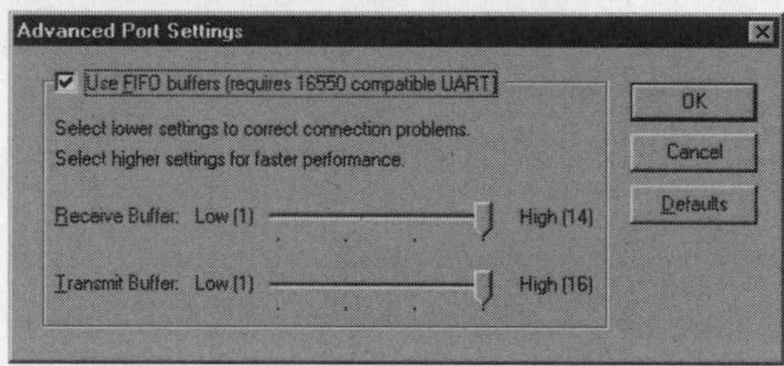

There are two types of FIFO buffers: the 16550 UART (Universal Asynchronous Receiver/Transmitter), which is standard on all 486 and later computers, and the 8250 UART. The 8250 is a much older standard, which allows a maximum rate of only 9600bps.

Advanced Connection Settings Clicking the Advanced button in the Connection tab brings up the Advanced Connection Settings dialog box, shown below.

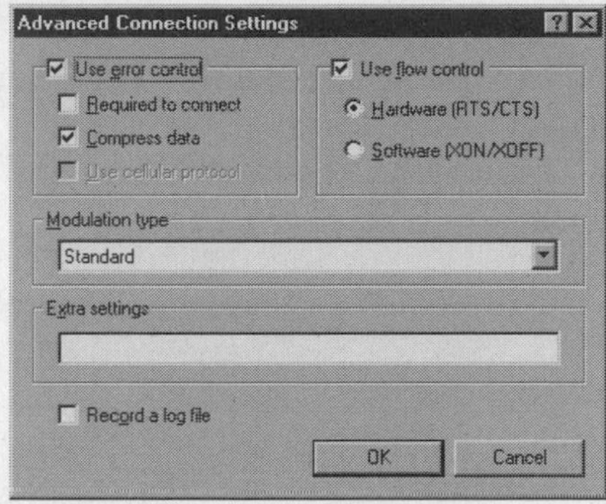

These settings allow you to modify what type of error control and flow control you use, as well as set a modulation type and enter extra settings:

Use error control Allows you to specify whether or not you use error control and compression. Windows 98 can support v42.bis compression and MNP/5 error correction.

Use flow control Allows you to specify whether or not the modem or the software handles flow control between the modem and your computer. The default is for the hardware to do this. (XON/XOFF may not work with certain programs.)

Modulation type Must be the same on both modems in order for them to communicate. If you are having trouble communicating with an older modem, try using the Non-Standard setting.

Extra settings Allows you to enter special modem initialization strings that older modems require in order to connect and communicate. These are strings like "AT&FE=S0." They tell the modem exactly how to behave.

Record a log file Allows you to record a modem log file called MODEMLOG.TXT, which will be placed in your \Windows folder. You can use this file to monitor the modem and for troubleshooting.

Running Modem Diagnostics

To find out which drivers are installed for which modems and to test your modems, use the Diagnostics tab of the Modems Properties dialog box, shown below. This dialog box shows all currently installed serial ports and attachments.

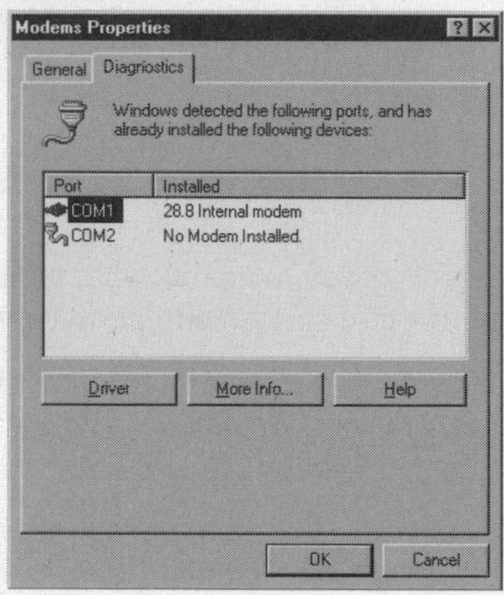

Clicking the Driver button brings up a dialog box that will tell you what driver that particular port is using.

If you have selected a port with a device installed on it and you click the More Info button, you will see information about that port. Windows 98 will send a standard set of AT commands to the port and then display your modem's response, as shown below. You can compare the responses with the documentation supplied with your modem to make sure that everything is working properly. The More Info dialog box shows the port's IRQ (interrupt) channel, base address expressed as a hexadecimal value, and UART type. You may also see information about the highest speed available on that port. If you choose a port that does not have a device attached to it and select More Info, you will get to the same dialog box, but it will not display any of the AT commands.

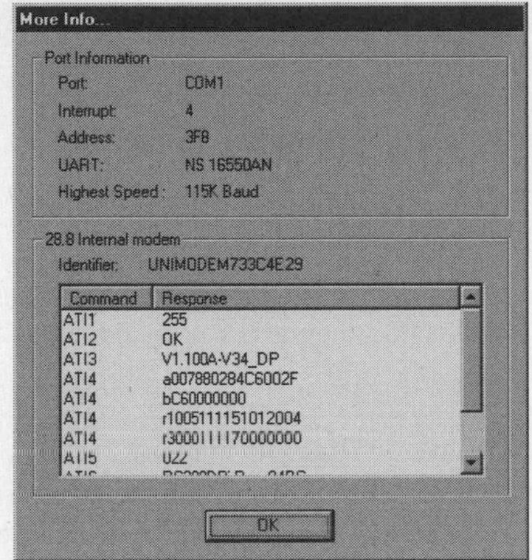

NOTE

The standard set of AT commands run from AT1 through AT17. AT+FCLASS=? will display a list of fax modem classes supported by this modem.

Clicking the Help button brings up troubleshooting information to walk you through some diagnostics.

Installing Printers

The procedure you use for installing a printer depends on whether or not you install a printer locally or across the network. The following sections discuss how to set up local printers and networked printers, including Point-and-Print setup.

Printer installation and management is handled through the Windows Explorer or the Printers folder, located under Start ➢ Settings ➢ Printers. From the Printers folder you can perform the following tasks:

- Install a printer (local or network)
- Share a printer (local printers only)
- Administer both local and remote printers and print queues
- Control printer configurations, such as default printer designation, font selections, spooler considerations, and orientation

Installing Local Printers If you have a Plug-and-Play printer, local installation is a snap. Simply attach the printer cables and turn on your printer. When you restart Windows 98, it should recognize the new printer and install the appropriate printer drivers for you.

TIP

If you don't see your printer in the Add Printer Wizard's list, check the printer manufacturer's documentation to see if there is a compatible driver you can select.

If you do not have a Plug-and-Play printer, you can easily install a local printer from the Printers folder. The Add Printer Wizard allows you to select the printer manufacturer and model. Follow these steps to install a local printer through the Printers folder:

1. Open the Printers folder by selecting Start ➢ Settings ➢ Printers.
2. Double-click the Add Printer icon to start the Add Printer Wizard.
3. You will be presented with a Welcome screen. Click Next to begin the installation process. This brings up a screen asking you whether this is a local printer or a network printer.
4. Choose the local printer option and then click Next. Windows 98 builds a driver information database and loads it into memory. The driver information database is a list of manufacturers and their printers, and the drivers needed to support those printers.
5. Choose the manufacturer of your printer in the Manufacturers list, and then choose the printer in the Printers list. If you do not see your printer listed, click the Have Disk button. The Wizard will ask you to put the floppy disk that shipped with your printer into the floppy drive. The next screen asks you to select the port where your printer is located.
6. Choose your printer port. In most cases, your printer will be hooked up through a parallel port to LPT1. If you want to configure your ports from here, click the Configure button. When you have made your selection, click the Next button to move to the screen that asks for a printer name.

7. Enter a name for this printer. This name can be up to 31 characters in length and is known as the "friendly name." Your friendly name must be unique. If you plan on allowing others access to your local printer from across the network, it may be safer to use a UNC-compatible name (so that the shared name and local name can be the same). From this screen, you also have the option to make this printer the default printer for your Windows programs. Click Next when you are finished.
8. The last screen of this Wizard gives the option to print a test page. This is a good idea. The test page will show you that the printer is hooked up and running properly, and it will tell you which printer drivers your printer is using and their version numbers. It will also print a sample graphic. If you are using a color printer, the Windows logo graphic will be in color. When you are finished, click Finish. Your new printer icon will show up in the Printers folder.

Installing an Infrared Device

If your infrared device is Plug-and-Play-compliant, all you need to do is install or attach the device to your computer, power the device, and then turn on your computer. Windows 98 will recognize the device and automatically begin the installation process. If the device is not recognized, you may have to activate the Infrared icon in the Control Panel. If the Infrared icon does not appear, press F5 to refresh the screen.

You can also use this icon to start the Infrared Monitor applet. This tool allows you to check the status of your infrared devices, enable and disable communication, set connection speeds, turn sounds on and off, and obtain identification information.

If your infrared device is not Plug-and-Play-compliant, then you should use the Add New Hardware Wizard in the Control Panel. Select Infrared device from the Hardware Types dialog box. For the device section, choose "Generic Infrared Serial Port or Dongle." All of the other infrared devices are Plug-and-Play-compliant devices. Set any other parameters that are requested.

Printing with Infrared To print to an infrared-enabled printer, simply bring your computer within range of the printer. If the printer has been installed, Windows 98 should detect it and install the appropriate drivers.

Otherwise, you may need to set up the printer manually. Once the printer is set up and Windows 98 recognizes it, you can simply choose to print as you would normally.

Transferring Files with Infrared When you install an infrared device in Windows 98, Windows 98 will add the Infrared Transfer program; this program allows you to move files back and forth between two infrared-enabled computers.

The Infrared Transfer program adds an icon to the My Computer screen and an Infrared Recipient menu item in the Send To menu. The Send To menu is activated when you right-click a file.

The first time you use Infrared Transfer, a folder called "My Received Files" is created, and your transferred files will show up there. There are a couple of methods that you can use to send your files. Here are the steps outlined in brief:

1. Double-click the Infrared Recipient icon in My Computer.
2. Select an available infrared recipient from the list of available recipients.
3. Click Send Files.
4. You will be presented with an Explorer-type interface where you can choose the files to send. Make your selections and choose Open.

You can also drag-and-drop files to the Infrared Recipient icon in the My Computer screen. Another method is to right-click a file and select the Send To menu item. You can then choose the Infrared Recipient sub-menu item to send your files.

You can use the Direct Cable Connection program over the "cableless" infrared channel. To do this, you must set up a Direct Cable Connection host at the other PC. You can then use the Direct Cable Connection applet on the guest PC to log in to a host computer. The connection will automatically be made over the infrared link and you will see the shared folders and printers on the host PC. You can then transfer information as you would over a regular network connection.

Installing Multilink

In order to install and use multilink capabilites with modems, you must first have created at least one Dial-Up Networking connection. For more information on Dial-Up Networking, see Chapter 27 on Windows 98 and dial-up connections. These are the basic steps that you need to follow in order to install and use multilink:

1. Open up My Computer.
2. Double-click Dial-Up Networking.
3. You can now make a new connection or edit an existing connection. Once a connection has been created, right-click the Connection icon and open the property sheet.
4. Select the Multilink tab.
5. Select Use Additional Devices.
6. You will now be able to add additional devices to your bundle to create the multilink.
7. With the Add, Edit, and Remove buttons, you can modify the properties of each of these devices. This includes modifying the phone number that each device will dial.

Using Multilink To use the multilink bundle, simply double-click the Dial-Up Networking connection as you would normally for a single device dial-up. The primary device will call and make a connection using the phone number for that connection. Once a connection has been made, Dial-Up Networking will then use the other devices assigned to the connection to dial the number for the connection, one at a time, until all devices have made a connection.

Once you have established your connections, you can view status information about your links by double-clicking the Communicating Computers icon displayed in the Taskbar. Status information will be displayed about the number of bytes sent and received and about the protocols and additional devices that are in use.

When you select a non-primary device you will be provided with a Suspend and a Resume button. The Suspend button allows you to disconnect that device and remove it from the bundled connection. The Resume button, when clicked, will reconnect the device so that it becomes part of the bundle again.

An advantageous feature of both the Suspend and Resume buttons is that they allow you to drop and connect without dropping the original connection. This can be especially useful as, most of the time, you can use your bundled modems to increase your connection speed. For instance, when all of your dial-up adapters are in use, you cannot send a fax or make a phone call on those lines. To remedy this problem, simply suspend the connection, make your call, and then resume when you are finished with that particular line.

Install and configure Microsoft Backup.

Windows 98 comes with a backup program that lets you easily and quickly back up and restore files to floppy disks, to tape drives, or even to a network server. Chapter 26 includes a more complete objective on backing up and restoring data using Windows 98. Because the "Back up data and the Registry and restore data and the Registry" objective in Chapter 26 is more comprehensive, a complete discussion of installing, configuring, and using the backup program (including the Backup Wizard and different backup techniques) will be covered there.

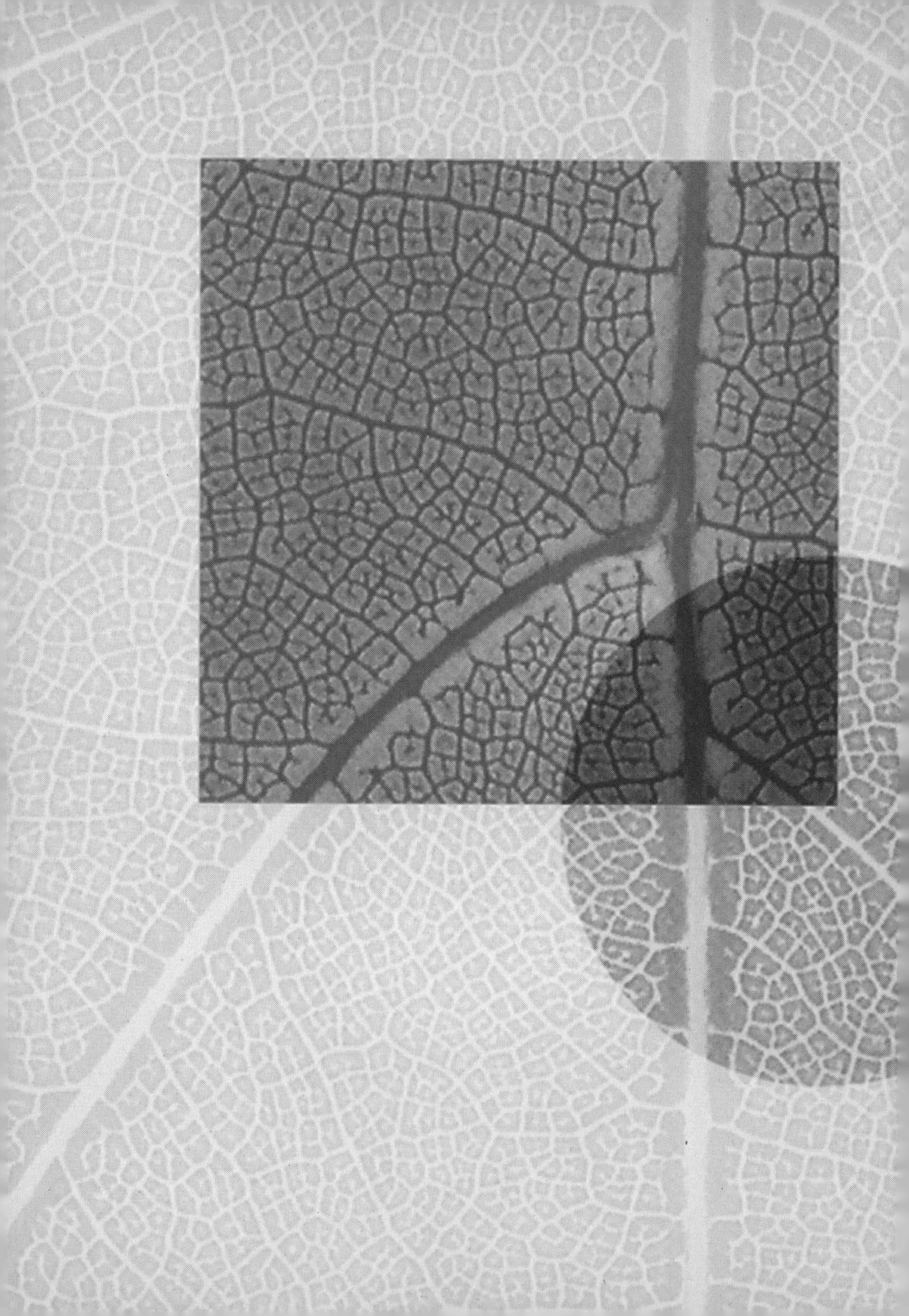

Chapter 26

Configuring and Managing Resource Access

This chapter focuses on creating and managing shared resources such as folders and printers. It also has to do with enabling user profiles and creating system policy files. Backing up data and the Registry, as well as restoring both, are discussed. Configuring the hard disk using compression, partitioning, and FAT32 conversion are also covered. Hardware profiles end the chapter.

Adapted from *MCSE Exam Notes: Windows 98* by Rick Sawtell and Lance Mortensen

ISBN 0-7821-2421-6 416 pages $19.99

Assign access permissions for shared folders in a Microsoft environment or a mixed Microsoft and NetWare environment.

Methods include:

- Passwords
- User permissions
- Group permissions

In this objective, we will cover the more practical points of creating shared folders, including setting security for shared folders. User-level security is inherently more secure as access to shared resources can be assigned to a validated account. Share-level security, while convenient, can be problematic because users can share resources without any passwords and secured passwords can get out.

Creating Shares Using Share-Level Security

When you share a folder using share-level security, you have three basic security options:

Read-Only Allows users on the network to see and run applications in that folder, and to see and open files.

Full Allows all of the above rights, plus gives users the rights to modify and delete programs and files, and to create new files and folders.

Depends On Password Allows you to set different passwords for Read-Only and Full access. You then give the appropriate password to users based on which rights you want them to have.

WARNING

If you select Read-Only or Full access and don't specify a password, the shares will be available to any and all users on your network—even those who have not been authenticated by any server!

These options are listed on the Sharing tab of a folder's ShareMe Properties dialog box.

Follow these steps to share a folder and set the security using passwords:

1. Choose a folder to share.
2. Highlight the folder and right-click. Sharing should appear in the pop-up menu if you installed the File and Printer Sharing service correctly.
3. Select Sharing to display the Sharing tab of the folder's Properties dialog box.
4. Select the Shared As button.
5. As the Share Name, leave the default name (which will be the name of the folder), or enter another name.

TIP

Note that if your share name ends with a $ (dollar sign), the share will be hidden from the browser. The only way to connect to this share will be to use the Map Network Drive command and type in the full UNC (Universal Naming Convention) path. UNC paths are entered as *ServerSharedResource*.**

6. Select Depends On Password.
7. Enter a password (like **readme**) in the Read-Only Password box.
8. Enter a password (like **fullcontrol**) in the Full Access Password box.
9. Retype the passwords when prompted.
10. Click OK to create the share.
11. You should now see the folder with a hand icon under it, signifying it is shared.

TIP

You can check all of your shares by going to the Network Neighborhood. Under your computer name, all the shares should be listed (except those ending with $). It might take up to 15 minutes for the new share to be listed in Network Neighborhood.

Creating Shares Using User-Level Security

Once you have switched to user-level security, you can share folders and printers based on a central network server. When you share folders with user-level security, you are able to grant rights to users or groups. The Sharing tab of the shared folder's Properties dialog box looks different from the one that has share-level security.

Setting Up a New Share with User-Level Security

The rights you can grant are Read-Only, Full Access, or Custom. You can grant rights to users or groups from the network, or to The World, which includes any valid user on the network.

If you choose Custom, you can set individual rights.

Custom Access Rights include:

Read Files Allows the user to open or run files or applications

Write to Files Allows the user to edit existing files

Create Files and Folders Allows the user to create new files or folders

Delete Files Allows the user to delete files or folders

Change File Attributes Allows the user to change file or folder attributes

List Files Allows the user to show files and folders

Change Access Control Allows the user to change security settings

Follow these steps to create a new share using user-level access and assign rights to users and groups:

1. Make sure you are using user-level security (see Chapter 24).
2. Select a folder, right-click it, and choose Sharing.
3. Choose the Shared As button.
4. Leave the default name of the folder as the Share Name or enter a different name.
5. Click the Add button.

6. In the Add Users dialog box, highlight a user or group and click the Read Only button to give them read access to the folder, the Full Access button to give them all rights in the folder, or the Custom button to selectively give them rights in the folder.
7. Choose OK twice to save your new share.

Managing Existing Shared Folders

To modify the properties of existing shares, return to the Sharing tab of the shared folder's Properties dialog box by right-clicking the folder and choosing Sharing from the menu. From the Sharing tab of a share using share-level security, you can change the share name, its access type (from Read-Only to Full), or its passwords. From the Sharing tab of a user-level security share, you can change the share name, how it is shared, or which users and groups have which rights to the share.

Create, share, and monitor resources.

Resources include:

- Remote computers
- Network printers

Windows 98 allows you to use many of the common system administration tools to manage remote computers. Many of the administration tools have prerequisites that must be met before they can be used remotely. The test focuses on which tool to use for a given situation and the prerequisites for each.

Remote Administration

There are several tools that you can use for remote administration of Windows 98 computers on your network. These include the Net Watcher, System Monitor, Administer, and Remote Registry Editor utilities. Before these tools can be used, the networked Windows 98 machines must be configured to accept RPCs (remote procedure calls) from the administrator's machine. Your administrative capabilities are also affected by the security level (share or user) that has been configured on both the remote PC and the administrating PC.

Four Windows 98 tools are useful for remote administration:

Net Watcher Allows you to administer shared resources on a remote workstation. This includes the ability to view who is accessing those shared resources.

System Monitor Allows you to view performance statistics of a remote workstation.

Administer Allows you to access a special hidden share called C$. C$ is the root directory of a remote workstation.

Remote Registry Editor Allows you to edit and modify a remote workstation's Registry.

Because System Monitor and Remote Registry Editor need access to a workstation's Registry database, they can be used only when user-level security has been enabled on both the remote workstation and the administrating computer. They also require Remote Registry Services to be installed.

The Net Watcher, System Monitor, and Administer tools are accessed from the Tools tab of the Properties dialog box for the Windows 98-based computer that you want to remotely administer. As shown in Figure 26.1, the remote computer is called "Gambit." You can access Remote Registry Editor from the Registry Editor program (REGEDIT.EXE).

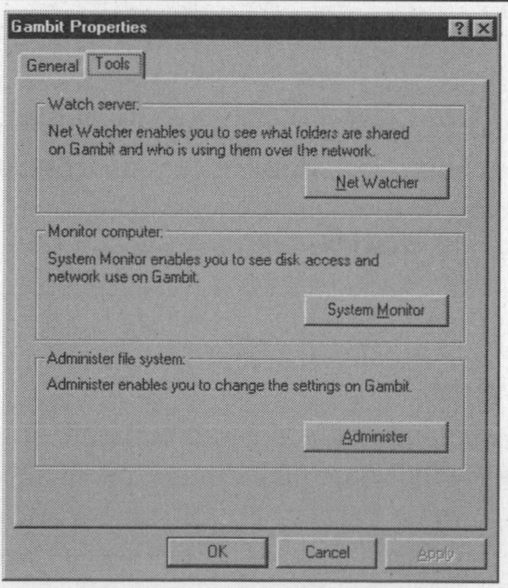

FIGURE 26.1: The Tools tab of a remote machine's Properties dialog box

Table 26.1 summarizes the requirements for running the remote administration utilities. The following sections describe each of these tools in more detail.

TABLE 26.1: Requirements for the Remote Administration Tools

Tool	Remote Workstation			Administrating Workstation	
	User/ Share	File & Printer Sharing Enabled	Remote Registry Services	User/ Share	Remote Registry Services
Net Watcher	Share	Yes	N/A	Either	N/A
Net Watcher	User	Yes	N/A	User	N/A
Administer	Share	Yes	N/A	Either	N/A
Administer	User	Yes	N/A	User	N/A
Remote System Monitor	User	Yes	Yes	User	Yes
Remote Registry Editor	User	Yes	Yes	User	Yes

Shared Printers

Windows 98 allows local printers to be shared across the network. To share printers, you must first have installed the File and Printer Sharing service. After a printer is shared, it can be connected to by various clients on the network, provided the clients have appropriate rights. Windows 98 supports a new feature called Point-and-Print printing, which means that clients automatically install the correct print driver when they connect to the network printer.

Point-and-Print from a Windows 98 Machine

Point-and-Print is automatically supported by Windows 98 machines and requires very little setup. All that you need to do to enable Point-and-Print on a Windows 98 computer is to install the printer and then share it.

NOTE

The printer drivers required for a Windows 98 machine to support Point-and-Print are specified in the MSPRINT.INF, MSPRINT1.INF, MSPRINT2.INF, and PRNTUPD.INF files located in the hidden directory C:\Windows\Inf. When you share a printer on a Windows 98 machine, Windows 98 will create a special hidden share called PRINTER$. This hidden share is used by other Windows 98 machines to copy the driver and configuration files from the server. The hidden share PRINTER$ has no password. It can be mapped through a network drive connection as *servername*\PASSWORD$.

Point-and-Print from an NT Machine

Point-and-Print installation for a Windows 98 client from a Windows NT machine is supported a bit differently than for a Windows 98 client from a Windows 98 configuration. This is because of the way Windows NT handles printing. When a printer is shared on a Windows NT computer, you can choose to also install drivers for other operating systems (such as Windows 98), which enables Point-and-Print for that particular operating system.

NOTE

Point-and-Print from a Windows 98 print server to a Windows NT client is not currently supported.

Point-and-Print from a NetWare Machine

To use a Point-and-Print setup from a Novell NetWare machine, the NetWare server must be running bindery emulation. A NetWare *bindery* is similar to the Windows 98 and Windows NT Registry in that it stores account and printer information. You must also have Supervisor Equivalent rights to set up Point-and-Print on a NetWare server.

Procedures for Remote Administration and Networking Printing

Enabling support for remote administration and networking printing is explained in the following sections.

Enabling Remote Administration

You enable remote administration through the Remote Administration tab of the Passwords Properties dialog box.

(If you don't see the Remote Administration tab, your computer might be using a system policy that does not allow this tab.) Follow these steps to enable remote administration on your Windows 98 machine:

1. Go to Control Panel ➢ Passwords.
2. Choose the Remote Administration tab.
3. Check the Enable Remote Administration Of This Server checkbox.
4. If this PC is using share-level security, set a password and then confirm the password. If the PC is using user-level security, select the users and groups who have permission to administer this PC.
5. Click OK.

Installing Remote Registry Services Since Remote System Monitor must pull information from the Registry, you must install Remote Registry Services on both workstations to allow remote administrators to see the Registry. Installing Remote Registry Services is also necessary for using Remote Registry Editor. See below for the screens involved in this procedure.

Follow these steps to add Remote Registry Services:

1. Go to Control Panel ➢ Network.
2. From the Configuration tab, click the Add button.
3. Select Service, then Add, then Have Disk.
4. Insert the Windows 98 CD-ROM and go to the \Tools\Reskit\Netadmin\Remotreg folder.
5. Click OK in the dialog boxes. You are told that you must reboot your system before these changes will take effect. (The folder that the Remote Registry Service is located in may be different in your version of Windows 98.)

6. Click OK and let the system reboot.

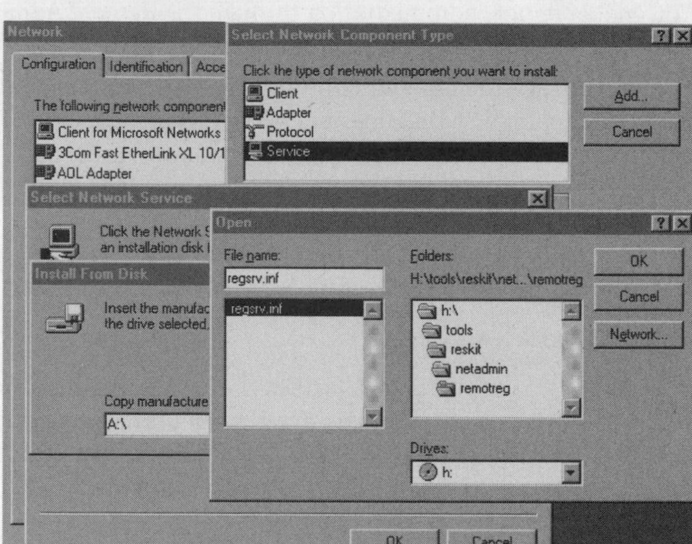

WARNING

Do not install the Remote Registry Service unless you need it, as workstations suffer a slight performance hit.

The Administer Utility The Administer utility gives an administrator access to the hard disks on the remote workstation. From the local computer, you can administer the file system as if you were sitting at the remote workstation. The Administer tool can be used with both user- and share-level security. Follow these steps to use Administer:

1. Double-click the Network Neighborhood icon on your Desktop.
2. Navigate to a Windows 98-based computer involved in remote administration and right-click its icon.
3. From the Context menu, choose Properties to open the Properties dialog box for that PC.
4. Choose the Tools tab.

5. Click the Administer button. The Administer utility starts and allows you to look at the remote workstation's C: drive. You can share resources and delete, create, and modify files as if you were sitting at that remote workstation.

Creating Shared Printers

Sharing a printer is relatively easy. To share a printer, follow these steps:

1. Install the printer as a local printer.
2. Make sure File and Printer Sharing is installed and enabled.
3. Go to the Properties dialog box of the printer (or right-click the printer icon).
4. Choose Sharing.
5. Select Shared As and enter a name.
6. Enter a password (if using share-level security) or assign users and groups to the printer (if using user-level security).
7. Select OK to share the printer.

Connecting to a Network Printer

There are two methods for connecting to a network printer.

Manual Installation: This method requires you to specify or browse to the network printer, and to choose the correct manufacturer and model.

Point-and-Print: This method only requires you to specify or browse to the network printer, as the correct printer driver will automatically be installed on your workstation.

Installing Network Printers Manually An advantage of Point-and-Print installation is that you copy the current printer configurations over to your workstation. With manual installation, you are using default, unmodified drivers and configurations. You may need to make changes to these configurations for paper size, fonts, orientation, and so on.

Follow these steps for a manual network printer installation:

1. Open the Printers folder by selecting Start ➢ Settings ➢ Printers.

2. Double-click the Add Printer icon to start the Add Printer Wizard.

3. Click the Next button to begin the installation process. This brings up a screen asking you whether this is a local printer or a network printer.

4. Choose the Network printer option and then click Next. The next screen asks you for the network path or queue name.

5. You can type in a UNC name, or you can click the Browse button to browse the network and locate the printer or queue. You also need to specify whether or not you print from MS-DOS–based programs. If you choose to print from MS-DOS–based programs, you will be presented with a screen that has a Capture Printer Port button. Click this button to capture the printer port. In the Capture Printer Port dialog box, select the port to capture from the Device list (usually you will choose LPT1), and then click OK.

6. Click the Next button to move to the manufacturers and printers screen. Select the manufacturer and the appropriate printer from the lists. Click Next to move to the screen that asks for a printer name.

7. Enter a name for the printer. This name can be up to 31 characters in length and is known as the "friendly name." Your friendly name must be unique. (For a local printer, if you planned on allowing others access to your printer from across the network, it might be safer to use a UNC-compatible name, which means your friendly name should be 15 characters or fewer. Since you can't reshare a network printer using Windows 98, you can use a longer name for your printer.) From this screen, you also have the option to make this printer the default printer for your Windows programs. Click the Next button when you are finished.

8. The last screen of this Wizard gives the option to print a test page. This is usually a good idea. The test page shows you that the printer is hooked up and running properly, and will also tell you which printer drivers and versions your printer is using and print a sample graphic. If you are using a color printer, the Windows logo graphic will be in color. When you

are finished, click the Finish button. Your new printer icon will show up in the Printers folder.

Installing Network Printers with Point-and-Print With Point-and-Print, you can install driver files for a networked printer in several ways:

- Drag the Point-and-Print printer icon from the networked PC to your Printers folder or Desktop.
- Select the Install option from the Context menu of the networked printer.
- Double-click the networked printer icon and begin the Point-and-Print installation.

You can also print to a networked printer by simply dragging and dropping documents onto the printer icon. If the printer hasn't been installed yet, this will initiate the installation process and then send the print job to the printer.

Set up user environments by using user profiles and system policies.

This objective has to do with creating profiles and policies that enable you to better manage your users. This objective is more about the actual installation and implementation of profiles and policies. Make sure you know the features that profiles and policies give you, as well as how to implement them.

Profiles

Windows 98 stores settings and preferences in a *profile*. By default, all users on the same computer use the same profile. Windows 98 has the ability to track individual profiles for different users, so preferences and settings can be maintained by multiple users of a computer. You can enable user profiles (they are not enabled by default) by going to the Passwords Control Panel and selecting the User Profiles tab.

Local profiles are stored on the local computer, and they don't follow the user around. Local profiles are held in the <*Windows Root*>\Profiles folder.

Roaming profiles are stored on a central server and are downloaded to a workstation when a user logs on. To enable roaming profiles, you must be using a 32-bit client (such as the Client for Microsoft Networks or the Client for NetWare Networks), and that client must be selected as the Windows 98 client's primary network logon. Roaming profiles are held in the User's home folder of an NT server, or in the SYS:Mail\User_Id directory of a NetWare server.

Roaming Profiles on an NT Server

Roaming profiles are held in the NT server's home folder. When a user logs in to an NT domain and profiles are enabled, Windows 98 will ask the user if he or she would like to enable profiles. If the user answers no, the default profile will be used. If the user answers yes, Windows 98 will do one of four things:

- If Windows 98 can't find a profile for the user, the default profile is copied into the user's profile.
- If there is a profile both locally and on the server, Windows 98 compares the date and time of the profiles and loads the most recent one.
- If there is no profile on the server, but there is one locally, the local profile is used and then saved to the server when the user logs out.
- If there is a profile on the server but not one locally, Windows 98 copies the profile from the server to the local computer.

Roaming Profiles on a NetWare Server

If you have NetWare servers as your main servers, you can enable the NetWare servers to store user profiles. On a NetWare server (2.*x* or 3.*x*, or 4.*x* or 5.*x* in bindery emulation mode), roaming profiles are stored in the Mail\User_Id directory on the SYS volume. If the NetWare server is version 4.*x* or 5.*x* and running pure NDS (not supporting bindery emulation mode), then the profile is placed in the user's home folder.

Troubleshooting User Profiles

If user profiles are not working correctly, here are some steps to take to see where the problem lies:

- Make sure profiles are enabled on the workstation.

- Make sure the appropriate client is picked as the default.
- Check the date/time/time zone of the workstation and server. Incorrect time zone settings are a major source of time synchronization problems under both Windows 98 and Windows NT.
- Check the NT server to ensure home directories have been assigned.
- Check the NetWare server for Mail\User_Id directories.
- Check the folders and files in the directories on the NT server to make sure profiles are being saved to the server.

WARNING

If a user is logged on to more than one computer, when he or she logs off from the first computer, the profile will be saved to the server. When the user logs off from the second computer (and the profile is once again saved to the server), the changes from the first computer are then lost.

- Any Briefcases that were created prior to enabling profiles will need to be re-created because the links in the Briefcase are not updated to reflect the profile.
- Programs that do not record their information in the Registry (such as 16-bit programs) will probably record their information in the WIN.INI or another INI file. As such, these settings are not stored in the user's profile.
- Check to ensure the users have appropriate rights to their home directories in NT or to their Mail\User_Id directory on a Netware server.

System Policies

The process for creating policies involves loading a template, modifying it to suit your needs, and saving it so Windows 98 can find it. This process can be broken down into the following steps:

- Enable user profiles.
- Decide on the appropriate policies for your company.
- Decide if policies will be based on group membership.

- Install System Policy Editor and support for group policies (if you decided to base policies on group membership).
- Load or create the appropriate template.
- Create policies for groups (if you decided to take this approach).
- Configure the order in which groups will take effect.
- Create default settings for users via the Default User.
- Create default settings for computers via the Default Computer.

NOTE

The Default User and Default Computer are part of default templates, called WINDOWS.ADM and COMMON.ADM, supplied by Microsoft. These templates are discussed later in this chapter.

- Create exceptions for users via unique user settings.
- Create exceptions for computers via unique computer settings.
- Save the policy as CONFIG.POL where Windows 98 will find it (by default in the NETLOGON share of a Windows NT primary domain controller, although you can change this).

Deciding How to Use Policies

Policies are flexible enough to do almost anything that you want, with respect to enforcing restrictions that may be required for your network. Some companies have even formed committees to look at the COMMON.ADM and WINDOWS.ADM templates (default templates that contain many common registry settings) and decide which restrictions should be enforced. If your network requires restrictions that are not present in the default templates, you can edit the templates or create a new one.

Policies can be based on group membership. Groups can come from either an NT server or a NetWare server. Support for group policies is not installed by default; you must install this support for every computer that is expected to load group policies. While it is relatively easy to enable profiles and create a system policy, you should practice doing it and become familiar with the various options for both.

Configuring Profiles

There are two basic types of profiles, *local profiles* and *roaming profiles*. The next section covers enabling and configuring both types of profiles.

Enabling Local Profiles

User profiles are not enabled by default. Everyone uses the same settings on a computer until profiles are enabled. Once profiles are enabled, everyone on that computer will be asked to log in so that Windows 98 will know who the user is and can load the appropriate profile.

The user will be prompted the first time he or she logs in and a profile is not found. If the user chooses not to create a profile, the default profile will be used.

Enabling Roaming Profiles

User profiles are *local* when they are created, in that they reside on the local hard drive. You can enable *roaming profiles* by configuring profiles to reside on a server, so the user profile will be available to the user no matter which computer that user logs in from.

Roaming profiles are stored on a central server and are downloaded to a workstation when a user logs on. You can enable roaming user profiles on Windows NT and NetWare servers.

Roaming Profiles on a NetWare Server

If you have NetWare servers as your main servers, you can enable the NetWare servers to store user profiles. On a NetWare server, roaming profiles are stored in the SYS:Mail\User_Id directory.

The procedure is essentially the same as the one for enabling roaming profiles on an NT server:

- Enable profiles on the User Profiles tab of the Passwords Control Panel.
- Synchronize the clocks of the client and server.
- Make sure you are using a 32-bit client.
- Make the NetWare client the primary network logon.
- Make sure the user has a directory under the Mail directory that corresponds to his or her ID number.
- Make sure the NetWare server supports long filenames.

When Windows 98 looks for a profile from a NetWare server, it compares date and time stamps and loads the most recent one (much as it does on an NT server).

Configuring Policies

If your system policies are going to be based on groups, you must not only install System Policy Editor on your machine (to create the policy), but you must also install group policy support on every computer in your network.

Installing System Policy Editor and Group Policy Support

Policies are created using System Policy Editor. This program is not installed by default; you must first install it from the Windows 98 distribution CD-ROM before you can create or edit policies. If you plan to use group policies, you must also install group policy support on the computer that creates the policy. System Policy Editor is located in the Tools\Reskit\Netadmin\Poledit folder of the CD-ROM.

Follow these steps to install System Policy Editor and/or group policies:

1. Go to Control Panel ➢ Add/Remove Programs.
2. Select the Windows Setup tab.
3. Choose Have Disk.
4. Type the path to the folder (Tools\Reskit\Netadmin\Poledit), or use the Browse button to point to the Poledit folder. If you use the Browse button, both the GROUPPOL.INF file and POLEDIT.INF file appear in the Open dialog box.
5. Windows 98 lets you select only the GROUPPOL.INF file (because it is the first INF file in the list). Choose OK after indicating the folder to open.
6. In the next dialog box, shown below, choose which components you wish to install: Group policies and/or System Policy Editor, as shown below. Then click Install.

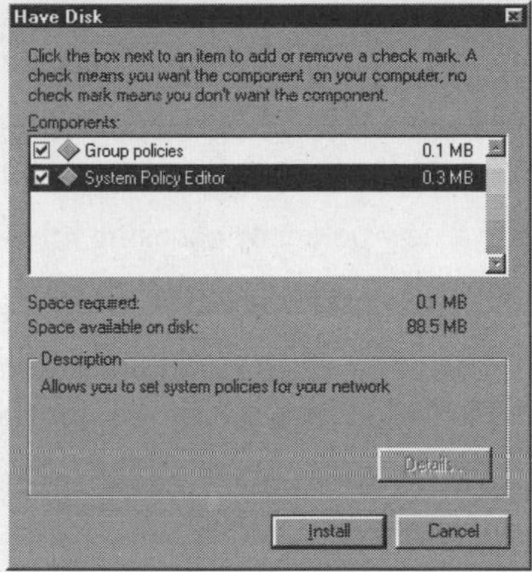

7. If you installed System Policy Editor, verify that it is installed correctly by selecting Start ➢ Programs ➢ Accessories ➢ System Tools. There should be an icon for System Policy Editor.

Loading Templates

Microsoft supplies default templates called COMMON.ADM and WINDOWS.ADM, which contain many popular Registry settings. These files are located in the (hidden) INF folder located in the Windows installation folder after System Policy Editor is installed. There are two major sections of each template: the Default Computer (which pertains to the Hkey_Local_Machine Registry key) and the Default User (which pertains to the Hkey_Users Registry key). You can view the Default Computer and Default User entries in System Policy Editor by double-clicking their icons in the System Policy Editor window.

Creating Policies for Groups

You can create policies for either NetWare or NT groups by adding a group and assigning policies to it. You can also change the order in which Windows 98 implements groups so that users who belong to more than one group can receive the rights of the group you choose.

WARNING

Windows 98 does not support group policies by default. Group policy support must be installed on the computer that creates group policies and on every computer that will implement policies based on groups.

After you have installed group policy support for all the computers that will be using group policies, you can create and modify group policies.

1. Start System Policy Editor by selecting Start ➢ Programs ➢ Accessories ➢ System Tools ➢ System Policy Editor.
2. Create a new policy by choosing File ➢ New File.
3. Create a new group policy by choosing Edit ➢ Add Group.
4. Type the name of the group (e.g., Sales). If user-level security is installed, you can browse for the group name.
5. Choose OK. Your policy should appear in the System Policy Editor window.
6. Highlight the Sales group and select Edit ➢ Properties, or double-click the Sales group.
7. Choose Control Panel ➢ System ➢ Restrictions, check Restrict System Control Panel, and check the Hide Virtual Memory Button box.
8. Save the policy as CONFIG.POL and close the Editor.

Setting Group Priority

When you use group policies, the policies for groups that come later will override those for groups that come earlier. To make sure that the desired group policy is applied, you can specify group priority, as shown in Figure 26.2.

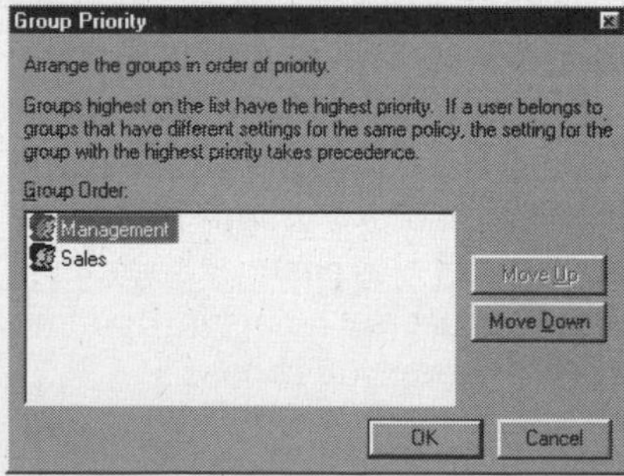

FIGURE 26.2: Specifying group priorities

We will resolve the conflicts in the example by giving the Management group priority.

1. Start System Policy Editor and load the policy CONFIG.POL.
2. Create a new group policy for the Management group by choosing Edit ➢ Add Group and specifying the Management group.
3. To set the order of the groups, select Options ➢ Group Priority.
4. Give the Management group priority over the Sales group by highlighting Management group and choosing Move Up until Management is on top.
5. Save the policy as CONFIG.POL and close the Editor.

NOTE

If a policy exists for a specific user, group policies are not applied for that user.

Creating Policies for Users

Policies set for the Default User apply to everyone except those who have a specific user policy. Follow these steps to make a policy for all users who lack a defined policy.

1. Start System Policy Editor and load the policy CONFIG.POL.
2. Select the Default User and make changes as appropriate.
3. Choose OK to save the settings.
4. Save the policy as CONFIG.POL and close the Editor.

NOTE

All exceptions to the Default User policies must be specified by adding a policy for each specific user or group you want excepted.

Adding Specific Users By creating entries for specific users, you can override both the Default User settings and any group policies that would have been enforced for that user. Follow these steps to make a specific user policy:

1. Start System Policy Editor and load the policy CONFIG.POL.

2. Create a user policy for a person by choosing Edit ➢ New User and entering their username.
3. Open the policy for the new user and edit the policy as appropriate.
4. Choose OK to save your changes.
5. Save the policy as CONFIG.POL and close the Editor.

Creating Policies for Computers

Policies can be set for all computers using the Default Computer specifications. Specific exceptions can be made by creating a separate computer entry for each excepted computer. Computer policies are based on the computer name. Follow these steps to make a policy apply to all computers that lack a specific policy designation:

1. Start System Policy Editor and load the policy CONFIG.POL.
2. Select Default Computer to open its properties.
3. Change the properties of the default computer as needed.
4. Choose OK to save the settings.
5. Save the policy as CONFIG.POL and close the Editor.

Adding Specific Computers By creating entries for specific computers, you can override the Default Computer settings. Follow these steps to add a specific policy for a computer:

1. Start System Policy Editor and load the policy CONFIG.POL.
2. Create a new computer account by selecting Edit ➢ Add Computer.
3. Enter the computer name, or use the Browse button to find it. (Notice that the Browse button allows you to browse the Network Neighborhood to find a computer name.)
4. Open the new computer account and make policy adjustments as necessary.
5. Choose OK to save your changes.
6. Save the policy as CONFIG.POL and close the Editor.

NOTE

Entries for the computer are based on the computer name and thus will not work if the computer name changes.

Saving Policies

After making the appropriate changes in System Policy Editor, you can save the policy and put it in the appropriate location.

Windows 98 looks for the CONFIG.POL file in one of two places:

- \\NT Server\NETLOGON share
- NetWare Server:SYS\PUBLIC directory

If the Client for Microsoft Networks is the primary logon, Windows 98 will look in the NETLOGON share of the domain's PDC. The NETLOGON share is usually in the <*NT Root*>\System32\Repl\Import\Scripts folder, which is also where logon scripts are stored by default.

WARNING

Windows 98 loads policies only from the PDC by default, which could cause a bottleneck in a large environment. To avoid such a bottleneck, you can enable load balancing, which forces Windows 98 to look on domain controller servers other than the PDC for the policy file. For this to work, all of the controllers in the domain must have a current copy of the profile (CONFIG.POL).

If the Client for NetWare Networks is chosen as the primary network logon, Windows 98 will look for the policy file in the public directory of the preferred NetWare server. Windows 98 can also be directed to load a policy by specifying the path and filename of the policy. This is called Manual Update mode, and the procedure is explained in the next section.

Specifying a Policy Path and Update Mode

You can specify a path for a local computer through the Path for manual update entry, as shown below.

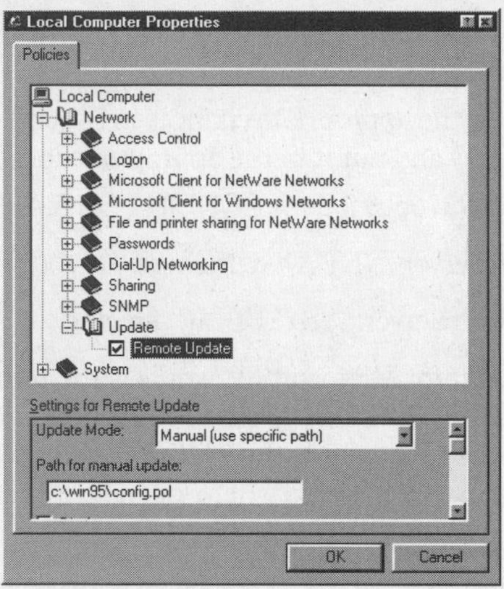

1. Start System Policy Editor.
2. Select File ➢ Open Registry. This will open the local Registry for editing, instead of making changes to a policy file.
3. Select Local Computer ➢ Network ➢ Update.
4. Check the Remote Update box, change the type to Manual, and add the path, including the policy name, to your policy file.

NOTE

Notice that you can also select Load Balancing from this menu.

5. Choose OK to save your changes.
6. Exit System Policy Editor. When you are asked if you want to save your Registry changes, answer Yes.

Back up data and the Registry and restore data and the Registry.

This objective has to do with the various options you have for backing up and restoring both the Registry and data on a Windows 98 system. You will also need to know the advantages, disadvantages, and techniques of using the various backup tools.

Backing Up and Restoring Data

Windows 98 includes a back up and restore program that lets you easily back up and restore files on your hard drive. Although there are many different programs you could use to back up your hard drive, the program that comes with Windows 98 has the advantage of being able to save long filenames; other programs may not preserve long filenames if they are not certified for Windows 98.

Backup Techniques

There are three general techniques you can use to shorten the time it takes to back up or restore data.

Full backup Doing a full backup entails backing up every folder and file on the computer system. While this is the slowest backup method, it is also the fastest way to restore data, as only the most recent backup set needs to be used. The archive bit is reset on every folder and file after a full backup is performed.

Incremental backup An incremental backup only backs up the folders and files that have changed since the last backup session, making it the fastest way to back up a computer (assuming a full backup is done occasionally). However, data restoration takes the longest, as the full set must be restored before each and every incremental set is restored in its proper order. The file archive bit is reset after performing an incremental backup.

Differential backup Differential backups are similar to incremental backups in that only the data that has changed since the last full backup is saved. The archive bit is *not* reset after a differential backup, which means that the backup set is a cumulative set of changes since the last full backup. Differential backups are slow to back up, but fast to restore, as only the most recent set has to be restored after the full backup set is restored.

Restoring Your Data

There are several reasons you may need to restore data: accidental erasure or editing of data; malicious erasure or editing of data; viruses; failure of a hard disk; or archive data loading.

There are several questions to ask yourself before you can restore your data: Do I have a valid backup? Have I solved the problem that is requiring me to restore my data? To where do I want to restore my data?

If you don't have a valid backup, you may need to send your hard drive to a professional repair service. (Recovering your data could cost you thousands of dollars.) If you have a valid backup and you have fixed your problem, then restoring your data is relatively simple. The Windows 98 Backup program also allows you to restore your data almost as easily as it backs it up.

Backing Up and Restoring the Registry

The Registry contains all of the settings for your computer, thus it is essential that it does not become corrupted or erased. Because the Registry is constantly being changed and added to by applications and hardware configurations, it is more likely to become corrupted or damaged than other, more static, files on your computer. By backing up the Registry, you can ensure that the latest changes and configurations can be restored in case of corruption or damage.

Another reason you may want to restore your Registry to an earlier state is if an application installs incorrectly, and thereby damages your Registry. The designers of Windows 98 realized that the Registry is extremely important and programmed Windows 98 to automatically back up the Registry. You can also manually back up the Registry to further ensure recoverability.

Automatic Registry Backups with Registry Checker

Windows 98 includes a new utility called Registry Checker which automatically runs at bootup. Registry Checker scans the Registry for corruption and backs up the Registry if there are no errors. The Registry backup is stored in a file called RB*XXX*.CAB, with the five most recent backups being kept, by default.

Registry Checker consists of two programs:

ScanReg A real-mode version of Registry Checker that allows you to restore the Registry from a command prompt.

ScanRegW A protected-mode version of Registry Checker that allows you to scan the Registry for errors and create a new backup of the Registry from within Windows 98.

Manually Backing Up and Restoring the Registry with Registry Checker

Registry Checker can also be started manually and can be used to make a backup of the Registry at any time.

Manually Backing Up and Restoring the Registry with Regedit

You can use the Regedit command to back up and to restore the Registry manually while within Windows 98. The Regedit program is contained on the Windows 98 Startup disk, so that if the Registry becomes corrupted, it can be restored.

Exporting All or Part of the Registry

Registry Editor can be used to export either the entire Registry or a selected part of the Registry to an ASCII file. There are two reasons why you might export the Registry to help avoid or troubleshoot problems:

- If you are preparing for (or expecting) trouble, you can export the Registry in order to have a current backup.
- If you have a computer with problems, you can import the subkey in question from a computer that works.

The Registry can be exported in its entirety by using the /e switch with the Regedit command from the command prompt, as explained later in the chapter.

Backup and Restoration Procedures

You will need to know how to back up and restore data and the Registry, and how to set various options of the Backup program.

Backing Up Your Data

The Microsoft Backup program was designed to be easy to use; it can back up any valid device, including floppies, hard drives, tape drives, removable media (such as Zip drives), or network drives. When you start the Backup program, the introduction screen prompts you to create a new backup job, open an existing backup job, or restore backed-up files. If you choose to create a new backup job, the Backup Wizard starts by asking you to choose to do either a full backup or a backup of selected files only.

NOTE

If you do not have the Backup program installed, use the Add/Remove programs applet of the Control Panel to install it.

If you don't use the Backup Wizard, the Backup program is relatively intuitive and allows you to specify what to back up or restore, and allows you to set various options for the backup or restore, including verification, compression, and overwriting on restoration. Follow these steps to backup or restore your data:

1. Create a folder on your C: drive called **Backups**.
2. Start the Backup program by going to the Properties dialog box of the C: drive and choosing Backup Now from the Tools tab, or by going to Start ➢ Programs ➢ Accessories ➢ System Tools ➢ Backup. The Backup Wizard will start, allowing you to create a new backup job, use a saved backup job, or do a restore. Choose to create a new backup job.
3. Select Backup Selected Files, Folders, And Drives, and choose Next.
4. Open whatever folder you wish to back up. Click the folder to mark it for backup, as shown here.

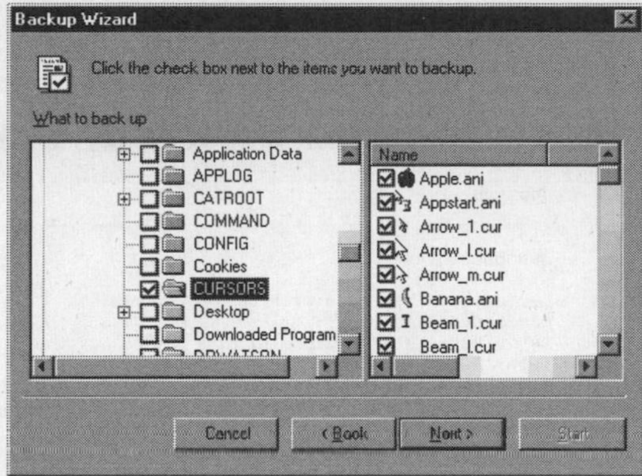

5. Click the Next button, choose All Selected Files, and then choose Next.

6. Click the Browser button next to the filename and browse to the C:\Backups folder so that the file will be saved as C:\Backups\MYBACKUP.QIC. Then choose Next.

7. Leave both of the next options selected in order to verify and compress the backup, as shown below. Click Next.

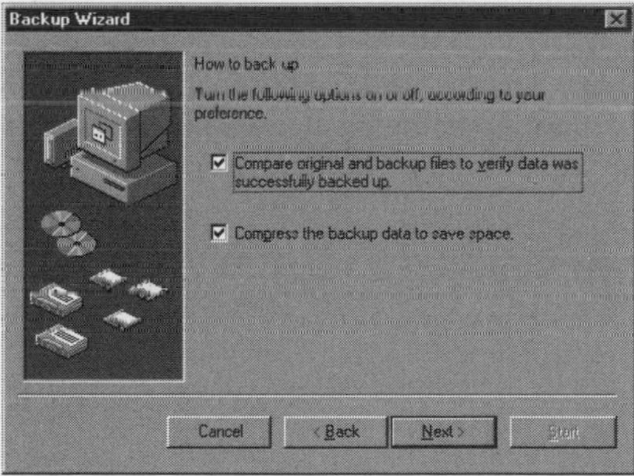

8. Give the backup set a name (such as **test**), and click Start. After a few seconds, the backup should finish. Click OK to close the prompt, but keep the main backup screen open.

9. Click the Report button to see a report of the backup. The report should look something like this:

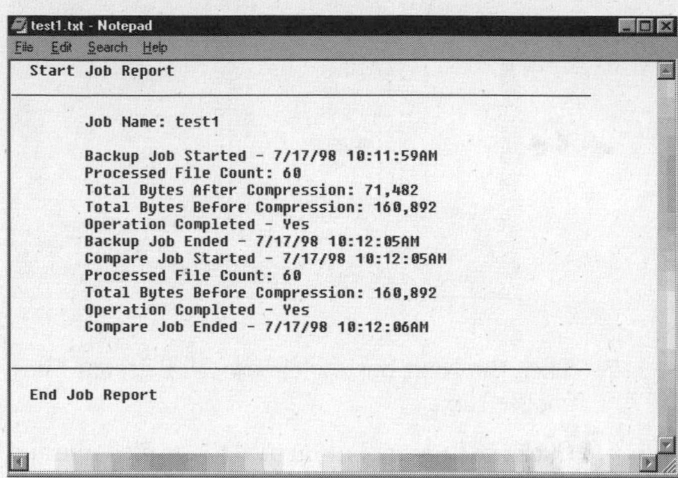
test1.txt - Notepad

File Edit Search Help

Start Job Report

Job Name: test1

Backup Job Started - 7/17/98 10:11:59AM
Processed File Count: 60
Total Bytes After Compression: 71,482
Total Bytes Before Compression: 160,892
Operation Completed - Yes
Backup Job Ended - 7/17/98 10:12:05AM
Compare Job Started - 7/17/98 10:12:05AM
Processed File Count: 60
Total Bytes Before Compression: 160,892
Operation Completed - Yes
Compare Job Ended - 7/17/98 10:12:06AM

End Job Report

10. Close the Report window and click OK to close the Backup window.

To restore your data, run the Backup Wizard and choose to do a restore or start the Backup program and choose the Restore tab, as shown below.

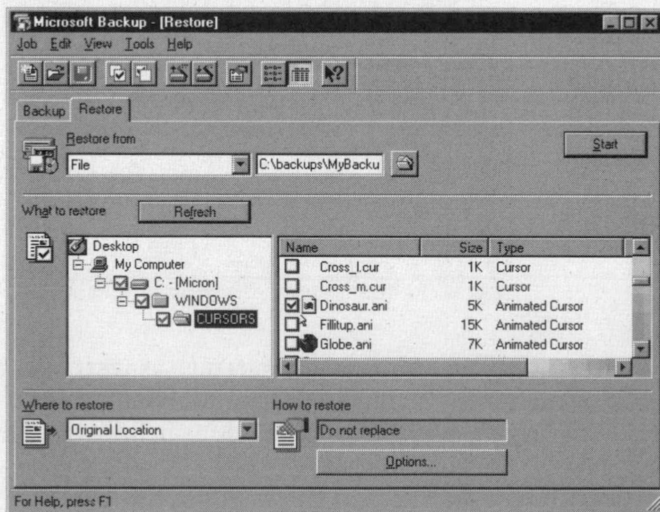

You can select to restore to the same drive and directory, or you can specify that data be restored to a different drive and directory. If you suffer a complete failure of your hard drive, but you have a backup on tape, you will need to reinstall Windows 98 and then use the Restore program to restore your drive to its previous state.

If you want your restored files to overwrite existing files, you need to change the default setting using the Options button before you start the restore.

WARNING

The Backup program that is included with Windows 98 is not compatible with any earlier versions from MS-DOS or Windows 3.*x*. If you have backup files that were made with an MS-DOS version of a backup program, you will not be able to restore them with Windows 98.

Backing Up and Restoring the Registry

Windows 98 automatically backs up the Registry every time you start Windows 98. You can manually check the Registry for errors by running ScanRegW at any time. If you need to restore the Registry, you must boot to MS-DOS mode or boot with the Windows 98 Startup disk. Run the SCANREG.EXE program, which will present you with a list of the last five backups of the Registry. Choose the backup you want to restore. Reboot Windows 98 to use that copy of the Registry.

Backups of the Registry will be labeled Started or Not Started. Started simply means that Windows 98 was successfully started using that copy of the Registry. Not Started means that, although the copy may be good, it has not actually been run, so Windows 98 is not sure if it is good or not.

To export the Registry to an ASCII text file, enter this command at the command prompt:

Regedit /e *file*.txt

To import into the Registry and overwrite the current Registry with the file that you indicate, use this command at the command prompt:

Regedit /c *file*.txt

Configure hard disks.

Tasks include:

- Disk compression
- Partitioning
- Enabling large disk support
- Converting to FAT32

This section of the test deals with disk partitions, compression, and FAT32 type partitions. The exam will test your knowledge of FAT32 in particular.

Compression

The primary benefit of using disk compression is that you can store more on a hard drive. The two disadvantages of using compression are a decrease in speed and the possibility that the entire drive will become corrupted. With prices of hard drives dropping rapidly in the last couple of years, compression makes more sense for computers that are hard to upgrade to larger hard drives (such as laptops) than for computers that are easily upgraded (such as desktops).

Windows 98 supports and comes with software-based, real-time compression of volumes and disk drives via a program called DriveSpace 3. By using compression, you can gain anywhere from 10 to 100 percent or more disk space. Windows 98 has new protected-mode compression drivers, but is also backward-compatible with older compression programs from Microsoft. Because compression is an integral part of Windows 98, both the paging file and Windows 98 itself can be kept on a compressed drive.

WARNING

Drives compressed under Windows 98 are unavailable to both OS/2 and to Windows NT. If you are dual-booting Windows 98 and NT, you should not use compression.

Windows 98 is compatible with DOS compression programs, including DBLSPACE and DRVSPACE. Windows 98 replaces the DBLSPACE.BIN or DRVSPACE.BIN files in the root directory with ones that it can unload, so that the 32-bit version (DBLSPACX.VXD) can be loaded.

The DriveSpace 3 compression program that comes with Windows 98 is fully integrated into the operating system. This means that Registry files, page files, and system files can all reside on a compressed drive. Compressed drives can hold long filenames and can be cached by Vcache.

Disk Partitioning

Before you can format a hard drive, it must be *partitioned*. The original version of Windows 98 allows a maximum size for primary and logical partitions up to 2GB each.

There are three types of partitions you can make using the Fdisk utility: primary, extended, and logical. Each of these partition types is described in detail in the following sections.

Primary Partition

The first partition you create on a hard disk is almost always a *primary partition*. A primary partition is required to be bootable in DOS. This is generally how the C: drive is partitioned. Older versions of DOS (5.0 and earlier) would allow only one primary partition per hard drive, but DOS 6.0 and higher allow up to four. (Other third-party utilities such as System Commander allow up to nine primary partitions.)

Extended and Logical Partitions

An extended partition can hold logical partitions within it, and these can be formatted as separate drives. *Extended partitions* exist because of the limitations that older versions of DOS (5.0 and earlier) had on the number and sizes of partitions. Older versions of DOS would allow only two partitions: one primary and one of another type. Older versions of DOS also would allow partitions of only 30MB or less. If you had a hard drive that was 80MB and were not using extended partitions, you could have only 60MB of your hard drive in use (30MB on each of the two allowed partitions).

Extended partitions can fill the remainder of the space left after the primary partition is created. Within the extended partition, logical drives can be created. In earlier versions of MS-DOS, creating many *logical partitions* within the extended partition was the best way to get around partition size restrictions.

By using logical partitions within extended partitions, DOS can get around its partition number limitations (two in earlier versions; four in Windows 98—for both the primary and extended) and size limitations. Size restrictions affect only primary and logical partitions, so the extended partition can be as large as is needed to fill the hard drive.

There is still a size restriction of 2GB with FAT16 partitions (discussed below), so being able to use primary, extended, and logical partitions is still useful. Figure 26.3 shows a typical hard drive, with a primary partition (C:) and an extended partition that has been divided into logical partitions D: and E:.

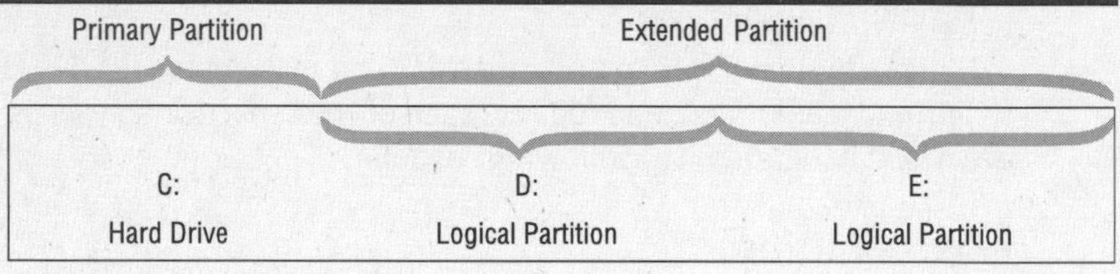

FIGURE 26.3: Disk partitions

FAT32 Partitions

Every copy of Windows 98 supports the latest partitioning scheme called *FAT32*, which helps reduce wasted space on a hard drive by supporting smaller partition clusters. When using Fdisk to make partitions, you can choose to create FAT32 partitions by enabling FAT32 at startup. Otherwise, FAT16 partitions will be created by default.

Converting to FAT32

Windows 98 comes with a program that will nondestructively convert a FAT16 partition to FAT32.

There are several issues that must be taken into consideration before converting a partition to FAT32.

- The name of the protected-mode Drive Converter program is CVT1.EXE, and the name of the real-mode program is CVT.EXE. Normally, you would use the protected-mode program.
- Windows 98 comes with a one-way conversion program. If you want to convert a FAT32 partition back to a FAT16 partition, you will need to use a third-party utility such as Partition Magic from Power Quest.

- Most third-party compression programs are incompatible with FAT32. If you are using such a program, you will be unable to convert to FAT32.
- If you convert a removable media drive, such as a Zip or Jaz drive, that drive can be used only by Windows 98 or by Windows 95B (OSR2).
- You cannot uninstall Windows 98 after converting to FAT32 (unless you use a third-party utility to first go back to FAT16).
- You cannot dual-boot with MS-DOS or Windows NT 4.0 (or earlier) after converting to FAT32.
- FAT32 is considerably slower than FAT16 when running in MS-DOS mode or Safe mode.
- Many older third-party disk utilities are not compatible with FAT32 and may need to be upgraded.
- Many programs (such as setup programs for various applications) will not show available space over 2GB on a FAT32 volume. This is a cosmetic bug and should not affect the operation of the program.
- Many laptops will have "hibernate" software installed, which may cause the Drive Converter program to either suggest not converting the drive or automatically cancel the conversion process. To override the defaults, run the CVT.EXE with the `/HIB` switch to delete any hibernation programs it finds.

The conversion program may take an hour or more. After the conversion, you should run Disk Defragmenter, which may take two or more hours to run.

Disk Management Procedures

Procedures you will need to know include compressing and decompressing a drive, partitioning a disk with Fdisk, enabling FAT32 support for a new partition, and converting a FAT16 partition to FAT32.

Compressing a Drive

When you compress a drive, you are actually taking the contents of an entire drive and putting them into one large file. The file is called a *compressed volume file* (CVF). The CVF usually has a filename such as DRVSPACE.000 or DBLSPACE.000. DRVSPACE.000 appears if Windows 98 reads an older compressed drive, and DBLSPACE.000 appears when Windows 98 reads a newer compressed drive or creates a new one.

When you compress a drive, the CVF is stored on the host drive, which is the original drive. The host drive letter is then changed to a higher letter, usually H:. Programs recognize the compressed drive normally, but Windows 98 is actually compressing and decompressing files into and out of the CVF (which is on the H: drive) and displaying the uncompressed files as the C: drive. You can choose to hide the host drive, which is a good option for users with less experience; in so doing, you will reduce their chance of damaging or deleting the CVF.

WARNING

It is absolutely essential that the CVF is not modified or edited by hand. Doing so could cause the entire compressed volume to become corrupted.

Compressing a Floppy Disk Drive Compressing a drive under Windows 98 is a simple process. When you run the DriveSpace 3 program and choose to compress a drive, it will display before and after compression information, as shown below. Follow these steps to compress a floppy disk:

1. Format a floppy disk or find one that still has some room on it.
2. Select Start ➢ Run and type **drvspace**, or go to Start ➢ Programs ➢ Accessories ➢ System Tools ➢ DriveSpace.
3. From the DriveSpace menu, highlight the floppy drive and choose Drive ➢ Compress. DriveSpace will then show you the estimated size of your new drive and ask you to confirm before it actually does the compression, as shown below.

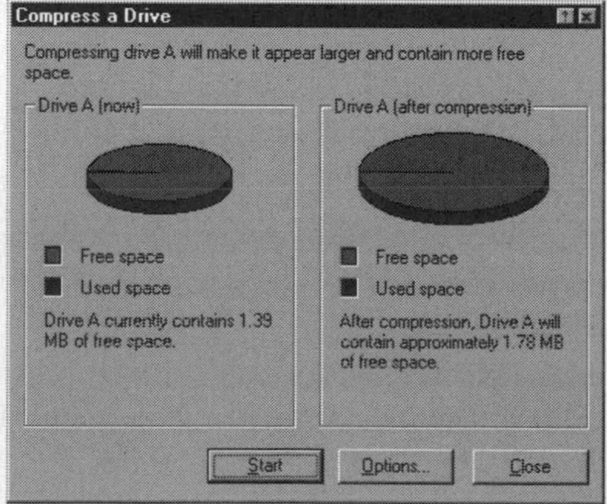

4. Click the Start button to begin the compression.
5. After compressing your floppy, you should get a status screen reporting on the compressed floppy drive, as shown below.

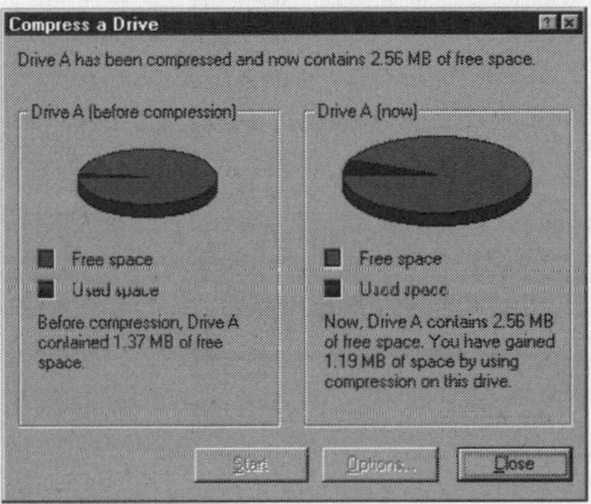

6. Click the Close button to close the window.

Compressing a Hard Disk Drive The above steps will also work on your hard drive, but you should back up any critical data before compressing or decompressing a hard drive. If you are compressing a hard drive, you can choose to compress the entire volume or just a part of the volume. Windows 98 will prompt you for a size to make the new drive, as shown below.

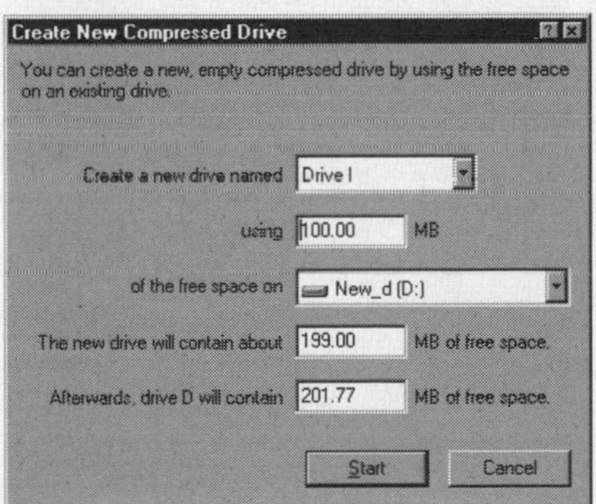

As you copy data to your new drive, you can check the status of your compressed files on the Compression tab of the drive's Properties dialog box, as shown in Figure 26.4.

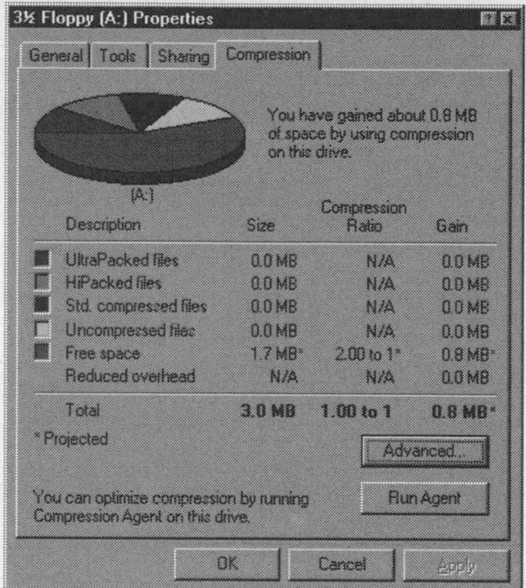

FIGURE 26.4: Checking the status of your compressed volume

If there are many uncompressed files, you can run the Compression Agent manually. Click the Run Agent button in the Compression tab to see the Compression Agent dialog box (see Figure 26.5). You can either activate compression with your default settings or you can change your compression settings.

Compression Agent - Drive A

Compression Agent recompresses your files according to the settings you specify. This might take a long time, especially on a large drive or if you have not run Compression Agent in a while.

You can pause or stop Compression Agent at any time without affecting the work it has already completed.

New compression format	Space gained by increasing compression	Space lost to improve performance
UltraPack	0 KB	0 KB
HiPack	0 KB	0 KB
None	0 KB	0 KB
Total	0 KB	0 KB

No change in disk space

0% Complete

Start
Exit
Settings
Overview

FIGURE 26.5: Running the Compression Agent manually

Decompressing a Drive You may want to decompress your drive at some future date. Windows 98 supports nondestructive decompression of the hard drive. When you run DriveSpace 3 and choose the Uncompress option, you will see before and after uncompression status screens, similar to the compression status screens.

Partitioning a Disk with Fdisk

Windows 98 does not provide a graphical partition manager. You must still use the DOS-based partition manager called Fdisk. When you choose to display partition information or desire to change your current hard drive with Fdisk, you'll see screens similar to Figures 26.6, 26.7, and 26.8, shown below.

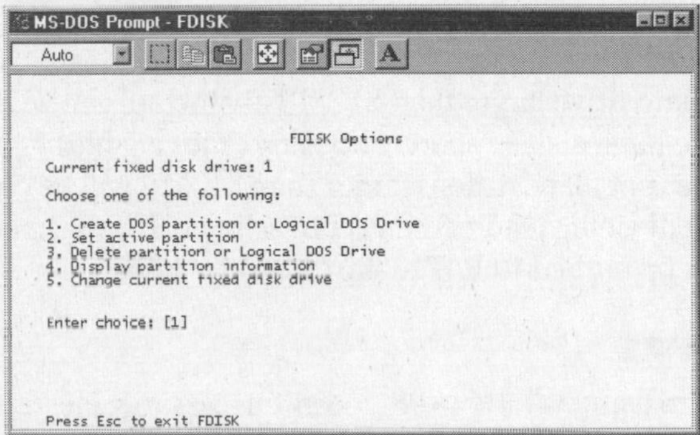

FIGURE 26.6: The Fdisk menu

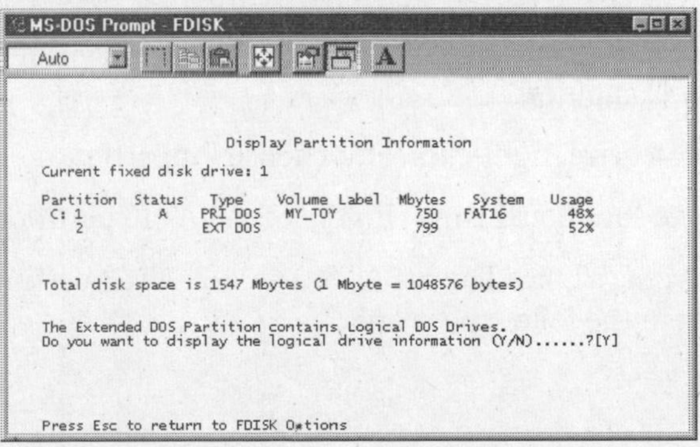

FIGURE 26.7: Fdisk partition information

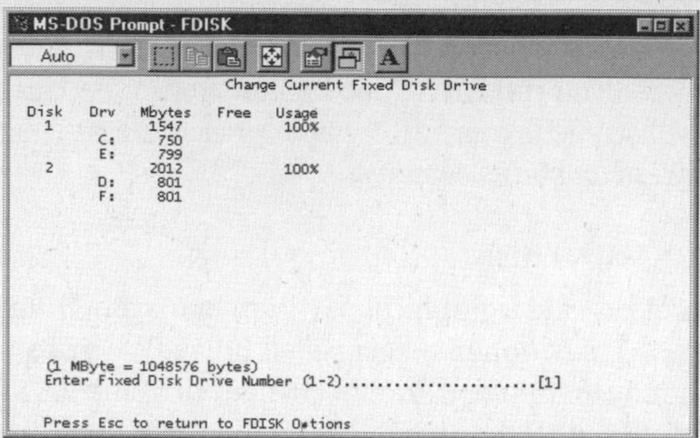

FIGURE 26.8: Choosing a hard drive to change

Enabling FAT32 Support

If Fdisk detects a hard drive larger than 512MB at startup, you will be prompted to enable large disk support. Choosing (Y)es enables FAT32 support and means that all partitions larger than 512MB will be created using the FAT32 scheme instead of the FAT16 scheme. If you choose (N)o, then you will be limited to FAT16 partitions.

Converting to FAT32

Just because you are using Windows 98 doesn't necessarily mean you have the benefit of decreased cluster size. Follow these steps to determine your partition status. If your hard drive was partitioned and formatted with MS-DOS or Windows 95(A) Fdisk and format, your partitions will be of the old FAT16 variety. You can convert to FAT32 with the new Drive Converter program.

1. Go to My Computer.
2. Highlight a drive, right-click, and choose Properties.
3. If the drive says Local Drive (FAT), it is a FAT16 partition.
4. If the drive says Local Drive (FAT32), it is a FAT32 partition, as shown in the following image.

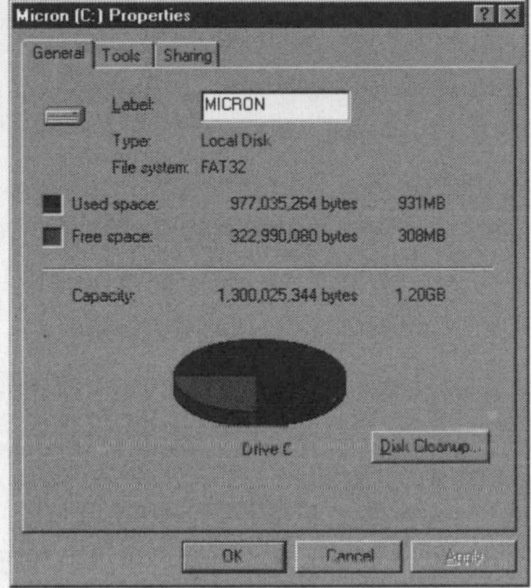

To convert to FAT32, run the Drive Converter program, as shown in the steps below.

WARNING

Converting to FAT32 could have undesirable results on your computer and older applications. As with any major system modifications, be sure to first back up any critical data!

1. Go to Start ➢ Accessories ➢ System Tools, and run the Drive Converter (FAT32) program.
2. Choose Next from the opening screen. Note that you can get more information about FAT32 by selecting the Details button.
3. Select the drive you want to convert.
4. Choose Next to start the conversion process. Answer Yes to any prompts verifying the conversion.

Create hardware profiles.

Hardware profiles are powerful tools that allow you to customize Windows 98 with various hardware devices. Windows 98 allows you to keep different sets of hardware device settings called hardware profiles. On a laptop with a docking station for example, you may have one profile with additional network, video, and SCSI drivers for when you are docked, and one profile for when your laptop is operating undocked. When a profile is created, the different sets of enabled devices are stored in the Registry under the Hkey_Local_Machine key.

Hardware profiles are created and managed using the Control Panel ➢ System applet in the Hardware Profiles tab. Once hardware profiles are enabled, you select which profile to use when Windows 98 boots.

Follow these steps to use a hardware profile:

1. Create a new hardware profile by copying an existing one.
2. Reboot Windows 98 and select the new profile.
3. Disable drivers as desired (see below)–your configuration will automatically be saved to the current hardware profile.

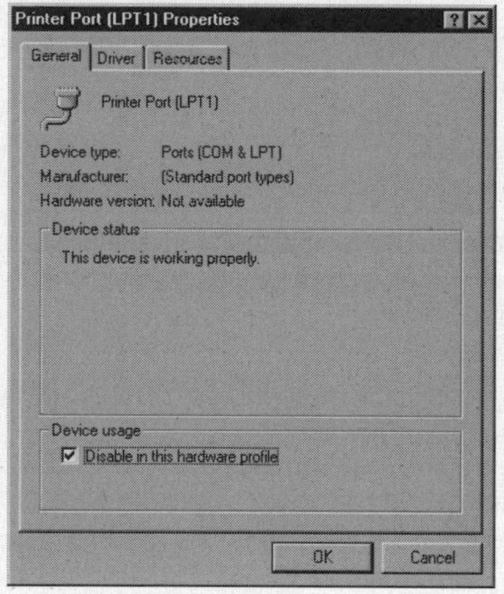

4. Reboot Windows 98 and select, modify, and test various hardware profiles.

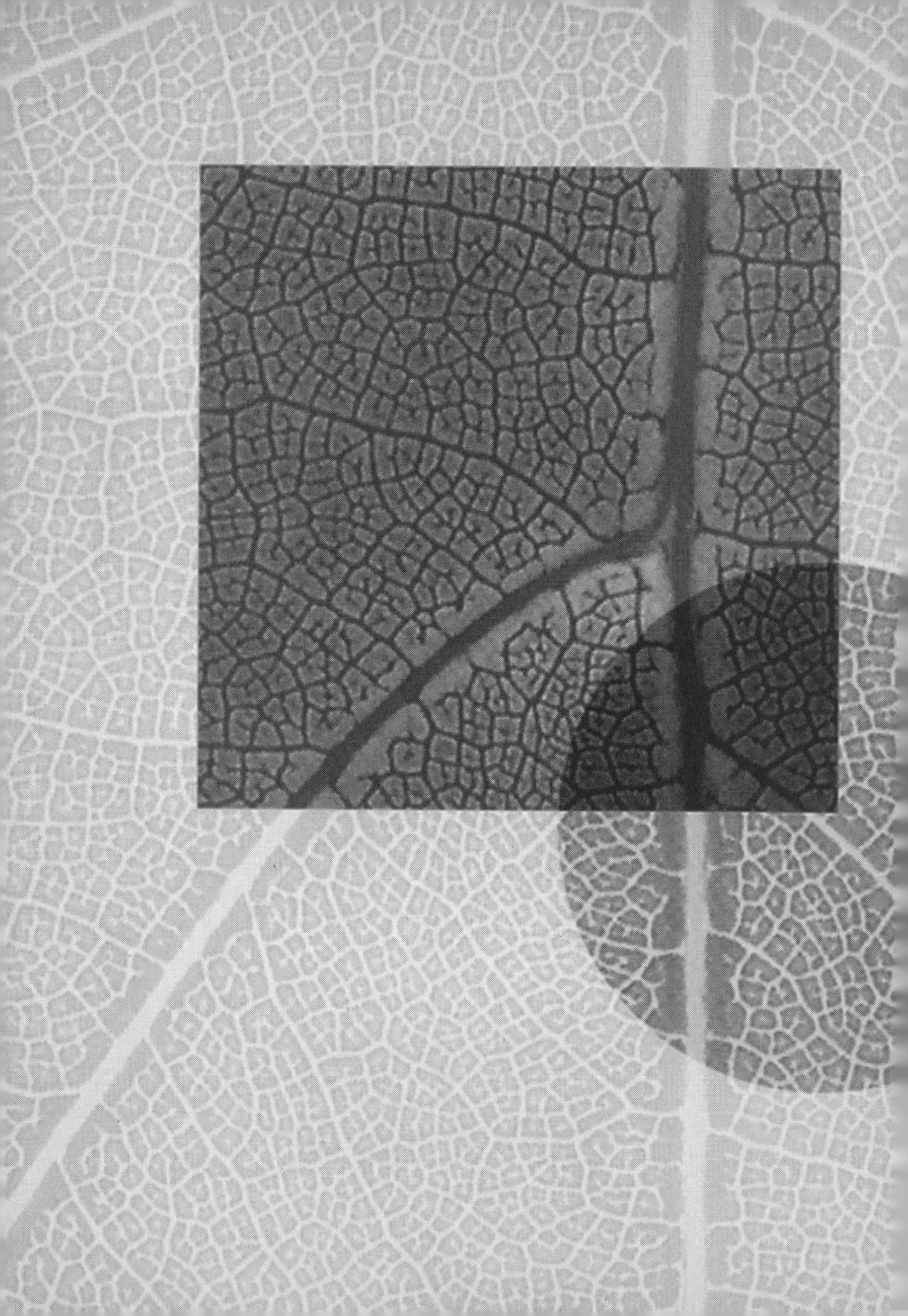

Chapter 27

Integration and Interoperability

This chapter deals with connecting Windows 98 as a client to a local network and as a dial-up networking client. Many of the topics covered in this chapter were covered in earlier chapters and will not be covered again.

Adapted from *MCSE Exam Notes: Windows 98*
by Rick Sawtell and Lance Mortensen
ISBN 0-7821-2421-6 416 pages $19.99

Configure a Windows 98 computer as a client computer in a network that contains a Windows NT 4.0 domain.

Several options can be configured for client software that affect the way connections are made. Options that can be set include the protocols bound to the network card and the client software (NetWare, NT, or another client) that Windows 98 loads and logs in to first. These settings are usually configured during initial installation of the computer and rarely need to be changed.

Logging in to a Network

An item that may need to be changed on a regular basis is the user password. Windows 98 will cache usernames and passwords that you use to connect various shared resources so it can automatically reconnect to those resources after you log in. You may want to disable the password cache for security reasons.

Choosing a Primary Network Logon

Windows 98 keeps a local database of usernames and passwords. If you are logging on to a domain or another type of server, you must choose whether to have Windows 98 first log you in to the domain and then the local computer, or first log in to the local computer and then the domain.

You have the following choices for primary logon:

- Windows
- Client for Microsoft Networks (if installed)
- Client for NetWare (if installed)
- Other clients such as Banyan VINES or DECNET (if installed)

You should set the client that you use most often as your primary client. Another reason you may wish to select a particular logon is to select which logon script and system policy files get loaded. Note that the primary client selected may not necessarily be the one used most often, as the first authenticating server is the one that supplies the login scripts, profiles, and policies. Some features of Windows 98 (such as roaming user profiles) work from a Windows NT server only if the client for Microsoft Networks is set as the primary client.

TIP

If security is not an issue, to keep Windows 98 from prompting you for a password, set Primary Network Logon to Windows Logon and make your password blank.

Logging in to an NT Domain

Another logon option you have is whether you log in to a workgroup or a domain. If you choose to log in to a domain, you must already have an account on that domain (usually created by a network administrator).

NOTE

A *workgroup* is a loose association of computers that has no central database of users, groups, or passwords. A *domain* is a logical grouping of computers that has one or more Windows NT servers acting as controllers. Each controller maintains a copy of the user database and can validate logon requests.

The benefit of logging in to a domain is that once you are validated by the domain, you should never need to enter your username and password again (during your session) to access resources on the network. The domain controller creates an access token when you log in that is used by all the servers in the domain. It is akin to getting your ticket stamped at an amusement park and being able to go on any of the rides (because you have been authenticated at one of the ticket windows).

Password Caching

Windows 98 can *cache*, or remember, the usernames and passwords with which you connect to shared resources. While convenient, caching passwords poses a security risk if the password file is de-encrypted. The caching of passwords happens if you select the Reconnect At Logon box when using a network resource. When you log in to Windows 98, the system uses the cached passwords to automatically reestablish all the drive connections you had the last time you logged off.

Password caching can be disabled by using a system policy.

Protocol Bindings

By default, every protocol is bound or used by every client and all server software installed on Windows 98. You may wish to have certain protocols unbound from certain services. For example, you may wish to have NetBEUI bound to the Microsoft Client so you can connect to various servers that are running NetBEUI, but you may wish to unbind NetBEUI from the File and Printer Sharing service because no NetBEUI clients will need to connect to your computer.

Network Logon Procedures

You will need to know how to configure the Primary Network Logon, set the Domain you will log in to, and change passwords, as well as be able to bind and unbind protocols from the various clients and services installed on Windows 98.

Configuring the Primary Network Logon

The Primary Network Logon setting is on the Configuration tab of the Network Control Panel, as shown below.

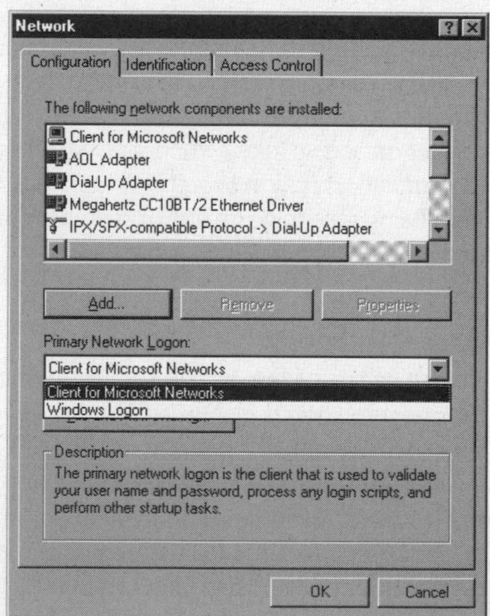

Follow these steps to choose your primary logon:

1. Go to Control Panel ➢ Network.
2. From the Primary Network Logon drop-down list, choose where you want to log on first. Select Windows Logon for a peer-to-peer network or Client For Microsoft Networks if you log in to an NT domain.
3. Click OK.
4. Reboot Windows 98.

Choosing to Log in to a Windows NT Domain

The option to log on to a Windows NT domain is in the Client For Microsoft Networks Properties dialog box.

Follow these steps to set up Windows 98 to log on to an NT domain:

1. Go to Control Panel ➢ Network.
2. Highlight Client For Microsoft Networks and choose Properties.
3. Put a check mark in the Log on to Windows NT domain box.
4. Type the name of the domain in the text box.
5. Click OK.
6. Reboot Windows 98.

Changing Your Password

You can change both your Windows 98 local password and your NT password from the Password Properties dialog box, shown below. Windows 98 will also allow you to change other passwords, such as those for screen savers, from the same Properties dialog box.

The steps for changing the Windows password, as well as the NT domain and screen saver password, are shown below.

1. Go to Control Panel ➢ Passwords.
2. Click Change Windows Password.
3. In the Change Windows Password dialog box, select the Microsoft Networking (to change your NT domain password) and the Windows Screen Saver boxes.
4. Click OK.

5. In the next dialog box, change your password by typing the old one once and the new one twice.
6. Click OK.
7. Reboot Windows 98 to use your new password.

Changing Protocol Bindings

To change protocol bindings, go to the properties of the individual protocols and then to the Bindings tab. Select (enable) or deselect (disable) the appropriate bindings.

Configure a Windows 98 computer as a client computer in a NetWare network.

This objective deals with configuring the NetWare client software for various NetWare servers and situations. NetWare servers communicate using a language called NCP (NetWare Core Protocol). By installing and correctly configuring the NetWare client software, you enable Windows 98 to communicate with NetWare servers.

NetWare Clients

NetWare 2.*x* and 3.*x* servers rely on a bindery to hold all user, group, password, and printer information. The bindery is essentially a flat-file database and is server specific. NetWare 4.*x* and 5.*x* servers use NDS (Novell Directory Services), which holds the users, groups, printers, and other resources in a hierarchical tree-like database. The same NDS tree can link many servers and is not server specific. Because many applications are not yet "NDS-aware," the NDS tree supports bindery emulation, which makes the 4.*x* and 5.*x* servers look and function like 3.*x* servers. True NDS support is preferred to bindery emulation because NDS is more flexible than bindery emulation.

You can choose from various clients for NetWare:

Microsoft Client for NetWare Networks This is a 32-bit, protected-mode client that can connect to NetWare servers. However, it is a bindery-emulation client and connects to NetWare 4.*x* and 5.*x* servers in bindery mode (it does not support NDS).

Microsoft's Service for NetWare Directory Services This is a true, protected-mode NDS client with a terribly long name.

This client is listed with the various services (instead of clients) and requires the Microsoft Client for NetWare to function.

Novell's VLM or NETX NETX is a real-mode MS-DOS client that was used extensively to connect to NetWare 2.*x* and 3.*x* servers. NETX is a bindery client and does not provide true NDS support. VLM came out when NetWare 4.*x* did, and it is a real-mode, true NDS client. NETX and VLM are loaded from the AUTOEXEC.BAT file as Windows 98 boots. As mentioned in the previous section, if you're using NETX or VLM, you must use ODI drivers (which also load from the AUTOEXEC.BAT file). Note that VLM and NETX do not come with Windows 98—you must obtain them from Novell.

Novell's Client for Windows 95 This is a 32-bit, protected-mode client that provides true NDS support. The Novell Client v2.5 for Windows 95 is also compatible with Windows 98 and supports the following versions of NetWare: 3.11, 3.12, 3.2, 4.10, and 4.11 (compatibility with version 5.0 is assumed, but was not verified by the authors). The Novell Client v2.5 for Windows 98 can be downloaded from Novell's Web site (`www.novell.com/download`).

Common Configuration Items

There are several items that commonly need to be configured for NetWare clients, including:

Preferred server When booted, NetWare clients broadcast a special packet to find a server. By specifying a preferred server you ensure that the client will attempt to connect to that server before it does a broadcast.

Preferred tree NDS records various resources in a database commonly referred to as a tree. Because there can be different trees on a network, the client can be set to look for a preferred tree.

NDS context A specific location in NDS (also known as an NDS container). A client can be configured to go to a particular context in a tree.

Printing options Various network printer settings that can be configured to enable/modify banner pages, form feeds, notification, and number of copies.

Frame type There are various frame types that NetWare servers and clients can use. Although a workstation will attempt to autodetect the correct frame type, you may wish to select a particular frame type for a particular client.

You need to know how to install and configure NetWare clients and change the various options for those clients.

You can set the preferred server and enable login script support in the Client for NetWare Networks Properties page.

If you are using the MS-NDS client, it will also be listed in the Configuration tab of the Network applet of the Control Panel.

Follow these steps to change the NetWare client settings:

1. Go to Control Panel ➢ Network.
2. Highlight the Client For NetWare Networks and choose Properties.
3. Enter the preferred server.
4. Turn off login script processing.
5. Choose OK to save your changes.
6. Highlight the Service For NetWare Directory Services, and choose Properties. You will then see the following dialog box, which includes settings for the preferred tree and default context for the workstation:

7. Enter your preferred tree and context. (Notice that we used **OAK** and **OU=SALES.O=ACME** above.)
8. Choose OK twice.
9. Reboot Windows 98 to have your changes take effect.

Configure a Windows 98 computer for remote access by using various methods in a Microsoft environment or a mixed Microsoft and NetWare environment.

Methods include:

- Dial-Up Networking
- Proxy Server

Windows 98 allows you to remotely connect to your computer at the office as a dial-up server and have the machine sitting in front of you use resources as if you were on the network. The modems at both computers act as the network cable. You can download e-mail, get those Microsoft Excel files that you forgot at the office, or play a networked computer game. You will need to know what Dial-Up Networking supports, as well as how to install it and create a connection. You will also need to be familiar with Proxy Server and know how to configure Internet Explorer to take advantage of it.

Dial-Up Networking Features

Dial-Up Networking encompasses many features found only in Windows 98 and Windows NT, including the following:

Compatibility As a dial-up server, Windows 98 can support Microsoft Windows NT, LAN Manager, Windows for Workgroups, LAN Manager for Unix, IBM LAN servers, and Shiva LanRover. When running as a dial-up client, Windows 98 can connect to systems supporting Microsoft RAS, Novell NRN, or SLIP, or servers running PPP. (See the discussion of line protocols in the "Dial-Up

Networking Architecture" section of this chapter for definitions of these protocols.)

LAN topology independent As a dial-up server, Windows 98 supports Ethernet, Token Ring, FDDI, and ArcNet.

Advanced security Dial-Up Networking allows the use of encrypted passwords to prevent their capture and use over public switched telephone lines.

Advanced modem support Dial-Up Networking supports all modems that work with the Windows 98 Unimodem driver system. This includes support for flow control and both software and hardware compression.

Slow links Dial-Up Networking exposes the slow link API to indicate to programs that they are running over a slow link. This is useful because programs will wait for a predetermined amount of time to receive data across the network. Since networks are so much faster than modems, most programs would issue a timeout error while waiting for the information to come across a slow link. Because programs know that they are using a slow link, the timeout waiting period is much longer.

Dial-up server Windows 98 can be used as a dial-up server. As such, Windows 98 can support one connection.

NOTE

If you install RAS (Remote Access Service) on a Windows NT Server machine, it can support up to 256 simultaneous inbound connections (versus just one for Windows 98).

Line Protocol Layer Line protocols are used to encapsulate data into a format suitable for transmittal over telephone lines or null-modem cables.

Windows 98 comes with support for the most common Line Protocol Layers. Dial-Up Networking in Windows 98 supports the following line protocols:

Windows NT RAS (Remote Access Service) An older protocol developed for Windows NT 3.1. It has been carried forward and is still available under NT 4 RAS uses asynchronous NetBEUI. This protocol is slower and less compact than SLIP and PPP, but it has the added advantage of being well tested and runs with few errors and even fewer opportunities for improper configuration.

SLIP (Serial Line Internet Protocol) A subset of the tools and utilities included with TCP/IP. SLIP should be used in a networking environment that requires machines to have their own unique IP addresses. SLIP is not installed automatically with Windows 98, as it is an older protocol that has been replaced with the more reliable PPP protocol. To add SLIP, use the Add/Remove Programs applet of the Control Panel. The files are located on your Windows 98 CD-ROM in the \Admin\Apptools\Slip folder.

NOTE

If you installed Windows 98 using floppy disks, the SLIP folder is not available. The \Admin folder does not ship with the floppy disk version.

PPP (Point-to-Point Protocol) A standard low-speed protocol that originated from TCP/IP. It has become the most widely used protocol because it is very flexible. Dial-Up Networking is compliant with the industry-standard PPP communications protocol. SLIP requires a preassigned IP address, whereas PPP can use a DHCP server and "lease" an IP address for a short period of time. (See Chapter 25 for more information about IP addresses and DHCP.)

PPTP/VPN (Point-to-Point Tunneling Protocol/Virtual Private Network) This new protocol allows a user to dial up an Internet Service Provider (ISP) and use PPTP to create a secure tunnel into the network at their office.

NRN NetWare Connect A proprietary connection protocol that allows a Windows 98 machine to directly connect with a NetWare Connect server. Novell's IPX/SPX network protocol must be used for this type of connection.

NOTE

NetWare Connect clients cannot connect to a Windows 98 dial-up server.

Wide Area Network Support

Dial-Up Networking can make use of the modem and TAPI (Telephony Applications Programming Interface) components to work over different types of wide area networks (WANs):

Public Switched Telephone Networks (PSTNs) The regular telephone lines that you use every day to make phone calls. The modem in your computer can use these same telephone lines to transmit and receive data.

X.25 A special packet-switching network. An X.25 packet is delivered to another X.25 node on a worldwide X.25 network. That node then forwards the packet to the next node, and so on, until the packet finally reaches a packet assembler/disassembler (PAD) at the other machine. The PAD takes the place of your standard modem.

Integrated Services Digital Network (ISDN) A standard for digital telephony. ISDN offers faster communications than you can get with a standard analog telephone line. ISDN speeds range from 64,000 to 128,800bps. ISDN requires a special digital modem and an ISDN telephone line to your home or office.

Security for Mobile Computing

Anytime you open up your computer system to the outside world, you take a chance that someone will try to break in and destroy information. When setting up your computers for dial-up access, you should consider implementing the following security strategies to prevent unauthorized access to your systems:

- Use user-level security on the server side. This forces the server to check both the user ID and the password before allowing access.
- Use system policies in conjunction with dial-up access. Windows 98 system policies can implement different levels of access to the computer resources based upon the login.
- Use encrypted passwords. This keeps outsiders from getting your password as it is passed along telephone networks.
- Use firewalls for large servers that allow Internet access. A *firewall* is a set of multiple layers of security strategies to keep outsiders out of your system.

- You might want to encrypt sensitive documents that you will be sending over the Internet. There is encryption software available from a variety of sources, including the Internet.

Data-Transfer Performance

There are several steps that you can take to improve your data-transfer performance. Here are just a couple of things you might try:

- Use compression. Windows 98 supports both hardware and software compression. This setting is available from the Modems applet of the Control Panel.
- Use System Monitor to check your performance. Look at the bytes read per second and bytes written per second under the dial-up adapter.

Proxy Server and Internet Explorer

A *proxy server* is designed to act as an intermediary between WWW servers and browsers so that it can cache frequently used Web pages. Proxy servers can also be used as firewalls and for protocol conversions. Proxy Server 2.0 for Windows NT is the current version available from Microsoft. Microsoft Internet Explorer (IE) can be configured to use a proxy server via the Connection tab of the Internet Options window.

Dial-Up Networking Installation and Configuration

The requirements for Dial-Up Networking include one or more compatible modems. You also need 2MB of free hard disk space to install the client, server, and administrative utilities. There are four parts to the installation process:

- Install Dial-Up Networking.
- Install and configure your modem.
- Create a client connection to a server.
- Create a dial-up server.

You install Dial-Up Networking using the Internet Connection Wizard or through the Add/Remove Programs applet of the Control Panel. The procedures for installing and configuring a modem were covered in Chapter 25. The following sections describe how to create dial-up connections and a dial-up server.

Creating Dial-Up Connections

Creating a connection places a connection object in your Dial-Up Networking folder. The connection object is analogous to an index card. It tells Windows 98 where to go to connect to the host computer and can provide details like a user ID and password to the host system that it is attempting to log on to. The New Connection Wizard guides you through setting up a connection, as shown below.

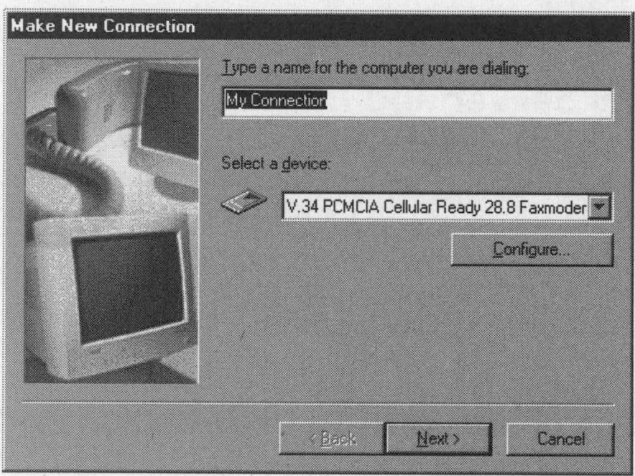

1. Select Start ➢ Programs ➢ Accessories ➢ Communications ➢ Dial-Up Networking to open the Dial-Up Networking folder.
2. Double-click the Make New Connection icon to start the New Connection Wizard.
3. If you see the "Welcome to Dial-Up Networking" screen, click the Next button. (Your version of Windows 98 might bypass this screen.) This takes you to the first Make New Connection dialog box.

4. In the "Type a name for the computer you are dialing" box (shown above), enter a name for this connection: **Groucho** (if you can't think of anything better).
5. Select your modem. If you haven't installed your modem yet, see Chapter 25. (The Configure button allows you to make configuration changes to your currently selected modem.) Then click Next to move to the screen requesting the telephone number that you want to call:

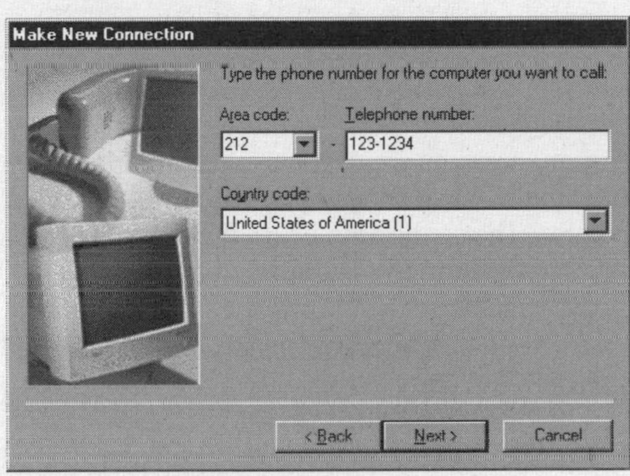

6. Type in the area code **212** and the telephone number **123-1234** (if you don't have a real connection number to use). Then click Next to go to the confirmation screen.
7. If everything looks correct on the final screen, click the Finish button. Your Dial-Up Networking folder now has a new icon in it called Groucho.

Making a Connection

When you select your connection icon in the Dial-Up Networking folder, Windows 98 presents the Connect To dialog box, shown below. The Dial Properties button in this dialog box will take you to the Dialing Properties dialog box.

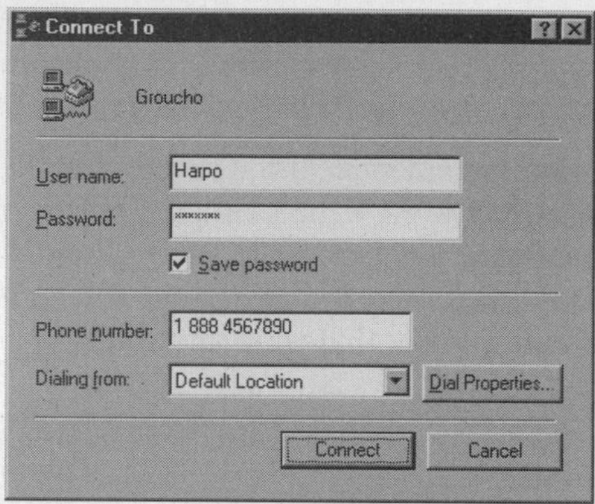

While you are connected, you can see what type of server you have connected to and which protocols you are currently using. In the example shown below, the connection is to a Windows for Workgroups and Windows NT server using the NetBEUI protocol.

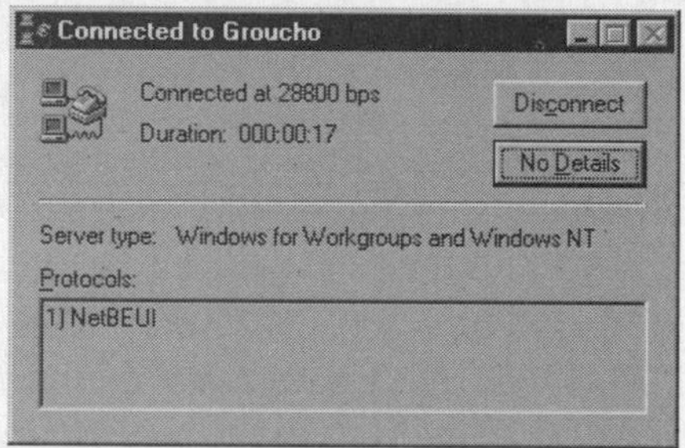

Once you have connected, you can use the resources on the dial-up server just as if you were working at the office. You can go to your Network Neighborhood and see the server there. If you have mapped drive letters to network resources, these should now be accessible through Windows Explorer or My Computer.

Configuring Internet Explorer and Proxy Server

On the Connection tab of the Internet Properties page, there are several options that can be set for proxy server connections, including when to bypass the proxy server to connect to intranet servers.

Advanced proxy server settings allow you to enable different proxy servers and ports for different applications, as well as build a list of sites and addresses that will cause the proxy server to be bypassed.

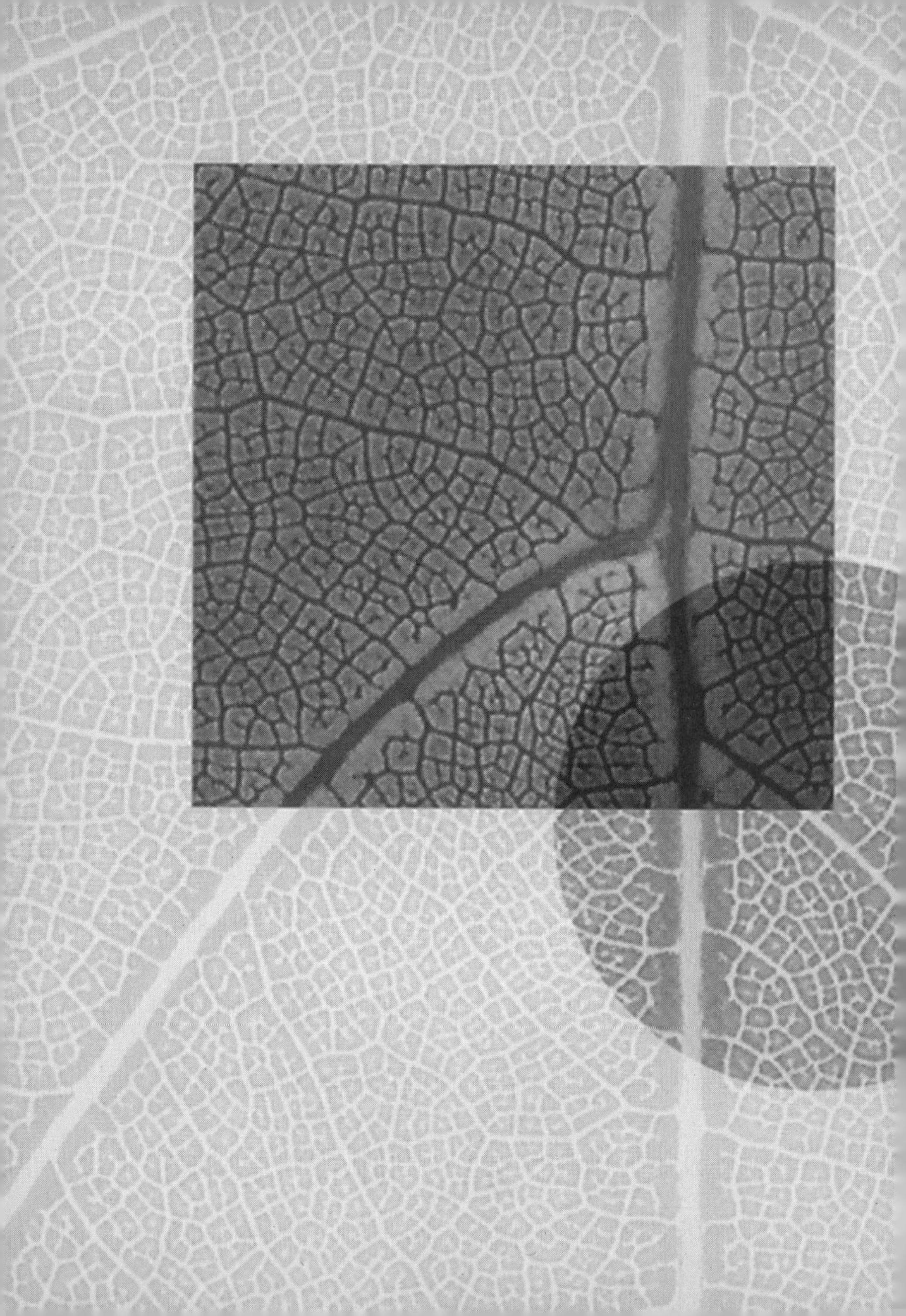

Chapter 28

Monitoring and Optimization

The objectives for this chapter focus on the administrative tasks of tuning and optimizing your Windows 98 computers. This is accomplished by a multipronged approach. Optimization can be applied to many different areas—ranging from hard disk management and working with shared resources to finding and replacing corrupted and/or outdated files.

Adapted from *MCSE Exam Notes: Windows 98*
by Rick Sawtell and Lance Mortensen
ISBN 0-7821-2421-6 416 pages $19.99

Monitor system performance by using Net Watcher, System Monitor, and Resource Meter.

The Net Watcher and System Monitor tools can report information on the status of your local PC as well as on the status of remote PCs. This exam objective not only emphasizes what these tools report, but the permissions required on both the administrating and remote PCs. The Resource Meter can only be used to track resource usage on your local PC.

Net Watcher

Net Watcher is an interactive tool for creating, controlling, and monitoring remote shared resources. Net Watcher can be run on remote computers using either share- or user-level security. However, if a remote PC is set to user-level security, the administrating PC must also be set to user-level security. You can also use Net Watcher to manage your local shared resources.

As an administrator, you can create, add, and delete shares, change resource properties, and monitor who is connected to which resource. Figure 28.1 shows an example of a Net Watcher screen.

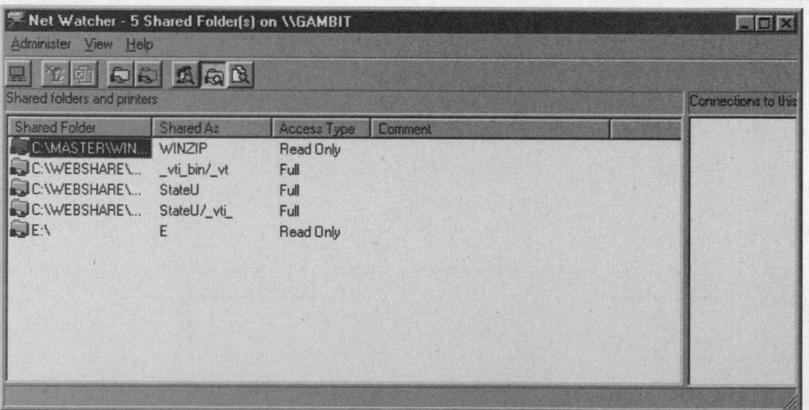

FIGURE 28.1: The Net Watcher tool allows you to manage shares.

Remote Net Watcher

If a remote computer has granted you sufficient rights, you can use Net Watcher to monitor that computer's shared resources. In order to monitor a remote computer, the user must first grant you permission. To do this, go to the Control Panel (see Figure 28.2), double-click the Password applet, and choose the Remote Administration tab.

NOTE

If share-level security is being used, a password can be assigned to the remote administration right (as shown in Figure 28.2). If user-level security is being used, you can choose to assign the remote administration right to individual users and groups.

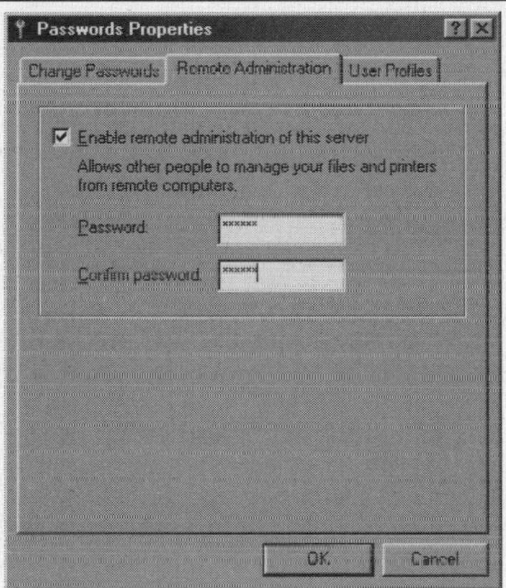

FIGURE 28.2: The Remote Administration tab of the Passwords Properties dialog box

NOTE

If you don't have Net Watcher (or any other system tool installed), you will have to add it using the Add/Remove Programs applet of the Control Panel.

System Monitor

System Monitor is a tool for tracking memory and other system resources for usage and possible problems.

TIP

You can run multiple instances of System Monitor side by side to compare the performance of different computers.

The following sections examine different ways to use the System Monitor's options in the File System, IPX/SPX-Compatible Protocol, Kernel, Memory Manager, Microsoft Client for NetWare Networks, and Microsoft Client for Microsoft Networks categories. The System Monitor options vary depending on what you have installed on the system, so you may not encounter all of the options described here.

File System

To work with System Monitor on your local system, choose Start ➢ Programs ➢ Accessories ➢ System Tools ➢ System Monitor.

To work with the System Monitor's performance counters, go to the Edit menu and choose Add Item. You can now choose from the following File System options:

Bytes read/second The number of bytes read from the file system each second.

Bytes written/second The number of bytes written by the file system each second.

Dirty data: The number of bytes waiting to be written to the disk. Dirty data are stored in cache blocks, so the number reported might be larger than the actual number of bytes waiting.

Reads/second The number of read operations delivered to the file system each second.

Writes/second The number of write operations delivered to the file system each second.

IPX/SPX-Compatible Protocol

If you are using the IPX/SPX-compatible protocol, choose Edit ➢ Add Item ➢ IPX/SPX-Compatible Protocol to view details of IPX/SPX activities. You can monitor the following items.

IPX packets lost/second The number of IPX packets received by the computer from an IPX network that were ignored.

IPX packets received/second The number of IPX packets received by the computer from an IPX network each second.

IPX packets sent/second The number of IPX packets sent by the computer to an IPX network each second.

Open sockets The number of free sockets.

Routing Table entries The number of known IPX internetworking routes.

SAP Table entries The number of known service advertisements.

SPX packets received/second The number of SPX packets received by the computer from an SPX network each second.

SPX packets sent/second The number of SPX packets sent by the computer to an SPX network each second.

Kernel

Choose Edit ➢ Add Item ➢ Kernel to view details of Kernel activities. You can monitor the following items:

Processor Usage (%) The approximate percentage of time that the processor is busy. Monitoring this setting will increase processor usage slightly.

Threads The current number of threads present in the system.

Virtual Machines The current number of virtual machines present in the system.

Memory Manager

Choose Edit ➢ Add Item ➢ Memory Manager to view memory details. Here are the memory-related items you can monitor:

Allocated memory The total number of bytes allocated to applications and system processes. This is the sum of the Other memory and Swapfile memory settings.

Discards The number of pages discarded from memory per second. These pages are discarded rather than swapped because the data on the page have not changed and, therefore, do not have to be written back to disk.

Disk cache size The current size of the disk cache, in bytes.

Free memory The total amount of free physical RAM, in bytes. This number is not related to allocated memory. If this value is zero, memory can still be allocated, depending on the free disk space available on the drive that contains the swap file.

Instance faults The number of instance faults per second.

Locked memory The amount of memory, in bytes, that is locked by the system or an application, and cannot be swapped out.

Maximum disk cache size The largest possible disk cache size, in bytes.

Minimum disk cache size The smallest possible disk cache size, in bytes.

Other memory The amount of allocated memory, in bytes, that cannot be stored in the swap file. This includes code from Win32 DLLs and executable files, memory-mapped files, memory that cannot be paged, and disk cache pages.

Page faults The number of page faults per second.

Page-ins The number of pages swapped from the page file to physical RAM per second.

Page-outs The number of pages swapped from physical RAM to the page file per second.

Swapfile defective The number of defective bytes in the swap file. These are caused by bad sectors on the hard drive.

Swapfile in use The number of bytes currently being used by the swap file.

Swapfile size The current size of the swap file, in bytes.

Swappable memory The number of bytes allocated from the swap file. This includes locked pages.

Microsoft Client for NetWare Networks

If the machine has the Microsoft Client for NetWare Networks installed, choose Edit ➢ Add Item ➢ Microsoft Client for NetWare Networks to view details about the NetWare network connection. You can monitor up to nine different items.

Burst packets dropped The number of burst packets from this computer lost in transit

Burst receive gap time The interpacket gap for incoming traffic, in microseconds

Burst send gap time The interpacket gap for outgoing traffic, in microseconds

Bytes in cache The amount of data, in bytes, that is currently cached by the redirector

Bytes read/second The number of bytes read from the redirector per second

Bytes written/second The number of bytes written to the redirector per second

Dirty bytes in cache The amount of dirty data, in bytes, that is currently cached by the redirector and waiting to be written

NCP packets dropped The number of regular NCP (NetWare Core Protocol) packets lost in transit

Requests pending The number of requests that are waiting to be processed by the server

Microsoft Network Client

If the machine has the Microsoft Client for Microsoft Networks installed, choose Edit ➢ Add Item ➢ Microsoft Network Client to view details about the Microsoft network connection. You can monitor the following items:

Bytes read/second The number of bytes read from the redirector each second

Bytes written/second The number of bytes written to the redirector each second

Number of nets The number of networks currently running

Open files The number of open files on the network

Resources The number of resources used

Sessions The number of sessions running

Transactions/second The number of SMB (Server Message Block) transactions managed by the redirector each second

Microsoft Network Server

If the machine has File and Printer Sharing installed for a Microsoft or NetWare network, choose Edit ➢ Add Item ➢ Microsoft Network Server to view details about the sharing connection. You can monitor the following items:

Buffers The number of working buffers used by the server

Bytes read/second The total number of bytes read from a disk each second

Bytes/second The total number of bytes read from and written to a disk each second

Bytes written/second The total number of bytes written to a disk each second

Memory The total amount of memory used by the server

NBs The number of server network buffers

Server threads The current number of threads used by the server

Microsoft Network Monitor Performance Data

If the machine is a Microsoft server on a network, choose Edit ➢ Add Item ➢ Microsoft Network Monitor Performance Data to view details about its performance. You can monitor the following items:

Mediatype broadcasts/sec The number of broadcast frames transmitted over the network adapter each second

Mediatype bytes/sec The total number of bytes transmitted over the network adapter each second

Mediatype frames/sec The total number of frames transmitted over the network adapter each second

Mediatype multicasts/sec The total number of multicast frames transmitted over the network adapter each second

Remote System Monitor

The System Monitor tool can be used to monitor performance statistics on a remote workstation. System Monitor uses values stored in the Hkey_Dyn_Data key in the Registry to get its information. If you wish to use the System Monitor to view resources on a remote computer, open the Network Neighborhood, right-click a computer, and choose Properties from the Context menu. Then click the Remote System Monitor button. Note that to use Remote System Monitor, you must have user-level security installed on both the remote PC and the administrating PC. You must also have Remote Registry Services installed on both PCs.

Table 28.1 delineates the software and permission requirements for administering remote PCs. You should study this table in detail. The exam will test your knowledge of which tools require which type of security.

TABLE 28.1: Remote Administration Security Summary

Tool	Remote Workstation			Administrating Workstation	
	User/Share	File & Printer Sharing Enabled	Remote Registry Services	User/Share	Remote Registry Services
Net Watcher	Share	Yes	N/A	Either	N/A
Net Watcher	User	Yes	N/A	User	N/A
Remote System Monitor	User	Yes	Yes	User	Yes
Remote Registry Editor	User	Yes	Yes	User	Yes

Resource Meter

Resource Meter monitors the system resources that are used by running programs. This includes System resources, User resources, and GDI resources; all three resources loosely correlate with the Win32 APIs.

The System resources item monitors Kernel32-related functionality. The Kernel32 provides the base for operating system functionality and includes support for file I/O, virtual memory management, threading, and thread scheduling. Kernel32 is also responsible for loading and unloading .EXE files and .DLL files.

The User resources item is analogous to the User32 portion of the API. The User32 handles Windows management, mouse movements across the screen, and other user-related inputs and processing.

The GDI resources item corresponds to the GDI32 section of the Win32 API. The GDI (graphical device interface) is responsible for monitoring all of the graphics on your system. This includes graphics that are rendered to your monitor as well as graphics (and anything else) that are sent to a printer.

At times, you may have a program that turns into a *runaway*. This describes a program that appears to function correctly, but continues to use up system resources when idle (as viewed by Resource Meter). Such a program may be scheduling more and more threads (System resources), generating graphics to be shown on your screen (GDI resources), or continually opening and closing different windows (User resources).

There are a couple of things to remember when using Resource Meter. When a new program is opened in Windows 98, the necessary system resources are allocated for that program. Your initial resource counts may be 85%, 87%, and 82% for System, User, and GDI resources, respectively. After your program opens, these resource counts may drop to 80%, 82%, and 79%, respectively. When you close the program and check your Resource Meter again, you may note that the resource counts do not return to their original values. This is not an error or cause for alarm. The resources remain allocated for that particular program in case you decide to reopen it. Then, when you do reopen the program, it will load much more quickly than it did initially. However, Windows 98 will release those allocated resources when other programs load and when those resources are required by other programs that are subsequently opened. The key difference here is that the resources are reserved for your program when the program is running, but are only allocated when you close the program.

Monitoring System Performance

In this section, you will work with the Net Watcher and the System Monitor programs to gather information about the resources you are sharing and the system resources being consumed on your computer.

Using Net Watcher

Follow these steps to use the Net Watcher tool. Of course, the remote workstation must be sharing resources, folders, and/or printers for this tool to be useful. If it is not sharing resources, nothing will show up in the Net Watcher window.

1. Double-click the Network Neighborhood icon on your Desktop.
2. Navigate to a Windows 98-based computer involved in remote administration and right-click its icon.
3. From the Context menu, choose Properties to open the Properties dialog box for that PC.
4. Choose the Tools tab.
5. Click the Net Watcher button. The Net Watcher application will start and display the status of shared resources on the remote PC (see Figure 28.1).

NOTE

When you use Net Watcher, two special shares are created. *Admin$* gives administrators access to the `\Windows` folder on the remote PC. *IPC$* is an interprocess channel between the two computers and acts as a buffer area for RPCs (remote procedure calls) to move between workstations.

If you disconnect a user from a shared resource, the user will reconnect to the resource immediately. To prevent this, you need to change the resource password if you are using share-level security. If you are using user-level security, you need to remove the user from the list of users who have been given access to that shared resource. This is also true when you are closing a file. The user will still have access to the shared folder, but will be momentarily disconnected from the file. The user will immediately reconnect to the file unless you do something to prevent it.

WARNING

If you are using share-level security and you change a password on a shared resource, everyone who is currently using that resource will be thrown out. They will need to supply the new password in order to reconnect.

Using System Monitor

To use System Monitor to observe items on your local computer, follow these steps:

1. Select Start ➢ Programs ➢ Accessories ➢ System Tools ➢ System Monitor.
2. Click the Edit menu and choose Add Item.
3. In the Add Item dialog box, choose the category and then the specific item you wish to monitor. Choosing the Explain button gives a (very) brief explanation of the item.
4. Click the OK button to add the item.
5. Add more items by the same method.
6. Change the interval time by choosing Options ➢ Chart.

Using Remote System Monitor

With Remote Registry Services installed and both the remote workstation and the administrating workstation using user-level security, you can run Remote System Monitor to view a remote computer. Figure 28.3 shows an example of the CPU utilization statistic on a remote workstation.

Follow these steps to use Remote System Monitor:

1. Double-click the Network Neighborhood icon on your Desktop.
2. Navigate to a Windows 98-based computer involved in remote administration and right-click its icon.
3. From the Context menu, choose Properties to open the Properties dialog box for that PC.
4. Choose the Tools tab.
5. Click the Remote System Monitor button. Remote System Monitor starts and shows performance statistics for the other workstation.
6. To look at different statistics, select Edit ➢ Add Item; then choose a category and click OK.

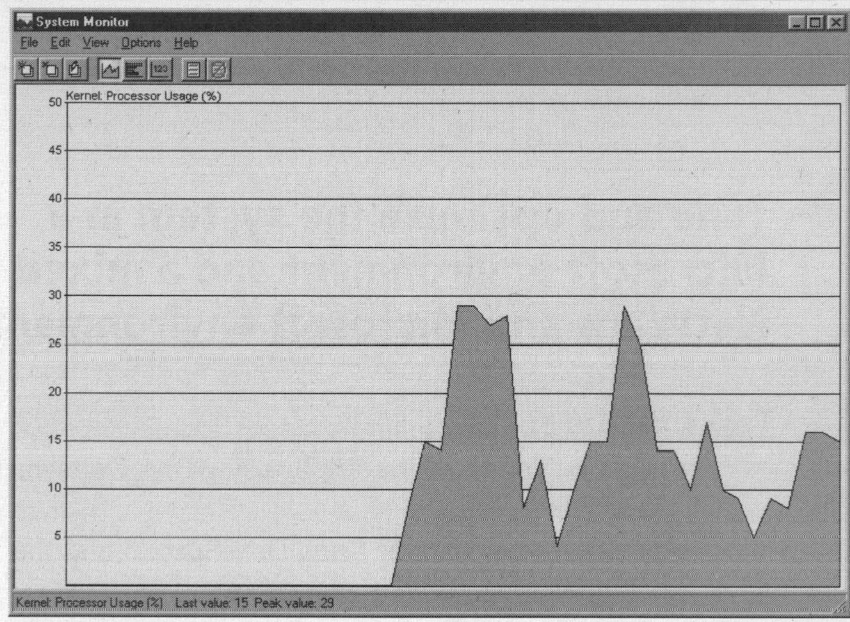

FIGURE 28.3: System Monitor can be used to view performance statistics on a remote workstation and local workstation.

Using Resource Meter

To use Resource Meter, follow the steps outlined here:

1. Close all open programs in Windows 98.
2. Open Resource Meter. You can find Resource Meter in Start ➢ Programs ➢ Accessories ➢ System Tools ➢ Resource Meter.
3. This will place the Resource Meter icon in your system tray. Open up the Resource Meter detail screen by double-clicking the icon, or right-clicking the icon and choosing Details.
4. Note the current resource settings.
5. Open up several applications and take a look at your resource settings.
6. Close the Resource Meter when you are finished.

NOTE

Keep in mind that Resource Meter can only be used to view resource usage on the local computer.

Tune and optimize the system in a Microsoft environment and a mixed NetWare and Microsoft environment.

Tasks include:

- Optimizing the hard disk by using Disk Defragmenter and ScanDisk
- Compressing data by using DriveSpace 3 and the Compression Agent
- Updating drivers and applying service packs by using Windows Update and the Signature Verification tool
- Automating tasks by using the Maintenance Wizard
- Scheduling tasks by using Task Scheduler
- Checking for corrupt files and extracting files from the installation media by using the System File Checker

These objectives discuss the techniques involved in optimizing your system. This includes optimizing your hard disks using Disk Defragmenter, ScanDisk, and DriveSpace 3 with the Compression Agent. You must also understand how to update drivers and verify the digital signatures of your files. Windows 98 allows you to automate maintenance and schedule tasks (like ScanDisk) to run on predefined occasions. Finally, you can keep corrupted files out of your system by using the System File Checker utility to search for and replace corrupted files.

Optimizing the Hard Disk

The Disk Defragmenter utility can be used to optimize both FAT16 and FAT32 hard disks. This section takes a closer look at the capabilities and features of Disk Defragmenter.

Disk Defragmenter

Over time, you may find that your computer doesn't perform as quickly as it once did. *Fragmentation* (a natural phenomenon that can easily be fixed) of your files may have occurred. Fragmentation happens as files are deleted and their space is used by new files. When files are saved, they are saved in sequential order on your hard drive. If a 10MB file is being saved, it will use free space as it finds it, not bothering to look for a contiguous 10MB spot it can use. When scattered over the hard drive, the file is more difficult to find and put back together, and may take twice as many hard drive revolutions to assemble as it would take if it were contiguous.

TIP

Windows 98 Disk Defragmenter not only defragments the hard drive, it places .EXE and .DLL files from the same application next to each other on contiguous sectors of the hard disk. This can cut load times by as much as 50 percent, especially when combined with FAT32 volumes.

Windows 98 includes a disk defragmentation program called Disk Defragmenter. The default settings will defragment your drive by making sure that files are stored in contiguous clusters and by consolidating free space so defragmentation is less likely to happen in the future. The defragmentation program will also run ScanDisk to check for errors before defragmenting.

Disk Defragmenter is available from the Tools tab of any drive's Properties dialog box.

TIP

You can also start Disk Cleanup from the General tab, and ScanDisk or the Backup program from the Tools tab of the hard drive's Properties dialog box. For more information about Disk Cleanup or the Backup program, please see the *MCSE: Windows 98 Study Guide* (Sybex, 1999).

You can also start the defragmentation program by going to Start ➢ Programs ➢ Accessories ➢ System Tools ➢ Disk Defragmenter. If you start the disk defragmentation program this way, you can change the settings for the program and specify which drive to defragment, as shown in Figure 28.4.

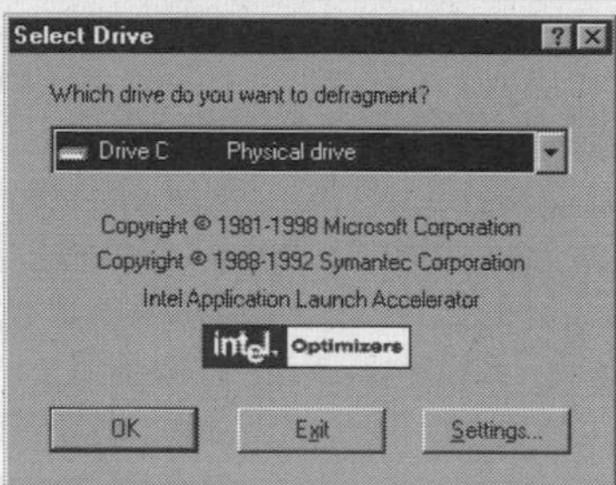

FIGURE 28.4: The Disk Defragmenter dialog box

The Settings dialog box changes the way the defragmentation program will work, but the default options are probably the best. The options you can set are:

Rearrange program files so my programs start faster. This places .EXE and .DLL files from the same application together in contiguous hard disk sectors to speed loading times as much as 50 percent.

Check the drive for errors. This runs ScanDisk before the Disk Defragmenter program runs.

This time only. The settings you picked are only used once.

Every time I defragment my hard drive. The settings are saved as the default.

You can also see a graphical display of the defragmentation process, as shown in Figure 28.5.

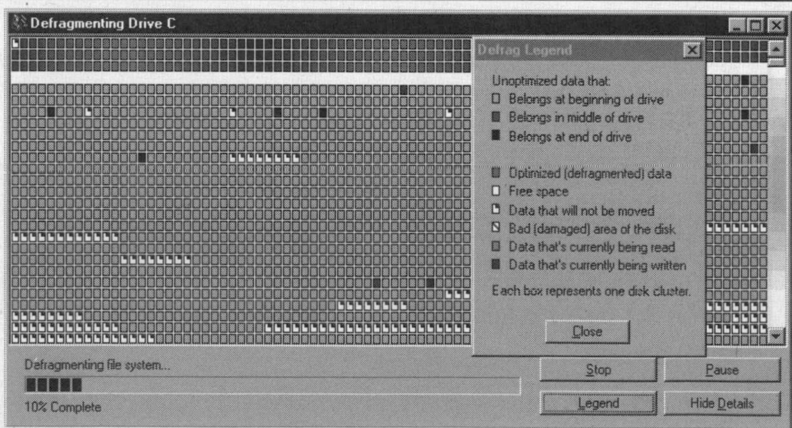

FIGURE 28.5: Disk defragmentation in progress

You will run the defragmentation program and look at the settings options as well as the graphical displays in the Necessary Procedures section.

ScanDisk

Although there is no software fix for your hard drive if the drive is failing due to physical defects, some hard drive problems can be repaired with software. Windows 98 comes with a program called *ScanDisk*, which can diagnose and fix many problems that it finds on your hard disk and/or floppy disks.

Common Disk Problems Several things can happen to files on your hard drive that might make them unusable. Some problems are easily fixed; others can be very serious. Here are some occurrences that could cause problems on your drive:

Crosslinked files This can happen when two or more files have become confused as to where their data reside. The cross-linked files both point to the same data area. This is one of the more serious errors, because one of the two files no longer points to the correct data area and will probably not be recoverable.

Bad sectors These can occur on either a floppy disk or hard drive and prevent programs or data files from working correctly. Bad sectors, or "spots," can happen naturally due to wear and tear on the drive, scratching the surface of a floppy by touching it, or by the drive head hitting the drive platter (usually because of dropping/banging the drive while in use). A bad spot can sometimes be read, and the data moved to a good spot, but a bad spot can also be completely unrecoverable. If the latter happens, the affected file is probably unrecoverable.

Lost clusters These appear when data areas have not been correctly identified as either in use or available for use by a new file. Lost clusters cannot be used for files until their status is resolved. They can either be correctly marked as deleted or be recovered as files in case something valuable was in those clusters. This is usually the least damaging problem that you will encounter on your hard drive.

Problems Addressed by ScanDisk As with any kind of troubleshooting, success is never guaranteed, but ScanDisk has a relatively good chance of fixing all three of the aforementioned problems:

Fixing crosslinked files Since ScanDisk can't tell which cross-linked file is the original and which one got attached by mistake, by default it fixes crosslinked files by taking the crosslinked data area and attaching it to both files. One of your files will be good while the other one will be corrupted. You can have ScanDisk copy the crosslinked data to both files, delete both files, or ignore any crosslinked errors through the Advanced Options dialog box.

Fixing bad spots Files that happen to be on bad spots can sometimes be read by ScanDisk and moved to a safe area. The bad area is then marked so that future files will not be saved there.

Fixing lost clusters Lost clusters can either be erased or saved as a file. If you save the lost cluster as a file, you can later look at the file and see if it contains any data that you still need. Seldom, if ever, do these files contain anything of use. You can change this option in the Advanced Options dialog box.

The ScanDisk program is available from the Tools tab of the drive's Properties dialog box. Click on the Advanced button while in ScanDisk if you want to configure how ScanDisk will run, and how it will deal with any errors it may find.

Disk Compression and DriveSpace 3

Disk compression has been around for many years. Some early versions of disk compression required that a hardware compression board be installed in the computer, while others were software-based. The primary benefit of using disk compression is that you can store more data on a hard drive. The two disadvantages of using compression are an overall decrease in speed and a greater likelihood that the entire drive will become corrupted. With the prices of hard drives dropping rapidly over the last couple of years, compression makes more sense for computers that are hard to upgrade to larger hard drives (such as laptops) than for easily upgraded computers (such as desktops).

Windows 98 supports and comes with software-based, real-time compression of volumes and disk drives. By using the compression program called DriveSpace 3, you can sometimes double your available disk space. Windows 98 has protected-mode compression drivers, but is also backward-compatible with older compression programs from Microsoft. Because compression is an integral part of Windows 98, both the paging file and Windows 98 itself can be kept on a compressed drive.

WARNING

Drives compressed under Windows 98 are unavailable to both OS/2 and Windows NT. If you are dual-booting Windows 98 and NT, you should not use compression. Although compressed removable drives created under Windows 98 have a README file that says that they require Windows 98, compressed floppies can be successfully read with Windows 98 on a Windows 95B (OSR2) computer.

Windows 98 is compatible with DOS compression programs, including DBLSPACE and DRVSPACE. Windows 98 replaces the DBLSPACE.BIN or DRVSPACE.BIN files in the root directory with ones that it can unload, so that the 32-bit version (DBLSPACX.VXD) can be loaded.

The version of compression that comes with Windows 98 is fully integrated into the operating system. This means that Registry files, page files, and system files can all reside on a compressed drive. Compressed drives can hold long filenames and can be cached by Vcache.

When you compress a volume, you have two choices:

- Compress the entire volume.
- Use some of the free space on the volume to make a new, compressed volume.

For example, if you had a 2GB drive (your E: drive) with 500MB of free space, you could compress the entire E: drive, giving you approximately 1GB of free space. Alternatively, you could use part of the 500MB (let's say 150MB) to create a new drive (call it your H: drive) that would have approximately 300MB of free space.

NOTE

Although DriveSpace 3 will recognize FAT32 volumes, it cannot compress them.

When you compress a drive, you are actually taking the contents of an entire drive and putting them into one large file. The file is called a compressed volume file (CVF). The CVF usually has a filename such as DRVSPACE.000 or DBLSPACE.000. DRVSPACE.000 appears if Windows 98 reads an older compressed drive, and DBLSPACE.000 appears when Windows 98 reads a newer compressed drive or creates a new one.

When you compress a drive, the CVF is stored on the host drive, which is the original drive. The host drive letter is then changed to a higher letter, usually H:. Programs see the compressed drive normally, but Windows 98 is actually compressing and decompressing files into and out of the CVF (which is on the H: drive) and displaying the uncompressed files as the C: drive. You can choose to hide the host drive, which is a good option for users with less experience; they will have less chance of damaging or deleting the CVF.

WARNING

It is absolutely essential that the CVF is not modified or edited by hand. Doing so could cause the entire compressed volume to become corrupted.

Compressing a drive under Windows 98 is a simple process. When you run the DriveSpace program and choose to compress a drive, it will display before and after compression information.

You should back up any critical data before compressing or decompressing a hard drive. You can choose to compress the entire volume or just a part of the volume. If you choose to take part of the free space to make a new compressed drive, Windows 98 will prompt you to specify the size of the new drive.

As you copy data to your new drive, you can check the status of your compressed files on the Compression tab of the drive's Properties dialog box, as shown in Figure 28.6. If there are many uncompressed files, you can run the Compression Agent manually. Click the Run Agent button in the Compression tab to see the Compression Agent dialog box. You can either cause compression to happen with your current settings or change your compression settings by choosing the Settings button.

You may want to *decompress* your drive at some future date. Windows 98 supports nondestructive decompression of the hard drive. When you run DriveSpace and choose the Uncompress option, you will see before and after uncompression status screens.

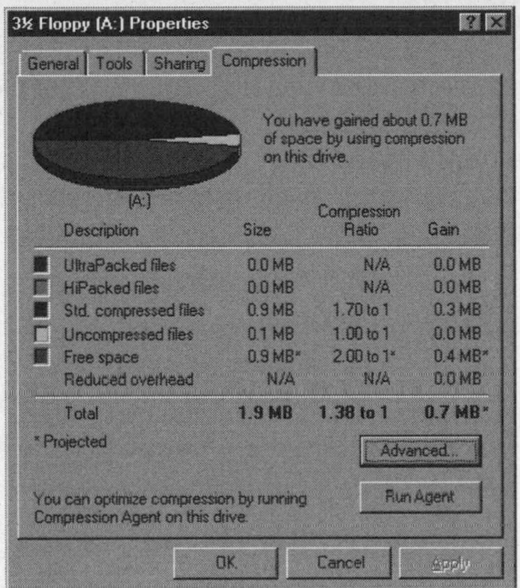

FIGURE 28.6: Checking the status of your compressed volume

Drivers and Service Packs

Service Packs are also known as *patches* and are generally used to update your DLL files, replace older drivers in your system, and fix problems in the original application.

The Windows Update Utility

Microsoft periodically releases service packs for different software programs. The service packs are used to do any of the following:

- Fix problems with current drivers, DLLs, and other files
- Add new features to drivers, DLLs, and other files
- Add new components to take advantage of more of the features already included in the current drivers, DLLs, and other files

Keeping track of all of these modified files can be cumbersome. Windows 98 comes with a utility called Windows Update that provides a central location where you can find product enhancements, new system files, device drivers, and any other additional features that have been added.

The Signature Verification Tool

With all of the information and files available on the Internet, the security of your system is quickly becoming a task that requires close monitoring. One method of guaranteeing that files downloaded from the Internet, or elsewhere, are from who they are supposed to be from is by applying a *digital signature*. A digital signature is really a digital certificate that has been applied to a file or e-mail message. When a digital signature is applied to a file, that file has the following characteristics:

- The file has not been tampered with since the digital signature was applied.
- The author of the file is known. To gain a digital certificate, you must apply for one through a Certificate Authority (CA). The CA verifies the author of the work and provides other services.

NOTE

Microsoft's Web site lists many of the currently available Certificate Authorities. Go to `www.microsoft.com/security/ca/ca.htm`.

The Signature Verification tool allows you to search for both signed and unsigned files in your system. To start the Signature Verification tool, open the System Information utility by clicking Start ➢ Programs ➢ Accessories ➢ System Tools ➢ System Information Utility. From there, choose Signature Verification Tool from the Tools menu.

The Signature Verification tool searched My Computer for signed files and identified several files to choose from. You can view general information about a selected file by clicking the Details button. If you click the Fine Print button you will get the copyright information for this file. Other tabs within the Signature Verification tool will provide you with additional information about this file and its digital certificate.

Scheduled Tasks and the Maintenance Wizard

Windows 98 includes a task scheduling component that allows you to automate certain tasks on a preset schedule.

NOTE

Windows 95 users have to purchase and install Microsoft Plus! in order to get the scheduling component, which is called System Agent.

You can add, edit, or delete scheduled tasks by opening the Scheduled Tasks folder now located in My Computer. To create a new task simply choose Add A New Task, which starts the Scheduled Task Wizard. You will then be presented with a list of the applications installed on your computer and prompted about when to schedule them and whether or not to start them automatically.

Windows 98 also comes with a Maintenance Wizard that schedules disk maintenance tasks (including Disk Defragmenter, Disk Cleanup, and ScanDisk) to be performed on a regular basis.

Once an application is scheduled, it is easy to change. Simply go to the Scheduled Tasks folder and double-click the task you want to edit. For example, Figure 28.7 shows a scheduled ScanDisk task that you can modify. The Schedule tab lets you alter the frequency of an existing task as shown in Figure 28.8, and the Settings tab lets you set various options for running the task (see Figure 28.9).

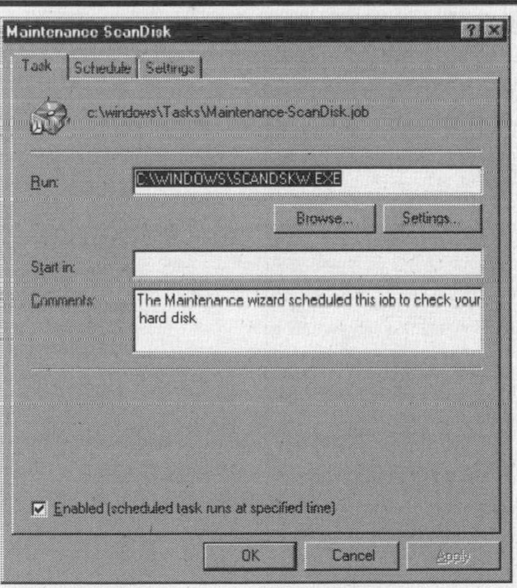

FIGURE 28.7: Editing a scheduled task

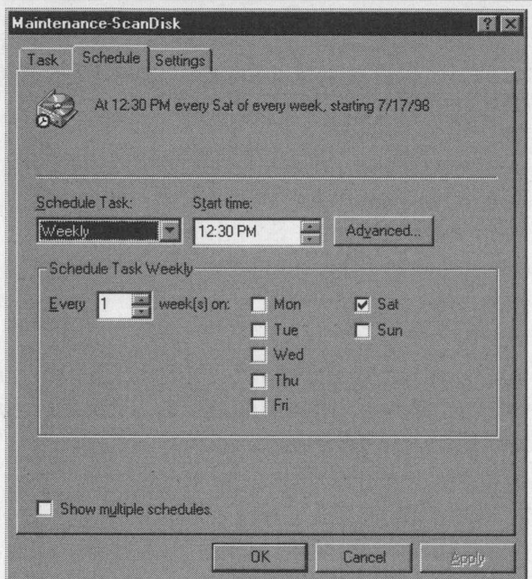

FIGURE 28.8: Changing the schedule of an existing task

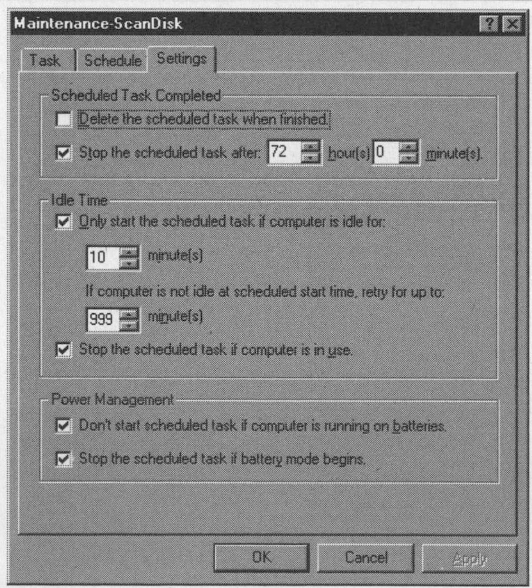

FIGURE 28.9: Changing the settings of an existing task

System File Checker

You can use System File Checker (see Figure 28.10) to verify the integrity of your Windows 98 system files. You can also use the utility to restore files when they are corrupted, as well as extract compressed files from your installation CD-ROM. System File Checker can also make backups of existing files before you overwrite them with the original files. To start the System File Checker utility, start the System Information utility. From the Tools menu, choose System File Checker.

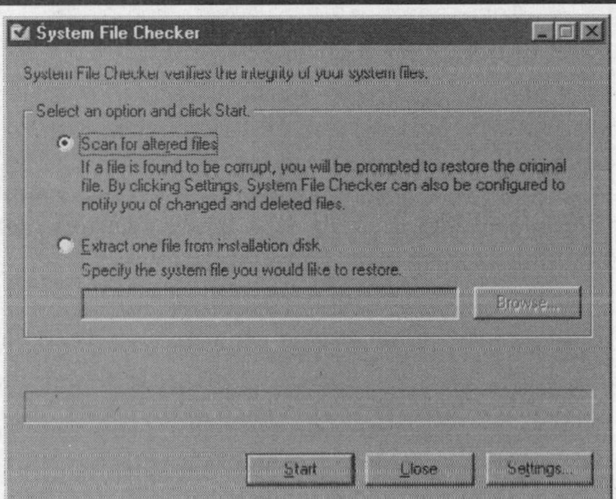

FIGURE 28.10: The System File Checker tool

If you click the Settings tab, you can specify backup options, like whether to always back up a system file before you overwrite it, prompt before backing up a file, or never back up a file. It is possible to modify the folder in which your backups will be stored. From the Settings dialog box, you can also specify whether or not you want to track these changes with a log file and determine whether or not the tool should check for changed and/or deleted files. This should be done prior to the installation of any new software on your Windows 98 system.

If you select the Search Criteria tab, you can determine which system files to look for and in which folders to look for them. You can also specify different file types to search for. The Advanced tab allows you to create a System File Checker template, but its settings are beyond the scope of this book.

Optimization Procedures

You can brush up on your administration skills by practicing with the Disk Defragmenter, ScanDisk, Windows Update, and compression utilities.

Defragmenting the Hard Drive

Defragmenting your hard drive is a task that you should perform on a regular basis. Follow these steps to defragment your hard disk:

1. Start the disk defragmentation program by clicking Start ➢ Programs ➢ Accessories ➢ System Tools ➢ Disk Defragmenter.

NOTE

If you start Disk Defragmenter by going to the Properties dialog box for any drive and choosing the Tools tab, you will not be able to change any settings—the utility will only run according to the default settings.

2. Click the Settings button to see how you can change the way defragmentation works. The default settings are recommended.
3. Start the defragmentation process by making sure the hard drive you want to defragment is selected and clicking the OK button.
4. While your disk is defragmenting, click the Show Details button for a graphical representation of your drive. Then click the Legend button to see the Defrag Legend box (shown in Figure 28.5).
5. After defragmentation is complete, close the window.

Using ScanDisk to Check the Hard Drive for Errors

In this next procedure, you will check your hard drive for errors by using ScanDisk. Follow these steps to run the ScanDisk program:

1. Go to the Properties dialog box for the C: drive, choose the Tools tab, and select Check Now from the Error Checking Status section of the dialog box.

2. Click on the Advanced button to see the default options. Click Cancel to go back to the main ScanDisk dialog box.
3. If you are in a hurry, choose Standard for the type of test and check the Automatically Fix Errors checkbox. If you have more time, choose the Thorough test and deselect Automatically Fix Errors.
4. Wait for ScanDisk to finish. If there are any errors, ScanDisk will either automatically fix them (if selected), or it will prompt you on how to fix them.
5. If you selected the Thorough test, ScanDisk will check your current files and will then check the entire hard drive for bad spots. This takes from several minutes to more than a half hour, depending on the size of your hard disk.
6. When ScanDisk is finished, close its information box.

Compressing a Disk

You can compress your hard disks as well as your floppy disks using DriveSpace 3 and the Compression Agent. Follow these steps to compress a floppy disk:

1. Format a floppy disk or find one that still has some room on it.
2. Select Start ➢ Run and type **drvspace** in the Run Program dialog box, or go to Start ➢ Programs ➢ Accessories ➢ System Tools ➢ DriveSpace.
3. From the DriveSpace menu, highlight the floppy drive and choose Drive ➢ Compress. DriveSpace will then show you the estimated size of your new drive and ask you to confirm before it actually does the compression, as shown in Figure 28.10.
4. Click the Start button to begin the compression. Select OK to accept the warning regarding the drive being inaccessible from Windows NT and OS/2. It may take a while (up to five minutes) to compress your floppy disk. Keep in mind that your hard drives are faster than floppy disks, but they will take much longer to compress because they are so much larger. For instance, a 6GB partition with about 1GB of used space may take as long as 45 minutes to compress.

5. After compressing your floppy, you should get a status screen report of the compressed floppy drive.
6. Click the Close button to close the window.

Decompressing a Disk

To decompress a drive after you have compressed it, you use the same DriveSpace 3 utility. Follow these steps to decompress your floppy disk:

1. Make sure your disk (floppy or hard drive) is large enough to hold the files it may contain after it has been decompressed by checking the Properties dialog box for your disk. Also make sure that the used space is less than the capacity of your drive after decompression.
2. Select Start ➢ Run and type **drvspace** in the Run Program dialog box, or go to Start ➢ Programs ➢Accessories ➢ System Tools ➢ DriveSpace.
3. Highlight the drive you want to decompress and choose Drive ➢ Uncompress. Windows 98 will show an Uncompress screen, with estimates for how much free space your drive will have after uncompressing it.
4. Click the Start button to begin the decompression process. Select Yes to remove compression.
5. After successfully uncompressing your drive, you will see a final status screen with new readings for used and free space for that drive.
6. Click the Close button to close the window.

Updating System Files

The Windows Update utility can replace DLLs and other files on your system with the most recent versions from Microsoft. You will need an Internet connection to accomplish this. Follow these steps to update files on your system with the Windows Update program:

1. Click Start ➢ Settings ➢ Windows Update. An Internet connection to the Microsoft Web site will be initiated as shown in Figure 28.11.

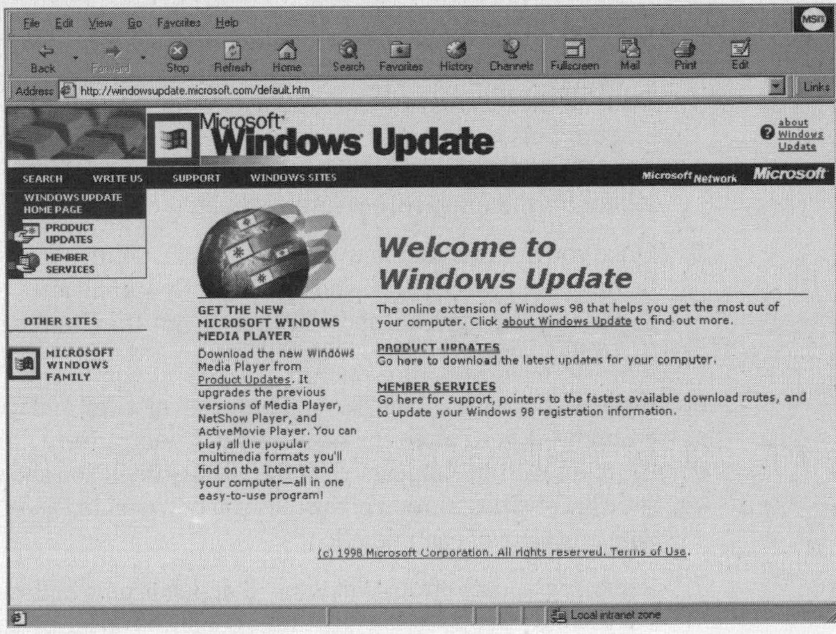

FIGURE 28.11: The Windows Update utility

2. From here, you should select the Product Updates icon on the left side of the screen or from the hyperlink in the middle of the page. At that time, you will be asked to allow a program to scan your system to determine what products you currently have. The information gained by the program is not sent to Microsoft. Once the program determines what has been installed on your system and what service packs, if any, are there, it will generate a list of available downloads that you can choose from. Some of these items will be listed as a Critical Update, Pick of the Month Update, or a Recommended Updates and Additional Files.
3. The Outlook Express service pack has been identified/chosen for download. Once you have made your update selections, click the Download Now item at the bottom of the Web page. This will initiate the download and installation process.
4. The download process will provide you with feedback in the form of a download and installation dialog box. If you choose to download and install multiple files during the installation

portion of the dialog, you may be asked to reboot your system. Microsoft recommends that you choose No. This will allow other programs to complete their installations as well. Once all the installations are completed, you can reboot your system. This will save you time as there may be several programs that require you to reboot your system. It's better to reboot once than to reboot several times.

5. Once you are finished downloading and installing, you will be presented with a dialog box that briefly summarizes the downloaded programs and whether or not they were successfully installed.

6. If you wish to view which files you have downloaded and used for updates, you can rerun the Windows Update utility. Once the main Web site appears, click the History item. You should see a list and description of the files you downloaded and the date and time of each download.

7. Removing updates from Windows 98 depends on whether or not you have a connection to the Internet. If you do have a connection, you can do the following: Start the Windows Update utility by selecting Start ➢ Settings ➢ Windows Update. You will be presented with the Windows Update dialog box. Choose the Program Updates tab and then choose the Device Driver item from the list of choices on the left. This will open the Update Wizard window, as shown in Figure 28.30. Click the Restore button. This will allow you to select updated drivers from the left panel. Once you have made your selections, click the Uninstall button, and your new drivers will be replaced with your old drivers. Your old drivers are saved to a backup folder each time you update them.

8. If you don't have an Internet connection, you can use the Update Wizard Uninstall utility. Click Start ➢ Programs ➢ Accessories ➢ System Tools ➢ System Information. This will start the Microsoft System Information utility. From the Tools menu, select Update Wizard Uninstall. This will start the Wizard. Then choose which files you wish to uninstall and click OK. The current files selected will revert to their previous versions.

Scheduling Disk Maintenance Tasks

You can use the Maintenance Wizard to schedule disk defragmentations, scandisks, and other tasks. Follow these steps to use the Maintenance Wizard:

1. Start the Maintenance Wizard by going to Start ➢ Programs ➢ Accessories ➢ System Tools ➢ Maintenance Wizard.
2. Choose "Change my maintenance settings or schedule" (see Figure 28.12) and click OK.

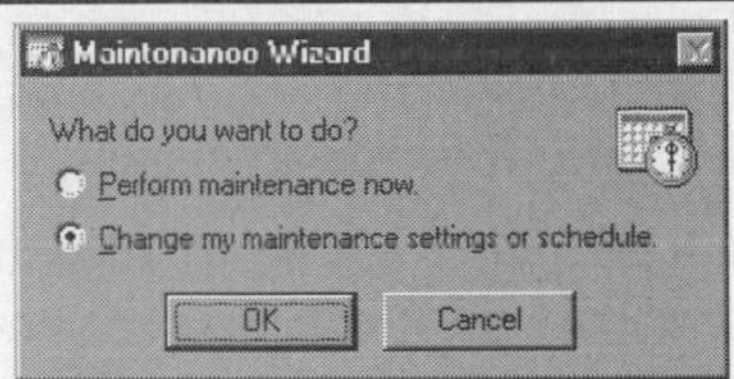

FIGURE 28.12: Using the Maintenance Wizard

3. Select Custom and then Next so you can selectively set up maintenance options, as shown in Figure 28.13.

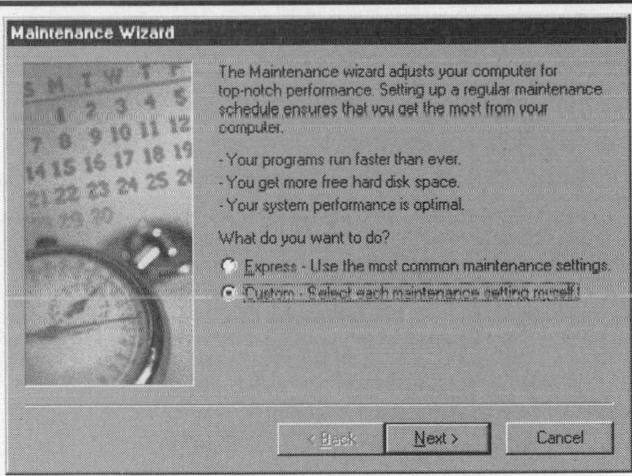

FIGURE 28.13: Maintenance options

4. You are then prompted to designate a time to run the selected maintenance tasks. Pick a time most appropriate for your computer and click Next.

5. The next screen shows you which programs are started automatically by Windows 98 and allows you to select or deselect a program. Choose Next when you are done.
6. The next screen prompts you for a time to run Disk Defragmenter. Select Yes to enable Disk Defragmenter; use the Reschedule button to change the time the program runs or the Settings button to change how it runs. Click Next when you are done.
7. The next screen prompts you for a time to run ScanDisk. Select Yes to enable ScanDisk; use the Reschedule button to change the time the program runs or the Settings button to change how it runs. Click Next when you are done.
8. The last screen prompts you for a time to run Disk Cleanup. Select Yes to run Disk Cleanup; use the Reschedule button to change the time the program runs or the Settings button to change how it runs. Click Next when you are done.
9. You should now see a completed list of your new scheduled maintenance tasks. Choose Finish to save the tasks.

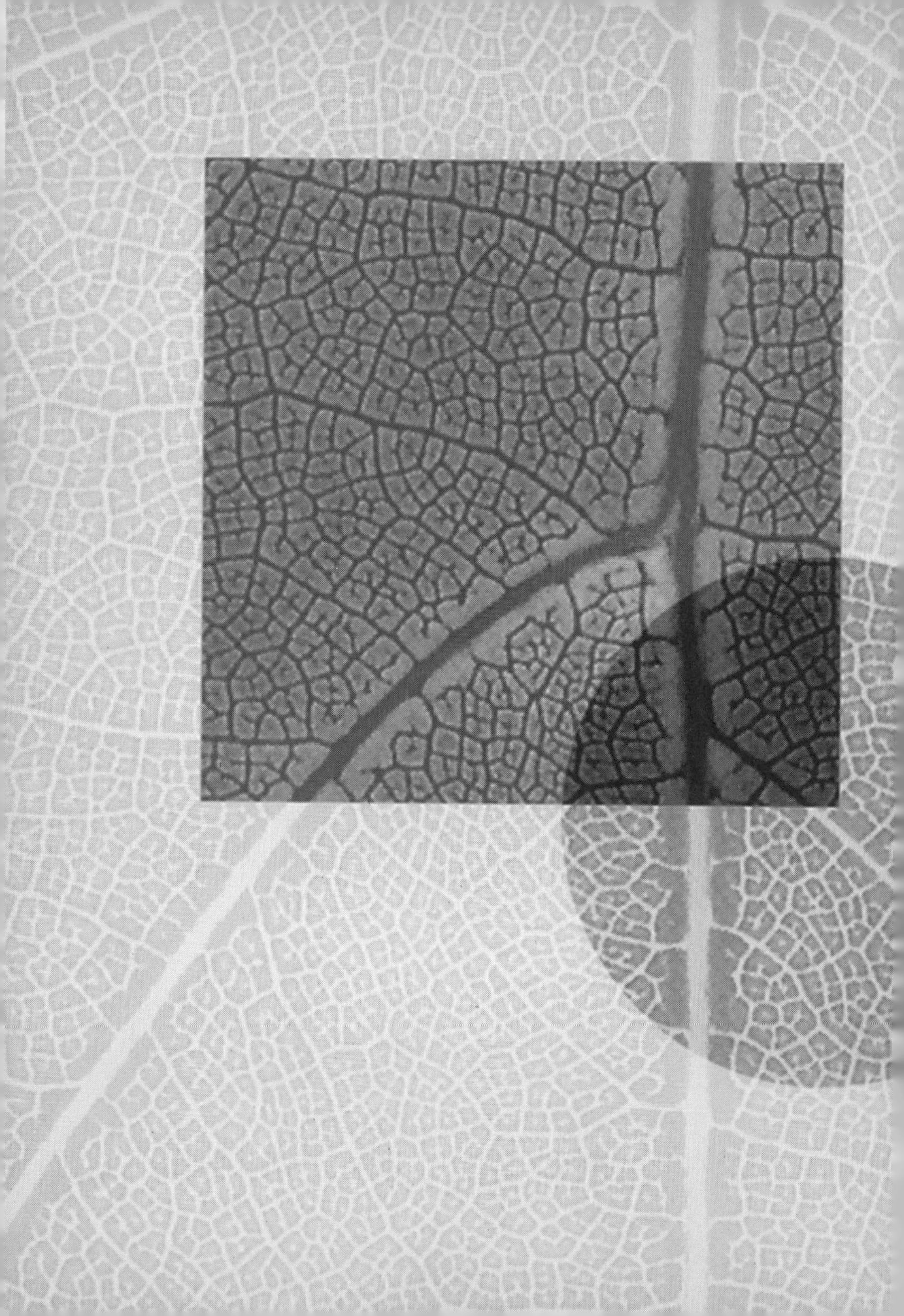

Chapter 29

TROUBLESHOOTING

The objectives for this chapter deal with the administrative tasks of troubleshooting your Windows 98 computers. Troubleshooting is an art form, and the best way to get better at it is through practice. Troubleshooting begins with defining the problem and identifying its cause. Then you need to know how to go about fixing it. This chapter will address what you need to do to fix a problem once you have discovered it. Let's take a look at the first troubleshooting exam objective.

Adapted from *MCSE Exam Notes: Windows 98*
by Rick Sawtell and Lance Mortensen
ISBN 0-7821-2421-6 416 pages $19.99

Diagnose and resolve installation failures.

Tasks include:

- Resolve file and driver version conflicts by using Version Conflict Manager and the Microsoft System Information utility

The Version Conflict Manager tool is just one in a suite of tools that are bundled under the System Information utility. The System Information utility is an invaluable resource that can be used not only for troubleshooting, but for point-and-click configuration of many different aspects of your Windows 98 environment.

Version Conflict Manager

The Version Conflict Manager is used to replace older versions of files that were updated when new software was added to your system. The older versions of the software were automatically saved to a backup folder by Windows 98. If a conflict is listed, you simply need to select the version of the software you wish to use from the panel in the window and then click Restore. This will replace the current version of the file with the backed up version. The current version that is being replaced will then be saved as a backup.

This type of conflict management generally occurs when you install software that has drivers older than the drivers on your system. Usually you will be warned and asked if you wish to replace your current (newer) drivers with these older drivers. Normally you would choose No. In some instances, however, the newer drivers may not work with the older software; in those situations, you could use the Version Conflict Manager to alleviate your problems.

Figure 29.1 shows the Version Conflict Manager screen. While version conflict problems do not occur very often, you do need to know how to respond to them for the exam.

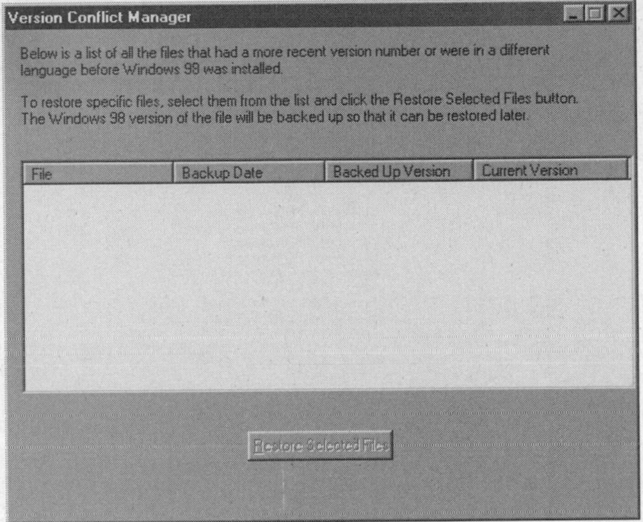

FIGURE 29.1: The Version Conflict Manager

The System Information Utility

Microsoft System Information is a very powerful utility for gathering information about the current configuration and layout of your Windows 98 system. Figure 29.2 shows a small sample of the information to be found in the base utility.

The utility offers an entire suite of tools that can be used to gather additional information about your system and do some troubleshooting. System Information tools include:

Windows Report This tool will generate a diagnostic report containing pertinent information about your system files and your computer that can be e-mailed to technical support engineers at Microsoft. The engineers can then look through the information and develop a troubleshooting solution.

Update Wizard Uninstall Use this tool if you installed a new patch or driver on your system with the Windows Update tool and want to uninstall it. Update Wizard Uninstall is very similar to the Version Conflict Manager in that it keeps backups of your patches and drivers installed through the Windows Update utility.

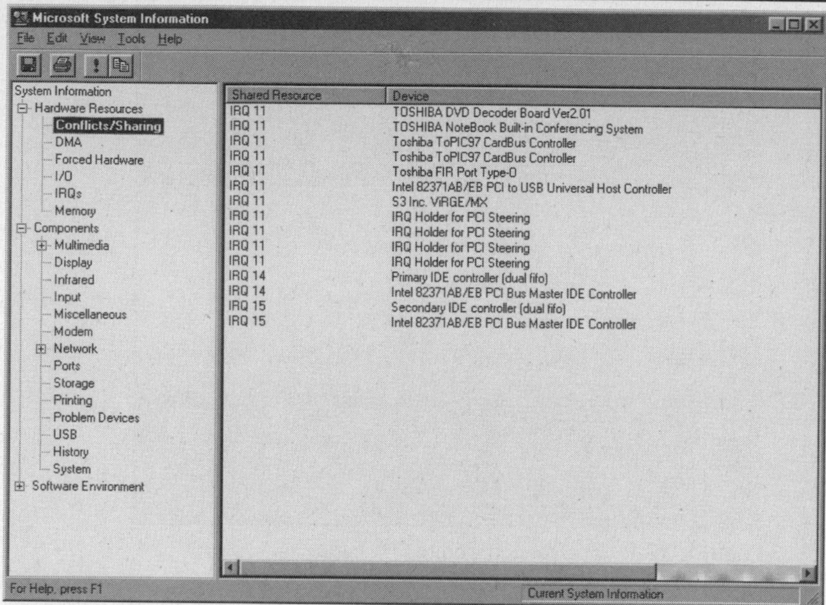

FIGURE 29.2: The System Information utility

System File Checker This tool will verify the integrity of your operating system files. If it finds corrupted files, it will extract clean files from the compressed cabinet (.CAB) files on your installation media. The System File Checker can also be used to back up existing files before restoring the original files.

Signature Verification This tool will search specified locations for both signed and unsigned files on your computer. Once it finds a file possessing a digital signature, it allows you to view the certificates and confirm that the file has not been tampered with since the digital signature was applied.

Registry Checker This tool will verify that your Registry isn't corrupted. If it finds corruption in the Registry, it will replace the current instance of your Registry with a backup copy.

Automatic Skip Driver Agent This tool will identify failures that cause Windows 98 to quit responding during a startup. The next time a startup is attempted, the agent will automatically skip the driver causing the problem. Any devices or drivers that failed to start will be listed in the Skip Driver Agent under Details. You will also be given suggestions on how to fix the problem.

Dr. Watson This tool is used as a diagnostic utility to take a snapshot of your system whenever a system fault occurs. The snapshot tracks information that is generally only useful to the developer whose program caused Dr. Watson to fire. Dr. Watson will identify the software that has faulted, provide a description of the most likely cause of failure, and often give suggestions on how to fix the problem as well.

System Configuration This utility allows you to point-and-click in various supplied checkboxes to modify your system configuration files, including WIN.INI, SYSTEM.INI, CONFIG.SYS, and AUTOEXEC.BAT. It is recommended that you use this utility to edit these files rather than the Notepad utility because the System Configuration utility permits you to work with all system files from one central location using a single visual interface. This utility will also create or restore a backup of your system files.

ScanDisk This tool will check your hard disk for both logical and physical errors and attempt to fix the damaged areas, or at least move information from the damaged areas.

Version Conflict Manager This tool allows you to manage different versions of your files and drivers. When a new version of a file is installed on your system, the old file is stored as a backup. You can then replace the current version with the backup version; the current version will also be saved as a backup version.

Knowing how to use these tools is not essential to passing the exam, but knowing *what* they do is. The best way to remember what these different utilities do is to actually try them out.

Using the Version Conflict Manager

Follow these steps to use the Version Conflict Manager:

1. Start the Microsoft System Information utility by clicking Start ➢ Programs ➢ Accessories ➢ System Tools ➢ System

Information. You should see something similar to the following screen:

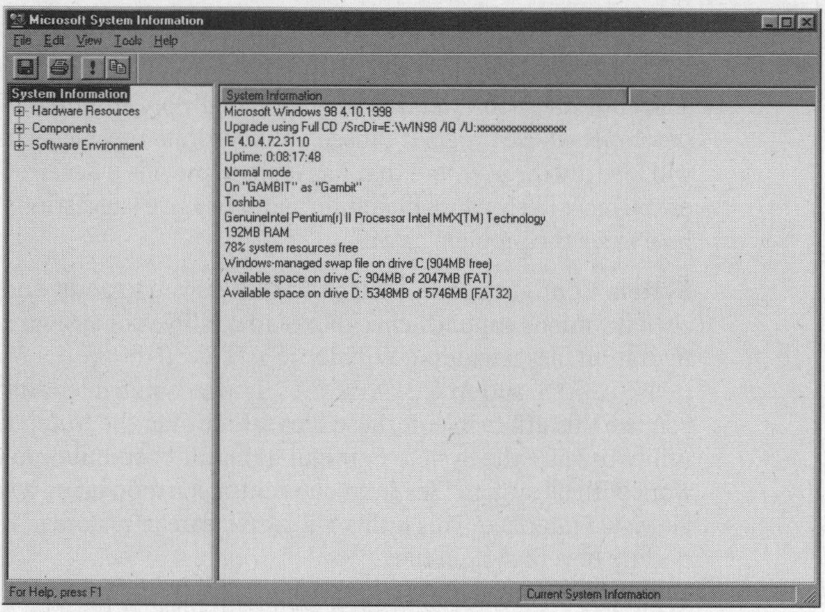

2. From the Tools menu, select Version Conflict Manager. You will be presented with a dialog box similar to Figure 29.1. If you have version conflicts, they will be displayed in the dialog box. Simply click the version of the files you wish to use and choose Restore. To revert to the original version, re-run the Version Conflict Manager, select the drivers that you just switched, and choose Restore.

Using the System Information Utility

The Microsoft System Information utility has many different associated tools; the preceding section provides a brief summary of each. Other chapters will cover these tools in more detail.

Diagnose and resolve boot process failures.

Tasks include:

- Editing configuration files by using the System Configuration utility

You can use the System Configuration utility to make visual modifications to the system startup files. This point-and-click environment can speed up the modification process and reduce the chance for errors.

System Configuration Utility

The System Configuration utility as shown in Figure 29.3 can help automate troubleshooting by walking you through the same steps that the Microsoft Technical Support people would follow to track down and diagnose problems.

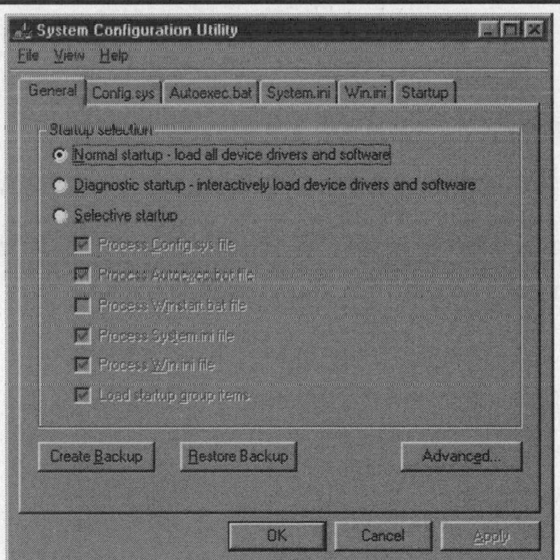

FIGURE 29.3: The System Configuration utility

With the System Configuration utility, you can modify the system configuration files through an easy-to-use, point-and-click interface. This saves you the time of editing the CONFIG.SYS, AUTOEXEC.BAT, MSDOS.SYS, SYSTEM.INI, and WIN.INI files separately. You can also create backups of the current system files before you begin making changes to them. In this way, you can undo any modifications that you make while troubleshooting.

Using the System Configuration Utility

To use the System Configuration utility, follow these steps:

1. Open the utility by clicking Start ➢ Programs ➢ Accessories ➢ System Tools ➢ System Information. Choose System Configuration Utility from the Tools menu.
2. You will see a screen similar to the one shown in Figure 29.3. Now you can select the different tabs and make modifications to the various files.

To better familiarize yourself with the System Configuration utility, take a quick look at what each of these different tabs has to offer. For more specific information on the tabs and their uses, please see the *MCSE: Windows 98 Study Guide* (Sybex, 1999).

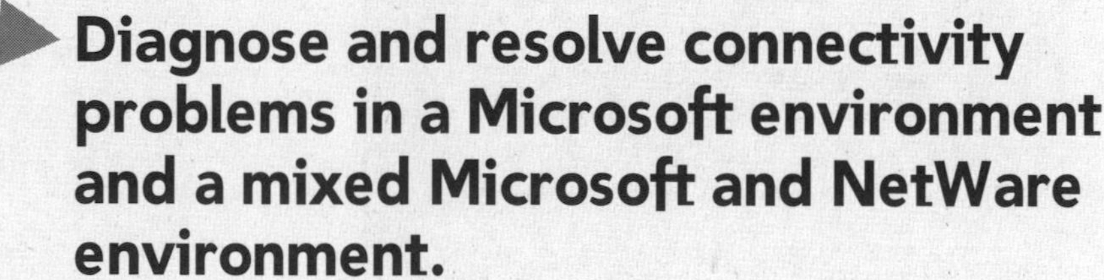

Diagnose and resolve connectivity problems in a Microsoft environment and a mixed Microsoft and NetWare environment.

Tools include:

- WinIPCfg
- Net Watcher
- Ping
- Tracert

Be aware that there are several utilities that come bundled with the TCP/IP protocol. You can use these utilities to check the status of your connection and ascertain how your data are being routed through the network.

TCP/IP Utilities

Several utilities and applications come installed with TCP/IP that can help with diagnostic functions:

WinIPCfg A GUI utility for verification of IP settings, such as IP address, subnet mask, default gateway, WINS server address, MAC address, DHCP server address, and DHCP lease status.

Ping For verification of configuration and connections.

Tracert For verification of the route taken to reach another host.

Route For viewing or editing a local route table.

NetStat For viewing protocol statistics and connections.

FTP A command-line FTP client. (File Transfer Protocol is used to break apart files into smaller packages that can be transmitted across the Internet.)

Telnet A GUI Telnet client that is used to work remotely with Telnet hosts across a network. (Telnet is an application that allows two computers to work with each other in a client-server environment.)

NOTE

The Winsock interface (version 2.0) will automatically be available, so it is not necessary to install a third-party Winsock utility such as Trumpet. It may be necessary to open the TCP/IP property sheet and fill in the IP address information manually if DHCP is not configured on the network.

Net Watcher

The Windows 98 Net Watcher tool allows you to create, control, and monitor remote shared resources. It can be useful for managing peer sharing in Windows 98. Net Watcher has easy-to-use icons that give you several options:

- Add a shared resource or stop sharing a resource on a local or remote system.
- Show all shared resources, connected users, and open files.
- Close any files that users have open.
- Disconnect a user.
- Change the properties of a remote shared folder, including its share name and access rights.
- For sharing a folder on any remote system, find out which users are connected to the shared resource, how long they've been connected, and which files they have open.

NOTE

File and Printer Sharing services must be installed and enabled to use Net Watcher.

Troubleshooting with TCP/IP Utilities

The following procedures outline how you can use the TCP/IP utilities for troubleshooting purposes.

Using WinIPCfg

To run the WinIPCfg utility, follow these steps:

1. Click Start ➢ Run.
2. In the Run Dialog box, type **WinIPCfg**, and click OK.
3. You will be presented with the WinIPCfg dialog box. Click the More Information button to view other vital statistics, as shown here.

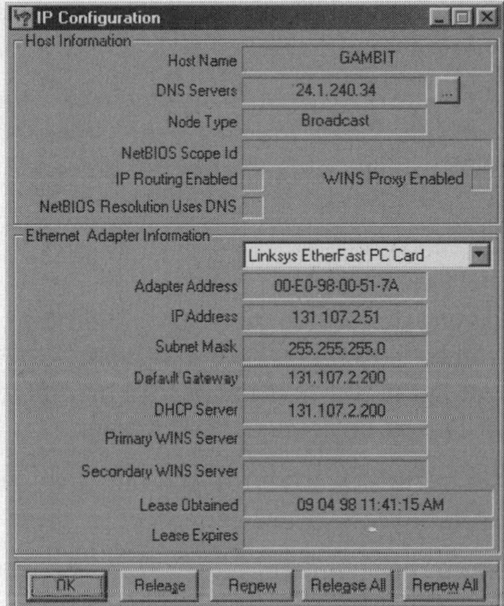

4. The Release button will release your current IP address, if you are leasing it through a DHCP server. The Renew button will renew your lease.

5. The Renew All button will renew leases for all network adapters currently configured on your computer.

Using Net Watcher

For information on using the Net Watcher utility, see Chapter 28.

Ping

You can use the Ping utility to send packets of data to a host. The host will then send the packets of data back to you. This whole process will also be timed. Follow these steps to run the Ping utility:

1. Open a command prompt. Click Start ➢ Programs ➢ MS-DOS Prompt.

2. From the command prompt, you can ping yourself (localhost) or you can ping another IP address on the network. Note: You can also ping another host on the network by their host name (computer name). Enter the following command: **ping localhost**.

3. You will get a response back from your local network adapter. The localhost has a default loopback address of 127.0.0.1.

4. If you are on a network, try pinging another computer on the network. When you are finished, type **Exit** to close the MS-DOS prompt and return to Windows.

Tracert

The Tracert utility is used to track the different routers that your packets of data are going through to get from your location to their final destination. This can be a useful tool when you want to determine network latency or configure your routing tables a bit differently. Follow these steps to run Tracert on some of your packets:

1. Go to an MS-DOS prompt. Click Start ➢ Programs ➢ MS-DOS Prompt.

2. From the command prompt, run Tracert from your location to Microsoft. For example, if you are hooked up to the Internet you can type **Tracert www.microsoft.com**.

3. The number of steps (or hops) between your current location and final destination, the amount of time it took from one location to the next, and the final destination are included in the feedback. A "hop" refers to the movement of your data from one network router to the next.

Diagnose and resolve printing problems in a Microsoft environment or a mixed Microsoft and NetWare environment.

One of the most frustrating problems is a printer that just won't print. Windows 98 has some built-in features that can help you remedy printer problems. What follows is a presentation of some of the most common problems and an introduction to the Windows 98 Print Troubleshooter tool.

Printer Installation Problems

Here are some tips for troubleshooting problems encountered while installing printers:

No printers are listed in the Print dialog box. If nothing appears in the dialog box when you are trying to install a printer, you should verify that the printer INF file exists. The PRTUPD.INF file is the built-in list of printer manufacturers and models. You may need an updated INF file from your printer's manufacturer.

Setup cannot find the printer driver files. The Add Printer Wizard will try to install the required driver files from the Windows 98 default installation drive and directory. If these files cannot be found, you will be prompted to designate a path to their locations. You can either enter the path to the required files or use the Browse button to search for them.

Copy errors occur during printer installation. If an error occurs while the system is trying to copy files during the installation process, a dialog box is displayed with the expected source and destination paths and the filenames that were being copied when the error occurred. Verify the proper locations of the files and retry the installation.

Printing Problems

There are several things you can try to resolve printing problems. The following sections provide suggestions for troubleshooting some of the most common problems.

The Printer Will Not Print

If the printer simply won't print, here are some ways to determine the source of the problem:

- Check to see that the printer is turned on, is online, and that all cables are connected correctly.
- Check to see that the printer has paper and is not jammed.
- Try turning the printer off, waiting a few seconds, and turning it back on. This will clear the printer memory buffer.

- Try printing to a file and copying the file to the printer port (local printers only).
- Try printing directly to the printer port without spooling. If this works, you may have run out of disk space on the drive that handles print spooling.
- Delete the printer and reinstall it.

Printing Is Delayed or Slow

Here are some techniques for troubleshooting delayed or slow printing problems:

- Check to see that spooling is enabled to EMF files.
- Restart in Safe mode and try printing.
- Make sure you have plenty of free disk space on the drive for spooling. Empty the Recycle Bin.
- Run Disk Defragmenter to create contiguous space on the drive for spooling.
- Check available space on the disk for temporary files.
- Check for low system resources.
- Delete and reinstall the printer driver in the Printers folder.
- Make sure that TrueType fonts are being sent as outlines and not as bitmaps (check the Fonts tab of the printer's property sheet).

Print Jobs Are Garbled or Are Missing Data

When your print jobs are not printing correctly, you can try the following solutions:

- Restart in Safe mode and try printing.
- There may not be enough printer memory. Try using a lower resolution or increasing memory.
- Try spooling in RAW format rather than EMF format.
- If available, try printing with a PostScript driver. If this corrects the problem, you probably have a corrupted UNIDRV.DLL. This file can be extracted from the Windows 98 CD-ROM.

- If PostScript fails, there is either a problem with the application or the GDI. Try printing from another application.
- Try printing one job at a time to avoid conflicting jobs.

Only Partial Pages Are Printed

When only part of the page is being printed, try the following techniques:

- There may not be enough printer memory. Try printing at a lower resolution or adding more memory.
- If it is a graphic, try printing it from a different document or application.
- Make sure that the font used is valid and correctly installed.
- Check the printable region of the printer by printing a test page.
- Try printing from a different document or application with the same font.
- Try printing from the same document or application with a different font.
- Enable Print TrueType as Graphics (an option on the Fonts tab of the printer's property sheet).
- Simplify the page by reducing the number of graphics or fonts.

The Print Troubleshooter

Windows 98 has a built-in tool to help remedy printer trouble called the Print Troubleshooter. You access it by selecting Start ➢ Help. When the Help dialog box appears, open the Troubleshooting book, and choose If You Have Trouble Printing. This brings up the Print Troubleshooter, as shown in Figure 29.4. You will then be guided through a series of questions, each answer leading to another set of questions, which will narrow down the problem and help you find a solution.

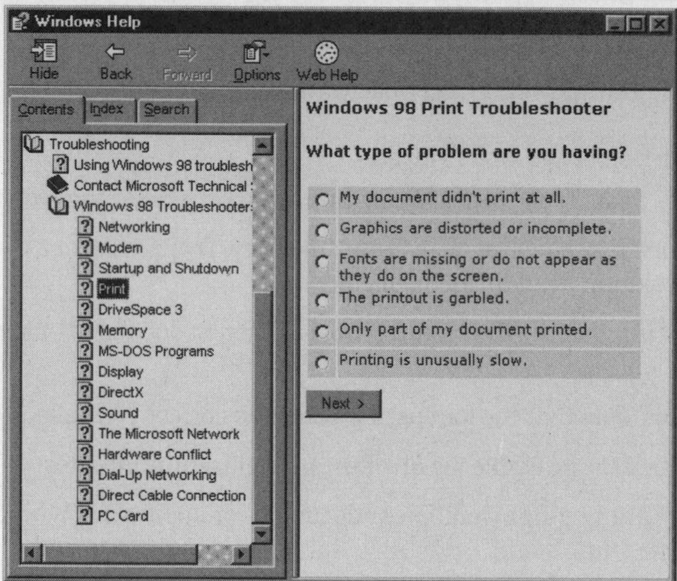

FIGURE 29.4: The Print Troubleshooter

Using the Print Troubleshooter

To use the Print Troubleshooter, follow these steps:

1. Click Start ➢ Help.
2. From the Windows 98 Help screen, click the Contents tab and drill down to Troubleshooting. In the Troubleshooting book, click Print. You should now see a Troubleshooter window similar to Figure 29.4.
3. To use the Troubleshooter, choose the option button and then click Next. You can walk through this process until you find the information you need.

Diagnose and resolve file system problems.

There may be times when you are having trouble with your hard disks. The ScanDisk tool is essential in tracking down and fixing (hopefully) these disk-related problems.

The ScanDisk utility is used to manage the integrity of your disk drives.

ScanDisk

ScanDisk allows you to check your hard drives for both logical and physical errors. The ScanDisk program itself (see Figure 29.5) is capable of fixing errors in most cases. It also contains options that allow you to delete or save lost data clusters and give them specific filenames.

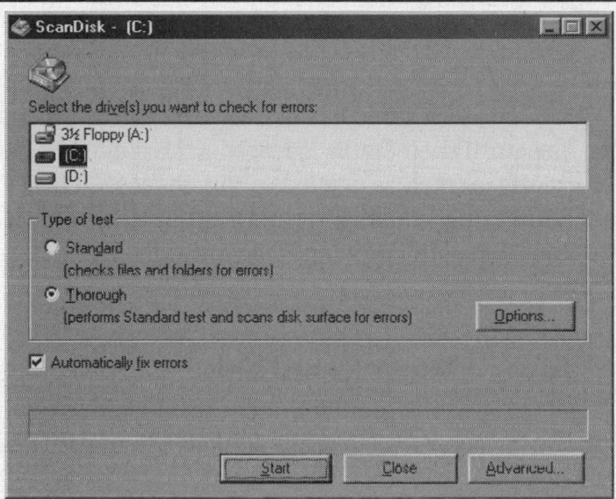

FIGURE 29.5: The ScanDisk utility

Although there is no software fix for your hard drive if the drive is failing due to physical defects, some hard drive problems can be repaired with software. Windows 98 comes with a program called ScanDisk, which can diagnose and fix many problems that it finds on your hard disk and/or floppy disks.

Several things can happen to files on your hard drive that might make them unusable. Some problems are easily fixed; others can be very serious. Here are some occurrences that could cause problems on your drive:

Crosslinked files This can happen when two or more files have become confused as to where their data resides. The crosslinked files both point to the same data area. This is one of the more serious errors, because one of the two files no longer points to the correct data area and will probably not be recoverable.

Bad sectors These can occur on either a floppy disk or hard drive and prevent programs or data files from working correctly. Bad sectors, or "spots," can happen naturally because of wear and tear on a drive, or can be caused by scratching the surface of a floppy by touching it, or by the drive head hitting the platter (usually because of dropping/banging the drive while in use). Bad sectors can sometimes be read and the data moved to a good spot, but sometimes a bad spot can also be completely unrecoverable. If the latter happens, the affected file is probably unrecoverable.

Lost clusters These appear when data areas have not been correctly identified as either in use or free. Lost clusters cannot be used for files until their status is resolved. Lost clusters can either be correctly marked as deleted or can be recovered as files in case something valuable was in those clusters. This is usually the least damaging problem that you will encounter on your hard drive.

Fixing Problems Using ScanDisk

ScanDisk can fix all three of the problems mentioned above. As with any kind of troubleshooting, success is never guaranteed, but ScanDisk has a relatively good chance.

Fixing crosslinked files Since ScanDisk can't tell which cross-linked file is the original and which one got attached by mistake, by default it fixes crosslinked files by taking the crosslinked data area and attaching it to both files. One of your files will be good, while the other one will be corrupted. You can have ScanDisk copy the crosslinked data to both files, delete both files, or ignore any crosslinked errors by using the Advanced button.

Fixing bad sectors Files that happen to be on bad sectors can sometimes be read by ScanDisk and moved to a safe area. The bad area is then marked so that future files will not try to save there.

Fixing lost clusters Lost clusters can either be erased or saved as a file. If you save the lost cluster as a file, you can later look at the file and see if it contains any data that you still need. Seldom, if ever, do these files contain anything of use. You can change this option by using the Advanced button.

To run ScanDisk, follow these steps:

1. Click Start ➢ Programs ➢ Accessories ➢ System Tools ➢ ScanDisk.

2. Select a drive as shown in Figure 29.5.

3. If you wish to work with some of the advanced options, click the Advanced button. You should see something similar to the following dialog box:

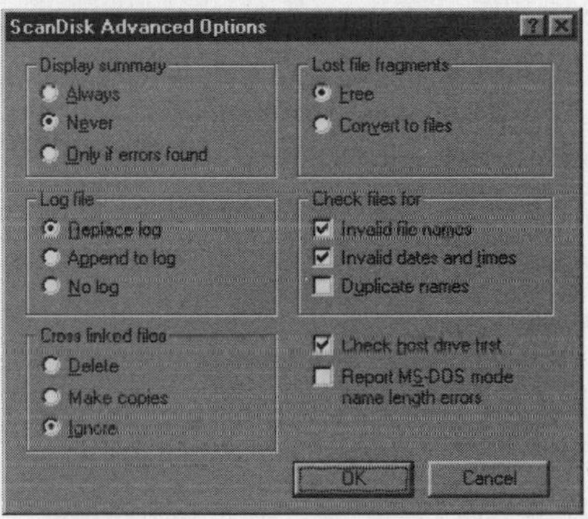

4. If you are in a hurry, from the ScanDisk main screen, choose Standard for the type of test and check the Automatically fix errors checkbox. If you have more time, choose the Thorough test and deselect Automatically Fix Errors.

5. Wait for ScanDisk to finish. If there are any errors, ScanDisk will automatically fix them (if selected) or it will prompt you on how to fix them.

6. If you selected a Thorough test, ScanDisk will check your current files and will then check the entire hard drive for bad spots—this takes from several minutes to more than a half hour depending on the size of your hard disks.

7. When ScanDisk is finished, close its information box.

Diagnose and resolve resource access problems in a Microsoft environment or a mixed Microsoft and NetWare environment.

This exam topic may seem very broad, but, in effect, it is really quite a narrow area of study. If you take a closer look, you'll see that resource access problems can only arise from three distinct areas.

The three distinct areas of resource access problems include: hardware issues, protocol issues, and no permissions.

Hardware Issues

Hardware issues include any of the following problems:

- Bad network card
- Bad network cabling
- Cable not plugged in
- Resources not plugged into computer or power
- Corrupted or bad drivers for your hardware

Most of these hardware issues are fairly easy to track down and fix. For example, you could use the Ping tool to check your local network card. You could then use Ping again to check a particular network segment by pinging a computer on the same segment.

Bad drivers can be located using the System File Checker utility as discussed earlier in this book. You can use Windows Update to see if newer versions of your software are available as well.

Protocol Issues

Protocol problems can arise from any of the following possibilities:

- Bad IP address
- Bad subnet mask
- No gateway

- Multiple computers employing different protocols

Most of your protocol issues can be checked quickly. You can use the WinIPCfg program to verify your TCP/IP information. You can use Ping to check to see if your computer can talk with another computer; if you cannot reach the other computer, verify that the correct protocol is installed and that it has been configured properly.

Permission Issues

Permission issues are probably the most common cause of your inability to access a resource. There are many problems that can arise with permissions. These include:

- You don't know the password to the resource (using share-level access).
- Your user account has not been given access to the resource (using user-level access).
- You didn't log in to a validation server (Windows NT or NetWare) when you started your Windows 98 session.
- Your user account has not been granted sufficient permissions to access the resource.

Diagnose and resolve hardware device and device driver problems.

Tasks include:

- Checking for corrupt registry files by using ScanReg and ScanRegW

You can use the ScanReg and ScanRegW programs to verify and fix your Registry database. Because the Registry contains all the settings for your computer, it is essential that it does not become corrupt or get erased. Because the Registry is constantly being changed and added to by applications and hardware configurations, it is more likely to become corrupted or damaged than other static files on your computer. Backing up the Registry ensures that the latest configuration changes can be restored in case of corruption or damage.

Automatic Registry Backup

Windows 98 includes a new utility called the Registry Checker, which automatically runs at bootup. The Registry Checker scans the Registry for corruption and backs it up if there are no errors. The Registry backup is stored in a file called RB*XXX*.CAB that is located in the Windows\Sysbckup folder; the five most recent backups are kept by default.

The Registry Checker consists of two programs:

ScanReg A real-mode version of the Registry Checker that allows you to restore the Registry from a command prompt.

ScanRegW A protected-mode version of Registry Checker that allows you to scan the Registry for errors and create a new backup of the Registry from within Windows 98.

Checking the Registry for Corruption

Windows 98 automatically checks the Registry for corruption in case of an improper shutdown. You can also manually begin the scanning process by starting the ScanRegW program from within Windows 98 or the ScanReg program from MS-DOS mode.

To manually test the integrity of your Registry and make backups or restorations, you should use the ScanReg and ScanRegW programs.

Manually Backing Up and Restoring the Registry with Registry Checker

Follow these steps to manually operate the Registry Checker utilities:

1. Registry Checker can be started manually by going to Start ➢ Run and typing **scanregw**.
2. Your Registry will be scanned for errors. If errors are found, they will either be fixed or you will have to boot to MS-DOS mode to load an old copy of the Registry using SCANREG.EXE.
3. If the Registry Checker has already backed up the Registry today, you will get a message like the one pictured below. Choose Yes to make a new backup.

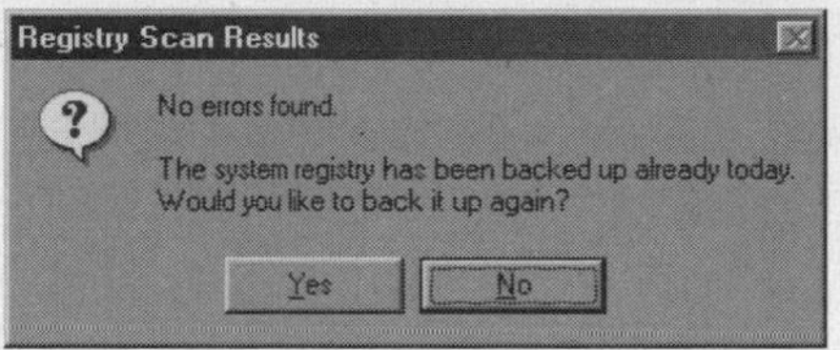

4. If you need to restore the Registry, you need to boot to MS-DOS mode or boot with the Windows 98 startup disk. Run the SCANREG.EXE program, which will present you with a list of the last five Registry backups. Choose the backup you wish to restore and reboot Windows 98 to use that copy of the Registry.

NOTE

Registry backups will be labeled Started or Not Started. Started means that Windows 98 was successfully started using that copy of the Registry. Not Started means that, although the Registry copy may be good, it has not actually been run, so Windows 98 is not sure if it is good.

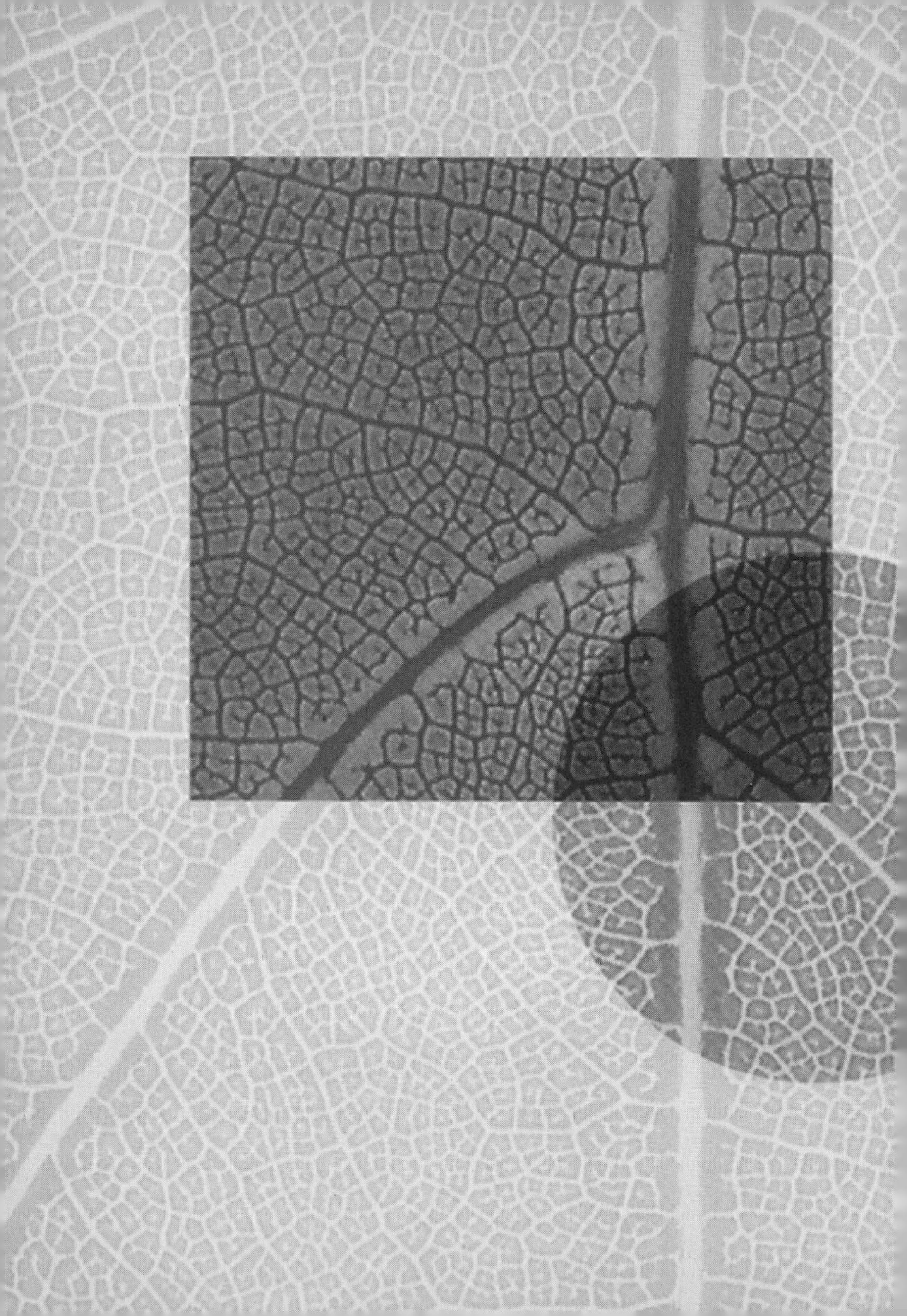

Part V

Windows 98 Practice Exam

1. You have three workgroups (Sales, Marketing, and Accounting) and two domains (Headquarters and Branch1). All users at your location log in to the Headquarters domain. The users from Sales would like to see the servers in their group when they first open Network Neighborhood. How do you set their computers?

   A. Make their computers members of the Headquarters domain, and set Network Neighborhood to the Sales workgroup.

   B. Make their computers members of the Sales workgroup.

   C. Put their user accounts in the Sales workgroup.

   D. Put their user accounts in the Branch1 domain and set Network Neighborhood to the Sales workgroup.

2. Your group policies don't seem to be working on certain computers. What is the likely cause?

   A. Users are logging in incorrectly.

   B. The policy file is named incorrectly.

   C. The users are not members of the group you have the restrictions set for.

   D. The group policy support DLL has not been installed on those particular computers.

3. You have three workgroups (Sales, Marketing, and Accounting) and two domains (Headquarters and Branch1). The Headquarters domain has two servers, HQ1 (the PDC) and HQ2 (the BDC). All users at your location log into the Headquarters domain. You wish to have your Windows 98 clients switch to user-level security in the Headquarters domain. What do you enter for the security provider?

   A. HQ1

   B. HQ2

   C. HQ1 or HQ2

   D. Headquarters

4. The Setup /d option prevents Windows 98 from doing what?

   A. Diagnosing real-mode problems

   B. Diagnosing hard-disk errors with ScanDisk

   C. Detecting virtual hard disks

   D. Detecting and using any previous version of Windows

5. Which program can automate the Windows 98 setup process?

   A. DBSetup

   B. Microsoft Batch 98

   C. NetSetup

   D. Microsoft Information Installer

6. A user wants to make a newsletter available to the entire company. What service can she install in Windows 98 to make this possible?

   A. An Internet browser

   B. IIS

   C. FPNW

   D. PWS

7. A user complains that he can't always connect to a certain NetWare 4.11 server because the connection doesn't always work. The user is using Microsoft Service for NetWare Directory Services. What could be the problem? (Choose all that apply.)

   A. The NetWare server could be out of licenses.

   B. The client and the server could be using different frame types.

   C. The client needs to install the Microsoft Client for NetWare.

   D. The client needs to install IPX/SPX.

8. Your network consists of MS-DOS and Windows 3.*x* NetWare clients and NetWare 3.*x* and 4.*x* servers. You want all of the clients to be able to access your computer so that they can look at old company memos. You intend to install the following components: File and Printer Sharing for NetWare Networks, Service for NetWare Directory Services, and IPX/SPX. Will this installation fulfill the requirements?

   A. Yes, all requirements are fulfilled.

   B. Yes, but only if you enable SAP advertising.

   C. Yes, but only if you enable the Browser service.

   D. No, this installation will not work.

9. You have a network across five routers that consists of NetWare and Windows NT servers. You also have HP printers with Jet-Direct cards in them that you want the clients to directly access. You want your clients to be able to access the Internet. Which protocol(s) should you install? (Choose all that apply.)

   A. DLC

   B. TCP/IP

   C. IPX/SPX

   D. NetBEUI

10. Some of your users complain that they can connect to some servers but not others. You find that the affected users can connect to servers in their department but not to those in other departments. You are using TCP/IP. What parameter is probably set up incorrectly?

    A. Subnet mask

    B. Default gateway

    C. TCP/IP address

    D. DNS address

11. If you can connect to a Unix HTTP server by address, but not by name, which software program is probably at fault?

    A. WINS

B. DNS

C. DHCP

D. NetBIOS

12. A user complains that her print jobs come out at the wrong printer if she forgets to change the printer before she prints a job. What can you do to fix the problem?

A. Set the printer to offline.

B. Change the printer device type.

C. Change the default printer to the one she prints to most often.

D. Install a new local printer on her computer and set it to offline.

13. Sue is using default security settings on Windows 98 and is sharing office memos. She wants to be certain that the sales team can read the memos, but only the sales manager can make new memos. How can she do this?

A. Share the folder as Full control and mark the memos Read-Only.

B. Share the folder as Read-Only, and then make a second Full control share.

C. Share the folder as Depends On Password. Give the appropriate password to the appropriate group or user.

D. Switch to user-level security.

14. Where can you start the Administer program so that you can administer the files and folders of a remote Windows 98 computer?

A. Control Panel ➢ System

B. Network Neighborhood ➢ Computer ➢ Properties ➢ Tools

C. Start ➢ Programs ➢ Accessories ➢ System Tools

D. Control Panel ➢ Network

15. Your Windows NT users are OK, but your Windows 98 users complain that it takes a long time to log in. What can you do to help speed the logon process?

    A. Disable ghosted connections.

    B. Enable load balancing for the system policy.

    C. Make roaming profiles.

    D. Enable load balancing for the roaming user profiles.

16. Which program is used to make partitions?

    A. Format

    B. ScanDisk

    C. Partition Manager

    D. Fdisk

17. A user just bought a new computer with an 8GB hard drive. Her hard drive has been split into four partitions. How can you convert it into one big partition?

    A. You can't without third-party software.

    B. Use the FAT32 conversion program and choose the Merge function during the conversion.

    C. Use the Fdisk utility to convert and merge the partitions to FAT32.

    D. Use Fdisk to delete all the partitions. Then create one large FAT32 partition and reformat it.

18. You want to build a profile for a user who has two modems. Sometimes they only have a single phone line to dial out. How would you set the profile for the second modem so that the second modem is not used when the single modem profile is selected?

    A. Disabled

    B. Deleted

    C. Changed IRQ

    D. Changed COM Port

19. You have a manager who uses a laptop at work and at home. She has a docking station at work with a network card but uses an external modem at home to dial in to the network. How would you set up the laptop so that she can use both configurations easily?

   A. Create two hardware profiles. Disable the network card for the work profile and disable the modem for the home profile.

   B. Create two hardware profiles. Delete the network card driver in the home profile and delete the modem driver in the work profile.

   C. Create two user profiles. Disable the network card driver in the home user profile and disable the modem driver for the work user profile.

   D. Create two hardware profiles. Disable the network card for the home profile and disable the modem in the work profile.

20. Users are complaining that they can't remember all of their passwords and keep them in sync. What tool can they use to change all their Windows passwords at once?

   A. Control Panel ➢ Passwords

   B. Control Panel ➢ Network

   C. Accessories ➢ System Tools ➢ Passwords

   D. Accessories ➢ System Tools ➢ Client Utilities

21. You have three NetWare servers in your company. The servers are called FS_Sales, FS_Mrktg, and FS_Acct for the sales, marketing, and accounting departments, respectively. What parameter should you set on your Windows 98 computers to make sure everyone is logging in to their appropriate server?

   A. Local server

   B. Master server

   C. Assigned server

   D. Preferred server

22. You wish to dial in to your computer at work so you can copy some files when you are at home. How do you get Windows 98 to act as a dial-up server?

  A. Install the Plus! Pack.

  B. Install the service from Add/Remove Programs.

  C. The service installs automatically when you install the dial-up client.

  D. Windows 98 cannot be used as a dial-up server.

23. You have a proxy server set up for your Internet connections. You have an intranet Web server called INSRV1 that has a DNS name of `www.insrv1.com` and is at `131.145.3.200`. What can you enter in the exclusion list so that the proxy server will not be used for the intranet Web server? (Choose all that apply.)

  A. `131.145.3.200`

  B. `www.insrv1.*`

  C. `insrv1`

  D. Select "Bypass proxy server for local (intranet) Web sites."

24. You have been using the Remote Administration tool on your Windows 98 machine to administer other network client PCs. You have just added an additional ten PCs to the network. You have enabled File and Printer Sharing on these new PCs and are sharing various folders and printers. You have access to these shares from all of the computers on the network, but when you attempt to remotely administer the new PCs, you find that you cannot. What else do you need to do to enable remote administration of these ten new client PCs?

  A. Add a new protocol to the Network property sheets.

  B. Add the Net Watcher program from the Add/Remove Programs Control Panel.

  C. Enable remote administration from the Passwords applet of the Control Panel.

  D. Run the Remote Administration applet of the Control Panel.

25. You are satisfied with the way your current applications are loading, but you are about to install a new, extremely large application. You want to prepare your drive so that the new application loads as quickly as possible. What is the fastest way to prepare your drive for the new application?

A. Run Disk Defragmenter with the Defragment Files Only option.

B. Run Disk Defragmenter with the Full Defragmentation option.

C. Run Disk Defragmenter with the Defragment Future Installs option.

D. Run Disk Defragmenter with the Defragment Free Space Only option.

26. You are having problems with some of your real-mode device drivers. To troubleshoot the problem, you decide to use the System Configuration utility to view your current settings and make changes to them. You begin by using the System Configuration utility to back up your current settings. You then make incremental changes and reboot until you find the problem. How would you rate this solution?

A. This is an excellent solution and appears to work.

B. This is a good solution, but you cannot make backups of your startup files from here.

C. This is a poor solution, but it may work.

D. This solution will not work. You should use other means to make these changes.

27. A user calls and says that when she booted her Windows 98 computer, she got an error message about her IP address, but she just clicked OK and continued. Now she can't see any servers. What program can the user run to find and reset her current TCP/IP address?

A. IPCONFIG.EXE

B. WINIPCFG.EXE

C. PING.EXE

D. LOGON.EXE

28. Your printer is sending you a message that it is low on toner. You have printed the first 60 pages of a 200-page document and don't want to rerun the entire print job. You decide to cancel the print job and then resubmit the print job from your application, beginning with page 60. How would you rate this solution?

A. This is an excellent solution and will work.

B. This is a good solution and will work.

C. This is a poor solution, but appears to work.

D. This is a poor solution and will not work.

29. Your Windows 98 machine seems to keep corrupting your files. You have run the Disk Defragmenter program and everything seems to be working properly. Whenever you run your ScanDisk program, it almost always finds lost clusters and crosslinked files. You decide that you need to check your hard drive more closely. What should you do?

A. Open the computer case and remove the hard drive. Take it back to the vendor.

B. Run the Disk Defragmenter program again.

C. Run ScanDisk with the Thorough test option enabled.

D. Run DiskFix with the low-level disk format and verify options enabled.

30. Your Windows 98 computer is configured with TCP/IP. You are getting your TCP/IP configuration from a DHCP server located on a Windows NT server. You have logged in successfully and can see other computers on the network. You can see a shared printer on another Windows 98 machine, however, you get error messages whenever you attempt to print. Which of the following would you check? (Choose all that apply.)

A. Run WinIPCfg and verify that you have TCP/IP configured properly.

B. Verify that you have permissions on the printer in question.

C. Verify that the printer is on and plugged in properly.

D. Verify that your print drivers are not corrupted for that particular printer.

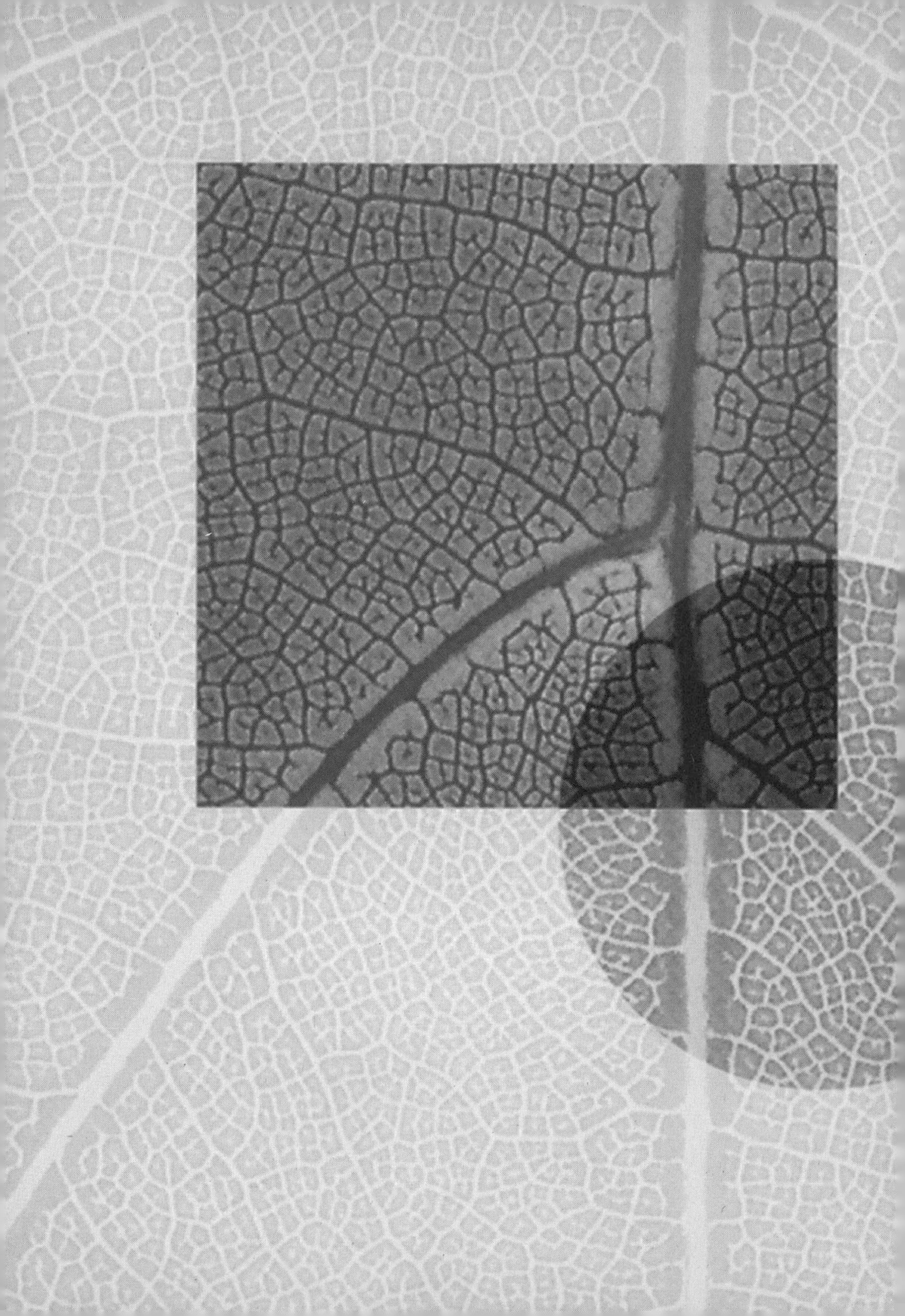

Appendix A

Exam Answers

Part I: Networking Essentials

1. Which of the following best describes the function of the token in a Token Ring network?

   A. Only the station that holds the free token is allowed to transmit a message on the network.

   Answer: A–On a Token Ring network, a computer must wait for a free token in order to transfer data.

2. As a consultant, you have been asked to design a network for a mid-sized accounting firm. Because of the data handled by the company, security is extremely important. The network must support 80 computers with easy expandability to more than 100 in the next few months. What type of network would be best for you to install at your client's office?

   D. Server-based

   Answer: D–A server-based network provides security and password access to logon, and is easy to use.

3. Which one of the following roles does the server play in a system that uses the client/server architecture?

   A. The server fulfills the requests from the client computer for data and other processing resources.

   Answer: A

4. Security is not a major concern in your company network. However, your boss wants to protect several resources with special passwords. Which of the following security models should you implement to accomplish this task?

   A. Share-level security

   Answer: A–There are two types of security models. Share-level security is also called password-protected shares. Each user has control of their shared resources by assigning a password to a resource of network as access control.

5. Which of the following is associated with connection-oriented communication?

   B. Assured delivery

Answer: B–With connection-orientated communication, the network takes responsibility for delivering packets in a reliable way that detects loss and data corruption.

6. Which of the following connectivity devices work at the Data Link layer of the OSI model?

   B. Bridge

   Answer: B–Bridges work at the MAC sublayer of the Data Link layer.

7. Which type of media access method is commonly used by Ethernet networks?

   C. CSMA/CD

   Answer: C

8. Which of following statements shows the benefits of both NDIS and ODI?

   D. They allow network adapters to be independent of any particular transport protocol.

   Answer: D

9. Which of the following cable types can be used for 100BaseT networks?

   D. Category 5 UTP

   Answer: D–Category 5 UTP supports transmission speeds of up to 100Mbps.

10. Which of the following refers to the signal overflow from an adjacent wire?

    B. Crosstalk

    Answer: B–Crosstalk refers to the signal overflow from an adjacent wire.

11. Which of the following are true of 10BaseT networks? (Choose all that apply.)

    B. They use hubs as the central point of connection

    D. They utilize category 3 UTP

Answer: B, D–10BaseT is a standard for transmitting Ethernet over twisted-pair cable.

12. Which of the following protocols cannot be routed? (Choose all that apply.)

    B. DLC

    C. LAT

    D. NetBEUI

    Answer: B, C, D

13. Match the definition to the networking term: This high-level network protocol provides file-sharing services on a network that uses NetBIOS.

    F. Server message block (SMB)

    Answer: F–SMB operates at the Application level of the OSI protocol.

14. Which of the following connectivity devices works at the Data Link layer of the OSI model?

    B. Bridge

    Answer: B–Bridges work at the MAC sublayer of the Data Link layer. The Data Link layer packages raw bits from the Physical layer into data frames. Routers work at the Network layer of the OSI model. Repeaters work at the Physical layer. Gateways work at all seven layers of the OSI model, especially the upper three (Application, Presentation, and Session).

15. Which of the following describes the difference between bridges and routers?

    B. Routers can choose between multiple paths

    Answer: B–Routers can choose multiple paths between network segments. Because routers can connect segments that use different data access methods, there will often be several paths available. Both devices are supported by Token Ring networks.

16. Which of the following best describes Frame Relay technology?

B. It is a point-to-point system that transmits variable-length frames at the Data Link layer.

Answer: B–Frame Relay is a point-to-point system that uses a private virtual circuit (PVC) to transmit variable-length frames at the Data Link layer. Frame Relay networks can also provide subscribers with bandwidth as needed that allows the customer to make nearly any type of transmission.

17. Which of the following should you implement to ensure that the data on a server is easily and quickly available in case of a server disk crash?

D. RAID level 1

Answer: D–Disk mirroring (RAID 1) can be set up to protect against the data being destroyed. In disk mirroring, all data written to the primary disk is written to the mirror disk. In case of a disk crashing in the server, the system uses the backup data from the image disk.

18. What can you do to make sure the data on a server is easily and quickly available in the event of a server disk crash with minimum down time?

C. Implement RAID level 5

Answer: C–In RAID 5 (striping with parity), data is striped across multiple drives and then its parity sum is calculated, which is also striped across multiple drives. A minimum of three drives is needed for RAID 5 implementation. When one disk fails, the data on that failed disk will be calculated from the parity sum disks.

19. Al has just plugged a new network adapter card into his computer, but the operating system failed to detect the network adapter card. Which of the following is the most likely cause of the problem?

A. The IRQ setting of the adapter card

Answer: A–If there is an interrupt conflict (it is the most common problem), the network adapter card cannot send a request to the computer because when the network adapter card sends a request to the computer, it needs to use an interrupt. Al should know which interrupts are available on his computer and check the card to make sure that the desired IRQ is set before installing a network adapter card.

20. Lorraine's computer consists of COM1, COM2, LPT1, and LPT2 with their default IRQ settings. The NE-2000 network adapter card is using IRQ3 and 0x300 as I/O port address. Which of the following devices is conflicting with the network adapter card?

D. COM2

Answer: D—The network adapter card has an interrupt conflict with COM2.

21. Which of the following uses 15-character names to identify computers on a network?

A. NetBIOS

Answer: A—NetBIOS is an application programming interface (API) used to create LAN applications for Microsoft and IBM networks. It provides a uniform set of commands for requesting the lower-level network services required to conduct sessions between nodes on a network. NetBIOS names are created when a computer is first set up or connected to a network.

22. Examine the following situation, desired result, and solutions:

You are designing a NetBIOS naming scheme for all the servers and client computers in your company. In the next two years, your company will install a WAN that will connect all its networks.

Required result: You need to setup a NetBIOS naming scheme for all the servers and client computers in one company's networks. The NetBIOS naming scheme at your location must continue to work after the WAN is connected.

Optional desired results: You want the NetBIOS name for each server to describe the server's department or function. You want each client computer's NetBIOS name to describe the computer's primary user or function.

Proposed solution: Assign each server a NetBIOS name that consists of the first eight characters of the server's department name, a five-character location code, plus a two-digit identifier to distinguish between multiple servers within the department. Assign each client computer a NetBIOS name that corresponds to the e-mail address of the computer's principal user.

Which result does the proposed solution produce?

A. The proposed solution produces the required result and produces both of the optional desired results.

Answer: A–Providing a NetBIOS naming scheme that consists of the server's department name, location code, two-digit identifier, and computer name that corresponds to the e-mail address of the principal user meets all the above requirements.

23. Which of the following functions is provided directly by Systems Management Server (SMS)?

C. Remote control of client machines

Answer: C–In addition to remote control and monitoring of client and server machines for troubleshooting, SMS provides software distribution and inventory management features. For example, any program can be run on any machine in the network using a central SMS server. It does not provide virus protection or an SNMP management interface, but it allows third-party products to interface with it in order to provide these services.

24. There is a frame type mismatch on your Novell NetWare network. It is only affecting one computer. Which of the following needs to be reconfigured?

A. The frame type on the client machine

Answer: A–For two IPX (or NWLink) computers to communicate, they must use the same frame type. The frame type is the format used to put together packet header and data information for transmission on the data link. The 802.2 frame type is the default and most commonly used frame type in Windows NT networks. If only one computer on the network is affected, then it would almost always be more appropriate to change its frame type rather than change the frame type of the server and all the other computers on the network.

25. You added one client machine on an IPX network, but the new machine cannot communicate with the other machines on the network. What may be causing the problem?

    C. Frame type

    Answer: C–All the protocols (such as TCP/IPand NetBEUI) deal with the packets themselves, except NWLink IPX. If your network uses TCP/IP or NetBEUI, you need to set up nothing on packets. In a Novell IPX environment, IPX is not tied to any particular frame type. In Ethernet, IPX supports four kinds of frame type, and Token Ring has two. Two computers with different frame types cannot communicate with each other.

26. After a long holiday, Barry reported that his computer is no longer connected to the network and he cannot get through. However, he can log on to the network on a coworker's PC. What should you check first?

    A. The network cable is detached from Barry's computer

    Answer: A–Remember the key words "no longer." This means Barry could log on to the network on his computer before the holiday. Answer B is not appropriate. He can log on to a network through a coworker's PC, so the network is operating normally. Answers C and D are not appropriate in this case.

27. The following is the configuration of a new computer on your network:

    Pentium-200 CPU MMX

    32 MB of RAM

    A 3.5GB IDE hard disk

    A parallel port configured as LPT1

    A mouse on COM1

A modem on COM2

SCSI host adapter for a scanner is using IRQ5

Sound card using IRQ11

Amy needs to add a new network adapter card into her computer. When Amy looks in her reference manual, the network adapter card will support only IRQs 2, 3, 4, 5, 10, and 11. Which IRQ should Amy use for the network interface card without creating an IRQ conflict with another device?

D. IRQ10

Answer: D–In most cases, IRQ2 and IRQ9 (EGA/VGA) are not available. COM1 and COM3 use IRQ4, while COM2 and COM4 use IRQ3. IRQ7 is used by LPT1. IRQ5 is used by LPT2 or a sound card. Normally, IRQ3 or IRQ5 can be used for the network adapter card. IRQ10 and IRQ11 are usually available.

28. Your network has been very slow for the past two days. You check the computer systems, cables, and the hub. You do not find any problems. You have concluded that the problem is broadcast storms. Which of the following tools can confirm your guess and troubleshoot the problem?

D. Protocol analyzer

Answer: D–A protocol analyzer, also called a network analyzer, has the functions of real-time network analysis, such as packet capture, decoding, and transmission.

29. Why does a high number of broadcast messages degrade overall network performance?

A. Broadcast messages are processed by every computer on the network.

Answer: A–Every computer on the network must process each broadcast message. This can potentially cause broadcast storms. A broadcast storm occurs if the number of broadcast messages on the network approaches or surpasses the capacity of the network bandwidth so that the network can no longer carry messages from any other computer.

30. Only Laura's computer on your network cannot connect to the network, but all other computers can access all network resources. Which of the following is the most likely cause of the problem?

   D. The network card on the client computer is faulty

   Answer: D–The problem seems to be local due to the fact that only one computer is affected. If more than one computer is affected, then it will be a network problem. It could be caused by the network adapter card on the client computer. A network adapter card could have I/O address conflicts, interrupt conflicts, or memory conflicts with other devices that prevent the computer from connecting to the network.

Part II: NT Server 4

1. Which of the following selections is a valid disk configuration?

   B. Three primary partitions–one set active, one extended partition

   Answer: B–Each disk can have a maximum of four partitions, only one of which can be an extended partition. Since the active partition is the one that the system will use for the boot process, only one primary partition can be set as active.

2. When assigning drive letters, in what order does NT perform the following actions?

   A. Starting with drive 0, assign letters to logical drives

   B. Starting with drive 0, assign letters to primary partitions

   C. Starting with drive 0, assign letters to the first primary drive on each disk

   Answer: C, A, B

3. A network administrator has noticed that network performance has decreased since 20 new workstations were added to the network. Which of the following services might help correct this problem?

B. WINS

Answer: B–By default, name registration and resolution are accomplished by broadcasting packets on the network. These packets can produce heavy traffic in some environments. One way to decrease the amount of broadcast traffic is to implement a WINS server. WINS clients direct their traffic to the WINS server rather than broadcasting on the network.

4. Suppose that your network consists of an NT 4 primary domain controller. It is configured with 50 CALs and set to use Per Server licensing. Your users continue to access the resources provided by your network, and it has become necessary to add a second server to provide BDC capabilities. Your client workstations include 35 NT 4 workstations, 5 Windows 95 workstations, and 5 Windows for Workgroups workstations. What would be the most cost-effective way to license the servers?

Answer: Since the scenario did not mention network growth, you can convert the PDC to Per Seat licensing and configure the new server to use the Per Seat mode as well. In this case, if you switch the PDC to Per Seat mode and configure the BDC to Per Seat mode, you would meet the objectives of the scenario.

5. When the change log fills up, which of the following things will occur?

B. Records will be overwritten

C. A complete update will occur in the next pulse

Answer: B, C–The change log records transactions to the domain SAM. If it fills up between synchronization pulses, the oldest records will be overwritten. Since this means that certain changes might not have been synchronized to the BDCs, a complete update will occur.

6. The /OX switch, when used in conjunction with the WINNT.EXE file, will do what?

D. Create three startup diskettes

Answer: D–The /OX switch will create three startup diskettes.

7. Suppose that you are charged with creating a distribution server. Which two subdirectories do you need to XCOPY from the NT installation CD to the distribution server?

   B. i386

   D. DRVLIB

   Answer: B, D–The two directories that should be copied to the distribution server are the i386 and DRVLIB directories.

8. Which of the following parameters should be configured for the IPX/SPX protocol?

   A. Frame type

   C. Network number

   Answer: A, C–The frame type defines how packets are formed–what headers will be included and in what order they will appear in each packet. The network number identifies the network segment.

9. When you install a network interface card, if you are using a 16-bit AT bus slot, what must the interrupt setting on the card be?

   A. Unique

   Answer: A–If you are using a 16-bit AT bus slot, interrupts must be unique.

10. Which types of licenses will License Manager track?

    A. NT Server client access licenses

    Answer: A–License Manager will track NT client access licenses. It does not track application licenses at this time.

11. Configuring a modem in NT can be done through:

    A. Control Panel

    Answer: A–Modem configuration can be done by using the Modems control panel.

12. Which of the following items are true for a volume set?

A. Adds together multiple sections of free space.

B. Data are written to each partition until that partition is full before moving to the next partition.

Answer: A, B–Answer C describes the process used by a stripe set. Neither a volume set nor a stripe set can hold NT's system or boot partition.

13. The basic Microsoft understanding of groups is as follows:

B. Global groups should be placed in local groups.

Answer: B–Microsoft recommends that you place all users in global groups and make global groups members of local groups.

14. Suppose that your boss is a control freak. He wants to make sure that each NT workstation has exactly the same system policies. Each workstation is attached to the network, and the users must always log onto the domain before starting work. How can you keep your boss happy?

D. Create a system policy file that will affect all end users and copy it to the NETLOGON folder of the PDC.

Answer: D–Create a system policy file that will affect all end users and copy it to the NETLOGON folder of the primary domain controller.

15. After you created a system policy and stored it in the NETLOGON directory so that people can access it, you find that the policy is virtually ignored by several systems on your network. What is a possible cause?

A. The computers may have a local policy that conflicts with the system policy.

Answer: A–If there is a conflict between a local policy and the system policy, the local policy takes precedence. Answer D is never an option, is it?

16. Given the default permissions assigned to groups, which groups would you need to belong in to create a share?

A. Administrators

Answer: A–Administrators can create shares.

17. Suppose that a user is a member of three groups–Administrators, MIS, and Apps_Acctg. There is a share created called Accounting. The Administrators group has Full Control permissions to the Accounting share. The MIS group has been assigned No Access permissions, and the Apps_Acctg group has been given the Change permission. What can the user do with the share?

    C. The user can attach to the share, but cannot see or do anything. This is a result of the No Access permission given to the MIS group.

    Answer: C–In the Microsoft security model, all bets are off when the No Access permission is granted. If you are given No Access permission because of your membership in any group or by an explicit assignment to your user account, you have no access to the share.

18. Which of the following items is loaded on client computers to allow direct access to Novell NetWare servers?

    A. CSNW (Client Service for NetWare)

    E. NWLink IPX/SPX Compatible Transport

    Answer: A, E–To allow a client to access a NetWare server directly, you must load both the appropriate protocol (NWLink) and a NetWare redirector (CSNW).

19. What is multilink?

    C. The ability to use more than one communication channel for the same connection

    Answer: C

20. Which of the Performance Monitor views allows you to save data for later analysis?

    C. Log

    Answer: C

21. On a file and print server, which of the four main components is most likely to be the bottleneck?

    A. Memory

Answer: A–Memory is used to cache users' data requests. If not enough memory is available, the system will spend too much time accessing its hard drives.

22. On an application server, which of the four main components is most likely to be the bottleneck?

B. Processor

Answer: B–Since most of the actual processing of data occurs at the server, the processor becomes a critical component.

23. What are the four phases of an NT boot (in the correct order)?

A. Initial, Boot loader, Kernel, Logon

Answer: A

24. A user is given the chance to use the last known good configuration in which phase of the NT startup?

B. Boot loader

Answer: B

25. Which of the five main registry subtrees holds file association information?

B. HKEY_CLASSES_ROOT

Answer: B

26. Suppose that a user has a big report due in the morning. They are trying to print that report to an HP printer that has an onboard network interface card using the DLC protocol. DLC is currently installed and working on their computer. Even after the user resets the printer, they still cannot print to it. What is the most likely cause of the problem?

C. Somewhere on the network, there is another computer hooked to the printer using DLC in continuous-connection mode.

Answer: C–If DLC is being used by another computer on the network in continuous-connection mode, no other system can connect to the printer.

27. All else has failed—it is time to read the log. Where are entries made for RAS logging?

    C. WINNT\System32\RAS\DEVICE.LOG

    Answer: C—The RAS log is kept in the WINNT\System32\RAS\DEVICE.LOG file.

28. How do you view the RAS log?

    A. Use Event Viewer

    Answer: A—The RAS log is viewed through the Event Viewer.

29. Which of the following items accepts and handles network requests that use UNC names?

    A. MUP

    Answer: A—MUP stands for multiple UNC provider.

30. Which of the following items accepts and handles requests not formatted using a UNC name?

    B. MPR

    Answer: B—MPR stands for multiple provider router.

Part III: NT Workstation 4

1. What is an unattended answer file used for during automated installations?

    B. It answers some or all user-supplied information during an NT Workstation setup.

    Answer: B—The unattended answer file provides some or all of the user-supplied information during a Windows NT Workstation setup.

2. What is the function of the SYSDIFF utility during an automated installation?

    C. It installs and configures software application suites.

    Answer: C—It helps to install and configure software application suites by taking a snapshot of the system before and after installation. It then creates a different file to use for the next workstation installation.

3. Which of the following file systems offer local file and directory level security?

   A. NTFS

   Answer: A–While network access to any of these file systems can be secured, only NTFS offers security against an individual with direct access to the computer.

4. Workstation performance and network acccss sccm to be slow. What is one way of improving performance?

   C. Change the protocol binding order on the workstation. Move the most widely used protocols to the top.

   Answer: C–The client controls the protocol selection. Moving the most widely used protocol to the top ensures that it is the first used.

5. You are installing NT Workstation on a computer that is currently configured to run NT 3.51. The workstation makes use of the High Performance File System (HPFS). How can you complete the installation?

   B. Convert the HPFS file system to NTFS before the upgrade.

   Answer: B–NT 4 does not support HPFS. You would have to convert HPFS to NTFS before the upgrade.

6. Which of the following methods can be used to delete an NTFS system partition?

   A. FDISK

   B. The OS/2 boot disks

   C. The NT boot disks

   Answer: A, B, C–The disk administration tool can remove any partition except the system/boot partitions.

7. Which of the following are recommendations for optimizing the virtual memory system?

   B. Do not place your paging file on the same disk as your operating system files.

C. Split the paging file across multiple hard drives.

Answer: B, C–Remember, you should split the workload across disks to optimize performance.

8. Which GUI-based utility can you use to copy the \i386 and the \DRVLIB folders to the distribution server?

D. Microsoft NT Explorer

Answer: D–Microsoft NT Explorer. XCOPY is not a GUI-based utility.

9. Which of the following tools is used to upgrade from Windows 95 to Windows NT 4.0?

D. There is no upgrade path from Windows 95 to Windows NT.

Answer: D–Because the registries are different, there is no upgrade path.

10. Bobbi has an account created on an NT Workstation that is a part of a network that has two separate domains. When the user account is created on the computer, how many domain user accounts are created?

A. None

Answer: A–Creating a user account on a computer does not necessarily mean that a user account has been created for the domain.

11. Your boss is a control freak. She wants to make sure that each NT Workstation has exactly the same system policies. Each workstation is attached to the network and the users must always log on to the domain before starting work. How can you keep your boss happy?

D. Create a system policy file that will affect all end users and copy it to the NETLOGON folder of the PDC.

Answer: D–Create a system policy file that will affect all end users and copy it to the NETLOGON folder of the Primary Domain Controller.

12. Given the default permissions assigned to groups, which groups would you need to belong to in order to create a share?

A. Administrators

D. Power Users

Answer: A, D–Administrators and Power Users can create shares.

13. Denise is a member of three groups: Administrators, MIS, and Apps_Acctg. There is a share created called ACCOUNTING. The Administrators group has full control permissions to the Accounting share, the MIS group has been assigned No Access permissions, and the Apps_Acctg Group has been given the Change permission. What can Denise do with the share?

    C. Denise can attach to the share but cannot see or do anything. This is a result of the No Access permission given to the MIS group.

    Answer: C–In the Microsoft security model, all bets are off when the No Access permission is granted. If you are given No Access permission from membership in any group, or by an explicit assignment to your user account, you have no access to the share.

14. Jack just started to work for your firm today as a temporary programmer. When you set up his account you made him a member of the following groups, each with permissions given to the share \NewApps: Everyone - List, Users - List, Developers - Full Control, and Temps - No Access. What will Jack's rights be to the \NewApps share?

    C. No Access

    Answer: C–No Access. When No Access has been granted to any group that the user is a member of, the user will have No Access to a resource.

15. The Windows NT Workstation that you are configuring contains a shared folder that resides on an NTFS partition. How is access to the folder determined?

    B. A user accessing the folder remotely has the same or more restrictive access permissions than if he were a local user.

Answer: B–The user accessing the system remotely will have the same or *more* restrictive rights than the user accessing the system locally.

16. The chief executive officer of your company comes to you and tells you that she has a problem. It seems that she and all the executive vice presidents print to the same printer, and quite frankly she is tired of waiting for their stuff to print. How can you handle this situation?

A. Create two printers printing to the same print device. Call the first one Boss and the second one NotBoss. Set the priority on Boss to 99 and the priority to NotBoss to 1. Connect the CEO to Boss and everyone else to NotBoss.

Answer: A–With a priority of 99, the Boss printer will take control of the print device.

17. Which of the following describe ways to add a computer account to the domain SAM for an NT Workstation computer?

A. Use Server Manager before installing the Workstation.

D. Choose the option to add the computer to the domain during the installation and provide an account/password for a domain administrator.

Answer: A, D–On the exam, Microsoft will often give an obscure method of accomplishing a task in the hope that you won't know it. It's best to know a couple of ways to accomplish anything.

18. Client Service for NetWare should be loaded on which of the following computers?

B. Any NT client that will need to connect directly to a NetWare server

Answer: B–Connecting to a Netware server is a common task and is heavily tested. You need to know how to configure for this connectivity.

19. Which of the following parameters must be configured on each TCP/IP client in a routed network?

A. IP address

C. Subnet mask

D. Default Gateway

Answer: A, C, D–DNS is an add-on service, not a mandatory component of a TCP/IP network.

20. What is multilink?

C. The ability to use more than one communication channel for the same connection

Answer: C–Multilink is the ability to use more than one communication channel for the same connection.

21. PWS provides which of the following services?

A. WWW

C. FTP

E. Gopher

Answer: A, C, E–WINS is an add-on service related to address resolution, not a function of PWS.

22. Windows NT Workstation assigns how much address space to each application?

D. 2GB

Answer: D–Each application receives 2GB of address space.

23. You are running a Windows 3.1 application that is performing slowly. How can you increase performance?

C. The next time you start the application, use the Start command with the /HIGH option.

Answer: C–You can run a Windows 16-bit application from the command line using the Start command and the /HIGH option. This runs the application at High Priority, giving it a larger percentage of the processor time.

24. Which of the following memory counters represents the number of pages that were not in RAM when requested?

A. Pages/Sec

Answer: A–Pages/Sec is one of the more useful memory-related counters, and is tested heavily.

25. Which of the following would be an appropriate fix for a system in which the network is the bottleneck?

    A. Add another NIC card to segment your LAN.

    B. Upgrade the NIC card to a faster type.

    C. Upgrade the bridges, routers, and other network devices involved in communication.

    Answer: A, B, C–Adding a processor probably wouldn't do much in this scenario—the problem (as described) is getting the packets to the processor, not processing them.

26. The Current configuration becomes the Last Known Good configuration at which point in the boot process?

    B. After a user successfully logs on

    Answer: B–An NT boot is considered successful when a user logs on at that computer. At that point, the current configuration is considered to be valid so it is written to the Last Known Good configuration.

27. Which of the following actions should you take if you encounter a media error when installing NT?

    A. Try another NT CD-ROM.

    B. Try another method of installation: across the network, copy the i386 to the local drive first, etc.

    D. Clean your CD-ROM drive.

    Answer: A, B, D–Although answer C might seem like the easiest method in the short term, it is not a Microsoft-recommended solution.

28. What permissions can be granted to a folder on a FAT partition?

    D. Folders on FAT permissions cannot receive permissions.

    Answer: D–The FAT file system does not have the ability to accept permissions. Only folders on an NTFS partition can have permissions.

29. Which of the following are methods used to back up the registry?

B. Use the Save Registry option in the NT backup utility.

C. Use REGBACK.EXE from a command prompt.

D. Update your Emergency Repair Disk.

Answer: B, C, D–Answer A is not complete enough to accept: The software must be Windows NT 4–certified.

30. In the driver information section of a stop screen, which of the following are included in the data shown?

B. Preferred load address

C. Creation date

D. Name of the driver

Answer: B, C, D–The driver information section shows information about drivers loaded–not the hardware they might control.

Part IV: NT Server in the Enterprise

1. If users in Domain 1 need access to resources in Domain 2, which of the following trust relationships should be created?

B. Domain 2 should trust Domain 1.

Answer: B–Trusts always refer to the users. Domain 2 should trust Domain 1's authentication of users.

2. When a disk fails in a stripe set with parity, you can expect which of the following things?

B. Users can continue to access the data stored on the stripe set with parity.

D. Performance will degrade.

Answer: B, D–The whole point of a stripe set with parity is to provide fault tolerance. If a disk fails, the system can re-create the data on the fly from the parity information. However, this will probably affect performance since the information must be recreated for each data access.

3. Which of the following protocols must be used to communicate with a Novell NetWare server?

   B. NWLink IPX/SPX Compatible Transport

   Answer: B

4. DHCP is used to perform which of the following tasks?

   A. Assign IP addresses to clients

   Answer: A

5. If you are placing domain controllers to facilitate the logon process, which of the following statements would be correct?

   B. Place domain controllers near the users that will need them.

   Answer: B–Users must access a domain controller each time they log onto the network. If all domain controllers are across a WAN link (from the users), authentication traffic will have to cross that WAN link every time a user logs on.

6. Which of the following items describes the purpose of a subnet mask?

   C. To define which portion of the IP address represents a network and which represents a host

   Answer: C–The subnet mask defines the number of bits that represent the network ID portion of an IP address.

7. Which of the following parameters should be configured for the IPX/SPX protocol?

   A. Frame type

   C. Network number

   Answer: A, C–The frame type defines how packets are formed–what headers will be included and in what order they will appear in each packet. The network number identifies the network segment.

8. The types of browser computers include:

   A. Domain master browser

   B. Backup browser

C. Potential browser

Answer: A, B, C–Computers can be a domain master browser, backup browser, or potential browser.

9. How many partitions can exist on a hard disk?

C. 4

Answer: C–Each hard drive can have a maximum of four partitions, one of which can be an extended partition.

10. Which of the following ARC paths would point to the second partition of drive 1 in the question above? (Assuming IDE disks.)

A. multi(0)disk(0)rdisk(2)partition(2)

Answer: A–Each component of the ARC path represents a piece of the path to a partition. If this is confusing, review the material for this objective.

11. In the world of NT, what is an HP Laserjet 5P?

B. A print device

Answer: B–When taking a Microsoft exam, read each question carefully. In printing, an HP Laserjet 5P is a print device. A printer is a software tool that operates at the client or workstation.

12. You notice that the NT workstation you are using communicates slowly on the network. What can you do to speed up communications?

C. Change the binding order of the protocols

Answer: C–Changing the binding order at the workstation may affect the speed of communications on the network. NT workstation uses the different protocols in the order they were bound.

13. Which of the following statements is true?

C. Local groups can contain members from multiple domains.

Answer: C–Global groups can contain only members from their own domains. Local groups can contain global groups from different domains; therefore, local groups can contain members from different domains.

14. How do you change a user profile to a mandatory user profile?

B. Change the extension in the NTUSER.DAT file to NTUSER.MAN.

Answer: B–If you change the extension in the NETUSER .DAT file to .MAN, it makes the user profile a mandatory user profile.

15. Remote administration is accomplished by:

D. Using a workstation running Windows NT Workstation

Answer: D–Remote administration can be accomplished from either a properly configured workstation running Windows 95 or a Windows NT workstation.

16. Given the default permissions assigned to groups, which groups would you need to belong in to create a share?

A. Administrators

Answer: A–Administrators can create shares.

17. Which of the following features are benefits of GSNW?

A. Only the server needs to load NWLink.

B. NetWare resources look like NT shares to your clients.

Answer: A, B–The server providing the GSNW service is the only NT computer that must communicate directly with the Novell environment. Thus, it is the only computer that must load NWLink. Since all NetWare resources look like a shared resource on that NT server, no retraining is necessary for your users.

18. When creating an NT Server-based TCP/IP router, in what order are the following actions taken?

A. Select Enable IP Forwarding.

B. Configure the NIC cards.

C. Install TCP/IP.

D. Install the NIC driver.

E. Assign each NIC an IP address.

Answer: B, D, C, E, A

19. What are the three RAS call-back options?

A. No Call Back

B. Preset

C. Set by User

Answer: A, B, C—The call-back options for RAS are No Call Back, Preset, and Set by User.

20. Which dial-up line protocols does RAS support?

A. PPP

C. SLIP

Answer: A, C—PPP and SLIP are the only two dial-up line protocols listed.

21. If the parameter %User Time is consistently over 80 percent, which of the following subsystems is most likely the bottleneck?

A. Processor

Answer: A—%User Time refers to the amount of processor time being used by user-mode processes.

22. Which of the following tactics would be used to reduce the amount of information presented in a Network Monitor capture?

A. Filtering the data collected by computers involved

B. Filtering the data collected by protocol

C. Filtering the data after the capture has occurred

Answer: A, B, C—The amount of information on a network can be overwhelming. Network Monitor offers many ways to limit the amount of information presented so that you can concentrate on a specific area.

23. On a domain server, which of the four main components is most likely to be the bottleneck?

A. Memory

D. Network

Answer: A, D–The function of a domain server is to handle network management tasks. Also, keep in mind that every connection to a server uses memory.

24. Which of the following actions should you take if you encounter a media error when installing NT?

A. Try another NT CD-ROM.

B. Try another method of installation–across the network, copy the I386 to the local drive first, etc.

Answer: A, B–Although answer C might seem like the easiest method in the short term, it is not a Microsoft-recommended solution.

25. The current configuration becomes the last known good configuration at which point in the boot process?

B. After a user successfully logs on

Answer: B–An NT boot is considered successful when a user logs on at that computer. At that point, the current configuration is considered to be valid, so it is written to the last known good configuration.

26. Which of the five main registry subtrees holds file association information?

B. HKEY_CLASSES_ROOT

Answer: B

27. Your RAS connection is using call back with multilink over a regular phone line. How many numbers can you configure RAS to call back per call?

B. 1

Answer: B–RAS can be configured to call back only one number using call back. Multilink is disabled when call back is set.

28. Which of the following items accepts and handles network requests that use UNC names?

A. MUP

Answer: A–MUP stands for multiple UNC provider.

29. Which of the following items accepts and handles requests not formatted using a UNC name?

    B. MPR

    Answer: B–MPR stands for Multiple Provider Router.

30. Which of the following parameters must you add to the BOOT.INI file to implement a memory dump?

    B. Crashdebug

    Answer: B

Part V: Windows 98

1. You have three workgroups (Sales, Marketing, and Accounting) and two domains (Headquarters and Branch1). All users at your location log in to the Headquarters domain. The users from Sales would like to see the servers in their group when they first open Network Neighborhood. How do you set their computers?

    B. Make their computers members of the Sales workgroup.

    Answer: B–Because the users wish to see the servers in the Sales workgroup, you should set Windows 98 to be in that workgroup. Network Neighborhood will then show all computers in the Sales workgroup at the first (default) level of Network Neighborhood.

2. Your group policies don't seem to be working on certain computers. What is the likely cause?

    D. The group policy support DLL has not been installed on those particular computers.

    Answer: D–Every computer that will use system policies based on group membership needs to have support for group policies installed on it.

3. You have three workgroups (Sales, Marketing, and Accounting) and two domains (Headquarters and Branch1). The Headquarters domain has two servers, HQ1 (the PDC) and HQ2 (the BDC). All users at your location log into the Headquarters

domain. You wish to have your Windows 98 clients switch to user-level security in the Headquarters domain. What do you enter for the security provider?

D. Headquarters

Answer: D–When you switch to user-level security and you are basing it on a domain, you need to enter the domain name, not the server name.

4. The Setup /d option prevents Windows 98 from doing what?

   D. Detecting and using any previous version of Windows

   Answer: D–This feature is used to prevent the setup process from detecting any other version of Windows on the hard disk.

5. Which program can automate the Windows 98 setup process?

   B. Microsoft Batch 98

   Answer: B–NetSetup was the Windows 95 utility; it no longer exists in Windows 98. DBSetup and Information Installer allow you to enhance or augment the setup process. The Microsoft Batch 98 utility allows you to create script information that automatically answers the questions that you are prompted with during the Windows 98 installation process.

6. A user wants to make a newsletter available to the entire company. What service can she install in Windows 98 to make this possible?

   D. PWS

   Answer: D–By installing PWS (Personal Web Server), HTML files can be shared via HTTP on the network, making Windows 98 into an Internet Web Server. IIS (Internet Information Server) and FPNW (File and Print Services for NetWare) only run on Windows NT computers, and installing a browser sets you up as a client, not as a server.

7. A user complains that he can't always connect to a certain NetWare 4.11 server because the connection doesn't always work. The user is using Microsoft Service for NetWare

Directory Services. What could be the problem? (Choose all that apply.)

A. The NetWare server could be out of licenses.

B. The client and the server could be using different frame types.

Answer: A, B–If the NetWare server is low on licenses, the client may be getting connected sometimes and refused other times. If the client is using a different frame type, he may be connecting to the server through a third machine that is acting as a router. If the third machine happens to be turned off, the connection fails. Service for NetWare Directory Services requires the Microsoft Client for NetWare, so it must already be present. MS-NDS also requires IPX/SPX, but we know the protocol is already installed because the connection works sometimes.

8. Your network consists of MS-DOS and Windows 3.*x* NetWare clients and NetWare 3.*x* and 4.*x* servers. You want all of the clients to be able to access your computer so that they can look at old company memos. You intend to install the following components: File and Printer Sharing for NetWare Networks, Service for NetWare Directory Services, and IPX/SPX. Will this installation fulfill the requirements?

B. Yes, but only if you enable SAP advertising.

Answer: B–You need to enable SAP advertising so that older (non-windows) NetWare clients can see your computer as a server.

9. You have a network across five routers that consists of NetWare and Windows NT servers. You also have HP printers with Jet-Direct cards in them that you want the clients to directly access. You want your clients to be able to access the Internet. Which protocol(s) should you install? (Choose all that apply.)

A. DLC

B. TCP/IP

C. IPX/SPX

Answer: A, B, and C–You need DLC to get to the JetDirect printers, TCP/IP to get to the Internet, and IPX/SPX to get to the NetWare servers. The Windows NT computers are not running NetBEUI because they wouldn't be able to see each other across the routers; they must be running either TCP/IP or IPX/SPX.

10. Some of your users complain that they can connect to some servers but not others. You find that the affected users can connect to servers in their department but not to those in other departments. You are using TCP/IP. What parameter is probably set up incorrectly?

B. Default gateway

Answer: B– The default gateway tells the computer how to access remote networks. With a bad gateway address, a computer can still contact other computers in its subnetwork, but doesn't know how to get packets out to the rest of the network.

11. If you can connect to a Unix HTTP server by address, but not by name, which software program is probably at fault?

B. DNS

Answer: B–DNS (Domain Name Service) is the service that resolves the friendly name of a computer with an IP address so the connection can be made.

12. A user complains that her print jobs come out at the wrong printer if she forgets to change the printer before she prints a job. What can you do to fix the problem?

C. Change the default printer to the one she prints to most often.

Answer: C–Each user should have the printer that they print to most often set as their default printer.

13. Sue is using default security settings on Windows 98 and is sharing office memos. She wants to be certain that the sales team can read the memos, but only the sales manager can make new memos. How can she do this?

C. Share the folder as Depends On Password. Give the appropriate password to the appropriate group or user.

Answer: C–Sue can make the shared folder Depends On Password, and give the Read-Only password to the sales group and the Full control password to the sales manager.

14. Where can you start the Administer program so that you can administer the files and folders of a remote Windows 98 computer?

B. Network Neighborhood ➢ Computer ➢ Properties ➢ Tools

Answer: B–The Tools tab of the target computer's Properties dialog box allows you to launch Net Watcher, Remote System Monitor, and Administer.

15. Your Windows NT users are OK, but your Windows 98 users complain that it takes a long time to log in. What can you do to help speed the logon process?

B. Enable load balancing for the system policy.

Answer: B–By enabling load balancing for the system policy file, the policy file can be loaded from the BDCs as well as the PDC. Answers A and C will probably make things slower, if anything, and there is no load balancing for roaming user profiles.

16. Which program is used to make partitions?

D. Fdisk

Answer: D–Fdisk is used to create partitions.

17. A user just bought a new computer with an 8GB hard drive. Her hard drive has been split into four partitions. How can you convert it into one big partition?

D. Use Fdisk to delete all the partitions. Then create one large FAT32 partition and reformat it.

Answer: D–There is no Merge function in either Fdisk or the FAT32 conversion program. You will have to delete all of the partitions, create one large one, and then reformat that partition.

18. You want to build a profile for a user who has two modems. Sometimes they only have a single phone line to dial out. How would you set the profile for the second modem so that the second modem is not used when the single modem profile is selected?

   A. Disabled

   Answer: A–You activate hardware profiles by disabling various device drivers, not by changing or deleting drivers.

19. You have a manager who uses a laptop at work and at home. She has a docking station at work with a network card but uses an external modem at home to dial in to the network. How would you set up the laptop so that she can use both configurations easily?

   D. Create two hardware profiles. Disable the network card for the home profile and disable the modem in the work profile.

   Answer: D–When choosing between hardware configurations, you need to create a hardware profile, not a user profile. You don't delete drivers in a profile, you just disable them. In this particular case, you would want to disable the network card driver at home and disable the modem at work to match the hardware configuration at each location.

20. Users are complaining that they can't remember all of their passwords and keep them in sync. What tool can they use to change all their Windows passwords at once?

   A. Control Panel ➢ Passwords

   Answer: A–You can change your password for Windows 98, as well as Windows NT and your screen saver, by using the Passwords applet, not the Network applet. There is no such program as System Tools ➢ Passwords or Client Utilities.

21. You have three NetWare servers in your company. The servers are called FS_Sales, FS_Mrktg, and FS_Acct for the sales, marketing, and accounting departments, respectively. What parameter should you set on your Windows 98 computers to make sure everyone is logging in to their appropriate server?

   D. Preferred server

Answer: D–The preferred server setting is used to tell Windows 98 which server to connect to during bootup.

22. You wish to dial in to your computer at work so you can copy some files when you are at home. How do you get Windows 98 to act as a dial-up server?

    B. Install the service from Add/Remove Programs.

    Answer: B–Windows 98 comes with the dial-up server software, but you may have to install it using the Add/Remove Programs applet.

23. You have a proxy server set up for your Internet connections. You have an intranet Web server called INSRV1 that has a DNS name of `www.insrv1.com` and is at `131.145.3.200`. What can you enter in the exclusion list so that the proxy server will not be used for the intranet Web server? (Choose all that apply.)

    A. `131.145.3.200`

    B. `www.insrv1.*`

    C. `insrv1`

    D. Select "Bypass proxy server for local (intranet) Web sites."

    Answer: A, B, C, and D–You can specify that Web sites be directly accessed (and avoid going through the proxy server) by specifying their TCP/IP address, their name, or their DNS name. You can also select to have the proxy server bypassed for intranet Web sites.

24. You have been using the Remote Administration tool on your Windows 98 machine to administer other network client PCs. You have just added an additional ten PCs to the network. You have enabled File and Printer Sharing on these new PCs and are sharing various folders and printers. You have access to these shares from all of the computers on the network, but when you attempt to remotely administer the new PCs, you find that you cannot. What else do you need to do to enable remote administration of these ten new client PCs?

    C. Enable remote administration from the Passwords applet of the Control Panel.

Answer: C–You enable and set the security for remote administration from the Remote Administration tab of the Passwords applet in Control Panel. There is no Remote Administration applet. The Net Watcher program only needs to be installed on the administrating computer. You can already see the new computers in the network, so adding a new protocol is not necessary.

25. You are satisfied with the way your current applications are loading, but you are about to install a new, extremely large application. You want to prepare your drive so that the new application loads as quickly as possible. What is the fastest way to prepare your drive for the new application?

D. Run Disk Defragmenter with the Defragment Free Space Only option.

Answer: D–You can quickly prepare for new installations by running Disk Defragmenter and choosing the Defragment Free Space Only option.

26. You are having problems with some of your real-mode device drivers. To troubleshoot the problem, you decide to use the System Configuration utility to view your current settings and make changes to them. You begin by using the System Configuration utility to back up your current settings. You then make incremental changes and reboot until you find the problem. How would you rate this solution?

A. This is an excellent solution and appears to work.

Answer: A–This is an excellent solution and will work. This is exactly what the System Configuration utility was intended to do. We strongly recommend that you use the utility's backup option before you begin making changes to the files. If the changes do not work or if they make your system unstable, you can choose the restore option from the utility to restore your backup.

27. A user calls and says that when she booted her Windows 98 computer, she got an error message about her IP address, but she just clicked OK and continued. Now she can't see any servers. What program can the user run to find and reset her current TCP/IP address?

B. WINIPCFG.EXE

Answer: B–IPConfig is used in Windows NT to view TCP/IP configuration information. Ping is used to check if another host is accessible across the network. Logon is used to log on to a NetWare machine.

28. Your printer is sending you a message that it is low on toner. You have printed the first 60 pages of a 200-page document and don't want to rerun the entire print job. You decide to cancel the print job and then resubmit the print job from your application, beginning with page 60. How would you rate this solution?

C. This is a poor solution, but appears to work.

Answer: C–This solution will probably work. However, canceling the print job after 60 pages have already printed will most likely print any additional pages that had already been submitted to the printer. Therefore, you will print duplicate pages. A better solution would be to pause the printing process from the printer's print queue, add toner, and then resume that print job.

29. Your Windows 98 machine seems to keep corrupting your files. You have run the Disk Defragmenter program and everything seems to be working properly. Whenever you run your ScanDisk program, it almost always finds lost clusters and crosslinked files. You decide that you need to check your hard drive more closely. What should you do?

C. Run ScanDisk with the Thorough test option enabled.

Answer: C–Running ScanDisk with the Thorough test option will check the physical media for any damage. Disk Defragmenter is used to consolidate free space and resequence your files. The Disk-Fix tool is an outdated DOS-based tool.

30. Your Windows 98 computer is configured with TCP/IP. You are getting your TCP/IP configuration from a DHCP server located on a Windows NT server. You have logged in successfully and can see other computers on the network. You can see a shared printer on another Windows 98 machine, however, you get error messages whenever you attempt to print. Which of the following would you check? (Choose all that apply.)

C. Verify that thc printer is on and plugged in properly.

D. Verify that your print drivers are not corrupted for that particular printer.

Answer: C, D–You know that your TCP/IP configurations are correct because you can access other computers on the network and you can view the computer and printer in question on the Desktop. You know you have permissions to use the printer–otherwise you would have been given an access denied dialog box. At this point you could check to see that the printer is attached and switched on. If that isn't the source of the problem, you may have a faulty or corrupted print driver for that printer.

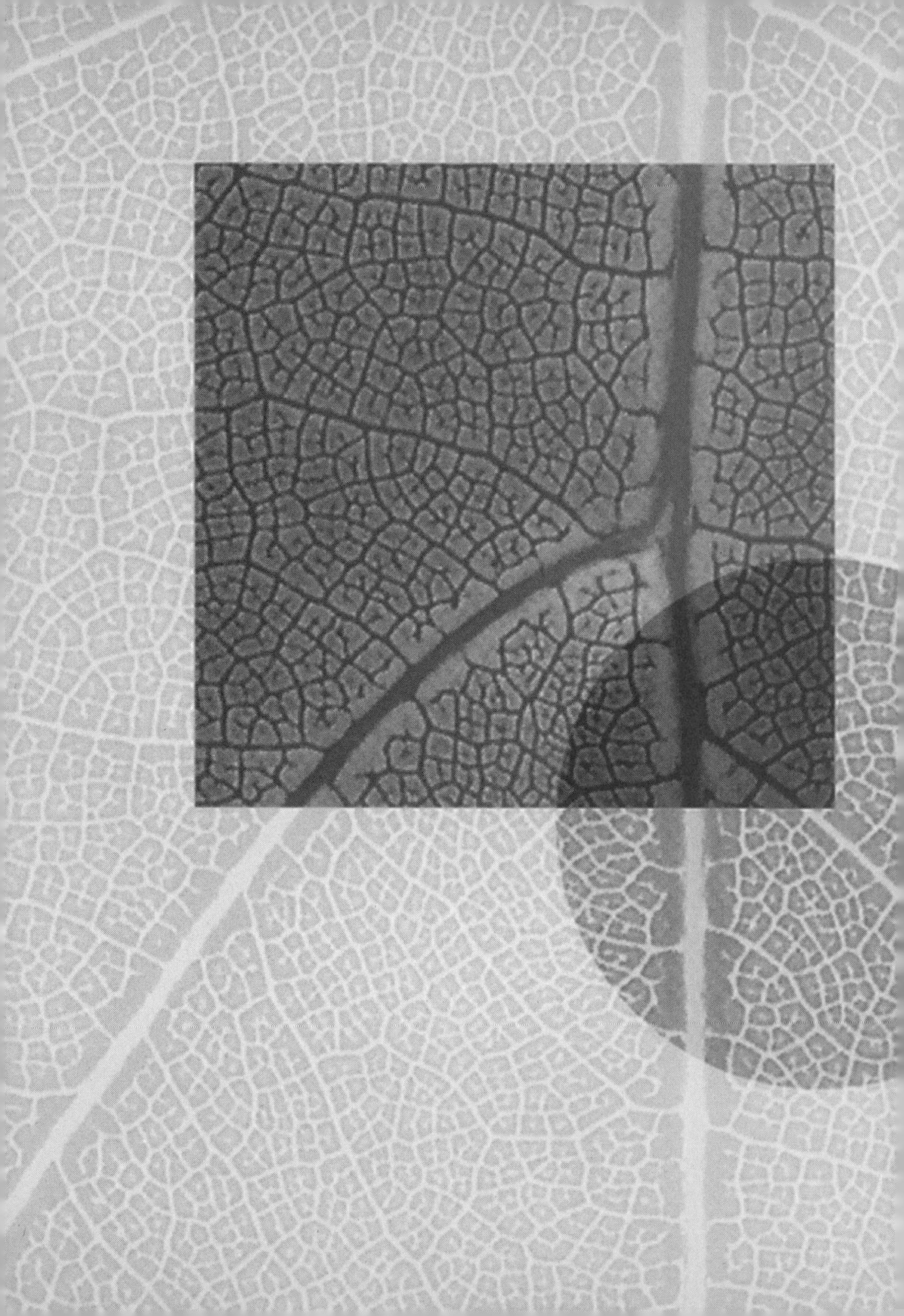

Appendix B

Glossary

\DRVLIB folder

A folder on the NT installation CD-ROM in which drivers are located. This is an optional folder that can be XCOPIED to the distribution server.

\i386 folder

A folder on the NT installation CD-ROM in which WINNT.EXE can be found. This should be XCOPIED to the distribution server.

\WINNT

Default root folder for the installation of Windows NT 4.

100VG-AnyLAN

A network standard that provides speeds up to 100Mbps and uses demand priority media access instead of CSMA/CD.

10Base2

A standard for transmitting Ethernet over Thinnet (RG-58) cable.

10Base5

A standard for transmitting Ethernet over Thicknet (1/2 inch round, 50-ohm coaxial) cable.

10BaseFL

A standard for transmitting Ethernet over fiber-optic cable.

10BaseT

A standard for transmitting Ethernet over twisted-pair cable.

5-4-3 rule

A rule that states that a network using coax cable can have a maximum of five cable segments with four repeaters where only three segments can be populated with nodes (computers or other devices).

Access control list (ACL)

Hard-coded list of users and groups with permissions to various hidden shares. Also, a list of users and groups that have been provided permissions or rights to a resource.

Access permissions

Network security model in which rights to access network resources are determined on the basis of security policies stored in a user-access database on a server.

Access Through Shares (ATS) permissions

Permissions granted at the share point, at the folder level.

Account disabled

Temporarily closing a user account.

Account policy

A Windows NT policy that establishes password security features.

Account synchronization

The process of the PDC updating the copy of the SAM database on a BDC.

Active hub

A central hub that regenerates as it retransmits messages.

Active partition

A partition on the drive that will be used to load the operating system.

Add and Read

Directory-level permission that allows the user to add information to a directory and see information already stored in the directory.

Add

Directory-level permission that allows the user to add information to the directory. With just the Add permission, the user cannot read any information from the directory or even see other files stored in the directory.

Address resolution

The act of resolving an IP address into the MAC (media access control) address for a node.

Admin$

This is a special share that points to the root of the Windows 98 installation. Because it ends with a $ (dollar sign), it is a hidden share.

Administrative alerts

Messages generated by the operating system to warn of security and access problems, user session problems, power problems, and printer problems.

Administrator

A default user created on an NT Workstation who has full rights to the workstation, the file system, and the resources.

Administrators

A default group created on an NT Workstation. Members of the Administrators group have full rights to the workstation, the file system, and resources.

AGLP

Accounts go into Global groups, which go into Local groups, which are granted Permissions.

Any-to-any connections

Describes packet-switching networks. Instead of paying for each connection between every two LANs, as with leased lines, a company only pays one fee for one entire network.

AppleTalk

The set of network protocols on which AppleTalk network architecture is based. When you set up Services for Macintosh, it installs the AppleTalk protocol stack on a computer running Windows NT Server so that Macintosh clients can connect to it.

Application server

A server that acts as the back end for a client/server-based application.

ARC path

A path to a particular partition, on a specific disk, on a computer.

Archive bit

Every file and folder has an attribute called the archive bit. The archive bit indicates whether a file or folder has been changed since the last full or incremental backup. When you execute a full or incremental backup, the archive bit is cleared (reset). When a file is modified the archive bit is set, thus allowing files that have been modified since the last full backup to be differentiated from those that have not.

ARP (Address Resolution Protocol)

A TCP/IP protocol that maps an IP address to a physical address.

Asynchronous transfer mode (ATM)

See ATM

Asynchronous transmission

A type of transmission that sends data using flow control rather than a clock to synchronize data between the source and the destination.

ATAPI (AT application programming interface)

This is a subset of the SCSI standard drivers.

ATM (asynchronous transfer mode)

ATM is a technology designed for the high-speed transfer of data, images, video, text, and audio through public networks.

Attachment User Interface (AUI)

Specifies how a transceiver is attached to an Ethernet device.

Attenuation

The degradation or distortion of an electronic signal as it travels from its point of origin.

Auditing

The process of tracking the use of network resources.

AUTOEXEC.NT

Configuration file in a Virtual DOS Machine that corresponds to the AUTOEXEC.BAT file.

Back end

The server component of a client/server system. It provides services to the front end (the client component).

Backup browser

A computer, appointed by the master browser, that holds a copy of the browse list for access by users.

Backup domain controller (BDC)

See BDC.

Backup Operators

A default group created on an NT Workstation. Members of the Backup Operators group have file system rights suspended so they can archive the files.

Bad sectors

These can occur on either a floppy disk or hard drive and prevent programs or data files from working correctly. Bad sectors, or "spots," can sometimes be read, and the data moved to a good spot, but a bad spot can also be completely unrecoverable.

Bad-cluster remapping

A process used by the operating system to mark bad sections on a hard drive so that they are not used to store data.

Bandwidth

The maximum amount of data that a medium can transfer.

Base I/O port

An address that specifies an I/O location through which the computer communicates with the card.

Base memory address

The starting memory address of a location in a computer's memory.

Base Priority

Setting between 0 and 31 to gauge an application's use of processor time.

Baseline

The process of gathering network performance statistics for use in later performance comparisons.

Batch 98

This program allows you to set up INF files for batch installations of Windows 98.

BDC (backup domain controller)

In a Windows NT Server domain, a BDC refers to a computer that receives a copy of the domain's security policy and domain database, and authenticates network logons. It provides a backup in the event that the primary domain controller becomes unavailable.

Beaconing

The process on a Token Ring network by which a device, in the event of a cable fault, determines the state of the network and the location of the fault.

Binding

To link components at different layers of the operating system so that they can communicate. More specifically, to link the NDIS NIC driver to a communication protocol.

Binding Order

A list that is used to determine the order in which protocols will be used in an attempt to communicate.

Bit

Short for binary digit; either 1 or 0 in the binary number system. In processing and storage, a bit is the smallest unit of information handled by a computer. It is represented physically by an element such as a single pulse sent through a circuit or small spot on a magnetic disk capable of storing either a 1 or 0. Eight bits make a byte.

BNC (British Naval Connector)

A connector for coaxial cable that locks when one connector is inserted into another and is rotated 90 degrees.

BNC T connector

A T-shaped coaxial connector that connects two Thinnet Ethernet cables while supplying an additional connector for a network interface card.

BOOTP

A protocol designed to carry client configuration information. It was first developed to be used in the boot process of diskless workstations. It is also used for all DHCP traffic.

Bottleneck

The slowest component in a system. Usually this definition is expanded to mean the slowest piece that is effecting the quality of service.

Bottlenecks

Situations that introduce delays into the flow of network traffic.

Bridge

A network device that filters traffic by using hardware (MAC) addresses and works at the Data Link layer.

Broadband

An analog transmission method in which channels can be used simultaneously.

Broadcast message

When one computer makes an announcement to all other computers on a network.

Broadcast storm

When there are too many broadcast packets on a network, usually caused by a malfunctioning network adapter card.

Brouter

A networking device that acts as a bridge and as a router.

Browser

The software running on the client that interprets HTML code received via the HTTP protocol and shows it as a graphical interface.

Built-in group

Administrative groups created during Windows NT installation. Each built-in group is automatically assigned certain rights that allow the performance of various administrative tasks.

Bus

A network topology in which all computers are connected by a single length of cabling with a terminator at each end.

Cable tester

An instrument used to test a stretch of cable for attenuation, resistance, and other characteristics.

CAL (client access license)

License that allows a workstation to access an NT server.

Call back

A part of RAS security. You can configure the RAS server to return the call of the system needing access.

Capture

The act of collecting packets for analysis.

Carrier Sense Multiple Access with Collision Detection (CSMA/CD)

A type of access control generally used with bus topologies.

Category 1 to 5

The EIA/TIA designations for unshielded twisted- pair cable.

CDFS

CD file system.

Cells

Data blocks used by ATM. Cells are exactly 53 octets long.

Centralized administration

A method for controlling and managing access to network resources from a central point of access and control.

Change

Permission that allows the user to read, execute, write, and delete folders, subfolders, and files at the share level and below.

Change log

A log of the changes made to the domain accounts database. Used to determine which records need to be updated on the BDCs.

Change permissions

An action that allows the user to change permissions to the file for others.

Channel Service Unit/Data Service Unit (CSU/DSU)

A hardware device used to connect a computer network to a digital line used in a WAN environment.

CHAP (challenge handshake authentication protocol)

Password security protocol used by RAS systems to communicate with non-Windows systems.

Circuit switching

A type of data transmission in which a circuit is established between endpoints and data is sent in a stream through a network.

Client

A computer that accesses shared network resources provided by another computer called a server.

Client for Microsoft

Installing the Client for Microsoft allows Windows 98 to be a Microsoft (SMB) client.

Client for NetWare

Installing the Client for NetWare allows Windows 98 to be a NetWare (NCP) client.

Client Services for NetWare (CSNW)

A Microsoft NT Workstation–based solution for connecting an NT client to a Novell NetWare server.

Client/server architecture

Client/server network architecture is designed around the concept of distributed processing in which a task is divided between a back end (server), which stores and distributes data, and a front end (client), which requests specific data from the server.

Client/server

An application process that is divided into two parts—the server code that does the actual request processing and client code that communicates requests to the server.

CMOS

Configuration information stored in a nonvolatile form that is used by the computer at boot.

Coaxial (coax) cable

A network wiring cable that includes RG-58 and RG-62. The 10Base2 system of Ethernet networking uses coaxial cable.

Collision

When two or more network devices transmit at the same time, through the same channel. The two transmitted signals meet and cause data to be destroyed.

Complete trust domain model

An environment where users and resources are defined in multiple domains. Each domain trusts all other domains.

Compression

The compression option of the Backup program allows you to put more data on a tape.

Compression agent

A program that compresses files in the background while Windows 98 is running.

CONFIG.NT

Configuration file in a Virtual DOS Machine that corresponds to the CONFIG.SYS file.

CONFIG.POL

The name of the file that stores system policies for Windows 95 client workstations.

Congestion

A condition in which a network transmission medium is overwhelmed with network traffic, causing network performance to decline.

Connectionless communication

A type of communication link that does not require a session to be established between the sender and the receiver before the sender starts sending packets (called datagrams) to the receiver. This method does not have the reliability of connection-oriented communication but is good for sustained burst transfers.

Connection-oriented communication

A type of communication link that establishes a formal connection between two computers before sending messages and data. It is reliable and assures delivery.

Contention

On a network, competition among stations for the opportunity to use a communications line or network resource.

Counter

Within Performance Monitor, a counter is a specific statistic of an object.

Crash dump

A process in which the contents of memory are dumped into a file for later analysis.

Crosslinked files

This happens when two or more files have become confused as to where their data reside. Each file is stored in clusters on the hard drive. One cluster points to the next cluster until there are enough linked clusters to store the entire file. Occasionally, a cluster from one file will point to clusters owned by another file. This is a crosslinked file. The orphaned clusters are now called lost clusters or allocation units. Both of these can be found with the ScanDisk program.

Crosstalk

When wires are close to each other, the magnetic field that each wire generates can interfere with normal transmission, or create crosstalk.

Custom user security

An option within user-level security that allows you to pick and choose the various permissions that are allowed in a shared folder.

CVF (compressed volume file)

The file that contains all the files resulting from compression.

Data link control (DLC)

See DLC.

Datagram

A term usually used to describe a non-directed packet on the network (broadcasts, acknowledgments, etc.).

Datagram packet-switched network

A type of network on which messages are divided into a stream of separately addressed packets. Each packet is routed independently. The packets are reassembled at the destination address.

DBSET

DBSET.EXE is a Windows 98 utility. It allows you to personalize the setup process by creating a setup database of user-specific information. This tool can also be used to customize Registry files and write environment variables.

Dedicated line

A transmission medium that is used exclusively between two locations. Dedicated lines are also known as leased lines or private lines.

Dedicated server

A computer that functions only as a server at all times. It is not used as a client or workstation.

Default Gateway

The IP address to which communication with remote hosts should be directed. This is also known as the Default Router address.

Default printer

When a printer is set as the default printer, it is automatically chosen for applications to print to. The default printer can be overridden within an application.

Delete

An action of deleting a file.

Demand Paging

The process of moving data from RAM to virtual memory.

Depends On Password share security

An option within share-level security that allows you to make a Read-Only password and a Full control password for your shared folder.

Desktop

The Windows 98 GUI. Documents, folders, and shortcuts can be stored on the desktop.

DHCP (Dynamic Host Configuration Protocol)

This service allows a client to request and receive a TCP/IP address automatically.

DHCP Relay Agent

A device that passes DHCP traffic across a router on behalf of clients.

Dialin Information

A user property that sets guidelines for the way the user will be treated when logging on to a Remote Access Service (RAS) Server.

Dial-Up Networking

Enables you to connect to a server via modems and common phone lines, allowing you to access anything you have rights to.

Dial-up server

A server capable of receiving dial-up connections and routing client requests to the rest of the network.

Differential backup

A backup system that starts with a full backup and is followed with daily backups of the data that have changed since then.

Digital volt meter (DVM)

An electronic measuring device that measures the voltage in a circuit or cable. It can help determine the continuity of a cable and the possibility of a short.

Direct Connected Printer

Printer devices that have onboard network interface cards, connecting the device directly to the network.

Disabling an account

Temporarily suspending access. The account can be reactivated at a later time.

Disk Defragmenter

This Windows 98 application can help files load faster from the hard drive by defragmenting the hard drive.

Disk duplexing

The process includes disk mirroring with the additional feature where each hard drive in the mirror set has its own controller card.

Disk mirroring

The process of providing a complete copy of one hard drive partition on another hard drive partition on another physical hard drive.

Diskless computers

Computers that have neither a floppy disk nor a hard disk. Diskless computers depend on special ROM in order to provide users with an interface through which they can log on to the network.

Distance-vector protocol

In distance-vector routing, each router advertises its presence to other routers on the network, along with the information in its own routing table. Then other routers can update their tables.

Distribution Server

An NT server configured to provide network access to the files normally found on the NT Installation CD-ROM.

DIX (Digital, Intel, and Xerox)

The first Ethernet connector. The connector used with standard Ethernet that often includes a cable running off the main, or backbone, coaxial cable. Also known as an AUI connector.

DLC (Data Link Control)

A protocol that must be used in conjunction with another protocol—TCP/IP, IPX/SPX, or NetBEUI. DLC is used to communicate with IBM mainframe computers and Hewlett-Packard (HP) JetDirect adapters.

DMA (Direct Memory Access)

A method for transferring data from a drive or other peripheral device, such as a network card, directly to the computer's memory, bypassing the CPU.

DNS (domain name system)

Sometimes referred to as the BIND service in BSD UNIX. Offers a static, hierarchical name service for TCP/IP hosts. The network administrator configures the DNS with a list of host names and IP addresses, allowing users of workstations configured to query the DNS to specify remote systems by host names rather than IP addresses. DNS domains should not be confused with Windows NT networking domains.

Domain

A situation in which one or more Windows NT servers are responsible for a central database of usernames and passwords, and authenticate users at logon.

Domain Controller

An NT Server that holds a copy of the domain accounts database. Because it holds the user account database, a domain controller can be used to authenticate users as they log on to the network.

Domain master browser

The PDC of an NT network. It acts as the master browser for its network segment and as a go-between for all master browsers in the domain, building and distributing a domain-wide browse list.

Domain name service (DNS)

A TCP/IP service used to resolve an IP address from a host name.

Domain server

A server that performs network management tasks.

Drivers

Small pieces of code that speak the language of a particular Windows interface and the language of the hardware device. They essentially translate information from Windows into something that hardware can understand.

DriveSpace

A compression administration program. The current version of the compression program that comes with Windows 98 is called Drive-Space 3.

Dual boot

This process allows you to boot Windows 98 or another operating system on the same computer.

Dual-boot system

A computer that is configured to boot into multiple operating systems.

DUMPCHK.EXE

A utility designed to verify the format and contents of a memory dump file.

DUMPEXAM.EXE

A utility designed to analyze a memory dump file and extract any pertinent information into a small text file.

Duplexing

A subset of mirroring in which each disk is attached to a different controller.

Dynamic Host Configuration Protocol (DHCP)

See DHCP.

Dynamic routing

An automated method used by a router to learn the paths of other routers.

EIDE (enhanced integrated device electronics)

Allows for drives of higher capacity. An EIDE paddleboard can handle a maximum of four devices.

Electronic eavesdropping

The ability to pick up signals passing through a medium made possible by its emissions.

Emergency Repair Disk (ERD)

A floppy that contains replacement copies of critical system files. This disk can be used to recover from boot problems caused by the deletion or corruption of these files.

EMI (electromagnetic interference)

A type of interference caused by emissions from external electrical devices, such as electrical motors and transformers.

Encryption

The encoding of messages for security reasons. The process of making information indecipherable to protect it from unauthorized viewing or use. A key is required to decode the information.

Error control

Can be required at connection. The two modems will agree on an error-checking protocol. The agreed-upon protocol will be used to determine whether the information received is the information sent.

Ethernet destination address

The MAC or physical address for which a packet is destined. A packet with the Ethernet destination address set to all *F*s denotes a broadcast packet.

Execute

An action of running or executing a file.

Expiring an account

Used for temporary or seasonal workers. You provide a date for when the account expires.

Extended partition

A type of partition that contains logical partitions. Extended partitions cannot be formatted until logical partitions are created.

FAT (file allocation table)

The original DOS-based format method of saving and accessing disk files. In an NT server, drives under 400MB should be formatted as FAT.

FAT16

The older partition type compatible with all versions of MS-DOS, Windows 3.*x*, Windows 95/98, and Windows NT.

FAT32

An improved version of the FAT file system. Windows NT cannot read FAT32 partitions.

Fault tolerance

When a networked system is designed to survive the failure of one of its components.

Fault-tolerant disk system

A disk system with redundant data storage, which enables it to continue to function in the event of hardware failure.

Fdisk

The MS-DOS–based program that creates and deletes partitions.

FDISK.COM

A DOS and Windows 95 command-line utility used to manage disk partitions.

Fiber Distributed Data Interface (FDDI)

A standard for high-speed fiber-optic networks using Token Ring.

File and print server

A server that provides data storage and print services to the network.

File and Printer Sharing for Microsoft Networks

This service allows you to create shared resources as an SMB server.

File and Printer Sharing for NetWare Networks

This service allows you to create shared resources as an NCP server.

File auditing

Configuring the server to keep track of various actions or events that occur to a given resource.

File permissions

File permissions work only with NTFS volumes and limit access to directories and files.

File server

Offers services that allow network users to share files. File services are the network applications that store, retrieve, and move data.

File system driver

Software designed to provide access to a file system.

Firewall

A device that keeps the public side of the Internet from connecting to the private internal network.

Flow control

How the modem will control the flow of information. Either software or hardware.

Format

The program that formats drives and disks in both MS-DOS and Windows 98. Formatting a drive prepares it for the particular type of operating system (such as Macintosh, MS-DOS–compatibles) that will use the drive or disk.

Fragmentation

Fragmentation happens as files are deleted and their space is used by new files that are scattered throughout the hard drive.

Frame

A package of information transmitted on a network as a single unit. Frame is a term most often used with Ethernet networks; a frame is similar to the packet used in other networks.

Frame Relay technology

Packet-switching network service that uses variable-length packets to provide high-speed data transmission rates.

Frame type

The definition of the industry-standard way to organize data and headers within a packet. On an IPX network, two computers cannot communicate unless they are using the same frame type.

Front end

The client component of a client/server system. A front-end application on a client that works with a back-end database on a server.

FTP (File Transfer Protocol)

Provides quick transfers of files via the Internet.

FTP service

A service that allows file transfers to and from a server.

Full backup

Initiating a full backup means that every file on the computer will get backed up, and every file archive bit will be reset.

Full Control

Permission that gives the user full rights to the share, including the permission to determine ownership.

Full control share security

An option within share-level security that allows you to share a folder so that anyone with the password (if a password was entered) can access it with full permissions.

Full control user security

An option within user-level security that allows you to specify the users and groups that have full permissions to the shared folder.

Gateway

A networking device that translates information between different protocols or different networks.

Gateway Services for NetWare (GSNW)

A Microsoft NT Server–based solution to connecting an NT network to a Novell NetWare network.

Global account

A normal user account in an NT domain. Most network user accounts are global accounts.

Global group

A group that can be used in its own domain's member servers and workstations, and those of trusting domains. In all those places, it can be granted rights and permissions, and can become a member of local groups. However, it can contain only user accounts from its own domain.

Gopher service

A service primarily designed to index files and directories.

Group

In networking, an account containing other accounts that are called members. The permissions and rights granted to a group are also provided to its members.

Group account

Groups gather users into manageable sets for configuration and control of numerous user accounts.

Guest

A default user created on an NT Workstation. The Guest account has no rights to any secured files, folders, or resources. For security purposes, the Guest account may be disabled.

Guests

A default group created on an NT Workstation. Members of the Guests group have the same rights and permissions as does the Guest user.

HAL (hardware abstraction layer)

A set of hardware-specific DLLs that allows the operating system to be independent of the hardware.

Hardware profile

A combination of hardware drivers and settings that can be chosen at bootup.

HCL (hardware-compatibility list)

A list of hardware that has been tested and approved for use with Microsoft Windows NT.

Hierarchical

A structure used to store information. The registry is a hierarchical database made up of keys and subkeys that hold values.

High

Switch used with the Start command to start an application with a Base Priority of 13.

Hive

A part of the registry made up of keys, subkeys, and values. A hive is stored in its own file, \\WINNT\System32\Config.

Hkey_Local_Machine

This is the Registry key that holds the various hardware profiles.

Home Directory

A unique folder for each user, where that user may store data.

Hop

In routing, a server or router is counted as one step along a path that a packet travels from a sending computer to the receiving computer.

Hop count

The number of routers a message must pass through in order to reach its destination.

Host computer

When debugging a fatal error, the machine running the debugging software.

HPFS (High Performance File System)

A file system developed for OS/2.

HTML (Hypertext Markup Language)

The text and codes that browsers interpret to show the graphical interface to WWW servers.

HTTP (Hypertext Transfer Protocol)

Provides data from the server that can be interpreted by a browser into a friendly graphical interface.

Hub

A connectivity component that provides a common connection among computers in a star-configured network. Active hubs require electrical power, but they are able to regenerate and retransmit network data. Passive hubs simply organize the wiring.

I/O port

The base input/output (I/O) port specifies a channel through which information is transferred between your computer's hardware (such as your network card) and the CPU. The port appears to the CPU as an address.

IDE

A hardware disk technology in which the controller hardware is placed on a circuit board attached to the drive itself. IDE devices can be disk drives or CD-ROM drives.

IEEE (Institute of Electrical and Electronics Engineers, Inc.)

An organization of engineering and electronics professionals; noted in networking for developing the IEEE 802.3 standards for the Physical and Data Link layers of LANs.

IEEE 1394

The IEEE 1394 specification is often referred to as FireWire because of its high-bandwidth capabilities.

IEEE Project 802

A networking model developed by the IEEE. Project 802, named for the year and month it began (February 1980), defines LAN standards for the Physical and Data Link layers of the OSI model.

Incremental backup

When you complete an incremental backup only the changed files (those with the archive bit set) get backed up, and the archive bit is reset.

INF Installer

The INF Installer program, INFINST.EXE, allows you to add device drivers, network drivers, and other third-party software to the setup process so that all of the drivers will be installed as though they were part of the Windows 98 Setup program.

Infrared

The portion of the electromagnetic spectrum immediately below visible light. Good for transmitting signals in a short to medium range (up to 40 km) for a point-to-point connection.

Intelligent hub

A hub that provides network management and intelligent path selection in addition to signal regeneration.

International Standards Organization (ISO)

An organization of standard-setting groups from various countries. The ISO works to establish global standards for communications and information exchange.

Internet Explorer

Microsoft's HTML browser.

Internetwork

Two or more independent networks that are connected, yet maintain independent identities, and are joined by interconnectivity devices.

Interrupt

Calls to the CPU for action or attention.

Interval

In Performance Monitor, a setting that determines how often data are updated.

Intranet

An internal network that utilizes the tools and techniques of the Internet to provide services limited to local network users. Most commonly refers to an internal Web or FTP server.

IP (Internet Protocol)

TCP/IP's network protocol, which performs addressing and routing tasks.

IP Address

A 32-bit value used to uniquely identify a device on a TCP/IP network. It is made up of two parts–a network address and a host address.

IPX

Internet Packet eXchange protocol.

IPX/SPX (Internet Packet eXchange/Sequenced Packet eXchange)

A set of protocols developed by Novell, used with NetWare, and supported by Microsoft operating systems. SPX is a guaranteed-delivery, connection-oriented transport protocol. IPX is a fast, connectionless network protocol.

IRQ (interrupt request lines)

Sixteen hardware lines, numbered 0 to 15, over which I/O devices, keyboards, and disk drives can send interrupts to the CPU. The IRQs are built into the hardware, with preassigned priority levels.

ISDN (Integrated Services Digital Network)

A switched digital communications network designed to bring the power of the digital network directly to the desktop.

IUSER_SERVER NAME

A user account created for IIS. Security assigned to this user defines the access allowed to anonymous connections to your Web server.

Key

A subtree that contains per-computer or per-user configuration databases.

LAN drivers

A workstation or server software module that provides an interface between the NIC and the upper-layer protocol software running in the computer.

Licensing based upon simultaneous usage

Software sold under the pretext that only a certain number of users will use the product concurrently.

Link Time Stamp

A driver's creation date and time.

Link-state protocol

Link-state routers broadcast their complete routing tables only at startup and at certain intervals, which reduces the amount of network traffic that can result from a distance-vector router.

List Permission

Directory-level permission that allows the user to see the contents of the directory, even if the user cannot gain access to the directory.

LMHOSTS

A text file, stored on each client, used to store NetBIOS names and their associated IP addresses.

Load balancing

The ability to have Windows 98 load the system policy file not solely from the PDC, but from the BDCs as well. By default, load balancing is *not* enabled for Windows 98 clients.

Local account

A user account provided on a computer for a user who does not have or does not wish to log into a global account.

Local area network (LAN)

A number of computers in close proximity linked together through network media.

Local File and Directory-Level Security

Security that applies to a user logged in at a computer and accessing files stored on that computer.

Local group

A group that can be granted permissions and rights only for its own resources. However, it can contain user accounts and global groups both from its own domain and from trusted domains.

Local printer

A printer that sends the print jobs it receives to disk. It then processes the jobs and forwards them to a printing device.

Local Profile

Information stored on a local computer that reflects how the end user has configured the system.

Log on locally

To access a computer directly rather than remotely across the network.

Logical link control (LLC)

The LLC sublayer is the upper sublayer in the Data Link layer that manages data link communication and defines the use of logical interface points, called service access points (SAPs).

Logical partition

A partition that exists within an extended partition and can be formatted for use.

Logon script

A set of commands run at logon from your initial server that can automate certain tasks such as printer connections or virus scanners.

Logon scripts

Batch files, executables, or another form of command structure attached to a user account to configure the environment after logon.

Lost clusters

These appear when data areas have not been correctly identified as either in use or free. Lost clusters can either be correctly marked as deleted or be recovered as files in case something valuable was in those clusters.

Low

Switch used with the Start command to start an application with a Base Priority of 4.

LPR printer port

A printer port configured to use TCP/IP print properties.

MAC (media access control) address

A unique address that identifies each node, or device, on the network. The network address is generally hardcoded into the network card on both the workstation and server.

Macintosh-accessible volume

Server-based share that is available to users of Apple's Macintosh.

Mandatory Profile

The process of setting a local profile that the end user cannot change.

Master Boot Record (MBR)

A section of the boot device that contains a list of the partitions on the disk and which partition is the active partition.

Master browser

Each workgroup or subnet must have one. Gathers information on services for the domain or subnet, gives the list to the PDC to include in the domain master list, and passes the list to the backup browser.

Member Server

An NT Server computer that does not hold a copy of the domain accounts database.

Memory address

The base memory address defines the address of the location in your computer's memory (RAM) that will be used by the network card to exchange information between your computer and the other computers to which you are connected. This setting is sometimes called the *RAM start address*.

Mesh

A topology with alternative paths used for redundancy.

Microsoft Backup program

A native Windows 98 backup program that can back up your hard disk to tape, to a local file, or to a network drive.

Microsoft Client for NetWare

The client supplied by Microsoft to connect to bindery-compatible NetWare servers.

Microsoft Service for NDS

The client supplied by Microsoft to connect to NDS-compatible NetWare servers.

Migration Tool for NetWare (MTFN)

A utility that migrates users, groups, files, and directories from a NetWare server to an NT server.

Mirroring

A disk configuration in which two disks hold the same data.

Modem

From modulate/demodulate. Computer hardware that will turn a computer's digital signal into an analog signal that can be sent over a phone line. The modem at the receiving end will then turn the analog signal into a digital signal that the computer can understand.

MSAU (Multistation Access Unit/MAU)

A hub-like device used for Token Ring.

MS-CHAP

Microsoft's implementation of CHAP. Default RAS selection. Used to provide secure password authentication between a RAS server and Microsoft Windows 95 or Windows NT clients.

MS-NDS (Microsoft Service for NetWare Directory Services)

Installing MS-NDS allows Windows 98 to be a true NDS client to NetWare 4.*x* and 5.*x* servers.

Multidisplay/multiple monitor support

The ability of Windows 98 to use two or more video cards (or one card with two outputs) to run simultaneously two or more monitors at the same or different resolutions and number of colors.

Multi-homed

A computer with more than one network interface card installed.

Multilink

The ability to use two or more modems so that their bandwidths are aggregated into one connection.

Multiple master domain model

An environment where multiple domains manage only user accounts, with other resource domains defined by departmental or geographic boundaries.

Multiple protocol router (MPR)

A user-mode component designed to route requests to resources that do not adhere to the UNC conventions.

Multiple UNC provider (MUP)

A user-mode component that interprets UNC names, passing them along to the proper redirector.

Multiplexer

A device that multiplexes signals for transmission over a segment and reverses this process for multiplexed signals coming from the segment. Multiplexing is a method that allows several channels to share a single medium segment.

Name registration

An action taken by the client as it joins the network. The NetBIOS client queries the WINS server to determine if its name is unique.

Name resolution

Before two NetBIOS computers can communicate, they must acquire each other's IP addresses. Name resolution is the process of asking a WINS server for the IP address of a particular NetBIOS name.

NCP (NetWare Core Protocol)

The language NetWare clients and servers use to communicate.

NDIS (Network Driver Interface Standard)

A universal specification for both real-mode and protected-mode network drivers.

Net command

A utility designed to allow administrative functions to be performed from a command prompt.

Net Watcher

This utility can be used to monitor your shared resources and list the users connected to them. Net Watcher can also be used to add and remove shared resources, as well as manage the permissions that have been granted on those shared resources.

NetBEUI (NetBIOS Enhanced User Interface)

A protocol developed by IBM for small interoffice networks. NetBEUI has severe limitations because it was designed for up to only 254 nodes and can't be routed.

NetBIOS (Network Basic Input/Output System)

An application program interface (API) that can be used by application programs on a local area network. NetBIOS provides application programs with a uniform set of commands for requesting the lower-level services required to conduct sessions between nodes on a network and transmit information back and forth.

NetBIOS Name

A unique identifier for an NT-based computer on the network. This name is used to direct communication to the correct computer *and* the correct service on that computer.

NETCONFIG.POL

The name of the file that stores system policies for Windows NT Workstations and servers.

NetWare Client32

A protected-mode, NDS client supplied by NetWare.

NetWare Core Protocol (NCP)

The language spoken internally at a NetWare server. Requests made of a NetWare server must be made using this protocol.

NetWare Directory Service (NDS)

Novell's X.500-compliant directory services. Basically, this is a management component of NetWare used to organize network resources.

NetWare server

Windows 98 can participate as a client or server in a NetWare environment. As a server, Windows 98 can access shared NetWare resources, as well as share its own resources with other clients in the NetWare network.

Network

Two or more computers and associated devices that are connected by communications facilities; a group of computers and various devices (such as printers and routers) that are joined together on a common network transmission medium.

Network adapter

Sometimes called Network Interface Card (NIC). It is a peripheral card that plugs into the motherboard of the computer and into a network cable.

Network Client

Software services run at the client workstation to provide communication with a server.

Network connectivity

Linking of segments of a single network.

Network Interface Card (NIC) Driver

Software designed to allow communication between the physical network interface card and the operating system.

Network Monitor

An NT utility used to collect and view packets on the network.

Network Monitoring Agent (NMA)

An NT service that must be installed and running to support network object counters in Performance Monitor and Network Monitor. NMA also sets password controls on which users are allowed to access captured data and data files.

Network Neighborhood

The icon that will first show you the servers and shared resources in your native workgroup or domain before showing you the entire network.

Network Number

A unique identifier for a network segment in an IPX/SPX network.

Network printer

A printer that the computer accesses via the network.

Network Redirector

Software capable of communicating with a specific type of network, that understands the process for accessing network resources.

Network-attached printing device

A physical device that connects parallel or serial printing devices to the network, or a printing device that has an internal NIC.

NetX

A real-mode, bindery client supplied by NetWare.

NFS (Network File System)

NFS is a TCP/IP application protocol that provides file services to Unix environments through the NFS file system.

NIC

Network Interface Card.

No Access

Users can connect to a share, but will not be able to access any resources.

Node

On a LAN, a device that is connected to the network and is capable of communicating with other network devices.

Noise

For electrical environments, noise is defined as a low-voltage, low-current, high-frequency signal that interferes with normal network transmissions, often corrupting data.

Non-Paged Memory

An area of memory that cannot use virtual RAM. Usually used by the operating system.

Normal

Default priority setting of 8.

NT Backup Utility

Utility provided with NT 4.0 that can back up local and remote computers. Backup will back up NTFS and FAT volumes.

NT Explorer

Operating system graphical-based utility that can be used to copy files and subdirectories. If you are using NT Explorer to copy folders and subfolders to a distribution server, change the default settings to allow the utility to show hidden files.

NTCONFIG.POL

The name of the file that stores system policies for Windows NT workstations and servers.

NTFS (NT file system)

NTFS is most efficient in drives greater than 400MB. In addition to other capabilities, NTFS allows for local file system security.

NTHQ (NT hardware qualifier)

Software that checks your hardware to ensure that all components are on the hardware-compatibility list.

NTUSER.DAT

The name of the file stored in the \WINNT\Profile*Username* directory that contains all the settings in the local profile.

NTUSER.MAN

The name of the file stored in the \WINNT\Profile*Username* directory that contains all the settings in the mandatory user profile. When you change the extension of .DAT to .MAN, it turns the profile file into a read-only file.

NWLink (NetWare Link)

Microsoft's implementation of the IPX/SPX protocol. Installed to be compatible with Novell networks. Can be used by RAS servers as a networking protocol.

NWLink IPX/SPX Compatible Transport

A standard network protocol that supports routing and can support NetWare client-server applications, in which NetWare-aware sockets-based applications communicate with IPX\SPX sockets-based applications.

OBDC driver

A set of DLLs that allows a service to access a data source created using another program.

Object

Within Performance Monitor, an object is a major component of the environment.

ODI (Open Driver Interface)

A specification by Novell for real-mode network card drivers.

Offline printing

When a printer is set as offline, print jobs are spooled up to the local hard drive. When the printer is set to online, all spooled jobs are then sent to that printer. This is very useful for laptop computers that may spend some time disconnected from the network.

Open Systems Interconnections (OSI) reference model

A seven-layer architecture that standardizes levels of service and types of interaction for computers exchanging information through a network. It is used to describe the flow of data between the physical connection to the network and the end-user application.

OS/2

Provides support for IBM's OS/2 operating system, in both OS/2 and DOS mode.

Oscilloscope

An electronic device with a CRT used to measure voltage in relationship to time. It is also used with a TDR to determine crimps and sharp bends in cabling, shorts, breaks, and problems with attenuation.

OSPF (Open Shortest Path First)

TCP/IP's link-state routing protocol, which is used to find the best path for a packet to travel through an internetwork.

Packet

The basic division of data sent over a network. Each packet contains a set amount of data, along with a header containing information about the type of packet and the network address to which it is being sent. The size and format of a packet depend on the protocol and frame types used.

Packet switching

A type of data transmission in which data is divided into packets. Each packet are then routed optimally across a network. Packets may or may not arrive in the correct order, but each packet is numbered for proper assembly.

Paged Memory

An area of memory that can be extended using virtual memory space.

PAGEFILE.SYS

A file on a hard disk used as virtual memory by Windows NT.

Paging File

A special file on a PC hard disk. With virtual memory under Windows NT, some of the program code and other information is kept in RAM, while other information is temporarily swapped into virtual memory. When that information is required again, Windows NT pulls it back into RAM and, if necessary, swaps other information to virtual memory. Also called a swap file.

PAP

Password authentication protocol.

Parity

Parity refers to an error-checking mechanism that can recreate missing data.

Partition

A physical section of a hard drive, set aside for the use of an operating system.

Partition Boot Sector (PBS)

A sector of the disk that contains specific boot instructions.

Partitioning the database

Breaking down an existing domain SAM and creating more than one NT domain in a given environment to support organizational boundaries or domain limits.

Passive hub

A central hub that only retransmits a message. Both of the cables from the source and destination computers are considered as one combined cable length.

Pass-through authentication

The process used to authenticate an account from a trusted domain.

Password

Part of the NT security schema to authenticate a user to the Security Account Manager (SAM) database.

PCMCIA (personal computer memory international association)

A set of devices used generally in laptop computers to provide peripheral support. Usually a network card or SCSI adapter.

PDC (primary domain controller)

An NT server that contains the master login accounts database for a domain. It performs login validation for all computers in its domain and synchronizes the account database with any and all BDCs in the domain.

Peer Web Services (PWS)

Web server software designed for small environments.

Peer-to-peer network

A network with no dedicated servers or hierarchy among the computers. Normally, each computer functions as both a client and a server.

Per Server licensing

NT server licensing method. In Per Server licensing, the CALs are assigned to the server. Each server will have a maximum number of connections.

Performance Monitor

A Windows NT utility used for graphing network performance related to a server or particular computer.

Permanent virtual circuit (PVC)

A virtual circuit in a packet-switching network using a permanent connection where devices are always on.

Permission

Windows NT settings you set on a shared resource that determine which users can use the resource and how they can use it.

Permissions

A set of rights granted to users and groups that controls the actions they can take on a file or within a directory.

Ping

Used to verify connectivity to a network host running TCP/IP. For example, you can ping localhost to test if TCP/IP is configured properly on your computer.

Plenum

The area between a drop ceiling and the real one; also any hidden space between walls.

Plenum-rated cable

A cable made from material that will not emit toxic fumes when it burns.

Point-and-click

The configuration mode of using the mouse to select options presented through a visual interface. This visual interface typically consists of checkboxes, option buttons, and/or lists of choices.

Point-and-Print

This feature allows you to install the print drivers on a computer with a shared printer so that when clients connect to the shared printer the drivers are automatically installed. Point-and-Print is automatically supported when a Windows 98 computer shares its printers with another Windows 98 computer.

Point-to-Point Protocol (PPP)

A protocol for direct communication between two nodes over a serial point-to-point link. PPP works with more protocols than SLIP.

Policy

Default settings for a variety of NT objects.

POSIX (Portable Open System Interface)

Standard programming interface that is independent of any operating system.

POSIX.1 compliance

POSIX is a set of specifications concerned with how some Unix programs access files. NT is compliant with the POSIX.1 standards.

POTS

Plain old telephone system.

Power On Self Test (POST)

A process run by the computer in which it determines the amount of memory installed and confirms the existence of required hardware.

Power Users

A default group created on an NT Workstation. Members of the Power Users can create shares to folders and printers.

PPP (Point-to-Point Protocol)

A data-link-layer transport that performs over point-to-point network connections such as serial or modem lines. PPP can negotiate with any transport protocol used by both systems involved in the link.

PPTP/VPN (Point-to-Point Tunneling Protocol/Virtual Private Network)

PPTP is used to make a secured, encrypted connection via the Internet. In other words, with PPTP/VPN enabled, the Internet can function as a WAN link for a secured, virtual private network (VPN) connection.

Preemptive multitasking

Several applications can be open at one time, but the processor will only work with one application at a time.

Preferred load address

The base memory address a driver requests when loaded.

Primary domain controller

See PDC.

Primary network logon

The selection from the list of possible server types that Widows 98 will connect to and log in to initially.

Primary partition

The first partition you create on a hard disk is almost always a primary partition. A primary partition is required to be bootable in DOS and is generally the partitioning scheme for the C: drive.

Print Device

The actual hardware that puts the ink on the paper.

Print driver

A print driver is the software that Windows 98 uses to communicate with a particular printer. Choosing the wrong print driver, or using an out-of-data or corrupted print driver, may cause problems.

Print Pool

A collection of similar printers attached to the same print server. The printers must use the same printer driver. Ideally, the printers will be in the same physical location.

Print Priorities

Providing the scheduling opportunities for one set of print jobs to print routinely before another.

Print server

Manages and controls printing on a network, allowing multiple and simultaneous access to printing facilities.

Print spooler

Temporary holding areas for print jobs. Print spooler files are stored in the \WINNT\System32\Spool\Printers folder.

Print Troubleshooter

The Print Troubleshooter is a Wizard that can be used to suggest different settings to check when troubleshooting printing.

Printer

A software device to which applications send print jobs. A Windows NT printer matches a name with a printer driver, an output port, and various configuration settings.

Printer options

Various printer options like PostScript or Printer Port may be changed to help solve certain printing problems.

Printer pool

A collection of similar printers attached to the same print server. The printers must use the same printer driver.

Printing device

The device that physically produces printed output.

Printing pool

A number of print devices that are connected to the same printer. The printer directs the print job to an available print device in the pool.

Priority

Setting that lets the user determine how much processor time will be allocated to a running application.

Private virtual circuit (PVC)

A logical connection made between two devices across a shared communications path. There are no dedicated physical circuits between the devices, even though they are acting as though there is one.

Profile

Settings that refer to how a user has configured a local computer.

Profile path

This points to the share where the Profile is stored.

Profiles folder

The folder where Windows 98 stores local profiles.

Protected mode

32-bit drivers.

Protocol

A protocol is a language that computers use to communicate with each other. There are three main protocols supported by Microsoft: NetBEUI, IPX/SPX, and TCP/IP.

Protocol analyzer

A device that monitors network activity, providing statistics you can use in determining baseline and optimum performance.

Protocol bindings

When a protocol is connected to a particular card, client, or service, it is considered bound to that item.

Protocol suite

A family of related protocols where higher-level protocols provide application requests, and lower-level protocols provide networking capabilities.

Proxy Server

Microsoft's firewall and WWW filtering and caching application. Proxy Server must be run on a Windows NT computer.

PSTN (Public Switched Telephone Network)

Plain Old Telephone System. The network of phone lines that can be used by Dial-Up Networking and standard modems to make a connection from the client to the server.

Publishing directories

The directories used to hold information that the selected service (WWW, FTP, or Gopher) makes available to connected users.

PWS (Personal Web Server)

Once installed, PWS allows Windows 98 to share HTML files via the HTTP protocol, thus turning it into a WWW server.

Queue

A holding area for print jobs received by a print server but not yet sent to the target printing device.

RAID (Redundant Arrays of Independent Disks)

A system of using several hard disks to allow a computer to recover from the failure of any one disk without losing data.

RAID level 0/stripe set

A disk system that allows a logical drive to span multiple hard drives.

RAID level 0/volume set

A disk system that allows a logical drive to span multiple hard drives.

RAID level 1/disk mirroring

A disk system that has a complete copy of a partition on a separate hard drive.

RAID level 5/disk striping with parity

A disk system that stripes data across multiple drives. In addition, a calculation is performed on each write, which creates parity information that can be used to re-create the data. This information is stored on another drive in the set, which allows the system to continue functioning if one of the drive partitions in the set fails.

RAS (Remote Access Service)

Service run on an NT Server that allows a dialup connection to the server.

RAS permissions

Front-line security to determine whether the user has the right to log onto the RAS server.

Read

Assigns Read and Execute permissions to the share, folders, subfolders, and files. Also an action of reading a file.

Read-Only share security

An option within share-level security that allows you to share a folder so that anyone with the password (if a password was entered) can access it with Read Only permissions.

Read-Only user security

An option within user-level security that allows you to specify the users and groups that have Read-Only permissions to the shared folder.

Real mode

16-bit drivers.

REALTIME

Switch used with Start Command to start an application with a Base Priority of 24.

Redirector

Software loaded onto a workstation that can forward or redirect requests away from the local bus of the computer onto a network. A server then handles these requests. This type of software is often called a *shell*, *requester*, or *client*.

Regenerate

To rebuild data on a replacement disk in a stripe set with parity.

Registry

This is the database that holds all of the settings for hardware, software, and user preferences. The Registry replaces the various INI files under earlier versions of Windows and is contained in two files, USER.DAT and SYSTEM.DAT, located in the Windows folder.

Registry Checker

The common name for both Scan-Reg and ScanRegW.

Registry mode

A way the System Policy Editor can be used to edit the registry of either local computers or other computers in the domain.

Remote Access Service

See RAS.

Remote Administration

There are several utilities built into Windows 98 that can be used to remotely administer other Windows 9*x* computers. This includes the Administer utility, Remote Net Watcher, Remote System Monitor, and Remote Registry Editor.

Remote printer

A printer that does not save to disk the print jobs it receives. Instead, it redirects its jobs directly to a print server.

Remote Registry

This feature allows you to view and edit the Registry on other computers.

Remote Registry Services

This service allows Registry Editor and System Monitor to be used remotely. It is not installed by default.

Repeater

A network connectivity device that boosts network signals to extend the distance they can travel.

ReplicationGovernor

A registry setting that controls the frequency of synchronization and the amount of data transferred.

Replicator

Default group created on an NT Workstation that supports file replication in a domain.

Rights

Define a user's access to a computer or domain and the actions that a user can perform on the computer or domain. User rights permit actions such as logging onto a computer or network, adding or deleting users in a workstation or domain, and so forth.

Ring topology

A network topology in which computers are arranged in a circle and use a token-passing protocol. Data travels around the ring in one direction, with each device on the ring acting as a repeater.

RIP (Router Information Protocol)

A distance-vector routing protocol used to determine the best path for a packet to travel through an internetwork. RIP is used by TCP/IP and SPX/IPX.

RIP for IPX

A protocol used by IPX routers to pass network information.

RJ-45

An eight-wire modular connector used to join a telephone line to a wall plate or some other device. It is similar to an RJ-11 telephone connector but has twice the number of connectors.

Roaming profile

Profile created for a user who accesses more than one computer. The user's look and feel will remain the same, no matter what computer is being accessed.

Routable protocols

Protocols that support internetwork communication.

Router

A networking device that filters traffic according to logical network addresses. It transfers messages to other computers as it uses these network addresses to find the best path. It can translate between different network architectures.

Routing

The process of finding a path between networks.

Routing table

A list of network segments available on your network and the routes to get to them.

SAP (Service Advertising Protocol)

Used by file and print servers on Novell networks to inform computers of services offered.

ScanDisk

This Windows 98 program examines drives for errors and *attempts* to fix damaged files.

ScanReg

This is a real-mode program that will scan the Registry for corruption. If corruption is found, a list of available backups of the Registry will be presented for your use.

ScanRegW

The 32-bit Registry Checker program that runs automatically when Windows 98 boots to check and back up the Registry. ScanRegW can also be run manually at any time.

Scope

A definition of the IP addresses and other configuration parameters that the DHCP server should send to clients as they initialize.

SCSI (Small Computer System Interface)

A type of hardware interface allowing up to 14 devices to be hooked up to a single controller card.

SCSITOOL

A tool provided on the NT Server installation CD-ROM that will return a list of the SCSI hardware in the potential server.

Sector sparing

A fault-tolerant method where data are moved from a bad sector on a hard drive to a good sector, and then the bad sector is never used again.

Security Accounts Manager (SAM)

The database containing information about users, groups, and computers defined in the NT operating system. The SAM used throughout the network is called the domain SAM, while the database contained by individual computers is called the local SAM.

Serial Line Internet Protocol

See SLIP.

Server-based network

A network in which resource security and most other network functions are provided by dedicated servers. Server-based networks have become the standard models for networks serving more than ten users.

Service pack

This is also known as a *patch*. These are generally used to update your

DLL files, replace older drivers in your system, and fix problems in the original application.

Share

To make resources, such as directories and printers, available to others.

Share name

A name that refers to a shared resource on a server. Each shared directory on a server has a share name, used by PC users to refer to the directory. Users of Macintoshes use the name of the Macintosh-accessible volume that corresponds to a directory, which may be the same as the share name.

Share permissions

Permissions to shared resources that only operate at the folder or directory level and work regardless of the file system being used.

Share point

A directory that has been made accessible to users over the network.

Share security

Security that applies to a user accessing files over the network.

Shared adapter memory

Memory on the card that also appears in the computer's main memory space.

Shared directory

A directory to which network users can connect.

Shared folders

Folders that clients can connect to across the network.

Shared network directory

See shared directory.

Shared printers

Printers that clients can connect to across the network.

Shared resource

Any device, data, or program that is used by more than one other device or program. For Windows NT, shared resources refer to any resource that is made available to network users, such as directories, files, printers, and named pipes. Also refers to a resource on a server that is available to network users.

Shared system memory

A portion of the computer's main memory to store and buffer data.

Share-level security

The default sharing model for Windows 98 is similar to that of Windows for Workgroups. Shared resources can be assigned a password, and only those who know the password can access the shared resource.

Shielded twisted-pair (STP)

A type of wiring that includes a pair of conductors inside a metal or foil shield. This type of medium can support faster speeds than non-shielded wiring.

SID (security identifier)

Code generated to identify a specific user or group to the NT security subsystem.

Simple Network Management Protocol

See SNMP.

Single domain model

An environment with only one domain.

Single master domain model

An environment where all user accounts are defined in a single NT domain, with all other resource domains defined by departmental or geographic limits.

SLIP (serial line Internet protocol)

An implementation of Internet protocol (IP) over a serial line. SLIP has been replaced, by and large, by PPP.

Small Computer System Interface

See SCSI.

SMB (server message block)

A block of data containing client/server requests at the higher layers of the OSI model.

SMB (server message block) protocol

The language spoken internally by the NT operating system. There have been several revisions (dialects) of this protocol released. The client and server must agree upon the dialect to be used before communication can occur.

SMTP (Simple Mail Transport Protocol)

An Application layer protocol that supports messaging functions over the Internet.

SNMP (Simple Network Management Protocol)

A TCP/IP protocol for monitoring network devices and servers.

SPID (service profile ID)

ISDN-required configuration information. The ISDN phone number.

Spooling

When a print job is created, it is cached on the local hard drive and eventually fed to the printer. Applications return from printing faster when using print spooling (the default).

Spread-spectrum radio

A form of wireless medium that switches among multiple frequencies.

SPX

Sequenced packet exchange protocol.

SQL Server

The Microsoft SQL Server is a relational database for managing and storing data. It provides distributed client/server RDBMS (relational database management system) components.

Star topology

A network topology in which all the cables run from the computers to a central location, where they are connected by a hub. Signals transmitted by a computer on the star pass through the hub to all computers on the network.

Start menu

The Windows 98 folder analogous to the Program groups of earlier versions of Windows. The Start menu holds subfolders, which hold shortcuts to various applications on the computer.

Static routing

The type of routing where a router is manually configured with all possible routes, including the routes from other routers.

Stop Screen

A term used to refer the data NT displays when it encounters a critical error.

Stripe set

When areas of free space on two or more drives are combined into one logical drive. Data will be written to each disk in turn in 64KB stripes.

Stripe set with parity

A set of three or more disks to which data are written in turn in 64KB stripes. For each stripe, a parity calculation is performed—the results are stored on another disk in the set.

Subnet

A number overlaid on an IP address to indicate the network number and the host number, which are the two parts that make an IP address.

Subnet Mask

A value that defines which portion of the IP address represents the network and which portion represents the host.

Switched Multimegabit Data Services (SMDS)

A telecommunications service that provides connectionless, high-performance, packet-switched data transport.

Switched virtual circuit

A virtual circuit that is established across a packet-switched network for the temporary connection between two devices.

Switching hub

A network device that works at the MAC sublayer, much like a bridge. The first packet destined for a particular address causes a dedicated circuit to be set up through which subsequent packets are routed.

Synchronization

The PDC holds the master copy of the SAM. When changes are made to the database, the process of synchronization updates the copies stored on the BDCs.

Synchronous Optical Network (SONET)

A set of specifications for synchronizing public communications networks and linking them together via high-speed fiber links.

Synchronous transmission

A type of transmission that uses a clock to control the timing of its bits being sent.

SYS.COM

A DOS/Windows 95 command-line utility used to make a disk bootable.

SYSDIFF

A utility found on the Installation CD in the `\support\deptools\i386` directory. This utility can be used to aid in the installation of suites of applications on a workstation.

System files

The files needed to boot the computer. New system files can be put on a floppy or hard disk without having to format the drive with the SYS command, or by choosing Copy System Files Only when formatting the disk.

System Monitor

This utility can be used to monitor various components of Windows 98, including processor usage, swap file size, and memory usage.

System Policy Editor

The NT Server-based utility used to create system policies. Available through Programs ➢ Administrative Tools ➢ System Policy Editor.

System policy file

A file that Windows 98 can look for and implement during the logon process. System policy files are basically modifications to the Registry that cause certain functions to be either ignored (left as is), enabled, or disabled.

System policy files

Another way of controlling the user's work environment or system configuration.

System Policy mode

The mode in which the System Policy Editor can be used to mandate registry settings throughout the domain. Settings changed in the system policy files will override local registry settings.

SYSTEM.DAT

This piece of the Registry holds settings that deal with hardware and core applications, and applies to all users.

Systems Management Server (SMS)

A Microsoft software program that helps manage a network. SMS functions include inventory management and remote monitoring of network clients.

Take Ownership

An action that allows the user to take ownership of a file.

Tape backup unit

See TBU.

Target computer

When debugging a fatal error, the target is the computer that is encountering the error.

TBU (tape backup unit)

A device used to archive data currently stored on a hard disk to a tape. The tape can then be stored away from the computer. This is called off-site storage.

T-carrier

A type of multiplexing, high speed, leased line. T-carrier service levels include T1, T2, T3, and T4. T-carriers offer transmission rates up to 274Mbps.

TCP/IP (Transmission Control Protocol/Internet Protocol)

A set of networking protocols that provides communications across interconnected networks made up of computers with diverse hardware architectures and various operating systems. TCP/IP includes standards for how computers communicate and conventions for connecting networks and routing traffic.

TDI (transport driver interface)

A specification to which all Windows NT transport protocols must be written to be used by higher-level services such as RAS.

Telnet

A TCP/IP protocol that provides remote terminal emulation.

Terminator

A device at the end of a cable segment that indicates that the last node has been reached. In the case of Ethernet cable, a 50-ohm resistor (a terminator) at both ends of the cable prevents signals from reflecting back through the cable.

Thicknet

A relatively rigid coaxial cable about one-half inch in diameter. Typically, Thicknet is used as a backbone to connect several smaller Thinnet-based networks because of its ability to support data transfer over longer distances. Thicknet can carry a signal for 500 meters (about 1650 feet) before needing a repeater.

Thinnet

A flexible coaxial cable about one-quarter inch thick. It is used for relatively short-distance communication and is fairly flexible to facilitate routing between computers. Thinnet coaxial cable can carry a signal up to approximately 185 meters (about 607 feet) before needing a repeater.

Thread

A thread is the lowest form of work that a processor can do.

Three-Finger Salute

Tongue-in-cheek reference to the Ctrl+Alt+Del key sequence.

Time-domain reflectometer (TDR)

A device that can determine the location of shorts and breaks in network cabling. It has the ability to send a high-frequency signal or pulse down the cable line and measures the time the pulse is reflected back to the TDR.

Token

A predetermined formation of bits that permits a network device to communicate with the cable. A computer may not transmit unless it has possession of the token. Only one token at a time may be active on the network, and the token may only travel in one direction around the ring.

Token passing

A media access control method in a Token Ring network that involves passing a data frame, called a token, from one station to the next around the ring. To transmit, a node must be in possession of a token, preventing multiple nodes from transmitting simultaneously and creating collisions.

Token Ring

A network that uses a token-passing protocol in a logical ring. A token is a small frame with a special format that designates that its holder (a network device) may transmit. When a node needs to transmit, it captures a token and attaches a message to it, along with addressing information. Token Ring transmits at 4 or 16Mbps.

Topology

A general term used to describe the physical layout of a network.

Transceiver

A device that connects a computer to the network. The term transceiver is derived from transmitter/receiver, so a transceiver is a device that receives and transmits signals. It switches the parallel data stream used on the computer's bus into a serial data stream used in the cables connecting the computers.

Transient

A high-voltage burst of electric current, usually lasting less than one second, occurring randomly. They are often referred to as spikes.

Translation Mode

Software utility that will allow an Integrated Device Electronics (IDE) hard drive that is greater than 504MB in size to work with an older system board.

Transport drive interface

See TDI.

Trust

A communication link between two domains that allows sharing of NT security data for permissions and accesses.

Trusted relationship between domains

A link between domains that enables pass-through authentication, in which a trusting domain honors the logon authentication of a trusted domain. With trust relationships, a user who has a user account in one domain can potentially access the entire network.

UDF (uniqueness database file)

While the UNATTEND.TXT file provides generic answers to questions, the UDF provides answers to questions that require unique settings.

UDP (User Datagram Protocol)

A connectionless TCP/IP protocol at the Transport layer that provides fast data transport.

Unattended installation

Allows a generic automated installation of NT Server. Answers are provided from a file called UNATTEND .TXT. There is a sample UNATTEND.TXT file on the NT Server Resource Kit; or, you can generate the file using the Setup Manager utility on the NT Server installation CD-ROM.

UNATTEND.TXT (Unattended answer file)

A sample of this plain-text file is found on the Installation CD in the `<driveletter>:\i386` directory.

UNC Path

An industry-standard method of naming and accessing resources on a network.

Uniqueness Database File

See UDF.

Universal naming convention (UNC)

An industry-standard method of naming resources on the network. All names begin with two backslashes (\\) to indicate a network resource.

Unshielded twisted-pair (UTP)

A type of cable usually containing four pairs of wire, each pair twisted to reduce interference. Commonly used in telephone and LAN cabling. A cable with wires that are twisted around each other with a minimum number of twists per foot. The twists reduce signal interference between the wires. The more twists per foot, the greater the reduction in interference (crosstalk).

Upgrade

The process of installing Windows 98 in the same folder as earlier versions of Windows and thereby retaining all of your previous settings, applications, and program groups.

UPS (uninterruptible power supply)

Supplies power during a power failure. May also condition power when the power is on.

User account

Consists of all the information that defines a user on a network. This includes the username and password required for the user to log on, the groups in which the user account has membership, and the rights and permissions the user has for using the system and accessing its resources.

User Name

Unique name given to a user to allow them to authenticate to the NT Workstation or to a domain. The

User Name may bear little or no resemblance to the user's real name.

User profile

Windows 98 can be made to track individual preferences and settings separately for each person who logs on to a computer. These preferences and settings are stored in a *user profile* which operates by building a unique USER.DAT file for each user.

User rights

Define a user's access to a computer or domain and the actions that a user can perform on the computer or domain. User rights permit actions such as logging onto a computer or network, adding or deleting users in a workstation or domain, and so forth.

USER.DAT

This piece of the Registry stores settings that are specific to a particular user.

User-level security

A security model that requires a user to first be authenticated by a network server or domain before the user can use shared resources.

Users

A default group created on an NT Workstation that contains all the users assigned to that workstation.

Value

Within the registry, a specific parameter's setting.

Vampire tap

A specific type of Ethernet transceiver on a Thicknet network. The vampire tap does not break the Thicknet cable, but instead pierces the jacket of the cable to contact the center conductor. The transceiver's DIX (DB15) connector provides an attachment for an AUI cable that runs from the transceiver to either the computer or a hub or repeater. Thick coaxial cable has bands on it every 2.5 meters (8 feet).

Variable

A string of data set to a value. This data can be used as a configuration parameter for a process.

Verify

When the Backup program checks the data it wrote against what was supposed to be written. Using verification takes longer, but helps prevent data loss.

Version ID

Each change in the change log is given a version ID (counter). The PDC compares the version ID of the last change replicated to the BDC with the version ID of changes in the log file. Changes with higher values need to be replicated.

Virtual circuit

A logical connection between two endpoints across a packet-switched network. The connection can be either temporary or permanent. With this method all the packets follow the same route.

Virtual Device Driver (VDD)

Software drivers designed to work with DOS applications in a Virtual DOS Machine.

Virtual DOS Machine (VDM)

Application support for applications from the DOS environment.

Virtual Memory model

A memory system that uses hard drive space as if it were RAM.

Virus

A dangerous or destructive program that alters stored files or system configurations, and copies itself onto external disks or other computers.

VLM (Virtual Loadable Module)

A real-mode, NDS client supplied by NetWare. The VLM client software is composed of many separate pieces that all load to create client functionality.

Volume set

When areas of free space are combined into a logical drive. Each segment will be filled with data before anything is written to the next segment.

Wide area network (WAN)

A computer network that uses long-range telecommunication links to connect the networked computers over long distances.

Win16

16-bit Windows application support for applications from the Windows 3.1 environment.

Win32

32-bit Windows support for applications written for Windows 95 and Windows NT.

Windows Internet Name Service

See WINS.

WinIPCfg

A GUI utility for verifying IP settings such as IP address, subnet mask, default gateway, DNS, DHCP, and WINS servers. WinIPCfg also allows you to release a dynamic address to the DHCP server and request a new address from the DHCP server.

WINNT.EXE

The executable that starts the Windows NT Installation Wizard from a non-NT operating system environment.

WINS (Windows Internet Naming Service)

An automatic service database of computer name-to-IP address mappings. The NetBIOS names are mapped to IP addresses. The network must be IP-based, and the client computer must know the IP address to use the service.

WINS partner relationship

A pair of WINS servers configured to trade their databases so that each server has a list of resources on the entire network.

Workgroup

A collection of computers that are grouped for sharing resources such as data and peripherals over a LAN. Each workgroup is identified by a unique name. A group of computers linked together to share resources. A workgroup is less sophisticated than a domain in that workgroups lack the central administrative capacities of a domain.

WOW (Windows on Windows)

A descriptive term for the way Windows NT runs 16-bit Windows Applications.

Write

The action of writing information to a file.

WWW (World Wide Web)

Servers that can share HTML pages via the HTTP protocol are considered WWW servers. They usually have `www.xxx.com` as their name, although this is not required.

WWW service

The service that provides Web pages in HTML format to users connected to your Web server.

XCOPY

Operating system command-line utility that can be used to copy files and subdirectories. Used with the /S parameter (copy subdirectories) to copy directories from the NT Installation CD-ROM to the distribution server.

INDEX

Note to the Reader: Throughout this index **boldfaced** page numbers indicate primary discussions of a topic. *Italicized* page numbers indicate illustrations

SYMBOLS & NUMBERS

A

B

C

D

E

F

G

H

I

J

K

L

O

P

R

S

T

U

V

X

Z